Sean Longden, through a series of groundbreaking books, has rewritten the history of the Second World War as seen through the eyes of those who were there. In *Dunkirk: The Men They Left Behind*, he exposed the story of the 41,000 who did not make it back from the battle lines and suffered at the hands of the Nazis. In *Hitler's British Slaves*, he explores the horrors of life in the PoW camps. *T-Force* revealed, for the first time, the story of the covert regiment created by Ian Fleming and Churchill to go behind enemy lines in 1945. *To the Victor the Spoils* follows Montgomery's 20th Army from D-Day to the liberation of Berlin. Sean Longden lives in London with his wife and two children.

Praise for *Blitz Kids*:

'The stories are by turns amusing, shocking and unbearably sad and Longden has done us a great service in allowing them to be told' *Sunday Express*

'This is a rich, human book' *Literary Review*

'. . . interesting, comprehensive' *BBC History magazine*

'Extensively researched and grippingly told, this riveting book uncovers an entirely new aspect of the Second World War' *Good Book Guide*

Also by Sean Longden

BLITZ KIDS

SEAN LONGDEN

CONSTABLE • LONDON

Constable & Robinson Ltd
55–56 Russell Square
London WC1B 4HP
www.constablerobinson.com

First published in the UK by Constable,
an imprint of Constable & Robinson Ltd, 2012

This paperback edition published by Constable, 2012

A copy of the British Library Cataloguing in
Publication data is available from the British Library

ISBN: 978-1-78033-552-0 (paperback)
ISBN: 978-1-84901-827-2 (ebook)

Typeset by TW Typesetting, Plymouth, Devon

Printed and bound by CPI Group (UK) Ltd, Croydon, CR0 4YY

1 3 5 7 9 10 8 6 4 2

For Sapper Arthur 'Paulus' Woodard,
a sixteen-year-old 'boy soldier' at Gallipoli, 1915.

To my parents, Roy and Margaret Longden,
whose memories helped to inspire this book
but who did not live to see its publication.

And to all the staff of the Primrose Unit, Pilgrim Ward
and Godber Ward, at Bedford hospital,
who cared for my parents between February and April 2011.

Contents

Preface

'a war of unknown warriors [in which] the whole warring nations are engaged, not only soldiers but the entire population, men, women and children.'

Winston Churchill[1]

So many times we have heard or read the story of children in the Second World War. Yet so often that story starts with the painful wrench of evacuation and goes little further. There are the stories of gas masks, of rationing, of separation, of loss. The traditional version of events tells us about the struggle of the nation's youth to combine schoolwork with collecting scrap metal, or working alongside their parents on allotments to grow their share of desperately needed food. That version of the story casts the children as observers to the conflict and the incredible changes it caused to British society.

But in that story there is something missing. The sadness and separation endured by the evacuees, and the terrible sufferings of the children of the blitzed cities, are only the beginning of the story. What about the thousands of other youngsters? Those whose parents refused to allow them to be evacuated? Those too old to want to be evacuated, yet too young to be conscripted? What of those who were active participants in war?

Theirs is a forgotten story.

As an historian who believes in filling the gaps left in the traditional telling of history, for me the wartime experiences of British children and teenagers was fertile ground. My aim was to uncover the tales normally told to friends or grandchildren, yet seldom collected by historians. I had no intention of writing another book about babies crying as they were placed inside gas masks or of tearful evacuees, when there were the tales of teenage sailors – some as young as fourteen – enjoying the pleasures of New York still waiting to be told. Their experiences of shopping for the latest American fashions or queuing to watch Frank Sinatra perform offer a perspective on youth in wartime that had been ignored for far too long.

For thousands of young Britons, war meant independence – from their families, their homes and their schools. It meant a fundamental disruption to their education, leaving them to enjoy – and exploit – their new-found freedom. Or it meant leaving school to work in armaments factories, earning high wages and enjoying the fruits of their labour. It was a period of taking pleasure wherever it could be found – regardless of bombs and bullets. As such, for this book, I wanted to rewrite the story of Britain's children and teenagers, to tell the story of those who were not just observers of life in wartime Britain but active participants in the conflict.

Prior to starting this project, I already had some idea of the independence offered by war. My father's story of leaving school (or more correctly, not bothering to go to school for his final year) and starting work earning a man's wage aged just thirteen had given me some idea of how war allowed children to grow up. I had not expected to discover that the small market town that was his home had also been the source of a significant proportion of the infections of American servicemen with sexually transmitted diseases. When I uncovered documents from a criminal case naming boys who spent their spare time watching the nightly antics of the local girls and American airmen on the town's riverbanks, I discovered the voyeurs were my father's contemporaries – boys living in the streets around him. Such details encouraged me in the pursuit of these forgotten stories.

Embarking on this project, I also thought of the story of my own grandfather who, as a sixteen-year-old boy, had gone to war in 1915 and suffered serious wounds fighting in the Middle East. So many times the experiences of the underage volunteers of the First World War have been publicized. Surely, now was the time for the experiences of child soldiers of the Second World War to receive similar exposure. These days, when we think of 'child soldiers' we inevitably think of the recent stories of children forced into African militias, sacrificing their childhoods – and often their lives – in some bloody civil war. Yet this is not just some Third World phenomenon. The pension queues and British Legion parades are full of our own one-time child soldiers whose story should never be forgotten.

As with my earlier books, I wanted this story to include the first-hand testimony of participants. Wherever possible I wanted my interviewees to be telling their story for the first time. And so began months of driving up and down the country to visit those who wished to tell their tales. Fortunately, I soon remembered that I had already collected the stories of a number of underage volunteers during my research for earlier books. Some of the stories included in this book are of veterans interviewed for my first book, *To the Victor the Spoils* (published in 2004). At the time I had not examined the significance of their having joined the Army while underage. Fortunately, I was able to go back to some of them to get further details of their experiences prior to being in battle.

This made me think that there must be many more veterans, from the Army, Navy and Royal Air Force, with similar experiences. And so I searched for the teenage boys – some as young as fourteen – who falsified their birth certificates to join the Army between 1939 and 1945. I soon realized that those who gave false ages were not alone and there were many youths who legally served under the age of eighteen. I had always thought that the Royal Navy's use of boys barely into their teens had gone out with the sailing ships. Prior to commencing my research, I did not realize that fourteen-year-old boys had served as buglers on battleships during the Second World War. So I tracked down former 'boy sailors' and Royal Marine bugle boys, the survivors from among hundreds who paid the ultimate price for their service at sea. Whilst many of their contemporaries were still at school, they had faced submarines, torpedoes and kamikaze attacks.

Now was also the time to remember the teenage boys that served in the Merchant Navy, who, in the nation's darkest hour, helped keep the United Kingdom from starving. Such job titles as 'Laundry Boy' or 'Pantry Boy' may not have been glamorous, but their jobs were vital and – to me, at least – a far more interesting element of the story of wartime children than stories of evacuees. The response from the veterans who answered my appeal in the Merchant Navy Association's newsletter showed they were eager finally to tell their tales of lifeboats, shipwrecks and Arctic convoys. It soon became clear that the veterans of the Merchant Navy still feel their wartime sacrifices have been neglected. Once I had come to appreciate the scale of sacrifice, I realized there must have been boys in the merchant fleet whose ships were sunk and who were subsequently held in prisoner-of-war camps. Therefore, I uncovered tales of boys who spent most of their teenage years in the misery of German camps.

That the contribution of these boys had been forgotten was something I noticed whenever I spoke with veterans. So often during my research I spoke with men who told me that in later years people had queried their 'war stories' and membership of veterans' organizations. They have spent years answering the challenge 'you were too young to have been in the war!'.

Soon it became clear that, in the midst of a total war, there were thousands of children, of all ages, whose endeavours were vital to achieve victory. From the Boy Scouts, who unloaded ambulances at hospitals, to the Girl Guides who assisted the victims of the Blitz. From teenage boys using what they had learned in the Army Cadets to help train the volunteers of the Home Guard, to the valiant messenger boys of the fire service. In an era when youths are so often criticized, it is refreshing to uncover stories of teenage girls who were awarded medals for their courage during the Blitz. It was an honour to meet the man who, as an eleven-year-old evacuee heading to the United States, had been decorated for heroism after the ship he was travelling on was torpedoed in the mid-Atlantic. Nowadays, it seems unthinkable that fifteen- and sixteen-year-old telegram boys were sent to deliver messages telling families of the death of a loved one. To listen as a former messenger recounted tales of breaking the news to bereaved parents, then waiting to see if there was a reply to the telegram, made me realize the 'stiff upper lip' had never been stiffer – nor was it the preserve of the gentleman.

On a darker side, I also wanted to write about those who were emotionally scarred by a wartime childhood, and so searched for those who had experienced the full horror of the Blitz. Thus I heard tales told through a mist of tears as survivors of the Bethnal Green tube station disaster recounted their memories, just yards from the spot where they had endured unbelievable trauma.

I also wanted to give a voice to the 'villains' of the period, those children who turned to crime to support themselves through the lean years, or the teenage girls who – lured by the bright lights of London and captivated by the glamour of men in uniform – fell into a life of prostitution.

What follows is the story of children and teenagers growing up in wartime Britain. It is a story of immense courage and sacrifice. It is the story of children who were forced to grow up amidst violence and horror: children who watched their world turn upside down. They were the bombsite boys and girls.

They were the 'Blitz Kids'.

Introduction: London, 1930s

As the crowds gathered, so too did the local children. There was the black van with loudspeakers fitted on top, surrounded by rough-looking men, all dressed in black. Maybe an orator was giving a fiery, heartfelt speech, or some martial music was playing, attempting to rouse the masses into action. Flags filled the air, black flags emblazoned with a symbol that meant nothing to the watching children. But they knew what the demonstration meant: trouble. From their vantage point perched on top of the wall, they could listen to the rhetoric and hear the cheers and jeers of the assembled crowd. Other flags appeared on the fringes of the crowd, clenched fists were raised in the air, voices chanted.

The children waited, all knowing what would come next. Suddenly a missile was thrown from the crowd, a punch, a surge, banners waving, flags falling, trampled under jostling feet. Gangs running at each other, a swirling mass of violence. Screaming women and shouting men. The sound of breaking glass. And on the walls, smiling children, non-partisan but urging on the fighting crowd.

And then whistles, the clatter of horses' hooves on the tarmac, swinging batons, a surge of blue-uniformed men striking at anyone in their path, clearing the street. Black shirts and even blacker

bruises; red flags and red blood on the streets. A violent sign of the
political divisions tearing Europe apart; a spectacle for the local
children. Another day, another Blackshirt rally, in London's Bethnal
Green.

Watching the spectacle was young Alf Morris and his schoolmates. This was just a couple of streets away from his house in
Prospect Terrace, so he could run home quickly if the trouble got
out of hand. Born in 1930, this was his area. Life was hard, times
were tough, but Alf was happy. He could run in the streets, play in
the park behind his house. That his parents were working hard for
little reward meant little. There was food on his plate, mates nearby
and all his family was in the area.

But then life began to change. Whilst the radio spoke about distant
troubles – what did the rise of a man named Hitler mean to a schoolboy
in Bethnal Green? – real troubles appeared in his own neighbourhood.
Whilst some adults concerned themselves with political crises, Alf and
his mates could watch politics acted out on their doorstep.

> When they used to march, they'd come through Bethnal Green. On
> the way past, they'd smash all the windows of the Jewish shops. The
> police tried, but they couldn't control it. As kids we didn't realize what
> it was about. We'd just see it, we didn't understand it.

Morris and his friends would sit on walls around a street corner
where demonstrations took place:

> We'd be watching the fights, shouting, 'Go on, hit him!' When it got
> out of hand the police were ready – they put police horses across the
> road to keep people away. And when it got really out of hand they'd
> charge. We'd look at the police and egg them on. It was fun for us kids,
> but it was serious – although we didn't realize it.

One night they were watching a fight when the action started to
come closer to where they were sitting:

We got up and ran. Behind them were police officers on horses with batons drawn, who started to knock people down. Me and my mates ran along and a big man grabbed us and put us into the porch of a house and put his body in front of us – so the horses missed us.

Once the danger had passed, the man shouted at them: '*Go on – go home! Bloody fools! Go home.*' The boys made their way home reflecting on how it had been fun – a violent and bloody spectacle, but fun nonetheless.

What Alf Morris had seen was mostly from organized groups – communists, Jewish groups, trade unionists – opposed to Oswald Mosley and his supporters who intended bringing the ways of Nazi Germany and Fascist Italy to the streets of Britain. But one night it was not the opponents of fascism who voiced their defiance. The Blackshirts were strong in the area and wanted more than to listen to speeches, flex their muscles and fight in the streets: they wanted to take real action. Their attempt to dominate the area was witnessed by Alf Morris. A crowd of Blackshirts gathered in his street and began threatening the Jewish family who lived next door: 'They tried their utmost to belittle these people. They filled the street and stood there calling at the Jewish family, "You Jewish bastards" and so on.' This was different to the demonstrations and street fights – things the local men often ignored or avoided – this was a deliberate attack on a local family. As Morris watched, the men of the street came out of their houses and confronted the Blackshirts: 'My dad was out there, the men from across the road were there. Some of them were veterans of the Great War – they were very hard men.' In no uncertain terms, they told the Blackshirts: 'Do yourself a favour and go. We won't mess about with you. There's no one here to protect you. Now you go!'

As the boy watched, the Blackshirts turned away and walked off. It was the defiance of everyday people who had defeated them. Within a few years, the entire country would stand defiant to the same threat. The attack would be bloodier and more violent, but the defiance would be stronger. For what lay ahead was a war in which the children of Britain would witness horrors they had never imagined, and go from being spectators to being active participants in the heroics, endurance and sacrifice of a nation at war.

CHAPTER I

The Coming of War

'In 1939 I was fifteen years of age, and I remember discussing with a friend whether or not there would be any fighting left for us when we reached military age. Unfortunately there was, and I have the scars to prove it.'

Peter Richards, Post Office Messenger Boy

'War had started and for us little boys it was a big excitement. I remember my mother crying and I said to her "What are you crying for?" Well, you know what little boys are like. I thought war was going to be great.'

Tony Sprigings, Merseyside

3 September 1939. It was a day that everyone knew was coming. Ever since the rise of the Nazis in Germany, many had been predicting war. After the Munich Crisis of 1938 it had seemed that the world was balanced on the edge of a precipice. Then, on 1 September 1939, Hitler's Germany invaded Poland and the world took a step into the unknown. For the next two days the people of Britain were on tenterhooks, knowing that war might be declared at any moment. Parents became withdrawn, veterans of the Great War grew quiet, fearful that their own sons might be sucked into a war every bit as horrible as the one they had known. For all the chatter about the likelihood of war, there was a dreadful silence about what it might mean.

For fifteen year olds Peter Richards and John Cotter, there was no reason why the declaration of war should interrupt their routine. 3 September was a Sunday and they would do what they always did: go for a cycle ride. The two boys had been firm friends since attending grammar school in Kingsbury, north London, where they had 'palled up' and stayed together.

After leaving school, the two boys had gone their separate ways, but kept in touch and met regularly. In February 1939 Peter and his family had moved to Camden Town and he found employment as a boy messenger with the Royal Mail, in central London. His family was relatively poor and, as such, every penny he earned – of his twelve shillings and sixpence weekly wage – was precious. On 1 September, with war looming, he had gone to the cinema to watch the latest Will Hay comedy. When told there was to be blackout that night he was unconcerned as he did not really believe there would be a war. He was convinced by newspaper articles claiming it would be averted. Like so many others, he had seen the film of the H. G. Wells novel *The Shape of Things to Come*, which fixed in his mind the vision of a London destroyed by war. Surely no one would risk such horrors?

Despite his seeming nonchalance, Peter Richards was a child of his time. Born in May 1924, for him the deprivations of the 1930s had inspired a fascination with politics that stayed with him all his life. He had watched the rise of fascism at home and abroad. And having followed the Spanish Civil War with interest, he was well aware of the horrors of modern warfare. The conflict drew him towards left-wing politics:

> I wasn't a convinced 'Labour' person at first, but the thing that shook me was the Munich Crisis. Then at fourteen I can remember going out for a walk with a friend of mine. Just by chance we went to a Communist Party meeting that was being held in a school. The main speaker was Wal Hannington, a well-known leader. He was the first person who put the idea into my head that the government wasn't

> doing the right thing. So I began to get interested in government policies.

His mate John Cotter was no less a product of the same times. He lived in Edgware in north-west London, having moved around during the late 1920s and early 1930s as his father struggled financially in the Depression. The two boys had become friends despite their political differences:

> We were at opposite ends of the political spectrum. Peter was a communist and I was thinking of joining the young fascists. I wasn't anti-Jewish, because I lived in a Jewish area. I was brought up reading the *Daily Mail*. It said that Mussolini ran the trains on time and everything worked well. They were also pro-Franco, which I was. On the way home from school I used to have fights with other boys about it: they'd be supporting the republicans, I supported the nationalists. So Peter would take me to meetings held by pro-Republican factions and I would sit there fuming. I was pro-Mussolini but I wasn't pro-German.

With youthful disdain for the lofty affairs of state the boys, whose political views seemingly mirrored the conflict that was about tear Europe apart, set out on their regular Sunday morning cycle ride, heading towards St Albans. As Peter later recalled: 'We were young. It was just a normal day.' They had not gone far when they pulled up at the roadside to buy a drink from a corner shop. By chance, the lady behind the counter called them over to listen to the radio. There they heard the words that would mean so much to their generation, as Neville Chamberlain told the nation: 'This country is at war with Germany.' This was followed by the dejected voice of the shop-owner: 'Oh no, not again.' Her dejection was not shared by the two youngsters, who cycled on merrily calling out to passers-by: 'War's declared! War's declared!'

Within minutes of the declaration, the air raid sirens sounded for the first time. It was a false alarm that sent most of London scurrying around looking for their gas masks before running off to the shelters. Indeed, pre-war Air Ministry estimates concluded that London would be hit by 100 tons of bombs on the first day of war. Blithely, the two teenagers continued on their way to St Albans, unconcerned by the potential realities of war. The reality felt by the older generation was not revealed until the boys returned home later that day, with Peter Richards being asked by his mother: 'Why didn't you come home earlier?' In the Cotter household it was similar: 'My father was in a bit of a funk. They'd had the air raid alarm, which we hadn't heard. He had got my mother, my sister and my brother ready to go to the air raid shelter and I wasn't there.'

And so the first day of the war came to an end and Peter Richards noted:

> On that day, apart from concerns over military service, a hundred & one questions quickly surfaced. Could London survive the expected air raids, would poison gas be used and how long would the conflict last? Would we get enough to eat? Such questions were answered with the agreed, 'we will have to wait and see!'. As night fell, people prepared for bed in a sober mood. The day seemed to have changed everything. In the small hours of the morning the air raid sirens wailed again, but it was another false alarm. Unknown to us the 'Phoney War' had begun.

The whole country experienced the outbreak of war on an individual level. The wide-ranging emotional impact of war differed from person to person, but fell into a number of general themes. The youngest children had no understanding of what it meant. For older children, buoyed by the natural exuberance of youth, the threat of war was easier to ignore, meaning many of the nation's teenagers were unmoved. They had a life to live. Whether still in education or out taking their steps into the world of work, they inhabited a world they wanted to enjoy. For the boys, there were girls to chase, sports and games to throw themselves into and a world to explore. For the girls, there were boys to impress, clothes to buy, make-up to experiment with and a similar world to explore. For teenage newspaper vendors, the first change to their routine was that Sunday newspapers rushed out special editions and they had to head out on to the streets to sell the papers to a concerned public.

For twelve-year-old Sylvia Bowman war seemed almost unintelligible: 'I didn't really understand what it meant. I knew it was a fight between countries for whatever reason, and they were short lived, maybe just a few weeks. The whole concept was too much for a youngster like me.' However, the situation became clearer when her father announced he was glad he had five daughters since women did not have to go to war. In Hainault, five-year-old Colin Furk was also too young to understand what was going on, but realized something had upset his grandmother, asking her: '"What have you done wrong?" She said, "I haven't done anything wrong. It's somebody else."'

Eight-year-old Sylvia Bradbrook was in a cake shop with her father when the news was broadcast. He grabbed her hand, barked 'Quick!' and they ran back to their house. As they ran, the sirens sounded. She had no idea what the sound meant. There was no Sunday lunch that day. Her mother was too occupied putting sticky tape across the windows, to prevent the shattering when bombs dropped, to bother about cooking.

In London's Bethnal Green, nine-year-old Alf Morris found the coming conflict confusing. No one he knew wanted a war; instead, everyone just wanted to get on with their lives. Men wanted to work to provide for their families, not go off to war to fight an enemy that had been defeated just twenty years before: 'I had no understanding of what it meant. Everyone said it would be over in a few weeks. The men who'd been in the First War said nothing would happen.'

Some older children were excited by the announcements. Young men were either concerned about how war might affect them or fired by a desire to do their duty. Older men, veterans of the earlier world war, felt their hearts sink, knowing the impact it would have on the younger generations. Women feared for their husbands and sons, whilst optimists thought it would all be over quickly and wasn't worth concerning themselves with. On the other hand the pessimists expected to die as soon as Chamberlain finished speaking. Fourteen-year-old Anthony Wedgwood Benn (as the politician Tony Benn was originally named) was immediately struck by the implications of the declaration of war: 'It was very frightening when the war began. I sat there with my two brothers – one who was going into the Air Force and I knew might be killed. He was.'

In Portugal, where he was on holiday from Winchester public school, sixteen-year-old Patrick Delaforce was struck by the tone with which Chamberlain spoke: 'I can remember very clearly the sad, dejected, defeated voice of Neville Chamberlain. I certainly thought, "This man is not a leader." I wanted to return to Winchester.' In north London, fourteen-year-old errand boy Stanley Scott was listening to the radio with his bus-driver father, a veteran of the Great War:

> We were listening to old dreary pants bloody Chamberlain. He said, 'This country is now at war with Germany.' I shot across the road because the family didn't have a radio. I banged on the door, the wife opened it: 'What's the matter, Stanley?' I went in and told old Joe – who'd lost his leg in the first war. His reaction was 'Gawd help us.'

But Stan Scott was enthused by the idea of war and had long dreamed of being a soldier. With his father having been a regular soldier, and his uncles all being veterans of the Great War, this seemed an ideal time to be living. As a child he had played with spurs brought home from the Army by his father, a former artilleryman, pretending the family's sofa was a horse. War, it seemed, was a time of opportunity for the military-minded. Though just fifteen, he was already determined to do his duty.

Others had a less optimistic view of war. In Huddersfield,

thirteen-year-old orphan Eric 'Bill' Sykes had some idea of what the conflict might mean:

> I was vaguely familiar with the events in Europe leading up to this moment, but I must admit that those words filled me more with a feeling of excitement, than a realization of the horrors that the world was about to witness. Due to my youthful optimism, or my lack of a realistic approach to the seriousness of the situation, I failed to recognize that in a matter of a few years I myself would be very much involved in a personal fight to survive the rigours of war.

Bill later recalled feeling exhilarated by the prospect of war. In many ways, this was a strange emotion. His own father had met a premature death brought on by wounds sustained in the Great War. Before he died, Sykes senior had taken his son to the cinema to see *All Quiet on the Western Front*: 'I think my father's objective was to show that war is not full of heroics like John Wayne dashing up a hill to plant a flag. War is bloodshed and killing.' Despite their differing experiences and outlook, both Scott and Sykes would later take similar steps towards playing their part in the conflict.

Whatever their position, those who were old enough to understand seemed to agree on one thing: the war was right. It was a case of standing up to the aggressor and protecting the weak. As Clydebank teenager Jeanie, a girl who lived in a cramped and crowded home in an area blighted by poverty, later noted:

> The outbreak of war was exciting. Everyone knew it was right. There was never any question that we shouldn't be doing this. It was the right thing to do. Nobody talked intellectually about the rights and wrongs – there was just a feeling that this was absolutely right.

The timing of the declaration of war – eleven on a Sunday morning – meant that many children first heard the news whilst at church. It was an appropriate setting to hear news that would inevitably lead to the deaths of so many. In Staines, twelve-year-old Bill Edwardes, whose school had just been evacuated from London, was at the local Catholic church when the service was interrupted:

> In the middle of the mass the big doors opened and there was the heavy clonk of footsteps down the central aisle. We all looked at this guy in his steel helmet, with his gas mask on his chest and an ARP armband. He walked up to the altar, whispered into the priest's ear, then walked out again. The priest walked to the front of the altar and said, 'I have some terrible news. We are now at war with Germany.'

The news was not a shock; after all, Bill Edwardes and his classmates had already been evacuated from London and had spent the entire preceding week going to school carrying bags of spare clothing in case a further evacuation was announced. But now reality hit them. As the priest announced the news, a shiver of excitement ran through the boys, whilst the adults were visibly moved. As he listened he could hear the sound of people crying: these were the people old enough to understand the true meaning of war. These emotions were not shared by Edwardes: 'Why are they crying? This is great!' Within minutes the air raid sirens sounded and they streamed out of the church, into a field, where they lay in rows. The Air Raid Precautions (ARP) warden reappeared, this time riding a bicycle and waving a rattle, telling them to put their gas masks on. Amidst the combination of excitement and trepidation, Bill Edwardes had but one thought in his mind: 'This is a big adventure.' In the years ahead, he would learn war was anything but an adventure and would discover exactly why the people in church had been crying.

Whilst most of Britain's youth listened to the announcement and wondered what effect this war would have on their lives, some of their contemporaries immediately realized that war was about to turn their world upside down. At Eastney Barracks in Portsmouth, fourteen-year-old Len Chester suddenly discovered what it meant to be on active service in wartime. The youth was part of a group training to be 'boy buglers', who were employed on warships to sound orders to the crew by bugle call.

The son of a south London policeman, Len had applied to join aged just thirteen:

> What was there for me when I left school in 1939? I would have been pushing a delivery bike around or working in shop. I wasn't brilliant at school. You could almost say I was a thickie. My brother was a marine and I'd seen them in displays. I thought: I can do that.

Volunteering for the marines had been simple. He collected papers from a recruiting office, filled them in, got his parents' consent and then was called to central London for a medical. For the first time, the thirteen year old entered a world far different to a sheltered life of school and home. He entered the world of men:

> It was very exciting. I went up to London for a medical at Great Scotland Yard. There were about six others there – eighteen year olds, who were joining as marines. I was four feet eight inches tall. I wasn't even tall for my age. I wasn't half the size of them.'

First of all, there was a medical to pass. Their vision was tested, then the would-be marines had to strip off and line up ready for inspection. As a boy among men, the physical differences were laid bare for all to see:

> That was traumatic. It was something I'd never done before. You have to strip off and a man prods and pokes you. All the others were eighteen. It was humiliating for me. I'd never seen anybody naked in my whole life! When the doctor got his torch out, I didn't know what he was looking for!

Having endured the humiliation of public nudity, Len Chester swore the oath of loyalty and took the 'King's shilling'. He was officially a member of His Majesty's Armed Forces. The pride this inspired was soon deflated. After he took the shilling, the Recruiting Sergeant informed him he had eaten a lunch costing one shilling and sixpence and therefore already owed the Royal Marines sixpence. Then it was home, back to the world of childhood, to await his orders.

On 3 May 1939, aged just fourteen years and twenty-eight days, he left home and travelled to Portsmouth to begin training as a bugler. He would serve for four years as a boy, then for twelve years as a marine. His father did not hide his feelings: 'He was as "Proud as Punch" to see his son going to fight the Hun.' Notably, his mother was less effusive. She kept her emotions hidden. Whilst everyone else was expecting a war, the thought didn't cross the youngster's mind. 'I had no idea or experience of war. Everything new is an adventure at that age. And I thought being a marine was going to be a big adventure.'

During the summer of 1939 Len Chester had watched many changes at Eastney Barracks. Reservists were being called up and arrived at the barracks dressed in caps, uniforms and equipment that seemed like relics of another age. They were time-served marines, men who had done their full service and retired. To the fourteen year old these men, most in their late thirties and early forties, appeared ancient. Yet the political crises that had caused their recall meant little to the teenager. His summer had been spent learning the bugle calls and drum rolls and trying to master the flute. For him, Sunday, 3 September was a special day: 'It was our Sunday church parade. It was the first time I'd been to it in full regimental dress. It was always a bit of a spectacle. The public were allowed in church and we used to do a bit of a show for them. But war was declared whilst we were in church.' The padre announced that the civilians should return home and the marines should return to their barracks. For Len Chester the announcement of the declaration of war was less important than the cancellation of his chance to perform in front of an audience. He thought to himself: 'Mr Chamberlain could have left it another hour!'

Returning to the barracks, Len had no idea what was going on elsewhere in the country. Whilst other boys his age were being evacuated, he was suddenly immersed in the world of war. Their first instructions came through almost immediately: 'Everyone thought there'd be bombs falling on us straight away. They were worried about rabid animals roaming around on the bombed cities. So we got our first wartime order.' The order they received was direct but shocking. It simply read: 'Drown all cats.'

CHAPTER 2

Should They Stay or Should They Go?

'They talk about the good old days . . . they were horrible . . . I was always hungry, I had holes in my shoes and my arse was hanging out of my trousers.'

Reg Baker, on growing up in the East End of London

For children like Bill Edwardes and his classmates, the threat of war had been hanging over them for a year. The Munich Crisis of 1938 had given children a taste of what was to come. For Roy Bartlett, living with his parents above their west London hardware shop, the impending conflict had little impact:

> The prospect of war was talked about in hushed tones. I became familiar with names like Hitler and Mussolini, and the Rhineland. But at nine years old, it all sounded rather exciting, I wasn't worried. I was more bothered about how many goals I scored in the playground kickabout – or *The Adventures of Tarzan* at the pictures. Until gas masks were distributed at school: I didn't like the look of them. I was under the impression that once they were issued, I'd have to wear it all the time – even in bed.

The sudden arrival of gas masks was the one thing that changed their world. From early 1937 factories had been producing gas masks at a rate of some 150,000 per month and these had started being issued in 1938. With their issue, war was no longer something that concerned only the adults. At Roy Bartlett's school, the distribution of gas masks was a less than formal occasion, despite the efforts of the instructor:

A very bossy lady arrived. 'Stand still! Line up! I'm going to show you how to put a gas mask on!' I can clearly remember it was a horrible feeling. There was the smell of new rubber and the claustrophobic feeling as the mica at the front misted over. I was pleased because it meant no one could see that I was crying. But there was some light relief because one of the lads realized that if you exhale harder, the air can't get out of the filter. Instead it makes the rubber vibrate and makes a farting sound. If you can imagine forty kids, all doing it! We loved it. This poor lady was jumping up and shouting 'Stop it!' The idea that this was supposed to save our lives didn't even enter our heads.

He and his classmates soon realized that gas mask cases had many potential uses: 'If you stood three on top of each other it became a cricket wicket. Stand them three yards apart and they were goalposts for football. Or you could chuck them up into trees and knock conkers down.'

Despite the light-hearted antics of children who were too young to understand war, there was a serious undercurrent that soon impacted upon them: evacuation. In preparation for war, some schools had embarked upon evacuations, moving their pupils into the countryside for safety. Born in July 1929, Colin Ryder Richardson was at Arnold House School in St John's Wood, London, at the time of the Munich Crisis. Suddenly the children were told the school was moving to Scotland:

We were told to pack some food and clothes and that we would be getting the night train. It was an enormous shock to me, my parents packed me off. We arrived in Scotland and went to a hotel on an estate. We stayed there a week whilst the school tried to carry on – turning a day school into a boarding school in a temporary location. Then Munich was resolved and we came back. But it left an impression on me and indicated to me that the political situation wasn't very stable.

For Roy Bartlett, the discussion of evacuation seemed somehow unreal:

All the chit-chat at school was about evacuation. I couldn't make head nor tail of it. It seemed to be a mad scheme where you were taken away from home, sent hundreds of miles away, to a place that was totally secret, to people you had never met in your life – and they said we'd have a good time. I decided to ignore the whole silly affair and tell my mother I wasn't going.

It was just the start of a process that saw some sixty million changes of address in six years of war, a remarkable figure considering the population stood at less than fifty million.

Despite the opposition of children who had no desire to be evacuated, the story of the children's war effectively began on Friday, 1 September 1939. The evacuation of the cities, ports and industrial areas began immediately. This was the starkest possible warning of what 'total war' might mean: the transportation of one-and-a-half million people out of danger. Never before had such a movement of population been attempted in the UK. There were 735,000 children who were separated from their parents and a further 426,500 mothers with young children. From London alone, 339,000 children left London in the government scheme. Many more left the city with private schools or with families who decided to relocate to the countryside.

All across London and the big cities, parents were faced with an uncomfortable choice. The government reaction, though extreme, was deemed logical. For all the tears it inspired, from children and parents alike, the threat of modern war was too great for anything else to be done. It was a terrible dilemma: should they lose their children to the safety of the countryside or risk staying – and possibly dying – together?

In east London's Bethnal Green, war had been prefaced by the rise of the Blackshirts and the conflict between them and many of the locals. Nine-year-old Reg Baker, who had watched the street fights in defiance of his parents, was under no illusion that the world was a violent place. The East End was a rough place, but his local community was close-knit and generous – those with spare cash would willingly lend their last pennies to a mate in need. His was a world of pawnbrokers and constant hunger, a world where a bus trip to Oxford Street seemed like travelling to another planet. Winter and summer, Reg wore the same battered woollen jersey, thread-bare trousers and worn-out shoes: 'You put cardboard in your shoe, but it's no good if you step in a puddle.'

He was under no illusion about the world he lived in. Even the most loving parents had little time to show affection to their kids. Often it was the women who suffered most from the frustrations brought on by poverty, as Reg Baker soon realized: 'They were such drab days – drink was the only way out. That's why men got violent.' The violence made an impression on the youngster:

> It was a Saturday night. He was skint – and he'd had a few. Mum was cutting up tomatoes. All of a sudden he's gone for her. She lifted up the knife and cut him across the wrist. The blood came out like a fountain. So my sister wrapped a towel round it and took him down Bethnal Green hospital.

The violence only stopped when Baker's elder brother had grown tall enough to intervene: 'I came home one night and my old man started on Mum. My brother came over and bang! He knocked him down. Dad sobbed – I think he was embarrassed that his son had hit him.'

When the time came for London's children to be evacuated, it was no wonder both Baker and his parents were happy for him to go. Having one fewer mouth to feed made a significant difference – even before rationing was introduced. And so, when the time came, Reg made his way to school alongside his classmates. In later years Baker was always struck by one thought: whenever he saw photographs of evacuees they seemed to be well dressed and carrying small suitcases or wearing rucksacks. That was not his experience. He was dressed in his normal ragged clothes and had travelled with a carrier bag containing little more than a tin of condensed milk.

The children gathered at their schools. The older ones were evidently enjoying the adventure, anxious to discover what life would be like in the countryside and keen to maximize the opportunity. Younger children held their mothers close. Family groups held hands, the eldest sibling urged not to let the others out of their sight. In Ealing, Roy Bartlett had voiced his opposition to evacuation and his parents had originally accepted his protests, agreeing he should remain at home. When they discovered the rest of his school were going away the decision was taken out of the nine year old's hands, his mother arguing that she did not have time to teach him at home. So he joined the classes assembling in his school playground at six in the morning:

> I'd been scrubbed and polished to perfection. All the dads stood to one side because emotion was never shown by men in those days. They certainly never showed tears. It was a bit different from the mums. All the mothers were crying. My mother was desperately trying not to cry. She told me not to worry.

As the mothers cried, the evacuees had labels tied to their coats, were given a 'goodie bag' of food for their first meal and lined up to board the buses: 'We were excited. It was an adventure. Which over-rides the fear. I was going with all my mates.' As they boarded the bus, the children could hear their mothers shouting to them: 'Don't forget to write! Don't forget to change your socks! Don't forget to wash behind your ears!' As Reg Baker left the East End for Oxfordshire he considered it an adventure. The most exciting thing was that they were given a bar of Cadbury's chocolate: 'It was supposed to last the whole day. I'd eaten mine by the time I left Bethnal Green. It was a real treat – I was always hungry.'

That Friday, as the children began their journey, there were awkward scenes the like of which the country had never seen. On the brink of total war, the children reached railway stations where they passed columns of soldiers heading off to join their units. The juxtaposition of the two was a stark reminder of the changes that were taking place. At stations, the evacuees climbed onboard one of the 1,500 special trains that had been laid on to carry them away from home. Around 600,000 were herded on to requisitioned buses and driven to their destination. The bright red of London Transport buses seemed incongruous in the country lanes as they weaved their way into the villages to unload their youthful cargo. On his bus, Roy Bartlett found the journey seemed to last for hours. It was all an illusion. By the time they reached their destination they had travelled just twenty-four miles. One lucky group of children were even evacuated from London to the Norfolk coast on a pleasure steamer more used to transporting holidaymakers on day trips.

In their excitement most of the children failed to notice that some faces were missing. In every class there were a few gaps, children whose families refused to let them join the exodus. In east London, soon to be one of the most bombed parts of the country, there were plenty who decided to take their chances. When the Morris family heard the news that young Alf was going to be evacuated the discussion was brief. Alf listened as his mother boldly stated: 'If I die, he dies with me.' The decision was final: the whole family would face war together, come what may.

The children arrived at their destinations, some clumped together with friends, others holding the hands of siblings. It was a pathetic sight to see these lost and lonely children nervously waiting to see what would happen next. The comics they carried, bought by parents as a going-away gift, seemed altogether sadder than when they had begun their journeys. The pages were crumpled, courtesy of so many eager hands. They had served their purpose, keeping the children occupied on the journey; now they were little more than a reminder of home. Likewise, those who had left in their best clothes, seemed dishevelled after hours of travelling. Above all, behind the little bravado offered up by some, there was a quiet air of caution – and not a little sadness – surrounding the evacuees.

As hundreds of thousands of children began the exodus from the cities, a vast army of helpers was recruited to help look after them. In some areas, schools organized their senior pupils and prefects to support the evacuation system. Boy Scouts and Girl Guides played a major role in helping to collect children from railway stations and then deliver them to their new homes. Girl Guides also volunteered to clean homes, many of which had stood empty for years, to be used for housing evacuees. Their work also entailed using their sewing and handicraft skills to make blackout curtains. In the opening days of the war, many Guides were fully engaged in war work: as well as cleaning houses, they were looking after children and helping to dig air raid shelters. Once the evacuees were selected, Guides who had passed their 'Child Nurse badge' volunteered to help at nursery schools that had moved to their area.

One teenage volunteer was Jean Redman. At fifteen years old, she was just one year older than many of the evacuees. The daughter of a dentist, Jean was selected to assist at Bedford Town Hall: 'I was seconded from school to help with the evacuation. The town clerk asked the Head if there was anyone who would be available to help with the evacuations. My friend and I had done our exams so we volunteered.' After mustering at the Town Hall, Jean and the other volunteers walked to the railway station where they collected the children: 'On the first train they were fairly young. Some were crying, but some were happy as they thought it was a holiday.' The children were marched through town, with adult volunteers trying to keep order. They were then deposited in the local Corn Exchange, where they awaited selection.

Jean Redman watched as the children were assessed by potential foster-parents:

> That was the worst thing. Then I didn't realize it – I was too young – but now I think that must have been absolutely terrible for those that were left at the end. I was watching them all being distributed. The nicest looking children went first ... then the best dressed ... it's human nature. People didn't want large families. Hardly any people even wanted two children together. If you were in the countryside you might find a farm big enough for two or three children, but the average family didn't have space.

Arriving in the village of Wooburn Green, Roy Bartlett and his classmates exited the bus with some trepidation, then were marched into the village hall:

> We were sorted out like dirty washing. My friend Ken and I were sitting on the floor and we were among the leftovers. Us two sweet angelic lads! We were put into this car to be touted around the village. I was absolutely petrified. We were huddled together. We didn't know what was going on. The car was surrounded by women, all peering in. They spoke funny! They had these country accents. Then a couple opened the car door and said, 'Would you like to come with us?' We hadn't got a lot of choice really.

After arriving in Oxfordshire, Reg Baker and his schoolmates had a similar experience as the children were separated, although in farming villages the emphasis was slightly different: 'The big boys were chosen first, for the farms. Then good-looking girls were next. The scruffy ones – like me – were left to the end.' Finally chosen by a blacksmith and his family who lived at the village forge, he began his new life. As they walked to his new home, Reg was shocked by his surroundings: 'It was a world I'd never seen before.' There was a village green with the obligatory stocks on it; the village pub faced the green. It was quiet, he could hear birds singing and the air was strangely clear. There was a vacant bus stop, where buses stopped every few hours: nothing like Bethnal Green, with its busy roads, constant noise and smoky air.

Those who assisted with the allocation of children – many being members of the Women's Voluntary Service (WVS) – found themselves scrubbing the heads of children who gleefully admitted to having nits. Others – including women and girls – were appalled and insulted at having their heads shaved. One woman was upset to see her young child having her teeth examined, calling out: 'Hold up – she's not a horse.' Foster-parents were shocked to encounter children without night clothing, who insisted on sleeping in their clothes, or refused to take a hot bath. Despite such complaints about the incoming children, the evacuees also complained about their hosts. Children from 'respectable' homes were appalled to be housed in draughty country cottages. One girl noted how she was unable to wash her hair for months and had to fetch all water from a pump at the bottom of a hill. Others found themselves billeted with drunks, the physically abusive and even paedophiles.

Having moved from Streatham in south London, nine-year-old Sylvia Bradbrook's experience of evacuation was unremittingly miserable. She was housed with a family where the mother ruled the house:

> The woman was terrible. But everyone thought she was wonderful, a pillar of the church, because she had ministers coming to lunch with her. My mum would come down to see me and bring me a parcel of food she'd saved like an orange. Mrs Morris would say, 'Oh look at that – isn't that lovely?' but as soon as my mum was gone she'd have it off me. My sister's firm was evacuated round the corner but she wouldn't let her come to see me.

Sylvia found she was treated like a servant rather than foster-child:

> I used to have to get up at 6 a.m. in the morning and cycle miles to
> Bracknell to do all the shopping. After that I had to cycle miles in the
> opposite direction to Woking where I went to school – and all that had
> to be done every day before school at 8.30.

In later years Sylvia realized her foster-mother's mood swings were
a symptom of the menopause:

> She was forty-five to fifty and she would rage. She'd beat her dog with
> a walking stick and I'd scream because any minute the walking stick
> might come down on me. She'd make me keep the same clothes and
> underwear on for a whole week because she didn't want to do washing.
> But she was nice when my mum came down and I was frightened to
> say anything.

Her hen-pecked husband seemed frightened to confront his wife,
spending the evenings in his chair, smoking his pipe and desperately
trying to avoid her wrath.

Sylvia also found she was given different food to the rest of the
family: 'The sandwiches I had were made out of something called
tomato jam – a bit like ketchup – it was so bad I used to throw them
in a stream on the way to school.' They were so unpleasant that she
was relieved to open her bicycle basket one day to find a rat was
eating them. The situation made Sylvia yearn to be back in London
– bombs or no bombs:

> All she wanted was the ten bob a week. I don't think there was a middle
> ground with evacuation: they either saw you as a child or a drudge who
> could do work. The house I stayed in had no electricity, just oil lamps.
> There was a bath in the kitchen with a wooden top. I never said
> anything to my mum because she would have been upset. I was glad
> to get home and I don't think I was alone. The country people thought

we should work for our keep. The abuse was under a cloak of religion. It was all very different from my life in London. I was only there for a year and it was the worst year of my life.

It was culture shock for both sides. Roy Bartlett was nervous of his guardians until he spotted the man's uniform: he was a member of the village's voluntary fire brigade. More importantly, the fire engine was kept in a shed at the end of the garden. However, when time came for their first meal, Roy and his mate refused to eat what the fireman's wife had prepared. As he later recalled, corned beef, biscuits and homemade jam was a less than appetizing meal. The nervousness of the boys continued that evening when they were told to have a bath. At first they refused to undress and then hid behind the bath: 'No way was a strange lady going to see our bits and pieces.' One foster mother was shocked when her new wards refused to sleep in a bed with clean white sheets. The children were from a poor home and, as they explained, their family only used crisp white bed linen for laying out corpses.

Bath-time also caused some consternation in Reg Baker's new home as the culture clash continued. When he was told to write home to tell his parents where he was, his adopted family were shocked that the nine year old could not spell his own name. Next, the blacksmith's wife was shocked when it was his turn to have a bath: as he undressed, and prepared to climb into the old tin bath, she realized he wasn't wearing any underpants. This was normal for the boy – he had never owned any. The situation was soon rectified.

Whilst the more nervous children, and those who were homesick, sat quietly in their new homes, others explored this unfamiliar habitat. They marvelled at the animals they saw in the fields. They had seen such creatures in picture books or at the cinema, but these were living, breathing creatures that seemed to be everywhere. New arrivals had to learn the way of the countryside, needing to be warned not to chase chickens since it would stop them from laying eggs. Reg Baker loved this new world:

The first three days they just let us roam. We chased the cows, sheep and horses. Then the farmer said, 'Don't do that, boys. The cows give us milk, the sheep give us wool and the horses are likely to bloody kick you.' So we settled down and started helping the farmers.

He started to learn about birds and flowers, and discovered how to grow vegetables. Back home their only garden had been a window box that was unable to support any life. When he first saw a hedgehog he thought it was a hairbrush. He climbed conker trees, ran in the fields, drank from streams and had fights with the local kids. Eventually, as the two sides – townies and yokels – learned to understand each other's accents, they settled down, played together and became friends. One of Reg Baker's highlights was being taken out for a drive by a local man who allowed the children to ride around in his car: 'I'd never been in a car, let alone a sports car!'

With so many children sent from the cities, there was an inevitable conflict between the hosts and the visitors. Bad manners, bad language and bed-wetting were among the many complaints heard by those who monitored the evacuees. Children complained of being mistreated by the children of the house in which they had been placed, whilst foster-parents struggled to cope with the strange habits of the evacuees.

Having helped administer the evacuees at Bedford Town Hall, Jean Redman was asked to continue working for the council. The fifteen year old had intended to go to a teacher training college, but with colleges closing after the outbreak of war, her options were limited. With her own school only giving lessons part-time, due to an evacuated school occupying the classrooms for half the week, she spent the rest of her time in the council offices, helping deal with the welfare of evacuees. She was soon asked to work full-time: 'The town clerk asked if I could go full-time at the council a few days a week. The Head said as we were only doing half-days schooling we weren't learning much so I may as well go full-time. So I did.' At first she assisted the billeting officer, dealing with issues raised by

both the evacuees and their foster parents. In reality she spent much
of her time acting as a messenger and making tea, hardly using the
shorthand and typing skills that had been the reason she was
originally selected for the task.

The most interesting part of the job was learning about the
behaviour of people with whom she would never have mixed
pre-war:

> I remember people who were looking after evacuees coming to the
> office and complaining. I remember one woman came in and she said,
> 'And he shit on the window sill!' I thought what is that? I had never
> heard of the word before – and I didn't know what it meant and I didn't
> dare ask. I knew it was something awful by the way she was going on
> to the billeting officer – she didn't want the child any more.

She also dealt with cases where evacuees were moved between
families. One example was a local woman who was unable to cope
with the family she had been sent and turned them out into the
street. The family, a Jewish woman from London and her young
children, was left standing in the street until a local woman took pity
on them and took them in. Although Ivy Woodard had three
children of her own to cope with, she happily made space for the
homeless Londoners. This constant mixing of people had a
considerable influence on all those who experienced it. Mrs
Woodard's six-year-old daughter Margaret was fascinated by their
guests. She watched in awe as they carried out their Friday night
preparations for the Sabbath. All crammed into the small front room
of a council house, the family lit their candles and said their prayers
before retiring. For a child living in a small market town, it was
exposure to a world she had had no idea existed.

Some children found themselves in curious situations. One boy
was sent from London to the Surrey countryside, where he was
billeted with a blind man. However, the man decided to move to
London and took his evacuee with him. In 1940 the boy found

himself, supposedly in a place of safety, actually living in a heavily bombed area of south London.

One of the private evacuees was Terry Charles. Born in June 1927, twelve-year-old Terry was the son of dancers and had spent most of his young life travelling around the UK. Wherever they had worked, he had gone with them, attending some fourteen different schools by the time war broke out. With the coming of war he was taken out of school and 'evacuated' to Cornwall. It was a private arrangement made by his mother:

> I went to my mother's old nanny. She had brought up my mother but was retired and living in Cornwall. But I got bored. It was a little village near St Austell. I would cycle to Newquay to go swimming. It was great fun. There was an old ruin of a monastery called Roach Rock nearby. It was marvellous for children.

For others evacuation simply meant their entire family moving from London and continuing their lives from a new base. In many cases, couples moved in with their parents and wherever possible fathers still commuted into cities to work. For the children, it was little different from spending a summer holiday with their grandparents. One of the children in this situation was ten-year-old Colin Ryder Richardson. In the summer of 1939 he was staying with his mother's parents in Lingfield, Surrey. His parents had kept the children in Surrey as a preliminary precaution as the war clouds gathered. The location was convenient: his barrister father was still able to travel into London for work. On 3 September Colin had been helping his grandfather to dig out an air raid shelter when the sirens sounded: 'Jesus Christ! Where's my gas mask?' were his first thoughts – war really had come swiftly.

The decision was taken that Colin would not return to London or to his school, which was being permanently evacuated. Instead he would stay in Surrey and attend a local school. This worked until he returned to school one day to discover that it too had been evacuated – to Cornwall. The school hadn't been able to contact his parents and was forced to leave Colin behind. He was unconcerned about the interruption to his education:

> Frankly, by 1940 I thought, 'Why have I got to learn French?' The Germans had occupied France, the French will have to speak German. I thought 'Why should I learn any language? I'm going to be shot. At my age, I will end up in the Army, I'll get a rifle and I'll be lucky if I survive.' We just thought about survival, getting extra rations, scrounging food. The whole structure of society was being geared for war.

CHAPTER 3

A Phoney War?

'War isn't fun, it's deadly.'

Len Chester, Royal Marines bugler at age fourteen

The coming of war was not greeted by a wave of overt patriotism, and portraits of the King and Queen were conspicuous by their absence. There was little flag-waving jingoism; instead, the people remained calm and, in many ways, stoical about their situation. This muted response was hardly surprising. So many factors influenced the emotions of a country that had endured four years of war, followed by twenty years of political, economic and social turmoil that inspired a wave of pacifism. Yet as one writer noted: 'the worst mistake of the Axis was to confuse the attitude of the mild, easy-going people of Great Britain with spineless selfishness'.[1] In the first month of the war, the British people might not have been fired up in a patriotic fervour but they were not about to submit to the aggressive intentions of the enemy.

But there was so much more to the story. Maybe it was the sudden change in the street scenes, with vast numbers of children already removed to safety. Maybe it was the horrors of war engrained in the minds of a whole generation of men who had survived the Great War only to see their sons threatened with the same fate. Or maybe it was simply the acceptance of war generated by years of waiting for conflict to come. As one diarist noted of Hitler's annexation of Czechoslovakia: 'So now we shall fight for England not, as I used to say, in Czechoslovakia, but in Middlesex.'[2]

Children, like their parents, threw themselves enthusiastically into the necessary preparations for war. As the entire country became covered in mounds of sandbags, boys eagerly joined their fathers in digging holes to fit air raid shelters and fill sandbags. Helping prepare and fit blackout curtains was a joy to children who wanted to be part of the war effort. When asked to put tape across windows to prevent the glass shattering when bombs fell, some children soon got carried away. They ignored the regular criss-cross network and instead stuck the tape in childish, random patterns that seemed so much more interesting.

It was not just the houses that were transformed. Within days the entire scenery of the country seemed to have changed. Suddenly men – and increasingly women – in uniform seemed to abound. Barrage balloons began to fill the skies. One of the first changes noticed by ten-year-old Colin Ryder Richardson was that female soldiers began inflating barrage balloons opposite his grandparents' home to protect Lingfield racecourse, where local units of the Territorial Army were being mobilized. For a child, it was a fascinating sight and watching these changes became entertainment for the youngster. He watched as pillboxes were built in the North Downs, ready to hold back an invading army intent on heading north into London. At his great-uncle's shop in Reigate a machine-gun post was set up on the first floor since it commanded a good field of fire along the High Street. A large triangle of cement was set beneath the window to act as a mount for the weapon. When their work was done, the soldiers thanked the bewildered shopkeeper and told him someone would return if and when the invasion came.

Even when he returned on day trips to London Colin was confronted by the new reality, watching taxis pulling water pumps for use in fire-fighting and seeing museum-piece fire engines out on duty. As he recalled: 'Already our lives were being totally changed.' One particular blow was felt by pet lovers: with dogs banned from air raid shelters there was a rush to have animals put down. In the first days of war some 400,000 domestic pets were killed by vets.

It was not just the military situation that changed the face of the country. It was the beginning of what seemed like a vast, if enforced, social experiment. The rattle of pram wheels on the paving stones and tarmac were conspicuous by their absence. Elsewhere, in country towns and villages, former city-dwelling mothers who had been evacuated with their young children tried to coax their prams along the rough roads and grass verges of the new homes. From the mud of the countryside to the steeply cobbled lanes of fishing villages, Britain's mothers had to learn to adapt.

Mothers brought the ways of the city to the villages. Shocking as it was for their hosts, some of the evacuated women tucked up their children for the night and then made their way to village pubs. Heads turned as the locals were surprised to see women casually ordering drinks just as they had done back home. In one Essex village London mothers changed the look of the whole area as the influx of more than 500 mothers and babies almost doubled the population.

It was not just the evacuees who changed the face of the countryside. In sleepy villages there was a wave of activity as the young women of the 'Land Army' arrived to take up the work of men who had gone to war. The arrival of these young women was a breath of fresh air in villages unchanged for so long. Likewise, families began to arrive in the countryside, spending their holidays engaged in agricultural labour. Village children were also drafted into the war effort, with over 30,000 working on farms, earning great praise for previously concerned farmers. Ken Durston – twelve years old at the outbreak of war – recalled the effect on rural Somerset:

Pre-war our village was very quiet – everyone knew everyone else. Suddenly there were WAAFs moved into the balloon sites and you got

to know more about the outside world. I'd never known anything
before that. We lived in a little cottage with one bedroom for seven of
us and I'd never been outside the village up to that point. Most of the
girls on the barrage balloons were only eighteen – and they were
looking for company. The young lads would creep round there at meal
times and get invited in for tea.

But if the arrival of children changed the face of the countryside, then
the lack of children changed the cities. Though thousands had defied
the order to evacuate, the authorities had made little provision for
those left behind. Their schools had closed, their teachers had left for
the countryside and their classrooms had been taken over for civil
defence purposes. In London alone, two thirds of schools had been
converted to civil defence facilities – such as first-aid posts and fire
stations – by authorities who believed all school-age children would
be successfully evacuated. More than 100,000 teachers had followed
the children from the capital. In Croydon, every school in the
borough was closed for a full six months from the start of war. Across
the country, some one million unevacuated children found themselves with no school to go to. With nowhere to go, in the first weeks
of war the children left behind experienced a new freedom – an
extended holiday that most relished at the time.

   For Alf Morris, what started as a welcome break became a lifetime
regret:

   I just stopped school. The air raid wardens took over the schools. I used
   to go to the park, take a few jam sandwiches and a bottle of water. I'd
   play football or have a game of cricket, and later, as soon as the air raid
   sirens went, I'd run home and get in the Anderson shelter. It was a
   strange life. Your whole life was taken up with sitting in an air raid
   shelter.

Even when the schools reopened, with crowded classrooms catering
for an often transient population of children, education was

sporadic. Even when schools were open, absenteeism was recorded at rising some 50 per cent on pre-war figures. This rupturing of normality was lost on the children, but was later of significance for boys like Alf Morris: 'That was the one thing in my life that I regret. Education was hit-and-miss. Sometimes you could go, sometimes they didn't let you in. I don't mind admitting it, I was a dunce when I left school at fourteen.' He was not alone: one pupil reported that every member of her class failed a scholarship exam. In Scotland pupils recalled their teachers assisting them by giving them the answers to exam questions: after all, it was not the children's fault they had not been in lessons.

Whilst boys like Alf happily played football and hung around in local parks, others were less innocent: in the early part of the war juvenile delinquency rose by 40 per cent. With just fifteen of 900 London County Council schools open in early 1940, there were attempts to bring wayward children under control. Many churches and social groups opened their facilities to local children, offering games and lessons in such curious subjects as Esperanto, in an effort to keep children occupied. Some councils opened dedicated rooms for children within their libraries, where children could listen to the broadcasts but also be encouraged to read the available books.

Yet whilst so many children were slowly attempting to settle into their new surroundings or enjoying their new-found freedoms, others were already embroiled in war. For some youngsters war immediately entered their lives, catapulting them into the front line. While history books reflect the 'Phoney War' that supposedly lasted until spring 1940, truth was far different and the cabin boys, galley boys and deck boys of the merchant fleet were suddenly at the forefront of the conflict. The Merchant Navy played a vital role for the UK. The country relied on exports to raise revenue and imports of food to sustain its population. In peace and war, it was the merchant fleet that fulfilled this task. As the Germans knew, if they could prevent the Merchant Navy from carrying out its duties, then Britain would surely fall.

As they began their dangerous mission they were protected by the Royal Navy, the one arm of the British military that could claim to be the equal of any service in the world. Just like the merchant fleet, the Royal Navy was home to numerous boys under the age of eighteen who, despite their youth, were considered old enough to be at the forefront of war. Kenneth Toop, who had joined the Royal Navy in 1938 aged fifteen, explained the most common reason for youngsters joining the Navy:

> When I left school, if you were extremely fortunate, you could get an apprenticeship. But you had to have money to pay for it. For a lot of us it wasn't possible. I couldn't even take up a scholarship. My mum and dad couldn't afford a school cap and blazer for me. We were more interested in earning a few shillings as an errand boy.

After initially working as a presser in a cleaning firm, Ken left Basingstoke with two mates and joined the Royal Navy.

Though most 'boys' in the Merchant Navy were aged between fifteen and seventeen, some were far younger. Among the youngest was twelve-year-old John Chinnery. Born to a teenage, single mother in Edinburgh in April 1927, John had known the depths of poverty through the 1930s. Despite the hardships of the time, he didn't let his situation affect him. He worked hard, delivering bread rolls around his local area at 5.30 each morning, before handing over his wages to his mother and going to school on an empty stomach. Yet he accepted his situation – after all, there were plenty of others around him experiencing much worse – and enjoyed spending long hours in a library, whiling them away alongside the older, unemployed men.

For John, the turning point came in the summer of 1939, just after his twelfth birthday. One day, he wandered down to Leith docks to look at the ships. As he stood on the dockside, staring at a ship, he was spotted by the ship's cook. Leaning out over the rails, the cook called him to come aboard and take a look around the ship. Out of curiosity, he accepted the offer. His escort soon realized that John was hungry and asked him to join the crew for a meal. The boy eagerly accepted, quickly emptying his plate. Then the cook spoke: 'We need a boy. Would you like to join the crew?' The offer had come out of the blue, John hadn't been looking for a job – after all, he was still at school. However, he went home and explained it to his mother: if he went to sea, he would be earning money and there would be one fewer mouth to feed. She agreed and happily signed the necessary papers allowing him to go to sea. And so, aged just twelve, John Chinnery made his first trip, sailing on a vessel that worked the Scottish coastal waters. Yet, just months after he joined the ship, war was declared and the schoolboy found himself heading off around the world at the mercy of enemy submarines and surface raiders. In the years ahead he sailed the Atlantic, the North Sea, Arctic and Mediterranean.

At first it seemed war did little to alter the ship's routine and it still travelled along the east coast of Scotland. Then one morning a German reconnaissance plane appeared overhead. The next day it returned, until it became such a regular occurrence that the sailors began to wave at it. One day the reconnaissance plane did not appear and in its place came a bomber that unloaded its deadly cargo towards the ship, with one bomb striking the funnel. For John Chinnery one thing was certain: his war had started.

More typical of the youngsters at sea was Ron Bosworth. Born in Bristol in May 1923, he had first gone to sea in 1938, making two trips to Jamaica on a 'banana-boat'. For fourteen-year-old Ron, the sea was a natural choice. His father and grandfather were both sailors and his mother was used to life as a seaman's wife: now she needed to get used to life as the mother of a deck boy. Like many youngsters, he had attempted to get an apprenticeship with a shipping company only to discover his family couldn't afford it. So, instead of going to sea to train to become an officer, he took the first job he could find. He later recalled joining his first ship, the SS *Carare*:

> First you signs on in the saloon room. Then you goes down to your cabin and are given your sleeping gear, a straw palliasse and two hairy blankets. You don't sleep in hammocks, it was cots. They were full of bugs. Every so often they used to take the bunks off and put them in boiling water to kill the bugs.

Heading off on his first voyage to the West Indies, he had watched as his mother cried on the quayside. Yet he had no fears as his mind was full of stories of adventure on the high seas: 'I was going to where all the pirates came from.'

Through 1938 and 1939, Ron was untroubled by the political crises engulfing Europe. As a teenager with money in his pocket, travelling back and forwards to the West Indies on a monthly basis, bringing home presents for family and Jamaican rum for his father, he was enjoying life. The storm clouds of war were of far less importance than the real storm clouds he encountered in the Atlantic. Just one day after the declaration of war he embarked on his fourteenth trip to the West Indies, returning a month later. On that first trip under wartime conditions there was little to report; they did their job as normal, sailed for the West Indies and returned laden with bananas. Next month he made a final visit to the West Indies before joining a new ship. It would be some years before the merchant fleet again found room for a luxury product such as bananas.

On 9 December 1939, aged sixteen, Ron joined the MV (Motor Vessel) *Eildon* at his home port of Avonmouth. Leaving port, the *Eildon* had only reached Ilfracombe on the North Devon coast when she ran into trouble:

> I was on the wheel when she struck a mine. I ain't never panicked in my life. We launched the lifeboats but the ship broke her back. One of the bunker chambers was empty, but it was filled with coal dust. They reckon when it hit the mine the explosion ignited the dust. That broke her in two. I can remember one chap on the starboard of the lifeboat. It up-ended and he was the only one we lost.

Rowing away from the sinking ship, they were soon picked up by an RAF launch and returned to shore. It was a journey that belied the existence of a 'Phoney War'. Like John Chinnery, Ron Bosworth's war had started early and it was the first of a number of sinkings before he reached his eighteenth birthday.

The boys of the merchant fleet were not the only ones coming to terms with being at war. The 'Phoney War' was also no more than hollow words for the sailors of the Royal Navy, which went to war immediately and took its boys with them. On 17 September 1939, exactly two weeks after the declaration of war, the aircraft carrier HMS *Courageous* was sunk, taking seven boys down with it.

Far to the north of the towns and cities that had evacuated their children was a small population of teenagers for whom war was already very real. Anchored at Scapa Flow in the Orkneys was the once-mighty battleship HMS *Royal Oak*. She was there to provide anti-aircraft defence to the other ships of the Home Fleet. On the night of 13 October 1939 a German submarine slipped through the defences and fired three torpedoes at the *Royal Oak*. Onboard were 165 boy sailors under the age of eighteen. After the first explosion, many of the boys jumped from their hammocks ready for whatever might come next. Within seconds the Chief Petty Officer entered the after mess deck and told the fifty boys within not to panic and to return to their hammocks. Trusting of his words, they settled down again. Then came a second, even bigger explosion. Some of the boys were thrown from their hammocks and immediately began to rush for the exits. Within seconds the lights went out and they could feel the ship turning beneath their feet.

Fifteen-year-old Kenneth Toop was sleeping when the first torpedo struck, but was awoken by the boy in the next hammock, who told him: 'You'd better get out, Lofty, something's happened.' Dressing in just his shoes and trousers, he made his way from the mess deck. At first he tried to escape through a route crowded with boys but abandoned it, choosing to move forward through the screen doors, reaching the deck by a clearer route.

As sixteen-year-old Henry Cox rushed for the exit he realized he was not wearing any trousers, turned back, collected his trousers and reached the deck just in time. One boy later recalled how he was fortunate to have the bunk beside the ladder, meaning he was first out on to the deck above. As the escaping sailors rushed for the next ladder, they were forced to stumble through the deck in complete darkness. Up the next ladder, the first escaping boys reached the open air. Looking back on the disaster, Bert Pocock, who had escaped because he was sleeping beside the escape ladder, thought of the horrors the boys left behind must have endured: 'They'd have struggled against each other to get out of the hatch, but in the pitch dark they wouldn't have known where to go.'[3]

Out in the darkness of the deck, the boys soon realized they had to abandon ship as soon as possible. One recalled crawling down the tilting deck carefully until he reached the water. Once in the cold waters of Scapa Flow he struck out as fast as he could, desperate not to be sucked under by the sinking ship. As Henry Cox reached the decks he was glad he had fetched his trousers. To reach the water he had to slide down the barnacle-encrusted hull. Without trousers they would have shredded his skin.

Another boy who was relieved to have put his trousers on was Kenneth Toop. As he reached the deck, the *Royal Oak* began to list to starboard and he clambered over the port side, moving along the hull towards the position where he expected the ship's drifter, *Daisy*, to be tied: 'Of course the *Daisy* had to cast off, as she would have floundered. I was left with no option but to move up the side towards the keel, until sliding into the sea was unavoidable. I entered into a thick covering of oil on a freezing sea.' Although not a strong swimmer, Ken struck out for a wooden frame he saw floating nearby. He climbed on to the floating frame, where he found some other exhausted members of the crew.

Within minutes the mighty battleship had slipped beneath the surface. Desperate sailors – men and boys – swam for safety through the oily waters, hoping to reach the rescue ships that had raced to the scene. Ken Toop waited for what seemed like hours, until the *Daisy* picked him up and took him to HMS *Pegasus*. Safely onboard, he began the long and hard task of scrubbing the thick, sticky oil from his body. It was a thankless task, but was better than the alternatives: of the 165 boys serving on HMS *Royal Oak*, 125 had been lost when she sank.

The next day the survivors were sent to the mainland and two days later they were taken by train to Portsmouth. As Ken Toop remembered, as he travelled, his hair was still thick with oil: 'It was awful. We looked like the seabirds you see after oil spills.' It was weeks before he was finally clean. Arriving in Portsmouth, he was given ten days' survivor's leave, then the fifteen year old was told to report to the dockyard where he joined HMS *Manchester* and headed off to war as a member of the crew of a six-inch gun turret. One year later he was torpedoed for a second time. As he later recalled of life at sea in wartime: 'It was awful – bloody awful. You spent long hours closed up below the waterlines, at action stations. I look back on it and it was indescribable. I just hoped I was going to get through it.'

As the survivors arrived in Portsmouth, it became clear to many that the so-called 'Phoney War' was a myth. In the Royal Marines barracks, there had begun a procession of boys arriving back from sunken ships. For Len Chester, seeing these first survivors was a pivotal moment in his understanding of the true cost of war:

> The thought of war suddenly became apparent. We were getting the first survivors coming back. Two survivors from HMS *Glorious* came back to the barracks. We talked to these boys and they told us about life at sea. So war became real to us. Then, two of my mates – Aubrey Priestley and Harry Mountford – were lost on the *Royal Oak*. Suddenly you realize there's a war going on.

And so it continued. As the weeks passed, more and more boys became casualties. By the end of 1939 almost 140 boy sailors had been killed in action. When the nation rejoiced at the scuttling of the German battleship the *Graf Spee*, they were unaware that the Battle of the River Plate had cost the lives of two boys, Ronald Hill and Ernest Squire. By May 1940, when the Germans invaded Western Europe, the Royal Navy had lost another fourteen boys. In the days following the sinking of the *Royal Oak* a diarist noted: 'The *Royal Oak* has been sunk. Last month it was the *Courageous*. I have heard there are thirty such ships. How many of them can we afford to lose and yet win?'[4] These haunting words, sensing the perils presented to the Royal Navy in face of the might of the resurgent German Navy, acted as a reflection to the country's situation: how many youngsters could the country lose to war before the whole strength of the nation sapped away?

As 1939 drew to a close and the first full year of war commenced, a sense of restlessness engulfed the nation. Following the first flush of excitement – the evacuations, the air raid alerts, the mobilization of thousands of men for war service – everything had seemingly gone quiet. Defying so many expectations, London hadn't been flattened by high explosive or chemical weapons dropped to poison the population. Instead, short of the sinking of a few ships, the world had kept turning. Yes, there were shortages in the shops and, yes, large parts of the population had been moved around the country, but daily life continued. It seemed that something had to change: either war would erupt or Britain would gradually drift back to its old familiar routines. At first it seemed the latter option was in the ascendance.

Once winter was over, there was a genuine change in the villages and country towns of Great Britain. After the harsh winter many of the evacuees were frustrated in the countryside. There was nothing to do, there had been no bombing of their old homes and conditions in their new homes were often cramped. Schools were overcrowded and teaching was anything but efficient. The authorities did their best, but it was simply too much to take entire cities, rehouse them in the countryside and expect life to continue as normal. Then there was homesickness. With many children pining not just for their parents but for the familiar streets of home, the trickle of returning children became a flood. More than 300,000 of the 734,000 evacuees chose to ignore the dangers of the wartime city and returned home by the start of 1940, and by March 1940 only around 300,000 evacuees remained in the countryside. At first the authorities attempted to stop the drift back to the cities. They tried to undermine the overwhelming sense of homesickness by offering cheap tickets for parents to visit their children. Some parents were even asked to sign contracts accepting they would not take their children home. In London newspaper adverts were placed, encouraging parents to send their children back into the countryside. But it was hopeless: the drift continued and when parents were officially asked to register their children for re-evacuation, some 100,000 refused.

Out in Oxfordshire, Reg Baker was happy to be in the countryside. After the poverty of his upbringing in London, the countryside was a welcome relief. However, he soon realized some of his friends were less enthusiastic about their new surroundings. One child had run away three times, only to be returned each time to the village. One unhappy child had been locked in the attic, whilst another had been locked in the shed: these were extreme measures to prevent the drift back to the cities. But Reg wasn't concerned: he was eating well, putting on weight and was loved by his foster-family. He knew it wasn't his real home but what little homesickness he felt was tempered by the knowledge that his hard-working parents would have little time for him back in London. On the occasions he felt like running back to London, he would sit on a wall and watch lorries passing by. Whenever he saw one bearing the name 'London Brick Company' he would think about jumping on and riding back to the city. He later discovered it would have been a foolish move: the 'London Brick Company' was actually based fifty miles north of London.

Those who did return to the cities entered a world that had changed, despite the absence of bombing. Parents happily received their kids at home but then discovered that there were few schools open to accommodate them. Their teachers remained in the countryside and at the officially evacuated schools, many classrooms remained in the hands of the ARP or the fire service. Those schools that were open were overcrowded and offered irregular classes. As a result, many of the returning evacuees simply spent their time in the streets. Cinemas and amusement arcades reported increasing numbers of youngsters hanging around with nothing to do. It was a welcome return home, but not a situation that could continue indefinitely. With increasing children to cater for, schools had to be reopened, but only after shelters were hastily dug in the grounds, with benches for the children to sit on and lights by which the teachers could read to the children. One teacher reported being unable to use a classroom since it had been converted into a mortuary in expectation of heavy civilian casualties. At one school, children were given a year's worth of class work and then told they should do it at home.

As the drift continued, pressure increased on evacuees remaining in the countryside. As his classmates drifted back home to Ealing, Roy Bartlett found himself increasingly wanting to join them. With fewer Londoners in the school, the evacuees were no longer educated separately, instead joining the main classes. It was an uncomfortable time: 'We were outcasts. "Cockney kids" was a term of derision.' Added to the fact that he had never even wanted to be evacuated, it was time to go home. After nine months his parents came to collect him, returning him to his old school in Ealing where he rejoined his classmates. Arriving home he found little had changed: there had been no bombing and his school was due to reopen. The one major difference was the cellar of his parents' home. They took him down the wooden stairs beneath the shop. Inside the stockroom were supporting pillars and beams, built-in bunks and a set of stairs leading to the pavement entrance. There were even doorways connecting to the adjoining shops. Now, instead of just being their home, it was a public shelter.

As the children returned to the cities, some adults began to disappear. January 1940 saw the call-up of the second batch of conscripts into the 'Militia', the draft of twenty-one year olds into the Army. At the same time, volunteers continued to arrive at recruiting offices and more reservists were 're-called to the colours'. In north London, fourteen-year-old Stan Scott noticed that his father had failed to return home from his work as a bus driver: 'Mum was worried. She thought he'd had an accident. So I walked to the bus station at Wood Green to look for him. They said he'd not been in that day and told me to try Finchley. So I humped it up to Finchley. They told me to try Wood Green!' Realizing his father had not been at work at all that day, he decided to search the Royal Fusiliers offices in Holborn, a place his father had taken him on occasions as a child:

> I was wandering around and suddenly a sergeant said to me, 'What do you want? Who are you looking for?' I said, 'My dad.' He told me to look on the board where there was a list of names of men who were being drafted. There he was. I thought, 'Shit, I'm going to have to tell Mum.' When I finally got home she asked me what I'd found. 'Mum, he's back in the Army.' A couple of days later we got a letter from him, marked 'BEF France'. 'Dear Rose, I'm back in the Army. I'm in France with the reserve.'

Meanwhile, for those youngsters who had not been evacuated, life continued as normal across much of the country. For Peter Richards that meant working in the Post Office by day and spending his evenings at his local youth club:

> What affected my generation was the National Association of Boys and Girls Clubs. Everywhere there were youth clubs. I used to go to one in Woburn Place. They were non-religious and carried out a number of activities. They did PE, gym, boxing and running. There were lots of competitions. There weren't enough days in the week. I was involved

in the Young Communist League and the youth club, and of course I
was working.

Sport dominated much of his spare time. He boxed in the gym and
went running in nearby Regent's Park. He also noticed how some
of the less active members of the youth club began appearing on the
sports fields: 'When they got called up they didn't want to be a
complete failure – they wanted to be reasonably fit.' He laughed to
see one newly animated colleague slow down after just 200 yards of
a run. Stopping, he pulled out a packet of cigarettes from his shorts
and exclaimed: 'I think I'll have a fag.'

His mate John Cotter had also by now left school. He had passed
a scholarship to continue at school but decided against it: 'I wasn't
doing very well. I just wasted my time. I was lazy. I was going to be
held back a year before I passed my matriculation so I thought I
might as well go and get a job.' His mother soon found a job for him,
securing a place in the civil service at the prestigious Colonial
Office, where he worked in a department licensing exports from
around the Empire and earned nineteen shillings and sixpence a
week. His mother believed this would be a good career move,
ensuring him a good pension in later life. However, in the winter of
1939–40, young men like John were not looking that far ahead.

Whilst youths like John Cotter did their best to ignore the war,
others found there was no escape. In October 1939, fourteen-year-
old Len Chester had mastered all the necessary bugle calls and
'passed out', ready to join a ship. In December he received orders
to go to Scapa Flow to join HMS *Iron Duke*. Travelling north, he tried
to prepare himself mentally for joining a warship. Arriving at the
ship, he discovered there were only two boys among the 1,000-man
crew. He also discovered this would mean living in virtual isolation:

Boys were not allowed to fraternize with the men. I wasn't allowed to
talk to them. I wasn't allowed to go on their mess deck. I had to live in
the sergeant's mess. I was mentored by Sergeant 'Lofty' Dewey. If I had

to speak to a trained soldier – I had to stand to attention and say 'Yes, Trained Soldier!'

Len soon learned that the strict rules were in place for a very good reason: 'It was partly for my own protection: Paedophilia was about in those days – it's not a new thing!' As part of his introduction to life onboard, the sergeant told him: 'Don't ever get yourself in a confined space with Marine so and so.' At first he was not certain what the sergeant really meant; after all, he had been sheltered from such matters until very recently: 'I didn't really have an understanding of it. To be frank, when I joined up at fourteen I still thought that babie's came from belly buttons.' Len later recalled that he grew used to a daily barrage of sexual innuendo – some of it innocent, some of it not – faced by 'Boys' on warships. It didn't take him long to gain an increasing awareness of what he had been warned about. It became clear the Royal Navy's reputation for 'Rum, Bum and Baccy' was based on fact:

One time, I was cleaning out the baggage store and I was cornered by one of the men I'd been warned about. But I was too fly for him. I was streetwise. I got out. He wasn't going to ask my permission: if I hadn't got out of there, it would have been a case of rape.

Traumatic though such experiences were, there were greater dangers awaiting Len Chester in Scapa Flow. In March 1940 German aircraft attacked the *Iron Duke*: 'My action station was beside the captain. And I ran messages for him. Everyone was rushing here and there. It was ever so exciting. I wasn't frightened. I didn't have time to be frightened. I was dashing everywhere.' As he moved around the ship, the ship's anti-aircraft guns were firing at the enemy planes:

One of the three-inch guns was just above the quarterdeck. I came out of an armoured door just as it fired. That gun was the worst in the Navy because it gave a 'crack'. It went off and blew me back through the door. I went deaf, but when it came back, I'd lost the hearing in my right ear. That never came back. We had no earplugs or ear protection. Later I saw men whose ears were bleeding from the noise of the guns.

Filled with adrenaline, Len ignored the very real dangers as he continued his duties:

The bullets were close. The captain had given me a message to take to another officer. I was on my way when I heard this plane coming down. So I started running. I got through the armoured door, just before the bullets hit. A bomb hit forward of where I was running. If the pilot had pressed the button a second sooner, then I would have been the youngest active service casualty of the war. I was still weeks away from my fifteenth birthday.[5]

When the raid was over, a sense of calm was quickly restored and everybody swiftly returned to their duties. But first Len decided to collect a souvenir of the air raid: 'I've still got the bullet that I dug out of the deck.'

The fourteen year old had come under attack for the first time. What made this attack notable was that after flying away from the *Iron Duke*, the German pilots bombed a nearby cottage. The only casualty, James Isbister, became the first civilian of the war to die on British soil. Just weeks later, Len Chester had his first introduction to death: 'It was the first time I'd seen a coffin in close proximity, let alone six of them.' On 3 May 1940 he was selected to play 'The Last Post' at the funeral of six seamen who lost their lives, some from a Royal Navy minesweeper, some from a Norwegian merchant ship. Arriving at the cemetery, he found there were many senior officers in attendance, led by Rear Admiral Harold Walker, better known as 'Hooky' because of the hook worn in place of a hand:

I was completely overawed and completely alone with my fear of all this ceremony with no one to tell me what to do. The mass funeral started and then it came to my solo piece, Last Post and Reveille. I started well, but halfway through I could feel my lips going like jelly, until eventually, I unashamedly burst into tears.

He was expecting to be in trouble for his emotional reaction. However, Admiral Walker laid his hook on the youngster's shoulder and said, 'Never mind, laddie.'

CHAPTER 4

Eruption – May 1940

'After Dunkirk, I was guarding vulnerable points, like radar stations. But I had no bullets for my rifle.'

Ted Roberts, a soldier at fourteen years old

On 9 April 1940, German forces attacked Denmark and Norway, where they finally came face-to-face with British troops. The next day Denmark surrendered, then on 3 May the British and French were forced to withdraw from Norway. One week later the Germans attacked Belgium and the Netherlands, and the British advanced into Belgium to meet them. Next, the assault on France was unleashed. After seven months of waiting, the so-called 'Phoney War' was finally over.

For John Cotter and Peter Richards, the German invasion of the Low Countries and France meant one thing: their cycling holiday to the Isle of Wight had to be cancelled. With war raging just across the Channel, the two boys were more concerned with spending a long-weekend in the saddle than with what was going on in Europe. Furthermore, Peter had something else on his mind: his sixteenth birthday and the Civil Service examination that would determine his future in the Post Office.

For some British children the German invasion of the Low

Countries had an immediate and violent effect. Sisters Yvonne and Julienne Vanhandenhoeve were living in the Belgian port of Antwerp with their English mother and Belgian father. Born in south London in 1928, Yvonne and her family left London after Mr Vanhandenhoeve's fur business had collapsed following the Wall Street Crash. Her sister Julienne had been born in Belgium in 1930. At home the two girls spoke English, whilst at school they spoke Flemish, and with their Belgian family they spoke a mixture of Flemish and French. As Julienne later recalled, she only spoke English until the day she started school, when she cried her eyes out in confusion to hear everyone speaking a language she could not understand. As both sisters recalled: when they were in Antwerp they thought of themselves as Belgians, but when they were in England, they thought of themselves as English.

With Belgium under threat from Germany, the sisters and their mother were uncertain of what the future might hold. Then, in May 1940, with the Germans advancing, eleven-year-old Yvonne became increasingly aware of the ominous situation: 'We didn't have much time to think about things. The war started and suddenly we were off. People were loading up carts. We saw people we thought had come from Holland. Maybe they were heading to France? We didn't know.' However, although she realized her parents were concerned, Yvonne was surprised to learn the decision had been taken to leave for England. Her mother was desperate that they should make the journey.

The first stop on their journey was the British Consulate where they were given the news that a ship – SS *Ville de Bruges* – was leaving for England on 13 May, but that only British nationals would be allowed to board. As a result, their father would have to stay behind in war-torn Belgium, with the intention that he would follow later. They rapidly packed up their possessions including clothing, paintings, photo albums, sheet music and the family silver. The girls even took their schoolbooks in the expectation that their education would continue in London. Next came the moment that the family

was divided. At 4 p.m. the girls and their mother left the family
home to begin the journey to London. As Yvonne recalled: 'It
seemed exciting. It was a surprise. I had to accept the idea. I wasn't
quite certain why we were going to England. But it did seem to make
sense.' Despite the sudden change, the girls were told by their
mother that they would be staying with their aunt in Morden, as
they normally did on their annual holidays. If anything, this journey
was even more convenient than the route used each summer. The
ship was heading directly from Antwerp to Tilbury: normally they
had to travel by rail to the Hook of Holland to board for the trip
across the North Sea. As the ship departed the girls felt they were
simply heading off on another summer holiday.

Having said goodbye and boarded the ship, their whole world
began to change. Only women and children had been allowed to
board, with the Consulate having told them no men would be
allowed to travel in order to ensure the Germans would not target
the ship. It made little difference. The next morning the vessel had
begun the journey along the River Scheldt towards the sea when it
was targeted by enemy aircraft. Standing on the upper decks, as
Yvonne Vanhandenhoeve remembered they were saying goodbye
to their home city, the civilians heard the ominous drone of
approaching aircraft. The sense of excitement that had greeted their
departure was soon submerged beneath the violent reality of their
attempt to escape to reach England. As the girls watched, German
planes opened fire with machine-guns, strafing the decks. As
Yvonne recalled: 'It was nerve-wracking because the noise never
stopped. The aircraft swooped down: it was the first we knew of the
troubles ahead.'

The girls and their mother rushed inside, sheltering from the
bullets that rattled off the decks, when they heard a terrible noise.
The staircase they were standing beside was torn open as a bomb
crashed through, exploding in a machine-room below decks. The
explosion killed a number of the would-be refugees. The girls'
mother later wrote of their ordeal:

> I have a nasty leg ... I was standing with the girls just at the front of the staircase. As a result [of the bomb] the banister broke down on top of my leg. I pulled my leg through all the woodwork to run up the few stairs on to the next deck where we all lay on our stomachs because we all expected the German plane to come back again and machine-gun us.

Surprisingly, there was little panic – it seemed the crew were more shaken than many of the passengers. As Yvonne remembered: 'We realized something was happening, but as children I don't think you panic so much. I think I panicked more afterwards.'

With the *Ville de Bruges* heavily damaged, the decision was taken to abandon ship. The lifeboats were swung out ready for the passengers to disembark. With the ship burning, the passengers were ushered on to the exposed decks, given numbers allocating them to lifeboats and told to prepare to disembark. However, there was another surprise for the Vanhandenhoeve family: 'Instead of looking after women and children, the seamen were more concerned about saving their own lives and they got into the boats before us. They weren't at all helpful. They weren't worried about the women and children. Everyone was looking after number-one.' As Julienne later recalled, their poor mother had to fight with the ship's crew to get help to board the lifeboat.

After a two-hour wait, the girls and their mother were able to board a lifeboat and were rowed to the riverbank. They were offered passage on a police launch back to Antwerp but refused, not feeling safe on the water. Disembarking, they faced a two-hour walk along the riverbank, through a tunnel and back to the docks, where they could board a tram to their home. As they walked back, they were struck by the sense of uncertainty. They had packed up their home, left behind their father, been machine-gunned, had their ship blown from under them and been lucky to escape with their lives. They had lost most of their possessions – including all their clothing and many treasured family items such as photographs. As their mother later recorded, the girls cried their eyes out when they realized how much had been lost, including their communion dresses, rosary beads and schoolbooks. To comfort them, she explained that there was only one thing that really mattered: it was a miracle they had survived the attack on the ship and had been safely reunited with their father. Now they were heading home. All Yvonne could think was: 'What will happen next?'.

The next big shock was for their father, as his wife and children returned to the family home. At first their mother hoped the family might be able to reach Ostend and find a passage back to England. However, she soon realized there was little chance of getting her girls on to another ship after what they had experienced. Furthermore, the girls were sick after the effects of the smoke onboard the ship. Before any such plans for escape could come to fruition, events overtook them. The city was heavily bombed by the Germans, forcing the family to take shelter in their cellar.

Within days the German Army occupied the city, moving in to requisition property and occupy homes. There was nothing the family could do to replace their possessions and no way of applying for compensation; after all, the British Consulate was now closed. Then came the question of their status: fortunately, their mother's dual nationality meant that the family were not interned by the Germans and were able to live in relative security.

During a similar evacuation of Britons from the Belgian port of Ostend, a group of British schoolgirls joined military personnel onboard a British freighter, SS *Abukir*. There were around 200 people onboard when she was attacked by German E-boats. The *Abukir* sank within a minute, with just twenty-one passengers and two crewmen being rescued. Among the casualties was seventeen-year-old William Blair of Belfast, an ex-boy of the Prince of Wales Sea Training Hostel in London's Limehouse.

Just four days after the Germans launched their assault westwards, the British government took the next step towards the full mobilization of the nation for total war. On 14 May the Secretary of

State for War, Anthony Eden, announced that he was forming a new force for the defence of the realm. The Local Defence Volunteers (LDV) was intended to be a voluntary militia of around 150,000 men aged between seventeen and sixty-five. Such was the clamour to sign up for this unit that some men were reported to have arrived at police stations before Eden had even completed his broadcast. In the first twenty-four hours more than 250,000 men and boys had volunteered, meaning that the authorities soon ran out of enrolment forms. By September, with the nation standing almost alone against the might of the Nazis and fearing imminent invasion, the newly christened 'Home Guard' had 1,700,000 volunteers.

In these early days men turned out for duty armed with whatever weapons were available: homemade 'pikes' little more than a length of wood with a bread knife tied to the top, golf clubs, heavy walking sticks – anything that might do injury to the enemy. Retired officers paraded with their old service revolvers, whilst shotguns and hunting rifles were common in rural areas. Those able to secure a little petrol constructed 'Molotov cocktails' or made primitive flamethrowers from stirrup-pumps designed for fighting fires. Units lucky enough to have machine-guns mounted them in carts that could be towed behind cars, giving them the semblance of being a mobile unit. Others were so badly equipped they initially equipped themselves with rotten potatoes studded with old razor blades. One young volunteer, who had just been turned down by the Army as too young, recalled his father appearing with a German rifle he had brought home from France in 1918 and fitting it with a bayonet that had spent the intervening years as a fire poker.

Yet whilst history has overwhelmingly concentrated on the image of doddering old men – veterans of the Boer and Great Wars – turning out night after night as impromptu heroes willing to sacrifice themselves to save the nation, there was another altogether fresher element to the force. Thousands of teenage boys heeded the call to arms. Often ignoring the official lower age limit of seventeen, youths flocked to join the Home Guard. One teenager recalled how he and his mates, all underage, joined the Home Guard because the officer was the father of one of his mates and decided they should join. He later recalled being refused beer in a pub due to his age. His officer confronted the landlord and told him that if a boy was old enough to wear a uniform, he was old enough to drink beer. One lad, who claimed to be the youngest member of the Home Guard, was just fourteen. He was recruited whilst working at the Admiralty, having got that job due to his membership of the Sea Scouts.

For all the jokes about the Home Guard, they played a serious role in the conflict. The very first Home Guard unit successfully to engage the enemy was an anti-aircraft unit on the south coast, two of whose members were sixteen years old. It was not just anti-aircraft gunners of the Home Guard who were in danger. In total, more than 1,200 members of the organization were killed whilst on duty or died of their wounds. Many were killed in air raids or in accidents with weapons they handled without adequate training.

Yet in the early days of the Home Guard, despite the very real threat of invasion, many of their activities seemed like a game. As one young recruit noted, it was, 'Like playing Indians but with a real rifle.'[1] The childish nature of events that summer was summed up by the experience of a unit that attempted to drill on a patch of waste ground. They were driven off by a group of cricket-playing boys who called out: 'But, mister, we were playing 'ere first.'[2] One youngster who joined the Home Guard was sixteen-year-old John Cotter:

There was a unit at the Colonial Office so I joined it. I think we were all expected to join. We all had to shuffle off down to Bisley to practise rifle-shooting. Initially, when I was on night duty at the Colonial Office, they gave me a baton. I presume they told me, 'If the SS appear at the end of the street, you wave the baton and shout "Stop!"' I was sixteen years old. I had no uniform, just an armband with "LDV" on it. I was supposed to defend the Colonial Office!'

Another sixteen-year-old volunteer was Geoff Pulzer, an account-
ant's clerk in the City of London. In the months leading up to war,
Geoff, a pupil at the Haberdashers' Aske's Boys' School, in
Cricklewood, north London, had taken little interest in politics. He
was also less than concerned by his studies, meaning the war had an
immediate effect on his life:

> I wasn't a brilliant scholar. The school was evacuated to Mill Hill and
> I had to go there twice a week. So my mother couldn't see any point
> in my staying on. So after the autumn term I was taken out. At first I
> worked in the East End making cases for barometers. I had this awful
> journey across London and all I did was sweep up wood shavings and
> make tea for the other workers. So my mother found me work as a
> clerk with an accountant in the City.

Though his academic work had been unremarkable, Geoff had taken
an interest in one element of public school life: the Officer Training
Corps (OTC). 'I had taken the OTC seriously enough. I wasn't
academic or a great sportsman. But I was very good with the rifle. I
was in the school shooting team. I shot for the school at Bisley and we
won the shield. I enjoyed it.' He soon began to realize this was one
talent that might be useful. Previously, he hadn't taken much notice
of the newspapers or the radio. In May 1940 Geoff suddenly realized
that the war was very real. Upon hearing about the creation of the
Local Defence Volunteers, he discussed it with a friend and decided
to volunteer: 'My mother wasn't very happy about me joining. At
first we just had the armband – nothing else. It was quite funny. It
seemed silly walking around with just an armband. But then we got
our first rifles – Lee Enfield 303s – our uniforms, hats and badges.'

With their rifles having arrived, Geoff was finally able to get fully
involved in the war effort:

> My training in the school OTC was very useful. My mate Derek
> Dashfield and I, who had both done our military training at school,

were telling the old boys – men in their twenties and thirties – how to march and how to do their drill. They were too young to serve in the Great War and too old to be called up in 1939. We instructed them in how to fire their rifles. And when the unit got a Bren gun, we had nimble fingers and learned to strip it down. So we acted as instructors for the others in the unit.

As Geoff later recalled, the older men seemed quite genuine in their willingness to receive military instruction from two boys just out of school: 'They were so kind to us, but they probably thought we were a pair of upstarts.'

There were other, even younger boys who assisted the Home Guard with their training. In West Wickham, thirteen-year-old Peter Tiling – whose father was a rifle shooting champion – trained the local Home Guard on a rifle range. In the period before systematic training of Home Guard recruits could begin, they had to get lessons wherever they could. Some LDV recruits were sent to public schools where senior pupils, usually NCOs in the school OTC, gave instruction on rifle ranges with the school's weapons. Some public schools, including Eton College, even established their own branches of the Home Guard, in which boys in their final year were able to serve, thus giving them additional military training in the final year before conscription. At Westminster School, Anthony Wedgwood Benn joined the Home Guard unit in 1941, aged sixteen, working his way up to the rank of sergeant:

> I joined the Home Guard in 1941 and was trained as a terrorist – how to use a rifle and throw grenades. I was well trained in the Home Guard – if the Germans had arrived I'd have thrown a bomb or a grenade in a restaurant. I don't know if I was any good at it – when you are that age it is just a lark but I was well aware that we might be invaded.

The initial period of inspired innovation, as shown by Home Guard units that developed their own weapons and used children as instructors, was what Geoff Pulzer referred to when he admitted: 'The TV series *Dad's Army* was brilliant. Everything they did was right.' He recalled how night duties were made more pleasant by his officer who was the manager of the local branch of Marks and Spencer and arrived on parade with sandwiches and cakes. Geoff also reflected on how much his life had changed since he had left school. At the end of 1939 he had been a schoolboy; by summer 1940 he was a part-time soldier, with a rifle in the cupboard at home, helping train men many years his senior ready for an invasion that was expected at any moment.

Despite its frequently comic appearance, the force played a genuinely important military role. The government acknowledged that the existence of the Home Guard made it possible to send desperately needed reinforcements to the Middle East. The role of the Home Guard included far more than simply parading in church halls and waiting for the enemy to invade. Frank Whitewood, a fifteen-year-old Home Guard volunteer, soon found his nights filled with activity. After a day's work, he returned home ready for evening duties:

> In those days it was called the Local Defence Volunteers, or the LDV. We called it 'Look, Duck and Vanish'. We were supposed to be defending this part of the Thames. The Home Guard and the Air Raid Wardens were in the old Greenwich Town Hall. We had parades and exercises against the Army. One night we were supposed to attack the college as part of a training exercise. They turned the hoses on us so we fixed bayonets. We got in trouble for that. Then on Blackheath, we used to be in the trenches or doing guard duties on the roofs of some of the big houses.

It was from these positions on Blackheath, with their commanding view across east London, that Frank watched the opening of the Blitz and the destruction of so much of the industry on the north bank of the River Thames.

For younger children, the formation of the Home Guard brought war one step closer. Fathers were soon sporting armbands, then caps and uniforms. Next came rifles and even machine-guns that were stored at home, much to the fascination of young boys. Many children watched as Home Guards paraded on the only available open spaces, often school playgrounds, where the children watched and wondered if this force could hold off invasion. When Roy Bartlett watched his local Home Guard he noticed the company had just one .22 rifle and two shotguns between them. It was hardly reassuring. Aged ten, he was starting to realize war was a serious business and there seemed to be nothing standing in the way of invasion. All anyone talked about was invasion and his parents were increasingly nervous for the future. Even for the children, it seemed the novelty of war had finally worn off.

Teenage evacuee Tony Moynihan, whose school was at Hartfield in East Sussex, joined the Home Guard as soon as he was old enough: 'I was the "Private Pike" – the youngest member of the platoon.' He soon grew accustomed to the struggle to provide sufficient weapons:

> There would be two of us on duty, walking up and down the village all night. There was Sir Dougal Malcolm, who had a magnificent shotgun in a leather case, whereas I had a rifle but no ammunition. One day when we were on duty, I asked to see the gun. We sat down and it took him about half an hour to get it out of the case and assembled. We were useless! I could have got my gun ready in seconds but had no ammunition. He had ammunition but it would have taken him half an hour to get it set up.

It was a strange existence for Tony Moynihan: he carried out Home Guard patrols by night, then went straight to school in the morning. He also experienced the rather haphazard way that Home Guard preparations were carried out:

One day they delivered huge barriers to stop tanks. They dug holes across the main road and put wood across the road. However, the weight was terrible – one of the men made a trolley with wheels for it – and finally we managed to take them. They were so heavy, but at last we managed to drop them in. However, we couldn't get them out again. The captain – who was the headmaster of a school – had to call out the Army to get them to take them out.

After struggling to erect the anti-tank barriers and then struggling to take them down again, they came to an interesting conclusion: 'We didn't know which direction the enemy would come from anyway.'

It was not just the Home Guard that readied itself for invasion. Whilst many teenagers who were not yet seventeen had been accepted into the Home Guard, there were other eager youngsters whose obvious youth meant they would never be accepted. For them, defiance of the enemy was displayed by joining the Army Cadet Force. One recruit was fourteen-year-old Reg Fraser who, whilst working as a gardener in Staines, volunteered for the Army Cadets. During the 1930s he had already been active against the rise of fascism:

I'd nick the eggs and throw them at the Blackshirts' office. They'd all come out and chase me. I had a big mouth. I'd shout at them, throw eggs and run off. They never caught me. I had seen them shouting at the old people, so I didn't like them. They were bullies.

Now ready for a more organized resistance to fascism, the only problem was that his unit had neither uniforms nor rifles. All they had were armbands and broom handles. Despite their lack of equipment, the boys paraded alongside the Home Guard, eager to show their martial qualities. The armband marked the first of four uniforms he would wear before the war was finished.

In London, sixteen-year-old Irish-born Bill Fitzgerald joined a branch of the Army Cadets based near Paddington Station. With his

mother and young sisters evacuated from London, he needed
something to fill the hours between work and the inevitable trip to
the air raid shelters. As he later admitted, he felt lost without the
family around him and with only his father for company in the
evenings. With so many friends displaced by bombing and others
having left the city, the evenings needed to be filled. After all, even
the local girls seemed to have been confined to their homes and
dates were hard to come by:

> I joined with my friend Jimmy. We were based at St Saviour's School
> in Shirland Road. I heard about it and wanted to know what they were
> doing – I just wanted something to do. When we got there we saw the
> uniforms – they were from the First World War! We had the flat hat
> and we wrapped puttees around our legs.

Though their uniforms were out of date, the boys remained
enthusiastic:

> That was our life. It meant there was something to do all the time. We
> trained with the cadets three nights a week. Over at Royal Oak station
> there was a Territorial Army barracks, where the Home Guard was
> based. They taught us drill and trained us with rifles. We used to go to
> Camden Town to do parades down there and we went on a firing range
> so we could get used to the kick of the rifle. As we got really into it, we
> went to the Home Guards and trained with them. It was strict but we
> really liked it. I learned what the Army was all about.

His father, an ex-regular soldier whose arm had been partially
paralysed in the Great War, was happy Bill had joined the cadets.
After all, by 1940 it was clear the war would not be over quickly and
that boys of his son's age would eventually be called up. At the time
the young cadets had no idea how soon their services might be
needed:

At that time, they still expected the Germans to invade. The Home Guard took us to Little Venice and showed us a house on the corner of Howley Place. They told us, 'This is one place you've got to remember.' We asked why. 'In case anything happens to the barracks, you'll find a lot of arms and ammunition here.' This was our unit's fall-back position in the event that the enemy invaded and captured our barracks. We could fight from this house. They had scattered the stuff around the area. So in the event of an invasion, we would have fought alongside the Home Guard.

The threat of invasion did not only impact upon boys who joined the Home Guard and Army Cadets. Girls also threw themselves into organized activities. In one Girl Guides patrol it was decided they would be prepared for invasion. Their plan was to use treetop lookouts to pinpoint the enemy, then signal by Morse code to those waiting on the ground, who would lure the Germans into clumps of nettles, and then attack the Germans with stinging nettles and penknives. It was lucky the girls never needed to put their foolhardy plan into action. In other locations, the Guides found more practical ways to be of assistance, acting as messengers for Home Guard units. In the event of invasion, their role was to cycle around alerting the men of the Home Guard and telling them to assemble ready to meet the enemy. Other Guides found themselves training Home Guard units in Morse code. One group, whose fathers were zookeepers who had trained the girls to use rifles, helped the Home Guards by challenging them to shooting contests: the Guides always won.

In May 1940, the British Army and its allies were unprepared for the scale of the onslaught that hit them. As they were relentlessly pushed back towards the English Channel, it became increasingly clear there was only one course of action: evacuation. Operation Dynamo, more commonly known as the Dunkirk evacuation, soon became legendary. The Royal Navy, valiantly supported by hundreds of merchant ships and the legendary 'little ships', was somehow able to rescue more than 300,000 servicemen from

France. It was little short of a miracle. Under ever-growing pressure from the enemy, British, French and Belgian soldiers boarded the ships that would take them to safety.

As with almost every military operation of the Second World War, the youth of Britain played an unheralded role in the operation. Almost all the merchant ships carried galley boys and cabin boys, whilst most Royal Navy ships also carried lads too young to be conscripted. One seventeen-year-old merchant seaman recalled travelling down from Liverpool to Dover and being assigned to operate a machine-gun on a merchant vessel. His role would be to offer a measure of anti-aircraft cover whilst his ship picked up escaping soldiers. Despite having no military training, he was put into a four-man team and given a Great War vintage Lewis gun. In the days that followed, he and his new mates manned the gun whilst his ship ferried thousands of sailors home.

Among the youngest of those to witness the miracle of Dunkirk was Albert Barnes, a fourteen-year-old cabin boy onboard a Thames tugboat, the *Sun XII*. When his boat was ordered to France to assist the evacuation, Albert went with it. Officially, because of his youth, he should not have sailed with the craft, but he was below decks when the news came to depart and the rest of the crew did not realize he was there. Once they had set off on the first stage of the trip, there was no chance to send him ashore. At Gravesend, they were given orders to tow two barges to the beaches of Dunkirk, where they could be loaded with troops and then towed back to England.

Across the Channel, Albert witnessed things he had never expected when he took a job working among the docks and wharfs up and down the Thames. With the sky lit by the flames of the town, he entered a world of sunken ships, their funnels sticking up through the waters of the port. Sixty years later he described it as a 'graveyard of ships'.[3] Everywhere were the bodies – some complete, some in pieces – of soldiers who had died whilst attempting to escape. It was the first time the youngster had even seen a dead body. After towing back one barge, the other having been destroyed by German bombing, the *Sun XII* returned to France towing lifeboats that were used to ferry soldiers from the beaches to destroyers offshore.

Once the evacuation was complete, Albert and his barge returned to London where the boy was met by his mother, who was furious that he had gone away without telling her. When he had first failed to return from work she had contacted his employers, only to be told he was away on 'government business'. When she asked where he had been, he replied: 'I've been in France, Mum.' Shocked, she asked him: 'You've not been to Dunkirk?' Yes, he told her, 'that's the place'.[4] Though later in the war he saw many other awful things, it was the horrors of Dunkirk – as witnessed through the eyes of an innocent fourteen year old – that had the greatest impact.

Of course, whilst the operation was a resounding success, not all the British soldiers made a successful escape from France. Around 40,000 – one for every seven men who escaped – were captured by the Germans in May and June 1940. Among them was Frank Norman, known to his family as John, who was a sixteen-year-old boy serving in the Royal Corps of Signals. He had joined the Army almost a year earlier, having claimed he was eighteen. His was a typical story: his home life had been hard. He was the youngest of five children and the only boy. As a result, he was blamed for everything that went wrong and received many beatings from his father. His father – a qualified engineer – refused to pay for his son to start an apprenticeship, preferring him to start work and immediately earn wages. After two years of odd jobs, John had had enough and joined the Army just after his sixteenth birthday. At the first recruiting office he was sent away with the words, 'Go home and grow up first.' Undeterred, he walked seven miles to another recruiting office and was immediately accepted.

Less than a year after volunteering, he was captured near the town of St Valéry as he and some other soldiers attempted to board a boat waiting offshore. He swam out to the boat, only for it to come under fire from the enemy. With the boat in flames, he was forced to re-enter the water and struggle back through the waves to the beach where German soldiers were waiting.

The prisoners were rounded up and sent on a forced march through northern France, into Belgium and then into the Netherlands, where they were put on barges and sent into Germany. John Norman later described the journey as a nightmare of deprivation and suffering. After days crammed below decks on the barges, he was transferred to a train and crowded into a cattle truck ready for the journey to a prisoner-of-war camp. A few days later, tired, hungry and uncertain for his future, the sixteen year old stepped down from the train and was marched into Stalag 8B, the camp in Silesia that was to become his home for the next five years.

The children of southern England, in particular in the ports of Kent, were the first fully to realize the implications of the evacuation of the Army from France. They watched and waved as trainloads of servicemen left the ports and headed off to Army camps to reassemble. The children were shocked to see the state of many of the returning men. They smiled from dirty faces, lined with the exhaustion of war. Some were bandaged, others wrapped in blankets. Plenty were without helmets or caps. Some were armed and in full kit, others were dishevelled, forlorn figures without rifles or equipment. They were unrecognizable from the Army that had departed for France a few months earlier.

Elsewhere in the country, there was an initial period when the evacuation was not public knowledge. At Bedford Town Hall, fifteen-year-old Jean Redman was shocked when she arrived at work one morning:

> There were soldiers everywhere: some lying on the floor, others sitting on the floor or walking about. The whole area was so crowded – I had to push my way through to get to the office. I tried to go upstairs – they were all along the corridor. I didn't ask where they had been. One of the soldiers gave me a cigarette lighter and another gave me his cap

badge. They were there all that day but I don't remember seeing them eating or drinking. They looked tired and despondent. I didn't know why and they didn't explain. They were still there that night when I went home but in the morning when I went back to work they had been completely cleared out. All gone: like I had dreamed it. Only later did I learn they were from Dunkirk. The public didn't know the Dunkirk story at that point.

In Wiltshire, Ena Steves was surprised when her father brought home two soldiers. One was dressed in just ill-fitting boots and trousers, with a blanket wrapped around his shoulders. One of the men kept repeating the same things over and over again and, even as a child, Ena recognized he was suffering from a mental trauma. When the soldiers had gone on their way, she naively asked her mother why the Army sent old men to fight wars. Her mother's answer was shocking: 'They are not old men, dear, that's what war does to young men.'

With France all but beaten and an invasion of the United Kingdom seeming likely, June 1940 saw a second wave of evacuation. Just as the tattered remnants of the British Expeditionary Force arrived back from Dunkirk, unloading from ships in ports along the south coast of England, the region's schools were also evacuated. With invasion threatened, the children needed to be cleared from the possible landing areas. These two groups, exhausted soldiers and excited – if apprehensive – children, passed through railway stations together, a clear indication of the totality of modern warfare. The children, most of whom were carrying sweets and biscuits given by loving parents, soon passed them over to the soldiers. They threw them across platforms, shoved them eagerly through train windows into the hands of men desperate for some measure of comfort.

This second wave of evacuation was carried out with even greater efficiency than the first. Lessons had been learned and arrangements were put in place to smooth the transition from town to country.

Dirty children were first sent to a hostel where they were bathed and reclothed before being placed in foster-homes. The problem children, including those who had a bad reputation from the earlier evacuation, were sent more permanently to hostels where they were cared for by trained social workers. Mothers with young children were also placed in hostels, which gave them a sense of independence and allowed them to feel they were not imposing on their hosts. To ease the evacuees into their new life, nurseries, entertainment centres, laundries and communal feeding centres were made available. Again, not all children joined the evacuation. In Dover, those who remained in the port, despite the dangers from enemy guns firing from across the Channel, were known as the 'Dead End Kids'. They roamed the streets, playing in ruined buildings, until schools eventually began to reopen.

As the Army returned from France, some soldiers went missing from the trains laid on to take them to Army camps. Instead, they headed home for a brief reunion before returning to war. Children were shocked to see the unfamiliar figure of their father opening the front door. It was a shock – and no small relief – for the man of the house to return so unexpectedly. Such visits were all too brief: there were hugs, kisses and tears of joy, maybe one night back in the marital bed and then the long, dull journey back to camp. In one tragic case, a returning soldier went upstairs with his wife but was soon disturbed by the sound of a shot: their teenage son had accidentally shot and killed himself with the soldier's rifle.

At home and with his schoolmates, ten-year-old Colin Ryder Richardson had followed the course of the German advance. Even as children living the countryside, war still engulfed their lives:

> It's the best 'school of life' you could ever get. We looked at photos of German uniforms: 'How to recognize a Hun'. We felt threatened. Especially when France fell, we couldn't believe that: the great French Army had been defeated. We looked at maps and watched as the arrows moved across Belgium and France. It's awful to say but it was

a good geography lesson! We watched with incredible fear because the Germans were so well organized. We heard about the bombing of Antwerp. It was ruthless. I was very aware of what was happening. Even now I have feelings about how the Germans bombed Rotterdam and Antwerp.

The defeat of the expeditionary forces in Norway and France, and the isolation of the British, led to some youngsters feeling that it was important that their sense of duty and desire to defeat the evils of Nazism should not be wasted. For fifteen-year-old Peter Richards, this helped him to continue on a political path that had started as a schoolboy at a Communist Party meeting in the wake of the Munich Crisis of 1938. He became more critical of the government and its policies:

> I became an increasingly hardened left-winger from a very early age. I worked very close to the headquarters of the Communist Party. So I used to go there to get pamphlets and a copy of the *Daily Worker*. They were very keen to see youths like me coming in. But no one tried to grab me and say, 'Come and join the Young Communists.'

Nonetheless, Peter started to attend meetings of the Young Communist League, and to read the *Daily Worker* – until it was banned in January 1941. Eventually, he joined the party. Unlike the common impression of 'young communists' being dour intellectuals with their heads buried in dreary political tomes, Peter Richards and his comrades enjoyed a normal social life:

> I used to go to this dancehall. There I got to meet various members of the organization. They were into dancing and looking for girls. They invited me to meetings that were held at people's houses. We had meetings and study classes on Marxism. It opened my eyes tremendously. Apart from the political ideas, it made me realize my English needed a lot of attention. I couldn't understand what the books were

about. When they were talking about chauvinism, I thought, 'What does this mean?' It made me realize I wanted to be educated so I could understand the arguments.

When the Luftwaffe finally arrived over Britain, it was not London that acted as their first target. Instead, German bombs fell on ports along the Bristol Channel, while Hull and Wick were subject to the first daylight raids on 1 July 1940. July also saw raids on Swansea and other towns in south Wales. By the time the Battle of Britain commenced on 10 July 1940, 300 civilians were already dead, courtesy of high explosive and incendiary bombs dropped by the Luftwaffe. These figures, shocking at the time, would soon pale into insignificance as the attacks intensified, bringing the war to almost every town and city in the country.

As the Luftwaffe began its daylight incursions above southern England, children discovered a great new game. Despite being encouraged to take cover, children ran out into the streets to watch the RAF confront the enemy. Often, there was nothing to see except dots in the sky or swirling vapour trails that showed a dogfight was taking place. They pointed to the sky in excitement whenever they saw parachutes descending and argued endlessly over whether planes were 'ours' or 'theirs'. As one writer put it: 'Who could sit in a shelter in the daytime when there was so much to look at in the sky?'[5] In Roy Bartlett's school there was a sense of additional excitement since they received advance warning of enemy raids. As soon as RAF fighters were scrambled from the nearby Northolt base, they roared over Ealing, to the cheers of the local children: 'It was wildly exciting. We could see the trails in the sky. Then the sirens would go. We were soon spending nearly all the time in the air raid shelters.' Although wanting to watch the action in the skies above, the children were rushed down the thirteen steps to the shelters that had been dug in the school playground. Earth had been piled over the trench to make a roof, where the school caretaker grew marrows. At first the children sat on the underground benches, stamping their feet on the duckboards, chatting, singing and messing about: 'Then some silly teacher had the bright idea that we ought to learn something.' In the weeks that followed the teachers tried to continue lessons underground, but failed to hold the children's attention. Instead, they introduced educational quizzes and games that they hoped might just teach the children something.

One of those who watched the activity in the skies was Terry Charles who had returned from Cornwall after getting bored with living in the countryside with a nanny. He figured that was no life for a thirteen-year-old boy:

> Every time I left London the air raids seemed to stop and every time I went back they started again. I'd look out of my bedroom window and watch the fighting. I could see the Spitfires and Hurricanes up in the sky trying to chase the bombers away. I could hear the pitter-patter on the roof as spent bullets and cartridge cases landed. As kids we went out and collected them.

One teenage girl living in Kent recalled her parents shouting to her to join them in their underground shelter. Instead, she stood outdoors with other similarly enthusiastic children and cheered the British fighters as they struck back at the Germans.

At Lingfield, ten-year-old Colin Ryder Richardson became fascinated by the aerial activity:

> I was a fairly switched-on kid. I knew that wings with crosses on were the 'baddies' and the ones with roundels on were the 'goodies'. We watched the fighters in the sky, we could see their trails. We knew what was going on because we saw the wreckage of planes everywhere. Gatwick was a tiny aerodrome. We biked down there to watch. A policeman appeared out of the hedge and told us to stop, the next moment we heard a roar of engines and these Spitfires raced off over our heads. Fascinating for kids. We were like train-spotters taking engine numbers – we took plane numbers. We could identify the squadrons.

In Kent, children who were working in the hop fields stopped work to watch the dogfights above them. When planes were shot down they raced through the fields to find the wreckage, often searching for souvenirs. Often it was a race between local policemen or Home Guard units and local children to see who could reach the wreckage first. Sometimes the children enthusiastically guided policemen to where they might find downed pilots and then watched as the unfortunate Germans were rounded up. For children, who had heard so much about the enemy, there was a genuine desire to see a living, breathing German close up. Were they the race of supermen that Hitler seemed to claim? Were they the vicious brutes claimed by propaganda? In truth, most of the children were surprised to see the enemy were simply very young, very ordinary and genuinely frightened.

Other children, similarly enthusiastic about the shooting down of an enemy aircraft, were more interested in seeing dead Germans. One teenage girl recalled hastily getting dressed – putting on her trousers back-to-front – in the rush to find a German plane which she and her father had seen shot down. Her desire was to see the dead body of a hated German. In Essex, one eight year old rushed home from a crash site, his chest festooned with belts of machine-gun ammunition he had retrieved from the German plane.

In Somerset, twelve-year-old Ken Durston watched as a fighter crashed in the vicinity:

> We used to have a lot of barrage balloons near us – because there was an aircraft factory nearby. The pilot of the Spitfire was a Canadian and got caught in the balloon cables – it brought him down and he was killed. Me and a couple of my mates were first on the scene. It was a summer's night. There was nothing we could do for him – he was already dead. Before you knew it the Home Guard and the police were there and it was all 'Move away, my son, move away.' They wanted to protect us from it but as a kid you just wanted to see what was happening. They wanted to recover the body which would have been nasty but we were too young to realize that.

These scenes were of far greater interest to most children than the classes their teachers still attempted to deliver. Evacuated to Devon from Kent, thirteen-year-old Jim Thomas recalled how war became more important than his final year of schooling:

> The school had no room for us, so we did lessons in the park. When it rained we had to go down to the local railwaymen's social club. So when the summer holidays came along we were told that if any of us had a permanent job to go to we could leave then, rather than wait until Christmas. Well, we weren't learning much – every time we heard an aeroplane we were looking up to identify it. We had things that were more interesting than school. Too much was going on to bother about lessons.

He soon found employment in a newsagent's shop before going on to spend three years working on a nearby farm.

In the final days of the Battle of Britain, the Luftwaffe began to bring greater terror to the cities, towns and villages of Britain, carrying out attacks on random opportunity targets. Fighter planes flew along railway lines, firing on trains. They swooped down on roads and machine-gunned cars, lorries, buses and even lone cyclists. One teenage girl, on her way to pick cabbages from her father's allotment, faced such an attack. She ran for her life and sheltered in a shop doorway as the plane opened fire on her. Then, as soon as the danger had passed, she ran out into the road to collect the bullets as souvenirs to show her friends. In Ealing, Roy Bartlett faced a similar attack. He was out with friends when the sirens sounded. The group dispersed to make their way to their homes to take cover:

> I could hear the thunderous roar of a German aircraft. I turned around in some alarm and there was a Heinkel, very low, behind me. I chucked myself off the bike, but didn't make it to the wall where I intended to take cover. Suddenly, as it passed, the rear gunner opened

fire on me. These bullets went straight up the middle of the road. They were chipping the tarmac and ricocheting everywhere. There were windows smashing in the houses around me. I was absolutely bloody petrified. I was shaking from head to toe and sobbing with fright. I went into an alleyway to sort myself out. As I stood there, two Spitfires went over. I ran out shouting 'Get them!'

When he got home his mother asked if he had heard the planes. He denied having seen the plane, knowing she would not let him out to play again if she knew the truth.

Fifteen-year-old Stan Scott found himself enthused and excited by the successes of the RAF in the Battle of Britain. He was also angered by the enemy's increasing aggression. After all, he had been brought up to believe 'If someone hits you – hit them back.' He decided that, if his father could run away from home to rejoin the Army, then he could, too. Furthermore, he asked himself: 'What had Dad done in 1914 aged fifteen? Joined the Army and served in France.' To serve his country seemed to be his destiny. One morning, he left home as normal for work, but did not take his usual route:

> I just had to do it. I was fifteen. I was part of a group of mates, they'd all gone and joined up. My other mates had been evacuated. Dad was back in the Army. So I was alone. I got on the trolley bus, up to the Seven Sisters Road where there was a recruiting centre. The Sergeant said, 'Hello, son, wanna join the Army?' 'Yes, sir.' I was all innocent.

The sergeant asked for his birth certificate but Stan told him he had forgotten it and, if he had to go home to fetch it, he would not get back before the office closed. Accepting his claim, he was sent to one side to sit with another group of would-be soldiers. As Stan Scott soon realized, most of the boys looked underage; the sergeant realized the situation, but no one said anything: 'The sergeant must have heard all the answers before.'

He was immediately sent in for a medical and then signed on – opting to serve in the Queen's Own Royal West Kent Regiment, in which his father had served during the Great War. When the formalities were completed, he was asked if he needed any time to conclude 'business' before joining the regiment. It seemed a ridiculous notion: what business could a fifteen-year-old boy have that needed urgent attention? He declined the offer, was given some rations, his first day's pay and a railway warrant, and then sent on his way to Tonbridge.

Arriving at the barracks in Tonbridge, he was taken into the office and was greeted by an officer: 'Welcome to the regiment. This is the Queen's Own Royal West Kent Regiment. I am the officer commanding the 70th Young Soldiers battalion. How come you joined our regiment?' Stan told him that his father had joined the regiment back in 1914 and considered it his family regiment. Dismissed from the office he was sent to the quartermasters and measured for his uniform:

> I thought I'd get a uniform. But I was given nothing. Then on to the armoury. They gave me a Lee Enfield rifle, it was covered in thick, hard grease from muzzle to butt plate. 'There you are, son, that's yours, get it cleaned up.' I thought, how am I going to do that? I had no cleaning gear.

Then he was sent to a hut, and given a palliasse and three scratchy blankets: 'I was a fifteen-year-old kid. What am I going to do with this rifle?' One of the other recruits in the hut sent him to the garage to get petrol and a brush. He then stood the rifle in a bucket and scrubbed it down: 'Took a bit of time, but I got it spotless. Then I stuffed the palliasse with straw. Got myself in the corner, undressed and got in bed. That was that. I was in the Army, I'd got a rifle, a bed, but no toothbrush, no uniform, no spoon – nothing!'

The next morning he was sent for breakfast, and was given a mug of tea, a bowl of porridge and some bread and jam:

I scoffed that down. Then it was running around. Down to quartermasters, get me kit. It was waiting for me. A set of battledress and a set of denims, and some 1908 pattern webbing – like they had in the first war. Went back to my corner, sorted out my kit and webbing. Changed into uniform. I was told to bundle up my clothes and chuck it into the quartermasters with my name and address on.

Fed, watered, armed and finally dressed in an Army uniform, fifteen-year-old Stan was ready to follow in his father's footsteps in the Army.

Back in London, with the RAF pilots emerging as the nation's new heroes, Peter Richards noticed a change in behaviour among some of his friends at the youth club. Just as the declaration of war had encouraged some to try to get fit ready for military service, so the Battle of Britain drew their attention towards the RAF. Whizzing through the skies gunning down enemy fighters became the dream of these young men, of whom Peter noted: 'People started to study. Some of my friends, whose main prowess at arithmetic was to "take the chalk" at dart matches, began to enrol in maths classes with the aim of becoming eligible for aircrew selection.'

But that summer was about more than just watching dogfights and celebrating the victories won in the skies above southern England. For Peter Richards there was still time for sport and leisure:

We had the lido nearby. It was a great place. In the summer of 1940 the Army had been kicked out of France, but the summer was good. We carried on life as normal. We had holidays at home. I also went down to Runnymede with John Cotter and a work colleague called Ted.

Despite his increasing links to the Communist Party, Peter kept in close contact with his would-be fascist mate, John. Nevertheless, they continued with their political arguments, with Peter having – for the moment – the upper hand following Mussolini's decision to declare war on Britain. At the end of August the two boys decided to take a cycling holiday to make up for the one that had been cancelled earlier in the year. This time they travelled to Exeter, staying overnight in youth hostels, enjoying the beautiful summer weather. For John Cotter, this trip helped him to understand the seriousness of the situation. At the youth hostels there were always a number of older people who seemed to discuss nothing except what would happen in the war. It made him realize the impact the war had already had on the older generation. The timing of the trip was serendipitous: in 1939 the two friends had missed the declaration of war because they were out cycling. In 1940 their trip to Exeter meant they were absent from London on the first days of the Blitz. It was an absence thousands of Londoners wished they could have shared.

CHAPTER 5

London's Burning

'A lot of life went on. Much depended on where one lived, or how young and silly one was.'

Peter Richards, a teenager in London

Saturday, 7 September 1940, marked a turning point in both the Second World War and in the history of London. From that day onwards the entire human geography of the city underwent change on an epic – and violent – scale. Thus far, only a number of RAF bases and a few ports and coastal towns had been raided and there had been death, but what was to follow was something different. As the teenage Bernard Kops later recalled: 'That day stands out like a flaming wound in my memory.'[1]

On that day 375 German bombers made their way across Kent and approached London, while below the population had no idea what was happening. In his parents' Ealing home Roy Bartlett heard a noise that concerned him. At first it was a dull throbbing, somewhere in the distance. Then came the crump of anti-aircraft guns. He ran into the shop and found his parents and their customers outside staring eastwards into the sky.

Across London and south-east England, people could see the RAF fighters attacking the bomber fleet, but still the planes kept coming. As German planes reached south-east London, the bombs began to fall. Woolwich Arsenal, Becton gasworks, the power station at West Ham, Surrey Docks, Millwall, Rotherhithe, Limehouse, Tower Bridge – a vicious blow at London's industrial and trade heartland. As the docks began to blaze, the sky lit up, acting as a beacon for the waves of bombers that followed. From eight that evening until four the next morning, a procession of 250 bombers unloaded high explosives and incendiary bombs on to the already flaming warehouses, factories and docks of east London.

Roy Bartlett ran to the top floor of the house: 'We had a panoramic view across London and on a clear day you could see the dome of St Paul's Cathedral. We didn't know what horror we would later see from that window.' As he looked across the city he watched the opening of a bombing campaign that would last for fifty-seven consecutive days. He was struck by the final realization of what war meant: 'This was real, this was it – it was the beginning of the Blitz and we were petrified. Although nothing was yet happening in west London, it was a totally new experience.' Roy, his parents and their customers all ran for the shelter where they sat as the enemy planes rained down incendiaries and high explosive bombs on to the East End. As he sat in the shelter, listening to the distant sounds of war, an ominous thought gripped him: 'Is this the prelude to the invasion?'

At the centre of the inferno were the Surrey Docks where enormous stacks of timber burned with an inconceivable fury. London's firemen looked on in dismay as they pumped water on to the burning timbers. The heat was so intense that the water soon dried out and the timbers once more caught fire. In some cases the jets of water they aimed at the flames simply vaporized before they hit the target. As the fires raged, thousands of people crowded into railway arches, some of which were official, reinforced shelters, others were just part of a vast, and uncertain, sanctuary where fights broke out over floor space and prostitutes plied their trade.

In scenes that seemed like Armageddon, the vast stores of goods in the vaults of the dockside warehouses were set alight. Stocks of tea, shipped from the other side of the world, burned furiously while fireman laughed at the reversed situation in which cold water was poured on hot tea leaves. The flames also consumed warehouses full of sugar and barrels of every conceivable spirit. In the basins of the docks, burning sugar floated on the water, all the time giving off a sickly, sweet aroma. As the fires spread, even the wooden blocks used to construct some roads caught fire, rendering streets impassable.

In the aftermath of the raid, many children poured on to the streets to see the terrible, if fascinating, results of the bombing. It wasn't difficult to locate: they simply followed the thick black plumes of smoke and the red glow that marked where the docks were burning. The temperatures rose as they got closer, until they reached the inferno. Flames were rising skywards and sparks were spitting out into the streets. Blackened and exhausted firemen were everywhere. The fires seemed to be alive, engulfing everything in their path. With the heat burning their skin and the fires threatening to suck them into the inferno, the children returned home.

That single Saturday afternoon and night cost the lives of 430 Londoners whilst a further 1,600 were seriously injured. Hundreds of homes were destroyed and business premises were razed to the ground. And it was just the beginning. The following night the raiders returned, killing more than 400 people, destroying more homes and businesses, and wrecking railway lines into the city. The Sunday night raid was the second day of what would be fifty-seven consecutive nights of bombing. That night, in nearby Bethnal Green, ten-year-old Alf Morris watched the results of the raid: 'That's when I realized how bad the bombing was going to be. When they set the docks alight. You could read a newspaper from the light of the fires. It came home to you what a frightening thing war was.'

Immediately as the Blitz on London commenced, new rituals of life arrived. In the shelters, female ARP wardens took care of children who had been separated from their parents, comforting them or occupying their minds with games and conversation, in the hope that the children might forget the world outside. In the wake of the bombers came the heart-rending search for family members – parents searched for their children as they tried to establish who had survived. In return, children traipsed the streets as they made their way from hospital to rescue centre in search of parents.

The morning after each raid saw whole families trudging through the streets laden with whatever they had salvaged from their homes – perhaps a clock, a few precious family photographs, a bundle of clothes or a few pots and pans. Parents carried small children or guided them by hand through the rubble, as prams were wheeled through the streets piled high with salvaged possessions. Children searched for their favourite toys, rescuing dolls and teddy bears from the rubble of shattered homes – just something to comfort them in the days ahead as they settled into their new surroundings – wherever they might be.

In the worst hit areas, in the East End and around the docks, it seemed everyone knew someone who had been killed. On the day after the first raid one East End boy went to find his playmates, the twin boys he had been playing with the day before and had only gone in for tea just before the bombers arrived. He discovered the entire family had been wiped out.

Bereavement became a daily issue. Children found their parents blasted by high explosive or shredded by shrapnel. One child found her dead mother slumped in front of her dressing-table mirror; a single shard of glass had slit her throat. For rescue workers, there was the heart-rending experience of having to rescue people from bombed homes. Awful as it was to pull dead and wounded adults from the rubble, there was the terrible issue of children's bodies. The twisted and burned corpses of children had an additional impact. Every father who did rescue work could not but imagine it was his own child or grandchild. Even when they pulled a live child from the rubble there was the dreadful need to offer comfort to a child who might not survive or might live with their injuries for the rest of their life. What could they tell a child whose leg had been severed?

The people of London had something more than the horrors of war with which to contend. By night and day they rushed into air raid shelters at the sound of sirens. In an instant life stopped. Whether at work, shopping, sleeping or in a classroom, normal life was put on hold until the 'all clear' had sounded. The old routines were obliterated by the violence of war. Even in areas where few bombs were falling, the daily rush to the shelters turned their world upside down. It didn't take long for the disruptions to take their toll on the people. All across London, people were seen sleeping in the daytime, having cat-naps as they tried to catch up on lost sleep. Roy Bartlett remembered the scenes in his school:

> Everyone was so tired, we were walking about like zombies. But we carried on going to school each day. It was not uncommon for pupils to fall asleep in lessons. On one occasion myself and some others had dozed off. I awoke, looked up and saw that the teacher was asleep. You couldn't keep your eyes open. It was night after night after night. Then life took on a degree of normality. It was extraordinary how soon we were able to cope.

Newly returned to London, Terry Charles settled into the strange new reality of life in wartime. He had returned from evacuation just in time for war to hit London:

> I only realized it later on that we had all adopted a frame of mind where you lived for the day. There was no future – tomorrow didn't exist. You might not be here tomorrow. If you were alive – good. But you couldn't think 'Come summer we'll go to the seaside.' It was one day at a time. No one made a conscious decision. We all just grew into the mind frame.

Despite the horrors of the Blitz, the nation's children found a new game: collecting shrapnel. After air raids, they liked nothing more than to go hunting through the streets for the jagged shards of steel that had rained down from the skies. For collectors, some parts were more popular than others. Many children went searching for the elusive tail fins of incendiary bombs. Indeed, many children who searched for the tail fins were not actually certain they even existed. As some recalled, if the bombs burned how could there be tail fins scattered across London streets? Furthermore, whilst the children thought the pieces they found were from German bombs, most of the shrapnel was actually fragments of British anti-aircraft shells fired over the cities in an attempt to bring down the raiders.

As one of the children who had remained in London when his classmates had been evacuated, and whose parents stopped him from leaving London once the Blitz started, Alf Morris had a 'ringside seat' for the destruction of the East End. He had watched the sky glowing as the docks burned and had grown to accept the regular wail of the sirens as they announced the imminent arrival of more death and destruction. His mother had warned him not to venture too far from home, so that he could reach the shelter during daylight raids. Even at the height of the bombing, when his father suggested the whole family relocate, his mother remained steadfast: 'No, we'll be all right. We'll rough it in the shelters. We're not going to be evacuated.'

With many children having returned from evacuation, the schools had reopened, meaning Alf Morris did have some opportunities for education. It didn't last long: 'We started to get air raids during the day. It didn't matter when we were getting one a day, but when we were getting seven or eight each day, the teachers wouldn't take the responsibility. So they sent a note home to say the school would be closed.' Once again he was left to his own devices. Even when the school was open, Alf would take time off from school to work. His mother simply sent a note to school: 'Dear Miss so-and-so, my son wants to go hop picking in Kent.'

And so life continued against a backdrop of war. He stayed close to home in the daytime, for fear of an air raid, then at night the

whole family took to the bunks of the Anderson shelter at the end
of the garden, which had been built in the lee of the tall brick wall
surrounding the local park. The Blitz, the casualties and the damage
became the centre of conversation as people shared news about who
had been killed, who was in hospital, who had been bombed out
and where they were now living. As a child, Alf Morris found it easy
to adapt to the uncertainty of living in a blitzed city: 'Some people
decided to leave the area, announcing, "I'm going to be evacuated."
You got used to it. People were being killed and buried. You got
used to that, as well.' As he later admitted, the barrage of
propaganda – Churchill's defiant speeches, the newspapers that
proudly announced 'London Can Take It', the newsreels – all
helped. It bolstered the one thing that stood between them and
disaster: their morale.

Then it was the turn of the Morris family and their neighbours to
become the topic of the daily conversations:

> A mine dropped in Meath Gardens, right behind our house. The mine
> dropped just behind the wall from our house. It hung in the trees and
> went off. Bang! It rocked the shelter. We all screamed and cried. When
> we came out, the house had gone. All the houses had gone. It had
> cleared the terraces all around.

Standing in the ruins of his home was an emotional experience for
the ten-year-old Alf: 'Everything was gone. I was crying and
screaming. Mum said, "Shut it! Shut up!" Dad said, "There's no
need for that. You're not dead. You're not injured. The house is
gone but it don't matter as long as we're all right."' Pulling aside
shattered wood, clambering over piles of bricks, roof tiles and
shattered masonry, his mother entered the house: 'She had a dresser
with all her wedding-present china on it. Every week she used to
take it down and clean it. The house had gone, all the furniture was
gone but that had survived.' The survival of their best china was
nothing short of a miracle, but they no longer had anywhere to

display it: 'So the next day Dad didn't go to work. We got boxes and recovered what we could from the rubble. We had to find somewhere to live.'

These were terrible times for children, as they saw the world they knew being torn apart. In the aftermath of air raids, Alf Morris saw dazed people wandering the streets, uncertain of what they should do or where they should go. After heavy raids, it became routine to walk through the streets, stepping over piles of rubble, tasting the dust in the air, feeling the heat radiating from charred buildings and watching dead bodies being carried from the ruins of homes. For children, there was something haunting about walking past bomb-sites they knew still contained the undiscovered bodies – and unclaimed souls – of so many dead.

The question of where bombed-out families could be rehoused was a constant problem and the establishment of rest centres offered some solution. During 1940–41, one sixth of all Londoners were bombed from their homes, either temporarily or permanently, and were moved to what were effectively refugee camps for the victims of the Blitz. For the Morris family, rest centres were not an option: 'There were rest centres, but people in the East End had their pride. They wouldn't go to them. They would rather go to relatives or close friends. It was a very close-knit community. So we stayed with a friend for the next night.' In many cases, the reticence to move to rest centres was understandable. Some were so overcrowded people were forced to use buckets as toilets. Also, they were in blitzed areas, meaning they offered no safety. Hundreds of 'refugees' were reported to have been killed when one such rest centre was bombed.

With so much damage in the East End, Alf's father found a house a few miles away in Leyton:

But my Mum said, 'I'm not living in Leyton!' So he said, 'Liz, please. I'm trying to get us sorted.' So we went to Leyton, but a little while later a bomb landed behind the house. It didn't hit us but it dropped in the gardens. So we were bombed out again and moved back to Bethnal

Green. We stayed in the crypt of St John's Church. It had been opened up as a shelter. The crypt was full of lead coffins. So we slept on the floor between them. At night we could still hear the bombs falling.

Within days his father had found them another home, a two-room flat in the nearby Gretton Houses, a short walk from the church crypt that continued to be their shelter. Alf was in the block next door to the one from where Reg Baker had been evacuated the previous year.

By the end of October 1940 some 60,000 homes in London had been destroyed, with a further 130,000 suffering bomb damage. In the borough of Stepney three-quarters of homes had been wrecked and across London some 250,000 people had been made homeless. One unexpected side effect of the bombing was that the impact of explosions sent expectant mothers into labour. In the south London suburb of Thornton Heath, the local midwife found herself increasingly busy, as her niece recalled:

> As soon as she heard the warning siren, she knew she'd have to go out. That was when babies were born. She was always out in raids. When Thornton Heath baths were bombed she had to deliver two babies out on the pavement. She was out in one raid on her way to a call, when an incendiary bomb went off right beside her. After the delivery she came back home and our mum said to her – you look different. It was then we realized what had happened – the shock of that bomb going off beside her had sent one of her eyebrows totally white. For years she had one black and one white eyebrow.

Although the East End initially suffered the most intense bombing, the Luftwaffe soon spread its attention. Perhaps imagining there was little left to destroy in east London, the bombing spread out across the capital. Suddenly, entire areas that had so far escaped unscathed faced shocking destruction. Whilst some poor areas had experienced what seemed like extremely violent slum clearance, the next stage of bombing also hit the city's more modern suburbs.

The southern suburb of Shirley, an area of mostly modern houses built in the inter-war years, was far from the typical image of blitzed London. Yet, like many other suburbs, it saw its share of the bombing, as the Luftwaffe brought terror to the entire population. One teenage girl recalled the bombing:

> I was in a house which was badly damaged by a German land mine which was dropped. You couldn't hear those coming as they came down by parachute. My father was on Home Guard duty and my mother, her friend and my younger brother were in the house. That house didn't have a shelter but my father had reinforced the windows with tape – that was what saved us.

Without a shelter, the children slept behind the sofa in the living room that their parents thought might offer some protection:

> All we heard was a crack – we thought whatever is that? Next moment there was a blinding flash – all the windows and doors were blown in – the ceilings came down – all the windows were smashed to smithereens. The tiles came off the roof and the house was completely wrecked. I didn't feel frightened. Suddenly we could see all the way down the garden – it was filled with lights where something was burning. It turned out to be the embers from the fire in one of the bombed houses. My brother and I weren't injured but we were covered in muck. My mother had slight wounds and bruising and our friend broke her arm. She was up at the time and had gone to the lounge door. It came off its hinges and knocked her down.

Within minutes, Canadian troops who were stationed in the area arrived to check on the family:

> They bandaged my mother and took the other lady to hospital. They took my brother and me to a house across the road which had a big shelter, and we stayed there until the raid was over. My father was on

Home Guard duty nearby, he got the news and came down to find us. I don't know what he thought when he saw our house wrecked. For the next few days I was terribly shaky and I couldn't sleep – my body reacted. I couldn't believe it: suburban Shirley had been bombed!

In Ealing, ten-year-old Roy Bartlett had grown used to long nights sheltering beneath his parents' shop. As the days and weeks passed, the people who used the shelter put up curtains to give privacy to their bunks. Family photographs appeared at bedsides and a new community began to emerge. Then the inevitable happened. On 19 October 1940 the shelter filled up with its normal residents, who were joined by a few new faces, including some soldiers who were trying to get back to camp, when the sirens had sounded:

> I was sound asleep in my bunk in the corner of the cellar. My first conscious awareness was that my head hurt. Why was everything dusty? Why was I on the cold stone floor? It was total confusion. I couldn't hear. I suppose my head hit the brick wall to my side. Everyone had been thrown out of their bunks and deposited on one side. As I was thrown forward, my leg jarred against the wall and crushed the cartilage in my ankle.

As he regained consciousness he could hear frantic voices calling out through the darkness: 'The coal dust from our coal chute had been sucked up. There was dust and dirt filtering everywhere. We were coughing, choking, spluttering. Handkerchiefs were being passed around to cover faces.'

Upstairs, his father found that all the windows had been shattered but that the blackout curtains had caught the glass. Along with the two soldiers, and a policeman who had been sheltering in the cellar, Roy's father stepped out from the shop-front. As he did so, he stepped carefully over a woman's severed hand. They were immediately confronted by a thick fog of dust and realized that the shop's stock was spread all over the road. Looking up, they saw a red glow opposite: two houses on fire. They quickly burned to the ground whilst the owner of one of the houses continued to shelter beneath the Bartletts' shop. Out in the street, they discovered the cause of the devastation: a parachute mine had fallen nearby, demolishing a row of seven shops, killing seven people and wounding twelve. A further three people simply vanished without a trace, obliterated by the blast.

Down in the cellar, Roy Bartlett was unaware of the destruction that had happened in the street outside. All he wanted to do was escape the dust and get out into the fresh air: 'I realized what had happened when I tried to stand up. I fell over again.' Staying in his bunk until morning, Roy then tried to reach hospital for treatment. At first he and his father tried to get a bus, but none were running due to the rubble blocking the street. Then they tried to get a lift, but there were no cars moving. So they walked, the youngster hobbling and hopping as he supported himself on his father's arm. Once at the hospital the youngster realized how lucky he had been. It was crowded with the wounded. He watched trolleys going past with bloodied people being wheeled in for treatment. One of the passing stretchers carried a body completely covered by a blood-soaked blanket. He soon realized his injured ankle was far from a high priority. By the time the doctors came to treat him they had run out of plaster and could not set his lower leg in a cast. Instead, it was wound with a thick, sticky bandage and he was told to rest it for a couple of weeks. With that he returned home, just glad to be alive.

In south London, another youngster found himself sheltering in the cellar of his home. For seven-year-old Fred Rowe, a self-confessed 'street urchin', the sudden arrival of war on his local area had an immediate impact. He was pleased that his mother refused for him to be evacuated, but missed his father who was away in the Army. He also enjoyed the disruption that meant school opening times were haphazard. Too young to really understand what war meant, it was only when the bombs began to fall that he realized war was not a game. He watched German fighters swooping down on shopping streets firing along the middle of the road, watched anti-aircraft guns firing from nearby Battersea Park and began to taste the warm, dusty air that swirled through the streets in the aftermath of air raids.

With the start of the Blitz, summer had come to an end and everywhere seemed dreary and dull:

> All of sudden there were bombs going off. These planes would come along, drop their fucking bombs and there'd be these explosions. The ground would shake and rumble as the bombs exploded. The noise was like something from another planet. Your ears were ruined for days. It was all new to me. I thought this was going to be it for the rest of my life. I was in a permanent state of fear.

As the bombing spread, Fred experienced the terror of modern warfare:

> We lived in a house with a coal hole underneath. It had a hole in the pavement, where the coal was put in. We used it as a shelter. Mum kept a few tins of food, a can-opener and some water down there in case we got trapped. One night the house two doors along got a direct hit and the debris covered over the pavement. Our house was wrecked. There was tons of masonry against the cellar door. So we were trapped in there. We couldn't get out through the coal chute and we couldn't get up the stairs, 'cause of the debris. Mum told me to start singing, so the ARP would know we were trapped in there.

With the house collapsed on top of them, the family had no idea what would happen next. They were beneath tons of rubble, that much was clear, but was it burning? Would anyone come to rescue them? Or might another bomb hit them? As he sat in the dim candlelight, Fred Rowe realized their predicament:

> The whole place was vibrating. I started crying, so did my sister. Eventually the all-clear went and we could hear movement above –

ARP blokes. Then we heard muffled voices. Mum started singing loud. Then they shouted, 'Are you down there?' She shouted back to them that we were in the cellar and they could reach us through the pavement. They cleared a way through and then we saw the torchlight through the dust. It was total fear. I thought I was entombed there and I was going to die.

Yet there were worse things than being rescued from the rubble of your home, as he soon discovered as he passed through bombed streets, looking up at homes that had the front sliced off, leaving rooms open to the world:

It was fucking horrible. There was a bloke next door who lived in the basement. A bomb had dropped on the house behind him, and he was blown out of his basement on to the railings outside. The railings had ripped him in half. All his guts and gunge were hanging out of him. I thought 'Fucking hell, Percy!' I was choking when I saw him. And his son, fifteen years old, was killed. He was lying in the road with no head, no arm and a bit of his shoulder was gone. I didn't recognize him. And I saw a body all blown apart, mixed into another body. It was a young girl blown into her mum or her dad, blasted together.

Though just seven years old he became horribly familiar with death: 'When you saw the dead bodies, their face was all blue. The skin was mottled. It was fucking awful.' More than ten years later, whilst serving in the Army in Korea, he was to discover one effect of the horrors of the Blitz: 'It prepares you for war.'

Whilst high explosive bombs had the obvious power to destroy buildings, smashing their walls and throwing debris all around, and incendiaries were able to set fires wherever they fell, there was a third weapon in the enemy's arsenal: blast. This was the most curious of all results of the bombing. Buildings that were untouched by bombs had their windows blown out. The awesome surge of air unleashed by high explosive could lift people from the ground and deposit them on the opposite side of the road. Bernard Kops recalled being lifted off his feet and dumped to the ground as he played in a passageway near his home. He had felt a rush of air but not heard a sound. He soon discovered it was the blast from a bomb that had fallen 200 yards away, destroying an air raid shelter in Columbia Road.

In some cases unwounded corpses were discovered with no sign of the malevolent force that had killed them. As Sylvia Bradbrook – having returned to London from an unhappy evacuation – recalled, she was always frightened to walk past a local fire station. Rumour had it that the entire crew had been found sitting around the table playing cards. Every one of them was still and silent, as if time had stopped. But it was no illusion: blast had simply stopped their hearts. However, it was another sight that intrigued her: 'A man in our neighbourhood was blown to bits – and afterwards an air raid warden had to go up a ladder with a bucket and pick all the bits of flesh up off the building.' Watching from the upstairs window of her friend's house, she saw the warden scraping lumps of flesh from the brickwork and scrubbing to remove the bloodstains.

More than anything, blast played bizarre tricks. Trees were found with their branches full of items that had been blasted into them. In one case a family looked out to see their garden trees had seemingly grown a new and bizarre fruit – cabbages that had been blasted out of the ground. When one rescue worker searched for a man known to have been in a bombed house, he could find no sign of him. Eventually the man's body was located: blast had sucked it up the chimney.

One morning, following an air raid, Terry Charles awoke and stepped into the corridor of his basement flat. As he looked towards the front door he was surprised to see it open. He then looked more closely: 'We had no front door. I looked outside but couldn't find it. I thought no more of it and thought I'd better get ready for school. I went to the bathroom but couldn't open the bathroom door. I thought that was funny.' Bemused, he went outside and looked through the bathroom window: 'Our front door was in the bathroom. The blast had blown it in, along the passage – without marking the walls – the bathroom door had opened, the front door had gone through and then the bathroom door had closed on it.'

The power of blast also became apparent to Roy Bartlett. Returning from school in the pouring rain, he noticed that water was spilling from the gutters at the front of his father's shop. He informed his father, who sent for a local handyman:

> I watched him go up the ladder and try to clear the blockage. Suddenly, he came hurtling down and was violently sick in the gutter. I was dead curious. Had he been in the pub drinking? I was quickly ushered out of the way, but I soon found out what had happened. He had got up there with his bucket to clear the down pipe. He pulled out this stuff that was blocking the pipe and realized it was a woman's hair attached to the scalp. It was from the woman from the butcher's shop that had been bombed on the night I was wounded.

Faced with terrible scenes, Londoners desperately searched for any place of safety. What they wanted was to get as far underground as possible. For those in central London, there was one obvious place of sanctuary: the Underground railways. The tube stations soon became the favoured place of refuge. Starting on the fifth night of the Blitz, when locals crowded into the tunnels and platforms of Liverpool Street station, the tube stations became a vital part of the fabric of wartime society. Although the practice was frowned on by the authorities, people began crowding into the stations, marking out a spot and settling in for the night. Staff tried to keep the crowds back from the platform edge as commuters got on and off trains. Every space was filled by families looking for somewhere safe for the children to sleep. Night after night they filed underground, into a subterranean world without beds or toilet facilities, where trains rattled past until late at night, where rats and mice scuttled around once the lights had gone out, running across the sheltering people as they tried to get a night's rest. One child who slept in a tube station later recalled how the noise of the trains kept them awake until the last train had gone. Then, with the movement of trains sucking air through the tunnels, the smell of the open toilets took over and made sleep difficult. None of that mattered: at least they felt safe.

For the people of Bethnal Green, the local tube station was a godsend. The station was unfinished, part of an extension to the Central line which had not yet opened. With no track yet laid, there was no dangerous live rail, meaning the people were not confined to the platform, but could also sleep in the pit intended for the tracks. Night after night, the locals queued up to enter this sanctuary. Alf Morris was among them, sent by his family to secure a space for them:

> We heard the tube had opened. So Mother said, 'Alfie, when you get back from school go to the tube station and line up – get us a place in the queue.' That afternoon, all the boys from school were there larking about. They opened the gates at 5.30. We went tearing down the stairs, then the escalators. Ran on to the westbound platform. Got a blanket and threw it down. Sat there. The blanket was your spot. Then Mother came down an hour later. She had blankets over her arms and had all her relatives with her. So we made the beds up.

With the opening of the tube station as a shelter came a new concern. Families sleeping on the tracks and platforms needed several blankets to keep themselves warm at night. This meant trudging around the area carrying piles of bed linen. A solution was found by two enterprising locals. Renting an empty shop near the station entrance, the men erected a sign, 'The Bundle Shop'. There, for a few pennies a day, families could store their bedding, receiving a ticket each morning for bedding that could be redeemed in the evening. This soon became part of the daily routine of children's duties. They would queue at the station, rush down to claim their spot, then they would return to the surface to fetch their bedding from 'The Bundle Shop'.

Alf Morris and his family remained regular visitors to the station for many months to come, watching as the station developed from a bare, unfinished tube station into a properly organized shelter that, for many, became a home-from-home. At first it was nothing more than an underground space, somewhere far safer than the railway arches or church crypts far above them:

> It was very dirty down there. At night, when it was quiet, rats used to come out and crawl over you. It was horrible, but what can you do? Better to suffer that than be upstairs. We'd see them crawling about. That was how we lived – it was part of life.

Whatever the conditions, people had to sleep there. The scuttling of rats was preferable to the crash of bombs. If the men and women didn't sleep, how could they work? If they couldn't work, how could the country produce the weapons with which to fight the war? During the night one of the disruptions was the ominous sound of the station superintendent calling for men to volunteer to rescue people from bombed houses.

It was during a heavy raid that Alf Morris witnessed an incident that led the local authorities to develop the space to make it more amenable to its inhabitants:

> In 1941 a bomb fell almost above us, outside a pub called the Falcon. It rocked the tube. It was like in a war film when they drop depth-charges on a submarine. That's how much it shook. I was walking along with a jug of tea in my hand. The tunnel shook from side to side. The light bulbs swung. Everyone – including the mums and dads – started screaming. I dropped the tea and ran to my mother. Everyone looked up thinking the roof was going to come in on us. The superintendent, Mr Hastings, came up, calling out, 'Keep calm. All right, ladies, don't worry.' The lights went down that night as normal

but we didn't sleep much. We still thought the roof was going to come down.

When they emerged the following morning they could see the vast crater where the bomb had landed and smashed through the road, destroying the sewer. The pub had been reduced to a pile of rubble. One thing was certain, they had been very lucky. The tunnel had survived the impact, but whether it could survive another one was anybody's guess. There had already been enough loss of life inside tube shelters. On 15 October 1940 a German bomb had landed directly in the road above Balham Underground station. The bomb opened a crater that soon collapsed, the earth falling through into the station where hundreds of people were sheltering. People scrambled for the exits as torrents of water entered the tunnel courtesy of a burst water main. Yet the falling earth had blocked an exit, trapping people within. Sixty-four people were killed, many of them drowned in the rising waters.

One person who narrowly missed the disaster was Royal Marine Bugle Boy Len Chester. On his way home on leave to his parents' home, his train was stopped due to the bombing:

> How was I going to get home? I'd got as far as Clapham South, they turfed us out of the train and said we couldn't go any further. I came out from the tube in the middle of an air raid. I stood outside and a woman came out and hailed a taxi. It was the middle of an air raid and the taxis were still running! She was going to Mitcham so she let me go with her. The raid was still going on!

The fifteen year old realized that London was more dangerous than being onboard a ship:

> The sirens were going every night. I was glad to get back to my battleship. When you are on a battleship, you can fight back. But in the raids on London you felt so helpless. You think every bomb is coming directly at you. You think the pilot of that plane is only looking at you.

Just over two months later another Underground station was hit, with 111 people dying when Bank station was bombed. To insure against a similar tragedy, but much to the consternation of those who took shelter there, Bethnal Green station was closed. However, they soon discovered the shelter was to be refurbished, turning it from an empty space into a modern shelter. When it reopened, the shelter had been fitted with concrete plinths to support the roof. A thick door had been installed to protect the platform from blast that might rush down the stairs. The gully for the tracks had been covered over, creating a flat concrete floor. The area had been divided by walls into three sections. In each section, three-tier bunks had been installed, as had toilets which, although they stank of chemicals, were preferable to open buckets hidden behind a curtain. Furthermore, every bunk had been numbered, allowing the would-be troglodytes of Bethnal Green to be allocated their own spaces. For Alf Morris this was 'a home-from-home. No more lining up, no more fetching your bundles.' The old chaos had gone and been replaced by a new subterranean order.

Although the people of Bethnal Green felt safe in their subterranean shelter, their homes continued to be bombed, burned and blasted. For Alf Morris who had already been bombed out of two houses, it was only a matter of time until it happened again:

> One morning we came home and our block had gone. A bomb had hit it. So we had to move again. So we went to Waterloo Gardens by the London Chest Hospital. We were there for months. It was a nice little house. But when you wanted a bath, you pumped the water up by handpump, heated it in a 'copper', then had your bath. That was my job. One night the Chest Hospital got hit. It was set alight. We got it as well. A church was hit and some of the streets around. It was all blasted. It was uninhabitable. So we moved again. What can you do? You aren't concerned about your home – just about the family.

For their family, the situation was aggravated by Alf's father's refusal to shelter with them:

My dad never used to go down the tube. He would take us down there, then leave us there. He was a very level-headed man. I won't say he wasn't frightened – we all were. So my dad was in the house in Waterloo Gardens when it was hit. When we came out of the shelter, all we thought was what has happened to him?

Luckily he was safe: he had escaped the area as the fires took hold. For the fourth time, he had to find the family another home.

Once in the new home, the routine continued with Mr Morris taking the family to the safety of the station before returning home to bed. As Alf explained, the whole family was frightened for him, but he had made his choice and intended to stick with it: 'One night there was a raid at about eleven o'clock. A stick of three bombs landed near my house where Dad was asleep.' The following morning Alf, his mother and his aunt came home fearing the worst. There was wreckage everywhere and the local area had been flattened. Approaching the house they realized it was not badly damaged, but all the windows had been blown out.

Making their way inside, Alf's mother began the search:

Mum called out, 'Where's Father? I can't find him!' I was shouting, 'I don't know!' She went in his bedroom and he was in bed with the wardrobe on top of him – he was still asleep! I can laugh now but I didn't laugh at the time. My aunt woke him up. He said 'What's the matter?' Mum swore at him. He just said, 'I didn't hear nothing, what happened?' He'd slept through it. He just said, 'Get this bleedin' wardrobe off me.' He was that placid, it didn't affect him.

It was only when he looked outside and saw the destruction that he realized how lucky he had been. As with every near miss and lucky escape, it made Alf Morris consider his situation: 'I realized we were lucky to still be alive.'

His father's reluctance to use tube shelters was understandable. For Peter Richards his local tube station became less attractive after he watched an old man empty a chamber pot on to the lines. He chose never again to sleep there. The overwhelming smell of body odour and stale urine was enough to convince him that Underground shelters were not the place to spend the night. He remembered the mass crowds and thought it was a good place to spread disease. The pandemonium as people fought for space was not conducive to a good night's sleep. Similarly, he was unimpressed to see his uncle heading to the tube station to shelter each night. His uncle had long told of his adventures in the trenches during the Great War. To the youngster it seemed wrong that a man who had seemed so heroic was reduced to sheltering in the stench of an overcrowded tube station. However, Peter later admitted he had been wrong to consider Uncle Bill a 'fallen idol': 'What a fool I was, and it was not long before I learned that one only has a limited amount of courage and can only stand so much ... I had not yet experienced the gut-wrenching fears that were to come as situations became ever more frightening.'

Rather than use the tube station or public shelters, Peter Richards and his father chose to take cover in the cellar of their home. For Peter the question was whether it was safer to sleep in the cellar and risk the house collapsing on him or sleep upstairs and risk falling with the house. In the end, he used both methods and counted himself lucky that his home was never bombed. One night, after returning from the youth club, Peter and his father took shelter for the night. Soon, the whole house was shaken by a nearby bomb that seemed to threaten to bring their house crashing down on them. Minutes later a neighbour entered, leading another man who was obviously dazed. It soon transpired his home had taken the brunt of the offending bomb: 'I remember him sitting in a chair and waiting for news. Of course, all the news was bad.' The man sat shocked and motionless, a glazed expression on his face, until the bombing lifted and he was able to make his way home to where the corpses of his wife and daughter were buried under the rubble.

With the new wartime routine of a troglodyte existence in shelters and cellars came a terrible sense of utter exhaustion. The days and nights seemed to blur into one another. Every man, woman and child living in the bombed areas seemed on the verge of collapsing. In the worst hit areas people increasingly moved in a sluggish manner. Too little sleep, too much fear and uncertainty took a toll on their senses. When they did sleep, people became increasingly difficult to raise. As a result some slept right through air raids, preferring the comfort of their beds to the discomfort of the shelter. One girl recalled watching her sister fast asleep. The older girl had a baby that she clung to at all times. On this night the child was not there, it was sleeping on the floor. Instead, the exhausted woman was hugging a pillow and sleepily whispering to it to offer comfort.

And so life went on. When the offices of *The Times* newspaper were bombed in September 1940, not a single issue failed to roll off the presses. Street markets operated in their familiar locations, with shoppers avoiding craters and piles of rubble. Shoeshine stalls continued to set up at stations and street corners to polish the leather of those who happily walked through the rubble to reach work and wanted to maintain their sartorial standards. Vicars held services in shattered and roofless churches. As J. B. Priestley wrote in the introduction to *Britain Under Fire*, published during the war years: 'Ordinary life goes on too . . . children play in side streets and fields; the girls and their boy friends rush off to dances or wait patiently outside motion picture theatres'.[2]

Whilst much of the population was coming to terms with life in an air raid shelter, there were large numbers of youths who had a role to play in the conduct of war. As a member of the Colonial Office Home Guard, John Cotter found himself on duty during the Blitz: 'That was the closest I came to being bombed. The building looked over on to Downing Street. A bomb landed just outside.' Although he was lucky to be living in the relative safety of Edgware, John Cotter began to understand the impact of the Blitz:

As the Blitz got going it used to be depressing travelling home at night. Once the Underground train got out of the tunnel at Hampstead, you'd see the searchlights and know that the sirens had gone. You could hear bombs and you knew you were in for a miserable night. Everything had changed, rationing had started – I couldn't get my sweets. I was smoking twenty a day and you couldn't get them. Things got a bit tight.

As a teenager in full-time employment, John enjoyed great independence in wartime London:

When I got back from work at night, there was nobody at home. My father was in a funk about the bombing, so he decided to take my mother and my sister by car from Edgware out to St Albans to a field. They parked in the field overnight. So there was me and brother left in the flat with our aged aunt who was a bit dotty and refused to go with them. She would go out on the balcony, shake her fist and shout, 'Bugger you, Mr Hitler.' We'd tell her to come in and close the blackout.

The irony was that the boys and their aunt were safe in their Edgware flat. However, the same could not be said for their parents: 'Out at St Albans, a bomb dropped in the field and shattered the glass in my father's car.'

One teenage girl, who started work in London in 1940 at age fourteen, recalled how the routine of her life continued:

I worked in London travelling to the Strand every day. You'd go up and overnight there had been a bombing – buildings had just disappeared. But life just carried on as normal, your daily routine was so disrupted. Sometimes travelling was difficult. If there was overnight bombing you'd get damage at the railway or station but I always managed somehow to get to work. Most of the bombing was at night – so there was either a train or there wasn't.

This sense of resolve would soon be named the 'Blitz Spirit'. To the people who experienced it, this was simply a case of carrying on with life as normal.

Now sixteen, Peter Richards was one whose life continued despite the bombing. Looking back, he recalled: 'My own reflections on the Blitz were how bloody stupid I was to take some of the risks I could have avoided.' If at home during raids he took shelter with his brother and father in the cellar; if not he carried on as if ignorant of the dangers. Rather than settle in at home each evening, awaiting the sirens, he continued to live a normal teenage life. He went to the cinema, to the youth club, to the gym or called on friends. He later explained how air raids could be treated with nonchalance: 'You become streetwise. You become wary of things.' If anti-aircraft guns opened fire, it was worth taking shelter to avoid the hail of shrapnel that rained down from the guns. Otherwise, just keep walking. If the drone of enemy bombers could be heard overhead, dive into a doorway and wait for them to pass – all the time hoping not to hear the whistle of falling bombs. Then, when the drone had passed, it was safe to continue on one's way. He later recalled: 'It was bloody stupid. I used to go out running in the middle of the bombing. It's not that I didn't worry, but we took a calculated risk. We ran from the youth club in Bloomsbury to Regent's Park or ran round Bedford Square.'

This disdain for the bombing was the product of youth. His parents could not influence his decision to take risks during the bombing:

My parents realized they couldn't do anything about it. They couldn't say, 'Stay in,' because if you stayed in there was always the danger that you'd get bombed. I just thought I'd be all right. It happens to other people – it wouldn't happen to me. That was the general feeling. But there was a time I can remember coming up from Kentish Town. There was a tremendous raid going on. I could hear the bombs coming very close. I flattened myself on the pavement and thought, 'This is the end.' So there were some scary moments. It wasn't all dancing around as if nothing was happening.

One particular evening stuck in Peter's memory, which he later recalled as: 'One of the hairiest episodes of my life.' He had been visiting a workmate in Edmonton, six miles from his own home. After an evening of chatting and listening to records, Peter got ready to cycle home. As he departed, the sirens began to sound. Rather than remain in Edmonton, he decided to keep going: 'It was a horrible raid, but what could I do? I suppose I could have gone into a shelter somewhere, but I'd have to leave my bike outside. It might have got pinched.' Realizing that nowhere was safe, he raced through the streets listening to the banging of anti-aircraft guns and the whistle and thump of falling bombs. At some points he cycled through clouds of smoke from newly burning buildings. Arriving safely at home he faced his greatest challenge: surviving the wrath of his mother who hated his going out during air raids. His mother's reaction was an indication of the generation gap: 'You believe you are immortal. You don't know any different. You've got the energy to do these things.'

His mate John Cotter took similar risks. One evening he could see activity in the skies and decided to head into central London to take a closer look:

> I got on the tube and went up to Tower Bridge station, by which time it was dark. There was nobody around and I went out on to Tower Bridge. There was a lot of bombing in the East End, I could see it. There was a tea factory burning just to the east of the bridge. A warden came along and said, 'You should be in a shelter, son.' I told him I was all right and he called me a 'Silly little sod' or something.

John watched as the sky lit up with explosions and burning buildings. He could hear the drone of enemy bombers and the bang of the anti-aircraft guns. It was a horrible, yet fascinating, spectacle:

> When I had seen enough I went back to the station, got on the District line then changed to head home to Edgware. The tubes were running

normally and underground everything seemed normal – apart from
the hundreds of people sheltering.

Looking back at the impetuosity of youth, he recalled: 'It was a thrill.
I didn't think of the danger – I didn't think it was going to affect me.
My parents didn't seem to worry about what I was doing. They let
me get on with it. My sister was still young, they were more worried
about her.'

Whilst parents fretted over the fate of younger children, the older
ones were more difficult to control. With a sense of defiance, they
did their best to continue with life. Some 40 per cent of
schoolchildren continued to visit the cinema at least once a week.
Of course, the spirit of independence shown by many youngsters
brought its own pitfalls. For Peter Richards, the cinema was a good
way to take one's mind off the reality of high explosive and
incendiary bombs. The only concern was where one should sit. Was
it safer to sit in the rear stalls and have the shelter of the balcony
above, or was that risking being crushed by a falling balcony?
Similarly, was it safer to sit at the front and only risk the falling
weight of the ceiling?

Parents fretted over absent children, whilst those youths who were
out and about knew the ominous feeling as they approached their
own street again, uncertain of what might greet them. In the south
London suburb of Mitcham, Peg – a teenage school-leaver – was
one of many who decided to ignore the dangers:

I used to go out in the evenings. We'd go up the West End. The sirens
would go, and my mother would say: 'You're not going out yet!' But I
couldn't care less. I told her, 'If it hits me, it hits me.' Life had to go on.
You've got to enjoy your young life. We'd go up to the West End, meet
some lads, go and have a coffee somewhere. We were having a lovely
time. I always wore high-heeled shoes. I'd be tripping down the road
with all this red-hot shrapnel falling around me. I didn't take any notice
of it.

She had dark hair and a Jewish appearance, and her family teased her about what would happen to her if the Germans came. This became her greatest concern: the fear of what might happen rather than the fear of what was happening.

Relief and horror were shared by thousands. For Terry Charles the realization of the true meaning of the bombing came after a night out at the cinema near his new home in West Kensington:

> Life went on. When the sirens went off you had a choice: stay or go. Some went and some stayed. It was a lottery – you could get hit by a bomb in the street or you could get hit in the cinema. One night, when I came home I found the end of my road completely blocked off. There were fire engines and ambulances there. The road was cordoned off and they wouldn't let me go down. I could see that the first three houses on either side were still standing but the rest of the road had gone. The last standing house was the one we lived in.

Desperate to find his family, Terry asked to be let through but was told the building was not safe, it might collapse at any moment. 'I had no idea where my mother was. Was she alive or dead? Nobody wanted to speak to a kid to tell me what had happened.' Such was the blur of activity that Terry could not remember how he actually located his family: as he later realized, he had probably blotted out the memory since it was so traumatic. Eventually he found they had been taken to the Hammersmith Hospital and were safe. When he finally got to speak with his mother she explained what had happened. The blast from the nearby bomb had come down the chimney and had thrown the fire into her lap, badly burning her. They had then scrambled under the Morrison shelter that acted as their table: 'Whilst they were there, the ceilings and all the upper floors of the flats above just collapsed on to the table. It saved their lives.' Despite the damage to the house, it was patched up and, after a period in temporary accommodation, the family moved back in.

The horrors inflicted upon London reached its symbolic climax on the night of Sunday, 29 December 1940. That night more than 20,000 bombs were dropped on London, including 127 tons of high explosive and countless incendiaries, most of which rained down on the City of London. The capital's historic heart – the Square Mile – was under attack. ARP wardens and firemen struggled to cope as the destruction mounted. The fire was concentrated in a semicircle from north-east to south-west of St Paul's Cathedral. As whole blocks were set ablaze, Christopher Wren's fabled dome was soon silhouetted against a viciously beautiful red sky. The white stones themselves reflected the flames, making the building stand out amidst the swirling plumes of thick black smoke that rose into the sky.

From his top-floor window in Ealing, Roy Bartlett, and the rest of the people from his shelter, watched the fires as they burned. They could see sudden bursts of flames as buildings collapsed into the fires that had engulfed them. Just as they had watched in terror on the first night of the Blitz, they watched as the heart of London was destroyed by flames. Even eight miles outside London, Sylvia Bowman was called out from the shelter by her father who pointed up at bright red skies above London and said, 'This is something you will never forget.' He was right:

I saw the night sky, burning red and black, the colours changing with the wind and the explosions. It was like a fire wall, I looked to the left and the right and the whole scene was the same. The silhouettes of the chimney pots made it seem like a vision. We could smell the sooty air. I was afraid.

Another witness to the bombing was Peter Richards. As usual, he had gone out to the cinema in central London. He listened to the wail of sirens from his seat but decided not to take shelter: 'We decided that the spectacle of song and dance that we were enjoying was preferable to the sights outside.' They finally emerged from the cinema to see the whole sky lit up. It was as if the sun was rising early over the East End and the City. Despite the horror of a city in flames, Peter had to admit: 'It looked fantastic.'

For other youngsters, the flames were more than something to be watched. Throughout the Blitz there were teenagers working in official capacities – in particular the messenger boys working for the police and fire service. In the streets around St Paul's Cathedral, seventeen-year-old Richard Holsgrove was among the teams of firemen fighting back the flames. He had joined the Auxiliary Fire Service as a messenger, aged sixteen, and had then been promoted to junior fireman at age seventeen. He first fought fires at Tilbury Docks, later recalling: 'People used to say you must have been scared, but it was exciting to me. I wasn't scared at that age.'[3] He had grown used to seeing the corpses of those hit by blast.

On the night of the City bombing, Richard and his fellow fire-fighters drove from Tottenham to Newgate Street near St Paul's. They were told to save the cathedral. As burning buildings collapsed around them, they aimed their hoses at the walls of the cathedral to cool them and prevent fire from reaching them. The youngster was one of the lucky ones: in a nearby street a wall collapsed, killing the firemen beneath it. He remained on duty in the City for three days before returning to Tottenham.

The next morning, Peter Richards made his way to work at the main postal depot in the City of London: 'I remember the looks of incredulity on the faces of office workers as they returned to the City from their homes in the suburbs. They could not reconcile themselves to the extent of the damage.' He picked his way through streets that had changed beyond all recognition. He went out to deliver mail to addresses that were no more than piles of smouldering ruins. In the previous weeks and months he had already seen the city change as familiar landmarks were destroyed and building after building disappeared. Then this one raid tore the very heart out of the City:

> I saw a remarkable change in this period. I was delivering express letters but word would come round, 'There's no point in delivering it

– they've been bombed out.' It was the gradual erosion of the city. The day after the big December raid the devastation was horrendous. Delivering any mail was touch and go. But I went out as normal and looked for places to deliver to. There was rubble all over the place and buildings still burning. The fire brigade were still hard at work. You couldn't go up some streets because they were cordoned off.

Later that day, as he took his lunch break in the Post Office canteen, he watched as a fellow worker complained that lamb chops were off the menu. At first he felt sorry for the man and then wondered why he was so concerned about food when the city was in ruins? He thought back to less than a year ago when he and his pal John Cotter had been so angry that the war had meant their holiday was cancelled. Just months earlier he had remained selfishly aloof from the realities of war. Now he was able to reflect on his own self. Was he now changing? Was he maturing enough to understand what conflict really meant?

CHAPTER 6

The Water Babies

'Never take your life jacket off!'

Colin Ryder Richardson's mother's instructions to him
before sailing for America

The busy port seemed a far cry from the streets of St John's Wood where Colin Ryder Richardson had lived pre-war, or the lanes of Sussex where he had spent the early months of war, or rural Wales where the family had then settled. However, as Colin and his mother emerged from Liverpool's Lime Street station, the contrast could not have been greater. The city had recently been blighted by the Luftwaffe. In peacetime a young public-schoolboy like Colin would probably never have had a reason to travel north to a grand yet tough city like Liverpool, which had become, for so many, the gateway to England. In a few short years its docks would become the entry-point for American servicemen heading to the Old World to join the struggle against Nazism. However, in 1940 it was still predominantly a port of exit, taking refugees like the eleven-year-old schoolboy across the Atlantic to safety.

Colin's parents had decided he would join the SS *City of Benares*, a passenger liner due to depart for Canada, and from there it was agreed he would travel to America's Long Island and live with a

New York banker for the rest of the war. The reasons for the family's decision to send Colin overseas were simple, practical ones. It was known that the Germans searched for Jews in occupied countries by checking who had been circumcised, making it likely the Nazis would use the same method if they ever occupied Britain. Colin had been circumcised and risked being wrongly identified as Jewish, so it would be safer to get him away.

However, such concerns were not upmost in the boy's mind. He was delighted, particularly at the thought that he was heading to a land of 'Cowboys and Indians': 'I thought of the sun and the hills. The cowboys – eating around campfires: "Ride 'em cowboy!" When they said I was going to New York, I thought I'd bagged another town! My only concern was fitting in with the American children.' Enthused by films, comic books and action stories, Colin believed adventure awaited him across the Atlantic. What he did not know then, however, was that the adventure – if it could be called that – would actually come in the cold, dark waters of that ocean.

The 485-foot long *City of Benares* was to carry 191 passengers, including 90 children – 46 boys and 44 girls – heading to North America to escape the incendiaries and high explosive raining down on British cities. Built in Glasgow, and launched in 1936, the *Benares* had served the imperial passenger trade between Liverpool and Bombay. Crewed by 215 sailors, many of them Indians, the 11,000-ton liner – with its fresh coat of paint and newly installed guns – was to be the home to children selected as part of a new evacuation scheme: the Children's Overseas Reception Board (CORB). It was a proposed scheme that had initially met significant opposition, not least from the Prime Minister, Winston Churchill, as opponents argued that dividing families and removing children across the Atlantic sent out a defeatist message. Churchill felt it was better to stand and fight together and damn the consequences. In 'Total War' children were, after all, a significant asset. Had King George himself not set such an example by keeping his wife and children at his side even as his capital – and eventually, his palace – came under aerial assault?

Despite such deep opposition, on 18 June 1940 the Cabinet had finally acquiesced and the scheme went ahead; it was ordered that all overseas evacuees should be between five and fifteen years old. The scheme proved highly popular as in just two weeks the CORB offices received more than 200,000 applications for just 20,000 places from parents eager to send their offspring to safety.

There was an emotional and rational dilemma for parents considering this option. Evacuating your children to the nearby countryside was a burden for most parents, but there was always the hope of weekend reunions. Those sending children overseas, however, would miss out on so much of their child's development. A teenage girl might return home as a woman – even a married woman if the war lasted long enough. Yet the child would almost certainly be safe from war in Canada. In the cases of the *Benares* children, the argument for safety had triumphed over that of separation. Better a distant yet living child than the chance to visit a nearby grave.

Colin Ryder Richardson was travelling independently but the CORB children on the ship had an orderly introduction to evacuation. They had been summoned to Liverpool by letter telling their parents they had been granted a place in the programme. A visit from a CORB representative had followed to explain the details and announce that the children would depart within a week. Those chosen had travelled by train to Liverpool, and then were sent to a local school where they could form into a group, establish relationships and meet their adult escorts.

However, it was during the two days they had spent at that school that Liverpool received its first visit from the Luftwaffe. As the bombs fell, the children listened to the pounding of the anti-aircraft guns and, for those who had not yet encountered modern warfare on their doorsteps, the impact of the bombs and the roar of the guns was a stark reminder of why their parents had applied for them to leave the country. On Thursday, 12 September, the gathered children left the school ready for their great adventure. The journey to the *Benares* took them through a landscape completely altered by war, as the city displayed the scars of the bombing. The children arrived at the dockside like the earlier evacuees, clutching small suitcases and gas masks, and with a cardboard label tied to their lapels. Some were already evacuation veterans who had been separated from their families at the outbreak of war.

From the moment the children walked up the gangplank to board the ship, they were in awe of their new home. The vast passenger liner, towering over the dockside, was an introduction to a world few had previously experienced. There was the mysteriously exotic crew of Indian stewards in their immaculately laundered jackets. Inside they found bunk beds, portholes, play rooms and deck games like something from Hollywood.

Dressed in a bright red jacket, Colin Ryder Richardson stood out from the other children. But it was no ordinary jacket. Instead, it had been specially created by his mother ready for his Atlantic journey. She had sewn a life jacket inside a red silk jacket, which in turn had been stuffed with kapok to provide extra insulation. As she had told him: 'Never take your life jacket off.' However, despite his mother's obvious concern, there was no emotional farewell between them. Colin had handed over his gas mask and then she had handed him his passport, telling him: 'There's your ship. Goodbye, Colin.' Then, she had given him a quick hug and departed, choosing not to hang around waving at the departing ship. In a way, the eleven year old felt relieved as he saw some of the other children engaged in tearful farewells which he knew were not for him.

The *Benares* was sailing into a dangerously uncertain world. Not only had the departure been delayed by sea mines dropped into the Mersey by the Luftwaffe two weeks earlier, but the very first CORB evacuation ship, the SS *Volendam*, had been torpedoed on the second day of its voyage. Luckily, all of its passengers, including 320 evacuee children, were saved. The impact of this near disaster had been obscured by the start of the Blitz. Every bomb that fell on British towns, blasting away the bricks and mortar across the land, threatened the nation's children, so the news of 320 shipwrecked survivors had failed to deter the CORB parents. Indeed, two of the *Benares* children were actually veterans of the *Volendam* who had been shipwrecked in the Atlantic, had returned to England to find their homes destroyed by bombs and as a result had immediately been allowed to seek evacuation on the next available ship.

Once the convoy was underway the children soon found ways to entertain themselves. In the days ahead, the *Benares*'s decks played host to games including tug-of-war, tennis and even a lassoing contest, all of which helped to occupy the evacuees. Coming from a land already feeling the pinch of rationing, the children were thrilled to find they could purchase sweets, chocolate and lemonade and at meal times they ordered whatever they desired, with no need to surrender their ration books. Meat and milk, fresh fruit and vegetables, freshly baked bread – everything appeared on their tables at meal times.

Colin Ryder Richardson settled into his cabin and started to enjoy the crossing. His mother had packed his travelling trunk and he was astonished to find he had a dozen pairs of underwear. He liked the food onboard, was thrilled by the sight of barefoot Lascar seamen wearing traditional white Indian clothes and was fascinated to discover the ship had a gun mounted on the decks, although the gunners manning it told him they didn't actually have any ammunition. He spent his time reading books and magazines in the library and playing games on the decks: 'It was quite windy and we got deckchairs and, using the seat like a sail, would try to get them to go from one side of the ship to the other. Sometimes they went overboard. We would roar with laughter.' Officially, Colin was sharing the cabin with Laszlo Raskai, a Hungarian journalist who was supposed to act as his guardian for the duration of the crossing. However, the two had little contact: Colin was free to do as he liked, whilst Raskai spent his time in the lounges and cocktail bar.

By 17 September, Convoy OB-213 and the SS *Benares* were 600 miles from land. Seemingly safe from German raiders, the Royal

Navy withdrew and headed homewards to protect shipping nearer the coast. With the convoy spread through the waters, and now seemingly alone in the ocean, the *Benares* headed into a storm. The clouds had come down, the winds and rains had gathered and the waves were rolling, all portents of the rising storm. By nine o'clock that night a force-ten gale was blowing, with squalls rocking the ship. Yet the real danger was not the storm, but what lurked beneath the waves.

That night Colin Ryder Richardson went to bed in his usual manner. Unlike some of the other children, who had followed the instruction that they could take off their life jackets, Colin had continued to heed his mother's warning and before retiring for the night, he pulled on the life jacket over his pyjamas. As he lay in bed reading a comic, the eleven year old listened to the rolling of a ball-bearing he had placed in his bedside drawer, beating out the movement of the ship. That night Colin's ball-bearing crashed from side to side, telling him the ship was in dangerously heavy waters.

Below the waves, the convoy was being trailed by *U-48*, a German U-boat, captained by Heinrich Bleichrodt. He was waiting until the sea calmed enough for him to launch his attack. Finally, he gave the order to fire and two torpedoes erupted from their tubes, surging through the water. The crew listened for the signature crash of an explosion but nothing came. Then the captain gave another order and a third torpedo was fired. The 500-pound, explosive-packed weapon sped towards the ship. It was three minutes past ten on the evening of 17 September 1940 when the third torpedo crashed home, piercing hold number five, directly beneath the children's quarters.

Colin Ryder Richardson remembered the moment the torpedo struck the *Benares*:

> It was a bit late for me to be up, but I was by myself and took the opportunity to do some reading. I was sitting up in bed reading a comic – the *Dandy* or the *Beano*. I was listening to the ball-bearing and

thinking we were another day into the journey, another day nearer America. But I knew we were going very slowly. Then I heard a bang. My first thought was that we'd collided with another ship. Then I smelled the explosives – it was an easy smell to recognize. That hastened me. I got out of bed.

Colin acted quickly. With his life jacket already on over his pyjamas, he stepped into his slippers and put on his dressing gown. He also grabbed the wallet his father had given him containing £10 and slipped it into his pocket.

Elsewhere, one of the girls awoke, uncertain of what had disturbed her, reached for the light switch and couldn't understand why it wouldn't work. But, stepping down from her bunk, she discovered why, as her bare feet were immediately submerged in a pool of water. Others heard the impact and were immediately stirred into action as the boat shuddered and shivered around them. The crashing and splintering they heard meant just one thing: they were in danger. The children who were quickest to react immediately roused their companions, forcing them from their beds, pressing life jackets into fumbling fingers and readying them for whatever awaited. Barefooted kids leapt from their bunks only to slice open their feet on broken glass, others fumbled in the darkness for their glasses. Some had to push debris away before they could rise. One boy was forced to break through the wall, hacking at the plaster with a chair leg, to escape his cabin.

As the children began to leave their cabins, older children began to assist the younger evacuees, checking their life jackets, hurrying them along corridors and making sure they knew where to go. Two of the older girls, Bess Walder and Beth Cummings, rushed to help Beth's roommate Joan Irving who had been injured in the explosion. It wasn't heroics: it was simply their duty.

Some of the survivors later recalled being gripped by a surge of adrenaline that spurred them on. Strangely, despite their fear, it just seemed like another new adventure. In the first days of the journey, despite some homesickness most of the children had been gripped by a sense of excitement at the thought of heading west but it was something far more violent and disturbing that now faced them.

Quickly, the children gathered at the prearranged points. Colin went up to the cocktail lounge where his lifeboat was to assemble. There was little panic. Instead, people were milling around wondering what had happened as the ship's alarm bells rang in the background. Colin kept quiet, not wanting to alert the adults to the fact the ship had been torpedoed. Each lifeboat had its own position where groups assembled to meet their fellow passengers and the sailors who were to assist them and crew the boats. Most looked around and noted how calm everyone seemed to be. There were no crying children, just boys and girls quietly standing and shivering in their nightclothes and slippers as the storm raged around them. Slowly, the situation began to worsen. The weather grew increasingly harsh, soaking the children, some of whom were without coats or shoes. Then as a number of injured children, bloodied and bandaged, were brought on deck, fear grew and a few began to cry.

As the CORB children gathered at their lifeboat stations, the private passengers waited in the lounge, Colin Ryder Richardson among them. Eventually he moved out on to the decks. At first he hadn't been frightened, but once on the deck the situation changed as he looked out to sea and thought to himself: 'It's going to be difficult for the lifeboats to get through that lot.' What also struck him was the sight of the other children: 'These little kids beside me – some of them were only five years old. They were in their dressing gowns with no life-belt, clutching teddy bears. They'd just woken up.' In the commotion not all the lifeboats could be safely lowered. Lifeboat No. 8 was the first to go. As it slipped down towards the water, the boat lurched, one end jerked downwards and was smashed by a wall of water. Passengers were thrown into the water and scattered by the swirling sea. In seconds, they were gone.

As he waited to board his lifeboat, Colin was reunited with Mr Raskai, his Hungarian guardian, who was told for the moment it was 'women and children first': 'Mr Raskai bravely helped me into the swinging lifeboat. This thing was crashing about against the ship and I had to climb over the rail. They didn't have anyone at the ends holding it steady.' Once filled, the lifeboat was quickly lowered into the raging seas. Whilst other boats were overturned, Lifeboat No. 2 stayed upright. However, it was soon filled with water as waves crashed over the bows and, as they tried to escape from the stricken ship, more poured in until the escaping passengers were sitting up to their chests in water. Only the lifeboat's buoyancy tanks prevented it from slipping completely beneath the waves. As Colin later recalled, it was like sitting in a giant bathtub filled with freezing water.

An elderly nurse called Colin to her side, hoping to protect the small, lonely child. However, the situation soon became desperate. The heavy seas soon washed away the mast and oars. The sailors attempted to get the handle working to start the propeller designed to move the boat to safety. However, with so much water in the boat, the handle was of little use except to give people something to hang on to.

Lifeboat No. 5 seemed to keep level during its descent to the sea, but this was an illusion. It was level with the side of the ship, not with the water. With one lurch twelve passengers were thrown from the boat and lost in the darkness. Other lifeboats surrendered people to the ocean, leaving children floundering in the waters. They were terrified as they trod water and looked up at the steel sides of the ship as the waves battered them. A few were lucky to reach out for rope ladders lowered down to them, climbing back to the decks where they shivered in their sodden clothes before being wrapped in blankets by crew members. However, the less fortunate were soon lost in the storm.

Once among the waves, the sturdy lifeboats were soon shown to be vulnerable to the power of the ocean. Having already lost some of its passengers, Lifeboat No. 5 soon took on water before being upended and its passengers were cast into the storm. In seconds

many disappeared, scattered by the surging waves. Two among
them, the evacuees Bess Walder and Beth Cummings, found
themselves struggling to stay afloat just yards from the upturned
keel. The desperate girls reached out for the boat, grabbed the keel
and hung on for dear life. As they took stock of their surroundings
they could see they were among a group of about a dozen survivors.

Those adrift in the waters were in immediate danger. At this
temperature they might be expected to survive no more than three
hours before hypothermia would set in and hasten their death. Some
of the children kicked out, swimming towards the lifeboats and the
twenty-two rafts that had been released from the decks. A few clung
to driftwood in the hope it might keep them afloat. One desperate
boy called out to his mother, seated safely in a nearby lifeboat.
Others tried desperately to tread water before surrendering to the
freezing water, their bodies washed away in the chaos. A fortunate
few of the children were saved by adults who dived from the safety
of their lifeboats, swam swiftly through the waves and pulled them
to safety. One man alone pulled thirteen evacuees to safety. Colin's
escort, Laszlo Raskai, swam to safety with a child clinging to him.
He then struck out to rescue another child but soon disappeared in
the swirling seas.

Children joined in the rescues, with one thirteen-year-old boy
helping to haul a child into the boat. Seconds later the boat was hit
by a wave, throwing the boy overboard. As his fellow passengers
reached out, more waves crashed against the boat and the hero
disappeared from sight. As the survivors scrambled for lifeboats,
clung on to rafts or desperately tried to steer the lifeboats away from
the stricken liner, the *Benares* finally slipped beneath the waters.
From the half-submerged Lifeboat No. 2, Colin Ryder Richardson
watched the scene:

> The ship's emergency lights were still on. You could see people
> running around on the decks. I could see people trying to get down a
> ladder into the sea. People were jumping. We were still quite near the

Benares when suddenly you could see she was sinking by the stern. It was extraordinary to see your temporary home sinking under the water. Up went the bows and down she went! Up until then we had the comfort of the ship in the water beside us.

It was a staggering sight for the children who had expected the ship to sweep them over the sea to safety. The liner groaned and stood almost vertical, its bow rising from the water; the emergency lights went out and then it was gone. The survivors were all alone in the storm.

Colin took stock of his situation. He was on a lifeboat submerged up to his chest in freezing cold water. At first those onboard had tried to bail out the water, but it was hopeless: as soon as water was thrown over the side, more crashed back in with the waves. The one consolation was that the water in the boat helped keep it steady, so it was not tossed as roughly as it might have been. Colin also realized he was better off than some of his fellow passengers, who were poorly dressed for their circumstances. He had his life jacket, with its buoyancy device sewn within padded silk, a balaclava that had been specially knitted for him and he had even found a pair of gloves his mother had put in his pockets. These would be essential in the hours ahead as he gripped the gunwales of the half-submerged boat.

As the night engulfed them, Colin noticed some of the Indian sailors shaking from the cold, their thin cotton uniforms doing little to protect them from the storm. The situation on the lifeboat seemed hopeless; they were all freezing and soaked to the skin. As Colin recalled, comfort only came from urinating in the water: for a few brief seconds he could feel a bit of warm water swirling around his legs. 'We couldn't sing at all. You couldn't communicate – you had to keep your mouth shut because of the water. The waves were pouring over us.' Within half an hour, Colin watched as four sailors slipped into unconsciousness and died. Now a grim task awaited the young boy as he helped release the corpses, pushing them quietly from the lifeboat and consigning them to a watery grave.

With the corpses pushed out, Colin turned his attention to a woman beside him: 'This elderly nurse sitting next to me – who had earlier been comforting me, as an elderly lady would do – became distressed. I realized she was sinking into the water so I put my arm around her and tried to keep her head above the water.' Colin held on to the nurse, comforting her in her hour of need. Stroking her hair and lifting her head, the brave boy did his best to preserve her morale and her life. He whispered to her, telling her that they would soon be rescued but he couldn't really do much for her. He was freezing cold, his balaclava helmet had slipped from his head and he couldn't pull the sodden wool back in place: 'I couldn't do much for her, I was only eleven and I had my own problems! Luckily I had string gloves so I could keep a grip.' Grip was exactly what he needed, as being a small child the waves were threatening to pick him up and wash him out into the sea. If Colin didn't hold on tightly he knew he would soon be lost.

During the night Colin looked out to sea and spotted a light. His spirits immediately lifted: surely it was a rescue boat. He was wrong. What he had seen was the conning tower of the submarine, which had surfaced to catch sight of the damage it had caused. As the night progressed, many of those who had escaped the sinking ship succumbed to the elements. Sitting in their sodden clothes, body temperatures began to fall. Those who succumbed to sleep soon joined the growing numbers of dead whose bodies were cast overboard. Aboard one of the lifeboats a freezing boy drifted into unconsciousness, lost his grip, and somehow slipped into the sea as the boat rolled on the waves. He was saved by a fellow passenger who, summoning up energy from somewhere, leaned over the boat's edge and dragged the boy to safety. However, his efforts were wasted, as within minutes the boy died. In a touching scene on another lifeboat, a sailor and one of the adult passengers were each seen bouncing some small children on their lap but it too was an illusion. The children had been travelling with their mother who was on the same boat. As the mother reached the end of her endurance, and appeared to give up the will to live, the men were attempting to raise her spirits. By seemingly playing with the children they hoped it might give the woman strength. She could not be allowed to know the truth: the children on the laps of the men were already dead. The ruse was unsuccessful, too, as the mother joined the growing list of the victims.

In some lifeboats children drifting into unconsciousness were revived with a nip of brandy. Soaked to the skin, battered by the winds and on the verge of freezing to death, this might have been just the thing to keep them alive. The spirit had an instantaneous effect, rousing them from their dangerous slumbers and giving them brief hope. Yet the change was fleeting: almost as soon as the brandy had brought them back from the verge of death, it helped magnify their exhaustion. Instead of shivering and shaking as they froze to death, they were soothed into a deadly sleep in an alcoholic haze.

As the hours passed and dawn finally broke, somehow Bess Walder and Beth Cummings had managed to cling on to the upturned lifeboat. Out of the dozen or so souls who had clung on to the keel the previous evening, just the two girls and two sailors remained. As every second passed it seemed it would be easier just to give up, let go and drift off to sleep in the water. However, between them their spirits helped maintain their strength, preserving their morale. It was clear to both girls that if one died, they would both die and somehow they maintained their grip.

As dawn rose Colin Ryder Richardson was still comforting his neighbour who was now silent and one of the sailors quietly told the boy the woman was dead. Eventually he realized there was nothing more he could do for her:

> The old lady died in my arms. By that time I had no strength to move, to let her go, because of the stiffness and the cold. Others suggested I push her away but I couldn't. Also she offered me a bit of physical support against the sea.

In the end he realized he would have to let her go:

> She was slipping down into the boat, lying on her back in front of me.
> Then she was moving in and out of the boat, with all the others who
> were dying, who were floating up on their lifebelts. They were floating
> out to sea and then floating back into the lifeboat. They were a bloody
> menace – they were like bits of flotsam you didn't want to be hit by.
> You didn't want a fourteen-stone corpse banging into you.

It was time to push the old lady overboard to join those who had
died in the night. The boy was hardly able to move. As he had
gripped the woman his arms had stiffened leaving him with hardly
enough strength to move himself, let alone shift the woman.
Somehow, aided by one of the sailors, he was able to lift her from the
water, ease her corpse over the edge of the boat and into the sea.
With so many bodies around them, the sailor in charge eventually
asked Colin to help him with the other corpses. The eleven year old
was worried about letting go of the lifeboat but also knew they had to
get rid of the dead. Not only were they a nuisance, but their close
proximity was affecting the survivors' morale. So Colin helped the
sailor push the rest of the corpses from the boat, and tried to get them
far enough away so they wouldn't float back in again: 'We were all
becoming very sleepy, delirious, just mentally drifting. This was
dangerous. I had seen this happen to others, who then succumbed.'

For Colin, this was a sudden and violent introduction to the
realities of life – and death:

> I had nothing on my mind except staying alive. I could see people
> dying around me. I felt worried, I felt drowsy and I knew that if I fell
> asleep I would die. I thought, 'Wake up, Colin! You must stay awake.'
> But it's a natural thing to want to go to sleep. When you are sitting still,
> there isn't much you can do to stay awake. I had an internal fight to
> keep myself active, awake and alive. Some others didn't seem to want
> to stay alive – they seemed irrational.

With the numbers of dead growing, the survivors clung to whatever small hope they could muster. Above all, it was the growing light of dawn that lifted their spirits. As the horizon slowly became clearer, Colin told himself he would live. Surely now a ship would save them. Yet the dawn brought something else: a clear knowledge of how perilous was their situation. In the light of day it was easier to see who was alive and who was dead. More than that, the lifeboats were drifting on a sea that revealed the true nature of the previous night's tragedy. There was wreckage floating in the water amidst swirling patches of oil. Worst of all were the floating corpses all around the lifeboats. Where the sea took the boats, so it took the bodies. Just to add to their misery, hail and rain continued to fall.

In this gloomy world, Colin's conviction they would be saved suffered many blows. The dawn saw just fourteen living souls in his boat, which had begun its journey with thirty-eight. They remained half-submerged with no way of bailing out the water. In the distance he could see other lifeboats, and he watched as one young man descended into madness, threatening his fellow passengers, screaming at those around him. Then finally, and mercifully, the man threw himself overboard.

As the day broke, Colin continued to believe that salvation would come but he also knew if he fell asleep he would die before the rescuers arrived. Every element of his being was thrown into staying awake. He concentrated on the brave singing of the adults around him, as they too attempted to raise their spirits. He continued with the grim task of pushing away the corpses that endlessly rolled from the waters into the ailing lifeboat. All the time he knew that a single heavy wave might be enough finally to submerge them.

By late morning the rains ceased and the survivors attempted to use the weak sun to dry their clothes and revive their numb flesh. Clothing and blankets were laid out to dry, ready in case the storm rose again. For some there was nothing to be done. Bess and Beth, the two girls hanging on to the upturned lifeboat, had no relief from the waters. There was nowhere for them to go. At one point they spotted a lifeboat and tried to call out, but could not raise a sound. Their exertions the previous night had left their throats dry. Yet they had been spotted, though as fast as the sailors on the nearby lifeboat attempted to work the vessel towards them, the waves beat them back. By the time the waves had finally subsided, the girls were out of sight again. Nonetheless, the girls hung on and were not alone in their fortitude.

In the aftermath of the sinking, many of the children had displayed mental and physical courage. Colin had amazed the adults by his efforts to help his fellow passengers and keep the dead from rolling back into the boat. Elsewhere, a girl urged her mother to keep awake and stay alive. The desperate mother suggested they take off their lifebelts, slip over the side of the boat and go to sleep in the water. It was a touching invitation to suicide, a way that mother and daughter might at least die together. Yet the girl shouted at her mother, urging her to see sense, insisting that rescue would come and they should be alive to see it. On one of the rafts, an evacuee and a sailor toiled to rescue a sailor who had slipped overboard. Grabbing the man under his arms they somehow managed to pull him back to safety. The sailor was amazed at the strength of the child who, despite a freezing night perched atop a life raft, had summoned from somewhere the energy to help pull the man to safety.

And so the day continued: some people died whilst others defied death, fighting back through the cold and the pain to keep themselves alive, just hoping a rescue boat might be on its way. All day, this thought filled their minds: stay awake long enough and surely a boat must come. It was simple: the mentally strong would live, the weak would die. Yet with the light slowly fading even the strongest among them began to wilt. Through the night and the morning, they had been pitching over the waves, desperate to be rescued, yet no one had come. Certainly some of the survivors claimed they had seen boats, whether they were real or imagined was anybody's guess.

Yet someone out there was searching for them. Detached from its convoy duties, HMS *Hurricane*, a Royal Navy destroyer, had been ordered to find the *Benares* survivors. The ship's captain had headed through the storm, coaxing as much speed as was wise to reach the position of the lifeboats. Spurring him on was the knowledge that so many children had been aboard the ship. Captain Simms ordered all lookouts into position and set the ship on a course to conduct a 'box search' that would cover the entire area in which survivors might be expected to be found.

At first the *Hurricane* found nothing but then the sea began to reveal a lucky few. The first boat to be spotted contained survivors from a merchant vessel that had been sunk the same night. As fortune had it, two of the children from the *Benares* were aboard the craft, the first of the evacuees to be rescued. The next lifeboat spotted from the *Hurricane* proved less encouraging. The warship launched her whaler, sending sailors to investigate. They struck out through the waves to reach the lifeboat, on which they had counted twenty survivors. But it was an illusion. The lifeboat carried twenty corpses: all had succumbed to the elements during the night.

However, as the search continued, the news began to improve and, one by one, the lifeboats were located. It was not a quick process, as a box search requires skilful navigation and endless patience, but it was worthwhile. The sailors steered carefully, ensuring the destroyer did not swamp the lifeboats and rafts as it approached. On one occasion, as it was alongside a raft while a young boy was being pulled up from below, a sudden movement of the warship swamped the raft, washing two sailors overboard. The two exhausted men were saved by a trio of sailors who dived overboard before the sea could sweep them away. The eight-year-old boy who had been lifted to safety was taken to the *Hurricane*'s engine room where he was revived.

On Lifeboat No. 10, just one child had survived and fourteen had died. As they reached Lifeboat No. 11, the sailors found just fourteen passengers had survived, with twenty having perished overnight, including nine of the eleven children who boarded from the stricken liner. One of the survivors was Louis Walder, the brother of Bess Walder who was still adrift, clinging desperately to an upturned lifeboat. The other was Rex Thorne, whose sister had perished as the *Benares* launched its lifeboats. He was not alone in his suffering: as the survivors were slowly lifted onboard the *Hurricane* a fortunate few were joyfully reunited with their families, while others had their worst fears confirmed.

When Bess Walder and Beth Cummings were finally rescued, the sailors were shocked to find the girls had survived their ordeal. They were so cold and exhausted their frozen and swollen fingers had to be prised from their grip on the lifeboat. It seemed the girls were on the brink of succumbing to exposure as they could hardly move and did not respond to obvious pain. They could not speak and their mouths and throats were filled with sores. It was intensely painful and they could hardly swallow the drinks they were offered – but they were alive.

Finally, HMS *Hurricane* reached Lifeboat No. 2 where Colin Ryder Richardson had somehow managed to survive. At first he couldn't believe it. He had been thinking he would see a ship but nothing had arrived. All he could think was 'Where's the bloody Navy?' But now the moment had come. Suddenly, the increasingly drowsy boy looked up and saw the *Hurricane*, his thoughts immediately changing: 'I thought, she looks so beautiful.' As they neared Lifeboat No. 2, the sailors were astounded to hear the survivors singing 'Rule Britannia'. The first to leave the half-submerged lifeboat was the eleven-year-old Colin. He had been told to climb up the scrambling nets to reach the decks, but he was too weak to do so. Instead, a rope was placed around him and he was pulled towards the deck. He was shaking with cold and could hardly control his body, feeling nothing below the waist. His skin seemed waterlogged and as 'soft as jelly'. Whilst he had been so brave during the night, his ordeal was over and finally his body and mind succumbed to the cold. He could no longer stand up and was immediately rushed to the engine room to join other survivors.

Once aboard, the survivors were washed down, cuts were treated to prevent infection and frostbitten limbs carefully cleaned. Many had skin that was swollen and split as a result of their prolonged immersion in water. As the children were laid down to go to sleep, they were watched over to prevent them slipping into a coma. Despite all efforts, three of the children died after being rescued.

Although the captain and crew of the *Hurricane* believed they had rescued all the survivors, they were wrong. The first boat they had found was not from the *Benares* but from the *Marina*, the merchant ship that had been torpedoed the same night and which had carried a number of survivors from the liner. Lifeboat No. 12 had been missed. With a large complement of sailors onboard, the craft had not remained on the same patch of water. Instead, they had set sail for the nearest land, the coast of Ireland, hundreds of miles to the east.

There were forty-six people on board, a combination of seamen (both British and Indian), passengers and six children. The six boys were thirteen-year-old Ken Sparks, eleven year olds Howard Claytor, Paul Shearing and Fred Steels, and nine year olds Billy Short and Derek Capel. The experience of the sailors was vital to any hopes of survival. Most importantly they could navigate, were strong enough, initially, to work the 'Fleming' gear to help move the craft through the waters and vitally could organize the precious food rations to ensure they could be distributed fairly and last for a week. The boys in the lifeboat were lucky to be under a canvas shelter, rigged up by the sailors to protect the youngsters from the elements.

The boys on Lifeboat No. 12 were in many ways fortunate. Unlike some of the other boats the passengers were dry, their boat not having been swamped by the waves like the other craft. That said, their ordeal was only just beginning. The other boats had been the scene of immediate misery, with sodden and shivering people just hanging on for survival. For Lifeboat No. 12 the sufferings took longer to start but endured for days after. The cold was something none who lived through it could ever forget. Even wrapped up in blankets and huddled in their shelter, the boys couldn't avoid the weather. The wind burned their skin, dried and chapped their lips. Salt particles formed in their clothes and matted their hair. Their mouths grew parched and dry, leaving them hardly able to swallow the biscuits they received for their meals. It was the ultimate agony, surrounded by water but dying of thirst. Each day they received seemingly miserly rations, yet these were doled out in such a way to keep them alive for as long as possible. A few sips of water and a mouthful of ship's biscuits, supplemented at times with thin slices of tinned fruit, did just enough to keep them alive.

There were a few moments of relief. The sight of whales skimming through the waters gave them something to occupy their minds for a few moments. One of the sailors cheered them by tirelessly undertaking daily swims, as if to prove that if he had sufficient energy to keep moving then so should they. To keep their minds off their misery, the one woman on the boat – a children's escort named Mary Cornish – made up stories. These featured the popular character Bulldog Drummond, a hero known for the sort of heroics popular in the period. She had no idea where her stories were heading – or, indeed, whether the boys would survive long enough to hear the ending – but she knew it was vital to keep their spirits up. She also attempted to calm the boys by stressing that they were, just like Bulldog Drummond, living through their own personal adventure. She told them that any number of other British boys would envy them their adventure.

Yet for all its initial excitement, this was not a glamorous escapade. Misery was heaped upon misery as the boys watched the adults around them suffer. There was a seriously ill priest curled up before them. Worst of all, some were reduced to madness with one suicidal sailor diving overboard and surrendering to the waves. Such incidents lowered their morale, with their spirits only lifted again when the ever-decreasing rations were issued.

As the days passed it was the boys' turn to be touched by madness. One of their number, Paul Shearing, was reduced to crying out as his desire for water took over. He screamed out in recognition of his own madness, his desperate desire for liquid to sate his thirst. Those assisting him noted how the boy's feet and legs were bloated and marked with sores. It was clear he was dying and a small extra measure of water was surreptitiously smuggled to him, helping ward off the effects of thirst and hunger for a few brief minutes.

Wrapping clothes around Paul's legs and body to raise his body temperature, the adults tried to clean and dress his swollen legs, soothing the sores that afflicted him. They rubbed the puffy flesh to aid his circulation, in the hope of warding off frostbite. It was desperate and seemingly doomed to failure, but it was all they could do in the circumstances. Yet for all it seemed the boy could not possibly survive, by the eighth morning Paul had somehow defied the odds. He was still on the brink of madness and death, but he was still there in the boat along with the five other boys.

Though the boys did not know it then, their ordeal was almost over. After more than a week adrift their supplies were almost exhausted. A little water remained but it was hardly enough to do more than just wet their lips. Some food was still available but without water there was little hope anybody could generate enough saliva to swallow it. Though only the sailors realized it, the inhabitants of Lifeboat No. 12 were facing their final hours.

Somehow, seemingly out of nowhere, salvation finally came. It was one of the children, Ken Sparks, who first spotted it. He spotted a dot in the sky. At first the others dismissed it as a bird, a cloud or a trick of the light – more likely a trick of the mind. From his parched throat came the cry, 'Plane!' Some ignored him but others followed his gaze. Next the boy was on his feet waving his shirt in the direction of the apparition. Soon it came closer, revealing its form: it was a plane. For the children, this soon took on an element of a favourite wartime game. All across Britain, boys had developed a deep interest in aviation, learning to identify aircraft by their silhouettes. In the summer of 1940 plane-spotting had become the number one pastime for many youths, developing childish rivalries of who could best identify the aircraft – both British and German – that filled the skies. Those who had studied seaplanes soon realized this was a Short Sunderland, an aircraft that hunted submarines across the seas around Britain.

Though the plane came close, there was still some time before salvation would come. Unable to land on the choppy seas, the crew instead signalled to the sailors by Morse code signalling lamp, telling them that another plane would soon be with them, to be followed by a ship. True to their word, the plane soon arrived, dropping food and water to the desperate passengers of Lifeboat No. 12. Within minutes they were gorging themselves in anticipation of the forthcoming relief. Then what had become unthinkable finally came: on the horizon appeared HMS *Anthony*.

As the warship came alongside, the children looked up to see sailors smiling down at them. Within minutes they were hauled to the decks and were soon ensconced in the mess drinking tea and orange juice, and eating porridge. Next came warm baths and a change of clothing, wrapping themselves in baggy uniforms offered by the crew. In a short time it seemed the boys, except Paul Shearing who was being treated by the ship's doctor, had recovered their spirits. To onlookers it appeared they had forgotten their experience. Like so many children growing up in wartime Britain, they seemed to be able to forget how much they had suffered. In their minds all that mattered was that the ship had come, and they had now moved on to the next stage of their adventure. They were saved. More than that, they had come back from the dead. Nine-year-old Billy Short was reunited with his parents and discovered a memorial service had already been held for him, but the true tragedy was that the service was also for his brother, Peter, who had been lost when the *Benares* had sunk.

In the aftermath of the disaster, the true price of war was evident. With the survivors safely returned to the UK, the staff at CORB began the ominous task of informing the families of the child victims of their fate. In Sunderland, eleven children had been sent overseas on the *Benares*, yet just one returned. Just two of the twelve Liverpudlian children had been saved. Twelve children from Wales had sailed, none had survived. Fifty-nine homes soon received the terrible news that the children they had believed were being sent to safety had been lost at sea. Seventy-seven children had lost their lives, with a number of parents receiving the grim news that more than one of their children had been lost.

For one family, it was particularly tragic. The Grimmond family from Brixton in south London received the terrible news that five of their children – Violet, Connie, Lennie, Eddie and Gussie – had perished on the *Benares*. Their parents, Eddie and Hannah Grimmond, had only sent them away after their home had been destroyed by bombs a week before the *Benares* had sunk. Initially Hannah had been reluctant to let the children go but her husband, who had fought in the trenches of Flanders and knew the true horrors of war, had been adamant. He won the argument but lost five children. Following the disaster he immediately volunteered to rejoin his old regiment, hoping to avenge his loss. He was refused frontline service and instead joined the RAF, serving throughout the war. However, in 1943 the Grimmonds received further bad news: another of their children had been killed on active service. Of a total of eleven children, six had been lost to war.

The sinking of the *Benares* had one significant impact: on 2 October 1940 the CORB evacuation scheme was cancelled. In the aftermath a few details emerged. The convoy's Royal Navy escort ships had left the merchant ships in mid-Atlantic, leaving them unprotected. More importantly, in the aftermath of the sinking, acting under standing orders, no ships had deviated from their course within the convoy and left the Royal Navy to pick up survivors as and when it could. To some it seemed this was unfair: hundreds of people, including many young children, were left adrift in the sea. The time it took for the Royal Navy to reach the survivors cost the lives of many of those aboard the lifeboats. It was a cold and seemingly heartless strategy but rules were rules. As the Admiralty explained in reaction to the criticism, 'We do not think it would have been proper to depart from orders on account of the children as this would possibly have endangered other ships.'[1] The words made one thing clear: this was total war and children were in the firing line. If they had to die in pursuit of victory, so be it.

CHAPTER 7

The Blitz Spreads

'My brother handed me a bundle – it was a dead baby – and asked me to look after it. I was now horrified as well as terrified.'

Ray Peat, teenage ARP messenger in Hull[1]

As London reeled from the shock of bombing, the Luftwaffe spread its targets to cities, towns and even villages throughout the country. Within a week of the first heavy raids on London, both Liverpool and south Wales were hit. The march of violence was unstoppable: Southampton, Portsmouth, Bristol, Cardiff, Birmingham, Belfast, Hull, Coventry, Swansea, Manchester, Sheffield, Plymouth – all were changed forever by the hail of high explosives and incendiaries. The later 'Baedeker Raids' – named after the famous German guidebooks – saw the historic centres of towns and cities such as York, Bath, Norwich and Canterbury devastated by bombs. If anything, whilst London faced the heaviest bombing, its size meant the destruction was spread over a wide area. In small cities, the destruction was concentrated, in many cases almost completely obliterating the central areas.

There was one city whose fate came to symbolize the horrors of aerial bombing: the East Midlands town of Coventry. The destruction of the city even gave birth to a new word, 'Coventried', which was later used by the airmen of Bomber Command to describe German cities they flattened. With London still facing nightly attacks, Coventry was chosen as a target because of the preponderance of armaments factories that had been established in the engineering works around the city. It was to be the biggest attack of the war so far, bigger even than those raids that had flattened swathes of London.

It was already a cold and crisp winter's evening on 14 November 1940 when the bombers made their first appearance in the moonlit skies over Coventry. Some of the children in the city beneath them were evacuees from London, children who were supposed to be in a place of safety. At 7 p.m. the first aircraft were overhead and, accompanied by the crash of anti-aircraft fire, explosions were heard across the city. At the start of the raid no one had any idea of what awaited them. Many youngsters were still outdoors when the sirens sounded, with some remaining there in hope of adding to their collections of shrapnel. One thirteen-year-old boy was outside in the hope of finding the brass timing device from an anti-aircraft shell – one of the most sought-after pieces for shrapnel collectors. Instead, he found himself in the middle of the raid as incendiaries rained down around him. Seeing the vivid glare of an incendiary bomb fall into the gutter, he ran out and dropped a sandbag on top to smother the blaze. As he did so it exploded. He was blinded by the explosion and within minutes was on his way to hospital in a neighbour's car. After a series of diversions he arrived at the hospital and was taken to a ward. Still unable to see, he heard a voice shouting that the ward was on fire.

All over the city buildings were burning and some children doing their utmost to keep their city alive. Teenagers helped the wardens by smothering the incendiary bombs, whether they landed in the streets, gardens or homes. Some boys were even brave enough to dismantle incendiary bombs that failed to explode, ensuring there was less work for the bomb disposal squads. Yet, for all their efforts, there were more victims than heroes that night. For all the desperate desire to assist others in their time of need, the most important thing was for people to look after their own families. One nine-year-old boy recalled being pulled from the rubble of his home by a man he did not know. The man picked him up and offered to take him to his own home to give him shelter. As they approached the man's home, that too was hit, disappearing into a cloud of flame and dust. The child was left in the middle of the street, abandoned by his saviour who suddenly had more pressing concerns – the safety of his own family. The boy soon found his own parents and they took the decision shared by so many that night. There was no point remaining in Coventry, so they walked into the countryside to seek shelter. However, sanctuary was still not found. They were dive-bombed as they walked through the streets, took shelter in a rat-filled bakery and then moved on to spend the rest of the raid in a pub cellar.

In the aftermath of the raid, Coventry was a changed place. Not only were so many buildings now little more than charred shells, and the roads blocked with rubble, and the air filled with the stench of smoke and death, but the people had changed. Many, quite simply, packed up their remaining possessions and trudged through the ruins, abandoning the town in search of safety. There were many heroes, whether those who rescued children from the rubble, fought the fires or simply helped collect the dead. Following such horror, simply keeping a shop open was an act of sheer defiance. But there was more. As one thirteen-year-old girl, the daughter of a policeman, later recalled, her father came home three days after the raid. He had not rested, slept or eaten for seventy-two hours. In an era when emotion was not readily shown, he did the unthinkable and burst into tears. It was the first time she had seen a man cry. Whilst grown men were reduced to tears, children came to help. The Girl Guides from local towns came to the assistance of the stricken population of Coventry. The Guides in nearby Leamington Spa collected clothes for people who had been bombed out. They also distributed socks, hats and gloves that they had knitted.

Nationwide, the Guides used their magazine to promote the collection of relief supplies for bombed-out families. In many bombed towns Guides were active in civil defence work. In Cardiff – where nearly 300 people died in air raids – two girls, aged twelve and fourteen, spent a whole night fighting fires with a stirrup-pump. In some towns Guides showed people whose homes had been damaged how they could make brick ovens, using materials salvaged from bombsites. Other Guides cooked for people who had been forced from their homes into rescue centres. One troop converted a horsebox into a mobile canteen that travelled between bombed cities to offer relief to rescue workers and bombed-out civilians. The girls were also employed to collect the sphagnum moss used to make natural wound dressings. Others collected sheep's wool from barbed-wire fences, sending it to be used for stuffing cushions for the Army, or collected acorns used as pig feed. However, probably the greatest contribution made by the Guides was the fundraising they carried out to purchase ambulances, including twenty presented to the Royal Navy and two air ambulances.

In some areas people tried to make the best of the horrific destruction of their towns. Whole slum districts were wiped out in air raids. Rather than dwell on this destruction, some local politicians looked to the future. As the mayor of one south-coast city said:

> At least we can say that the Luftwaffe did for us in twenty seconds what we have been trying to do for twenty years. It removed the slum dwellings. And fortunately, with very little loss of life since our evacuation arrangements had been working for some time and empty buildings were hit. Now we can plan for the future that will bring hope and better conditions to untold thousands.[2]

Then it was Liverpool's turn. Living in a port city that faced westwards into the Atlantic and was vital to the convoy system that was keeping Britain alive, the people of the city could not have expected anything other than to face the full fury of the Luftwaffe. For seven nights the bombing continued without reprieve, setting alight areas that burned for days. The bombing of a school shelter killed 160 people, whilst there were 60 casualties when a hospital was bombed. A whole swathe of the city centre was simply obliterated and more than 1,400 people lost their lives. By the end of 1941, more than 4,000 people had been killed on Merseyside. As in London, the bombing caused a mass exodus as families streamed out of the city each night.

For thirteen-year-old Tony Sprigings, the war finally began to have an impact upon his life. At first he had been excited by war, and then unimpressed since nothing had happened in his area. Even after Dunkirk, with the threat of invasion looming, he never felt threatened. As he told himself, even if the Germans invaded, surely they would be stopped before they reached the north of England? In later years he found it difficult to explain to people that for much of the time war had been a non-event, hardly affecting his day-to-day life. Yet in 1941, things began to change. He kept away from the city, believing the bombing too dangerous to risk taking the Mersey ferry. From his hilltop bedroom he could watch the city burning and soon realized the horrors of what was happening just a few miles away across the water: 'Looking across I could see miles of fire. It was amazing. I thought nothing could survive. One ship in the port blew up when it was carrying ammunition. It was the most enormous explosion you've ever heard.' The exploding ship caused six other vessels to sink and parts of the ship were found up to two miles away. Despite the suffering inflicted on Liverpool, Tony recalled that he remained excited by what was happening: 'It was a terrible period. But as little boys it was very exciting, even though a lot of my friends lost their parents and relatives.' In the city, some 70,000 people were made homeless by the bombing.

Then the dangers came closer to home as the Nazi bombers inflicted their share of suffering on the people of the Wirral. It was Tony's turn to face the enemy bombers:

We were bombed one evening. It was very close. My grandfather was sitting in front of the fire and all the windows came in on him. I ended up under the settee. I don't know how I got there, I think it was from the blast. It was horrible – the blast, you can never forget it. The blast hit me like a brick wall. You wouldn't think air could be so strong. That was really frightening. It was damn close, just 300 feet away from the house.

Despite the bombing, life continued and Tony Sprigings made his way to school as usual, cycling quickly through the streets of Birkenhead, ready to share his experiences with his mates: 'I was all excited about this stick of bombs that had landed. The next morning I went to school to tell them all about this, only to find that all the roads on the way to school had been blasted. So I had nothing to say.' A few nights later, his father returned home during an air raid and shared a macabre story. He had been on duty at an air raid wardens' post as the bombs fell on the area. Concerned about his family, he rushed through the streets to check they were safe. Just as he reached the front gate a bomb fell nearby. As he reached out to push open the front gate, something flew past him. He looked down and found a severed hand resting on the front gate. He went indoors and told the family. It was a story that remained in his son's mind for many years.

The country's ports remained the focus of the raids. In Hull, air raids killed more than 1,000 civilians and left some 40,000 people homeless. In March 1941 Ray Peat and his brother Jim, who had joined the ARP as messengers after local Boy Scouts were asked to volunteer, were called out in heavy bombing. Ray Peat later admitted he was terrified as he cycled through the bombs to reach his destination: 'I set off in thick fog; the guns and machine-guns were firing and you could hear the shells going over you and bombs and shrapnel were dropping.' Arriving at the site of the bombing, he soon realized it was nothing like training, which he had found to be fun: 'My brother handed me a bundle – it was a dead baby – and asked me to look after it. I was now horrified as well as terrified.' He had to put the baby into the back of an ARP car then move to the next incident.

It was a terrible night for the teenager. He saw a frightened youth trying to rescue a woman trapped in rubble. The youth ran off as Ray approached. He then set to work to pull both her and her baby free from the ruins of their home. The terror continued: he went to bombed houses and found dead people. At a bombed shelter he helped the injured to leave. As he did so, one lady was so badly injured that her daughter saw her and had to be taken to hospital in shock. Whilst they were working, a wall collapsed, injuring two of the ARP workers. It only got worse. Hearing screams, he went into a house:

> A man was trapped and on fire. We got a stirrup-pump and sprayed him with water. The man said his daughter was in the house but we said we couldn't see her. He said to my brother, 'You are standing on her.' We found the girl, who lived, but her father died.[3]

Such experiences were difficult for all who lived through them, regardless of age. It was made worse when the casualties were fellow rescue workers. In May 1941 Ray Peat found the corpses of men who had been killed whilst fire-watching. He also saw the corpse of an ARP man lying dead in the road. When Ray arrived back at the ARP base he watched as his fellow workers sat around crying. After an awful night, the youngster went home and then had to go to work.

Things only got worse. Early in the morning of 11 June 1941, the sirens sounded so Ray and his brother Jim made their way to the first-aid post to await instructions. They were there when a bomb hit:

> The floor opened and I went downwards and the school came down on to us. I was completely buried; my legs were underneath me and I lay absolutely covered. My helmet must have caused a gap that

enabled me to breathe because my mouth and nose were blocked with dirt and this made it impossible for me to shout. My arms and legs were trapped and I was unable to move at all. I was totally buried.[4]

As he lay trapped in the rubble, he wished for a bomb to drop to blow away the debris. He could hear screaming from another room but there was no sound nearby. Eventually rescue workers dug through to where he was. Water was poured over his face to clear the dust and dirt that had been making it difficult for him to breathe. A doctor then gave him a shot of morphine. As Ray's leg was dug free from the rubble it started to bleed again. With the wound now dressed, the rescue worker had to sit on him to work free his other leg. He was lucky: his brother, and six others, had died in the bombing.

Portsmouth also fell target to enemy bombers. In January 1941 the raids hit the city, bringing the usual destruction and costing the lives of 756 people. As in so many other locations, the local youth were soon at the heart of the efforts to save the city. Fourteen-year-old Arthur Harvey witnessed the bombing, which followed him from home to work. Born in November 1925, he was typical of the youths who had thought little about war, drifting along with the circumstances as they changed. By August 1940 the biggest change in his life had been his father being called up into the RAF and that, in 1939, his education had come to an abrupt halt. However, living and working in the city centre, he was soon affected by the bombing. He had first seen bombers overhead as he delivered newspapers in the suburbs. Then he experienced fire-watching at his workplace as the Germans attempted to bomb the dockyards. As he later recalled, even when homes in his own street were bombed, he wasn't frightened:

I don't think I was old enough to appreciate it. At night I'd walk down the main street and see the city still in flames. It was just part of life. If you lived in Portsmouth, you couldn't avoid it really. You started to wonder if we were going to win.

He soon became more closely associated with efforts to defend the city:

> One night we saved the local pub, the Tramway Arms. We were in a big public shelter. They came in and said an incendiary bomb had landed and the storeroom of the pub was on fire. So me and some soldiers went round there. We put the fire out. But I was too young to get a drink for it.

Whilst his first rescue work had been relatively easy, his later endeavours were more daunting. On 24 August 1940 German bombers struck as children settled down to watch a matinee at the Prince's Theatre, a cinema in the city centre. The bombers were overhead for just five minutes. By the time they had gone the cinema was a smouldering wreck, with many children – the living and the dead – still trapped inside. Arthur Harvey and a friend rushed to help. Though just fourteen years old, they set to work shifting rubble, helping to make space for the rescue teams and first-aid teams to do their work. There was little the boys could do, but they continued, making sure they weren't a nuisance to the emergency services. As Arthur recalled: 'We done what we could.' He also noticed that, though appreciative of the assistance, the men made sure the two youngsters were kept away from the horrors of what was found in the wreckage: eight children had been killed in the cinema. For Arthur one thought soon came into his head: just months before, he had been a schoolboy attending matinees in the same cinema.

Despite the legendary comradeship of life on the 'Home Front', Arthur Harvey witnessed the dark side to the war. When the war had started Arthur had been part of a gang of eight schoolmates: 'One was killed when an ARP post near our old school was bombed. He was aged fourteen. One was lost when he was serving in the Army. One became a bugle boy on HMS *Hood.* He was on it when it went down. Just four of us survived the war.'

For the population of Portsmouth, the close proximity to death became part of everyday existence. Each time bombs hit the city, it seemed someone from the street had been killed. With so many local men away at sea, every maritime disaster seemed to affect another local family. Yet the people's spirits remained high. Arthur watched his mother and the other women from the street. Their husbands were away – mostly in the Royal Navy or the merchant fleet – and those remaining were working in the docks that were the target for enemy bombers, yet they seemed undeterred: 'Life went on, there was a wonderful spirit. You could go out and leave your door open – mind you, we didn't have a lot for anyone to pinch. People were resilient. They didn't have a lot in life, but they had a comradeship that was fantastic.'

The sense of defiance, as espoused by those who refused to go to the shelters during air raids, was noble. But for some it was a practical necessity, rather than out of any sense of duty. When fourteen-year-old Reg Fraser moved to Plymouth to be with his mother and grandparents he found his grandmother unable to use the Anderson shelter in the garden: quite simply, she was too fat to get through the doorway. Instead, she remained in the house and he chose to stay with her, rather than leaving her alone or making her walk uphill to the nearest public shelter.

The effect of the bombing of Plymouth was far-reaching, with more than 1,000 fatalities. At the height of the bombing some 50,000 people were believed to have left the city by night. They were known as 'trekkers'. Some went to relatives in nearby towns and villages each evening. Unofficial convoys of lorries, tractors and delivery vans ferried the population to safety in the countryside. Policemen were seen stopping cars and telling drivers to give lifts to the transient population.

If it were not enough that the boys of the Merchant Navy faced the full fury of war at sea, they also experienced it when ashore. Many were originally from port cities that were a frequent target for enemy aircraft. Even those from other areas had no choice but to pass through ports on their way to and from their ships. As ship's apprentice Alan Shard recalled:

Things changed on 20 March 1941 whilst anchored in Plymouth and I experienced a Blitz. I had just returned from four days' leave and as I stepped out of North Road station an incendiary bomb landed across the street. I beat a retreat and went in the tunnel under Platform 6 along with about fifty others. Shortly thereafter a bomb landed at the entrance of Platform 8 and filled the tunnel with blue acrid smoke. Fortunately no one was hurt. The 'all clear' went at 0130 and I went up to the street. It was devastation with fire hoses strewn all over. There were no taxis and I had to hump a sea bag over my shoulder and, with an attaché case in one hand, headed for the dock a mile away. It could have been worse: it might have been raining. At the dock I had to wait for the ship's boat to pick me up at 0700.

Alan had been lucky to reach his ship in safety: that night 250 enemy bombers had hit Plymouth, dropping more than 150 tons of high explosive and 30,000 incendiary bombs on the port city. Christian Immelman had a similar experience in Liverpool:

The worst experience I had of air attack was being in dock across the river in Birkenhead the week the Liverpool docks had their worst air raid of the war. After that experience I came to the conclusion I'd rather be out at sea tucked in the middle of a large convoy than be in a big UK city during heavy air attacks.

Fortunately for Glasgow, much of its industry was spread out along the banks of the Clyde, meaning that the heart of the city was saved from the appalling fate of other cities. However, one local town, Clydebank, did become the target of the bombers. On the night of 13 March 1941, seven-year-old Moyra Reid was asked to accompany her father to his post as a fire-watcher on the roof of a school outside Glasgow. As the sirens sounded, Moyra and her father climbed the stairs to the roof. She felt uncomfortable wearing the heavy steel helmet, but excited to be going upstairs rather than down to the shelter. One thing she could never understand was why her father would take a young girl outside to witness an air raid. 'My father was a gentle person – and why he decided to take me out there that night I'll never know. I think he said something about me seeing what it was really like. I think he wanted for me to see the carnage. He never took me again.'

What she saw from the roof was unforgettable:

> I was terrified – the noise was tremendous. I could hear the incredible noise of the anti-aircraft guns and I could see the glow and the searchlights. I know I was scared, but I didn't really know what I was scared of. I'd heard about people being killed in air raids but at that stage I couldn't really understand being killed or dying.

As the guns fired, the searchlights waved through the skies and the bombs fell, seven-year-old Moyra stood and watched, her head weighed down by the steel helmet: 'I can still see it now – the red, red glow of all the fires.'

What she had seen was the result of 236 enemy aircraft attacking the nearby town of Clydebank. Their targets were the shipyards and factories of the town, both vital to the war effort. First came planes loaded with incendiary bombs to mark the targets for those that followed, dropping their high explosive on the town. It was one of the most concentrated raids of the war. Around 400 bombs fell within two square miles, right in the heart of the town, with a further 96 falling on oil storage tanks to the north-west of the town.

Though there was damage to both the factories and shipyards of the town it was the residential areas that suffered the most. The devastation was appalling, with whole streets blasted or burned out. Even the sturdy stone tenements that made up so much of the town's housing stock were no match for high explosive. Inside one such tenement was eight-year-old Ella Flynn. With her was her young cousin Sheila, who had been sent from London to Clydebank to escape the bombing:

> My dad was listening to the nine o'clock news on the radio. I heard the
> siren go off and told him but he was so busy listening to the wireless
> that he didn't hear it. So I ran over and switched it off so he could hear
> – and it was then we heard more than just sirens – bombs were already
> falling.

They rushed downstairs to the middle-floor flat that her father believed would be safer:

> When we got there other people were already in the lobby of the flat
> – as the windows had already been blown out the lobby seemed the
> safest place.
>   We were there for some time before my mum and sister joined us –
> they had had a terrifying struggle along the streets from the cinema as
> bombs were already falling. Mum insisted on going back up to our flat
> to get proper clothes for us and collect the big bag in which she kept
> the insurance policies and other valuables. Just as my mum returned to
> the house, the door was blasted off its hinges on top of her.

As the children watched, the adults discussed what to do next and decided to move to the ground-floor flat of the building next door. They ran from the safety of the house into the street:

> My dad sheltered my sister, putting his coat over their heads – and my
> mum put an arm around me and Sheila, trying to prevent us from
> seeing the flames which were roaring up from the houses opposite,
> where our friends lived. I will never forget that sight or the noise, the
> terrible noise of the bombs falling on our town.

Also witness to the carnage was a local teenager, Jeanie,[5] who was living in the heart of the bombed area. She had seen the hard times in the town, growing up when unemployment was high and prospects low:

> We came through the Depression – there were lots of men standing on street corners with nothing to do. We lived in a tenement on Gordon Street. We had one room and kitchen on the top floor. Even as tenements go it was a poor one. There were three families on the landing – sharing a single lavatory – but it never seemed a problem to us. You didn't know it was tough times.

And if the 1930s had been tough, the 1940s were about to get tougher. So far war had not touched the town, indeed the biggest change was that the shipyards were working at full capacity. The prospects for the local population were actually quite good, as Jeanie remembered:

> War had started but we were unaffected except that everyone in the shipyards had work. That was a good thing about it. There was a confidence in the town – no more men hanging round street corners. I knew bombing was happening elsewhere but there were no visuals – you just heard about it and used your imagination.

On 13 March 1941, Jeanie was at home when the bombing started:

> I ended up in the concrete open close of our tenement – under the stairs. Out the back, there was a washhouse. On that night the close was crowded from front to back with people who lived in the tenement. Things had started to happen. Some people went in the washhouse to shelter thinking if there was a problem at least they wouldn't have a whole building land on them. They thought it was more secure.

She listened as bombs whistled down and exploded. Blasts came from near and far. They could hear the awful sound of buildings collapsing and the crackle of flames as other ones burned. As it grew worse Jeanie went to the front door to see what was happening outside:

> I remember looking up Bannerman Street and that was on fire. The sky was alight – it was yellow and orange. Looking up, it was like a picture. It was all black but there were squares with orange flames shooting up from them. I remember thinking I mustn't ever forget this.

Within minutes she was no longer a spectator:

> There was noise all the time you could hear bombs dropping. There was no fire where we were, just dust and dirt. You were enveloped in it. There was a man in the close. I thought he was dying but he was asthmatic and he couldn't get his breath because of the dust. He was all right in the end, but I thought he was dying.

Suddenly there came a crash as a bomb landed outside. Next came the shouts: 'They've all been killed in the washhouse.' It soon became clear it had taken a direct hit. People attempted to help those within and Jeanie was given a grim task:

> I was handed a dead baby from the washhouse. Someone had gone out and brought the baby in. I suppose they wanted somebody to hold it, but the baby was dead. I didn't know the baby; it looked about 6 months. As far as I know the mother had died.

Looking back on the incident, Jeanie tried to understand why she had been chosen to cradle the dead child, after all, she was herself just a teenager:

> I can remember women being distressed but there was no panic. There weren't many men there. I wasn't scared because of my age. It wasn't that I was being brave about holding the dead child. It was probably

that I would be less affected than a mother would have been – they had their own children to look after.

As the bombing continued, Ella Flynn's family tried to make themselves comfortable in the crowded flat. Sitting in the dark, they listened to the falling bombs, and the crackle of the fires as the houses opposite were engulfed in flames. Mrs Flynn tried to keep spirits up by singing. There was nothing more they could do but await the morning.

The bombing seemed to continue all night, as Jeanie cradled the corpse. The following morning it became clear why there had been so much dust in the tenement: 'The top of the tenement, where our flat was, had collapsed.' She was lucky: had the building not been constructed of solid stone, the bomb might have penetrated to the floors below, killing them all. All she was able to salvage was her own birth certificate – everything else was lost: 'We knew our house had been destroyed and it was too dangerous to go back. I had absolutely nothing with me, just the clothes I was standing in. I felt nothing about losing my possessions – people weren't so interested in personal possessions then.'

That morning, as the people of Clydebank stepped out into the street, they were stunned by what they saw. Stone tenements had been gutted by fire, their roofs gone and just their walls still standing. A cloud of dust and smoke hung over the town, making the air thick and difficult to breathe. In the aftermath of the raid, workers rushed around the town trying to shore up buildings that had been damaged and were in danger of collapsing. Their task should have been made easier by the presence of a large timber yard in the town. The only problem was that it too was on fire.

The world had seemed to turn upside down. This small town, far from urban centres, had its heart ripped out by the bombing. Nothing was normal. Children were carried over the rubble in blankets, looking at the charred remains of their hometown. Policemen helped people break up hoardings to provide wood for boarding up windows. One rescue worker even came across the curious sight of two goats sitting in armchairs within a bombed house.

As daybreak came, Ella Flynn and her family left their shelter:

> We went back home – there were no windows and the doors were off their hinges. The new carpet we had just got was standing in the middle of the floor like a wigwam. My mother kept saying, 'O ma hoose, ma hoose,' which my dad reprimanded her for – as we still had our lives which was more important. My mum put Sheila and me into bed after shaking off the glass and other debris – but then the siren went again and we had to get up – though this time the 'all clear' went shortly afterwards.

In all, around 500 people had perished in the bombing. It was a staggering number for a small industrial town. More than seventy of the casualties had been children, including one teenage boy who died whilst on duty fire-watching. Every school in the town was damaged, with six being completely gutted by fire.

Yet amidst the chaos there was a strange sense of calm and organization. Having finally put down the dead child, Jeanie stepped out to discover that the whole of the town centre was being evacuated:

> I was fascinated by the organization the next morning. There were coaches ready for us. They turned up and all the women and children went into them. Again there was no panic. We knew we were being taken away. I thought we were going to the country and that it was going to be beautiful and there would be lots of greenery. I found it exciting – I was an inexperienced youngster. If I'd been an adult it would have been different.

Not everybody left the town that morning. As the buses headed off into the countryside, Ella Flynn and her family tried to settle back to normality. Her father cleared out the brick air raid shelters that had remained unused during the bombing. Certain that the bombers would return, he even found wood to make benches within the shelter. Ella watched as the firemen continued to fight the flames. Her mother even apologized to the men for not being able to make them any tea: there was no water and no power. The only water the family had was what they collected from the river, ready if the bombers returned.

Whilst Ella remained at home, her sixteen-year old sister decided she had to do something positive:

> My big sister made her way down to the Town Hall, where she worked all day witnessing terrible scenes of displaced people and lost children, frightened and bewildered. She told my parents she just had to offer to help in any way she could – and her assistance was gratefully received.

That was one of the greatest horrors of the bombing: children searching for parents and parents desperately searching for missing children. Whenever there was a positive outcome it lifted the spirits of the relief workers; the rest of the time they were numbed by the overwhelming sense of tragedy.

On the night of 14 March the bombers returned. Ella and her family spent another sleepless night huddled in the shelter her father had spent the day clearing. In their exhausted state, it seemed the bombing went on forever, and each blast seemed to emphasize the hopelessness of their situation. The following morning the decision was taken to flee the ruined town:

> My parents decided to get out if at all possible. My dad was a motor mechanic and had managed to get a car from somewhere. He bundled us, and everything we could carry, into it. But it was impossible to drive with tram lines in mangled heaps and rubble strewn everywhere. It was a scene of devastation and progress was painfully slow as the path had to be cleared bit by bit.

Eventually they escaped into open country, and drove towards Glasgow where it seemed they had entered another world: 'What seemed amazing and cruel was that people were out and about their business. Our world had been turned upside down and they were shopping like nothing had happened.' Although the family home had only been damaged, not destroyed, they never returned to Clydebank. Her father's and sister's workplaces had both been destroyed so it seemed there was nothing to go back to. They settled in Glasgow and attempted to build a new life.

Despite the intensity of the experience, Jeanie felt a sense of relief and excitement. She had lost everything but considered it an adventure to move to the town of Renton. She had spent the night holding a corpse but could only feel pleased her home had just been bombed, not engulfed in flames:

> I was in the middle of an adventure – it's terrible to say that when people had died but that was how you felt as a youngster. It was only after you heard about all the deaths you realized how bad it had been. I didn't know what had happened to my school friends.

Within days Jeanie returned to work: 'I still had the same clothes on as when we had been bombed. I was blonde and when I got to the office one of the girls said that I suited my hair dark.' But she hadn't dyed her hair: 'I realized I hadn't washed my hair since the raid and it was clogged with soot, dust and dirt! Things like that are normally important to teenage girls but after the bombing it hadn't seemed important any more.' Within a year Jeanie joined the Army, serving on anti-aircraft guns, allowing her to help prevent any more horrifying air raids such as the one that had destroyed Clydebank.

In the days that followed, little news was released about the bombing. It seemed the scale of destruction, on such a small town, needed to be hidden from a population that was already struggling to cope with war. Many parents also attempted to conceal the truth of the severity of the bombing from their children. In the cities that faced the worst of the Blitz, children found themselves being moved from shelter to shelter. They were often confused as to why they should leave a place of safety. Only later did their parents reveal that they had left because the building above the shelter had been bombed or was burning. Yet there were sights the children could not be protected from. As they left the often stinking and overcrowded shelters, they entered a new, and horribly unfamiliar, world.

No amount of parental protection could conceal the glow of burning buildings that filled the skies above Coventry, Liverpool or Portsmouth. These were visions of hell. There was no hiding the reasons they had to step over endless fire hoses laid out in the streets, or step around bomb craters, or cross the road to avoid flaring gas mains. No child could miss the taste of dust in the air or the stench of shattered sewers. Nor could they avoid the sight of tarpaulin-covered bodies piled at the roadside. There was a realization that their town or city, as they had known it, was gone forever. Most tellingly, there was no escape from the reality of rescue workers – policemen, firemen and ARP wardens, their faces blackened with smoke, who had worked till they dropped – who were now crying over the horrors they had witnessed. For many children, this was the end of their innocence.

In the aftermath of raids, the heroes were many. In Manchester, one eleven-year-old boy awoke some hours after he had been blasted into unconsciousness to find himself buried beneath his own bed. Thinking not of his own condition, the boy dug through the rubble to find his two brothers. First he found his six-year-old brother, and then together – battered, bruised and swathed in dust – they dug out their baby brother. Then the two boys began calling for help, their shouts joined by the cries of the baby. All three were pulled from the rubble, with their rescuers admitting they had thought them all dead. Then they received the news – their mother had been killed.

All through the towns and cities of the country, children had their own way of dealing with the emotional and psychological impact of bombing. Whilst younger children took comfort in their favourite teddy bears or dolls, clutching them to their chests as they listened to the wail of bombs and the crash of high explosives, older children found their comfort elsewhere. Teenage girls retreated to the shelters clutching their favourite dress, or prized pair of shoes, refusing to be parted from the things that brought glamour to their lives and distanced them from the vicious reality of war.

For some parents there was an added issue to dealing with children in air raids. The parents of some teenage girls had not only to deal with the very natural fear of death, but with the way the pressure of air raids added to the everyday issues of dealing with teenage hormones. For teenagers the disruption of everyday life – in particular the lack of sleep – and the way that parental concern over the bombing often curtailed their burgeoning sense of independence led to girls arguing with their parents. Shelters were the scene of blazing rows between girls and their parents. Some stormed out, others were thrown out by parents. One girl recalled spending the night in the toilet outside the public shelter after the psychological pressure of the air raids caused an outburst of hysteria. It would be the last night her family stayed in the shelter, preferring to seek sanctuary in the cellar of their home.

As the country fell victim to incendiaries and high explosives, new organizations emerged to deal with the ongoing crisis. Civil defence became a national issue rather than a local one. The 1,451 local fire brigades were reorganized into 42 regional fire forces that covered the entire country while a Civil Defence Staff College was opened to train instructors to spread their knowledge. More than 1.25 million men, women and youths served on a part-time or full-time basis in the Civil Defence Services. The full-time men worked a seventy-two-hour week, although at the height of the Blitz time meant nothing and they simply worked until the job was done – or they passed out from exhaustion. By the middle of the war there were more than 2,500,000 places in rest centres. Some were in hutted camps near to locations expected to be bombed. London alone had 140,000 places ready as emergency accommodation. Every town of more than 50,000 people established feeding centres capable of serving at least 10 per cent of the local population, in case heavy bombing destroyed food stores or cut off gas supplies.

By mid-war, London had 2,500 large air raid shelters with canteen facilities, capable of accommodating nearly one million people. Eighty of the city's underground railway stations had been equipped with canteens and around 25,000 homes in the areas surrounding the capital had been requisitioned to provide emergency accommodation for homeless Londoners.

The ever-spreading bombing meant education suffered across the country, just as it had suffered in London. One Bristol girl was shocked that after hours of doing little at school, a history teacher finally asked the four children who had made the effort to reach school to hand in their homework. The boys made an excuse, claiming that the bombing had stopped them from doing it. The teacher was not sympathetic, telling the boys that they had all weekend to do their homework but there had only been air raids on the Sunday. They were given detention and made to complete the work. Elsewhere in Bristol, twelve-year-old Alfred Leonard, who had been bombed out from his home, remained philosophical about his situation: 'As a young person it was quite exciting to be bombed.' Despite the dangers, the streets remained a playground for him and his mates: 'We collected shrapnel and we went out picking up unexploded incendiary bombs. We'd swap them with the other boys. It was exciting. It was also dangerous, but we didn't realize that.'

It was not just the big towns and cities that suffered. Even small country towns like Newmarket suffered attacks. Just as elsewhere, the nation's youth responded to the challenge. One ARP messenger later recalled hearing the air raid sirens whilst at school. As the rest of his class sheltered, he jumped on his bicycle and raced to his post. With serious damage to the local high street and the destruction of the town's telephone exchange, the ARP remained on almost constant duty for the next three days. Rather than return to school, the teenage messenger remained at his post, carrying messages around the town. One of his duties was to take a message to the mortuary, where he was confronted with the sight of the air-raid victims laid out in rows.

The burden of the Blitz had been shared throughout the country. Though the population grew to accept its horrors, and found the views across the new inner-city wastelands a familiar sight, others were shocked by how much the country had endured. In Southampton the destruction had been heavy, leaving row upon row of bombed and burned-out homes and more than 500 people dead. Later in the war, American serviceman passed through the city by train. They were all laughing and joking until they looked out of the window and saw the scale of the destruction. The soldiers fell silent as they realized the price paid by the inhabitants of the city and finally understood exactly why they had been sent across the Atlantic to fight a war so far from home.

CHAPTER 8

Heroes and Villains of the Blitz

'There is no doubt that the great mass of young people are anxious to have the opportunity to help the national war effort.'

Interdepartmental Conference on Training for Boys,
November 1941[1]

Almost as soon as the Blitz commenced, the nation's youth were active in defying the enemy. The common public perception of children sitting inside the safety of shelters or as evacuees out in the countryside belies the true contribution of large numbers of youths who played an essential role in saving lives, preserving morale and keeping the country running. When the story of the children's contribution to the war effort is told, the focus is normally on wastepaper collection, salvage of scrap metal and efforts to help their parents grow vegetables. Though these were all vital activities, there were plenty of youngsters whose role was far more active – and dangerous.

Even before war was declared, there were youths all over Britain who were preparing to do their duty. Many Boy Scout troops were integrated into ARP units to offer their services as messengers and lookouts. Girl Guides had assisted in the distribution and fitting of gas masks, showing children how to ensure the seal fitted correctly.

They stepped up first-aid training, ready to assist in the aftermath of raids. The instructions they received were both graphic and gruesome, illustrating how to deal with the seriously wounded. The Guides also offered their equipment for ARP use, converting canvas latrine cubicles into gas decontamination facilities. Losing their latrines didn't matter, as once war started many of the Guides' tents were requisitioned by the Army, so there were few opportunities for camping.

One month after the declaration of war, the government decreed that children under sixteen should not be allowed to serve in ARP posts. This did not curtail the activities of Scouts who continued to assist by helping families to erect air raid shelters. Nor did it stop girls like Patricia Knowlden of West Wickham in Kent. She had actively assisted the ARP since 1938 when she helped her father distribute leaflets. By 1941, aged fourteen and still too young to join the ARP, she sat – and passed – the ARP warden's examination. In 1944, when she reached her seventeenth birthday, she was finally officially able to commence civil defence work. In Swansea, teenage ARP volunteers were even shown how to use petrol bombs, in case they became the last line of defence against invasion.

In the east London borough of Stepney, local teenager Sidney Ties began preparing for war almost as soon as he left school in 1937. Born and bred in the area, Sidney had attended a local school where the limited curriculum left him with few opportunities. However, deep down he harboured a dream:

> I really would have liked to be a surgeon. But it wasn't possible since I had no education at all. My school was awful. You got hit for even moving in the classroom. I didn't learn anything and it was not a happy time. It was difficult for people who had potential – you never got a chance to fulfil it. My father was a market trader, selling curtains and things from a stall near Elephant and Castle.

Despite knowing the dream was impossible, Sidney Ties was determined to maintain his interest in medical matters.

Whilst his background offered no openings in the medical profession, Sidney retained an enthusiasm that determined his immediate future. After joining the Boy Scouts as a twelve year old, he had learned first aid, earned his first-aid badges and become his troop's first-aider: 'I soon got beyond that and went to a London County Council [LCC] night school where I studied first aid. By the time I was about fifteen I was doing advanced first aid.' Having learned to treat cuts, bandage wounds, stem bleeding and fit splints, he soon possessed skills that were expected to be in great demand if and when war came. As part of his training he even attended a local hospital where he joined groups of trainee doctors, watching surgery and getting used to the sight of serious wounds. In the final months before war broke out he was even asked by the LCC to offer instruction in first aid: 'I was sent to see the taxi drivers to train them in giving first aid because a lot of them became auxiliary firemen. Can you imagine a fifteen year old giving lessons to a taxi driver? I was showing them how to stem bleeding and so on.'

Though he had no practical experience of treating serious wounds, he was considered a vital part of the local emergency services:

> I was sixteen years old. On the day war was declared I was just told by LCC, 'Go to the hospital and see what you can do.' This was the local children's hospital that had been closed down and evacuated. I was on duty with one nurse and three girls. The sirens went off and I went up to the roof with my helmet on, with my gas mask, carrying a stretcher and my first-aid kit. I was expecting the worst. Thank God nothing happened because we weren't ready.

The local medical services were far from ready to deal with what would come in the years ahead, but the enthusiasm of youngsters like Sidney Ties was a sure sign that there were many in the country ready for whatever challenge might arise.

Whilst youths like Sidney prepared for war, others found

themselves co-opted in working in civil defence. In late 1939, thirteen-year-old Roy Finch was out cycling with a friend when he was 'volunteered' for service. He was of the age group that felt too old for evacuation, yet were too young to leave school. However, with all the schools in the area closed, Roy found his days were somewhat leisurely. As they cycled past their closed school, Roy looked across at their former classrooms: 'Look, it's all been sandbagged!' The boys noticed there was plenty of activity going on:

> There was an ARP post with a copper outside. He called us over. We said, 'But we haven't done anything!' He said, 'You've got bikes and we're looking for messenger boys. Come on in.' So we went inside and the wardens told us what they wanted us to do.

For Roy Finch this seemed like a golden opportunity to get involved in the war effort. He had already been a member of the local Army Cadet Force, his local unit running a junior group that included boys too young to join the main force. He had even won the award for best-dressed cadet, which he thought was due to his father showing him the correct way to tie his puttees. However, his new role as an ARP messenger did not include a uniform:

> We had a whistle and a bicycle and we had to pedal around the area, blowing the whistle and shouting, 'Air raid warning! Take cover!' Everyone thought we were bloody ridiculous. But we thought we were great. We had a proper tin hat and a gas mask. Then we'd cycle back to the warden's post and wait in a classroom until we had to go out again.

It was an interesting role for the boys, who felt they were making a genuine contribution to the war effort. They were not alone: all over the country, children volunteered their services to the ARP. Scouts and Guides acted as 'spotters', scanning the sky for bombers then looking out for fires that started in the aftermath of raids. Some boys even established their own informal 'Junior ARP' posts, establishing lookout posts, constructing HQs and erecting signs highlighting their role. With homemade armbands and 'tin helmets' purchased from local shops, they prepared themselves for war. Some schools also established ARP, fire-watching and observation posts, with children going on the roofs to watch for enemy aircraft. Using signal flags they were able to relay information to messengers who could in turn pass it on to the ARP. All across the country, Boy Scouts, Girl Guides and members of the Boys Brigade made sure their first-aid kits were filled and ready to assist with the expected casualties bombing would bring.

One of the earliest targets was the outer London suburb of Croydon, chosen by the Germans because of its airport. As was later discovered, the Germans' method for locating the airfield was simple: they were guided by Luftwaffe pilots who knew their way from their pre-war careers as commercial pilots who had landed at Croydon airport. On 16 August 1940 the Luftwaffe bombed Croydon. However, in nearby Norbury, Roy Finch's ARP career got off to an inauspicious start: he was at home when he first heard the sound of aerial attack. It was only after the sound of explosions and machine-gun fire had faded, and the drone of the attacker's engines had long passed, that he actually heard the wail of the siren to warn of a raid.

In those few minutes, bombs had hit the airfield, some houses and the factories nearby, causing many casualties among workers who were rushed to hospital. With hospital staff unable to cope with both treating the wounded and carrying out ARP duties, they needed a source of labour. To meet the shortfall local Boy Scout troops volunteered their services. In the late 1930s many Scout troops had assisted in civil defence exercises, often playing the role of the injured, allowing the emergency services to hone their rescue skills. Now, in the hour of need, the Scouts made practical use of their experience. In Croydon, Boy Scouts over the age of fourteen were asked to volunteer to assist at the hospitals, a duty they continued throughout the Blitz. The boys became stretcher-bearers, fire-watchers, telephonists and messengers. They were given steel helmets and trained in fire-fighting, learning how to operate the stirrup-pumps, fire hoses and hydrants. Those over sixteen were stationed on a tower above the hospital to act as observers, watching for the fall of incendiary bombs. Others waited at the hospital with their bicycles, ready to act as messengers. When seriously injured people arrived at hospital, the messengers were sent out – ignoring the falling bombs and the shrapnel of the anti-aircraft guns – to notify next of kin.

In addition to the Boy Scouts, the Croydon hospitals also had assistance from other teenagers. The local Red Cross and St John Ambulance had formed three teams of girls aged between fifteen and eighteen. Many of these volunteered to work in the hospitals or at the blood transfusion service. Assistance was also provided by the teenage boys of the Air Defence Cadet Corps, an organization set up in 1937 to train boys keen to join the RAF. They volunteered to assist at hospitals by filling some 600 sandbags used to protect the casualty department.

The dedication of the Scouts meant that they also assisted with the unloading of ambulances, helping to move the injured into the wards and operating theatres. They helped doctors by pointing out wounds. One fourteen year old later reported that he had to take an amputated leg for incineration. When not dealing with the badly wounded, the Scouts helped to move patients to places of safety: one of their duties included carrying newborn babies down to the air raid shelters. Their efforts were recognized when the town council gave them a commendation in a special resolution to acknowledge their bravery and energy during the bombing. Croydon's Scouts were also recognized by the scouting authorities. The Scout's Gilt Cross medal was awarded to Eric Martin and the Certificate of Gallantry was won by John Dyne and Peter Standen. All were recognized for their work at Croydon Town Hall when it was bombed.

These raids were just a taste of what lay ahead. Even light
bombing brought casualties rushing into hospitals for treatment,
straining the emergency services. Once the raids grew heavier, so
too did the need for all available medical assistance. When the sirens
sounded in London on 7 September 1940, sixteen-year-old Sidney
Ties led his mother, grandmother and two aunts from their home in
Jamaica Street to the safety of the street's brick-built shelter. So far,
after a year of war, his contribution to the war effort had been to
continue training, giving instruction and setting up an aid post in the
basement of the dental technicians where he worked. As they made
their way along the street, Sidney made sure he had his small
first-aid satchel slung from his shoulder. After four years of training,
this would be his chance to prove that all those evening classes had
not been wasted.

Sitting in the shelter, he could hear the whine of bombs, the
banging of the anti-aircraft guns, the crash of explosions and the
ringing bells of ambulances and fire engines. Some 250 enemy
bombers flew over London that night. Though Sidney was unable
to see what was happening outside, it was clear that the full fury of
war was being unleashed:

> War started for me when they hit the docks. It really was tough. But
> when you're sixteen you just get on with it. You don't think about it.
> We just sat there listening to the banging of the bombs and then when
> the 'all clear' went, I went outside and helped.

As he made his way outside he noticed that the street was sticky with
a greasy yellow liquid. He looked down and realized it was melted
butter that was running out from a nearby bombed warehouse: 'I
had no official duties. I had no Red Cross armband or anything. I
was straight out into my street. My first patients were people in the
next street. I did whatever I could.'

Everywhere he looked there seemed to be buildings burning and
firemen attempting to quench the flames. The sky was lit up with a

red and yellow glow from countless warehouse fires: 'The air was full of smoke and dust. It was murder. The fires raging. The docks were alight. The glow lit up the sky.' And yet Sidney Ties did not stop to marvel at the scenes, instead he did all he could to help the injured:

> I wasn't affected by the horror and didn't find it difficult to cope. I had already got an idea of blood and open wounds from observing at the hospital. But there was not much I could do with my small first-aid kit. But I did help by digging people out – this was in my own streets.

That first night was a taste for what was to come. As the raids continued, Sidney made sure he took his first-aid kit with him to the shelter and did all he could to help. He soon grew used to the sights, sounds and smells of a city being pounded with high explosive and showered with incendiary bombs:

> When you go into a bombed area, the first thing you notice is that everything is white. There is dust everywhere. You are looking through all this dust on the person's body before you can even work out where they are hurt. They were so covered in white dust, you could hardly tell if they were alive or dead.

The dust he described surprised all who experienced it, thick clouds of dust and debris that had, in some cases, lain undisturbed for a hundred years or more.

In the battered and burning streets of his home borough, Sidney went out night after night to offer assistance to the wounded. In the first few weeks of the Blitz he went from being a youth with a basic understanding of rudimentary first aid to having a deep understanding of the horrors of modern warfare. Pulling the wounded from the ruins of their homes, treating them and helping them to ambulances, he was doing what he could to defy the enemy. All the time his experience was growing:

You'd find some people without a mark on them. Then you'd have a look, and they were dead – killed by the blast. They looked perfectly fine but were dead. I soon learned that if they had a small wound, the shock stopped it from bleeding too much at first. But if a main artery had gone you hadn't got much chance of saving them – the blood would spurt up to the ceiling. If you are not there to press the pressure point immediately, they hadn't got a chance.

His work was made worse by the fact that the bombing had disturbed the vast communities of rats that lived in the warehouses around the docks. As the fires raged and the buildings collapsed, the rats swarmed everywhere. Despite his dislike of vermin, Sidney worked on; this was no time to be squeamish.

After a month of seemingly constant bombing, the war came even closer to Sidney Ties. One night, as they waited for the all clear, the shelter was rocked by a tremendous blast and engulfed in dust. Immediately the people within began screaming, but Sidney was quickly to his feet, shouting into the darkness: 'Shut up! You're not hurt, are you? You're still alive.' Remaining calm, he checked and discovered that no one was injured. By taking command of the situation, he managed to calm the screaming women, helping them settle down as the bombing continued. The shelter had somehow survived a near miss. With order restored, Sidney once more waited for the all clear when he could safely search for people to assist.

Days later, his career as a first-aider in his home streets came to an end. Leaving the shelter as the air raid came to an end, he stepped out into the street:

I came out of the shelter and saw a big hole. Our house had been flattened by a parachute mine. I didn't have a thing of my own after that. All my clothes had gone. My mother just saved one photograph of me at school. We met a policeman who sent us off to a rest centre on Mile End Road. We had nothing. Our clothes were in a terrible state, full of dust and blood. We just sat there on the floor, then someone brought us tea. I have no idea how long I was there.

They could not stay in the rest centre for long as there were already too many other homeless people in the area:

They put us on to buses and drove us away in the middle of an air raid. There were bombs going off around us. There were bangs to the left and right, but I was not looking at anything. I was keeping my head down. They took us out to Guildford.

Though this marked the end of his first-aid work in the East End, it was not the end of his medical career.

Although Sidney had been forced out from his home, other young volunteers remained in the area. At Watson's Wharf in nearby Wapping a volunteer fire service was formed by a group of local youths. The gang was led by a local docker, Patsy Duggan, who had wanted to serve in the military but was in a reserved occupation. The gang included: Frank Pope, aged 13; Freddie Pope, 16; Oswald Bath, 15; and Jackie Duggan, 17.[2] Adopting the name the 'Dead End Kids', the boys formed into teams of four and used a handcart to transport their meagre fire-fighting equipment to wherever it was needed. They didn't have fire axes, but carried iron bars to force open blocked doors. They had a ladder to access windows and buckets of sand to snuff out flames and incendiary bombs. When the sirens sounded the boys watched from the rooftops to see where incendiary bombs were falling, then raced off to deal with them. When they found the smouldering bombs, they tied ropes around the tails, dragged them away and dumped them in the Thames. The boys charged into bombed and burning buildings to rescue the inhabitants and were spotted escaping from buildings with their clothing smouldering. Two of the boys were reported to have died when a burning building collapsed on them.

As the Blitz raged, Britain's youth played their part in keeping the country running. The Auxiliary Fire Service had accepted large numbers of teenage boys – officially from age sixteen upwards but often much younger – to act as messengers. Equipped with either bicycles or motorbikes, they raced around their local areas, delivering messages, fetching fire crews from one area to another as their services were needed. Some of the boys were shocked – and secretly surprised – to find themselves working as messengers in fire stations which had curiously been issued with antique rifles to defend against invasion. Added to that, they were allowed time off school to carry out their duties. As such, the jobs were greatly prized by youths who knew their mates envied them. During the Battle of Britain, one downside was that they had to remain on duty and could not race off to watch dogfights in the skies above them. Instead, their work took precedence.

Scouts and Guides played an increasing role during the bombing. Guides with 'Pathfinder' badges volunteered to use their knowledge of local areas to show people through blacked-out streets to reach shelters. Boy Scouts went out during raids to show firemen where they were needed. Their youthful enthusiasm for the task was sometimes met by officials who did not make their lives any easier. One teenage ARP messenger was cycling through the nightly air raid when he was stopped by a policeman. The constable then asked him, in all seriousness, whether he realized he was riding a bike at night without lights. As they were talking a bomb fell nearby and both the constable and the boy threw themselves to the ground. The policeman stood up and continued: did the boy know he was on the wrong side of the road? More bombs whistled down and yet the policeman continued, lecturing the boy on road safety.

This sense of duty was displayed by thousands of youths who braved falling bombs to ensure they 'did their bit'. In north London, seventeen-year-old Home Guard volunteer Geoff Pulzer and his mate Derek were sent to guard a local reservoir:

It was about 500 yards away from my house. My mother was quite upset because I had to walk up there. The planes were overhead bombing and the anti-aircraft guns were firing, but we had no tin hats. When we got there, there was a guard hut covered in sandbags. That was when we were given a steel helmet – there weren't enough to go round.

This shortage of helmets was initially a problem in most Home Guard units. One section commander was forced to join a queue in a department store in order to secure two helmets. He queued alongside children who were buying the helmets to wear when playing at soldiers.

Despite the twin dangers of enemy bombing and shrapnel from the anti-aircraft guns, the two boys decided to relieve the tedium of guarding somewhere that did not seem to be a target for anyone: 'It was quite boring, just standing there, so we used to drill each other. We would take it in turns to march up and down, whilst the other was shouting orders.'

Whilst older boys were serving in the Home Guard, the Boy Scouts became active in civil defence. Some sixteen-year-old Scouts helped to collect the corpses of those killed during air raids, stacking the bodies ready for collection and identification. Younger Scouts helped collect and transport furniture from bombed houses, moving it into storage until families were rehoused. Others helped the elderly to erect air raid shelters. In tube stations, Boy Scouts supported morale by leading sing-songs among the underground population.

Some teenagers paid the ultimate price for the dedication to duty. One of these was sixteen-year-old Kenneth Wiggins, a member of the Boys Brigade, who was a fire-watcher with the ARP. One September morning he was on his way to work at the Boys Brigade London headquarters when the sirens sounded. Rather than taking cover, he continued on his way and was killed when the street was struck by bombs.

The story of the destruction of Coventry touched the hearts of a nation, but that one night of bombing was not the only time German bombers visited the city and was not the only time that the heroism of its inhabitants was displayed. Three weeks earlier, Betty Quinn, a member of the St John Ambulance, had been called on to do her duty. She later described the events of that night:

> The bombing that night began with a shower of slow-burning incendiaries. We all ran around putting them out with sand and earth. Then a man ran up to me and told me one was smouldering on his roof. He asked me if we could get a ladder and go up into his loft before the house caught fire. I hated heights and was really nervous, but between us we managed to put out the flames with the help of a bucket and a stirrup-pump. Then, as I walked home the main shelling suddenly started. It was very dark, the sirens were wailing and our anti-aircraft guns were blazing as the bombers dropped their high explosives.

As seventeen-year-old Betty neared home, a small girl suddenly appeared, calling out for help:

> Something was obviously terribly wrong and I told her to run on to the ARP post to get help while I dashed down the road. As I ran I looked ahead and realized a bomb had made an almost a direct hit on an Anderson shelter. As I got near I realized our neighbours, the Worthington family, were all trapped inside. Instinctively I started digging into the rubble with my bare hands. It was too slow to work like that and I frantically looked round for something to use. Remarkably I found a spade lying nearby. I remember hearing moans from inside. I also remember there was no shouting, no screams.

Amidst the bombing a young boy on a bicycle suddenly appeared and Betty sent him into the house, through the back door which had been torn from its hinges, to collect blankets:

> I can still see his frightened face. I told him 'just go and do it' – then other people started arriving to help. We all worked together, fumbling

around in the dark with only light from the shells exploding overhead. Together we got the family free. There were Mr and Mrs Worthington, their daughter Joan, who was a friend of mine, and I think two other sisters and two other girls. Amazingly they were all alive but injured. I helped to give them first aid. One of them was cold and I just pulled off my brand new black coat and laid it over them.[3]

As anti-aircraft guns continued to fire and bombs continued to fall, Betty comforted her neighbours as they waited for help to arrive. For all her efforts, the entire family died in hospital. The only survivor was the girl who had first alerted Betty. For defying the bombs to save the family, Betty was awarded the George Medal. She received the award at Buckingham Palace in 1941. When she later met Winston Churchill he poked at her chest, moving the lapel that half obscured her medal, telling her: 'Show your medal . . . be proud of it.' With typical modesty, Betty Quinn later said: 'I still don't necessarily think I deserved it. I was only brave because we had to be'.[4] To her, she was simply 'in the right place, at the right time'.[5]

Another brave teenager was West Bromwich schoolgirl, Charity Bick. She had been desperate to join the ARP but, as a fourteen year old, she was too young. She had attempted to volunteer but, arriving at the depot and giving her true age, she had been sent away. Determined to serve, she pestered her father – himself an air raid warden – until he agreed to lie about her age. Returning to the depot he informed them that she was sixteen and she was accepted as a messenger.

During air raids, her job was to take messages between various ARP posts, ensuring they knew where their services were needed. Despite the falling bombs, Charity continued to carry out her duties:

There were times when I was close enough to be put off my bike but I don't think you really get frightened at that age. I'd just jump back on and we'd talk about it when I got back from that message. I suppose there were times when I could have died but you didn't think about that. The message had to get through and that was all that bothered you.[6]

She also dealt with incendiary bombs, moving them away so they could burn without doing any damage. In September 1941 Charity was awarded the George Medal for her work in the Blitz. She was the youngest ever recipient of the award.

Charity Bick and Betty Quinn were not the only teenage heroines. In September 1940, sixteen-year-old Rose Ede (later Rose Taylor) crawled into the ruins of the farmhouse at Buttons Farm, Wadhurst, East Sussex, which had been demolished by a German bomb. Earlier she had gone outside to investigate a bomb that had landed in her vegetable patch. As she did so she was blown off her feet by a bomb landing on her neighbours' home. Along with her father, Rose rushed through the rain to the house: 'It was pitch black and there were aeroplanes flying overhead so you couldn't see or hear anything. We found two of the children quite quickly but one of the girls was still missing.' One child was found still in her cot, which was perched on the edge of the bomb crater. A second was found in the wreckage but the third was buried. As her father lifted a beam, Rose crawled through the wreckage to find the girl: 'I was crawling around on my hands and knees for a long time and then I suddenly felt a foot. It was such a relief. If they hadn't been in their beds they would have been dead.'[7]

The children were pulled clear, but they were unable to save the mother. Rose later admitted:

> The sight of the wreckage is something I'll never forget. No one realizes the damage a bomb can do until they see it . . . If I had thought about what I was doing perhaps I would have been afraid but I just went into the demolished building and that was it.[8]

She was awarded the George Medal for her heroism, first hearing of the award when her name was read out on the radio. Rose helped the children's father care for them for two years until she was called up for military service.

In Canterbury, fourteen-year-old June Mackenzie was travelling on a bus when it was bombed during a daylight raid on Canterbury. She was wounded and her Girl Guides uniform was covered in blood, but she used her first-aid skills to help the wounded. First she covered up the body of the dead bus conductress, helped other passengers from the bus and then set about bandaging the wounded with strips of sheeting. When assistance arrived it came in the form of a Boy Scout carrying a first-aid haversack and wearing a tin helmet. She received the Guides' Silver Cross for her courage.

As well as having its shipbuilding industry outside the centre of the city, Glasgow's geographical location, far to the north-west, saved it from the level of attention afforded towns like Coventry. That said, it faced its share of raids. One of the city's heroes was fifteen-year-old Peter Brown, a grocer's boy who had volunteered as an ARP messenger. Like so many other youthful ARP messengers, it was his role to keep communications open to allow civil defence work to continue through the air raids. It was whilst he was on duty on the night of a raid that calls came through requesting that rescue squads be sent out to bombed buildings. Then came the awful news that a large basement shelter had received a direct hit. Before the message could be relayed to a rescue squad the telephone line went dead.

This was the moment Peter, like so many other boys, had been waiting for – his chance to prove himself. With the bombs still falling, he set out on his bicycle to find a rescue squad and direct them to the shelter. He made his way through shrapnel-strewn streets, dodging the flaring flames from burst gas mains and taking shortcuts to avoid blocked roads. His route was lit by the flashes from bombs and anti-aircraft guns, and by burning buildings. He could hear the screams of people in these bombed buildings, knowing that some were probably people he knew – maybe his own school friends – all the time fearing that his own home, and his own family, might be victims of the bombs.

Eventually came the one sound he feared above all – the whining of a falling bomb. The blast flung the fifteen year old from his bicycle, smashing him into a wall. Dazed by the blast, he picked himself up and began the search for his bike. He found it nearby, a mass of useless twisted steel. It seemed strange that the bike should be so damaged when he had suffered no more than a deep cut to his arm and bruises to his legs. Despite his wounds, Peter still had a job to do. Dazed, and with blood dripping down his arm, he began to run through the streets. As he ran past his own street he could see devastation where his home had stood. But there was no time to stop. He ran on until he reached his destination and found the mobile rescue squad. He was able to direct them to the bombed shelter before he fainted from loss of blood.

Now safely outside London, Sidney Ties remained keen to resume his contribution to the war effort. His family had been housed in Guildford and he had found a job. Eager to get involved in the war, he volunteered for the RAF, aged seventeen, but was turned down due to varicose veins on his leg. Frustrated, he decided that he would find another way to serve, quit his job and joined the ARP on a full-time basis, initially as a stretcher-bearer before soon being promoted to squad leader.

Though Guildford was spared the attentions of the Luftwaffe, Sidney Ties and his squad were soon called to support the emergency services in Southampton and Portsmouth that were swamped by their workload following heavy raids. Their first destination was Portsmouth, following a police convoy along the A3, towing trailers containing six stretchers behind their cars. As they drove through the night, it was difficult to see where they were going since they had covered headlights that offered little more than a pinprick of light. As they approached the city their headlights became irrelevant: 'The sight of the fires was awful. When we entered the town the roads were covered in fire hoses and debris. The destruction was terrible.' Sidney then saw something he would never forget: a bus that had been blown into the air and was hanging out of the front of a building.

Arriving safely in Portsmouth their first job was to evacuate a hospital that had an unexploded time bomb beneath it:

> That was quite hairy. We couldn't use the lifts, so we had to carry them down. On the top floor were people who were a bit mental. So we had some troubles carrying them down on the stretcher. And all the time we were thinking of this bomb under the hospital.

From there, the squad went out to rescue people from the ruins of their homes. Unlike his experiences in Stepney, there was no waiting for the 'all clear' before starting to search for survivors. Instead, they worked as the bombs continued to fall. Armed with a small torch, he searched through dust-filled ruins for those who could be saved. When they found a survivor, their role was to ensure they reached hospital as quickly as possible:

> You looked for casualties. You picked up someone covered in dust, had a quick look: if they were alive, you put a label on them saying where they were bleeding from, and put them in an ambulance and sent them to the hospital. You didn't have time to put splints on or anything like that. Very basic, you just dressed what you could.

Whatever the severity of wounds, Sidney and his team had to ensure they reached hospital: 'In first aid you never said someone is dead until a doctor had told you they are. So sometimes you had to move people who were dead already. Of course, sometimes you used your own discretion: if it didn't have a head, you didn't need to worry.'

In both Portsmouth and Southampton, Sidney Ties and his 'First-Aid Party' worked almost constantly, with the days merging into each other:

> When we went in there we just had our clothes. We didn't take anything off for days. We didn't have a wash. We had nothing to eat. I just remember the Salvation Army. Wherever we were, they

appeared with a cup of tea and a bun. We were there for about a week.
Then we came home.

Somehow, despite so many hours crawling through bombed
buildings and dressing the wounds, the seventeen year old managed
to remain calm and complete his duties:

> I didn't get cynical – but I didn't get involved. In that situation you treat
> it as a job and just do the best that you can. You have to be detached.
> The worst thing was dealing with children. Coming back after picking
> up a dead child changed everything, everyone was quiet. That affects
> you, because they hadn't had a chance to live their life.

Youngsters up and down the country enthusiastically joined in with
civil defence duties, whether officially or unofficially. Having moved
from London to Oban in September 1940, Anthony Wedgwood
Benn joined the local ARP unit where the local men deferred to
him: 'I was fourteen-and-a-half and the only one who'd ever seen an
air raid – so I was considered an expert.' In Ealing Roy Bartlett, still
not yet a teenager, began attending the local ARP post with his
father. He listened to a lecture on aircraft recognition and attended
lessons on the operation of stirrup-pumps.

In 1942, he finally got an opportunity to put his training into
practice:

> I always dreaded having to fight an incendiary bomb. It was my job to
> be the 'hose boy' on the stirrup-pump. My parents' biggest concern was
> the paraffin oil we kept for heating. We had two fifty-gallon barrels in an
> outhouse. So we had buckets of sand everywhere to fight a fire. So it was
> also my job to keep all the fire-fighting appliances in the shop topped
> up. I had to make sure the pump worked and the buckets were filled.

One night the sirens started and he made his way to the cellar. As
he waited for his mother to join them, he heard a noise from above:

'Mum was shouting and yelling. I went up the cellar steps and she was shouting, "Incendiary in the back garden!" I went out and, thankfully, the bomb hadn't landed on the paraffin tanks. But the garden fence was already alight.'

As his mother pumped, he directed the jet of water: 'However, the magnesium was too hot to put out – it just reignited. And we couldn't use sand because you can't cover a vertical surface.' He realized he needed to obliterate the supply of oxygen with a constant fine spray of water, as he had been taught at ARP lectures: 'Now was the moment of truth. Dad was out, there was no one else to do it. Just Mum and me, twelve years old. I began to direct the spray and it was working, but a bucket of water doesn't last too long.' One of the women from the shelter soon joined them, tripping over buckets of water in the dark: 'I yelled out, "Water, we need more bloody water!" Then the woman chucked sandbags over the remaining bits of the fire.' Soaking wet with both water and sweat, he had carried out his duty, extinguished the fire and stopped it from reaching the oil tanks: 'I felt proud of myself till Mum called me aside and said, "I don't want you using that type of language!" Her sense of propriety didn't fail.' Eventually, in 1944, having reached the age of fourteen, Roy made it official and joined the ARP. Having prepared for so long, attending so many classes and lectures, he joined just in time to work during a single air raid, running messages between the local ARP posts.

In north London, fifteen-year-old Stan Scott found himself back at home during the Blitz. Even if they didn't have any ammunition for their rifles, he had been enjoying training at the barracks in Tonbridge until he was called to the company office:

'How old are you, Scott?' 'Eighteen, sir.' 'I'll ask you again – how old are you?' 'Eighteen, sir!' 'Don't tell me bloody lies! I've got a letter here from your mother. You are fifteen. Nice try, son. Hand your kit in and come to the office and get a railway warrant back to London.

The disappointed youth discovered that when he had been issued his uniform, his civilian clothes had been sent to his home address. As soon as his mother had found out where he was, she requested his release. As he travelled home he read the official paper that showed he had served ten days but been released on the grounds of 'Making a mis-statement as to age on enlistment.' As he later noted: 'It was October 1940 and I had the one thing thousands of men wanted: release papers from the British Army!'

He returned home, angered by his mother's actions, and only became angrier when his sister's boyfriend greeted him with the words: 'Here he is, England's last hope!' When he saw his mother he told her she should not have told the Army his true age. Undaunted, Stan volunteered for the Home Guard – despite being two years underage – and dreamed of the day when he would rejoin the Army. In the meantime he had to deal with living in a blitzed city: 'I didn't go into the Anderson shelter. With me mum in there? With all me sisters? It was like a cathouse. Every time there was a bang, they were shrieking.' Instead, he sat outside in the trench, surrounded by sandbags. He preferred the noise of anti-aircraft guns and falling bombs to the shrieking of the women.

One night his mother sent him and his sister indoors to fetch cushions to make the shelter more comfortable:

We were coming out of the back door and we heard a whizz and a crack. It was an incendiary basket exploding. My sister went loopy, she dropped the cushions and started screaming. I grabbed her, shook her and got her back into the bloody shelter. Freddie from next door came out. We got shovels. There were incendiaries burning everywhere, all over the allotments out back. We put them out. There was a builder's yard, full of timber. We had to climb over the fence to get in. We dug holes, scooped up the incendiary bombs, put them in, covered them with earth and patted it down. We were running all over the bloody place. Then we went back to the shelter.

They were not there for long. He heard a banging on the front door and answered it. A neighbour shouted to him that a nearby house was on fire. Incendiary bombs had crashed through the roof and ignited among the rafters. Stan Scott and his neighbour Freddie again ran to help:

> There was an old couple renting the house. We banged on the door. They couldn't hear us. Freddie said, 'Stand back!' He ran at the door and kicked it in. We went in and found them sitting in the back kitchen listening to the radio. They knew there was a raid on, but didn't know their house was on fire! We got 'em out.

Once the couple were safely outside, Stan returned to the house:

> I went in the front room, opened the window and started chucking out their chairs, rugs, vases – everything that could move went out the window. Freddie shouted, 'Get out, the roof's gonna cave in!' I went out of the window, then a few seconds later it all came down. Next morning it was all burned out. Just the walls were standing.

As they surveyed the scene, the owner of the house asked who had put everything in the front garden. Freddie and Stan, expecting thanks, said they had done it: 'You bloody idiots! Look what you've done to the garden! You've ruined it!'

Even out in the rural areas, children played an active role in civil defence. Outside the village of Bleadon in Somerset, a decoy airfield had been constructed to divert the enemy's attention from more important targets. However, this brought bombs to the village. Twelve-year-old schoolboy Ken Durston recalled the incident:

> One night they dropped incendiaries on our village. The house next to ours had an incendiary bomb land on the roof and it caught fire. We had the Auxiliary Fire Service and the ARP come round but because we were close to it – my dad said to me, 'Come on, my lad, come and

help us.' I remember manning the old stirrup-pump that night. I was twelve and a weakling but I could do a little bit – and as long as I would do what I was told and I was doing what I could, they were happy. It was exciting for a young lad.

The achievements of the nation's youths during the Blitz were not only about heroism, but also about taking a responsibility beyond their years. One youngster who took on an adult's role was fifteen-year-old John Osborne. Whilst working as an errand boy in July 1940, he met a girl, Gina, the daughter of one of his customers. He was immediately attracted to her, but there was one problem. He was not yet sixteen yet she was already eighteen. He decided that, being relatively tall, he could pass as being older and told her he was almost eighteen. The couple began 'courting'.

However, after less than a month John was thrown into a difficult situation. In August 1940, a lone German bomber dropped its bombs on the factory in Wimbledon where Gina's father worked. He was among the seven casualties:

> That hit me hard. I had only known her a fortnight and there was no other male around to accompany her and her mother as they went to try and find out what had happened. So I took it upon myself to take them to his workmate's house to find out which hospital he had been taken to. That's where we found out he had been killed and taken to the mortuary.

Taking on the role of the only male, John acted as their escort, taking responsibility for the two women as they tried to cope with their grief. Although just a boy himself, since he had told Gina he was eighteen he could hardly avoid the role of their protector.

In the months that followed, the couple grew closer but, with nightly air raids, their social life was limited:

> We did our courting in her air raid shelter. There'd be her gran and her mother, and the two of us sitting there holding hands – all the time

checking how high the water was rising from the floor of the Anderson shelter, then bailing it out with a saucepan. We used to hold hands, maybe have a little kiss in the dark. And there was a terrible smell of a paraffin lamp. How romantic it was!

Since it would not have been seemly to stay the night, John waited as long as possible and then walked back through the air raids to his parents' house – all the time listening to the 'Ping! Ping!' noise as shrapnel landed around him.

At Christmas 1940, just before his sixteenth birthday, John Osborne went to Godalming, where Gina was staying with relatives. On 29 December, the night of his birthday, the couple went out for a walk. In the distance, to the east, they could see a yellowy-orange haze in the sky and wondered what it was. It soon became clear: London was being bombed. 'The next morning I had to go to work. By this time I was working for the Electric Light Company in the City of London, reading electricity meters. I caught a train to Waterloo then walked to Aldersgate Street.' What he witnessed as he walked to work was an unforgettable sight. It seemed the whole city had been razed to the ground. Whole swathes of the streets that he knew were now smouldering ruins. Some buildings were still burning. There were bemused office workers wandering the streets, weaving in and out of the rubble and the mazes of hoses, avoiding the burst water mains and flaming gas pipes. Familiar landmarks had gone: only St Paul's stood unmarked: 'There was this terrible stench, there were hoses all over the road. The area I knew, around the Guildhall, where I did my meter reading, was in absolute ruins.' As he made his way through the ruins just one thought occupied his mind: 'What will I find when I get there?'

He was lucky: his workplace still stood and the staff were ready to start work. He was immediately shifted to a new position:

That was when they switched me from meter reading to being an electrician's mate. I was palled up with an older man and we went round the bombed buildings taking away the electricity meters and cutting off the mains supply. We went on to do this all over the City and in Southwark. We had to make sure there was no live current in bombed buildings.

One of their jobs was to cut off the power in a soap factory that had been bombed. John and his colleagues had to step carefully across the sticky, soap-smothered floors, where the factory's product had melted and then mixed with the water from fire brigade hoses. Elsewhere, they struggled to identify buildings in streets they knew well:

> We had written instructions to go to addresses to turn off the electricity so we'd try to work out which building we were supposed to go to. Sometimes we'd have to guess – you couldn't work out which number the building was. So we'd go in and do the job and just hope it's the right building. And hope it didn't collapse on us.

John Osborne later noted that his role was insignificant: 'I was called an electrician's mate, but all I did was carry the toolkit and hold the torch. My cleverest thing was fitting a battery into a torch.' Though he downplayed his role, John was fulfilling a vital task: the mains had to be isolated to prevent accidents and further fires. Their role was not without dangers. They had to negotiate rickety, charred stairways and search through wrecked buildings to find fuse boxes.

Unlike many other workers in the City, the sixteen year old was unsentimental about what he had witnessed:

> I felt a certain pride in the City of London, and it was shocking to see the City like that. I was old enough to understand the destruction. But it needed doing: the City was an old place full of narrow lanes and courtyards. Some of the buildings were horrible – it was a dirty old place. I was happy to see the old buildings got rid of, then replaced with something new.

Whilst boys like John Osborne were tasked with making safe the bombsites of the City of London, there were others whose intentions were less honourable. One fifteen year old was convicted of stealing coins from the gas meter of a house whose occupants were seeking safety in a public shelter. The boy's crime – though minor – was symptomatic of a growing number of children who used the chaos to their own advantage.

Though housebreaking increased as a result of the long hours of night that people spent in shelters, the one crime to make the most impact was looting. In September 1940, magistrate Sir Robert Dummett queried why looters were being brought before him charged with theft. Since looting could be punished with death or penal servitude for life, it was hardly a deterrent to charge looters with a lesser crime, one for which they faced a maximum sentence of three months. Of course, the reality was that many looters took little of any value; they simply picked up small items that they found in the streets. One man was charged with the theft of a few bars of soap from a bombed factory, others for taking enough coal to light their fires or taking a tin of sweets from a shop.

Among the opportunist looters were some who made the crime a habit. The professional criminals were joined by a number of children, who copied their antics. In the East End of London a group of children were caught stealing toys from a bombed warehouse; elsewhere youths disguised themselves as ARP wardens to commit their crimes. Though, for many, this was no more than childish high spirits and a desire to relieve the drab monotony of rationing and wartime shortages, for some it was the beginning of a career in crime.

The opportunities thrown up by the Blitz tempted even the youngest children. One who was unable to resist was seven-year-old Fred Rowe. With his father away from home serving in the Army, his mother struggled to make ends meet. Whenever the family was short of money she simply defaulted on the rent, loaded a cart with their possessions and did a 'moonlight flit'. Having moved from

Pimlico to Battersea, she had taken the family into an area of heavy bombing. The devastation may not have matched the levels seen in the East End, but the violence marked a turning point in young Fred's life: 'It was months of destruction and death. It used to do my head in. I thought, I can't deal with this!' Amidst the violence of the aerial assault on London, he soon found a way to occupy himself.

Leaving a public air shelter in the aftermath of an air raid, he noticed the results of local shops having been blasted:

> I got the idea that there were all these shops with their windows blown out. We were skint. You'd see all this food everywhere, all over the pavement. There wasn't much, but it was grub. And it was more than we had. So I thought, if I can get out of the shelter a bit quicker, I can get a bit of the grub for Mum.

A thought that was conceived to get a bit of extra food on the table had a profound effect on his life.

Having made his plan, Fred made sure he carried a bag with him ready for the next air raid:

> The air raid warning went so I ran away and I hid somewhere. So I could be the first one out. These bombs fell quite near. They suck the air out of you! I was running down the street because I could hear these planes coming. And the blast knocked the legs from under me and pushed me against a wall. It seemed like ages before I could catch my breath. I was gasping. My ears were fuckin' ringing for days afterwards.

Despite having been blown off his feet, the seven year old soon got to work:

> There was a butcher's and a grocer's shop that had been hit. So I filled my bag up with food and ran home to Mum. She asked where I'd been. I told her I'd got her some food. She said, 'You shouldn't have done that, they shoot looters!' I said, 'They won't shoot a little boy!' She told

me they would, because it was wartime. But she still took the bag of food.

This set the pattern for the weeks and months ahead: his mother told him not to steal food; he stole food and justified it by saying the food would otherwise go to waste; she took the food, cooked it and warded off their hunger.

Fred had to take risks by hiding outside during the bombing and there was one factor that he had not expected when he decided to be the first person out in the streets: 'The air raid wardens were great: when the "all clear" went, they were straight out there clearing away all the bodies. They knew it would upset people. But because I was never in the shelter – I was hiding outside – I saw it all.'

The things he encountered on the streets of his home area shocked him, revolted him and stuck with him forever:

> It was terrible. There were fuckin' body parts everywhere. The first thing I saw was a shoulder and an arm on the street. People had been blown up into trees. There was legs and heads around. I saw a torso in a tree with all the blood dripping down. The worst thing – the one that really got me – was seeing dead babies. I saw babies in the street that had been blown out of windows. They were horrible. I saw women ripped apart, with half the head blown off. The dress was the only way you'd recognize it was a woman. It was the people that wouldn't leave their houses to go to the shelter. The blast would blow them out of the houses.

On one occasion, as he ran from the shelter, he was followed by his elder sister. As soon as she saw the bodies she screamed and ran back. Yet Fred continued his work. As he later admitted: 'I was too young to understand what I was going through.'

He took incredible risks to search the streets for food, running through the streets whilst bombs were still falling, taking shelter when he thought it was too dangerous, then scampering out to bombed shops as soon as there was a lull. He began to realize that one of the greatest dangers he faced was blast: 'When you were in the shelter it would rock, and the ground would rumble, but when you're out there, standing by a tree or something – the blast throws you. One time it threw me six feet.' Recognizing the dangers, but unable to resist the lure of free food, he continued looting. One time he ran across a road to grab food he had spotted. He was later confronted by a local ARP warden, who shouted: 'You're fucking mad, Freddy. I saw you out there running across the road to get that bit of meat! You're a nutter! I was sheltering behind the wall and you're out there collecting meat! I wouldn't go anywhere near that.' For all the horror and the dangers both from bombs and of being caught, Fred was excited by it. The sense of excitement he felt from putting himself in danger would later influence his entire life.

Despite the looting, Fred was also conscious of the need to help people who had been wounded. As soon as he had run home and stored his loot, he returned to the scene of the bombing and offered what help he could. As the emergency services patched up the survivors, Fred asked what he could do to help:

> They'd ask us to go to the local hospital, fetch a box of dressings and run them back to them. I did it. But I also nicked sheets from the hospital. There were sheets, blankets and pillows on the beds they had for people who'd been bombed out – I nicked them. Mum didn't say it was right to do it, but she didn't refuse them – our sheets were worn out. This was my life. I was just a fuckin' little street-urchin. I didn't know any better.

When Fred Rowe met a friend who admitted he was always hungry, he offered to take him with him after the next air raid. They hid, then ran out into the streets and collected food from the street, filling their bags with tinned corned beef, tins of beans, biscuits and bread. It was the only night Fred met any opposition: 'One ARP bloke stopped us. He asked what was in the bags. We said, "It's food. We're starving." He said, "Get on your way. I'll say I ain't seen you." So we ran home.' It was a close escape, but it did not deter him from further expeditions. Instead, the next day his mate said, 'My mum thinks you're a hero, Freddy.' Further encouraged, Fred decided to continue to risk being caught. Although he never stole from houses, he soon graduated to taking more than just food. One night he spotted a wrecked car standing in the street. Inside was the driver who had been decapitated and had one arm blown off. Unaffected by the sight, Fred approached the car: 'I nicked his watch.'

Even a child like Fred Rowe, a determined and expert looter, had shown that he was prepared to help out in the aftermath of air raids. Like so many others, he had played a role in helping out when the emergency services were hard pressed to cope with the effects of the bombing. However, he was too young to play any real role in the fight back against the enemy. Others were not. There was a whole generation of boys who went from acting as first-aiders, messengers and fire-watchers in blitzed towns to being active participants in the conflict.

Like so many British teenagers, fifteen-year-old John Longfield was determined to do his bit for the war effort. Intelligent and self-confident, but too young to be called up for military service, there were plenty of other things he could do and so he volunteered for the National Fire Service. Working as a messenger, the youngster soon found his spare time was fully occupied.

On top of regular evening and weekend duties, at least once a week John did an all-night shift at the fire station. Even when he was off-duty, as soon as the air raid siren sounded, he jumped on his bicycle and pedalled furiously to the station to see if he was needed. Whilst there were plenty of false alarms, sometimes he found himself far from home dealing with the aftermath of German bombing raids. Though fewer and far less destructive than the raids of 1940 and 1941, each night of bombing reminded him of the importance of his duties.

As part of the nation's collective war effort, these long nights and hard work were one small cog in the mighty wheel that had seen Great Britain survive its darkest years. But for all his efforts, not everyone was impressed. As he later recalled: 'All this may have been good for the war effort, but it didn't exactly help my studies. However, I did manage to pass my school certificate and went on to the Sixth Form.'

By January 1943, John, aged seventeen, was on a collision course with his headmaster. While the youngster was proud to be a fireman, his headmaster had chosen to offer his evenings to another branch of civil defence. As an Air Raid Warden, the headmaster searched for those breaking the blackout laws. One evening his rounds took him to the fire station where his pupil was on night duty. Banging at the door, the irate headmaster shouted that a light was showing from the building. As the door opened, the headmaster was confronted by a fireman who swiftly replied: 'Piss off!' Frustrated by the response, but not waiting to pursue the matter, the headmaster walked off, displeased by the sight of his teenage pupil smirking from behind the fireman. It was a brief victory for John.

The following morning he was called into his headmaster's study where he was berated for dedicating his time to his fire duties, rather than concentrating on his studies. The pupil found it difficult to understand the headmaster's reasoning: after all, in less than a year he would be called up for military service where his schoolwork would be irrelevant. Deciding he could not agree with the headmaster, John interrupted: 'Don't you know there's a war on, sir?' Shocked, his headmaster replied: 'If that's how you think, then you should join the Army!' Taking the bait, John asked if he could borrow his headmaster's telephone, called his father at his work and asked: 'Dad, is it OK if I join the Army?' Receiving his assent, he left school, travelled to Leeds and volunteered at the local recruiting office. He was then sent home to await notification to commence training. The following day he returned to his school and told his pals: 'You can call me Private Longfield.'

CHAPTER 9

Boy Soldiers

'Some people did it just to get a uniform, because if you didn't have a uniform you were nobody. Others did it just to get extra food, meaning there would be one fewer mouth for Mum to feed at home.'

Roy Finch, seventeen-year-old soldier

'I was young and stupid and up for it.'

Stan Scott, fifteen-year-old volunteer

At the outbreak of war, there was a rush of young men volunteering for service. However, with the Army wanting to control its intake by calling up men according to their age group, officials tried to limit volunteers. With the pre-war Army having increased through the call-up of territorial units and members of the reserve, followed by the conscription of the nation's twenty-one year olds during 1939 and early 1940, it could not cope with an uncontrolled rush of volunteers. Attempts were made to encourage would-be volunteers to wait their turn. That said, the volunteers kept coming.

At the start of the war no man under nineteen years of age could serve overseas, while the minimum age for conscripts was twenty. However, the Army soon found it had a wave of keen eighteen-year-old volunteers, who were legally old enough to join the Army but not old enough to serve overseas. Another source of volunteers was from among the even younger boys who ignored the age restrictions, including youths as young as fourteen.

The Army had a long tradition of accepting 'boy soldiers' – at one time it was drummer boys and buglers who started their careers as children. By the 1930s the Army continued to recruit boys as musicians and for training in technical trades. However, the threat of war ended the recruitment of boy soldiers, since the Army needed men to serve overseas. The end of the training schemes for boys meant the ambitions of some who dreamed of a career in the Army had been thwarted. They longed to be soldiers but suddenly, with war underway, they would have to wait to 'do their bit'.

One such would-be soldier was fourteen-year-old Ted Roberts. Raised amidst the slums of London's King's Cross, Ted was eager to join the military. His late father had been a veteran of both the Boer War and the Great War. Both his brothers were already overseas as regular soldiers. Left alone at home with his mother as war began to engulf Europe, he was ready to serve. There was just one problem: 'In my heart, I wanted to be in the Army as a career, but then the war broke out. So you couldn't join up on "Boy Service" like you could in the 1930s. So I just joined as a man.' He also had to change his preferred unit: 'I loved horses and intended going in the Household Cavalry or the Royal Horse Artillery. But when war broke out, the horses became tanks and no way would you get me into a "sardine tin".'

In early 1940, with six months to go until his fifteenth birthday, Ted made his way to his local recruitment office and said he had come to volunteer for the infantry:

> I didn't have any trouble joining up. I didn't even think about whether I looked old enough. I just walked in and said, 'I want to join.' They said, 'OK, get in the queue.' So I got in the queue, had a medical and – bang, bang – I was in. They didn't ask me for any birth certificates – nothing.' He was uncertain whether anyone at the recruitment office

had guessed his real age, but no one asked and so he remained silent: 'I'd always been a fairly big fella, but in those days if you were standing up and you were warm, you were in. Simple as that.'

With the paperwork completed, Ted returned home to await instructions to report for training. Ted was lucky to be accepted: had the recruiting sergeant asked to see his identity card, he would have been thwarted. All under-sixteen year olds had a brown ID card, whilst adults carried them in green. Whilst it was simple to change the date of birth on identity papers, changing the colour would have proved impossible. Three weeks later papers arrived telling him to report to the King's Royal Rifle Corps, a unit with a long and distinguished history that considered itself to be among the elite of the British Army.

Despite his youth, Ted Roberts knew that his mother would not try to stop him. She had been a soldier's wife and had two sons serving in the Army – how could she expect her youngest boy not to follow in the family career? As Ted recalled: 'My mum knew that if I wanted to join I was going to join. She didn't want me to – but she accepted it.'

It was easy to see why the Army accepted underage volunteers. In the rush of new volunteers and conscripts they were simply lost in the crowds. With the country desperate to create a modern army capable of defending the island from invasion, resources were fully stretched. As the historian David Fraser later wrote: 'there was conscripted every resentful or maladjusted misfit, provided he pass the simple medical test imposed'.[1] In summer 1940 almost 300,000 men were conscripted into the Army in just three months. Seeing the country's desperate plight, it was little wonder so many recruiting sergeants turned a blind eye to the forged documents and smooth faces of eager young volunteers. Furthermore, most pre-war soldiers were familiar with the recruitment of boys, with many NCOs having originally joined as boy soldiers.

There was also a division between regulars and conscripts, with regulars bewildered by the lack of enthusiasm initially shown by many conscripts. Army life was generally perceived as dirty and brutal, suited only to those unable to secure any other employment. The High Command was sufficiently aware of the lack of enthusiasm on display by conscripts that it even produced a training film, *The New Lot*, showing how even the most reluctant civilian could become a good soldier. But veterans could at least recognize their own keenness in the volunteers, regardless of age. The experienced NCOs and officers saw that the youngest volunteers were unaffected by the wave of pacifism and anti-militarism that had gripped the nation in the preceding years. In many ways, the teenage volunteers were the perfect recruits: too young to be affected by the Army's negative image, young enough to be swayed by the notion of glory and old enough to endure months of hard training.

Around 600 boys of eighteen and under volunteered each month during 1940 and 1941. To cater for them, it was decided to create a series of 'Young Soldier' battalions. These were designed as training units for the eighteen year olds who had no intention of awaiting conscription. The plan was for 'Young Soldiers' to remain with the battalion until the age of twenty then, fully trained, they would be transferred to their parent battalions as other men of their age group were conscripted, creating a cadre of potential NCOs to guide their contemporaries through basic training. It was with high hopes that some greeted the establishment of these units, with one officer reporting to the War Office: 'These battalions are the means of training and disciplining the youth of the country for after the war or for the final victory.'[2] These units, given the designation of '70th Battalion', proved to be a great lure. However, there was one problem: significant numbers of the volunteers were far younger than they claimed.

As envisaged by officials, would-be soldiers could serve in the Army Cadets from fourteen to seventeen, then they could join the Home Guard for one year until they were eighteen, then volunteer for a 'Young Soldiers' Battalion. As the President of the Board of

Education acknowledged, the policy was aimed both at preparing boys for military service and: 'ensuring that boys, after leaving school, should be kept under some measure of discipline and supervision'.[3] At first the Army had lobbied to allow under-eighteens to volunteer, with the intention of using them to man air defence positions in the UK, freeing up older conscripts to go overseas to fight. Churchill had supported the scheme, hoping it would help bring potentially wayward youths under control: 'Under present conditions, with little discipline and many opportunities for earning high wages, boys of this age were in grave danger of becoming demoralised.'[4] However, this was dropped in favour of utilizing Home Guard units as anti-aircraft gunners, with the Cabinet discussing lowering the Home Guard recruitment age to increase its strength.

The government preferred to keep the boys working in industry and training part-time as cadets. During 1941 there was even discussion of making pre-conscription military training compulsory. With around 220,000 boys between fourteen and eighteen already undergoing training in cadet units, there were a further 1,159,000 who took no part in military training. Compulsory recruitment was rejected on the grounds that the Army was hard pressed to cope with the men it already had, without trying to train hundreds of thousands of boys. As was noted, there were too few qualified instructors available, with senior officers admitting that indifferent leadership and training might prove worse than none at all. Furthermore, as was admitted by the War Cabinet, compulsory military training for boys would arouse 'considerable, if not violent, opposition from certain quarters'.[5]

Once in barracks, Ted Roberts adapted to a new life surrounded by youths, some of whom were four years his senior. It was a world where there were plenty of 'tough guys' with something to prove. Ted was certainly not alone in being under the official recruitment age of eighteen, but he was among the youngest of the boys who had been accepted: 'It was hard being so young. And I still had to have my fights with the other people. You always had a few who were on the bolshie side, but you had to stand up for yourself.' Since he had been an enthusiastic visitor to his local gymnasium, he was at least prepared for the physical side of the training, even if the weight of the Lee Enfield rifle was a shock.

Ted was largely unconcerned about living amongst boys and men years older than him: 'I enjoyed every minute of it. The only people I didn't like were the ones who put you on these stupid charges.' The finer points of discipline were his one difficulty with Army life: he was happy to follow orders and train to the best of his ability but he hated being shouted at for no reason. He was promoted four times, but each time lost his stripes after an altercation with his superiors. It started whilst in the King's Royal Rifle Corps. Falling asleep after a twelve-hour guard duty, he failed to shave before parade and was sent before his company commander: 'The punishment was cold water baths for five days. The sergeant got up each morning to make sure I got in that bath. I had to sit in it for five minutes until he let me out.'

As war came closer, the battalion was sent out to guard 'vulnerable points' – including radar stations – from invasion. The country was desperate: there were no bullets for a fifteen year old's rifle and little real hope of holding back an enemy invasion force. As he later recalled: 'Since I had no bullets, if the Germans had come – I'd have had to talk them to death.' He remained with the training battalion for six months until news of his true age somehow became known to the authorities and he was discharged. His brother – serving in the Royal Artillery – was brought to the barracks to escort him home: 'I didn't like it. But I couldn't do nothing about it. I couldn't make a fuss, I had to accept it.' The situation was particularly galling since he knew some of the other boys were younger than him.

The question of age was a difficult one. Many recruiting sergeants were happy to turn a blind eye to teenagers well below the age of eighteen coming to their offices. Even senior officers admitted to the problem, without taking steps to remedy underage recruitment. As the Secretariat of the Army Council reported: 'It is the natural tendency of youths to pretend that they are older than they really are.'[6] One battalion reported discharging 100 underage recruits. The 70th Battalion, Royal West Kents reported having to send home forty-five boys who were found to be underage, including fifteen-year-old Stan Scott. The headquarters of Southern Command even requested that the age limit be dropped to seventeen: 'in point of fact, many boys now serving improperly are below this age'.[7]

Every young man beginning military service went through a certain rite of passage. As one later recalled, joining the Army was like the initiation rite of some primitive tribe and 'the shedding of adolescence for manhood'.[8] Whilst this was true for all recruits, it was doubly true for the boys who joined underage. They underwent this initiation, not as their duty, but out of a sense of willing and eager defiance of the rules of the tribe. They were breaking the rules in order to join organizations that prided themselves on making sure their members obeyed the rules. Perversely, it was these youngsters that were prepared to break the rules who were often happier to accept military discipline than conscripts who waited to be called up.

As the situation settled down and it had become clear invasion was no longer imminent, there still remained a core of youngsters intent on serving their country before they reached the call-up age. As a result, many youngsters who were thrown out of the Army for being underage simply signed up again and joined other regiments. Stan Scott and Ted Roberts were among those who failed to be disheartened and returned to the recruiting office to re-enlist for training.

For Stan Scott, the decision was easy. He was keen to be a soldier and, since the Army was desperate for recruits, why shouldn't he serve? Furthermore, he was bored by the lack of interest shown by his fellow members of the Home Guard:

They were all old boys, '14–18 veterans. For them, the Home Guard was an excuse to get together to have a beer and swap all the old yarns about Passchendaele and all that. I expected to do something. We sat around with these useless American P14 rifles. I wanted to get stuck in, wanted to learn it all properly. I was enthusiastic, [the] rest of them weren't bothered.

After a lecture on their new machine-gun, Stan asked the instructor a number of questions. Afterwards, he was told: 'You want to learn about it? Well, you can carry the poxy thing!'

Disillusioned with the Home Guard, in February 1941, aged sixteen, he returned to the recruiting office: 'I didn't tell my mum. I got there, and it was the same bloody sergeant! "Hello, son, wanna join the Army?" By that afternoon I was up at Ipswich with the Royal Suffolk Regiment.' Once there, he restarted the training that had been curtailed the previous year. He saw the medical officer for a series of injections – not telling him he had been inoculated just months earlier – received a new rifle, uniform and kit, and headed to the barracks:

I sorted my kit out quickly. I put the webbing together, banged in two nails and hung it tidily on the wall – that was the correct method. So I was sitting there doing nothing. All the other blokes are cursing, 'Where does this go? What do I do with this?' In walks the sergeant, 'Come on, Scott, get your gear sorted out!' 'I've done it.' 'Who taught you to do that?' I said, 'Dad was in the Army, he taught me.' 'Well, don't just sit there, go and help the others!' I helped them sort their kit, sewed on my badges and then charged the others to do their sewing.

It wasn't long before the sergeant realized that Stan had previous training and soon began to give him extra responsibilities. The first job was to march the platoon up to the mess hall for their dinner. He soon found himself as a 'local unpaid lance corporal'. This was exactly what the Army had hoped for: the enthusiasts shone through and were promoted in order to form a future cadre of non-commissioned officers.

Having been thrown out of the King's Royal Rifle Corps, Ted Roberts tried hard to adapt to life in Civvy Street. But with the Blitz underway, life in London was none too comfortable:

> I didn't like air raid shelters. I just stayed upstairs and went to bed. If you got a direct hit on the shelter you were done for. If you got a direct hit on the house, it was the same. So what was the difference? If you are doing to die, you are going to die. You can't do nothing about it.

Bored with civilian life, he decided to rejoin the Army. He returned to the recruiting office, signed up as a 'Young Solider' and was called up into the London Irish Rifles.

For a second time, Ted went through the paces: relearning the drill, reacquainting himself with infantry weapons and learning to 'hold his own' in the barracks when confronted by older boys. Restarting his training, he went through all the same routines as before. He never told anyone he already had six months' training. There were two good reasons for his silence. Firstly, he did not want to alert anyone to his true age. Secondly, he didn't want to set himself apart from the other volunteers: 'I didn't want people to think I was showing off. I didn't want to seem big headed. I thought if I showed what I could do, the others wouldn't like me.' However, once again, his dreams of being a soldier were thwarted: 'There was a rumour that we were going overseas. So I told my brother and he told my mother. She said, "You're not going overseas at your age." So, she wrote to the regiment and that's how I got kicked out for the second time.'

In the aftermath of the Blitz there was plenty of work for youngsters in the cities. With the initial fury of the bombing having subsided, labourers set to work clearing the bombsites. Demolition gangs pulled down the blasted and blackened walls of ruined buildings. Whatever could be salvaged was salvaged. Reusable bricks were pulled from the rubble and stacked up, the few surviving sheets of glass were carried away. Buildings that might be saved were shored up to await the attention of builders. The overall impression was that the blitzed cities were undergoing a transform-ation.

For sixteen-year-old Fred Walker this was a perfect opportunity to make some money. From a poor family in London's King's Cross, Fred had left school with few job prospects. He found work at Smithfield market and gave most of his wages to his mother. In 1941, armed with pick, shovel and sledgehammer, he started working for a local company, pulling down bombed buildings around the City of London, clearing the sites ready for future development. The work was hard and heavy but it was summer, the weather was good and he was working outdoors. There were dangers – collapsing buildings and the possibility of unexploded bombs – and there was the chance of unexpected encounters – packs of rats or unmoved corpses – but the money was good for a youngster.

It was whilst clearing a bombsite near the Old Bailey that something occurred to change the course of his life:

> It was a very hot summer and me and my mate were sunbathing, trying to get our little bodies brown. The foreman came along and he said 'Oi, you two! Go and get your cards!' We were sacked for sunbathing. We wanted to have a go at him, but he would have murdered us. So off we went and had a cup of tea at Lyons Corner House near the Angel. I said to my mate. 'Come on, we'll go and join the Navy.'

It wasn't just being sacked from the demolition gang that had spurred Fred on. He was an only child, whose step-father was a violent man who had often beaten the youngster as he was growing up. At the age of fifteen, Fred had struck back at him but this had only served to strain the relationship. It seemed an obvious opportunity for a change of scenery:

So we went to Euston Road where the recruitment office was. We went in and saw this sergeant sitting there. He said, 'Hello, boys.' We told him we wanted to join the Navy. But he said, 'Don't join the Navy, lads, get into the infantry.' We didn't know what he was talking about.

They were not asked to provide proof of their age, only needing proof that they were not in reserved occupations. Having received their 'cards' at the building site, they were ready to join.

However, first came a medical examination. This proved a stumbling block for Fred. The examination revealed numerous scars on his body, the result of childhood operations that seemed to rule him out from military service: 'I wasn't passed because I only had one kidney. I was devastated.' However, the doctors were sympathetic and allowed him the chance to prove his one kidney was working. He was sent to a doctor's surgery in Harley Street. Over the course of the next few days he was made to drink water and then have his urine tested. He was passed fit for service: 'So I was in. It was a funny time. In those days they wanted anybody.'

Officially, Fred Walker should never have been employed in clearing bombsites in any case. According to the Ministry of Labour, such employment was not considered suitable for under-eighteens. In 1941 contractors working for London County Council were informed that youth labourers were not to be kept on. Another youngster working on bombsites was sixteen-year-old Walthamstow boy, Ron Leagas. His job was working as a plumber's mate, but with the plumber called up into the Army, Ron was given other tasks such as clearing damaged roofs. It was after a day's roofing that he made the decision to join the Army:

It was a shop with painted slates on the roof – they spelled out the name of the shop. I had to replace the tiles after a bombing. I got fed up, it was like a jigsaw. It would be bad enough if you knew what you were doing – but I knew nothing, I wasn't a roofer. It was a hot summer's day. I thought, I've got to do better than this.

Thoroughly disillusioned with his work, he soon had another experience that convinced him he needed a change. Arriving home from work, he asked his mother what was for dinner: 'It's stew,' she told him. 'Mum, I don't want stew, I want egg and chips!' His mother protested, telling him that eggs were rationed and such a meal was impossible: 'We only get one egg a week!' He then offered her his wages to buy him eggs. She refused, asking again: 'So you don't want the stew?' he shook his head. Disgusted, she shouted: 'If you don't want to eat it, you can wear it!' Recounting the incident, Ron laughed: 'So she picked it up and threw it over me. I was covered head to foot in stew! It was made from tinned soup and pearl barley. I told her, "That's it, Mum, you've done it. I'm going to join the Army!" And I did.'

With his mind made up, his next problem was actually joining the Army without revealing his true age. But he had a good plan:

> He asked, 'How old are you, son?' I told him I was eighteen. 'You don't look it. Have you got any proof?' I didn't have anything so I had to start telling lies: 'When we were bombed out we lost all the papers.' So he told me to go home to get my father to send a letter confirming his name and date of birth.

Having fought in the trenches and become a prisoner of war in the Great War, his father was very anti-war and Ron realized he would not sign the papers. He was also certain his mother wouldn't sign, so he decided to forge the letter. Sitting in the cubicle of a public toilet, he took a page from his work notebook and wrote: 'To whom it may concern, This is to certify that my son, Albert Ronald Leagas of 5 Exmouth Road, Walthamstow was born on the 1st June 1923.' He then went to the Post Office, purchased an envelope and delivered the letter to the recruiting office.

He was again confronted by the doubting sergeant:

> He said, 'Where do you live, son?' I told him and he said, 'How did you get there? Did you have a bleeding Spitfire?' I think he knew what

was going on. I pointed across the road and told him that Dad was across the road having his break from work. That's why it wasn't on proper paper. I had to make lots of excuses. The sergeant said, 'All right, in you go.' I had my medical and was told I'd be called up in six weeks.

The next step was to break the news to his father.

I sat in the front window of the house, I was shaking – I was dreading him coming home. He had a temper, more than once he'd chased me up the road with his belt. I was dreading it when the door opened. Mum said, 'What do you think Ron's done? He's joined the Army?' Dad said, 'Get off – he ain't old enough!' So she showed him the paperwork. He read it and said: 'He's made his bleedin' bed, let him lie in it!' That was it. Nothing else was said.

Another boy whose father had held anti-war sentiments was Eric 'Bill' Sykes. Born in December 1925, he was the son of a Great War veteran whose death had been hastened by war wounds and whose mother had died soon after. A bright child, he could have gone to college to continue his education except that his small bursary was insufficient to meet the costs. He found employment in a factory making Army uniforms, but this was not enough to satisfy him. As an active and headstrong youth, with no parents to deter him, there was one outlet for a youngster with limited educational or employment prospects.

In summer 1942, at the age of sixteen, Bill travelled from his Huddersfield home to nearby Leeds. His first port of call was the office of the Royal Marines, where a towering sergeant told him: 'You've changed your birth certificate, lad. Come back and re-apply when you're eighteen.' The forgery had been an obvious ploy, one used by many eager youngsters, but the unmasking of his efforts had not dampened his spirits:

Being a somewhat street smart kid, I wasn't going to be deterred by what I considered to be so insignificant a thing as a birth certificate. So, I walked along a passageway into the Army recruiting office. There sitting behind a desk was a very relaxed and amiable recruiting sergeant. The warm glow emanating from this very red-faced individual attested to the fact that he was obviously feeling no pain from his encounter during the lunch period with several pints of the local brew.

The sergeant looked up at him and asked: 'Come in, son. Do you want to join up?' Bill asked if he needed to show his birth certificate but was relieved to hear the reply: 'No, son, you look old enough to me. Just sign on the dotted line, here, here and here – here's your five shillings, you are now a member of His Majesty's Forces.'

In some cases, recruiting sergeants seemed unconcerned about the truth of a boy's age even when presented with reliable evidence that a boy had deceived them. In 1943, having been an Army Cadet, an ARP messenger and a Home Guard, seventeen-year-old Roy Finch took the next step: he added a year to his age and joined the Army. His thinking was simple: his elder brother had fought at Calais in 1940, had lost three fingers and four toes, and then been a prisoner of war for three years. In late 1943 he had been repatriated to the UK with other disabled soldiers. With his brother home, Roy was set on doing his bit, and getting some measure of revenge for what his brother had gone through:

I'd gone stupid, so I went to the recruiting office and joined the regular Army – seven years with 'the colours' and five on reserve. When my brother heard about it, he took me back to the recruiting office and told them I was too young. But they said, 'Sorry, he's signed the papers and taken the King's shilling, he's now a soldier.' He gave me hell. But I told him, he'd served in the Queen Victoria Rifles, I was going to serve in the King's Royal Rifle Corps. We did it because we were patriotic. I never regretted it.

With his brother having failed to convince the recruiting sergeant to release Roy, the next step was to tell their parents. The reaction was surprisingly positive: his mother accepted that since her elder son had returned safely, it was only fair that Roy, despite his age, should replace him in the Army. His father chose his words carefully, telling him: 'If you've got to go, you've got to go. Keep your head down and your braces up! Behave yourself.'

When Roy Finch arrived in York to commence basic training, he assembled at the station with a group of other volunteers. He noticed that four of them had, like himself, reported for training wearing their Home Guard uniforms. They were immediately singled out, called to the front and told they would lead the rest of the lads on the march to the barracks: 'So we marched smartly at the head of the column with all the others shuffling along behind in their civilian clothes.'

With his papers in hand, sixteen-year-old Fred Walker took the forty-five-minute train journey from St Pancras station to Bedford, where he was to join the 70th Battalion of the Bedfordshire and Hertfordshire Regiment. Arriving in the town, he walked to the somewhat daunting, Victorian, red-brick Kempston Barracks. Safe in the knowledge that he already had a mate who was two weeks into his training, Fred approached the entrance where he was met by a guard who called out to the fresh-faced boy: 'What are you doing here?' Putting down his case and pulling out his papers, Fred – bold as brass – answered: 'I've come to join the Army.' As he later recalled: 'I was a little bit cocky – well, you are when you're a kid.'

Whilst many underage volunteers, such as Ted Roberts and Stan Scott, faced the ignominy of being discharged from the Army when their true age was discovered, others were allowed to continue their training. Ron Leagas was sent to train with the East Surrey Regiment and immediately felt that everyone knew he was underage: 'No one said anything, but there was an atmosphere where I was treated differently. The Sergeant always called me "son" – he never said that to anyone else. He was careful to show me how to do everything.' After five weeks the matter came to a head when his commanding officer received the inevitable letter, sent by an aunt, revealing his true age. He was called into the office and asked: 'It's come to our attention that you are not as old as you say you are. What do you have to say to that?' Ron kept up the pretence, telling the officer he had been born in 1923. He was told: 'I'll give you a chance. You can leave now if you want, because you are not old enough to be in the Army.' Although he realized it was pointless to argue about his age, he pleaded with the officer: 'But I've joined and I want to stay in.' He was lucky. The officer simply stated: 'You do? You want to stay? Well, good luck then.' Then the sixteen year old was ushered out and allowed to continue his training.

At the end of his training, Ron requested he become a driver. His motivation was simple: he already had driving experience and had enjoyed it. At the age of fourteen he had taken a job as a driver's mate. Since the driver often turned up drunk for night shifts, Ron had driven the lorry around London. As he saw it, he had been an underage driver in Civvy Street so he might as well be an underage driver in the Army.

For the first three months after joining the Army, Fred Walker threw himself into his training. Then, hardly feeling like a fully trained soldier, he and his mates were told to pack their kitbags and be ready to leave. As they marched back through town to the railway station, crowds lined the roads, cheering them on and throwing cigarettes. It seemed they were being feted as they made their way to war. The reality was hardly so exciting: 'All we did was go by train to King's Lynn where we were guarding aerodromes. It was a Wellington bomber station. We were lucky. The Germans never attacked our aerodrome.' With so few fully trained personnel available, the Army couldn't spare any men from the front-line units to guard what were known as 'VPs' – Vital Points. Instead, the 'Young Soldiers' – including so many who had falsified their age to join the Army – had their training curtailed to mount guard around the country. Following the bombing of Coventry the 70th Battalion,

South Staffordshire Regiment was sent into the city to help clear the damage.

Serving with the 70th Battalion of the Royal Suffolk Regiment, Stan Scott found himself guarding an aerodrome in East Anglia. Upon arriving at the RAF base, they discovered it had recently been raided. There were wrecked planes around the airfield and the guard hut had been destroyed. He soon discovered why the enemy attack had been so effective: the air defence consisted of four Lewis guns mounted together. With the British Army so short of weapons, Stan Scott was told that they were to defend the airfield with an assortment of equipment:

> We had a solid-tyre lorry with a concrete blockhouse on the back. It had a flamethrower inside it. We did exercises with these bloody things. We could run faster than they could drive! We built defences at the airfield. There was French 75 mm gun with no ammunition. We had to lower the limber to make it work. A Hotchkiss machine-gun – how the French Army used them, I don't know. They were horrible things. You fed them with a strip of bullets and had to be very good to use them. Eventually they changed our American P14 rifles for Lee Enfield Mark IIIs. When we got our first Bren guns, then we were happy. We started to get all modern stuff. We were the last battalions to get the modern weapons.

His was a common experience. Initially, many of the 'Young Soldiers' (YS) battalions could only provide the most basic uniforms and equipment to the volunteers. In one YS battalion, a sixteen-year-old recruit recalled being issued a Canadian Ross rifle, a battledress uniform but no gaiters and a service respirator. He was lucky: the rest of his mates were issued with civilian gas masks in cardboard boxes, which were carried on a length of string. Others in the unit were initially issued with wellingtons instead of boots. Some complained of receiving First World War uniforms and equipment, some of the uniforms bearing obvious signs of repair.

The boys joked that some even had bullet holes in them. In the 70th Battalion, Leicestershire Regiment, C. T. Framp recalled: 'Out on the march we resembled nothing so much as a ghost battalion of 1918.'[9] Serving with the 70th Battalion, Essex Regiment, J. McGeouch later wrote: 'I often wonder to whom the webbing had initially been issued and whether or not he had survived the Great War.'[10]

The use of YS battalions to guard aerodromes and carry out other duties was not universally popular. Whilst there was a need to protect such locations in the event of invasion, sending the 'boys' out on such duties before they were fully trained undermined their training. One War Office report described the duties given to these keen volunteers as being of the 'deadening kind'. It was felt that they caused discontent and cramped 'the style of youngsters straight off the streets and bursting with energy and enthusiasm'.[11] That said, the duties gave the boys an opportunity to fight back whenever airfields came under attack. The 70th Battalion, Essex Regiment manned anti-aircraft guns defending North Weald aerodrome. Between summer 1940 and early 1941 they were regularly attacked. Indeed, nine young soldiers were killed and a further sixteen wounded during one raid.

The training missed by the boys guarding aerodromes was of scant concern compared to the major issue troubling the War Office. During 1941 a series of reports were carried out to ascertain the quality of officers and training staff in the YS battalions. It was widely recognized that the first weeks of a soldier's training left an indelible imprint upon him: if he received poor instruction he was likely to remain a poor soldier. The results of the survey were not encouraging. In many units, ageing officers with a limited concept of modern warfare were in charge of training the keenest young men in the entire Army. They were often of low mental and physical quality, lacking in leadership qualities. Many were in their forties, veterans of the Great War who were in a 'fixed groove' with limited knowledge of modern weapons and tactics.

One regiment described 60 per cent of the officers as being unsuitable, whilst one commanding officer was described as lacking 'the drive, initiative, and experience necessary to make a real success of a unit in which he is supported by subordinates of indifferent training and experience'.[12] Another battalion was reported as having five officers who had last undergone military training in 1919. In the words of a senior officer, the commanding officer of one of his training battalions was, 'physically incapable of entering fully into the training and games of the youngsters' and 'merely a bad example and a bad influence'. As the officer noted: 'Modern youth has little respect for grey hairs, and should be led by youth.'[13] One officer trying to command a battalion of teenagers was reported as arthritic and in one battalion thirteen officers were returned to their parent units as being unsuitable. The commander of one battalion went as far as to describe his subordinate officers as 'misfits', with one company commander being 'useless'.[14]

It was an officer of his training battalion that caused Stan Scott to receive an early transfer from a YS battalion to a regular unit. Whilst on guard duty he was confronted by the wife of his company commander who requested to be allowed to enter the camp by a side gate. He spoke with her briefly, then broke the rules by admitting her to the camp. The next day he was called before the company commander for daring to talk to his wife. The officer told him: 'If I had my way, I'd take off my jacket and give you a bloody good thrashing.' Stan rose to the challenge: 'Go on then – try it and I'll show you what a boy from Tottenham can do!' The enraged officer threw him out. Within minutes, Stan had returned with a letter requesting a transfer back to his original regiment: 'That paper hardly touched his desk. Straight away he gave me a rail warrant and orders to go to Deal to join the Royal West Kents.'

It was not just the officers. Many of the NCOs were also unsuitable. One commanding officer rejected an entire batch sent to him. Another rejected six from a draft of ten, telling his superiors they were 'obviously unsuitable'.[15] In the Bedfordshire

and Hertfordshire regiment (the 'Beds and Herts'), the standard of
NCOs was described as 'deplorably low'.[16] One sixteen-year-old
volunteer later recalled the low standard of some of his instructors:

> Some of the old training instructors were as thick as two short planks.
> We had one who took us out on map reading exercises. We'd ask him,
> 'Where are we, Sarge?' He'd get his big thumb, put it on the map,
> covering about ten square kilometres and say, 'Just about there.' He
> didn't have a clue.

In other units, recruits were genuinely pleased by the quality of their
instructors, being impressed by the experience of veteran soldiers.
Stan Scott found himself being trained by a veteran sergeant-major
who earned his respect. One night the sergeant-major caught him
entering the camp after 'lights out', by crawling under the perimeter
fence. The sixteen year old was expecting to be put on a charge but
gave an honest answer when asked where he had been: 'Over the
road for a pint.' The NCO told him that he had given the right
answer, since he had seen him in there. Stan was sent back to his hut
and no more was said of the incident.

The issue of ineffective staff meant that unsuitable volunteers
caused disruption. In one report sent to the War Office, it was noted
that the 'boys' would feel let down by the Army if high standards
were not achieved: 'We did not give them a fair start-off as the COs
were below standard, and many of the officers and NCOs quite
useless. The small number of young criminals exercised an influence
out of all proportion to their numbers owing to inefficient NCOs.'[17]

The types of boys joining the Army were a genuine concern to all
involved in developing the scheme to produce what was hoped to
be the next generation of NCOs. As the headquarters of Eastern
Command reported to the War Office, at the start recruiting officers
had accepted young volunteers: 'without reference to birth certificates, moral character, police records or criminal tendencies, large
numbers of boys whose inclusion among lads of an impressionable

age had a deplorable effect on discipline'.[18] The Black Watch complained that many of its young soldiers were criminal types from the slums of Glasgow and one Scottish commanding officer had to discharge a gang of what he described as 'razor slashers'.[19] One volunteer noted the unexpected friendship between a ex-student from Balliol College, Oxford, and an ex-Borstal boy. Private, later Captain, Collister noted: 'The average soldier in our battalion was 18 to 19, had left school at 11, had a spell in a reform school, or possibly a Borstal, had had intermittent employment, and had seen enlistment as a heaven-sent opportunity for escape and subsistence.'[20] Another volunteer, C. T. Framp, described some of his fellow 'young soldiers' as: 'anti-police, anti-authority and, not to put too fine a gloss upon it, anti-social'.[21]

With so many volunteers coming from the cities, the High Command received reports that many of the boys lacked physical strength, due to having been raised in poverty and having endured poor diets. Southern Command noted that many of their 'Young Soldiers' were not genuine volunteers, but boys who had been bombed out of their homes in London and needed somewhere to go, complaining that many of these were 'hooligans of low mentality and discipline'.[22] Elsewhere it was reported that many of the boys were orphans who left children's homes to volunteer. In Stan Scott's unit there was one youngster who, having volunteered for the Army, had changed his mind and was attempting to get thrown out. His chosen method was to refuse to wash and to wet the bed every night. Another boy who changed his mind attempted to give himself ulcers by drinking polish.

The senior officers of the 70th Battalion, Beds and Herts were concerned that too many recruits were 'boys of the Borstal type' who were a bad influence on the good lads: 'I have heard them described by various people as dirty, lazy, insubordinate and thoroughly bad soldiers'. In an uncharacteristic display of disloyalty, the commanding officer of the training centre even told former officers of the regiment that the presence of teenage criminals meant

they should not send their sons to the 70th Battalion of the Beds and
Herts. The Welch Regiment reported problems of theft, blamed on
the 'young gangsters'[23] who had been recruited.

Whilst the types of youngsters volunteering for service caused
initial concern, the situation soon settled. In late 1940 it was decided
that all 'Young Soldiers' with criminal records would be discharged.
The Royal Norfolk Regiment reported that a number of the recruits
had come from Borstal or reform schools but gave no trouble and
that two of the worst offenders became the smartest lads in the unit.

Despite the problems with the character of some volunteers, the
units were useful for the assessment of potential officers. There were
suggestions that such recruits should be segregated from the training
units. However, this was dismissed by the High Command, which
recognized it needed officers who understood the men they would
command. By allowing them to undergo a full period of service as
'Young Soldiers', they would mix with boys from all classes,
learning about all the varying types of men in the Army. Only after
completing their time in a 70th battalion were those who had shown
potential sent to an officer selection board.

In an attempt to provide the infantry with a high calibre of junior
officers, posters were displayed in schools encouraging boys to
volunteer for service as soon as they were old enough, hoping this
would encourage educated boys to prepare themselves for the
battles ahead. Genuine efforts to encourage schoolboys into the
Army to serve as officers were also needed to stave off competition
from other quarters. As one War Office report noted, the number of
young soldiers deemed suitable to train as officers had declined,
lured 'no doubt to the attractions of the RAF'.[24]

One potential officer discovered within a 70th battalion who more
than fulfilled the expectations of the War Office was Anthony
Farrar-Hockley. He ran away from school aged fifteen to join the
Army, only to be discharged when his age was discovered.
Undaunted, he signed up again aged seventeen, served in a YS
battalion, was promoted to sergeant whilst still just seventeen,

selected for officer training and commissioned just after his eighteenth birthday. He served in Italy, France and Greece with the Parachute Regiment and was promoted to company commander by the time he was twenty. In later years he served in Palestine, Cyprus, Aden, Egypt and Korea, where he was captured and held prisoner for two years. By the time he retired, he was General Sir Anthony Heritage Farrar-Hockley, GBE, KCB, DSO & Bar, MC, one of the country's most noted soldiers and a respected military historian.

Less highly ranked, but no less well known, was another graduate of a 70th battalion, Charles Whiting. Born in December 1926, he volunteered for the Army in 1943 having added two years to his age. Just days after his eighteenth birthday he found himself heading for the front in a train that came under attack by German aircraft. He served with the infantry in the final five months of the war, using his experiences as the basis for the books that later made him famous. By the time of his death in 2007, he had written around 350 books – both novels and works of non-fiction – almost exclusively on the Second World War.

Despite the desire of so many youngsters to be on active service, the early stages of the war saw continued opposition to any soldier under twenty going overseas. When pressed in Parliament, Churchill highlighted that mistakes were not easy to remedy, telling the house: 'One does not want to pull perfectly fit young men of nineteen and upwards out of their sections and platoons, and they themselves would be very much offended if they were so treated.'[25] Those who challenged the errors were swimming against the tide of necessity. As the manpower situation became increasingly stretched, the rules on conscription changed. In late 1941, conscription age was lowered from nineteen to eighteen-and-a-half. In January 1942 the age at which conscripts could be sent overseas was reduced to nineteen-and-a-half. Then the conscription age was lowered to eighteen, as was the age for overseas service. To allow for youngsters to continue to receive advance training, the recruitment age for YS battalions was dropped to seventeen-and-a-half.

However, this meant they had just six months' advantage over men of their own age group, rather than the eighteen months they had enjoyed at the start of the war.

From June 1942 the way the Army trained its recruits changed. Training was taken out of the control of individual regiments and standardized as part of the General Service Corps. Under this new system, all recruits received their initial six weeks' training at a Primary Training Centre, before facing a selection board to decide where they should serve. This had an impact on the YS battalions, which from October 1943 no longer carried the names of individual regiments. Many young soldiers disapproved of the change, objecting to wearing the 'General Service' badge and preferring to wear the badge of the regiment for which they had volunteered. This was considered a matter of pride, particularly those who volunteered to serve in 'family' regiments.

Having twice been denied his dream of becoming a soldier, Ted Roberts was forced to wait until he could legitimately sign on for service. In 1942, reaching the age of seventeen he was finally able to join a YS battalion without the constant dread of his date of birth being discovered. This time he made a choice that took him far from his London home: the Highlands of Scotland. Having already served in two light infantry regiments, he was well acquainted with the drill methods and high-speed marching practised in such regiments, and had no desire to learn a new and unfamiliar routine. However, with both of his former regiments not accepting new volunteers, he was forced to look elsewhere. With only the Highland Light Infantry looking for a new intake into its YS battalion, Ted headed north of the border.

Arriving at the barracks with a group of other volunteers, Ted was shocked to hear the air raid sirens. Luftwaffe 'raiders' had come across the North Sea and were above the camp. Seeing a gun pit with twin Bren guns on an anti-aircraft mounting, Ted was tempted to run to the position and open fire. After all, he had been trained to fire the guns during his previous stints in the Army. However, realizing that demonstrating his ability with machine-guns would raise questions about his past, he decided to keep still and allow trained soldiers to man the guns.

On his first day in Aberdeen he collected his kit and was allotted a space in a barrack room: 'It was all Scotsmen in the barracks, I couldn't understand a bloody word they were talking about.' Despite his concern, the next day brought some relief: 'There was a new intake and it was all English blokes.' Then, when he first went on parade, he was relieved to discover that even his corporal was a Londoner.

Having already undergone a considerable amount of training, Ted Roberts found himself able to daydream whilst his fellow recruits listened to their instructors:

> The corporal was teaching us the rifle drill, which obviously I knew inside out, having done it all before – twice. But as far as the Army was concerned I was a raw recruit – a rookie. I was sitting in the hut, with all these photos of naked girls on the wall, and the corporal was talking about the rifle. So I was just looking at the photos of the girls. The corporal saw me and says, 'You! I want you out here! What have I been talking about?' So I ran through the rifle drill – bang, bang, bang – all correct.'

The corporal took him outside and called the sergeant over: 'The corporal says, "We've got a Home Guard here who thinks he knows it all." I said to the sergeant, "Can I speak to you in private?" And I told him I'd never been in the Home Guard, I'd actually been in the Army twice.'

The sergeant immediately arranged for Ted to be promoted to lance-corporal and put him on barrack duties whilst the others continued basic training. He helped out by teaching the recruits fieldcraft and showing them how to use cover. Already proficient with small arms, Ted helped out on the rifle range, showing the recruits how to aim and fire their weapons. He was again enthused by Army life and soon became proud of serving in a Scottish regiment:

> Come rain, shine, we'd do these twenty-mile route marches. It was tough. But we had to do it. You'd get back to within a mile of the camp and you'd be 'on your knees'. Then the piper started playing – your back goes straight and you march in step. It was amazing!

He noticed how much better armed, equipped and trained the Army was compared to 1940 when he had been sent on guard duty with an unloaded rifle:

> We did forced marches in full battle order, with the small pack on our back. We had a respirator and Bren gun pouches with six magazines. And a bandolier of fifty rifle rounds. We ran for ten minutes, then marched for five – over and over again. Then on the way back we stopped at a rifle range. At 600 yards we fired five rounds 'application' – which meant firing at the bull. Then to the 400-yard range to fire five rounds 'grouping' – getting all the bullets together. Then to the 200-yard range to do ten rounds rapid fire. Then we fixed bayonets, 'doubled' 200 yards and charged at a straw dummy.

With his training completed, Ted was given a choice of units to go to and was offered either a commando unit – the Lovat Scouts – or the Glasgow Highlanders:

> Being young and stupid, I thought I'd go to the Lovat Scouts. That sounded different. So I put me name down for them. Then a rumour came round that they were being trained as ski troops. Well, snow and me never mixed. No way! So I pulled out and went to the Glasgow Highlanders.

It was with this regiment that he eventually went to war.

CHAPTER 10

Going to Sea

'It changed our lives. I was sixteen when I took a gunnery course to fire the ship's guns. Now I look at kids of that age and think they would never stand it.'

Alfred Leonard, Merchant Navy

'We were still children, in a man's world.'

Royal Marine bugler Len Chester,
who played at his first wartime funeral at age fourteen

Whilst those under-eighteen year olds who wished to serve in the Army or RAF were forced to falsify their age, there was one place where boys could legally join the anti-Nazi crusade: the sea. Both the Royal Navy and the Merchant Navy accepted boys for service.

From the age of sixteen, hundreds of boys legally signed on with the merchant fleet, though by giving false ages and submitting forged letters claiming they had their parents' permission, many fourteen and fifteen year olds were also able to serve 'under the Red Ensign'. It was the least glamorous of all choices, but that meant little: the sufferings and sacrifice of the merchant seamen equalled that of any service. They may not have worn glamorous uniforms or fought in instantly recognizable battles, but without them the war could not have been won.

When the only thing keeping the nation fighting were the sea routes to the United States and the British Empire, it was the Merchant Navy that kept the flame of defiance alight. Without them, the speechmaking of Winston Churchill would have counted for nothing. It was aviation fuel shipped across the Atlantic that powered Spitfires in the Battle of Britain. Without the men and boys of the Merchant Navy, the tanks that ensured success at El Alamein would never have reached Egypt. And the UK would have been starved into submission long before D-Day. Yet, as Winston Churchill admitted in 1945, the Merchant Navy was: 'so rarely mentioned in the headlines'.[1]

The ships and sailors came from all four corners of the globe. There were merchant ships and crews from all the seagoing nations of occupied Europe, including the mighty Greek merchant fleet. There were Dutch and Belgian barges – that had escaped from their homeports and were vital in the Dunkirk evacuation – working the coastline of the UK. There were seamen of every race, creed and colour of the Empire. And there were eager teenage boys from all over the UK who had taken the decision to go to sea. Whether from a sense of patriotism or adventure, or simply because they were from seafaring families, they helped save the nation.

The Merchant Navy was the easiest of all the services to join – in many cases it involved little more than a trip to the local dock office – and it was also the quickest route into the thick of the action. Whilst joining the RAF meant many months of flight training, serving in the Army entailed at least six weeks' basic training, followed by months of battle training, joining the Merchant Navy as a deck boy could mean heading out to sea within days or even hours. As a result, whilst a fourteen-year-old boy who joined the Army after Dunkirk might not actually see action until after they had turned eighteen in 1944, a boy who joined the Merchant Navy at the same time would have been a hardened veteran by then if he lived to reach eighteen. It was the one service where boys were made to grow up fast.

It was a dangerous job, but one that had to be done. As ships were bombed and torpedoed around the globe, new blood was needed to crew the new vessels leaving the world's shipyards. Despite the loss of so much shipping, there were plenty of boys willing to step into the shoes of those who had been lost at sea. Douglas Morse, who gave up his job as a milkman to volunteer for the sea at the age of seventeen, and who had earlier been bombed out from his south London home, recalled the sense of fatalism that gripped the families whose sons chose to serve at sea:

> My brother had already been called up and my mum thought, 'There's another one going.' She was worried but the situation for us all was if you survived you were lucky. There was a fear – but you had to go on. We thought, 'We've got to fight.' It was desperation really.

One important factor helped support the Merchant Navy through the dark times. In an era when Britannia truly did 'rule the waves' – with a fleet totalling almost one-third of all the world's merchant shipping – the UK supported the sea-going services through an historic network. There were dockyards producing merchant vessels, staffed by communities with a long tradition in shipbuilding. Most importantly, Britain was blessed with training facilities. All the port cities had maritime training schools and some, like London, were home to many such establishments. Since Victorian times, these schools had provided the merchant fleet with well-trained boys ready to serve at sea. With the vast fleet plying its trade around the world, the sea had long been the place for boys in search of adventure.

One such candidate was Bernard Ashton, a fifteen year old from the Kent coalfields whose miner father insisted he should never go underground. The family had travelled south from Yorkshire in the late 1920s to find work. They settled in Deal and young Bernard quickly took to the coastal life. He soon began working among the fishermen:

> I was always on the beach. At nine years old, I'd be down on the beach
> – when they brought in the herrings and sprats – helping the fishermen
> with their catch. I would sell sprats on the seafront. They'd sell the rest
> to the local canning factory. I had learned to gut a fish. I wanted to get
> on the boats and work, but I was too small to reach the sails.

In the summer holidays he also helped out on the beach, setting up deckchairs and helping the local boatmen take out holidaymakers keen to do some fishing.

Falling in love with the sea, Bernard knew he never wanted to be a miner. After leaving school he worked briefly on the surface at the colliery, then on a farm, but neither inspired him. His desire to travel was fired by the books he read. He consumed tales of adventure and books on how the British expanded the Empire. Inspired by these tales, and in love with the sea, he took the obvious step. In the summer of 1939, with war looming, it was arranged for him to join the Prince of Wales Sea Training Hostel (later the Prince of Wales Sea Training School) in Limehouse, east London.

In an era where many young men remained at home until they married, often in their twenties, boys training for sea had to become independent. Before he left for London, Bernard's mother gave him instructions in how to darn socks, a skill that would be useful at sea. Arriving in the capital to begin his training, Bernard was met by two boys from the school. They were dressed in smart blue serge uniforms and impressed him with their attire. They travelled to Limehouse by bus, taking the new recruit through the streets of an area that was home to London's Chinese community. Bernard was excited. He had been inspired by exotic tales of life in foreign parts and here he was, not yet started his training but already entering a world he had not experienced before: 'I'd read about the Chinese in my books and the night before I'd been dreaming about Chinamen with their knives.'

He was immediately absorbed into a new world. He was impressed by the sights of the area: 'I went to the docks and saw all the ships. It was amazing.' He soon took in his surroundings: the school had a central square with a ship's mast in the centre and there was also a platform with a rotating compass for the boys to learn navigation. The course was a short one: just six months and then boys would be found a ship in which to start their career. With so much to learn, their days were full:

> There was no time to be homesick. There was so much to be taken in. Our training was very good, and very strict. Our working gear was canvas uniform. We got up at seven and had our own 'cleaning station' in the morning. Then we had breakfast of porridge and jam – or an egg on Sundays. Then it was blackboard lessons, in a classroom – drawing diagrams of every part of the ship. Then it was Morse code class and signalling. Some days we marched to West India Dock and learned to row. Six boys rowed and one sat in the stern, steering by compass and bridle.

On washing days, the boys had to scrub their uniforms by hand, then hang them out to dry. They weren't allowed to use clothes pegs. Instead, they used 'snotters', a length of twine used to tie the clothes to the washing line. It was just another opportunity for the boys to practise tying knots. Each day they attended afternoon parades, where everything had to be just right. The boys worked hard to prepare their bell-bottom trousers which had to be made up in six-inch squares, folded back and forward, then put under the mattress to crease rings into them. At the end of a long day it was 'lights out' at nine-thirty. In the summer of 1939, Bernard Ashton spent many long evenings sitting out on the balcony, smoking with his mates, and listening to the music and chatter from the nearby pub.

With their working days full, the boys were allowed some free time at weekends. On a Saturday, some boys were escorted to the local cinema by the matron, where they surreptitiously passed forbidden cigarettes along the row. Those not going to the cinema hung around in local parks, showing off their smart uniforms to the local girls. On Sundays they put on their best uniform, complete with 'Trafalgar Collar', and went to church.

Whilst sea schools such as the Prince of Wales were shore-based establishments where the emphasis was on teaching them about seamanship in the classroom, others were more 'hands on'. Elsewhere, boys – quite literally – 'learned the ropes' whilst living and working onboard a ship. Many of these were obsolete wooden vessels that had once sailed the seven seas. One such ship was Training Ship *Exmouth*, owned and operated by the Metropolitan Asylums Board and used as a Poor Law Training School, which was moored in the Thames at Grays in Essex. Famous ex-boys included Eric Morley, the founder of the Miss World contest and Charlie Chaplin's brother, Sydney. The original ship arrived at Grays in 1876, remaining there until 1903 when she was found unfit for further service. Her purpose-built replacement arrived at Grays in 1905 and remained there until 1939, when – despite her age – she was used as the headquarters for fire-fighting ships on the Thames. In 1942 she was towed to Scapa Flow and used as a depot ship for minesweepers.

The staff of the training ship were all former Royal Navy officers and petty officers, and the ship was run with strict discipline. Each Sunday, the captain inspected the boys and their messes, running white-gloved hands under work surfaces to check for dust and dirt. Having joined the *Exmouth* aged twelve, Reg Osborn enjoyed his time onboard. He found there was an enthusiasm among the boys, all wanting to be the smartest on the ship. To achieve this they had some interesting, if arcane, rituals:

> I still have fond recollections of the sight and sound of dozens upon dozens of twelve- to sixteen-year-old boys gathered around mess tables on the long open mess decks . . . bent over their carefully arranged blue serge bell-bottom trousers with one of their issued plimsolls in hand and with a mouthful of water which they would spray over the location

of the intended crease and, when satisfied that the area was suitably dampened, would then begin to thump the plimsoll down with as much force as they could muster to form the very much desired 'tiddly' creases.[2]

For boys on TS *Exmouth*, the ultimate sign of their nerve and ability was to climb to the top of the foremast and stand on the 'button', the highest accessible point on the mast. As Reg Osborn later wrote, the 'mast would sway alarmingly as the ship was moved by the wash of passing liners and merchant ships, of which there were many in those pre-war days'.[3] As a boy at another training ship recalled: 'These days, the health and safety people would have a fit. We would go aloft, without any safety nets. But at the time I thought it was normal.' Reg himself admitted he never plucked up sufficient courage to reach this point and win the accolade of being a 'button boy'.

As a purpose-built, twentieth-century, steel-constructed training ship, the *Exmouth* was actually fairly modern compared to some of its rivals. The Thames Nautical Training College, based at Greenhithe in Kent, was centred on a much older vessel, HMS *Worcester*. By the time war broke out in 1939, the *Worcester* had been a training ship for more than sixty years and had been joined by the *Cutty Sark*, which was also used for training the boys. Among HMS *Worcester*'s former cadets were the multimillion-selling author Dennis Wheatley and the 'Nelson of the East', Japan's Admiral Togo Heihachiro. She had started life in the 1830s as the *Frederick William*, a 110-gun Royal Navy ship. She was finally launched in 1860 but, with the Navy converting to 'iron-clads', the *Frederick William* became obsolete almost immediately and was converted to a training ship.

The coming of war meant that many sea training establishments were relocated. The cadets of HMS *Worcester* left for Foots Cray Place in Kent, with their ship being taken over by the Royal Navy, although the boys continued to take some classes on the *Cutty Sark*.[4] The cadets' new home was somewhat grander than an obsolete

Victorian warship. The grand Italianate villa, complete with marble floors, provided both the classrooms and the sleeping quarters for the cadets. The cadets slept in bedrooms, in two-tier bunks, rather than the draughty mess decks of a rolling ship. There were bathrooms and additional shower rooms. With additional classrooms in wooden huts in the grounds, it looked more like a minor public school than a sea training school.

Despite moving ashore, life continued with military precision. A bugler raised the cadets from their beds each morning. There were physical exercises and uniform inspections before breakfast. After breakfast there were classes, training visits to the *Cutty Sark* and practice lifeboat drills. The cadets learned both basic seamanship, such as knots, as well as more advanced arts of navigation and signalling.

Having been 'less than brilliant' at school, and already having an interest in ships, Bromley-born Derek Tolfree trained at the *Worcester* between 1940 and 1942: 'My father said I needed to do something about my education since I was just digging holes for air raid shelters and filling sandbags.' His father pointed out the obvious advantages of the training: 'If you wanted to be a ship's officer you had to do four years before you could sit for your first mate's certificate. If you'd got the leaving certificate from the college, that knocked the apprenticeship down to three years.' He was further convinced by the head of the local ARP, whom he had met whilst working as an ARP messenger. Her husband had been a ship's captain and her stories of his experience helped to inspire the teenager.

Discipline at the college was strict and the training was of a high standard. There was the usual routine of learning to climb the masts and rigging of sailing ships. As Derek Tolfree explained, the boys were trained to a high standard:

It was old-style training. No radar or electronics. We did a basic wireless course, but I learned most of that when I was at sea. We did school classes in maths, trigonometry, science, ship stability, meteorology and marine engineering. We learned seamanship by boat work on the river: knots and splices, rigging. The seamanship was basic but the navigation was deep: astronomical navigation, reading the stars. It was up to the standard needed to be a Master Mariner. When you became an officer, you didn't need to know any more navigation to get your Master's ticket. *Worcester* boys could have navigated ships in Nelson's fleet.

The boys also learned that life at sea was regulated with ranks, something that was enjoyed by some of the cadets:

Discipline was very strict. The greatest crime was smoking: it was forbidden on a wooden ship. The first move was for senior boys to become a badge cadet, their recreation was at the fo'c'sle. The 'heads' – or toilets – were in the fo'c'sle deck. So you would have to ask for permission to go to the heads. If you weren't walking smartly or dressed right, they'd find some reason not to let you. Or they'd get a stick out and give you a whack. And the chief cadet was like a head prefect. He used to administer corporal punishment if your sea chest was untidy or you were late.

This hierarchy extended to mealtimes:

We ate lots of rabbit stew – I think it was caught in the grounds. We sat at long mess tables, twelve boys to a table. It was seated on seniority. When grub turned up, the senior boys got the best pickings. They took their share then passed it down, and so on, till the junior boys had what was left.

Although such conditions were an annoyance to the junior boys, they also served to encourage them to keep working and advance until they moved up the table.

The wartime evacuation of training ships took the TS *Vindicatrix* from Gravesend to Sharpness on the Gloucester and Avon Canal. Between 1939, when she arrived at Sharpness, and 1966, when the school closed, some 70,000 'Vindi-Boys' trained there. The ship had been launched in 1893 as the *Arranmore*, sailing around the world on an eighteen-month maiden voyage. After being sold to a German shipping company and renamed the *Waltraube*, she spent the Great War as a depot ship for the U-boats. In 1920 she returned to England as reparation for wartime shipping losses, was renamed the *Vindicatrix* and became the training ship for the Gravesend Sea School.

Having been rejected by both the Army and the Royal Navy, Bill Ellis decided the merchant service was the place for him – after all, they did not discriminate against small youths. A friend named McNair suggested he join since there were plenty of opportunities for youngsters to replace men being recalled to the Royal Navy. He chose to train on the *Vindicatrix*:

> We were housed onboard the ship – and I didn't mind it. As I had no mum or dad, I already had a sense of independence. You'd learn knots, sailing, lifeboats and basic sailing in little boats there. You had the choice to go as a steward or a deck boy – and I wanted deck.

With money short, Bill had to find ingenious ways of earning extra:

> The pay was 6s/6d a week but they charged you for everything – haircuts, shoes, shoe repairs – so there was hardly anything left. You had to try and make some extra money. Some of the boys would get their mums to send them cakes, which they'd cut up and sell for 1d a slice. Others would sell single cigarettes out of a packet of Woodbines. There was this girl I'd been going out with – I wrote to her and asked her if there was any chance her mum would bake me a cake – and she did, so I had something to sell.

When his friend joined the training ship, the two boys found other ways to make their lives easier:

We all had to do our own weekly washing. McNair had an idea – we passed our washing on to somebody else. Everyone had a pile of stuff to wash and we dropped a bit on to each person's pile. It would then all get hung out on the line together – and we would say we'd lost something and get it back. It worked until the officers realized that instead of washing we were standing around smoking – after that we were given the officers' shirts to do too as well as our own.

Another ruse the two boys used was when they rowed upriver to collect bread for the kitchens. As they unloaded the loaves, they threw a couple into the bushes and collected them later.[5] They also attempted to get extra food by stealing swans' eggs from nests on the banks of the canal: they were chased by the swans and broke the eggs in the rush to get away.

Bill and McNair were not the only boys who used ruses to make their lives more comfortable:

There was a bloke who wanted a fag off me but I wouldn't give it to him. So he said, 'If you don't I'm going to throw the ship's cat in the water!' I felt sorry for the cat and gave him a fag. He did this all the time – it turned out the cat was a pretty good swimmer!

Life onboard *Vindicatrix* was less than comfortable as Ron Singleton, who joined as a sixteen year old in 1944, recalled: 'It was rough. It was terrible. They told us the food was the worst you would get on any British merchant ship. If you could stick it on the training ship they said you could stick it at sea – on any ship. It was designed to make you tough.' The basic conditions were also a fitting introduction to life on some of the Merchant Navy's older vessels, as Tony Sprigings recalled of the first ship he joined as an apprentice: 'It was an old ship, with no new instruments. We just had sextants, a barometer and a chronometer. Nelson would have been happy with it.'

With war looming, the Royal Navy took over the premises of the

Prince of Wales Sea Training Hostel to train gunners to serve on merchant ships. The school was then evacuated to the Ingham Old Hall in Norfolk, where training continued. With the outbreak of war many parents decided to take their sons out of the school, fearing for their safety at sea. When Bernard Ashton's parents asked whether he wanted to return home he refused the offer: regardless of the dangers, he wanted to finish the course and go to sea.

Despite the change in location, training continued as normal. As Edward Ford, who arrived in late 1939 aged fourteen, later recalled, the school was a complete culture shock: 'Life at the school was something new to me. I had never lived away from home and here I was with other boys from all over the country, all with a different way of talking. One lad from Glasgow I could not understand.' He later recalled being taken to Ingham Old Hall by his mother and then crying himself to sleep that night. Six months later this self-confessed naive and unworldly boy had his first leave. His friends soon realized how much the sea-training had done for him, telling him he had gone away a boy and returned home as a man.

Having left their mothers, and the protection of home, the boys needed discipline. Edward Ford remembered the routine:

> The sleeping was in bunk beds in dormitories twelve to a room. All the cleaning was done by the boys and one spent a week at a time on each job. If your job was not done to the satisfaction of the officer of the watch then you did a second week, this seemed only to apply to jobs nobody wanted to do. Laundry, you had to do your own and time was set aside for the purpose. The day was governed by the ship's bell and was divided into watches.

It was good practice for living in the cramped conditions of a merchant vessel.

Of course, the boys were more interested in learning the rudiments of seafaring than making beds and mopping floors: seamanship, sail-making, rope work, Morse code and semaphore were what they had volunteered for. Bernard Ashton felt proud to have gained his signallers badge, having become competent in sending Morse code with an Aldis lamp and learning all the international signalling flags. Having come straight from school, most of the boys enjoyed the fact that this was a different type of schooling: there were no more spelling tests or pointless geography lessons, whilst maths was put to a practical use.

As boys approached the end of their six-months' training, they were given new duties, working in the office, being sent out to collect new boys from railway stations and holding the rank of petty officer. In the final days before departing they had to make their own sea bag. Under instruction from a retired Royal Navy sailmaker, they cut the canvas to the required size and shape, then stitched it together. It was a rite of passage that showed they were ready to join their first ship.

Although some youngsters clamoured to get to sea in wartime, for other teenagers war was far from their minds when they had signed on for service. Among them were boys whose decision to go to sea was made by chance. In July 1939, fifteen-year-old Christian Immelman was asked by his father what he intended to do with himself after leaving school:

> I only knew I did not want to work in an office. At the time my dad was taking a cigarette from a packet of Players with a picture of a seaman on the cover. I said, 'I'll be a sailor.' My dad was a commercial traveller, and he returned from his next trip to the north of England with all the details about apprenticeships.

He was soon granted an interview with the marine superintendent of the Anglo Saxon Petroleum Company (part of Shell). Christian was told he was to follow the orders of the deck officers and that he would learn all that was needed to become an officer upon completion of a four-year apprenticeship. To the fifteen year old, this all seemed very serious but he was relieved to hear the wages were to be sixty pounds for four years service: 'It didn't sound too bad for someone who'd been on a few pennies a week pocket money. And I would get a shilling each month washing allowance.' However, apprentices were not, he was told, permitted to 'frequent ale houses or taverns'.

With the interview concluded, and his indenture signed and witnessed, Christian and his father left the office and went to nearby Dock Street where they went on a shopping spree to buy the gear he needed for the sea. He was also given the titles of two books, *Nicholls's Seamanship* and *Principles for Second Mates,* and told he should read them before joining the ship. It was all the instruction he would receive before going to sea: 'The closest I'd been to the sea before were daytrips to Southend, summer holidays at Porthcawl, south Wales, and one trip to Scout camp in Guernsey.' He was fifteen years old, about to join his first ship, when the news came that Britain was at war with Germany.

Within a few weeks Christian Immelman received instructions to join his first ship, the *Dolabella.* He knew nothing practical about seafaring and was about to have a crash course on life in the Merchant Navy. He travelled from London to Newcastle on a train filled with service personnel. The sight of so many men in uniform made him feel like an imposter. Upon arriving, he asked directions to the platform to take him to the Hepburn shipyard:

> The porter directed me to go along the platform for the local train and turn to port at the end, I went ahead and turned right but received a shout from behind saying, 'I said port not starboard.' I gave him a wave and did a 180-degree turn and learned my first nautical terms.

In January 1940, aged barely sixteen, Bernard Ashton travelled by train to Southampton to join his first ship as a deck boy: 'As a deck boy, I was known as the "Peggy". It comes from a sailor with a peg leg – he can't go aloft, he can't do most of the jobs. So he becomes the general dogsbody.' With war underway, there was no time for the boys to go home first. Instead, Bernard telephoned his parents, telling them to meet him in Southampton before he shipped out. As his mother cried, he carried his sea bag and small suitcase on to the *Rochester Castle.*

With the coming of war, a career in the Merchant Navy was no longer seen by many parents as what they wanted for their teenage sons. The resistance displayed by some parents was fully justified. Ron Singleton's mother had no desire to see a second son go to sea:

> I hadn't been planning to go to sea. I lost my brother Gordon in the Merchant Navy. He was killed on his second trip. Like a sixteen year old I thought, 'Right, I'll go away to sea and kill a few Germans!' My mother didn't agree with it. She wouldn't sign the papers at first. She wasn't very happy. But I told her that if I didn't go to sea they'd send me down the mines. It wasn't true, but it worked.

This fear of being conscripted into coal mining was shared by many youngsters. When Bert Taylor made the decision to join the Merchant Navy in advance of conscription, his mates told him: 'You could end up in the Navy, Air Force, Army or down the mines. Better the Merchant Navy than take your chances in the mine ballot.' He had another reason for deciding to sign on for service at sea: 'Chaps I knew were starting to get the call-up for the military – they could be sent anywhere and I wasn't too keen on the military. The option of the Merchant Navy gave you a bit more freedom.'

In many cases, parents were never offered an opportunity to decide on their sons' career choice. In Portsmouth, fifteen-year-old Arthur Harvey, who had earlier helped fight fires and rescue younger children from a bombed cinema during the Blitz on the city, had become frustrated with working in a factory. In early 1941, eager to find adventure, he began to search for alternative employment. Working close to the docks, he soon discovered an opening:

I wasn't happy at work. I found out there was a fleet tanker in the dockyard that wanted a cabin boy. So on the spot I decided to go for it and went down to the Board of Trade office for an interview. They offered me the job. But they asked me my age. He said, 'You are over sixteen, aren't you?' I said yes even though I was only fifteen. Then they said that my parents had got to sign for me to go to sea. So I said, 'OK,' and took the papers. I went out of the office, round the corner and came back half an hour later with a signature. I hadn't told me mum I was going to go to sea, so I just signed her name on the paper and handed that in.

Like so many parents, Mrs Harvey was less than keen for her young son to leave home. With a husband already away with the RAF, she didn't want to risk losing someone else. Yet she didn't reckon with her son's spirit:

It was a Friday that I'll never forget. I went home and said to my mother, 'Have we got a suitcase?' She said, 'Yeah. Why?' So I told her I'd got a job and I was going away to sea. She said, 'You can't do that!' I said, 'I can!' And I packed my one suit into the case. Then I went down to the docks the next morning and joined the ship. She was very upset but grew to accept it.

It was not even as if he had given any warning to his mother, never having shown any interest in going to sea. As he later admitted: 'It was on a whim.'

For some, the Merchant Navy was an obvious place to go after leaving school. For sixteen-year-old Tony Sprigings it seemed the sea was the only place for him. His father worked for Cunard in Liverpool, and his bedroom looked out over the Mersey with its miles of docks and never-ending procession of ships heading off to join convoys. Like so many youngsters of his generation, he had dreamed of joining the RAF. However, that required qualifications.

He had entered Birkenhead public school in September 1939, just as war started. Not having attended prep school, he immediately struggled to keep up with his classmates. By 1944 he began to realize a career in the RAF was becoming increasingly unlikely:

> A fighter pilot was the most glamorous thing to be. But you needed good qualifications. You needed your school certificate. But I took it and failed the bloody thing. That was July 1944. I was coming up to sixteen. There were no re-sits. So I couldn't stay at school and I didn't have qualifications to join the RAF.

Thus the sea seemed his only option. At first his father, whose work entailed helping organize the convoy system, tried to talk him out of it. He had heard enough about the horrors of the war at sea and didn't want his son exposed to them, telling Tony: 'Don't go – you'll be killed.' But the youngster couldn't be convinced: he had heard plenty of reports of the terrible experiences of merchant seamen and seen the battered ships limping back into Liverpool, but displayed the typical arrogance of youth: 'I was excited by the prospect. Like any young boy of that age you think you are invincible: you are never going to die. It's not going to be you. I wanted to see what it was like at sea. I'd always been attracted by adventure.' Accepting his son's decision, Tony's father found him an apprenticeship with Brocklebanks, a Liverpool-based shipping company. His father's influence was important, as he later recalled: 'I didn't have the qualifications for an apprenticeship. But they were so short, they would take anyone.'

If the Merchant Navy was to successfully keep Britain supplied, these young volunteers, and the ships they crewed, needed the protection of the Royal Navy. Like the Merchant Navy, the Royal Navy had a long tradition of taking boys to sea, and whilst war ended the official recruitment of 'Boy Soldiers', the Navy continued to send under-eighteens to sea. With the Royal Navy offering a start in life to youngsters, boy service continued to be popular. It was a

way for people from impoverished backgrounds to break away from
their homes and make their own way in the world. Going to sea had
always been a lure for boys in search of glamour and excitement.
To them, the sea meant adventure, getting away from home and 'a
girl in every port'. In an era before the mass arrival of Americans in
the UK, it seemed that there was nothing more attractive than the
sight of a sailor in his bell-bottoms, Trafalgar collar and white cap
worn at a jaunty angle. When HMS *Royal Oak* was torpedoed in
1939, costing the lives of some 125 boys, many of those who lost
their lives came from similar backgrounds to survivor Ken Toop
who had volunteered to escape the poverty of his home life.

One boy who left home in search of adventure during 1939 was
Albert Riddle. Born in the small Cornish village of Quethiock in
1924, the fifteen year old had always dreamed of escaping the
village and going to sea. He did not live beside the sea, nor have
seafaring 'in his blood' – he just felt drawn to the ocean and had no
intention of joining his father on the farm: 'From the age of seven
or eight, when I was asked what I was going to do, I always said I
was going to go into the Navy. There was lots poverty around –
not much money in the village. So I was looking for a way out.'
His parents agreed: 'They felt I'd got a chance to get somewhere in
life.'

Eager to get to sea, he signed on with the Royal Navy aged
fourteen, telling them he was fifteen. However, his true age was
discovered and he was not called up until after his fifteenth birthday.
On 15 January 1940, along with a group of twenty other boys, he
arrived in Devonport to commence training at HMS *Impregnable*, a
land-based training establishment. Ushered on to the parade
ground, he was introduced to life as a boy in the Royal Navy:

> There was a Chief Petty Officer parading up and down in front of us,
> like a turkey cock. I'll never forget his words: 'No matter how good a
> horse you think you are, you'll find there are better jockeys in here.' I
> lived to find out that was true. It was tough going.

Albert realized just how tough it was when they were called from their hammocks in the morning: 'The Chief Petty Officer was a real bastard. He had a hat-pin and he'd stick the bugger in your arse as you were asleep. You soon got up. I thought, "What have I let myself in for? What have I done?"' As the boys also discovered, the Royal Navy had not yet abandoned corporal punishment: 'The third offence of smoking was ten lashes with a whip – I didn't get it though. I thought that isn't for me. I'd seen too many with their arses red from being birched. When the poor buggers came back – my God.'

Remembering the words uttered by the Chief Petty Officer that first morning, Albert soon realized that, if he was going to make a career in the Royal Navy, he would have to play the game, keep out of trouble and not break the rules: 'If you obeyed the rules it was OK. If you broke the rules, there was no way you could win. The instructors were old boys – petty officers – who'd done their time at sea. There were some bad buggers among them – like in any walk of life.' For minor infractions, the boys were sent on to the parade ground with a sack containing a concrete block or carrying a .303 rifle above their heads. Albert recalled the punishment:

> That's not a light thing. In my day, they did things you couldn't get away with now. I was a boy – not yet nine stone. I didn't carry a lot of flesh. It was hour after hour, until you collapsed. So when you had to keep running around the parade ground carrying this rifle it made you realize, 'I'm a mug doing this.' Some tried to buck the system but you had to come in line at the end. You didn't do anything wrong again!

The main feature of *Impregnable* was the impressive, if daunting, mast: 'It was 175 feet high and on three levels. We went up through the rigging, through a trapdoor, on to the deck, then out on the beam. The boys went up the levels, right up until a tiny boy went out on to the button, at the top.' Albert recalled the endless sessions of climbing the rigging: 'Up at six in the morning, in heavy boots, going up and over the rigging. In any weather. And the last boy had to go over again. That was bloody stupid because someone had to be last. But you had to take your punishment.' Another relic of the past was a row of cannons that the boys were paired up to polish each day.

Apart from endless sessions up in the rigging, the boys learned to tie knots, handle boats, and send Morse code and semaphore signals. They were also taught crafts, learning how to sew and make rugs. As Albert Riddle recalled, even mealtimes were regulated: 'They were meticulous about the way you held your cutlery.' And they learned to clean, scrubbing the mess, their classrooms and under the hammocks in their sleeping quarters until they were spotless. More exciting was the gunnery training, learning to load, aim and fire the heavy guns. As Albert recalled, he soon realized he was learning far more than he had ever learned in the classroom of his village school. There was a good reason for this: 'You learned more than at school because it was bloody beaten into you.'

After twelve months of training, sixteen-year-old Albert and his mates were sent to their first ship. Going north by train, they arrived in Scotland. Carrying their kitbags and struggling with the weight of their heavy canvas hammocks, they reached the dockside where their new home was revealed. Out of all the possible ships, they had been sent to the newest battleship in the entire fleet, the pride of the Royal Navy: HMS *Prince of Wales*. She was more than 227 metres long, with a top speed of 29 knots and was armed with ten 14-inch guns, sixteen 5-inch guns and fifty-six 20 mm and 40 mm anti-aircraft guns. Albert was immediately struck by the sight of the as yet unfinished warship: 'It was an impressive sight – a wonderful ship. We were thrilled to be going onboard.' He was just one of more than 150 boys who joined the ship ready for its sea trials.

Conditions on the ship were good, especially compared to some of the ageing, cramped ships in service at the time. The ratings slept in hammocks rather than bunks but this did not worry them. After all, they had grown used to hammocks whilst training and most found them warm and comfortable. For Albert Riddle, the biggest shock was how the boys seemed to spend most of their time: 'We were always scrubbing the decks. In the Navy you scrub everything – even if it has just been scrubbed.'

There was a shock in store for the sixteen year old when they first left port and headed out to sea: 'I soon discovered I was the world's worst sailor. I had terrible seasickness. I never got my "sea legs". I was always sick.' He spent long hours stretched out, wishing he could die: 'People made fun of me. I'd be stretched out in a locker room, sick as anything. They'd kick me – I couldn't do anything. I was useless.' Although he did not yet realize it, his seasickness would have a significant effect on his life at sea.

Some of the boys who left Merchant Navy training ships did not join merchant ships. Whilst training at the *Worcester* all boys were enrolled in the Royal Naval Reserve (RNR), the force composed of professional seamen who augmented the Royal Navy in time of war. It was very different from the Royal Naval Volunteer Reserve (RNVR), as *Worcester* boy Derek Tolfree explained: 'In the RNR we were sailors trying to be gentlemen. In the RNVR they were gentlemen trying to be sailors.' Upon completion of training at the college, the boys had the choice of resigning from the RNR and finding a merchant ship or remaining in the reserve and awaiting call-up by the Royal Navy. There was another option: leaving the RNR, taking a civilian job and awaiting conscription. Very few of the boys choose that route.

In 1942 Derek Tolfree left the *Worcester* and chose to remain in the reserve: 'I got mobilized straightaway as a midshipman, Royal Navy Reserve, and was sent to a battleship, HMS *Nelson*. I was sent to the Royal Naval College at Greenwich for a couple of months. I had to learn boat handling – turning and berthing motor yachts.'

At the start of the war, the Royal Navy still relied on bugle calls to relay orders onboard its ships. On smaller ships, the bugler would simply blow the required notes to change watches, call the crew to action stations or abandon ship. On large ships, tannoy systems

were used, with a bugler playing beside a microphone. History
decreed that the bugler should not be a sailor but a member of the
Royal Marines. Boys could join the marines aged fourteen, signing
on for twelve years. The twelve years only started when boys
reached the age of eighteen, meaning young recruits signed up until
they were at least thirty years old. At the age of eighteen, boys could
choose to remain as a bugler or join the ranks as a marine.

The continued use of boy buglers meant that throughout the war
the Royal Marines recruited a stream of teenage boys who were
trained at Eastney Barracks in Portsmouth. If the youngest boys
'passed out' as buglers, within months they could be sent to a ship
almost immediately, meaning fourteen-year-old boys joined the
crews of warships. Being able to join at such a young age produced
a great sense of excitement – and no little trepidation – as the boys
left home and began their training. Fourteen-year-old volunteer Len
Chester recalled arriving to commence training: 'Up to then I'd
lived with other children. I had a child's mentality. Suddenly I'd
entered a world of men, which was another traumatic experience.
I'd never been amongst men before.'

Another youngster who volunteered as a 'boy bugler' was
thirteen-year-old Robin Rowe. He was asked by his father if he
would like to follow his elder brother into the Royal Marines after
running away from home in an attempt to reach Plymouth, 'whence
embarked all great English seafarers'. When asked, he did not take
long to make up his mind: 'I thought about it for at least thirty
seconds. There was a war on and I could be part of it at sea. Not
everyone got killed and the Royal Marine uniform looked great.'[6]
It was a curious choice of career: his elder brother had volunteered
as a marine and had been lost at sea just months before. Robin went
through the process of medical tests and, just like Len Chester back
in 1939, was embarrassed by his nudity. Completely unclothed, he
was told to jump up and grab an overhead bar, and he then had to
pull himself up till his chin reached the bar. At that point a doctor
grabbed his testicles and told him to cough.

The insular world of a military base was far different from the discipline of school. Even those who had been raised in poor neighbourhoods were not ready for the atmosphere in a barrack room. Len Chester recalled how difficult it was to adapt:

> Suddenly I was in a barrack room with about thirty other boys. They'd been in a bit longer than me and were a bit more streetwise. In all my innocence, I went there and the others were saying words I'd never heard before. They were talking about things that I never knew about. It took a couple of weeks to realize what they were talking about. They came out with expressions I'd never heard. Also there were all the accents – Scots, Welsh, Irish. It was traumatic.

Such was the impact of this unfamiliar world, that Len felt homesick: 'When we went to sleep, all you could hear was boys groaning, breaking wind, talking in their sleep and – if you listened carefully – you would have heard me softly crying. What had I let myself in for?' When Robin Rowe arrived at Eastney Barracks – still aged thirteen – he did not have the same sense of uncertainty as other boys in a similar situation. He had been a pupil at a number of boarding schools and was used to being away from his family, living amongst other boys.

All new boys were taken for haircuts, given the ubiquitous short back and sides that was no more than an inch long on top. Next came the uniform. When Len first joined, he was just four feet eight inches tall. At that height, he had to wait until a uniform and a pair of boots could be specially made for him. With uniforms fitted, recruits were given a stamped identity disc and a 'type'. This was a wooden strip with their name carved into it, used to mark their kit.

New buglers had much to learn, including the unfamiliar language of the sea. If they asked what 'the heads' were, they heard the terse reply 'the shithouse'. Words had strange meanings: 'shit in it' meant 'shut up'. Swear words and curious words for body parts had to be memorized. They had to get used to drinking from deep

round-bottomed bowls that were used instead of cups. They had to
learn how to make their beds up in the correct manner. The iron
'truckle' beds came in two sections, meaning it could be broken
down and stored in daytime, with the straw palliasse and straw-filled
pillow stored on top. Just filling the palliasse with straw was an art
that had to be learned, filling it with just the right amount so that it
could still be folded but was thick enough to be comfortable. As one
young marine described it, sleeping on a mattress of fresh straw was
like sleeping on a hedgehog.

Life in the barracks was fast paced. There was little time for
introspection. Each morning they were roused from their beds at
6 a.m., with just minutes to break down their beds and store them
correctly. New recruits were surprised when reveille sounded at
6.30. They were woken half an hour early each morning in order to
clean their room to the highest standard. Next the floor had to be
polished and the whole room cleaned, with each boy allotted a task.
One would be cleaning out and polishing the fireplace, another
cleaning the windows, whilst the rest of the boys got down on their
hands and knees and polished the floor until they could see their
faces in it. The wooden table and stools were scrubbed white.
Cleaning was followed by a wash, then breakfast, then it was time
to polish buttons, buckles and badges, shine their boots and be on
parade by 8 a.m.

After all these duties, there were endless bugle calls and
drumbeats to be memorized. Every part of the day's routine was
sounded on a bugle: when to get up, when to eat, when to parade,
when to go to sleep. The buglers needed to recognize all these
commands just to be able to function in the barracks. And that was
before they themselves began to learn all the calls they would give
– both in the barracks and on ship.

Before they could think of boarding a ship, the boys needed to
master the bugle. Len Chester recalled that becoming proficient as
a bugler was done without learning to read a note of music.
Everything was learned by rote:

I joined in May '39, and passed out as a bugler in October. In that time I'd learned 150 bugle calls, plus drumming and the flute. So the training must have been intense and very good. And it was painful – your lips get sore. At first you can't blow a bugle, you have to train your lips and muscles.

Instruction was often given by older boys who had already earned the right to wear tassels on the end of their bugle cords. First the trainees learned how to position their lips, almost spitting into the bugle to get the required sound. To learn the individual calls they remembered a set phrase: if they could remember the phrase, they could remember the call. One favourite was the 'Rum Call': 'Oh Lucy, don't say no, For under the table you must go, Up with your petticoat, down with your drawers, My little winkle just fits yours.'[7]

Drum training added to their burden. They had to learn to keep time and also to march whilst playing a drum. That was made difficult by the swinging of the drum as they walked. Some developed a swing of the left leg to ensure the drum stayed in place. This gave them a gait recognizable to all in the Royal Marines. The method for learning drumbeats was sometimes harsh. One recruit recalled the instructor beating out the rhythm on to his shoulders, ensuring that he could not forget it. Similarly, when the boys did flute practice, the instructor kept a cane handy for whacking the hands of those whose fingering was incorrect.

There was always a certain amount of violence between the boys, although the sergeants quickly clamped down on trouble. Most boys were eager to pass on their knowledge to others, advising them on the best types of polish to use and how best to get a mirror-like shine on the toecaps of their boots. Len Chester soon noticed that life in barracks had changed him: 'You gradually absorbed things and eventually you got to be like them. If you don't change you won't survive.' As he put it: 'If you go into Fagin's kitchen, you learn to pick pockets.' Part of the rite of passage in joining up for service was to abandon childish ways and adopt a man's lifestyle:

I wasn't a smoker before I became a marine. My dad would have
beaten the living daylights out of me if he had caught me smoking. We
weren't allowed to smoke until we went to a ship but I started smoking
surreptitiously. When we went to a ship we got all our cigarettes duty
free. It was so cheap, we couldn't afford not to smoke.

Whilst training, the only way the buglers could get cigarettes was to
wait outside the 'wet canteen', where beer was served to the senior
marines, and scrounge them as the men left.

The boys noticed there was little sympathy for the sick. If they
could stand, they were expected on parade. The treatment given in
the sick bay was also guaranteed to prevent any malingering. Len
Chester recalled how his treatment consisted of a nurse administer-
ing an enema. Just like the medical he had been given when he
signed on, he found the experience embarrassing: 'That matron had
the biggest fingers you've ever seen. I'm only glad she kept her
fingernails short. I wonder how many children nowadays have even
had an enema.'

The boys of the Royal Navy and Royal Marines were genuinely
proud to walk out in their uniforms. Whilst Army uniforms were
drab and shapeless, the Royal Navy continued to be dressed in its
traditional outfit of flared trousers, blue smock, Trafalgar collar and
white cap. Similarly, the bugle boys of the Royal Marines wore a
formal blue tunic and cap when on leave. The smartness of their
clothing was impressive for the others and a mark of pride for the
boys. As Len Chester recalled of his first leave, aged fifteen: 'I felt like
a man when I went home. In barracks I'd felt like a boy. But after a
few months onboard the ship, you grew up. You felt like one of them.
You were there to do a job. You had lost your youth. You'd seen
man's things and become a man.' Despite this sense of pride, his
wages remained so low there was little he could do. His old school
friends were mostly working and he spent most of his leave at home.

However, being in uniform meant that – despite his youth – his
father could take him to the pub:

I was proud to be in uniform, but my dad was even prouder. Embarrassingly so. There was a song around at the time with the words, 'Oh little drummer boy, you are all the world to me.' When he used to take me out for a drink, he used to sing this song to everybody in the pub. It embarrassed me, but it was nice that he was so proud. I shouldn't have been allowed in the pub. It was only the uniform that got me in. A pint looked enormous to me at that time. The old ladies would come over and say, 'Oh, isn't he sweet!' They'd say, 'He's so young, it shouldn't be allowed.' At that age I was embarrassed.

In December 1939, Len Chester travelled to Scapa Flow to join his first ship, HMS *Iron Duke*. The twenty-nine-hour journey north by train became a regular feature of his life in the period he was based at Scapa Flow:

> I was so small at four feet eight inches they used to put me up in the luggage rack. The scenery was beautiful, but I never saw any of it. We had no food, but the men would get as much beer as they could and drink that. We relied on the Salvation Army for food at stations. It was usually soya-link sausages and powdered mashed potatoes – but at least it was food. Everywhere, there were thick clouds of tobacco smoke. There were kitbags and rifles everywhere and not everybody had a seat. To get to the toilet was like an obstacle course. There was usually somebody sitting in the toilet, 'cause it was the only free seat.

The biggest shock upon arriving onboard ship was the smell of oil that seemed to pervade it. Each morning he had to tour the ship, sounding 'Call the hands' to raise the sailors from their hammocks. His arrival was usually greeted with a barrage of swear words, with which the youngster was becoming increasingly familiar. When he first arrived onboard the *Iron Duke*, Len found it difficult to remember all the necessary bugle calls. The first time the ship came under air attack, rather than sound 'Air Raid Warning Red', he called 'Alarm to Arms – Repel Boarders'. It hardly mattered, as within seconds a bomb had hit the ship and no one needed to be warned they were under attack.

The *Iron Duke* remained at Scapa Flow, meaning that Len Chester did not go to sea for almost two years. However, living onboard a battleship, with few onshore facilities, meant he went for almost a year without setting foot on dry land. When this was discovered, the captain sent him ashore with a sergeant-major who took him on a ten-mile route march. There was one problem: as a growing teenage boy, Len's feet had outgrown his boots, meaning he was soon in agony. By the time he returned to the ship his socks were red with blood and within days he'd lost a number of toenails.

During this period, Navy boys still faced corporal punishment. Len Chester faced the prospect after he was put on a charge of mutiny for refusing to clean the ship's bell. He had already cleaned it once but the damp weather meant it tarnished almost immediately. When taken before the captain he was given the option of taking the captain's punishment or being punished by warrant. He chose the captain's punishment since 'punishment by warrant' meant being caned. Instead, he was punished with extra cleaning duties.

The Royal Marines' policy of recruiting fourteen-year-old boys meant that the former buglers eventually became the youngest veterans of active service in the Second World War. Someone who was an eight-year-old schoolboy at the outbreak of war could be on active service by war's end. One such boy was Stuart Henderson. Born in March 1931, he had been evacuated from Middlesex to Scotland, where he lived near the Royal Navy dockyards at Leith. Seeing the large ships, armed trawlers and minesweepers moving in and out of the Firth of Forth influenced his desire to join the Royal Navy: 'In those days wherever you were uniforms abounded and like most young boys they fascinated me.'

In 1945, a chance encounter with a sixteen-year-old marine gave him an opportunity to get into uniform:

He told me you could join at fourteen which was only a couple of months away at that stage. I was fascinated and wrote away post haste without telling my father. The papers were returned for completion and an interview and medical at Charing Cross Road in London. My father finally caved in and signed the papers, warning me that it wasn't all about uniforms . . . I couldn't wait to get the papers off.

Just days before the war in the Far East came to a close, Stuart reported for preliminary training.

CHAPTER 11

Flyboys

'The medical officer hinted that it would be better if I joined the German Air Force!'

John Osborne, on joining the RAF at age sixteen

While it was relatively simple for boys to change their age to join the Army, the Royal Air Force was rather a different proposition. The glorious and glamorous antics of 'The Few' meant there was no shortage of eager recruits for pilot and aircrew training. Everyone, it seemed, wanted to share in that glory. For most, the issue was that pilots required a certain standard of education. While the Army seemed prepared to accept anyone with two eyes and a full complement of limbs, the RAF needed volunteers who could operate intricate technical equipment, navigate by the stars and react with lightning reflexes, and have the physical strength to handle the controls of a heavy bomber and the mental strength to command a crew on long operations over enemy territory. As a result, the selection process was more rigorous than that for the other services. Whilst a recruit to the Merchant Navy had to do little more than turn up at port and look for a ship, most would-be RAF pilots needed to have their paperwork in order. For most, this meant examination certificates, showing the attributes they had displayed whilst at school. For those who had not passed their school leaving certificates, let alone matriculation papers, this was a hurdle. It effectively prevented any boy whose family could not afford for him to remain at school until the age of sixteen from being accepted for pilot training. As a result, a majority of pilots were from fee-paying or grammar schools.

Despite the entry requirements, plenty of boys brazenly attempted to join the RAF while underage. One sixteen-year-old recruit lasted all of ten minutes in the RAF. The problem came when the recruiting officer asked for his date of birth: 'I gave them the date, got a thick ear for my trouble and was told to come back in about nine months' time.'[1] Others were luckier. Having already lied to his girlfriend about his age, telling her he was eighteen when he was really fifteen, John Osborne saw no reason why he should not do the same with the Royal Air Force. His decision to join was a simple one:

> I was working in the City reading electricity meters and I had to read a certain amount each day. So I would read as many as possible in the morning, then have the rest of the day free. I was in Islington and went to the cinema. The film was *Target for Tonight*, about the RAF. I watched this film and was quite inspired.

The film got him thinking: he wanted to do something for the war effort and, just as importantly, his parents were on the verge of breaking up. The atmosphere at home meant it would be good to get away: 'So, out of the blue, I presented myself at a recruiting office near Euston station. The film was still in my mind so I plumped for the Air Force.' They asked what he did for a living and telling them that he was employed as an electrician's mate they put this down on his enlistment papers. He was exactly what the RAF thought they needed, a trained electrician. They didn't realize they had got an unskilled sixteen year old who had added fifteen months to his age. The limit of his skills was not yet apparent. He was told to go home and he would be sent for: 'I went home and told my parents. I rather fancy I had done them a favour by going into the RAF. It saved them from having to stay together for my sake.' He expected to receive his papers, be called for a medical and selection board, then be sent home to await the call for training. His papers soon arrived, but events did not play out as expected: 'I said to my girlfriend, "I'll be back in three days." I didn't get home for five months.'

Arriving at RAF Cardington for training, John was lucky; since he was tall for his age he was able to pass as an eighteen year old and was careful not to mention the truth to any of his fellow trainees. However, he soon met a serious hurdle to any hope of becoming a skilled member of the ground crew. During initial tests he was discovered to be colour blind. He was told that he could not be an electrician since the mass of colour-coded wiring within modern aircraft would confound him: 'The medical officer hinted that it would be better if I joined the German Air Force!' And so he was selected for general duties. He was not disappointed: he had not joined the RAF out of any desire for glory and he already knew his lack of education would prevent him being selected for aircrew, let alone pilot training. Instead, he was simply happy to 'do his bit'.

For some, the decision to join the armed services was not born out of patriotism and the desperate desire to contribute. In many cases youngsters had much simpler reasons to volunteer for service. For John Cotter, now seventeen years old, the decision was made in February 1941: 'It was a miserable winter – so miserable that I decided to join the Air Force.' An influencing factor was that John had attended a party and met an old friend in RAF uniform, who was training to be a wireless officer. John asked him one question: 'Can you get cream cakes and buns in the RAF?' For a youngster with a sweet tooth, who yearned for the luxuries missing from wartime shops, it was an important question to which he received a positive answer: 'The NAAFI is full of them!' He decided the Air Force was the place for him.

He spoke with his fifteen-year-old brother Paul, who was working for a film production company in Soho, and told him of his plans. Paul immediately decided he would also volunteer. The decision made, they marched off to the recruiting office, declining to tell their mother what they were doing: 'I had to falsify my age to accommodate my brother. The minimum age was seventeen-and-a-half – my age – so I had to put my age up to nineteen so that I could have a seventeen-and-a-half year-old brother. The RAF knew what we had done.' Together with an eighteen-year-old friend, the brothers signed on: 'They accepted my brother and myself without a birth certificate but sent the eighteen-year-old home to collect his birth certificate. The recruiting sergeant obviously knew what was happening.'

At the office the sergeant asked John Cotter what he wanted to do in the RAF. He told him he wanted to be a pilot and was then asked to what level he had been educated. John replied: 'Matriculation level.' It was almost true: 'I had been educated to that level but I hadn't passed it.' The lie clinched it and secured his future as a trainee pilot. However, Paul had only been to the elementary school so he was selected for air-gunner and wireless-operator training. The next day the brothers took a bus to Uxbridge, attested and were put on deferred service. In July 1941 John received his papers and was called to Lord's cricket ground to report ready for duty. A year later Paul Cotter, just sixteen years old, received his papers and commenced his training.

From July, John Cotter waited at Lord's, taking his meals at London Zoo, until he was called to RAF Brize Norton where he began initial training. Later he was moved to a hotel in Brighton where he got used to living in a crowded room, sleeping on mattresses crammed into every available space. It was an eye-opener for him:

I had my first experience of how unpleasant life can be with a whole lot of other fellas. There were six of us in the room, sharing one washbasin. One night, one chap got up and peed in the basin. I told

him, 'You can't do that!' Well, my mother had never taught me to
behave like that. He told me, 'Mind your own bloody business!' So I
thought I'd better shut up.

It was a period when his life began to change. His new mates started
taking him out to pubs and advising him on what to drink. He also
started to go to dances: 'But I still didn't have any luck with the girls!'
He was then sent to Canada to commence pilot training. There was
a certain irony to this: he had joined the RAF because of a miserable
winter in London; now he was in Canada in the midst of a freezing
winter. There was one consolation: on the first night on the base he
sat down to a large plate of bacon and eggs. He knew he had made
the right decision.

One result of this widespread desire to join the RAF was a
burgeoning of membership in the Air Training Corps (ATC). The
organization had started life pre-war as the Air Defence Cadet
Corps (ADCC). Cadets received general instruction on how to
dress, how to behave, physical fitness and, of course, basic air
training. In the early years of the war, cadets volunteered at RAF
bases, working in offices, acting as messengers, filling sandbags and
handling stores. In 1941 the ATC was established as a replacement.
Eventually one in five sixteen to eighteen year olds joined the ATC.
As Mr Lindsay, the Member of Parliament for the Combined
English Universities, later noted, why did boys of sixteen work a
nine-hour day, then cycle for two hours to reach a class in
navigation? 'It was because they wanted to pin "wings" on their
breast, preferably with the DFC beneath.'[2]

Having moved from Staines to Plymouth, Reg Fraser gave up
Army Cadets and joined the Air Training Corps. Like so many
youngsters he had been attracted by the glamour of the 'flyboys' and
thought he would try to join the RAF. However, on a weekend
course at an aerodrome he soon discovered it was not the life for
him. Taking him for a spin in a training aircraft, the South African
pilot brought the plane down: 'He crash-landed the plane. After-

wards, he said to me "So, are you going to join the RAF?" After that landing, I thought, no, I'll join the Army. So I went home and joined the Plymouth Dockyard Home Guard.' Another boy who was unable to progress in the ATC was Bernard Ashton. Whilst on two months' home leave following the sinking of his ship, sixteen-year-old Bernard started going to Air Cadets training with some of his old school friends. On a visit to a nearby RAF aerodrome, he got a close look at a Hurricane fighter. As he looked over the plane, one of the Air Training Corps instructors approached him. He asked about the badge he was wearing on his lapel. Bernard pointed out it was a Merchant Navy badge and was immediately told he should quit the ATC since, as a serving seaman, he would never be allowed to join the RAF.

As the war progressed, the RAF remained the most attractive service for youngsters. In 1940 it had been the pilots of Fighter Command that had been seen to save the nation, then, while the Army was seemingly still impotent, Bomber Command had begun to strike back at the enemy's heartland. It was a long, slow, costly campaign, but the public enjoyed the spectacle of German cities sustaining the same horrors that had been endured across Britain. There was a glamour attached to their blue uniform that was seldom shared by the other services.

And so RAF recruitment levels continued to be high, with sufficient volunteers replacing the casualties endured on the long, arduous flights over Germany. As the war progressed, and with flight training schools turning out replacements in sufficient numbers, the RAF found itself less eager for recruits than the other services. This had an impact upon the youngsters who hoped to learn to fly. One willing volunteer was Eric Davies of Carmarthen, west Wales. A grammar-school boy from a modest home, Eric had flown in pre-war pleasure trips from Heathrow airport when visiting London with his grandfather. Like so many of his contemporaries, he had ignored the lower age limit and joined the Home Guard in 1940 aged fifteen. He had also volunteered for fire-watching, carrying out his duties from the roof of a local shop where he worked part-time. Those early pleasure flights had inspired him to make the decision to join the RAF. Mindful of his father's wounds from the Great War, which had caused his premature death in the 1920s, he thought flying preferable to being an infantryman.

In February 1942, having just turned seventeen, Eric Davies went to his local recruiting office and applied to join the RAF as an air-gunner/wireless operator:

> Much to my surprise, I was called immediately to Penarth, near Cardiff, for a four-day assessment course. At the end of the four days I was told I had passed. When I asked when I would be called up, they said, 'Go home for a while as we have plenty of people at the moment.' This was not good enough for me. So on the way home, I stopped off from the train at Swansea and volunteered for the Army.

Eric found himself immediately called up and sent to an Army training camp. It was a decision that would have a long-reaching effect.

Whilst many young soldiers waited to be drafted overseas, or continued with years of training in preparation for the eventual opening of a 'second front' in Europe, the young volunteers in the RAF were able to immediately strike at the enemy. From bases across southern and eastern England, the bombers of the RAF were able to attack German cities. Returning to England in autumn 1942, eighteen-year-old John Cotter had got his wings and was ready to take the final steps to being a bomber pilot. Back in September 1939 he had wondered whether the war would last long enough for him to get involved. Three years on he was fully trained and waiting to take responsibility for a bomber and its seven-man crew. It was a heavy burden and one he felt he was lucky to have been allowed:

> I wasn't a natural pilot. I don't know how I got through training. You were allowed twelve hours' training before you went solo. After that

you were failed. I was the last, I got to twelve hours and was allowed a two-hour extension. I still hadn't made it. So they gave me another two hours. Then I made it. Nothing was holding me back – I just wasn't up to it. I didn't reward them for their patience with me. After I'd gone solo, I was landing with a friend alongside and I landed on top of him. Why they didn't chuck me out there and then, I don't know.

Having slowly increased in confidence, he joined Bomber Command as a Pilot Sergeant. He became the pilot of a seven-man crew, flying a Halifax bomber in 158 Squadron, arriving in June 1943. He was still nineteen years old and had the responsibility of taking his crew to war:

> You were young and you didn't think anything would happen to you. My first operation was on 24 July 1943, to Hamburg. I was very nervous but I got over the target and saw it all lit up in front of me. I got over the target, with the bomb aimer guiding me to the target markers. I pulled the lever the wrong way and the bomb-doors didn't open. So we couldn't release the bombs.

They flew on in the direction of Lübeck until they could circle the target and return to release the bombs. As John later admitted: 'Later on in my flying career I'd have never thought of doing this – I would have just released the bombs anywhere. Although we were alone, nothing happened to us and we were able to drop on target.' In the week that followed, John and his crew returned to bomb Hamburg on two further occasions.

In November 1943, John Cotter was commissioned. He went on to bomb Berlin, Frankfurt and Peenemünde, where the Germans were developing V1 rockets. He flew thirty-four operations and on 22 April 1944 he completed his 'tour', even volunteering to carry out a second tour, a request that was declined. He was pleased that his final operation was to Düsseldorf. He felt it appropriate to finish on a German target. He later noted that he was extremely lucky to survive. During those operations twenty non-regular crew members had joined him on operational flights. Only seven of those men completed their tours, seven were later killed in action and three became prisoners of war. In September 1944, just after his twenty-first birthday, he was called to Holyrood House in Edinburgh where he received the Distinguished Flying Cross from King George VI.

Whilst John Cotter had a successful, and lucky, RAF career his younger brother was not so fortunate. Paul Cotter, who had volunteered for the RAF aged just fifteen, tragically never completed his training. Their mother had always been concerned about John but not about Paul. He died in a training accident at Boundary Bay in Canada in 1944.

For John Osborne, the war was relatively unexciting. Having been transferred to 'Motor Transport' he spent much of his time driving officers around. At one point he found himself driving for Group Captain Percy Pickard. This was a surprise for John: back in 1941 it had been Pickard who had starred as the pilot in *Target for Tonight*, the film that had inspired the sixteen year old to volunteer for the RAF. However, John couldn't bring himself to tell the officer the effect his role had on him: 'I was still a youngster, and I was so in awe of him. I didn't have the courage to tell him.'

In early 1944 the truth about John Osborne's age was finally revealed. Now nineteen years old, he had asked his girlfriend Gina to marry him and she had accepted. However, he now needed to apply for a marriage licence and a married man's allowance. Having filled in all the necessary forms, he was called to the adjutant's office: 'Your two sets of papers don't seem to tally – there is a discrepancy in your ages.' The youngster explained the truth: that he added fifteen months to his age when he volunteered and that no one had asked to see his papers. Whenever he had been told to produce his National Insurance card he simply claimed he had misplaced it and would bring it at a later date. The officer accepted his story, telling him: 'I suppose it's a bit late to do anything about it now.'

Although the need for qualifications meant that fewer youngsters were able to find their way into the Air Force than into the Army or Navy, some did manage it. One eager youngster was Ted Wright from Winnipeg in Canada. Born in November 1928, he had added three years to his age when he volunteered for the Royal Canadian Air Force in 1943, just days after his fifteenth birthday. Upon completion of his training, he was posted to England as an air-gunner. Arriving in July 1944, he was sent to '26 Operational Training Unit', where he flew in Wellington bombers. During this period the fifteen year old flew on a number of operations over Germany. He was later transferred to 428 Squadron, where he became the tail-gunner in a Lancaster bomber. On 30 April 1945, less than one week before the end of the war in Europe, Ted Wright was killed when his plane crashed on a routine training flight over Staffordshire. It was only when the Commonwealth War Graves Commission contacted his parents about the inscription for his grave that the truth of his age was revealed.

CHAPTER 12

Fighting Back

'You go in as a boy and come out as a man.'

Seventeen-year-old Fred Walker, No. 3 Commando

For those boys who volunteered in the early years of the war, there were few chances to strike back at the Germans. If their units did not get drafted overseas then they had to wait in the UK, training, mounting guards, drilling, scrubbing barrack-room floors and trying to enjoy life on a pitiful wage. Even if their battalion was sent overseas, in the early years of the war anyone under the age of nineteen was forbidden from going with it. Instead they were transferred elsewhere and told to wait until they were old enough. In many cases, boys who volunteered in 1940 waited until 1944 to see action.

For some young volunteers, this was not enough. They had joined the Army for action and were keen to see it. For these boys there was one thing to do: volunteer for the commandos. When the commandos were first formed in 1940, they accepted only the fittest, keenest, most able soldiers. The physical training was intense, meaning only those able to complete the most rigorous feats of endurance were deemed suitable. Endless route marches in appalling weather; long cross-country runs; live firing exercises; obstacle courses; swimming tests; little food; little rest: these were the hurdles ahead of all potential commandos.

Volunteering for the commandos was not for the faint-hearted; as a result, large numbers of underage soldiers applied. Fred Walker made the decision to join the commandos whilst serving in the 70th (Young Soldiers) Battalion of the Bedfordshire and Hertfordshire Regiment. His unit received a visit from Captain Peter Young, a commando officer who was formerly a member of the Beds and Herts. Young had a clear idea of the calibre of soldiers he wanted for the commandos and was certain of his ability to identify the right types. He was in no doubt youth was a determining factor: 'Young soldiers are good. They have no wives or children. They follow you out of innocence.'[1]

There were plenty in the 70th Battalion of the Beds and Herts who fitted that description. Having put his name down for commando training, Fred Walker was called before Captain Young. Having just finished shovelling coal, Fred was covered in coal dust and dressed in his filthy, ill-fitting denim fatigue uniform. He hardly looked like a potential recruit for the Army's newest, most elite unit:

> Captain Young asked, 'Why do you want to join the commandos? You know you won't live very long.' But I was a bigheaded so-and-so and so I said, 'Well, I'll take me chances.' I was seventeen years old. I told him, 'I like the idea of the extra money.' He said at least I was honest.

Accepted for commando training, Fred was sent north to Scotland to endure what would be the most intense period of physical activity he would ever know.

The entire period of training was designed to weed out those unsuited to serving in a commando unit. Any mistake, any failure to meet the physical standards or any reticence was likely to result in being 'Returned to Unit' (RTU). Arriving at the station in Scotland the new recruits expected to see lorries waiting to take them to camp. Instead, they had to run. Those who could not complete the run were immediately rejected. Living conditions were tough: some lived in barrack huts but others were in tents. As Fred Walker remembered: 'It was always wet. We were under canvas.' Food was basic, but hot and filling. Breakfast included a dustbin full of porridge that the men dipped their mess tins into. Washing facilities were a stream; in winter they broke ice to shave in cold water.

If that was not enough, the training was enough to test even the fittest and most dedicated volunteer. They were sent on endless speed marches – carrying heavy kit, loaded with rifles and ammunition – running 200 yards, then marching for the next 200 and so on for mile after mile. They scaled terrifying rock-faces, then abseiled down. They climbed ropes, swung across raging mountain gorges, swam rivers, crawled through mud and tackled assault courses whilst instructors fired live rounds above their heads. They learned to handle rowing boats, boxed and practised infantry drill. And always, just when they thought they could do no more, there would be more to do. Most days ended with speed marches, sometimes as far as twenty miles. Fred Walker recalled the intense sessions of pounding up and down the country lanes:

> The speed marches were horrible – especially when you were carrying the anti-tank rifle. It weighed 36 pounds. We had to pass it along between us. Or the Bren gun – that was 23 pounds. That was on top of all your other gear. They got us going against each other – to see which of the troops was the best. It makes you close to each other. You can't buy comradeship.

It was a life in which being cold, wet, exhausted and hungry was the norm. Despite this, enthusiastic teenagers like Fred Walker remained resilient:

> The training was very hard, but I thought I'd get through it. I wasn't an athlete or nothing, but I was fairly fit – young and foolish – and they really got you at it. That was part of the game. A lot of people hear the

name commandos and they think you were some kind of 'he-man'. It wasn't like that. You just had to keep trying.

For those unable to meet the required standards there was an inevitable sense of failure: 'I saw blokes cry when they got "Returned to Unit".'

Eventually it was all over. Those who had lasted the course were granted their coveted green beret and posted to a commando unit. Having 'passed-out' from the commando training centre, Fred Walker was sent to No. 3 Commando. He had just reached his eighteenth birthday when the unit was sent to the south coast of England to prepare for a raid on France. Though the commandos did not realize it at the time, the operation was to go down in history: it was Operation Jubilee, the raid on Dieppe.

Officially not yet eligible for overseas service, Fred Walker was unfazed by the thought of going into action: 'I was up for it. I was under orders – I was young.' Leaving by boat from Newhaven, he realized that many of the others were youngsters who had given false ages to join the Army. One of his mates, John Tupper, also a former member of the Beds and Herts regiment's Young Soldiers training battalion, was just sixteen years old. Fred was not concerned by the stark reality: had he waited to be conscripted, he would still have been anticipating his call-up papers or undergoing basic training.

The plan was for their unit to land at Berneval near Dieppe and engage a coastal battery, preventing it from firing on the attacking landing craft. Waiting off the coast, the commandos cheered as they watched what they thought was a German fighter plane crash into the sea. Picking up the pilot from the water, they realized he was actually a Spitfire pilot. It was an ominous sign. As Fred Walker later recalled, any thoughts of a first glorious engagement against the enemy were swept away as they drew nearer the French coast:

I didn't land at Dieppe. I was in a gunboat with Lt-Colonel Durnford-Slater – he was the guv'nor. We were towing these little boats to get on. But the German E-boats got amongst us. They opened fire and rattled our boat. You start worrying when the stuff starts coming at you. The tracers came at us and rattled the boat. Lots of sailors were killed – we joke about the Royal Navy, but they were marvellous.

As German fire raked their boats, casualties began to mount among the commandos. Fred Walker was given a vicious introduction to how cheap life had become:

They killed my mate 'Blondie' Newell – he was in front of me. He was a man compared to us – like a father to me. He'd been on a couple of raids before and said to me, 'Keep with me, son, you'll be all right.' But he got it straight in the back and was killed outright. He was the first man I saw get killed.

Despite seeing his mentor and would-be protector killed in the opening minutes of the battle, Fred soon learned how combat had an immediate effect on the psyche: 'You think, "He's unlucky." But I was just glad it wasn't me.'

Whilst some members of No. 3 Commando reached the shore and attempted to attack the German battery, Fred's boat remained offshore. Unable to reach the coast they could not fulfil their role:

All we did was pick up wounded Canadians who swam out to our boat. They were telling us how awful it was on the beach but we didn't believe it. We thought they were moaning – we didn't realize how terrible it was. We said, 'Shut up, you're all right!' But we didn't really mean it.

As they would later discover, the stories of the carnage were true. The scale of the tragedy only really struck Fred when he returned to England: 'It's sad to see who never made it. I saw the empty beds of the men who didn't come back. That's when it hits you: it was a disaster.'

Though his role in the action had been brief, and the assault had been costly, Fred remained proud. On leave, he could hold his head up high:

> You felt good to be walking around in your uniform. I liked the girls and they liked me. Being a commando made me grow up. Young kids around King's Cross would come up to me and say, 'Hello, Freddie.' Of course, no one knew I had been at Dieppe – not that I did anything, but I was there when the shit was flying around. And I'd survived.

Like for so many young soldiers, the uniform seemed to give its wearers an unassailable feeling of confidence. The uniform had the ability to mask individuality, but also to act as a shield. As another youngster admitted, his uniform gave him the confidence to chat up shop girls, something he never dared as a civilian.

It was not only the elite of the British Army who were fighting back. When the Germans attacked Crete in May 1941 they were faced by one unlikely enemy: seventeen-year-old Merchant Navy cadet officer, J. H. Dobson. He was one of a group of survivors from the freighter *Dalesman* that had been sunk by German aircraft off the north coast of Crete. The survivors had been formed into anti-paratroop patrols by the Army units on the island, using them to look out for the enemy. Following the fall of Crete, Dobson was taken prisoner but was able to escape after he snatched a machine-gun from his captors, turned it on them and ran off with a number of his shipmates. The group made their way inland, hiding in the hills, before teaming up with some New Zealand gunners. The ragged bunch eventually reached the south coast of the island, found an abandoned ship and headed out to sea. With Cadet Dobson navigating, they were eventually able to reach Egypt. Dobson, who had been on only his first voyage when the *Dalesman* had been lost, was awarded the British Empire Medal for his role in the daring escape.

Transferred to the 4th Battalion Royal West Kent Regiment in early 1942, Stan Scott remained desperate to serve overseas. Although not yet eighteen, he was no longer in a Young Soldiers battalion and his papers showed him to be nineteen; therefore, he was officially eligible to see active service. As such, he was hoping to see action. As a result, he was disappointed upon arriving at the regiment not to be asked about his military training but about whether he played football. His first orders were to be ready for a football match the next morning. The teenager immediately thought to himself: 'What am I doing here? I didn't sign on for this!'

His fears diminished in the following weeks as he was selected for the battalion's 'battle patrol' – a quasi-commando unit that was trained to carry out reconnaissance patrols and specialist tasks. The explosives training and instruction in setting booby traps were exactly the sort of specialist training he relished. For Stan Scott, being a soldier meant being the best soldier he could be. If that meant relinquishing spare time in pubs or the NAAFI, so be it: 'I was never a bullshit soldier, but I was never scruffy. I enjoyed it when we did fifteen-mile speed marches. I always made my kit up properly and I was always practising and learning.'

Yet for all his hard work, more disappointment was to follow. After a period of intense battle training and an inspection by the King, the unit received orders to go to North Africa. However, Stan's name appeared on a list of men detailed as the rear party, whose role was to make sure all the unit's spare equipment was safely returned to stores. After an unofficial stopover in London with his family and a run-in with the Military Police, a frustrated Stan found himself transferred to the 2/7th Battalion, The Queen's Royal Regiment. He immediately felt he did not fit in and was unable to settle down. However, there was one advantage to being in a unit he disliked: he was finally sent overseas.

More frustration was to follow when he discovered they were going to be far away from the front lines, guarding oil pipelines in Iraq. The posting did offer Stan his first opportunity to use his weapons in action, firing on buildings occupied by gangs responsible for stealing from the British Army, but it was a far cry from what he had volunteered for. Eventually, the good news came that the battalion was to be sent to North Africa. However, once again Stan was called before his commanding officer who announced that his real age had been discovered and he was being sent home. During censorship of the mail between Stan and his family, his true age had been revealed. Frustrated, he was sent by train to the coast, then by ship to India. He was further frustrated to find himself in the company of servicemen far less eager than him: 'I was cursing. I went back on a train with two RAF blokes, and all they were interested in was skiving. At Basra it was all base wallahs and shit-house wallahs. People who weren't interested.' After a long and circuitous journey, he arrived back in England in April 1943.

Upon arriving in the UK, Stan was transferred to Maidstone, where the 13th Infantry Training Centre was based: 'I must have been the youngest instructor in the British Army. I was eighteen years old!' The role of the training centre was to prepare newly conscripted men for infantry service: 'I enjoyed it. They came to us after they'd done their six weeks' basic training. We taught them: skill at arms; assault courses; and fieldcraft.' But whilst Stan was a well-trained soldier, and someone who had prided himself on learning everything he could about the weapons he had been trained to use, training others had not been his intention when he volunteered aged fifteen. After a few squads had passed through the unit, he realized he was going nowhere and began to think of ways he could see active service.

With more volunteers having joined No. 3 Commando to replace the men lost at Dieppe, Fred Walker found himself in the Mediterranean ready for the assault on Sicily and Italy. In July 1943, his unit landed on the Sicilian coast at Scoglio Imbiancato, before advancing on the town of Cassible. Fred later described the night landing and the attack as 'a doddle' and recalled how, despite having been in the Army since 1941, it was his first chance to really strike back at the enemy:

The first time I fired my Tommy gun in anger was at a group of five
Italians who were about thirty yards away. I looked up and unloaded
a full magazine – twenty rounds – at them. Then they all stood up – I
never hit one of them! I was panicking as I reloaded, but I took them
prisoner. I was going to shoot them but our captain came up and
stopped me. I'm glad that I didn't kill them.

In the days that followed Fred found himself in his first real action.
Dieppe had been an introduction to the chaos of war, but now he
was about to find out about the intensity of combat. Advancing on
a German-held bridge that the commandos needed to capture and
hold, Fred found himself as the lead scout. As he later recalled: 'I
think they were trying to get rid of me!' As they approached the
bridge they saw German vehicles coming across from the other side.
One of his mates fired a Projector, Infantry, Anti-Tank (PIAT) gun
at the column. The bomb went straight through the first lorry and
hit the one behind. It was full of ammunition and immediately
exploded and burst into flames. With the enemy realizing their
position was under attack, the commandos were hit by intense
defensive fire.

   As the battle wore on, Fred found himself crouching behind trees,
unable to dig into the solid earth and fighting back against increasing
odds. As the battle reached its conclusion, it was clear their situation
was hopeless:

   We were waiting for relief by the 8th Army, but they left us in the shit.
   We'd had about five officers killed, and twenty-three other ranks. We
   were getting shelled, and our captain – Captain Lloyd, an Australian –
   got hit. He was a lovely man. He went into a pill-box and it was hit by
   a round from an 88. The situation was so bad, Peter Young said, 'Every
   man for himself!'

Whilst some escaped inland, Fred joined a group that made for the
coast:

Four of us were on the beach. It was 13 July 1943 and I was just coming up to my nineteenth birthday. We saw a little boat, about six foot long, so we put our guns inside and tried to push it out to sea. We wanted to hide there overnight. But the boat was rotten so it sank. It was so hot we decided to have a swim. So we swam for about 100 yards. But along came an Italian light tank that opened fire on us. My mate had to stand up and wave his white vest.

They quickly surrendered to the Italians and felt a sense of terror as the Italian officer put a gun to the head of one of the commandos. He froze, expecting to be murdered. They were lucky, the Italian was only trying to scare them and they were quickly handed over to the Germans for interrogation. Thinking quickly, the commandos, who had lost their uniforms when the boat sank, claimed they were merchant seaman whose clothes had been lost when they were shipwrecked. They had rowed ashore. The ruse was unsuccessful: 'This German paratrooper said, "You are No. 3 Commando." They knew all about us.'

That night the commandos were able to slip away from their captors. Using the cover of darkness they found a small ditch and crawled along until they found a cave on the beach. There they fell asleep. In the morning they saw a German officer standing outside: 'I went up to him and asked for food, cigarettes and water. They just gave us cigarettes – the Germans had nothing else. They were in trouble themselves.' With German resistance finally failing, Fred was able to reach Allied lines.

With the commandos having sustained heavy casualties, efforts were made to find reinforcements. With the commandos expecting to play a major role in any invasion of France, good quality soldiers were needed to fit into the most heavily trained units in the British Army. In September 1943, commando representatives arrived at the 13th Infantry Training Centre in Maidstone to find volunteers from among the most recent batch of recruits. Instead, they encountered a former 'boy soldier' on the staff of the training centre, who remained keen to get into action.

Stan Scott had originally attempted to join the commandos whilst still sixteen years old and serving in a 'Young Soldiers' battalion, but had been refused on the grounds of age. Listening as the officers told the recruits about the exploits of the commandos in the Mediterranean, he felt encouraged to volunteer again. At the end of the talk there was a call for volunteers to step forward. No one moved: 'I thought, "This is a chance to go into action." I marched up, halted and saluted – dead regimental – "I'd like to put my name down." He told me sorry, but as an NCO on the strength of this training unit, he couldn't take me.' Frustrated but not disheartened, Stan asked what he would have to do to be selected and discovered he would need permission from his commanding officer: 'I went down that hill to his office like a bloody rocket.' Within minutes he had seen the regimental sergeant major, been granted permission to see the colonel and been given written permission to be released: 'I went up that hill so fast. I got to the gym and they were still there. I composed myself, marched up and told him the colonel gave his permission that I may volunteer for commando service.' Within days, his orders came through and he made his way to Achnacarry in the Highlands, where selection and training took place.

At Achnacarry, Stan went through the same punishing routine that had been experienced by Fred Walker and his mates two years earlier: 'It was unbelievable. You cannot imagine it: it was winter in Scotland – I thought I wasn't going to get through it. We would do a fifteen-mile speed march, then do more training when we got back to the camp.' It rained every day, they were sleeping in tents, but Stan Scott enjoyed it. Unlike some of the other units he had served in, everyone was there because they wanted to be. They were all volunteers, all dead keen and all did their best to meet the expected high standards. As Stan recalled: 'After the first week, I'd have stood in the way of the *Flying Scotsman*, I felt that strong.'

It was on one of the intense speed marches that Stan came closest to failing the course:

> I got blisters on my feet, I was in agony. All of a sudden they got nice and easy: they'd burst. My boots were filled with blood. It was raining, there was blood and water coming out of the eyelets of my boots. But I had my mates around me. One got hold of my belt, the others held my arms – so my feet were hardly touching the ground. We got back in the camp, went up the hill and had to fire ten rounds at the targets. Then we had a foot inspection. The medic said to me, 'You've had it. It'll take a couple of days to get back on your feet.' That meant I'd be 'back-squadded' – meaning I'd have to do it all again.

It was a prospect that did not appeal.

He asked the medic if there was anything that could be done to speed up his recovery:

> He got these funny-shaped scissors and some liquid. He said he was going to cut all the skin off, then said, 'Hold on to the arms of the chair. This is going to sting. I'm going to bathe them in surgical spirit.' I thought, 'That ain't bad.' Bloody hell, it stung! I can still feel it now! But it worked, I was back on parade the next morning.

His return to training was also aided by some advice from a fellow commando. He was told to get boots that were a size smaller but in a wider fitting: 'Then I had to pee on them before I put them on. He also told me not to wear socks. It worked. I never got another blister, they fitted me like gloves.' The advice meant his feet survived the course, he received his green beret and was posted to No. 3 Commando. On his first leave after completing commando training he realized why he had endured all the hard training: 'I was wearing my No. 3 Commando and Combined Operations badges – with my "green lid" [beret]. I went to the Railway Tavern for a drink and met my dad. I felt on top of the bloody world!'

Having failed to achieve his aim of joining the RAF, Eric Davies had left his Carmarthen home and joined the Army. After training he was sent to North Africa where he joined a carrier platoon with

the 1/5th Battalion of the Queen's Regiment, part of the fabled 7th
Armoured Division – 'The Desert Rats' – as they landed in Italy in
September 1943. Having made the fateful decision to join the Army
just after his seventeenth birthday, rather than await either the call
from the RAF or conscription after his eighteenth birthday, meant
that he was fully trained by the time he was eighteen-and-a-half.
Had he waited for his call-up he would have still been in the UK.
Instead, he was about to go to war.

For Eric, the campaign started slowly: the enemy troops his
battalion met were mostly Italian who were eager to surrender and,
as Eric told himself: 'life was not too bad'. And then things began to
change. War engulfed his life, taking over every element of his
existence: 'We realized this was not a nine to five job. Once it
started, it never ended. There were attacks during the day and
patrols at night.' The first time he came up against German troops,
the sky seemed to be full of aircraft, there were shells flying through
the air – both Allied and enemy – and enemy infantry in plain sight.
Worst of all, there were the 'monstrous' enemy tanks that put the
fear of God into him:

> It was terrifying and we knew this would be no walk-over and that our
> life expectancy would be measured in seconds. We had spoken among
> ourselves about what it would be like to kill. We very soon learned that
> it was kill or be killed. Little did I realize that I would be killing, in one
> way or another, for the next two years. Thankfully my first kills were
> at a long distance with a machine-gun. So I didn't know how many
> Germans I had actually hit.

It was not long before he found himself caught up in house-to-house
fighting in the Italian town of Scafati, as the Germans repeatedly
counterattacked their positions: 'This was close fighting where you
saw the whites of their eyes before killing them.' It was not just the
killing that had a profound effect on the eighteen year old. He was
horrified to see a pack of rats descend on a corpse in the rubble of

an Italian home. As he watched, the rats began to strip away the
dead flesh. He saw his first case of shell shock as one of his comrades
jumped up and ran away during a mortar barrage. As the campaign
continued he grew to accept death: 'By now I had lost a few friends.
Because I had stopped and spoken to them as they lay dying – and
had hugged some of them – their blood had got into my clothes, and
it smelled.' This smell of death seemed to linger with him for the
next two years.

One consequence of these casualties was that there was rapid
promotion for the survivors. As the old hands – who had fought in
France in 1940, been evacuated through Dunkirk, and then fought
through North Africa and into Italy – were killed or wounded, it was
up to youngsters such as Eric Davies to replace them. Just eighteen
years old, he was promoted to corporal, then to sergeant. As the
division was withdrawn from Italy in late 1943, Eric realized those
brief months fighting had made him one of the veterans. He tried to
absorb what had happened to him since he landed in Italy:

> This was the end of an era. I don't know how I was able to stick it,
> every day and every night, with hardly any rest. I am sure that if I had
> not been an NCO I would have gone AWOL. The worst part is the
> middle of battle, when there is a lull and you sit down. When it was
> time to move on, you had to whip them, and yourself, up. You are
> sitting there nodding off and they expect you to get up and go and kill
> or be killed.

With the invasion of France not far off, it would soon be his turn to
impart his knowledge to a new wave of conscripts – boys of his own
age – and teach them how to stay alive.

CHAPTER 13

The World Turns

'If this is war, why am I enjoying it so much?'

Seventeen-year-old British girl[1]

'My main concern was to obtain supplies of Brylcreem, a hairdressing product particularly popular with young men.'

Peter Richards, sixteen-year-old Londoner[2]

For all the early hopes of war being 'over by Christmas' – which became a sort of annual mantra – the war went on. The air raids had come, gone and returned, and had spread across the country in a seemingly endless ebb and flood. The innocent teenagers of the early war years had matured into fighting men. And for the youngest of the children, those who could hardly remember the pre-war years, peace appeared an abstract concept. Truly, the world had been turned upside down. For the teenagers, their life seemed predestined: from spring 1942, youths aged sixteen had to register for training in preparation for war service. Although registration was compulsory, there was nothing to force anyone into training. However, with the RAF glamorized by the Battle of Britain, boys flocked to the 'Air Training Corps' in the hope of eventually gaining their wings. For teenage girls the 'Girls Training Corps' was established.

The experience of war had an enormous impact upon the nation's youth. For many, it seemed normal teenage pursuits had been put on hold. As John Cotter recalled: 'You couldn't meet girls. I'd been to one or two dances but never had any success, so I didn't think it was my scene. I stopped going until I joined the Air Force.' In West London, Bill Fitzgerald – who was employed in a factory making tents for the Army – had a similar experience of teenage life:

> All the young children had disappeared – as had all the boys over eighteen. There was just us teenagers left. At first we couldn't go out at night, because you spent all your time dodging bombs. And the men kept a close eye on their teenage daughters. Going to work was my social life. As soon as I came home in the evening, the bombing started and you had to make a dash for the shelters.

In south London, one teenage girl recalled how the bombing meant she did things she would never have previously considered:

> I was going to work in London during the Blitz. I had to get two buses to Tooting Broadway, but if the sirens had gone the tube trains wouldn't go under the Thames. You'd be stuck in the tunnel, in the dark. It was hot and you could hardly breathe. It was awful and you didn't know what was happening. Sometimes tube stations had been bombed, like when they bombed Balham. So I had to get out of the train and find a way to get to a different station. I hitched lifts on lorries to get past one station, to start again. Pre-war, a fourteen-year-old girl would never have thought of hitching a lift on a lorry. It became normal. Basically, I knew nothing about the real world at the end of the war.

Army Cadet Bill Fitzgerald realized the strange situation he was in: 'We were the innocents. We did army training with rifles, but weren't mature about sex.' It was an experience recognized by Anthony Wedgwood Benn, who had joined his school's Home

Guard unit aged sixteen: 'When I was in the Home Guard I was trained to kill – but I had no knowledge of girls. I missed out on what I would have had if I had been at home but I can't imagine my childhood being anything other than the war. It took over everything.' At least Bill Fitzgerald was working in an environment where he had daily contact with young women:

> At sixteen, I didn't know anything about sex and I couldn't ask my dad. I fancied the older girls in the factory, but I didn't really understand it. I didn't think I wanted to go to bed with them – I just liked them. I couldn't think about going out with girls or kissing. It was an innocent world: with bombs falling around you, shooting a rifle, training with the Home Guard. Then I started going out with girls at about seventeen. Just to kiss a girl was marvellous. But that was as far as you thought.

As he later admitted, real life seemed to be on hold: 'I was just waiting for my call-up papers to land on the door mat.'

Yet, this also had a liberating effect as attitudes to life changed. One probation officer reported on the behaviour of teenager couples, noting how they made their beds up together on the floor of public air raid shelters, with the full knowledge of their parents. As the authorities noticed, children and teenagers embraced their independence. Having returned from evacuation in 1941 aged nine, Sylvia Bradbrook found she had acquired an unexpected amount of freedom:

> Mother worked, my sister had been called up and I was at school in Norbury. We were all split up – and were getting caught up in different air raids. I was on my own most of the time and I'd have to go down to the shelter in the park on my own. I never thought of the danger. At the end of Melfort Road – there was a green with an air raid shelter on it. Me and my friend would cycle down that way to school in Norbury with our tin hats on. One day we decided to do it while a raid was still

on. We got round the corner and came face to face with an air raid warden. He shouted to us, 'What do you two stupid girls think you're doing? Get off those bikes and come over here.' Just because there was a raid on that wasn't going to stop us, we'd take a chance.

As war progressed, attitudes to life soon changed. It was difficult for children to retain a wide-eyed innocence as death became increasingly prevalent. Even the loss of family members, regardless of whether the death was war-related, failed to make the impression it had just a few years before. For Merseyside teenager Tony Sprigings, even his mother's death from tuberculosis in 1941 failed to affect him as much as one might have expected: 'Because there was so much mayhem going on you didn't get any sympathy from anyone. If you'd lost a parent, people thought, "So what? I've just lost mine." So we were brought up in a tough kind of way. No one gave you time to get over things.'

There developed a desperate desire, especially among the young, to seize the moment and enjoy everything – and anyone – available. In towns and cities where death had become a constant companion, youngsters became eager to gain some experience of life while they still had one. The constant threat of death combined with the increasing drabness of everyday existence to generate a sense of openness. When they went to cafes they found spoons fixed to the counter, rather than handed out to every customer. Pubs had beer but few glasses as industry was unable to meet consumer needs. Instead, some pubs insisted customers bring their own and beer drinkers resorted to hanging a jam jar on a string hung around their neck so that no one could steal it. Food was rationed and bland. Clothing was drab and worn out. Cosmetics were hard to find. And city streets were smoky, dusty and dirty. Those who worked spent long hours in their factories and offices. It is no wonder that, when they went out for the night, they were determined to enjoy themselves.

To overcome shortages of stockings, women were encouraged to go bare legged whenever possible. Younger women were advised to return to wearing ankle socks, something that did not appeal to a generation of teenagers who were enjoying the fruits of early maturity brought on by the freedom of the war years. To cope with shortages of cosmetics, girls collected exhausted lipsticks, melted down the remnants and re-formed them in usable sticks. Cold cream was mixed into lipstick to create a makeshift rouge. Eyelashes were brightened by brushing them with castor oil, whilst shoe polish and burnt cork doubled as mascara. In aircraft factories, female workers used varnish from the paint shops to paint their nails.

Despite the parental concern shown for many girls, plenty developed an independence that seemed nurtured by war. Jean Redman, who as a fifteen year old had worked in the evacuee administration department of Bedford Town Hall, found war had opened her eyes to opportunity. More than anything, war meant she had begun to mix with a wider circle of people than she could previously have imagined:

> The whole thing was exciting to me at that age. I had lots of boyfriends. The boys my age from a school evacuated to the town, also the boys in the Treasurer's office at the Town Hall where I took messages. The police station was next to the Town Hall and I used to take messages there. There were young cadets there, so I got a lot of attention. I enjoyed the war years. People came and went all the time. You met airmen and soldiers from different places. They'd ask you to write to them for a while, then they'd go overseas. We corresponded with a lot of men. It meant a lot to the chaps.

One of her friends even met and married a member of Glenn Miller's band that was billeted in Bedford during 1944.

Jean also developed a spirit of independence. In 1940, aged sixteen, she and a friend cycled the fifty miles to London where they booked into a youth hostel and enjoyed life in the capital. Every day they travelled into central London, soon becoming familiar with the tube stations crowded with shelterers. It was a strange, slightly unreal, sensation – being on holiday in London whilst it was the target for enemy bombers, but she enjoyed the freedom and the excitement of the city in wartime: 'London had just been bombed but we didn't care.'

The trip encouraged her to seek more adventure. Too young to be conscripted into the services and convinced her parents would refuse permission for her to volunteer at seventeen, she chose an alternative route:

> I was sixteen-and-a-half when I joined the Land Army. I had a wonderful time. I'd wanted to go into the forces but my parents wouldn't allow me – and I needed their permission. But my elder sister had joined the Land Army and I discovered you didn't need parents' permission to join that. So I was naughty. I went and joined and told them afterwards – when it was a fait accompli. I feel bad about that now – I can remember my mother crying. But one just wanted to be part of things. I wanted to get away from home and be grown up. That's why I did it. You had to grow up as you were on your own.

Having escaped the gaze of her parents, Jean Redman ironically found her new employers were even more concerned for her welfare. Working on a farm outside Windsor, she soon befriended local labourers, many of whom were Romany gypsies. They accepted the former public school girl with open arms, inviting her to their encampment where she shared meals around their campfire, surrounded by horse-drawn caravans. It was a far cry from the world she had known back in Bedford where her comfortable existence would never have exposed her to such a stratum of society. Whilst Jean enjoyed the company of her new friends, her employers considered the gypsies unsuitable companions for a well-educated, middle-class girl. She was soon switched to a new position within the estate where she witnessed a very different world: each day as she made her way around the farm a car passed her carrying the

royal princesses, Elizabeth and Margaret, and she became a familiar
sight to the princesses who started waving to her as they passed.

Working on a poultry farm, Jean found the job rewarding:

> You felt that you were doing something for the war effort. It was
> exciting to do different work – any work would have been exciting. I'm
> glad now I didn't go into the Army or Navy. The poultry farm was in
> the orchard. The farmhouse was right by where I was and I could go
> in there and drink. I had my own toilet facility and I sat in a huge shed.
> There was a boy from the house next door who'd come and a man
> came in the morning to light the boiler. He made the mash for the
> chicks – then I sat alone all day. At weekends the boy would come and
> help clean out the pens. There was no break – including Saturday and
> Sunday – as we were working with animals.

In more normal times Jean Redman would have been following her
intended career path, to be a teacher. But these were not normal
times. All across the country, education had been disrupted by the
pressures of wartime conditions. One Croydon boy estimated that
he attended around fifteen different schools in the six years of war,
as his family moved around and he was bombed out of his home:
'Some were just for a matter of weeks. It was chaotic and I had no
time to build up friendships. My education probably suffered but
everyone was in the same boat.' Returning from evacuation in
spring 1944, ten-year-old Kathleen Stevens was shocked by seeing
the condition of education in south London: 'On the first day the
headmaster looked at my mother – then looked at me – and asked,
"Can she read?" I thought, "What on earth is he going on about?
Of course I can read. I am ten!" I was completely gobsmacked.' She
was amazed when the headmaster pulled out a book containing lists
of words:

> I had to read these words. I couldn't believe it. I could read stories and
> everything. When I got to the class I saw why he did it. I had to read

stories to the whole class – nobody else could read! The headmaster was so used to teaching children whose education had disintegrated.

It was not just in the urban areas that education had been placed under a strain. Schools throughout the country were cramped and crowded, as they attempted to cope with the influx of evacuees. In Somerset, Ken Durston experienced the changes that included having two evacuees in a home already occupied by five children. If that were not enough, when the mother of one evacuee was killed in the bombing, his father came from London and moved in with them:

> We went to school in Weston-super-Mare, but there were so many children in the classes they couldn't control us. We'd catch the 8.30 bus from the village – then when we got to Weston we'd walk the half a mile along the sands to school. Mostly we'd dawdle along the sands and wouldn't reach school till after nine. In the classroom the teacher would say, 'Sit down,' but we were all wedged in. We were all crammed up. You didn't have a single desk; it was all doubles – we'd sit two to a desk. There should have been a passage-way between each row – but they put two rows together – so instead of four gangways between the desks there were only two, and that way they got an extra row of desks in. In the summer they'd try to get rid of us – if the weather was good, they'd send us up the fields to play cricket. As a result my education was very poor from twelve onwards. Mostly it was just mucking around with my mates.

It was easy to see why so many children had neglected their studies. War had engulfed their lives: the youngest schoolchildren had known nothing except war; the next group had experienced the disruption of bombing; and the teenagers realized their destiny was conscription. With war raging, maths and geography hardly seemed to matter any more.

For those at public schools, the changes were not as drastic. There

was no need to evacuate many of the schools since they were already
in the countryside. Where boys boarded, the schools continued as
before. The big difference was that many schools increased the level of
military training given to the boys. Most gave training for boys from
the age of fourteen to sixteen, followed by progress to the school's own
Home Guard unit. Cadets were given tests, earning 'War Certificate
A' in recognition of the military skills they had learned. At Stowe
School, boys aged fourteen were trained in 'intelligence scouting' and
taught how to gather intelligence. The headmaster of Winchester
College wrote to the War Office to request that training in schools be
more closely integrated with official training regimes in order to
prepare cadets to the standard the Army required. He noted the
enthusiasm shown by the boys: 'The rifle and uniform, to say nothing
of the Bren gun etc, makes the 15 year old feel that he is a real soldier.'[3]
He also requested assistance in teaching 'fieldcraft' to his boys on the
grounds that officers often found such skills difficult to pick up.

A potential source of fieldcraft training came from another youth
organization. In 1941 the Boy Scout Association wrote to the War
Office to offer its assistance in three areas: teaching fieldcraft to
members of cadet units; by offering fully trained Boy Scouts to the
War Office to help training in fieldcraft; and by encouraging Scouts
to remain members of the Organization even if they joined an Army
Cadet unit. The concentration on moving cadet units away from the
parade ground and on to more practical skills was noted by the
leader of a school cadet unit: 'the difficulty of holding a rifle is
considerable for boys of this size'.[4] In north London there was even
a 'Junior Commando Unit' organized to train enthusiastic boys in
commando skills, in anticipation of their conscription.

At Winchester College, Patrick Delaforce was active in the Officer
Training Corps (OTC) where membership was compulsory for the
pupils:

We had a school armoury complete with a tough, uniformed sergeant
and soon a Bren gun and 2-inch mortar for practising stripping and

assembly. The OTC was under Major Parr. We had uniformed drills,
'Field Day' manoeuvres against other schools, blank firing training,
setting ambushes. It was great fun.

The vigorous training was encouraged by Patrick's housemaster
who had been gassed in the Great War and had no love for the
'Boche'.

In 1940 Winchester College established a Home Guard unit for
the senior boys:

> The transition to the Home Guard was easy. I'd already learned battle
> drill and tactics on the meadows and trained on Bren gun and mortars
> – alas without ammunition. The school had a .22 rifle range. There
> were night manoeuvres on the hills, the theory being that we would
> take on German parachute troops – and some of us actually had 'Battle
> bowlers' [a commonly used name for steel helmets]. We were excellent
> amateur soldiers.

It was an experience Patrick later found to be of immense benefit
when he was called up into the Army. At Eton College the Home
Guard unit paraded in school uniform, complete with top hat and
Lee Enfield rifles. At Whitgift School in Croydon, the OTC
developed a specialist intelligence training course for its senior
pupils.

Apart from preparing the boys for war, Winchester College was
also at the forefront of the movement to encourage youngsters to
work on the land. Patrick Delaforce remembered the summer
months in the fields of Hampshire: 'The school ran several
agricultural camps, living under canvas, to bring in the harvest. We
were "stooking" corn, driving tractors, building haystacks, drinking
cider and ogling the Land Girls – a truly marvellous time.' As early
as 1939 Winchester pupils took part in summer harvest camps,
prompted in part by the recruitment of thousands of young men into
the militia, leaving many farms short handed.

To cope with the restrictions on imports vast tracts of idle land were utilized for raising crops. By 1941, two million acres of grassland had been converted into arable land, including an additional 43,000 acres planted with wheat and 128,000 extra acres of potatoes. With farm labourers called up into the Army, and a fall in numbers of Irish labourers coming to the UK, 1940 saw the need for 100,000 extra labourers in the countryside. With fewer than 12,000 girls serving in the Land Army, children were employed to meet the shortfall. By 1942 some 300,000 children were needed for agricultural duties.

During 1940 some 8,000 children – predominantly boys – took part in nearly 250 harvest camps. The children had to pay their own transport costs and contribute towards their keep, often meaning there was little left from their weekly pay. Schemes were also established in which children bombed out of their homes were sent to live in the countryside where they combined agricultural work with classroom education. In many ways, the schemes were like a legally sanctioned version of the selection process by which farmers chose the biggest evacuees to live with them in order to help out on the farm.

Children across the nation soon gained a taste of rural life. They rose early in the morning, had breakfast and then headed off to the fields. The hours were long and the work didn't stop in bad weather. Many found themselves at the limit of their endurance after eight full hours of heavy work. They ate their meals in barns that were swarming with rats. The children ate basic food, often cooked outdoors on improvised stoves, and endured a lack of privacy in the camps. Most were housed in tented camps, usually of no more than thirty children, although some slept in huts and barns. In addition to volunteers organized via schools, Girl Guide troops also assisted on farms, offering their services to farmers whose labourers had been conscripted. The arrival of girls was a welcome sight. Some 4,000 of the older boys were given instruction in tractor driving, meaning regular tractor drivers were freed for other work. Elsewhere, children plucked poultry, caught rats and threshed corn. Schools used spare land to grow crops or raise pigs. Teachers took children into woods to collect nuts and berries; some even established beehives and produced their own honey.

To meet the demands of the farms, school holidays were shifted to allow the children to be available when they were most needed. In some areas local authorities granted extra holiday time to pupils who volunteered to assist with picking the potato harvest. The use of children on farms was also formalized for term time, allowing them to work a maximum of twenty half-day shifts in the course of a year. What had been an unofficial pre-war practice for village children became a way of life for children from towns and cities. This scheme was believed to have resulted in around one million extra acres of potatoes being grown between 1941 and 1944.

Other youngsters volunteered to help in the countryside. In summer 1941 a group of twenty Liverpudlian Boy Scouts went to Scotland to do forestry work. They took saws and axes with them and imagined themselves as lumberjacks. When they arrived, the Forestry Commission explained their duties: they spent the entire two weeks weeding between rows of saplings. Though disappointed by the work, they were pleased to receive their 'National Service' badge.

These types of activities were an ideal tool for those in authority who believed that 'boys will be boys' and thought they needed to be given 'some outlet for their love of adventure, gang loyalty and so on'.[5] In East Suffolk a Youth Service Corps had been established in July 1940, an idea that soon spread to fifty other areas. The youths were engaged in tasks directly useful to the war effort and were centred on work, but increased to include physical training, technical and general education, and social recreation. By 1941 the Home Office had recognized the success of the Youth Service Corps. It noted that the groups had reacted to the local situation and sprang from a natural desire of children, both boys and girls, to assist the war effort. In Suffolk between 64 and 77 per cent of the members were kids who had never previously joined youth organizations. In one area, a group was established deliberately to attract the local 'tough guys'. The policy was a success, with youths being attracted to the lack of regimentation within the organization. The only problem with this success was that it actually bred a sense of respectability for the groups. Having attracted one group of the 'rougher type of boy and girl' who then became respectable, the scheme no longer attracted the next age group of 'undisciplined youth of the streets'.[6]

In Suffolk the scheme was credited with cutting juvenile crime. The most widely perceived reason for the success of the scheme was that youths were attracted by the lack of outside control, preferring these freedoms to the regular supervision of most youth clubs. It was in keeping with the feeling that war had increased their freedom and they wanted to expand their horizons and enjoy their independence without the influence of adults. Despite the genuine success of the scheme, it was believed such organizations would be difficult to replicate in urban areas. In particular, whilst in rural areas youths could be employed on manual tasks, in the big cities the main work available was on bombsites and the Home Office did not want to see younger boys working in demolition squads, for fear of the horrors they might encounter.

Nonetheless, children threw themselves into myriad tasks to support the war effort. Scrap collection and recycling were particularly appealing to boys who liked nothing better than scrabbling over waste ground and rifling through long forgotten hidey-holes. The task was sold to them with interesting facts. Government publicity highlighted how twenty-four rusty old keys would give enough metal to make a hand grenade, whilst forty-two would be enough to make a steel helmet. They were fascinated to hear how, if every household in the UK gave one key in to be recycled, it would be enough to build twelve tanks. Such details allowed youngsters to realize that they, in their own small way, were making a genuine contribution to the war effort. The only downside was that they were encouraged to hand over their own precious collections of shrapnel. The enthusiasm of some children was misplaced. One eager child arrived at a collection point with 'scrap' brass and lead he had found in a church. It turned out he had simply taken all the church vases.

Another favourite activity was taking part in savings campaigns. Many youth organizations arranged their own savings clubs. Organized and encouraged by the National Savings Committee, which had been established during the Great War to raise funds for the war effort, schools encouraged their pupils to pay into the savings schemes. In one case in northern England, a headmaster was asked how much his pupils could raise for a 'War Weapons Week' savings drive. He replied that they would raise £50. The organizer told him this was not very much and then asked the children what they could raise. The children fixed a target of £500. In the end they raised the staggering total of £5,000.

As the time approached for Patrick Delaforce to leave school and go into the Army, he made a conscious decision that he felt would help keep him alive. Winchester College had an established connection with the King's Royal Rifle Corps. Already, Patrick had heard the sad news of boys he knew from the years above him at school who had been killed in action whilst serving in the regiment: 'By chance I made my odds of survival better. My loyalty was to the Royal Horse Artillery – dashing, dangerous and smart, but not as dangerous as the "Greenjackets" which had, for officers, a very high death rate.'

As regiments that considered themselves to be the finest in the British Army, the King's Royal Rifle Corps and the Rifle Brigade actively recruited from some of the country's top public schools. Officers of the regiments toured the schools, attempting to find boys willing to sign up to eventually become the next generation of subalterns. Ken Hardy, a former secondary school boy who served with the King's Royal Rifle Corps and was believed to be a suitable officer candidate, recalled: 'They were a snobby lot. They made it quite clear I wasn't going to be commissioned into them.'

In his final year at Charterhouse, John Bendit recalled a visit by officers of the regiments:

> A colonel and Major Dick Cave, of King's Royal Rifle Corps and the Rifle Brigade, had been going round all the public schools actively recruiting – basically they were creaming off who they considered the most suitable candidates for their two regiments. The socialists created quite a stink about the issue in Parliament.

A pupil at Rugby School, Michael Howard was also inspired by the visit of a Rifle Brigade officer:

> You knew you were going to have to serve in one capacity or other. On 14 June 1943, just after the one o'clock news, I had heard a story about the 2nd Battalion of the Rifle Brigade at 'Snipe' in El Alamein. It was the most amazing action – which had come down to four men doing extraordinary things. Having listened to that I said to myself if I have to serve I'd like to serve with men like that. In fact, there already was beginning to be a tradition in my house at school that you went from there to the Rifle Brigade. In the event, Vic Turner, who had got the VC at 'Snipe' and was badly wounded, came to our school to recruit possible officers. It was he who recruited me. I felt I was fated to go into the Rifle Brigade. Of course, in my opinion it was the best regiment in the Army.

He cycled from school into Coventry to volunteer on his seventeenth birthday. During training, he noticed the result of the regiment's careful selection policy: 'All the others were people like yourself – who came from the same background: the finest public schools in the country. You felt you might end up marrying one of their sisters.'

Even the younger children were affected by the changes. Born in 1937, Anne Paton had already experienced the anxious conditions of life in Jersey in the final days before the German invasion.

Accompanied by her mother and sister, she had escaped on one of the last planes out of the Channel Islands. Yet, as a three year old, her main concern had been to get the necessary documents to be allowed to take her pet cat with her. The family settled in west London, where they were joined by Anne's father, Angus Paton.

It was Mr Paton's involvement in secret war work that brought Anne one of the most curious memories of her young life: 'We had an au pair. She had her own room in the house. I remember her standing at the top of the stairs – the telephone was in the hall on a table. I could see her shadow – and when the phone rang she'd be out on the stairs.' Even as a child, Anne thought it strange that the au pair would stand in the dark, halfway up the stairs, to listen to telephone conversations. The reason for her strange behaviour was finally revealed:

> My dad caught her going through the things in his desk. She was presumably looking for information on my father's work. He kept that in his study. Evidently she knew all the local factories: how many people worked there, clocking on times and all the rest of it. She was locked up until the end of the war. She was obviously gathering information – there was no reason why she should have known all that information about the factories. I don't know if she'd been planted with us or just used the opportunity.

The reason for the au pair's interest only became evident in later years when Anne discovered that her father had been the chief engineer on the construction of the Mulberry Harbours, the prefabricated concrete ports that had been secretly constructed and towed to Normandy to act as temporary ports on the invasion beaches.

For Yvonne Vanhandenhoeve and her sister, Julienne, the circumstances of being trapped in Belgium made life dangerous. They were British citizens living in an enemy-occupied city, never knowing what their fate might be. The uncertainty of life in an occupied city was magnified when she noticed children arriving at her school wearing the Star of David and 'J' insignia that identified them as Jewish. Initially, she did not know the implication of these signs – except that they signified the religion of the girls. Eventually, they disappeared from classes, never to return. As she recalled: 'It was known what was happening but there was nothing you could do about it.'

For Yvonne there was some measure of excitement in this life. She recalled how, as she travelled by tram to school, people would demonstrate their opposition to the occupying Germans by surreptitiously using cigarettes to burn holes in the Germans' clothing. It was a small but symbolic sign of resistance. This excitement was undermined by the genuine fear of what the Germans might do to them. Their English mother, a keen pianist, would open the windows of the family home and play patriotic songs like 'Land of Hope and Glory' and 'Tipperary'. Again, it was a small – but dangerous – sign of defiance. Added to the burden was the fact that their step-brother returned illegally from a forced labour camp in Norway. He was pushed into a lawless existence of living on forged papers. It was an experience, his younger sister recalled, that sent him 'off the straight and narrow', since he had no choice but to live a rootless, and dubious, existence in order to survive. For Yvonne, her greatest fear was that she would reach her eighteenth birthday with the Germans still occupying Antwerp. In those circumstances, as a British national, she would have been interned and sent to Germany.

Yet these concerns were submerged under the daily fight to find enough food to survive. As the war progressed, rations diminished, forcing the family to take risks to feed themselves. Their only choice was to buy food on the black market or smuggle it into the city. As the elder of two teenage girls, Yvonne assisted her father in hazardous trips to purchase food:

I accompanied my father to Holland to buy cheese and bread. My father had a waistcoat with all these little pockets that we used to fill.

We would get Edam cheese and sell some of it at an inflated cost. It wasn't safe because there were Germans sentries all along the border: we had to sneak through. I think my father had a contact who kept an eye out for sentries. If you got caught they would shoot you. I know I was scared.

It was an experience that she had to be careful about, never telling her friends what she had done in case they informed on them. Yvonne learnt to trust no one – in particular the Flemish nationalists – not even her classmates. Only family members or very close friends could be confided in.

Above all else, the lives of children in wartime were shaped by the changing roles of their parents. It was not unnatural for fathers to be away from home on military service. For many children, fathers were often remote figures who worked long hours, played little role around the house and seemed distant from their families. War service just seemed like an extension of that distance. Yet mothers had been a constant factor in the lives of the majority of children. It was mothers who gave them their meals, bathed them, took them to school and sent them on errands. With so few women in full-time employment pre-war, the housewife – stereotypically scrubbing the front step or beating a rug whilst chatting over the fence to a neighbour – was a bedrock of British society. But war changed the balance, meaning that for many children their mother became a figure almost as remote as their absent father.

There was a rapid expansion of day nurseries as working mothers needed somewhere to send younger children. By early 1943, a total of 1,800 nurseries had been opened or were in the planning stage. For a small fee, working mothers could drop off their children who would receive breakfast and then spend the rest of the day alternating between playing games, doing basic lessons, eating lunch and resting – all under the gaze of trained nursery staff. There were also residential nurseries which could house children whose fathers were away at war and mothers were working in factories. Another experiment that distanced children from their parents were 'County Camp Schools'. There were 38 residential schools, in which 250 children and their teachers lived in rural camps. In addition to their normal school lessons, children learned gardening and looking after animals. They were also taught to look after themselves, keeping their dormitories tidy and making their own beds.

For some of the children, although they had less contact with their mothers, war had positive benefits. For children of poorer families, whose pre-war diets had been woeful, nurseries provided wholesome well-balanced meals. Similarly, the National Milk Scheme gave free or subsidized milk to more than four million children, ensuring they received a daily dose of calcium at schools or nurseries.

It was not that women wanted to neglect their children: it was simply that they had too much else in their lives. The daily routine, regardless of work commitments, involved long hours queuing outside shops. When water supplies were cut off by bombing, there was the queue at the standpipe. Then there was washing and cleaning, with far less soap than pre-war. Not forgetting trying to feed a family on limited rations. Then when clothing was rationed, women had the added burden of patching, darning and swapping clothes with friends and neighbours as children grew, and unpicking old jumpers to reuse the wool. Others had allotments and vegetable gardens to tend. Add to this the burden of salvage collections and knitting 'comforts' for the troops, and it was clear that the women of the nation were fully engaged with the war effort. It was little wonder, with their worlds turned upside down by war and their parents occupied for so many hours just to get by, that some of the nation's youth began to run wild.

With war engulfing the entire nation, it began to touch everyone's hearts. There was hardly a family who did not have one or more family members in uniform. Whether they were at sea, above the clouds in fighters and bombers or out on the battlefields, millions were on the front line. Big cities, small towns, even villages had been blitzed. Death was everywhere and the fear of receiving bad news became an accompaniment to everyday life. As such, there were no more unpopular figures in wartime Britain than the messengers who delivered telegrams. Whether the telegram boys were delivering innocent messages or the ominous envelopes announcing the death of a loved one, nobody wanted to see them in their streets. As one later joked: 'Everybody was pleased to see the back of me.'

Peter Richards was one of those selected for the burden of being a telegram messenger. He had applied for a transfer to a position that would allow him to ride a motorcycle. In January 1941, aged just sixteen, he was transferred to a depot at Mornington Crescent, not far from his home in Camden, north London. Receiving a smart new dark-blue uniform, leather gauntlets and a motorcycle, he was tasked to deliver telegrams around the streets of the area. He could feel a sense of deepening gloom each time he entered a street. Many women gathered in their front gardens to chat, yet as he passed he could sense a deadly silence descending as they watched to see where he might draw to a halt. As he passed them he could sense the women's relief as they told themselves: 'Thank goodness, it's not for me.'

Though most of his messages were innocent, there inevitably came a time when he was resigned to being the bearer of bad tidings: 'When I first started I didn't realize the effect I would be having on people's lives. But I quickly learned. The trauma was delivering telegrams telling people their husbands or sons had been killed.' The first recipient was a woman to whom he handed a telegram informing her that her son had been lost at sea. It was an awful experience for Peter, he could show no emotion even though he knew exactly what the telegram contained. It was a horribly formal way of breaking bad news. Following protocol, he waited to see if there was a reply, watching as the distraught woman collapsed in hysterics, with another son attempting to console her as tears streamed down his own face. The sixteen-year-old messenger was haunted by the sight of the hysterical woman collapsing to the ground and screaming: '*No, no, no!*'

It was a terrible burden for a teenager to bear:

> We could show no emotion. But we never had any type of counselling
> and we weren't told what to do. Sometimes though we were warned,
> the supervisor would say, 'This one's a loss of life letter.' It was
> shocking. I don't know who else could have broken the news but it was
> done in a very bad way. I can remember asking the head man if we
> could always be told what we were delivering, because sometimes it
> was a complete shock. But he was a real stickler for the rules and said
> no. It was a horrible system. It gave me a new dimension on the mental
> suffering of war. It matures you.

A few months later he was on duty on a Sunday morning, delivering
messages around the Mill Hill area. He approached a house in a
leafy suburban street where a middle-aged man was tending his
front garden. Peter handed over the letter telling him his son had
been killed in an air training accident that afternoon. In contrast to
the woman who had collapsed in tears, with quiet dignity the man
thanked the young telegram boy and then turned to go inside to
break the news to his wife. It was an awful spectacle that remained
with Peter throughout his life: 'That was sixty-odd years ago but I
can still remember him – it just sticks in your mind. It had a real
effect on me. It made me realize the terrible cost of war.'

CHAPTER 14

Merchantmen and Boys

'Never, never, ever, ever, volunteer for f*** all! That's mandatory. [It] shows he is not a selfish person, for by not volunteering he leaves room for the keener and more deserving matelots to offer their services.'

Reg Osborn, who trained at TS *Exmouth*[1]

The boys of the Merchant Navy became the unsung heroes of the Second World War. Whilst war saw the evacuation of thousands of fourteen year olds, taken to the safety of the countryside, hundreds of their former classmates escaped the dangers of British cities for the far greater perils of the sea. The continual need for new boys to go to sea with the merchant fleet was shown by one stark figure: despite being civilians, the merchant fleet suffered a higher casualty rate than any of the armed services. Whatever their status, they shared the common experiences of a life – and often death – at sea in wartime.

Some of these youths were already experienced sailors. Not disheartened by the sinking of his first ship in late 1939, Bristol-born Ron Bosworth soon signed on with another ship, the *Port Dunedin*, sailing to Australia in early 1940. In the months that he was away, the British Expeditionary Force was defeated in France, Britain stood alone facing invasion and then it defeated the Luftwaffe in the

Battle of Britain. In almost five months at sea, Ron's luck had held. It continued to hold after he returned to England. The *Port Dunedin* docked in London's Victoria Docks on the second day of the Blitz. The whole of the docks seemed to be on fire, hundreds of ships were hit by bombs, yet the *Port Dunedin* suffered just minor damage when an incendiary bomb landed on a forward hatch. And through the chaos, Ron Bosworth was discharged from the ship, crossed London and headed back to Bristol by train – all in the lull between the bombing raids.

His next trip, on the Atlantic convoys, saw Ron witness an infamous incident. In November 1940, as it returned from Canada with a cargo of meat, Convoy HX-84 encountered the German pocket-battleship *Admiral Scheer.* An escort ship, HMS *Jervis Bay,* took immediate action. Knowing the odds were hopeless, the captain of the *Jervis Bay* gave orders to attack. It was a suicidal action, but the sacrifice was not in vain. Ron watched as the *Admiral Scheer* bombarded the *Jervis Bay.* As the German warship mercilessly pounded its escort, the convoy scattered, escaping the scene in a desperate bid to reach the safety of home. With the Germans focusing their attentions on the Royal Navy, all but six of the merchant ships were able to escape. Ron, like all his fellow seamen, could not forget the price paid by the sailors who had sacrificed their lives to allow them to escape.

After a short break, he returned to sea on the *British Fidelity* in early 1941. This time his luck changed:

> I was on lookout on the fo'c'sle head, looking for floating mines. Just out of Bristol, in the Channel, we hit an acoustic mine. It was a new German weapon, set off by the vibration of the propeller. As she exploded, the bows went down, I went up in the air and grabbed the stays above me – and held on. She began to sink by the stern.

Fortunately for seventeen-year-old Ron, the ship – a tanker – was empty, as it was making its way across the Atlantic to collect fuel.

The mine did only minor damage and the ship was saved. The captain dropped anchors and used them to steady the vessel, allowing time for the pumps to work:

> Out come the tugs from Cardiff. We slipped our anchor and they towed us in. We had two days and nights working hard to keep her afloat. The pumps were going all the time, the tugs also had their pumps working. It was worth it to save a ship like that. Then we had to sail her into dry dock. Within a few hours we were paid off. We were finished with her.

Less than two weeks after being paid off, Ron found another ship, the *Port Townsville*, a modern ship – a far cry from the banana-boat he had started the war in. The crew slept two to a cabin, not twelve to a room. The luxury did not last long as they headed out into the Atlantic. He was at the wheel when they came under attack. Looking up into the sky, he could see two aircraft approaching: 'Suddenly two German bombers came out of the sky. I remember the first bomb – it went down through the fore-part of the bridge. It killed one of the passengers. The skipper said, "You'd better go down and get your mate out."' Ron raced below decks to his cabin where he found his friend asleep in his bunk:

> I pulled him out of his bed and chucked him on the floor. I said, 'Come on, Billy, we've got to get going.' As we got out on the deck, the planes were machine-gunning us. A splinter hit me in the face. Me and Billy got our lifeboats away. It was difficult because there was a big hole in the side – we could see fires burning inside.

Braving heavy seas, they managed to get clear of the ship before she slipped beneath the waves. The next question was, how long would they be left in the sea. Fortunately, there were two vessels in the area: 'There was a coaster coming. The skipper said, "That's an Irish boat. If it picks you up, you'll be interned" – 'cause the Irish were neutral. But there was a French corvette coming, so we rows to that. You'd never credit it, but the French crew gave us vino to drink.'

Having seen his last two ships sunk from beneath him in just a matter of months, Ron returned to the *Port Dunedin* – a vessel he considered a 'lucky ship'. He had spent his eighteenth birthday at sea and then left her on his nineteenth birthday, already a veteran of convoys that had taken him around the world.

With so many ships sunk in the opening years of the war, controversy arose over the treatment of merchant seamen. As thousands discovered, they had their wages stopped as soon as they left ship: regardless of whether they had been paid off in port or torpedoed in the middle of the Atlantic. It had become a source of great disquiet that men who spent days – sometimes weeks – adrift in lifeboats, did so in the knowledge that their wages had been stopped. The seamen felt they were being neglected and their sacrifices were unappreciated. After all, a pilot did not have his wages stopped once his plane was shot down, nor did a soldier lose pay if his unit ran out of ammunition. To remedy this, a new act went through Parliament to make life more bearable for them. The 'Essential Work Order for the Merchant Navy' (EWOMN) came into effect in May 1941. Once the new law was in effect, the men had security of pay, but were effectively in the job 'for the duration': as essential workers they could no longer pick and choose when to work. Instead, they joined a Merchant Navy 'Pool', which found crews for ships using the men available in the area. They were allowed to reject two ships, but if they rejected a third they were called up for military service.

All new boys shared the experience of joining their first ship with little idea of what to expect. Even if they had attended sea schools, the world of an ocean-going ship, with its crew of old hands, was a daunting prospect. For those going to sea as cadets or apprentices with shipping companies, there were formalities to be observed. Seventeen-year-old Alan Shard was indentured as an Apprentice to the Counties Ship Management Co. of London on 18 June 1940:

The Company promised to pay me for four years the sum of £60 in the following manner: £10 for the first year; £12 for the second year; £18 for the third year; £20 pounds for the last year. Furthermore, it was agreed that I would provide wearing apparel and necessities. With this generous stipend the company promised to teach this apprentice the business of seamanship as practised in steamships. There were several conditions to this. I had to faithfully serve my masters, keep their secrets, not damage their property, not to embezzle, not to absent myself nor frequent taverns, alehouses or houses of ill repute.

As Alan noted, his wages were too low to indulge in such luxuries.

Apprentices had one final port of call before they joined their ships as many shipping companies had strict dress etiquette. They were sent to an approved outfitters, which provided them with everything they needed. One sailor recalled entering a shop as a sixteen year old and being kitted out in an astonishing array of clothing that he took onboard in a large travelling trunk. First came a formal blue doeskin uniform, which looked incredibly smart until he moved or attempted to do any work, then it creased beyond belief. For formal occasions in winter he received a greatcoat complete with shining brass buttons. For winter work, there was a duffle coat and 'whites' for use in the tropics. His tropical kit even included a 'solar topee'. As he later recalled, most of these items remained unworn throughout his wartime service. As the most junior member of the crew, he spent most of his service in overalls.

First-time sailors had to settle into a life that was different from anything they had previously known. Yes, those who had been on training ships knew all about the cramped conditions on a sea-going vessel, but they were still unprepared for the combination of this with having nowhere to go and nothing to see except sky and open waters.

For all the dangers and privations, life onboard a merchant ship was a fantastic experience for the boys. They were thrown into a world of men the like of which most had never met before. The crewmen were from all over the world: Lascars, Chinese, West Africans, West Indians and Norwegians were all common on British ships. Some boys sailed on foreign ships, which were working from British ports after the Germans had occupied the ship's home ports. Many boys found working on them a difficult experience as the men were often withdrawn. Unable to return home, and in enforced separation from their loved ones, they were prone to depression and bouts of melancholy.

Seamen who had already travelled the world were used to exotic tastes unknown to teenagers, like Christian Immelman, from the London suburbs: 'That first breakfast had me wondering whether I had made the correct career choice in coming to sea, the main item on the menu being called curry and rice, its main ingredient being reconstituted dried salt fish.' The curry was not the only exotic commodity onboard. Many of the ship's crew were Chinese and he discovered they had unexpected tastes: 'I had to pass through their accommodation to get to the steam pump: I still remember the smell of opium some of the older seamen used.' Glasgow-born Bert Taylor had a similar experience when he joined his first ship: 'There was a South African in our cabin who smoked hashish – I didn't even know what it was – I just thought it was a funny smell. This guy was always away with it.'

Whoever they served with, the boys spent many long hours listening to tales of the sea, especially those told by the men who had been at sea in the days of sailing ships. Bernard Ashton listened in awe to the stories of an ageing Norwegian seaman who recounted the tale of how he had once got drunk and woke up at sea to discover he had been shanghaied on to a four-mast sailing ship. The same Norwegian pointed out the blue-eyed, black-skinned children in West Indian ports, describing them as 'Norwegian Fucks'.

Despite the differences in expectations, once aboard, the apprentices shared much the same experiences as other crew. Though the cadets and apprentices were there to learn a trade, with the aim of becoming an officer, there was plenty of hard work to be done along the way. Before they could advance, they had to sweat with the rest of the crew and 'learn the ropes'. If they had expected to be swanning around in a navy blue jacket and white silk scarf, they had a shock coming. Christian Immelman, joining his first ship aged fifteen, described how he and the other apprentices, 'lived as officers but worked mainly with the crew'. As Alan Shard recalled of joining his first ship:

> We introduced ourselves to the chief mate and were told to get into working gear and report to the bosun. From then on it was all downhill and for the next two years I never saw the workings of the bridge. Uniform was only worn ashore to differentiate yourself from a conscientious objector and prevent getting abuse from passers-by.

For seventeen-year-old Norval Young, his arrival as an apprentice on a fuel tanker, the MV *Athelvictor*, was similarly inauspicious:

> I'd got my uniform and thought I was a smart little boy. The mate says, 'Get your shoes off and scrub the alleyways!' So I had to get my boiler suit out and get changed. I thought it was going to be glamorous. I thought I'd be on deck with a telescope. I was only ever in the wheelhouse to scrub the floor and polish the brass.

It was not long before he received another shock when the mate heard the noise his boots were making:

> My father had made me put a lot of metal segs [studs] in the soles so that they would last a long time. He went frantic and told me not to take even one more step. I was ordered to remove my boots and when he saw them asked me if I was trying to blow the ship up? I immediately proceeded to the chippy's shop where I was told to remove every seg. One spark would have been enough to blow us to kingdom come, as they were 'gas freeing'.

He later admitted that his youth meant such incidents did not worry him as much as they should have:

> It was always an excitement for me. I got a bit more sense later on. Young boys aren't aware of how dangerous it is. If a spark had got us, the whole ship would have blown up. But you are there for an adventure. I never thought anything was going to happen to us. I thought it was a big joke.

Another teenage seaman serving on a tanker also realized the dangers of a gas-filled tanker:

> We had been carrying high-octane aviation fuel for the RAF. I had to go down the gas-filled tanks to clean them, knowing that we could be bombed at any time! What's the difference, if we were torpedoed in that state we would just explode, so it didn't matter if you were in the fuel tanks or in your accommodation: you're still going to die!

However, he found there was a good side to the experience: 'You'd go down into the hold and there'd be gas down there – it was better than taking drugs, you'd be light headed. When we came up, the mate gave us a bottle of rum: it helped clear your system.'

The first few days at sea were a shock to all new boys. Many were without the months of training that characterized service in the Army, Royal Navy or RAF, or the careful training for sea as taught in sea schools. Instead they had to learn everything from scratch. One galley boy found himself unable to light the stove to prepare breakfast for the ship's crew. As he struggled to get a fire going, he was approached by two old hands who made him an offer: they would come up from the engine room to light his fire if he would find them some extra food. It was a deal. At 5 a.m. each morning they came to the galley with a shovel full of hot cinders. Both parties were satisfied: the stokers got their extra food and the galley boy got a few extra minutes in his bunk.

Joining his first ship, the *Rochester Castle*, in January 1940, Bernard Ashton soon adapted to life at sea. In his final weeks at sea school he had been one of the senior boys; days later he was the most junior member of a ship's crew working under the watchful eye of the bosun:

> At quarter to seven in the morning I collected dry stores for the breakfast. I had to have the coffee ready for the crew. I learned to make coffee by putting the grounds in and boiling them. Then I threw cold water on top and that made the grounds fall to the bottom of the pot. I could make a tin of milk last for ten days.

His days were spent making coffee and tea for the watches as they changed, washing down the showers, cleaning the toilets and scrubbing the alleyways. He was introduced to eating curries and rice, foods that were not exactly common in the Kent mining communities. He was also learning to look after himself, not letting the older men take advantage of his inexperience. As the product of a socialist miner's household, Bernard could hold his own in discussions on politics and risked fights with sailors who made excessive demands for food. Although able to stand up for himself, he was still a boy and, following gun drill, he was only allowed a bottle of shandy when the other sailors received a tot of rum.

Like most boys he was watched over by the captain, who was concerned with his welfare: 'The "Old Man" was like God.' Each Sunday, Bernard had to parade before the captain, who inspected his hands and feet to make sure he was looking after himself. And he watched in amazement as the captain ran white-gloved hands over the tops of cupboards to check for dust: it was something he had seen at the training school, but had never expected to see it at sea. Mindful of the temptations of a port, whenever the *Rochester Castle* docked, the captain forbade him from going ashore unless he had a suitable chaperone.

There was little room for privacy onboard ships and the boys had to get used to the sights, sounds and smells of living in crowded conditions. With washing often limited to stripping off and using a bucket of water, there was no time for modesty. For fourteen-year-old Tony Springings, life was basic and sometimes unpleasant. If he wanted a wash, he took a bucket of cold water and heated it with steam. The bucket was wedged into the rim of the toilet seat, allowing him to strip off and wash. Three apprentices shared a cabin, sleeping in bunks. There was no running water, just a washbasin with a bucket underneath to catch the water. One night, someone was sick into the basin. Rather than emptying the sink and washing it down, he left the vomit. Later that night, the senior apprentice rose for his shift on watch. Seeing that the basin was full, he reached in and bathed his face in vomit. He went mad, shouting for Tony and blaming him for what had happened. As he later recalled, that was the way of life at sea: Tony was the most junior, so he took the blame and had to clean up someone else's mess.

Like all first-timers, Tony found himself given the most menial tasks. Long hours were spent on watch; the rest of his time was spent polishing brass, painting and sweeping up. Whilst undertaking a twenty-one-day journey from Liverpool to Port Said, he made a serious error that might have undermined his career as a potential officer:

> I was in charge of sweeping up the wheelhouse and chartroom. Swinging in front of me was a barometer. Only a young fool would have done what I did. At the bottom was a screw-cap. So I turned it and thirty-two inches of mercury poured out on to the chartroom floor. I nearly died of fright. I tried to get it back in with a dustpan and brush, but it was useless. I thought this was the end of my career. The captain went mad and screamed at me and chased me out of the chartroom.

For most boys, there were far greater concerns than the wrath of an irate captain. Life at sea in wartime offered a swift, and often vicious, introduction to the horrors of modern warfare. One seventeen year old joined his first ship in June 1940 and his first voyage took him through the English Channel. Passing through the Dover Straits he was shocked to see corpses floating in the water, victims of the desperate evacuation of the British Expeditionary Force from Dunkirk. As Raymond Hopkins recalled of going to sea after just two weeks at a training school: 'We were on the front line as soon as we left port.'

Throughout the war, the U-boat menace was ever-present and there was always the danger of the sudden, unheralded arrival of a torpedo. Setting off on his first voyage, sixteen-year-old Ron Singleton experienced the emotions shared by so many: 'I thought I'd never see home again. Especially when I heard the first depth-charge explode. The escort was dropping them about three miles away but you could feel it. That unnerves you. You know there are U-boats about.' Later on that first trip across the Atlantic he spent his nights on the deck, sheltering beneath a lifeboat: 'I was so frightened, I couldn't sleep. It's difficult, especially if you are a youngster like I was.'

Tony Sprigings, on his first voyage and already unpopular with the ship's captain, found a chance to redeem himself when his ship faced danger. Whilst on lookout, he spotted a mine ahead, caught on a wave coming towards them on the starboard bow. He rushed into the saloon to see the captain as he was eating breakfast. In a moment that seemed straight out of a farce, the captain simply looked up and said, 'Take your hat off when you are in the saloon.' Despite the captain's indifference, he soon arrived on deck to watch the mine. The situation descended further into farce as a gunner on another ship opened fire on the mine. He couldn't depress the guns far enough and sent high-calibre anti-aircraft rounds over the heads of Tony and his captain, piercing the ship's funnel. Calm was restored when one of the Royal Navy escort ships safely detonated the mine. As Tony later recalled, it was the most exciting moment of his life.

Of course, war did not interrupt the normal routines of life at sea.

Instead, it just added to the burden endured by the crews. For much of the time the young sailors were too preoccupied with work to worry about the realities of mines and enemy submarines. 'The war wasn't something constantly on my mind – there was always plenty of work to keep me busy,' recalled Christian Immelman.

> It was work, with the crew on ship maintenance, chipping, scraping and washing paintwork; sewing canvas awnings, splicing ropes and wires, learning to steer. On the bridge, keeping lookout in freezing rain, envying the mate on watch – cosy in the wheelhouse with the doors shut.

As apprentice Alan Shard recalled of his first voyage: 'The first day we hit heavy weather in the Atlantic we were on our hands and knees scraping the poop-deck planks smooth with an iron. Normally this would already have been done by the shipyard, but in wartime they were in a hurry to get the ships out.' Nor was there any time for queasy first-time sailors to be indulged:

> The ship was prancing about like a racehorse and we were feeling the results. Hancock, the other apprentice, threw in the sponge and took to his bunk followed minutes later by an irate bosun. After threatening to make him eat some greasy bacon on a string (a favourite tactic for first trippers feeling seasick), the bosun gave him an hour to get back to work. Strangely enough, on practically every trip I made until I quit, I was slightly seasick for a couple of hours. I tried my first cigarette and immediately got queasy and could not turn up for work. The bosun was irate and gave me a severe bollocking that put me off smoking forever, for which I am truthfully thankful.

One similarly seasick apprentice recalled carrying a bucket around his neck on a rope, ready to collect his vomit. As many found, cleaning up their own mess helped them control their sickness.

Whilst most boys were thrown straight into the 'front line' of the war at sea, fifteen-year-old Arthur Harvey spent his first four months

John Cotter *(left)* and Peter Richards *(right)* on holiday in 1941. Cotter, a would-be fascist, and Richards, a member of the Communist party were unlikely friends.
(Peter Richards)

Peter Richards as a telegram delivery boy. The impact of delivering news to bereaved wives and parents had a significant impact on the sixteen year old.
(Peter Richards)

Eleven-year-old Colin Ryder Richardson *(centre)* and other survivors, in Glasgow, after being rescued following the sinking of the SS *City of Benares*. (Colin Ryder)

By the KING'S Order the name of
Edward Colin Ryder Richardson,
Passenger, s.s. "City of Benares,"
was published in the London Gazette on
7 January, 1941,
as commended for brave conduct in the
Merchant Navy.
I am charged to record His Majesty's
high appreciation of the service rendered.

Winston S. Churchill

Prime Minister and First Lord
of the Treasury

The commendation for 'brave conduct in the Merchant Navy' received by Colin for the courage he displayed whilst in a lifeboat. (Colin Ryder)

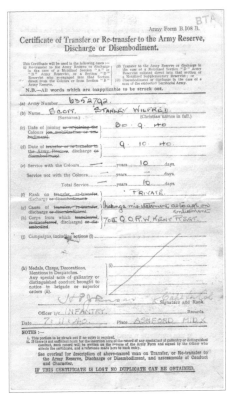

(above left) Ted Roberts not long before he was thrown out of the army a second time for being underage. He first volunteered aged just fourteen. (Ted Roberts)

(above right) The release papers given to fifteen-year-old Stan Scott after his true age was discovered just ten days into his army career. (Stan Scott)

(below) The three stages of a typical teenager's military service: Reg Fraser in the uniforms of the Air Training Corp, Home Guard and Army. (Reg Fraser)

(above left) Albert Riddle *(centre right, behind sailor in foreground)* and other boy sailors acting as look-outs on the Air Defence Platform of HMS *Prince of Wales* in 1941. (Imperial War Museum)

(above right) Riddle in Singapore after, once again, narrowly escaping death when the HMS *Prince of Wales* was sunk in December 1941. (Alfred Riddle)

(below) Boy cadets from the Bernhard Baron Company, 1st Battalion Royal Fusiliers, stand to attention. (Imperial War Museum)

Boy bugler Len
Chester, who
first played at a
funeral aged just
fourteen.
(Len Chester)

Fifteen-year-old
Peter Baxter,
who survived the
sinking of HMS
Barham. 841
other members
of the crew were
not so lucky.
(Len Chester)

(*above left*) John Chinnery in 1943 aged sixteen. He joined the Merchant Navy in 1939 aged twelve and served throughout the war. His traumatic experiences at sea drove him to the brink of suicide. (Daphne Chinnery)

(*above right*) A young merchant seaman making model aeroplanes at the Merchant Navy hostel. He is wearing the lapel badge which indicated that the wearer – though not in uniform – was 'doing his bit' for the war effort. (Imperial War Museum)

(*below*) Cadets at the Thames Nautical Training College, at its wartime home at Foots Cray Place, Kent. They are carrying cadet Matthews, that year's winner of the King's Gold Medal. Matthews was killed at sea later in the year. (Derek Tolfree)

(above left) Seventeen-year-old Leslie McDermott-Brown after two years in Milag Nord, a German internment camp for captured merchant seamen. (Mark McDermott)

(above right) Frank (John) Norman who, aged sixteen, was one of the youngest British Army prisoners of war. (Sylvia Norman)

(below) A cabin boy of the SS *Lustrous* being interviewed by a German naval officer after capture. (Author's collection)

(above left) John Osbourne and his wife Gina on their wedding day. When he asked for permission to marry her, his commanding officer discovered that he had added two years to his age when he first joined the RAF. He also had to tell Gina he was three years younger than she believed him to be; he was just fifteen at the time. (John Osbourne)

(above right) Yvonne and Julienne Vanhandenhoeve, in Antwerp, during the war. The half-British sisters were trapped in Belgium when the ship bringing them home was attacked by German bombers. (Julienne Pulzer)

(below) Sixteen-year-old girls at a London employment office, registering for National Service. All sixteen year olds had to register, in advance of 'call-up', when they reached eighteen. (Imperial War Museum)

on a tanker, refuelling ships in the waters around Portsmouth. One month before his sixteenth birthday he was paid off and joined one of the more glamorous ships in the merchant fleet. In October 1941 he joined the *Highland Princess*, a ship belonging to the Royal Mail line, whose pre-war run had taken passengers between England and Buenos Aires, carrying Argentinian meat on the return journey. Arthur joined the ship as a pantry boy, one of six lads on the ship. On the first morning they reported to the saloon where the steward gave them six buckets, six cloths and six scrubbing brushes so they could scrub the whole of the saloon until the floors and all the furniture were gleaming.

With the ship cleaned and ready for service, nearly 3,000 troops were loaded on, including 500 officers who were housed in cabins. Arthur was shocked to discover that, even in wartime, the officers received the same standards in the dining room as pre-war passengers. Each day they sat down to breakfast, lunch and dinner, sometimes receiving a seven-course meal. While the officers relished their good fortune, the ship's boys were less enamoured with the situation: 'My job was to wash up all the pots and pans. We were down there from seven in the morning till eight at night just washing up.'

The drudgery of kitchen work soon gave Arthur Harvey an incentive to seek alternative employment: 'I soon realized what I wanted to do – and it wasn't kitchen work. So I got to know the bosun. He was a good lad. I went before the first mate and I was able to switch over to the deck crew. That was the start of my career.' The change in employment also meant he moved from the overcrowded boys' cabin, complete with straw mattresses, into a deck with more space to relax. Not that he had much opportunity to relax: working four hours on and four hours off, he never got more than three-and-a-half hours' sleep at a time. There was no time to do anything apart from work, eat and sleep.

Once, returning from South Africa, Arthur was given an unexpected duty:

We took 100 high-ranking German officers – including some generals
– who'd been captured in North Africa. We took them to New York.
They were guarded by sailors from the Royal Navy. There was one
guard on deck with me. I was a seventeen-year-old seaman and I had
four or five of these German officers with buckets. I showed them what
to do and then watched as they scrubbed the decks. That was a good
job.

The experience of war soon changed the boys and, as most later
admitted, it turned them into men. Onboard the *Highland Princess*,
Arthur Harvey found that his duties took him to the most exposed
positions, undertaking tasks that would have been unthinkable a few
months earlier:

She had a permanent lookout post on the mast, halfway up. Further up
was an apple barrel and we had to go up a rope ladder to the top one.
We did two-hour shifts up there, lashed to the mast. There was no
telephone so we had to shout and wave. It was nice in the tropics, but
not so nice in winter. The rolling of the ship didn't bother me, although
I was 80 to 100 feet above the water. You could certainly see a long way.

On one trip to South Africa, Arthur was given an introduction to the
bitter realities of life onboard a troopship. Carrying thousands of
troops, it was almost inevitable there would be a number of casualties
during the journey, with accident or sickness taking their toll on the
passengers. One day, Arthur received a call from the bosun:

The bosun said to me, 'Come on, you've got to learn your trade.' I went
to do my first one. He was an RAF officer who had committed suicide.
It wasn't a very pleasant job, but it had to be done. I had to sew him
into canvas with a few fire-bars to weigh him down.

The youngster helped place the corpse into the canvas sack, then
listened to the bosun's instructions, sewing the sack shut. The officer

was then taken to the deck, covered in a Union Jack and, after a short service, was buried at sea.

However, Arthur's worst job came on his return to the UK from Argentina. Unbeknown to the crew, during the Atlantic crossing the refrigerators had failed:

> We went into Swansea and, when the dockers opened the hatch, they refused to discharge it. So we had to sail out into the Bristol Channel. We were out there for about two days unloading all this rotten meat and throwing it into the water. The stench was unbelievable. We had to go down and open the hatches for them. 1,000 tons of meat went into the water. Afterwards we had to clear up, and scrub down the hold – there was no one else to do it!

Whilst most of the youngsters who signed up for service at sea started at the bottom of the ladder as cabin boys or deck boys, others started at the bottom of the ship. When Raymond Hopkins signed on he gave his age as eighteen, rather than his real age of sixteen. It meant he got a man's wage – with the additional £10 a month 'War Risk Payment', rather than the £5 paid to boys. He was also given a man's work. He started service below the decks. It was a hot and dirty introduction to work: 'I didn't know anything about firing boilers, so I started off feeding coal down a shaft to the stokers. I had to make sure the lumps weren't too big. Then I moved on to the boilers. I was looking after three of them, making sure they were all burning.'

The sixteen-year-old stoker – part of what was known onboard as 'the black gang' because of the coal dust that encrusted them – soon got used to the routine of throwing shovelful after shovelful into the boilers, dripping with sweat but all the time building up his strength:

> It was heavy, dirty, sweaty work but I got stuck into it. On one ship I had four boilers. You'd let one die down, so it could be cleaned out by the man at the start of next shift. I'd go off shift and get a couple of

hours' sleep at a time. You couldn't sleep much. We were a dozen to a room and there were people coming and going all the time. My dad had said, 'You've made your bed . . .' He was right, but I didn't really have time to lie in it.

For those unused to working below decks, the heat was a particular issue, especially in the tropics. When Tony Sprigings arrived in Calcutta at the end of his first trip to sea he was given a depressing task:

We had to paint the coal bunkers, which had been completely emptied on the way across. It was a job for the apprentices and we worked in stinking heat. It was 140°F. We were right in the bowels of the ship. It was hell. I thought, 'It can't get worse. I'll never survive.' They tell you that it's character-building: if you can stand that you can stand anything.

Though the new boys found themselves carrying out all the menial tasks, many also found there were plenty of opportunities to learn. Whilst apprentices expected that they would have to learn all the jobs onboard, others were grateful for the opportunities to increase their knowledge and work towards becoming an ordinary seaman (OS) and then an able-bodied seaman (AB). Sixteen-year-old Bernard Ashton took his first steps towards advancement on his first voyage:

On Sunday afternoons, I had wheel practice with the bosun. I had learned the compass at sea school and knew the basics of steering. So when the 'AB' on the wheel wanted a smoke, I would take over. I soon learned that every ship was different and you had to compensate for the wind as it affected every ship differently. The sides of the ship acted as a sail. Also you learned that how you steered a ship depended on the type of engine it had.

At the end of this first voyage, Bernard was paid off in Liverpool and received his first wage packet: 'I got a big white £5 note – I couldn't believe it, I'd never seen one in my life.' Having successfully survived almost eight months at sea, he was determined to progress. Working on the coastal trade he learned all the necessary skills to become an ordinary seaman. He could work the derricks on deck, loading and unloading cargo. He already knew how to steer a ship, could do deck work and had spent many long hours on lookout. Returning to Liverpool, he decided to leave the *Rochester Castle* and join a ship as an OS. Leaving his suitcase and sea bag at Lime Street station, he went to the shipping office to find work. He found there were large numbers of experienced men all crowding around the grille, behind which sat the representative of the Board of Trade and a ship's captain, all looking for work. As a sixteen year old with just a few months of experience he knew he would need to be confident and stand firm, otherwise he knew he would be returning to sea as the 'Peggy': 'I wasn't afraid of anything.' He pushed his way forward and when the call came for able-bodied seamen he shoved his seaman's book forward, shouting out: 'I'm an AB, I can steer and splice!' Despite Bernard's obvious youth, the captain took his book and told him he would take him as an ordinary seaman. He was then given a rail warrant to go to Hull and an advance on his wages. He had taken his first step forward towards a career at sea.

Going to sea was a shock for all boys, but for some the first trip was the worst they would ever make. Having attended a nautical school in Hull, Alan Simms went to sea as soon as he reached his sixteenth birthday. In March 1942, along with a former classmate, he joined a brand new ship, the *Empire Cowper*. As they set off on their first voyage they had little idea of what awaited them: 'My first trip was my bad one: it was a real baptism of fire. We didn't know we were going into the thick of things.' Joining a convoy that formed up in Iceland, the *Empire Cowper* began the dangerous journey to the Russian port of Murmansk:

We got to Murmansk without really any bother – apart from the ice. The wire rope was about an inch thick, by the morning it was about

three inches thick, with all the ice that formed. But at Murmansk we
were getting bombed every night. A warehouse fifty yards away on
dockside was hit. We were sheltering in the cabin hoping everything
would be all right, whilst stuff was hitting the ship. They knew we were
in the port. It was an experience for us kids.

As both Merchant Navy and Royal Navy crews knew, Arctic
convoys were the most dreaded assignment. If they thought the heat
of the Middle East was unbearable, it was nothing compared to the
freezing conditions in the Arctic seas. Preparing for his very first
convoy, Anthony Longden recalled loading special equipment on
to his ship: duffle coats, scarves, balaclavas, gloves, thick woollen
socks and heavy leather boots. He soon realized they were headed
to the Arctic. Ice formed on every surface, meaning the crews had
to work tirelessly to clear it away: if they left the ice, the weight made
the ship dangerously top-heavy. If they touched exposed steel, their
hands froze to it, and tearing them free would pull off the skin.
Frostbite was an ever-present fear and men discovered their
eyelashes could freeze together when on lookout. They knew to
enter the water meant they had just minutes to live. All these
difficulties were bad enough on calm seas. When storms rose, their
chances of the sea defeating them increased. As ex-*Vindicatrix* boy
Bill Ellis recalled: 'One time we were on a Russian convoy and a
huge wave hit us – sinking four ships in the convoy. The water came
through the wheelhouse a foot high – we were all out of our bunks
and it was freezing but we didn't sink.' On his first trip, Anthony
Longden found an Arctic convoy was an ideal time to grow up: 'I
spent most of 26 December 1943 at action stations, in a full gale, on
the bridge Oerlikon gun. In these northern latitudes, it was only light
for about three hours a day, so it was a memorable seventeenth
birthday.'

Having arrived safely in Murmansk, Alan Simms sheltered from
the German bombing. However, other boys worked through the air
raids. When the SS *New Westminster City* was bombed, three of the

ship's apprentices carried the wounded from the ship, wrapped them up to keep them warm, placed them on 'skids' and pulled them to hospital. They then returned to their ship to help fight the fires.

Whilst it had been exciting – if dangerous – in port, sixteen-year-old Alan soon discovered the journey home would be far worse than the outward trip. Leaving Murmansk in early April, the ship made the return journey with an additional group of seamen onboard: ominously, these were all men who had been rescued when their ships had sunk on the outward journey. These shipwrecked seamen were soon back in the thick of the action: 'Eight o'clock next morning a German plane appeared – a Focke-Wulf Condor – flying round and round just out of gun range.' At midday Alan headed to the galley for lunch and then decided to have an afternoon nap:

> Luckily I didn't get undressed. At about quarter-past-one the alarm sounded and I went on to the deck to see what was happening. There were German aircraft coming in from all over the place. We were lagging behind the convoy, so we were a target. It all happened so suddenly, we had no time to be frightened. In the first attack, three bombs fell astern, doing no harm, but about twenty minutes later, two more planes attacked with machine-guns and bombs. I was standing aft, I didn't hear a bang – I just saw all this muck flying about. The bombs caused the ship to catch fire. Strangely enough, I wasn't frightened, I was excited. As the dust cleared I was looking at one of the aircraft, shouting, 'We got it! We got it!' as it dived down into the sea.

With the ship sinking, the lifeboats were swiftly lowered. In the haste to lower the boats, one tipped up, sending two men into the water, never to be seen again. Alan Simms was lucky to make his way safely off the ship. After an hour they were picked up by a trawler, HMS *Blackheath*, manned by a Royal Navy crew: 'It didn't bother me that we had been sunk. One of the crew took me and my friend and gave us jobs to do, so we were learning again. But we were soon getting attacked again. There were ships still getting sunk around us.' Eventually Alan returned home on three weeks' leave, his first voyage complete and his first ship lost: 'We got home and everybody thought we were heroes. We had our pictures in the local paper. But I'd lost all my clothing and had to go out in my dad's jacket. I was only sixteen and at that age you think it's quite exciting.'

The experience of having a ship sunk from under them – or watching the horrors of men drowning in the seas around them – had a profound effect on most boys. Having survived sinking on his first voyage, Alan Simms moved from Arctic convoys to the Atlantic:

> That's when I started getting nervous. On Atlantic convoys you knew it was going to happen but didn't know when. My heart used to bleed. You could hear ships going up. There were all the ships protecting the tankers in the middle. When one got attacked it was terrible – the sea was a mass of flame. You could hear people shouting and screaming. There was oil and fuel all over the water. They had no chance.

This sense that one's ship had to get hit at some point generated a sense of fatalism among even the most optimistic youngsters. It also served to change their behaviour, meaning they remained unable to relax for days on end, as Alan – who preferred sailing in rough seas because the waves deterred U-boat attacks – recalled:

> One ship I was on had been fitted with ASDIC for detecting submarines. When they got a 'ping' on the machine we didn't dare go to bed, 'cause we knew there were U-boats about. We took those 'Purple Heart' pills and we'd be awake all night. But we tried to keep life going normally – getting attacked was just a part of life.

Despite this acceptance that U-boat attacks on convoys were inevitable, it was always a shock when it happened: 'One night I went to have a wee overboard and was looking out at the next ship immediately to one side. All of a sudden, bang: she was hit. Her bow came up and she sank in about five minutes.' At the time Alan thought little of what had happened, it was only later he was struck by a sobering thought: 'I realized if that ship hadn't been in position, that torpedo would have hit us.'

Similarly, Arthur Harvey recalled how all seamen needed good fortune if they hoped to survive: 'We didn't have time to think about the dangers. I saw tankers get hit and the ruddy sea caught fire! It's not very pleasant but at least it was in the distance, you can just see the lads jumping over the side. I was lucky – it was just the luck of the draw.' The mental turmoil of life at sea in wartime put pressure on all crew members – regardless of age. As Tony Sprigings remembered, on his first voyage the fresh food soon ran out, leaving them eating hard-tack biscuits. He recalled looking into the huge ice-box that had carried their rations as they left Liverpool. After twenty-one days there were just a few soggy lettuce leaves and some sorry-looking tomatoes floating in the tepid water: 'I thought, "What have I let myself in for?" It was horrifying.' However, for some onboard, the pressure became too much:

> As the voyage progressed the temperatures went up and up. I went on watch one night, and as I headed towards the bridge I heard a blood-curdling howl coming from the boiler room. This Indian ran up and jumped over the side. He was one of the firemen. I shouted out that a man had gone over the side, but they said that we would never find him. So we didn't stop, we didn't go back. We couldn't – we were in convoy. It was the heat. There was no relief for the men working down below, it was unbelievably hot. They were shovelling 77 tons of coal into the boilers each day to keep the engines going. Seeing that happen makes a real impression on you at that age.

However, he was able to put the experience into context: 'It was just another person dying. We'd come from the UK where people were dying every day.'

Though Britain's merchant fleet sailed the world, defied the enemy and saved the nation from starvation, there was one element of the sailors' lives that could not be erased from the minds of many people on shore: homosexuality. The endurance of long weeks at sea meant sailors had long faced a reputation for homosexual behaviour, regardless of whether the reputation was deserved. For most, it was a subject that was hardly ever spoken about. Some received timely warnings when joining a ship. Twelve-year-old John Chinnery, who had joined his first ship just before the outbreak of war was lucky to be warned about the dangers a boy could face onboard a merchant ship. He was lucky to be treated like a son by his first captain, whilst the bosun offered him some good advice: 'Johnny, you've got nice legs. Just be careful of so-and-so and so-and-so. Keep clear of them.' As John later noted: 'The homosexuals sorted themselves out, they knew "who was there just for the ride".'

For teenage apprentice Alan Shard, his encounter with a crewmate's penis was a comical, rather than threatening, moment which occurred as he stood on deck with his hands behind his back:

> Suddenly to my complete and utter surprise an engineer came up from behind and placed his private member into my hand, hoping no doubt to get a good laugh out of the audience, but I turned the tables in a flash, kept a grip and towed him along the deck with the crowd laughing at him. He ran in step screaming blue murder. It reminded me of the tiger's tail. How was I going to get free without being thumped? As I neared the mast-house I let go and ran swiftly to the ladder with him in hot pursuit. Without much thought, I shinned up the vertical ladder aft the mainmast, praying to God he would not follow me. Discretion proved to be the better part of valour and he did not. When his temper cooled he realized his foolishness and nothing further was said.

In the fury of war, the boys did not only crew the ships: they saved them. They manned lookouts, sent vital signals, fought fires and manned anti-aircraft guns. Christian Immelman was on the bridge of the *Dolabella* when she came under air attack. Crewing a fully loaded tanker, he knew he had to do all he could to protect the ship:

> This fighter-bomber was coming directly towards us. I ran to the Lewis gun, but the third mate beat me to it. The 12-pounder aft was fully manned, so I grabbed the only weapon left, a .303 rifle. I went to the open deck above the wheelhouse. The main thought in my mind at the time was not fear but just being able to get something with which to shoot back. The plane was coming directly for us across the convoy at mast height, all the ships in its path shooting at it. The plane was close enough to see the pilot. It was above the ship in the next column when it suddenly veered left, gained height and flew off.

They were lucky: their combined fire had driven off the enemy bomber.

Ex-*Vindicatrix* boy Bill Ellis found himself manning a 12-pound gun in the middle of the Atlantic: 'Suddenly the ship in front stopped and there was an explosion – hit by torpedoes. You couldn't stop to help, you had to keep on going. I looked to see if the other ships were there – when a submarine suddenly came up out of the water.' It was time to put his limited gunnery training into practice:

> I was on the gun and there were two blokes who had to line it up – but they weren't sure of the charges. They used a huge charge and it went in the general direction but from where we were we couldn't tell if the shell had gone miles beyond the submarine. Everyone else in the convoy opened fire on the submarine but it dived.

That night another ship was lost: the next day another. Then one of the escort ships was sunk as it picked up survivors. Bill's ship made its way safely home. Reaching port they saw large numbers of Royal Navy destroyers and corvettes. As they entered port, Bill shouted at the ship's crews: 'What are you doing here? You ought to be out there!'

Of the 6,500 awards for gallantry awarded to the Merchant Navy, many were given to boys who had demonstrated a heroism that belied their years. In November 1940, the SS *Windsor Castle* was attacked by a German bomber, four 100-lb bombs hit the ship, smashing the propeller shaft and rendering the ship helpless. However, one of the bombs did not explode. With the unexploded bomb threatening the ship, two of the crew rushed forward to help: the laundry boys John Wiggins and Andrew McLellan. The two boys helped pack the bomb with sandbags to minimize any blast. They then showed great courage in rushing to fight fires. Both boys received commendations for their bravery.

October 1941 saw the torpedoing of a Dutch ship, MV *Tuva*, one of the many merchantmen from occupied Europe that operated from British ports. Ronald Cyril Green – a mess room boy from Dagenham in Essex – was commended for his bravery after a torpedo struck. The explosion trapped three men and Ronald risked his life to rescue two of them. He was attempting to free the third when he was forced to abandon ship, only just escaping before the ship went under. Though the third man was lost, Ronald's courage had saved two lives.

'Galley boy' was certainly not the most glamorous title to hold on active service. However, such a title did not minimize the heroism of the boys who carried it. One who received a commendation for his bravery was Galley Boy Leonard James Dumbridge of the SS *Yewcrest*. In August 1940 the ship's steering mechanism broke, forcing the captain to drop out of convoy. Alone on the seas, the *Yewcrest* was confronted by a submarine which proceeded to shell it. Whilst under fire, Leonard showed great courage in fetching ammunition for the ship's guns to return fire. Eventually they were forced to abandon ship and the crew escaped in lifeboats. Following a convoy to Russia in mid-1942, Galley Boy John Conroy from Edinburgh, serving on the SS *Zaafaren*, received the British Empire Medal. The ship was sunk during an enemy attack, yet John remained cool and courageous throughout the incident.

In July 1941, sixteen-year-old Harry Cromack of Hull was serving as a deck boy on SS *Dallington Court*. He received a commendation for bravery following an aerial attack on the convoy. Harry manned the Lewis gun, a weapon he had never been trained on, and managed to hit the attacking aircraft. The plane crashed into the sea as a result of the combined fire from a number of ships. Another brave deck boy was Gordon Hissey, serving aboard the SS *Elisabeth Massey*. He was commended for brave conduct in February 1942 after helping to rescue the crew of an American ship, the *Pan Massachusetts*, which had been spotted in flames in US waters. Gordon was part of the crew of the *Massey*'s rescue boat that searched the increasingly rough seas for the American crew. He was responsible for saving the life of one exhausted American who was unable to reach the ship's ladder.

Whilst some of the boys were recognized for their courage, the heroism of many others went unrewarded. In October 1941 the *San Florentino* was attacked by a German U-boat, *U-94*. Hit by four torpedoes, the ship remained afloat and fought a five-hour duel against the submarine in heavy seas. Eventually a second U-boat joined in and the *San Florentino* was abandoned. An official report on the incident noted: 'After merciless assault, the tanker sank. But she had left her mark on the foe, and the spirit of her people never wavered.'[2]

Among her crew was seventeen-year-old Tommy Burt of Glasgow. Whilst a number of the crew received awards for their actions, Tommy's contribution was not recognized. A crewmate complained that this was unfair, writing to the Admiralty to press for recognition of the boy. He pointed out that the rest of the crew had called Tommy 'a Nelson' for his defiance. When the tanker went down, the seventeen year old escaped in a half-submerged lifeboat and was 'the hero of the swamped lifeboat'. He remained standing all night, calling instructions to his crewmates, 'Steady to starboard, steady to port', as necessary. At the end of the long night he said, 'I done my best for you, boys. Oh, boys, I done my best to cheer you.' Then he smiled and fell down dead, one of twenty-two fatalities. His fellow seamen felt he had saved them.[3]

This was the violent reality of the war at sea. With most merchant ships carrying at least one boy, more than 500 under-sixteens became casualties of war. They were too young to vote, too young to volunteer for the Army, too young to marry or buy a beer: but they were old enough to die. Of the ex-boys of the Prince of Wales Sea Training Hostel who served during the Second World War, eighty-five died. Among these were fourteen boys still under the age of eighteen. There was one very sad side to the enthusiasm shown by some of the youngsters who went to sea. Some underage boys gave false names when they signed on, having run away to sea without the knowledge of their parents. When the SS *Coracero* was lost in 1943 eighteen-year-old 'J. J. Elder' was lost with her. Back in England no trace could be found of his next of kin. When his parents were finally traced it was discovered he was actually a fourteen-year-old boy named Robert Yates whose parents had no idea he had gone to sea.

Having a ship sunk from under them became a routine part of life for most of the boys who served in wartime. Just nine months into his career as a seaman, and on his first voyage as an ordinary seaman, sixteen-year old Bernard Ashton was sunk for the first time. His first ship had been newly built, with clean cabins for the crew. His next ship was less comfortable: 'To reach my sleeping quarters I went through the fo'c'sle head, to the chain locker. And my bunk was next to the hawsepipe, where the anchor went out.'

As he soon realized: 'I had been spoiled on the *Rochester Castle*. I didn't know what was going to come later.'

Within days of leaving Hull, Bernard found himself on lookout, standing forward of the winch:

> I heard the noise of an aircraft. I looked back to the bridge. In the moonlight I could see everything, and everyone on the bridge was

looking around. The next moment I felt strange, the hairs on the back of my neck stood up. I turned and, nearly on top of us, coming down, was a twin-engine bomber. It had a blue light in the cockpit and I could see the two men inside. And then I saw a bomb falling. It hit amidships. I hit the deck as the explosion went off. Within minutes it was ablaze. The men came running out.

Most of the crew got away on a lifeboat that had been quickly lowered. However, the blaze meant Bernard could not reach it.

He found himself alongside two able seamen and the bosun:

On the rigging was a life raft held in place by a bar and two rope strops. I had my sea-going knife but I couldn't cut the ropes. So we had to chop it away with the fire axe. We got the raft into the water, climbed over and stood at the rail. It was pitch black. The bosun shouted, 'Jump!' and jumped into the water. But one of the ABs put his arm across me.

Rather than jumping, his companion suggested running along the deck, climbing down the ladder and waiting for the lifeboat to come alongside. He was right, it was much safer – and warmer – than jumping into the Atlantic.

Within half an hour the crew were picked up by a rescue boat and sent below decks to rest after their traumatic experience. Bernard happily climbed into the top bunk and went to sleep. The next morning he realized the rest of the crew were less able to forget their experience. He had enjoyed six hours' sleep, the rest of the crew had sat up all night drinking and smoking, trying to relax. He soon realized it was his youth that allowed him to treat the incident so lightly. For him, it was just another step on the way to becoming a professional seaman: 'I'd been shipwrecked, I was now like one of the old hands.' Others were not so happy about his adventures. He arrived back at his parents' home wearing a new suit, hat, shoes and a white raincoat, courtesy of a charity for distressed seamen. He looked far different from the boy that had gone off to sea. When he told them of his experiences, they were incredulous and could not imagine their little boy acting as lookout in mid-Atlantic.

Even before reaching his fourteenth birthday, John Chinnery was torpedoed. Though the crew had been warned that, in the event of hearing the order to abandon ship, it was 'every man for himself', John's crewmates ignored the orders. Instead, they rushed to find the boy, throwing him over into the lifeboat where he found himself in nothing but the pair of underpants, wrapped in a blanket and clutching a packet of Woodbines. After being rescued, John was returned to Glasgow. He arrived in the port dressed in just a mackintosh and the pair of underpants. He had no documents or proof of identity. He was quizzed by Military Police who couldn't understand why a virtually naked thirteen year old was in the port asking for a travel warrant to return home to Edinburgh.

It was not John Chinnery's last experience of scurrying for a lifeboat. In a later sinking, he was again helped by older men who made sure he was safe before they themselves jumped to safety. In one case, the youngster was onboard a fuel tanker that was hit and soon engulfed in flames. He later admitted it was an experience that had always stayed with him, giving him a fear of fire that lasted all his life.

There were other boys of John's age who suffered at sea. Fourteen-year-old James Campbell was serving on an Arctic convoy when his ship, the SS *Induna*, was sunk. He and another boy spent five days in an open lifeboat before being rescued by the Russians and taken to hospital in Murmansk. There, his right leg, left foot and left fingers were amputated as a result of frostbite.[4] Another boy from the ship, sixteen-year-old James Anderson, is buried in the military cemetery in Murmansk.

Though all the deaths were tragic, none were more dreadful than those of the fourteen year olds who died whilst serving at sea.[5] Whilst thousands of their age group had been evacuated to safety, these boys paid the ultimate prize for the sense of adventure that had taken them into the front line. For many years, it was believed that the youngest of all casualties was fourteen-year-old Raymond Steed. Born in Newport, south Wales, in October 1929, he joined the Merchant Navy in December 1942. In April 1943 his ship, the *Empire Morn*, struck a mine off the coast of Morocco. Raymond and twenty other crew members died, their bodies taken ashore and buried at Ben M'Sik military cemetery outside Casablanca. He was just 14 years and 207 days old when he died.

It was later discovered that another boy had the dubious honour of being the youngest casualty. He was Dewsbury-born Reginald Earnshaw, just 14 years and 152 days old when he died. He was below decks in his cabin on the SS *North Devon* when she came under attack by German aircraft in coastal waters between Edinburgh and the River Tyne. As the engine room burned, the flames reached Reginald's cabin, trapping him despite rescue efforts. His body, along with the other six seamen who died that night, was taken to Edinburgh and buried in an unmarked grave. It was not until 2009 that he finally received a headstone and recognition of his status as the youngest casualty of the war at sea.

There were tragedies that had an impact on close communities. In December 1941 four former classmates from Walton, Merseyside – John Barret, sixteen; Freddy Hall, seventeen; Patrick Gallagher, sixteen; and Tommy Kavanagh, fifteen – died when their ship, Blue Star Line's *Almeda Star*, was lost en route to Argentina. Even greater tragedy had only been avoided when Tommy Kavanagh's thirteen-year-old brother Jimmy had been prevented from going by their father who decided he was too young.[6] Another terrible tragedy was the sinking of SS *Fiscus* in October 1940. Onboard were two brothers, Raymond Lewis, aged fifteen, and his fourteen-year-old brother, Kenneth. They were thought to have forged a letter stating that their father had given them permission to go to sea.

Whilst enemy aircraft and submarines were a constant threat to all wartime seamen, they also faced another enemy: the weather. The great irony was that heavy seas deterred enemy submarines, but they put all shipping at risk. Whilst those on modern, well-maintained ships were relatively safe, those manning old 'rust buckets' were in constant danger. Having been spoiled on his first ship, and bombed off his second, Bernard Ashton joined the *City of Oxford.* She was an old tramp steamer, hardly fit for the sea. In November 1940, the *City of Oxford* sailed from Liverpool. Within twenty-four hours of leaving port, they hit a gale. At four in the morning, he came off watch. There was no hot food or drinks available since the galley had closed due to the rolling of the ship. He made his way to his bunk only to find the whole ship shaking. Trying to sleep, he heard the steering chains above him rattling and he braced himself so that he wasn't thrown out. He soon realized there was little chance of sleep:

> They called, 'All hands on deck.' The starboard lifeboat was hanging in two pieces. As the sea increased we had to go on the boat deck and swing the other boat back in to secure it. As we worked, the sea was breaking over the front of the bridge. There were concrete plates from the front of the bridge being washed off.

The captain realized they were being blown off course and had the deck crew try to take soundings. It was an impossible task. Though tied on, the crew felt they could not survive. Water was running over the decks, the power of the sea tearing off boards and hurling them towards the crew. Bernard found this more frightening than enemy bombers or submarines: 'I was looking out at the front of the ship and the waves were like mountains. I was new to this. I've never been so frightened in my life. This was more frightening than a torpedo. All of a sudden there was a terrific bang as a wave hit us.' It seemed they could not withstand much more: 'All of a sudden she gave a lurch. We were carrying machinery for export. This shifted and the ship gave a 27-degree list.' To Bernard it seemed like the next wave would surely sink her. Then a miracle happened: the storm began to subside. Listing dangerously, and hardly able to fire the boilers, the ship limped back to port.

After more than two years at sea, Christian Immelman finally experienced the one thing all wartime merchant seaman knew that fate had in store for them:

> After the day's work chipping, scraping and painting I was in the toilet in my underwear when there was this massive double explosion. I went to look out over the main deck but couldn't see anything but a cloud of smoke. I thought I wouldn't be able to do much in underwear and barefoot so returned to my cabin to put on slacks, cap, jacket and a pair of shoes.

Back out on the boat deck, the smoke had cleared enough to let him see that his ship was listing heavily to port:

> The submarine surfaced out on the starboard bow. Captain Cuthill said, 'Some of you get into this boat and get it away.' I got in with a good proportion of the deck crew. Because of the list we had a job getting it down, having to lever it away from the ship's side all the way. When we hit the water I took the tiller. We pushed off, pulled clear of the ship, then rested awaiting developments.

He watched as the submarine's crew opened fire on the stricken tanker, its shells hitting the hull near the engine room. The *Darina* finally slid beneath the surface, stern first. And so the crew of the *Darina* were left in the open waters. Christian found himself in a boat under the command of the third mate, who took charge of rationing the supplies:

> We attempted to keep the boats together but a breeze came up, it got a little choppy so we separated to keep the boats from being damaged. We had to do a bit of bailing during the night. Daylight next morning there was no sign of the other boats. We stepped the mast, hoisted the sail and set course for the USA, about 600 miles to the west. Later that morning we saw a ship in the far distance, a tanker. We tried to catch

their attention, waving shirts, flashing with a signalling mirror, to no avail. Our boat had a good supply of food, hard biscuits, chocolate, barley sugar, malted milk tablets, water and pemmican. The sea was a little rough for two days then the wind eased and it calmed down, nice sunny days but cold at night.

After six days in an open boat, salvation came in the form of a Norwegian ship, the *Dagrun*, heading from Cape Town to New York: 'The Norwegians were a great crowd. They had to put up with us for twenty-eight days, they fed us mainly on ship's bread and canned fish balls and there was always a big urn of good coffee to be had on the galley stove.'

In March 1942 Bernard Ashton and his seventeen-year-old friend Peter Pickett joined a tanker sailing for Texas. He was at the wheel as the ship zigzagged to avoid submarines: 'Crash! A torpedo had hit us. All the glass on the bridge smashed. My life flashed before my eyes.' The captain immediately arrived on the bridge, asking, 'Everything all right?' Bernard told him they were steady on course. The captain then called the engine room and told the 'chief' he was going to make a dash for it. As the captain gave the order 'Full speed ahead' the crew heard a shout, 'Boat away!' The starboard lifeboat had been lowered by the first mate. Although the mate had defied orders, Bernard was convinced he was right: 'We couldn't have got away. The ship would have broken in two.'

Despite the dangers, it seemed to Bernard that the entire crew remained calm. The engines stopped and the ship went deadly silent. The only sound was that of the blocks as they launched the lifeboats. It took twenty minutes to get the boats ready, with the crew loading extra supplies, in excess of the emergency provisions already stored onboard. Then the peace was broken by another shout of 'Boat away!' Bernard watched as the chaps on the decks seemed unhurried: they didn't rush to the boats. Instead they just walked along the deck. As the boats moved away, with Bernard safely onboard, he heard a dull thud as the bulkheads gave way and the tanker began to sink. Next came a bang and a puff of smoke and she slid beneath the surface. Since he was dressed in just soft boots, football shorts, and a vest, he was given a one-piece rubber survival suit to protect him against the cold of the night. As he sat in the lifeboat, Bernard listened to the captain's hushed conversations. The fifteen-year-old cabin boy had been lowered into their boat with an injured ankle, caused by the explosion. The captain was talking about knives and was considering amputating the boy's foot if they were not rescued before infection set in.

With the ship still 1,000 miles from the West Indies, it was decided that the three boats would separate but stick to a predetermined course. By their reckoning, if one boat was rescued, it would be able to estimate a position for the others. At first light after the sinking, the sails were raised and they began the long, slow journey towards the West Indies. Once again, Bernard was not unduly concerned. He took his turn on the tiller, was warm in his survival suit, and felt they were making good speed. He was confident in the captain's ability to keep on course. Even when he spotted a ship which seemed to notice them, then turned away, he was not downhearted. The next day, an aeroplane appeared above, but did not approach.

Salvation came on the third day. They were spotted by an American merchant ship, the MV *Idaho*. Bernard was shocked as he climbed aboard: after just three days in a lifeboat, he felt weak and his legs were wobbling. The incredible sense of relief was heightened when he realized how good living conditions were on the *Idaho*: there were even water fountains on the walkways and he could get iced water in the galley. Like most teenage boys, his first thought was, 'I wonder what they've got to eat?' The captain's plan for separating the lifeboats had worked and within two hours they had picked up the others. The following evening, they landed in Puerto Rico.

Having survived a number of voyages without incident, seventeen-year-old Edward Ford found himself on a Dutch merchant

ship, the *Alchiba*, when it was sunk by a Japanese submarine 600
miles off the coast of Mozambique. With two lifeboats destroyed, the
survivors escaped in tightly packed boats. Their chances of survival
were not great:

> food and water were in short supply as the boat had more people than
> was catered for and we had no idea how long it would take us to reach
> land with the wind so light. Rations were quarter of a cup of water, a
> slice of corned beef and one biscuit twice a day. The days were hot and
> the nights cold. We were all in shorts with only a shirt on top. The
> morning of the second day dawned with no sight of the other boat,
> progress was very slow with just the fin of a shark following the boat
> from time to time.

After four days, they were rescued by another Dutch ship, landed at
Beira in Portuguese East Africa and sent by train to Cape Town.

One year later, Edward Ford was torpedoed for a second time,
this time on the SS *Alderamin*, as part of a convoy homebound from
New York. He was one of seventeen who were able to escape on a
life raft, which was soon discovered to be leaking: 'We drifted
against an empty life raft which we managed to get hold of. The
twelve of us that were able got on to the raft so we were able to sit
with our legs out of the water, the five that were left in the boat were
believed to be dead.' The following morning they were taken
onboard a rescue ship. As Edward later recalled, he doubted
whether the twelve remaining men could have survived another
hour on the raft. When they landed in Glasgow, Edward was given
a rail warrant and a piece of paper reading 'Mr Ford states that he
is a British subject and is permitted to land in the UK' to show to
waiting immigration officers. The next time he returned to the
shipping office the staff laughed and said they did not want to give
him another ship since his last two had been sunk.

After four weeks in Puerto Rico and two weeks in New York,
Bernard Ashton found work on a Dutch-registered ship. The captain

was due to sail to the Pacific and needed a crew since many of his Chinese crew had jumped ship in New York. Eager to get home by any route, he accepted a $35 advance on his wages and purchased new kit – jeans, overalls, oilskins, boots – ready to resume work. Sailing from Hoboken, New Jersey, the ship made its way south along the East Coast of the United States.

On 3 May 1942, they had reached Florida, as had a German submarine, *U-109*. Bernard was just about to come off watch: 'I was in the galley. Bang! A torpedo hit beneath where I was. The stove lifted off the floor and I nearly shit myself. I opened the door, stepped out. By the time I got to the boat deck, they were all in the boats.' Eager not to be left behind, he rushed for the lifeboats. However, he soon realized he was not alone:

> I saw a hand come up the ladder from below, I heard a yell and this bloke – an Australian – fell back down the ladder. So me and this other man went down and found him unconscious. You could feel the ship beginning to go down. So we had to carry him up to the deck. By the time we got there the lifeboat had drifted away from the ship's side. We'd just got there, when there was this almighty bash. Another torpedo had struck on the port side. The smell and the heat of the flames was terrible. It all happened so fast. I didn't know what happened to the chap we were carrying. We looked at each other, climbed on to the bulwarks and jumped. We swam like mad for the lifeboat. I got to the boat and who was there? It was the Australian we'd been carrying. I don't know how he got there before me!

The man he had rescued just minutes earlier returned the favour, pulling Bernard into the lifeboat.

As he sat in a lifeboat – for the second time in less than two months – Bernard Ashton looked back on his experiences at sea. He had been lucky: yes, it was his third time being sunk by enemy action, but it was only his first time in the water. He also thought of everything he had bought for himself in America: his new suit, his hats and shoes, which he had been looking forward to wearing to impress the girls back in England – they were all gone. At least he was fortunate to be just one mile from the shore. They rowed the lifeboats to the beach. As the 'distressed seamen' walked up the beach, they noticed local people – who had been disturbed by the sound of the explosions – filming them with cine cameras.

Whilst the Merchant Navy was best known for its efforts to transport goods and men around the world, its role went far deeper. The seamen also crewed hospital ships, ferrying wounded soldiers from land to sea, to be treated in floating hospitals. When the Allied armies landed in Sicily and Italy in 1943, the hospital ships provided a lifeline for wounded soldiers. Ex-*Vindicatrix* boy Bill Ellis served on HS (Hospital Ship) *Leinster*, ferrying the wounded by landing craft. His time on the *Leinster* exposed him to the full horrors of war:

> Running wounded back to the ship was pretty nasty. The worst wounded person I saw was someone who'd stepped on a mine – and it had taken his face off and his eyes were blown out. Fortunately, he didn't know what had hit him – he just lay there with a tube for breathing. He was dead the next day. The orderlies could be pretty wicked – one time they told me to come and have a look at this injured bloke. I followed him into this cabin – and there was an injured bloke head-to-foot in bandages like a mummy. He'd been hit by a flamethrower – he didn't last long.

He witnessed burns victims with huge blisters on their skin. He saw every imaginable injury: men with bullet wounds, amputees, men with crushed limbs. In time he grew used to the scenes and eventually went to watch the ship's surgeons at work: 'I saw him operate on a bloke who had shrapnel in his head – cutting it all out. When I first used to watch it was terrible but I got used to it.' When another hospital ship, the *Newfoundland*, was damaged by German bombers whilst on its way to Italy, Bill was among the landing-craft crews sent to rescue the medical staff, including a group of American nurses.

Following the Anzio landings in early 1944, the *Leinster* again provided hospital facilities. However, as it waited off the coast, the ship became the target for enemy aircraft:

> I was on watch at the time when all of a sudden planes started dropping bombs on us. A fireball came down the side of the ship – and my landing craft was blown apart. Those landing crafts had 100 gallons of petrol on them so it made quite an explosion. I got into one of the boats on the other side of the ship and thought, 'I'm going to get myself off.' It was chaos.

The *Leinster* was not the only hospital ship to be a target for the enemy bombers:

> Just then the *St David* reappeared. It had taken a direct hit and was sinking. We had to go in a landing craft and pick them up. As I was picking them up – I got hold of this bloke in the water and asked him if he spoke German – he said, '*Ja, ja.*' The others told me to let him go – so I did. We only had one boat and there wasn't the space for all of them.

As he rescued some American nurses from the water, pulling them safely on to his landing craft, he noticed that one was familiar. He discovered that the nurse, Ruth Hindman, was someone he had rescued from the sea when the *Newfoundland* had sunk.

The horrors of war had a profound effect on the youngsters. Having experienced being torpedoed in mid-Atlantic and the desperate rush for the lifeboats, John Chinnery found there were moments onboard a ship in the middle of the ocean that made him think clearly about his situation. Standing on deck on watch, he was struck by how alone he seemed. Staring out to sea, with nothing to see but the horizon, made him realize he couldn't be small minded. For him, the sea was like a rite of passage: he had started the war as a twelve-year-old boy and had grown up quickly. He had learned to accept the ways of the men around him, learned to live with their foibles and accepted the role he had chosen. He kept this in mind whenever tempers frayed. He realized how, on long and arduous journeys, a terrible atmosphere could engulf a ship. He watched vicious arguments erupt among men who played games of Monopoly that lasted for days. On one trip, a sailor was lost overboard. It was officially an accident but the teenager feared it was murder, the result of arguments among the crew. For a boy among men, it only served to increase the tension he felt.

In 1943, after four years at sea and aged just sixteen, John Chinnery decided he'd had enough. He had braved U-boats in the Atlantic and the ice of the Arctic convoys where he had suffered frostbite on his eyelids. He had escaped from the decks of a flaming tanker. Following a stressful Atlantic convoy, which had left him shaking with fear and unable to work, he knew that enough was enough. Back in Edinburgh, he found himself standing on a bridge looking down and feeling that he just wanted to throw himself off and end the incessant psychological pressure. It was the final straw. He returned home and informed his mother he would not return to his ship.

But the decision was not his to make. After a few days the police arrived to return him to the ship. He refused to leave, was arrested, taken to court and jailed for one month. Whilst detained, his fellow prisoners were appalled at his treatment: here was a courageous boy, whose nerve had gone, being treated like a criminal. To protect him, his fellow prisoners arranged for him to work in the prison library, where he was able to rest and finally experience some peace.

Freed after a month, John was sent to a rehabilitation centre on the west coast of Scotland, where he spent three months on a farm. As he later admitted, it was one of the best periods of his life. He loved the fresh food – devouring the platefuls of swede, mashed with butter and pepper, that the farmer's wife served for him. After enduring the horrors of the war at sea he delighted in getting close to nature: just watching as piglets were born helped him to reacquaint himself with the beauty of the world. It allowed him to reconnect with a more peaceful way of life after the stress of the Atlantic convoys. But it could not last forever: his three months were soon over and he returned to the Merchant Navy. Like so many of the boys in the Merchant Navy, he had volunteered and – despite his youth – he was no longer free to make his own choices.

CHAPTER 15

Boys Behind the Wire

'My teenage years were fantastic. If you can imagine it, all boys together. All the same age.'

John Hipkin, fourteen-year-old cabin boy and prisoner of war

With teenage boys active in every campaign of the war – on land, at sea and in the air – it was little wonder some under-eighteen year olds found themselves in the uncertain world of German and Italian prisoner-of-war camps. The world endured by POWs, of all ages, was far removed from that which they had earlier known. Those who had served time in civilian prisons or spent their youth at boarding schools, knew something of the enclosed atmosphere, but life 'behind the wire' in a POW camp went a step further.

An almost constant threat of death hung over them and, as many stressed, even inmates of civilian gaols knew the length of their sentence. The inmates of POW camps had no idea how long their ordeal might last; no idea when they would next see their families; no idea when they would next walk freely down the road arm-in-arm with a girl. Added to this was the burden of work, often in appalling conditions, something that was endured by all prisoners under the rank of sergeant.

Following the defeat of the British Expeditionary Force in France in 1940, some 40,000 British soldiers fell into the hands of the enemy. They joined others already captured in Norway earlier that year and by a constant stream of sailors and airmen. By war's end nearly 200,000 servicemen had endured life in German captivity. One of the first boys to arrive in a prisoner-of-war camp was sixteen-year-old John Norman, who was captured in France in 1940. He had attempted to reach a boat off the coast at St Valéry, only for it to be attacked and sunk by the enemy. He swam to the shore and was taken into captivity. After arriving at Stalag 8B after days of travelling in a cramped cattle truck, John was exhausted, hungry and uncertain of what fate had in store for him.

After being registered as a prisoner and allotted a bunk in a hut, he attempted to settle down to his new life. Youth had its advantages and disadvantages: being young he had no wife and children to worry about; he had the mental stamina and adaptability found in people too young to truly understand their situation; he was also fit and healthy and able to endure hardship, unlike some of the older prisoners whose bodies had been weakened by the hardships of the depression. Soon after arriving in the POW camp, John was selected for a working party – an *Arbeitskommando* – sent to mine in the nearby coalfields. For nearly five years, from the age of sixteen to twenty-one, he worked as a coal miner.

The work was hard and heavy. The shifts were often twelve hours a day, while all the time the prisoners lived on starvation rations augmented by occasional Red Cross parcels and whatever they could beg, borrow, steal or trade from the German and Polish miners they worked alongside. More than once, John Norman was thrown into solitary confinement, locked up on a diet of bread and water, for daring to defy the guards. On one occasion the teenager attempted to protect a mate who had been attacked by a German miner, who hit the prisoner with a metal rod. John punched the man and knocked him out. For his trouble, he received a beating from the guards who hit him until he was unconscious and dragged him off to the cells where he was left in total darkness. He remained in the darkness for two weeks, with the cell door being opened just once a day as the guards gave him a small ration of food and water – just enough to keep him alive. As he later admitted, at that time his mind was empty of the normal thoughts shared by teenagers: 'Forget about girlfriends – all I dreamed about was a large plate of bread pudding.'

From the start, British children played an important role in providing home comforts to the prisoners. They contributed to fundraising drives organized by the St John Ambulance, Red Cross and other independent groups. Some were the children of men who had been captured, others just wished to help. Though many contributions were small, every penny was gratefully received. The Red Cross recorded their efforts: five Girl Guides in Bishop Auckland donated £8 raised from a jumble sale; five-year-old Wendy Watson sold her doll's cot; a Sunday School in Cumberland donated the takings from a nativity play; William Northmore constructed a model aeroplane, selling it for £7; in Chorleywood three girls, Elizabeth and Jill Sanger and Sheila Buck, put on a production of *Ali Baba*, raising £21; eleven-year-old Betty Frosch of Stoke Newington donated eight shillings, the proceeds of the sale of a tulip she had grown; nine-year-old Norman Hudson raised £3 from a private library. Three enterprising schoolboys in Foulridge raised £20 through a whist drive. They then encouraged their girlfriends to try to match the amount and the girls raised a further £80.

Children also played an active role in supplying something else for the POWs. Girl Guides collected 5,000 used cotton reels. These were handed over to the authorities, without the girls understanding what they were for. The reels were stuffed with small silk escape maps, refilled and given fresh labels and then posted to POW camps to be used by escaping prisoners. But escape maps and other such ruses were part of a glamorous image of life in a prisoner-of-war camp. The reality was far less exciting.

Whilst Britain's children were raising funds for prisoners of war, they were unaware that some recipients were themselves little more than children. With so many merchant ships lost at sea, around 5,000 men and boys serving in the Merchant Navy found their way into the prisoner-of-war camps of Germany. Unlike soldiers who felt an almost universal sense of dejection upon being taken prisoner, merchant seamen had more mixed emotions. Most had survived the sinking of their ship only to be rescued from the water by their attackers. Thus, their captors were also their saviours. In a conflict where the sea often seemed the real enemy, the survivors of sunken merchant ships had a genuine reason to feel grateful to the Germans who had pulled them from the waves.

One of the early prisoners was Leslie McDermott-Brown, a fourteen year old from Glasgow. In 1939 he had been evacuated to Troon but had returned home after just two months, describing the town as a 'one eyed dump'.[1] He had worked in a solicitor's office and then gone to a nautical school, finding a position with a shipping company as a cadet. On 28 May 1940, he joined SS *Kemmendine* that left Glasgow for Rangoon via Cape Town. On 13 July, whilst in the Indian Ocean, Leslie was below deck heading for a wash, when he heard a bang: 'My first thoughts were that something had gone wrong down below in the engine room but, when the banging persisted and our Lascar baker came running along the alleyway making his life jacket secure, I immediately followed suit.'[2]

Reaching the deck, he saw the quartermaster in his pyjamas wearing a steel helmet. Next he spotted Lascar seamen praying. He knew it was time to get into the lifeboat. Rowing away from the sinking ship, they were taken onboard the German raider, the *Atlantis*, that had attacked them. They were taken below decks where they joined survivors from other vessels sunk by the German raider.

He was soon transferred to the *Tirranna* – a prize ship captured by the *Atlantis*. He was onboard for eight weeks and was nearing France when he was sunk for a second time. The *Tirranna* was torpedoed by a British submarine and Leslie dived overboard and swam to escape the sinking ship: 'Would I ever come to the surface again, was my thought, as the gurgling water filled my head. It seemed unending but at last my head broke surface.'[3] Whilst the teenager got away, 100 people on the ship were drowned. He began to swim for the coast, hoping he could avoid the wood from the wreck that burst through the surface of the water. He supported himself on a piece of wood, then swam towards a raft, struggling against the sea. He believed it took over two hours to reach the raft and eventually was transferred to a lifeboat that was then picked up by a German boat. Once ashore he was sent to Royan, where he was given an old French Army uniform, and then sent by bus to Wilhelmshaven in Germany. He was held at a navigation school, where he was interrogated. Next he was sent to an internment camp where he was registered as POW No. 1058.

From there he was sent to Sandbostel, 'a large dismal-looking camp'[4] that was home to 25,000 prisoners. The camp was built on an expanse of sandy ground. This was a world of endless food queues, surrounded by prisoners of all nationalities. On the first night Leslie and the other men from his ship bedded down on the floor. They then moved into a barrack room, twenty-six feet long, fifteen wide and eleven high. It was filled with wooden bunks in three tiers, built in blocks of twelve. As he later noted, they were each issued with a mug, bowl, knife, fork and spoon. However, he soon realized that a spoon was all he needed for the weak stews and soups that were their daily rations.

Whilst in the camp, Leslie joined in football matches played between crews of ships, in a league where each team bore a ship's name. Since there were only two others from his ship in the camp, the teenager joined the team formed by the crew of SS *Lustrous*. On 22 February 1941 the tanker SS *Lustrous* had been sunk two weeks into its journey. Among the crew was fourteen-year-old, Newcastle-born John Hipkin, known to his friends and family as Jackie. A keen Sea Scout, he had already told his schoolteacher that he intended to go to sea. One day in late 1940 he was sent on an errand but did not return home until late that night:

I got in touch with H. Amos shipping company, which had three vessels, and asked if there was an opening for a cabin or deck boy. I had to go to see a doctor in North Shields. I've never known a medical like it in my life. He lifted up my shirt and I had to drop my pants, cough – and that was it. I was declared fit for service. I never heard of anyone who failed that medical. They were so short of seamen during the war I think they would take anyone.[5]

Upon arriving home he told his parents that he had signed on with a merchant ship and was going to sea as a cabin boy. As he later recalled: 'It was just a question of leaving school at fourteen and living on Tyneside. It was a big shipping area, so there was always a demand for seamen.' Remembering how appalled their son had been when Germany had attacked Poland, his parents agreed that he should go to sea. They believed that this one trip would cure his desire to be a sailor and he would then return home. Their hopes were soon thwarted.

Also onboard *Lustrous* was fifteen-year-old John Brantom. In December 1940 John had had a fight with his brother at their Swansea home. The furious boy mounted his bicycle, rode to the docks where he spotted a ship advertising for a crew. He took his chance, signed on as a galley boy on the SS *Roy* and went to war. Immediately regretting his rash actions, and putting himself in considerable danger, the teenager thought about jumping ship in North America and seeking his fortune. His thoughts were typical of a generation of boys brought up on the action and adventure of cowboy films and comics. Instead, he left the ship at a far less glamorous location: Newcastle, where he went ashore and accidentally missed the sailing of his ship. After spending Christmas in a hostel for seamen, John Brantom found a position on the *Lustrous*.

The *Lustrous* left Newcastle on 13 February 1941, headed for the Dutch Antilles. Onboard were a total of four boys: John Hipkin, John Brantom, Nicky Holmes and Lewis McMahon. As they headed to sea, John Hipkin was struck by the reality of what he had signed on for:

I knew there had been lots of ships sunk but it wasn't until we'd sailed
from the Tyne during the night and up the Northumberland coast that
it struck home. I couldn't believe what I was seeing. There were masts
and funnels sticking out of the water all the way up to Scotland.[6]

Heading north, the *Lustrous* joined a convoy that was escorted by a
Royal Navy destroyer, but once out in the open waters of the
Atlantic, they were on their own. John Hipkin later recalled the
shock of discovering their situation: 'Came up on deck one morning
and our ship was alone. The convoy had been split up overnight.'
What came next was even more disconcerting.

Ten days into the journey, one of the lookouts spotted a shape in
the distance: the German battleship the *Scharnhorst*. It was part of
'Operation Berlin', a campaign to send raiders into the Atlantic to
sink merchant shipping and slowly starve the British Isles. With
nothing but a four-pound gun to defend itself, and unable to match
the battleship for speed, *Lustrous*'s fate was sealed. Coming up on to
deck John Hipkin was shocked to see the German raider in the
distance. As a youngster on his first trip to sea, John was uncertain
what would happen next. Fortunately, one of the older men was
quick to react: 'The cook said to me, "Get yourself back to your
cabin. Get some nice warm clothes on. We are going to be in trouble
soon!" He was right.' He rushed to his cabin and pulled on warm
clothes. As the order to abandon ship was given, John Hipkin was
still in his cabin putting on his life jacket. With no time to think, he
grabbed a carton of cigarettes he had purchased as a present for his
father. Taking nothing else, he made his way to the lifeboats,
worried the enemy might sink them as well.

The fourteen year old re-emerged on deck just the *Scharnhorst*
opened fire. With no means of defending their ship, the crew were
told to abandon ship and, as they did, a shell from the *Scharnhorst*
hit the radio shack, hastening their departure. As John Hipkin
watched the shells from the *Scharnhorst* landing in the sea around the
Lustrous, he became convinced the Germans had deliberately fired

wide in order to force the tanker's crew to make good their escape before their vessel was destroyed. It was what he later called 'the comradeship of the sea'. The experience made him realize he was lucky their attacker had been a battleship in daytime and not a U-boat at night. The three lifeboats were hastily rowed to a safe distance as the *Scharnhorst* blasted the *Lustrous*, sending it sliding, bow first, beneath the waves. As the crew wondered what would happen next, the *Scharnhorst* sailed away to continue its attack on the convoy, leaving them alone. To their great relief, she returned a few hours later to pick up the survivors who were hauled from the lifeboats by German sailors.

As they climbed up rope ladders on to the decks of the *Scharnhorst*, the relieved seamen were greeted by a German propaganda film crew who recorded the events. In the film it is easy to spot the fourteen and fifteen year olds among the prisoners – their bright but nervous young faces standing out from the old hands around them. Once beneath decks, John Hipkin began to think about what had happened to him. As he later recalled, it was a confusing, frightening and somewhat surreal situation: 'I was fourteen years old – at that age it's strange to be a prisoner onboard a German ship.' At the same time he was able to remain youthfully optimistic about what had happened: 'It was great. I was a fourteen year old among all these seaman. But after a while, there were about thirty or forty boys of our age – galley boys, cabin boys and so on.'

Whilst onboard, the crew of the *Lustrous* were questioned by their captors, who seemed surprised to see such young faces among the prisoners. Seventeen-year-old Lewis McMahon, who had joined the Merchant Navy as a fourteen year old, was singled out by his captors and was spoken to by the captain of the *Scharnhorst*, Kurt Hoffman. Lewis later admitted he had told his captor 'a pack of lies'. John Hipkin was asked his age and then taken to the galley where German sailors gave him sweets and cakes. After four days below decks, the prisoners were transferred to a German supply ship, the *Ermland*, before landing at La Pallice in France. Ironically, the camp had been built by the French in 1940 to house some of the thousands of Germans they had expected to capture. From there, the seamen were sent to a filthy transit camp before being transferred to Paris and then sent on a four-day train journey to Germany.

At first, the survivors of the *Lustrous* were sent to Sandbostel. Each morning they were woken at 6 a.m., given a breakfast of bread and water, and sent to work in the fields on twelve-hour shifts. As John Brantom later recalled, if they dared to slack, the guards beat them with sticks. John Hipkin was appalled by conditions at the camp, recalling that although the British were crammed 100 to a room, conditions for Yugoslav prisoners were even worse. It was hard to imagine such cruelty and so he would allow the Yugoslavs to dip their mugs into the British soup as he carried it between compounds. Similarly, John Brantom threw bread rations over the fence to the starving Yugoslavs. On one occasion, John Hipkin watched as a German guard took offence at seeing Yugoslavs sharing British food. He shouted to the prisoners and, as the Yugoslav ran away, the guard raised his rifle, fired and killed the man. As John Hipkin later recalled: 'I'll never forget that murder. All over a stinking bowl of soup.'[7]

Officially, the merchant seamen were non-combatants and should have been treated as internees, not as prisoners of war. Instead, they were placed in a special camp known as Milag Nord or Marine Internierten Lager, at Westertimke near Bremen (Royal Navy personnel were imprisoned in the nearby Marlag camp). In the case of merchant seamen under the age of eighteen, international law stipulated that they could not be interned. Instead, they should be repatriated. However, these rules were seldom adhered to and so Leslie McDermott-Brown, John Hipkin, John Brantom and many other boys were transferred there from Sandbostel.

When the first batch of internees arrived in the camp they discovered that the huts had been made from damp wood that had been left out in the snow all winter. Such was the poor construction of the huts that the wind whistled through the walls. For the incoming seamen, the first winter was a time of cold, hunger and uncertainty. As they soon learned, the loose sandy soil plagued them in the dry summers, coating their clothes in a fine layer of dust. Then, in winter, it soon grew thick and damp as it was churned up by thousands of footfalls from bored internees as they trudged around the perimeter.

Teenage merchant seamen from all parts of the British Isles ended up within the camp, meaning that they could share their time with others their own age. Also, just as most had experienced on their ships, the boys had the protection of older men who looked out for them. The boys met people from all four corners of the globe: aged mariners who had lived all their lives from port to port, fathers and sons who had sailed and been captured together, men of every imaginable nationality, race and religion. For the youngsters, it was an education just to listen to these men. They had travelled the world and their knowledge seemed infinite to teenagers fresh from home. John Brantom grew friendly with an older man, an experienced sailor who was a talented artist and was like an uncle to the teenager. He also befriended a musician who had been sunk the same day whilst crewing a separate ship. Unfortunately, the musician died of cancer and his sixteen-year-old friend had to dig his grave.

Despite this sense of camaraderie, at times the boys found life difficult to endure. Like all prisoners of war they often felt lonely despite living in cramped conditions amidst thousands of fellow seamen. John Hipkin wrote home requesting photographs of his family and friends, hoping they might help curb the inevitable sense of homesickness felt by all prisoners. At times John Brantom, whose teenage years were passing in captivity, considered climbing the perimeter wire and meeting an inevitable death. He regularly moved huts and found it difficult to settle amongst his countrymen. Feeling like an outsider, he spent increasing amounts of time with foreign sailors, including Jamaicans and Nigerians, who were sometimes shunned by the British sailors. For John Hipkin, the emotional turmoil of captivity was suppressed beneath a desire for education. Whilst a prisoner he became an avid student, spending many of his spare hours studying – just as many of his contemporaries were continuing their studies behind school desks across the United Kingdom.

With time, conditions slowly improved. Sailors in the adjoining Milag thought the merchant seamen were living a life of incredible freedom. There were rumours of widespread rackets, gambling syndicates, drinking and even women being smuggled into the camp. Whilst the issue of discipline among men who were interned rather than held prisoner, and who were not under military discipline, meant that life might have been easier than for their counterparts, life in Milag was far from a holiday camp existence. Although labour was not compulsory, some chose to work on local farms, which helped provide some fresh vegetables for the internees. By early 1943 there were nearly 3,000 merchant seamen interned in Milag Nord. The senior British officer in the camp recorded the former positions of the boys in his camp. He counted: seventy-four cadets; thirty-five deck boys; sixteen galley boys; fifteen cabin boys; six saloon boys; one steward's boy; one pantry boy; one engineer's boy; and one lift boy.[8] Red Cross reports indicated that the camp was sufficient to house them, except that the toilet facilities were substandard and there was insufficient equipment for private cooking. It was also recorded that they had just one hot shower per month. The seamen slept on straw-filled palliasses in two-tier bunks, with each man issued with two blankets. As one man wrote home: 'these boards do get hard'.[9] In 1943 it was recorded that each internee had just one good outfit of clothes. The men also complained that parcels from home were infrequent.

In July that year, a seaman wrote home:

> We are situated right in the middle of a very pretty farming district, pine woods completely encircle us in the distance. Half the fields are cultivated, wheat, potatoes, cabbages etc, the remainder is lovely

grazing pasture. Between our village and the next runs a stream, where paddle the local ducks; we can follow its course from our window by the willow tree.[10]

However, that rosy impression of life in the camp was far from the memory of others. Bill Manningham, who entered the camp aged seventeen, later recalled:

The first camp commandant was an elderly man named Prush. He hated us like we were poison and if anyone didn't go to work, he used to punish them. One of the punishments was to stand us beside the barbed wire with the guard watching us for two hours at least. We couldn't move and weren't allowed to smoke or drink. Sometimes we were kept there ten hours. He was in charge of the camp for about two-and-a-half years and was classed as one of the worst we had. There was nothing in his mind but work and punishment.[11]

Conditions at the camp annoyed Bill and his mates: 'We went on strike once because of the soup. We hadn't received any parcels and the soup was just like water. We only got it once a day so we were practically starving, but the strike ended when the commandant threatened to have us all shot.'[12] Such threats were genuine. One of Leslie McDermott-Brown's friends was shot and killed by a guard whilst attempting to trade food. With increasing numbers of cabin and galley boys falling into German hands it was decided they should all be housed together within the camp. As John Hipkin remembered it, the Germans had hoped the boys would be a good influence on each other:

As more and more boys came in, the Germans found us such a nuisance they put us all into one barracks in the camp. You do that with boys and they'll get up to everything. We became master thieves. So they gave us special jobs to do. We went out picking crops. We were expert at going into a spud field. We wore British army battledress which is baggy but buttons tight at the waist. You could get a stone of spuds inside there. So we became adept at stealing food. The German guards soon got sick of our antics. Whatever job was given to us, we made an ass of it.

John recalled the work details: 'The work I liked most of all was the forestry gang. You would spend a whole day working in the forest with just a few guards. We were felling trees so they had to be a safe distance away. I liked that because you could kid yourself you were free.'[13]

As a teenage boy, John soon grew to recognize that youth had its advantages:

Milag was probably the most cosmopolitan of prison camps, with seamen of all nations there, ranging from 14 year olds to men in their late seventies who had gone to sea as boys in the days of sail. It was easier for us as boys than for the men. One of the problems of captivity for men was the worry about wives and children back home, while those courting used to get 'Dear John' letters. That sort of stuff went over our heads.[14]

With help from groups back home, including the Merchant Navy Officers' Training Board, John Hipkin was able to restart his education. In 1944, after three years as an internee, he wrote home to his mother:

I hope my sister Betty is doing as well at school as I am here. I learned algebra and geometry last winter, and now I'm in the matriculation classes. I've also started learning Spanish, and am surprised how easy it is! A fellow named Stan Hagill, who has been travelling around a bit, is teaching me Spanish, and another man, Chinese and Japanese.[15]

In the camp, John also studied for the RAF entrance examination, using books sent to him by the Red Cross. His mental strength was also supported by a growing religious faith which he first encountered courtesy of the teachings of a padre who had been sunk in the Atlantic.

Not all teenage prisoners of war were held captive by the Germans. Some crews of merchant ships found themselves at the mercy of neutral powers. In some cases their treatment was far worse than that given by the enemy. Born in Blackwood, Gwent, in August 1925, Wilfred Williams was the cabin boy on a merchant ship, SS *Allende*. He had been working at a forge when war broke out and was upset that he could not join the Army aged fourteen. When he later saw a work colleague wearing a Merchant Navy badge he spoke with him and discovered that he was now old enough to join the Merchant Navy. He told his parents that if they did not allow him to go, he would run away to sea.

Wilfred joined the *Allende* in February 1941 aged fifteen. As a mess room boy he made breakfast each morning, did the washing up and laid the table for meals. One year on, the ship was eighteen miles off the coast of Liberia when a torpedo hit the ship. Wilfred was thrown from his bunk, hitting his head on the ceiling. When he got outside, the deck was already tilting and he could hear the cargo shifting beneath him. As he looked around, the deck was littered with debris from the explosion. One man narrowly avoided being hit by a lump of the engine.

Taking to the lifeboats, the crew did their best to get away. In a heavy sea, with rain pouring down, the lifeboats soon filled with water. They tried to bail out the boat, but without buckets they could do little. Facing the prospect of being sunk, and noticing the *Allende* was still afloat, the crew decided to row back to fetch buckets. As they approached, a second torpedo struck, sending the ship to the bottom. They were forced to continue bailing out as best they could. As the seas calmed, the men in the lifeboat were able to finish bailing out and get the boat under control. However, having been soaked all night by the rain, in the morning the sun scorched them. After two days in the lifeboat, they were washed upon the coast. They attempted to row ashore, hoping they could crest a wave and be deposited on the beach. However, the lifeboat was caught by a wave: the men were thrown from it and washed up on an empty beach.

There was no sign of life in the area, with the beach acting as a narrow strip between the sea and a thick jungle. The decision was taken to walk along the beach in search of a village. After the ordeal of the sinking, most of the crew were barefoot. Wilfred Williams tore strips from his trousers and bound his feet. Eventually they reached a fishing village and discovered they were in French Guinea. The local gendarme was fetched and the crew were taken into captivity. It did not take the shipwrecked sailors long to realize the local authorities were loyal to the pro-German Vichy regime in France and were vehemently anti-British.

Not knowing what to expect, the crew were put on lorries and sent inland by dirt road. By the time they arrived in Daloa in the Ivory Coast, most of them were already suffering from dysentery. The police doctor gave them a cursory medical inspection but, despite their sickness, they were pronounced fit to travel. As they climbed back into the lorry, the weakest of the sick seamen had to be lifted onboard. They had to remove their shirts to rig up a shelter to protect them from the burning rays of the sun as they travelled.

For two months they were shuttled from place to place by the French authorities. They survived on rations of half-cooked rice and black bread, washed down by cups of weak coffee. When they were not being scorched by the sun, they were soaked by tropical rains. Meanwhile, their families had been alerted that the ship was lost, but there was no word of any survivors. It was months before the French authorities told the Red Cross that the surviving crew were safely ashore in Africa.

Eventually, they were taken off the lorries and sent by native canoe along the River Niger. Sitting in the cramped boats, the men were plagued by insects and some of the men started to show signs of malaria. As a result of their ordeal, Wilfred Williams suffered from pellagra, a condition brought on by a deficiency of vitamin B. It caused his tongue to dry, making swallowing difficult, and also affected his eyesight. They were on the river for eleven days and by the time they reached Timbuktu, Wilfred found it a struggle to walk. Despite his suffering, the sixteen year old did not give up hope.

In Timbuktu they were put into a prison and for the next sixty-three days they shared their meals – usually just rice – from one large bowl, with all the prisoners dipping their filthy hands in to scrape out what food they could find. They could do little except attempt to shelter from the sun, and curse their chapped lips and exhausted bodies. They were reduced to sprawling on straw, plagued by lice and flies. Wilfred developed open ulcers on his legs and rapidly weakened. Only the extra food given by his shipmates, who recognized that a growing boy needed extra food to sustain growth, saved him. By this stage he had dysentery, pellagra – that had given him dry, scaly skin – and open, pus-filled ulcers. Whilst in the prison two of the crew died of sickness.

Eventually, just when it seemed hopeless, the French authorities had a change of heart and announced the men would be sent home. They were once more loaded on to lorries and moved back in the direction they had come. After a while they were put on a train, sent through Senegal and into the British colony of Gambia. By the time they reached safety Wilfred Williams had reached the stage where he was unable to stand. Finally able to receive treatment, they were taken to a hospital in Freetown, Sierra Leone. Wilfred was then sent home on a hospital ship, arriving home in August 1942, six months after the sinking. After a further six months of recuperation, he returned to the sea and continued his career in the Merchant Navy.

In the Far East a number of youngsters became prisoners of the Japanese. Some were captured at the fall of Singapore, including some of the boys who had survived the sinking of HMS *Prince of Wales* and HMS *Repulse*. Having been put ashore in Singapore, they were among the thousands of men unable to escape when the garrison surrendered to the Japanese in 1942. Among them was

Gordon Cockburn, a seventeen-year-old survivor of the *Prince of Wales*. He was held first in Bicycle Camp in Java, then in the notorious Kuching camp (also known at Batu Lintang camp) on the island of Borneo. He soon learned that the only way to stay alive was to keep quiet and obey orders. The one occasion he did disobey the guards to go to the toilet, he was kicked so hard his shin shattered and the bone penetrated his skin. Such a wound might have proved fatal had it not been for the fellow prisoner who made sure he kept maggots in the wound to eat away the infected flesh.

Recovering from his wounds, Gordon returned to work, building runways for Japanese aircraft. Every day seemed to bring more death, with Gordon and his fellow prisoners almost constantly burying the men who died from exhaustion and disease or who had been murdered by the guards. The experience had a profound effect on the youngster, who – on the eve of the fiftieth anniversary of VJ Day – admitted:

> My wife says I'm cold and can't really show my emotions. And those four years certainly made me able to accept death. I also tend to have very little sympathy for people who are sick or ill. During the years when I should have been growing up and going to dances like other teenagers, I was staring death in the face every day. I learned to become an expert at closing my mind down and keeping my feelings to myself. And I suppose I never learned to open up again. I have no regrets about fighting for my country – except for those who were less lucky than me. Those are the people I'll be thinking about tomorrow.[16]

Not all of the boys of the Merchant Navy remained resilient. Two of their number – Ronald Voysey, an Australian-born cabin boy who had been serving on *British Advocate* when captured, and Kenneth Berry, a fourteen year old onboard a tanker, SS *Cymbeline* – both volunteered for the 'British Free Corps' following a visit to Milag by William 'Lord Haw-Haw' Joyce. The Free Corps was the SS unit raised from British and Commonwealth prisoners that the

Germans hoped to use against the Russians as part of an anti-Bolshevist crusade. After his capture in 1940, Kenneth Berry's youth meant he had been allowed to live in Paris in the care of a British woman. Then, aged seventeen, he had been interned at the St Denis camp, north of Paris. There he was exposed to German propaganda, causing him to volunteer. He was detained by the Gestapo for a number of weeks and interrogated about his decision to volunteer. Then he was sent to Berlin, where he resided in a lodging house, joining the Free Corps in November 1943.

One of Kenneth's first tasks as a member of the unit was to begin a recruitment drive among fellow merchant seamen at Westertimke. In May and June 1944 he was successful, recruiting two men, one of whom had mainly been swayed by the prospect of extra food and tobacco. However, exposed to loyal sailors on his visits to the camp, he realized his mistake and attempted to extricate himself. On the advice of the camp leader, Kenneth visited the Swiss embassy in Berlin and to seek assistance. Failing to get help from the Swiss, he continued to attempt to recruit for the Germans. His next visit to Westertimke netted two more renegade volunteers. In early 1945 Kenneth was among the small British Free Corps detachment finally to reach the front lines, being sent to the armoured reconnaissance battalion of an SS division. The unit never actually saw action, being withdrawn and given a transport role behind the front lines. In the chaos of the final weeks of war, most of the unit managed to head west and avoid capture by the Russians. When Kenneth finally returned to the UK he was sentenced to nine months' hard labour for his youthful treachery.

At the mine in Silesia that was both home and workplace for John Norman, the conditions did not improve as the war progressed. The prisoners continued to live in fear and suffered continual deprivation. Every mouthful of food was savoured and every moment of rest was enjoyed. Anything was better than the long hours spent underground. Life as a coal miner was dirty and dangerous, as he found to his cost. One day, he reached up to hang his lamp on an overhead wire, not realizing it was a live wire, part of the electrical system used to haul the coal wagons. With the electrical current surging through his body, the teenager was unable to let go. Thinking quickly, one of his fellow prisoners lashed out at his hand, releasing his grip. Free from the current, he was thrown several yards along the tunnel. He was carried from the mine and, with his hand burned, swollen and bruised, was unable to work for two weeks.

In the winter of 1944 the conditions for prisoners grew increasingly intolerable. At Milag Nord Leslie McDermott-Brown recorded his experiences in his diary. In January 1945 he wrote: 'Cold and miserable, wood gang not functioning, making wood issues scarce. German food rations have been cut again and Red Cross parcels issued fortnightly.' A few days later the American sailors were allowed to leave the camp and a number of the sick were repatriated, as Leslie noted: 'This has an even more depressing effect on the camp.'[17] The youngster grew sickened by the rumours – all of which seemed to promise a swift return home. With thick snow on the ground, the camp was a miserable place. It was not until the end of January that they received their Christmas parcels. Leslie noticed how few of the prisoners ventured outside. Instead, they stayed indoors huddled around the meagre fires in their stoves. Even when the fires were left unlit, due to fuel shortages, they still crowded around them. With the fields frozen and covered in snow, there was no work on the farms and thus no opportunity for the prisoners to trade with the local farmers.

By the middle of February the food shortages had got so great that the prisoners went without food in the evenings. Cigarettes were running short and power shortages meant there were no lights in the huts during the dull winter afternoons. Worst of all, there was no coal for heating and they were forced to burn damp wood in the stoves. At the start of March the only good news was that American Red Cross parcels had arrived and thus the parcel ration increased to one per man, per week. The effect of parcels was that prisoners started smiling again. As Leslie noted, when parcels arrived it became impossible to see across the room for smoke.

By early April the tension had increased and he wrote in his diary, 'I wish to hell the troops were here . . . my nerves are in a terrible state.' Each entry to his diary emphasized how desperate the prisoners at Milag Nord were becoming:

> something I can't explain at present predominates over the Lager. Everybody is just watching, waiting, listening but nothing happens. It seems like the calm before the storm I wonder? What lies ahead we would like to know . . . It's torture waiting on them coming.

As the Allies advanced ever closer, Leslie was relieved to hear towns to the west being hit by artillery fire and towns to the east being bombed: 'Hell, I wish they'd hurry up and get here.'[18]

CHAPTER 16

A Boy's Life on the Ocean Wave

'I got in the water, but she was going down. The suction was pulling me back.'

Seventeen-year-old Albert Riddle, HMS *Prince of Wales*

Right from the outbreak of war, the youth of the Royal Navy were in the front line. From the Battle of the River Plate to the Dunkirk evacuation and from the North Atlantic to the Indian Ocean, boys as young as sixteen played their part in the war at sea. The terrible losses on HMS *Royal Oak* were only the beginning of what was to be a violent and dangerous war for the boys of the Royal Navy. Every major maritime operation involved boys. When HMS *Gloucester* was sunk during the evacuation of Crete in 1941, 44 boy sailors were among the 700 casualties.

War meant that youngsters who had joined up for the peacetime Navy had to suddenly adapt to the pressures of combat. All felt this pressure, but few were honest in admitting the intolerable strain it created. One who did was William MacFarlane Crawford. Aged seventeen, he was among the crew of HMS *Hood* when she sailed from Rosyth in March 1941. Since 1939 he had seen plenty of action, but a brief leave in Edinburgh had convinced him he did not want to return to sea. On the day they departed, he wrote to his mother: 'It took me all my time not to cry as we came down the river . . . God knows how much I didn't want to go back today, Mum.' He even asked that she write to the Admiralty to see if a position on shore could be arranged for him: 'I don't suppose it will do any good, but it might . . . Don't pay much attention to the letter, Mum, I'm just getting things off my chest, but everything is true. I'll get over this rotten feeling through time, I guess. But it's hit me hard this time.'

The following day he wrote another letter: 'I don't know what's wrong with me, but I feel sick, tired and in every way fed up.' He even admitted he had considered going absent and not joining ship: 'The first chance I get, Mum, I am leaving for good, as I honestly feel yesterday something died inside me, and now I don't care much about anything . . . I feel I'll go nuts if this carries on much longer.' A third letter revealed the sense of homesickness he endured onboard: 'I always feel like crying, Mum, and there is a permanent lump in my throat.' Poignantly, he asked his mother to make sure his little brother did not try to volunteer for the Royal Navy. Three days later he wrote a final letter home: 'We haven't been away very long, but we have had some tense times since I left. And now that Germany has started sending her warships out, there looks as if there will be action for the fleet soon. Anyway, the sooner we get them the better.'[1]

Two months later HMS *Hood* was sunk by the *Bismarck*. There were only three survivors – William Crawford was not among them. It was the Royal Navy's most infamous sinking of the entire war and cost the lives of numerous boys. Of the three survivors, Ted Briggs was a former 'boy' who had joined the Navy aged fifteen. When the *Hood* was sunk, he had just reached his eighteenth birthday. As he struggled to remove heavy clothing, a surge of water dragged him under. Resigned to death, he was suddenly hit by a pocket of escaping air that propelled him to the surface. As he emerged, Briggs looked up to see the bows of the *Hood* slipping beneath the water.

Another survivor of the disaster was William Dundas, a sixteen year old who had joined the Royal Naval College at Dartmouth in 1937 at the age of thirteen. When the *Hood* was sunk he was serving as a midshipman and was stationed on the compass bridge. As the *Hood* slipped beneath the water, William kicked out a window to escape. As she went down, he too was somehow carried away by a blast of escaping air and blown to the surface, from where he was able to swim to safety.

Adrift amidst the floating wreckage, he managed to reach a small floating raft and dragged himself aboard. Soon he found two others had also boarded rafts. All three attempted to keep together as they watched the battle continue, seeing HMS *Prince of Wales* steaming past. Adrift in the icy waters of the Atlantic, William helped his fellow survivors, singing 'Roll Out the Barrel', keeping them awake in the freezing conditions. After two hours, and with the oil-soaked, frozen sailors all but giving up hope, and two of them suffering from hypothermia, the destroyer HMS *Electra* appeared and pulled them aboard.

In total 1,415 sailors had perished with the *Hood.* Of these, more than fifty were aged seventeen, whilst an additional seventeen boys were aged just sixteen. They were all boys who had volunteered for the Royal Navy and were still some time away from being eligible for conscription. The youngest victim was sixteen-year-old Thomas 'Bernie' Sammars, born in Hampshire in 1925. The *Hood* was his first, and last, ship.

With the *Hood* lost, it was the turn of other ships to join in the pursuit of the *Bismarck.* Next to engage the German warships was the pride of the Royal Navy, HMS *Prince of Wales.* As she searched for the *Bismarck,* sixteen-year-old Albert Riddle had to fight against his seasickness. At least he was out in the open where the fresh air helped settle his queasy stomach. As both Albert and his officers knew, he was useless below decks, where every movement sent him reeling. So he had been posted to the air defence platform where, along with other boys, he scanned the horizon with binoculars, in search of enemy warships, submarines and aircraft.

The *Prince of Wales* had thrown itself into battle, opening fire on the *Bismarck*, yet now had become the target for both *Bismarck* and *Prinz Eugen*. The end of the sea battle came in an instant. With astounding accuracy, a fifteen-inch shell struck her bridge, exploding as it passed out the far side. On the air defence platform, just above the bridge, young Albert Riddle was standing beside Lt Esmond Knight. The contrast between the two couldn't have been greater: the sixteen-year-old boy who had gone straight into the Royal Navy, and the thirty-five-year-old actor, a star of stage and screen who had volunteered for the Royal Navy at the outbreak of war. The noise and heat of the shell was something Albert was never able to forget: 'Esmond Knight was my officer, he was in charge of all the lookouts. He was standing just behind me. This shell went between us – just inches away – and blinded him.' The shell exploded beneath them on the bridge.

Albert went quickly down to the bridge to see if he could help. He was confronted by a scene of absolute carnage: 'Captain Leach was a wonderful man. He was the only one left standing. He and the gunnery officer were the only two who survived.' The youngster looked at the rest of the men on the bridge: 'They were blown to bloody smithereens. It was a terrible shock. It's not a thing I've ever talked about. These people were absolutely blown to bits.' They had not suffered the type of clean death so often portrayed in the films of the period: 'The voice pipes, leading down to the engine room, were full of flesh and blood – bits of people's bodies – there was blood all over the floor.' Despite the carnage, the captain remained calm: 'I can still see Leach now, he said, "Is there anybody who can stomach cleaning this up?" He was looking for volunteers. I was quite happy with it. It didn't sicken me. I just got cracking. Some people couldn't do it. I was always fine with that sort of thing.' Looking back nearly seventy years later, Albert was able to explain why, despite his youth, he had been able to help clear up the shattered corpses: 'I think it was coming from a farm, I was more used to the idea of blood and mess. I used to help sheep give birth, or help the horse when she was foaling.' The shell had killed fourteen seamen, with two of the casualties just seventeen years old.

Having narrowly escaped injury, for Albert Riddle the war continued, but it did not get any better. In August 1941, the *Prince of Wales* took the Prime Minister, Winston Churchill, to Newfoundland where he met with US President Franklin D. Roosevelt. With Albert having celebrated his seventeenth birthday, they then escorted a convoy from Gibraltar to Malta. In October the orders came for the *Prince of Wales* and the *Repulse* to head to Singapore. The intention was that the presence of the ships would deter the Japanese from attacking Malaya and the East Indies. What had seemed sensible on paper soon turned into a disaster. As Albert Riddle recalled: 'They told us the *Prince of Wales* was unsinkable. The Japanese soon put an end to that myth!'

On 10 December 1941, as the ship set out to intercept the Japanese fleet, it came under attack. It was a tremendous shock for the crew; they had done battle with two of Germany's most powerful warships, but the attack by Japanese bombers was, as Albert Riddle recalled: 'Intense. By Christ, you wouldn't believe it. I saw torpedo tracks in the water and I could see the planes in the sky.' Albert was lucky; as they went to action stations he took up his position in one of the 5.25-inch gun turrets. This meant he was at deck level, with the door leading into the turret directly from the deck. He watched others going below decks: 'All the hatches and doors are closed and locked. That's it, you are down there and you are not coming up. If the ship goes, you go with it.' He knew exactly why he had been selected to man one of the upper turrets: since he was still so badly seasick, he needed to be somewhere with more air and where he might have a chance to see the horizon.

Whilst this was one of the mightiest ships in the Royal Navy, there was little the crew could do after the first torpedo struck:

> I heard the explosion – it would have been even worse below, they would have known they were trapped down there. That's a terrible

thing. It was the only time I was bloody glad to be seasick. I can laugh about it now, but there was no laughing about it then.

What Albert did not know was that the torpedo had hit in the worst possible place: 'They did the thing that buggered us completely, they hit us in the screws [the propellers].' No longer able to steer, without light, without power to many of its turrets and without power for many of the pumps, the *Prince of Wales* was all but helpless. Though her anti-aircraft guns kept firing, they were in a hopeless situation.

With no idea of how bad the damage was, Albert kept working:

> All I knew was the sound of the gun, and the recoil and the stench of the cordite. I couldn't see what was happening outside. You hadn't got time to think. I was in the turret with eight men, all handling the shells. We were trying to keep the lifts working. The ammo was being fed from the magazines, into the hoists. They came to us vertically, then into the breech. When the ship started to list, the shells were toppling over – that's when it gets dangerous. The mechanics eventually went wrong, so we had to handle the shells.

As the bombers kept up the attack, and more torpedoes struck, the ship began to sink, listing to port: 'We had finished firing by then, we couldn't do anything at all, the electrics had gone.' With the anti-aircraft guns useless, and the fate of the ship sealed, Albert listened as Captain Leach – an officer for whom he had great admiration – gave the order to abandon ship, then said a prayer: 'Lord, I shall be very busy this day and may forget thee, but do not thou forget me.' It didn't offer Albert much comfort: 'It frightened the life out of us. It sounded like we were already on the seabed.'

Realizing it was time to leave, Albert stepped out on to the deck. He got a sudden shock: 'The water was coming over the guard rails. I thought, this isn't going to last much longer.' Strangely, he felt little fear: 'All I had to do was to step off into the water.' However, what concerned him was that he had always been instructed that he should leave a sinking ship on the opposite side to the one that was going down. The thinking was that the undertow would be worse on the side that went down first. However, to leave from the opposite side would mean heading up the deck.

By now the situation was getting desperate: 'A bomb went through close to me, I could feel the heat from the bloody thing. I can't believe I was so lucky.' However, the blast caught him:

> My clothes were all blown off me. I was as naked as a jaybird. All I was wearing were white overalls, I had nothing on underneath. It was so hot in the turret, so I just had the overalls and white gloves and the anti-flash helmet. After the blast, they were tattered, so I couldn't swim in them.

Casting off the remnants of his overalls, he prepared to enter the water. There was something else to do first: 'I gave my lifebelt to a stoker who came up on deck, he'd been injured by steam. I wasn't thinking I'd need it as much as him.' It was whilst waiting to leave the ship that Albert encountered another boy: 'It was one the twins, James and Robert Young. I wanted him to leave, but he wouldn't go because his brother was injured. So he stayed and they were both lost.'

Uncertain of what to do next, Albert's mind was made up for him:

> For a moment, I thought I couldn't go because of all the other poor buggers still on the ship. So many of them were badly scalded, they were the engine room staff. They got hell from the steam when the pipes went. A hell of a lot of them had bad burns. What made me think it's time to get off was that suddenly she gave a lurch. A big life raft came tumbling down the deck and splashed into the water. I thought, 'I really ought to be going.' It was every man for himself.

As he headed into the water, his troubles were only just beginning: 'I got in the water, but she was going down. The suction was pulling me back. I was pulled back on to the quarterdeck. That was frightening. The strange thing was that there weren't many people about. I don't know if I was one of the last to get off.' Using all his strength, he was able to get away from the sinking ship, but there were other dangers: 'There was oil on the surface, you had to make sure it didn't get into your lungs. That killed so many of them. But I was young. I could swim like a bloody fish. I was fine as I swam away.'

Eventually he got away. He clung to some netting that gave him some support, thinking, 'If this bugger goes down, I'm going with it.' Getting as far away as possible, Albert turned to look as the *Prince of Wales* stood upright and then slid beneath the surface. He noticed there was a motorboat not far away and swam towards it. He spotted that the ship's gunnery officer was onboard: 'He was standing on the stern of this motorboat with the tiller between his legs, and all he had on was a shirt. No trousers and no underpants! For one of our senior officers to be like that, it struck me as funny – even at the time.' The smile was soon wiped off his face when he noticed that the water was full of injured men – many of them badly scalded: 'You couldn't touch them – the skin would come off in your hands.' The motorboat came closer and loaded as many survivors as possible.

Unable to take any more men, the motorboat moved away to unload the men on to a nearby destroyer. Albert waited in the water for a further two hours before the boat returned to pick him up. By the time it returned there were very few other survivors in the water around him. Surprisingly, he was not overwhelmed with fear: 'You haven't got time to think of yourself. If you are feeling well, you get a sense of well-being.' He had good reason to feel confident: he was a good swimmer, young, strong and uninjured. Most importantly, he hadn't swallowed any of the oil. In other words, he was in a better situation than so many of the others who had gone into the water that day.

Eventually, he was picked up and transferred to the destroyer.

There the survivors were crammed on to the red-hot decks. There was hardly any room to sit, and anyway the steel deck was too hot to sit on – especially since many of them were naked – but it hardly mattered. They were alive. As Albert Riddle recalled, all he could think was: 'That was a close call.'

Although Albert had got away safely, twenty-five boys were lost on the *Prince of Wales*. A further twelve were lost on the *Repulse*. Five days later, another seventeen boys were lost when HMS *Galatea* was torpedoed in the Mediterranean. Two days later, twenty-seven boys lost their life on HMS *Neptune*, when it entered a minefield in the Mediterranean. There was just one survivor from the 764-man crew. December 1941 had been a bad month.

The ordeal for the boy survivors of the sinking of the *Repulse* and *Prince of Wales* was far from over. Arriving in Singapore, the survivors were marched to the nearby shore establishment, HMS *Sultan*. For Albert it felt like a 'walk of shame': he, and many of the others, were black with oil and still naked. Reaching the base, their first task was to try to get clean. It wasn't easy, there was little hot water and not enough soap to go round. So they scrubbed and scrubbed in a desperate effort to rid their skin of oil. Even when they were clean, they struggled to find enough spare uniforms to get dressed.

The survivors of *Prince of Wales* and *Repulse* remained in Singapore until the Japanese started their attack on the city. First came the aerial attack. Coming so soon after the sinking of the ships, many of the survivors were seriously affected by the bombing.

> Being bombed and docks being bombed, that was bloody frightening. I thought, 'Christ, after all that, we're going to get hit by a bomb. After all we've done to get off the ship, and all those poor buggers who lost their lives, now we're going to die here.' It gets you. Very nervous – most likely suffering from shock.

The effects were shown as soon as the sirens sounded on the base:

We ran off to the jungle like a bloody rocket – hundreds of us. The guards, the sentries on the base, were trying to stop us. We said: 'Get out of the way, we're going!' There'd be hundreds of us hiding in the undergrowth. When the 'all clear' sounded, we'd sneak back to barracks. It took several days to get over that.

Once recovered, the survivors were given new duties and Albert was one of the lucky ones. He was sent to a golf club where the commander-in-chief had established his headquarters. There he worked as a signaller, although effectively he was little more than a messenger since he spent most of the time running messages around the HQ. He noticed that some of the defences were just dummy gun emplacements, with holes containing angled telegraph poles, designed to look like heavy guns from the air. It didn't give him any confidence in their situation.

When the city fell to the Japanese in February 1942, Albert, along with staff from the HQ, was sent to the docks and boarded an escaping boat. Arriving at the docks he noticed British and Indian troops trying to control crowds of Australian soldiers who were attempting to storm the port to board the remaining ships. He realized the desperate situation when the British and Indians were forced to open fire to control the crowd. Glad to be out from the chaos, Albert soon realized the boat he was on was not going to get them very far. It broke down and he was transferred to a ship that escaped. Another group of the boys boarded a merchant ship, the *Ping Wo*, as it left Singapore on the day the city fell to the Japanese. For sixteen days, they sailed through heavy seas that damaged the ship's steering gear. Eventually they reached the safety of Freemantle in Australia.

Others were less fortunate. Eight boys were killed when the Japanese captured the shore establishment of HMS *Sultan*. Some of the boys who had survived the sinking of the two battleships – including Albert Riddle's friends – were formed into a shore party that was armed and sent to the front to fight the Japanese. Those who survived the fall of the city spent the rest of the war as prisoners, building the infamous Burma-Siam railway. Many never returned home.

Also part of the desperate escape from Singapore was the merchant ship *Empire Star*, whose eight-man crew included five boys between the age of fifteen and eighteen. When she left Singapore the cargo ship, designed to carry just twelve passengers, was carrying over 2,000 refugees from Singapore, including civilians, soldiers and RAF personnel. The day after leaving Singapore, she was attacked by Japanese dive-bombers. Two bombs struck the ship, killing some twelve of the military personnel onboard and wounding many more. The crew immediately set to work extinguishing the fires that broke out, aided by volunteers who were led by two cadet officers, seventeen-year-old Redmond Faulkner and fifteen-year-old Raymond Perry. The two Liverpool lads were both commended for their bravery in helping extinguish the fires. The initial attack by six bombers was followed up by a two-hour assault by a total of forty-seven Japanese planes. Through a combination of good fortune and brilliant seamanship, the *Empire Star* somehow avoided the bombs and made its way safely to West Java. Eight months later, the *Empire Star* finally met her end, torpedoed in the Atlantic by a German U-boat. Among the casualties was Cadet Raymond Perry, who was last seen onboard a lifeboat that disappeared at sea.

After escaping from Singapore, Albert Riddle was taken to Indonesia, then to Colombo in Ceylon, now Sri Lanka. After a period of rest, he was sent to the Maldives, where he worked on a small supply ship. The twenty-seven-man crew were given the task of supplying the Royal Navy positions around an atoll, which was defended to prevent its use by the Japanese. Though the job was boring, and he never saw a woman in the whole sixteen months he was there, Albert relaxed and was able to clear his mind. After a year of danger and disaster on a battleship, it was exactly what he needed. He eventually returned to England in 1944, just in time for D-Day, and was posted to a warship supporting the invasion.

In March 1942 Royal Marine Bugle Boy Len Chester left HMS *Iron Duke* and returned to Eastney Barracks. Three years earlier he had been a new boy, uncertain of what to do and how to behave. He returned as a veteran, a sixteen year old who the younger recruits looked up to as 'an old soldier with many a tale to tell'.[2] He knew how to clean and polish, could strip his bed with ease and had earned badges of which the young recruits still dreamed: 'We lorded it over the new recruits coming in. We were "old seamen". We knew the ropes.' For the next six months his time was filled with parades and fundraising events in which he played with the band. One of the boys still training when Len returned to Eastney was Robin Rowe, who had volunteered aged thirteen following the death of his brother on HMS *Hood*. He recalled how Len appeared so old and experienced following his two years on the *Iron Duke*. The new boys were particularly impressed by that fact that he was wearing a pre-war uniform and carrying pre-war equipment. It was a sign that he was of an earlier generation and the new boys could learn much from him.

In June 1942, now aged fourteen, Robin Rowe joined HMS *Howe*, a newly commissioned battleship. Prior to joining her, he went on leave and underwent the traditional rite of passage for boys going to war: his father took him to the pub and gave him a beer. Arriving at the ship, he realized the crew was to be a mixture of newly trained men and experienced seamen. As he went to board the ship, he struggled to carry his equipment, since he had two kit bags, the larger being just nine inches shorter than him. Once onboard, he went through the routine of learning the rules of living on a mess deck, complete with historical idiosyncrasies such as marines never sitting or lying on a mess table, whilst sailors were allowed. The rules were strict: never wear a hat on the mess deck; always wear a shirt at mealtimes; never touch anyone else's equipment; never clean equipment at the table. Heading out to sea, Robin Rowe quickly learned the realities of life as a Royal Marine. He learned that in wartime rubbish was only dumped overboard at night, so as not to alert enemy submarines. He noticed how the sea changed colour from grey-green to blue-green as they moved out into deeper ocean waters. The fourteen year old soon realized that the marines maintained strict standards in order to show they were different from the other services: they believed they could soldier as well as any unit in the Army and were just as good sailors as anyone in the Royal Navy.

September 1942 saw Len Chester, at the grand old age of seventeen, posted to HMS *King George V.* There was one pleasant change onboard the battleship. The *Iron Duke* had carried a crew of regular sailors and endured harsh pre-war discipline. On the *King George V* many of the crew were 'hostilities only' who would never accept the same harsh standards. Another good thing was that the ship was fitted with a tannoy. Rather than run around the ship sounding calls, he remained on the bridge and sounded the bugle calls into a microphone.

His first trip was a sea-going convoy to the Arctic, escorting merchant ships to Murmansk. They seemed to be constantly under observation by long-range German aircraft and under constant threat of air attack. His life became an endless round of 'four hours on, four hours off' watch duties on the ship's bridge: 'You didn't have time to think about the dangers. When you came off watch all you wanted to do was sleep. Then you have something to eat and go back on watch again.' The old world of precise creases and perfectly tidy uniforms had gone. To make life bearable they wore whatever they could find, anything to keep out the cold. After two years on a static ship, the winter seas were a shock: 'The waves were as high as the bridge. You'd look out and see them. A forty-foot wave doesn't sound much, but every wave has a trough. So in the trough, the wave is eighty feet above you.' Even when he was off duty and safely ensconced below decks, he could not escape the sound of waves hitting the side of the ship. It gave him a sense of mortality to think there were just three inches of steel between him and a torpedo – and certain death.

His worst experience was when the ship encountered hurricane conditions en route to Russia, escorting Convoy JW-53. The ship took such a battering that even the men below decks suffered:

> All the ventilators faced forward and were ripped off by the heavy seas, as were the bow ack-ack guns. After that, every wave that came over went down the vents and into the mess decks. So we were flooded. We had to eat our meals with our trousers rolled up and up to our ankles in freezing water.

The experience gave him an enduring admiration for the merchant seamen who sailed the route:

> It was so bloody cold. To me that was the most bitter of all the campaigns. There was the weather and the danger. If you've ever seen an oil tanker blow up, you think, 'Who the hell would volunteer to serve on one of them?' That's why I've always had a deep regard for the Merchant Navy.

HMS *Howe* sailed as escort to the same convoy, giving Robin Rowe his first taste of extreme conditions. All men were cleared from the upper deck and all doors and hatches were closed to prevent flooding. Robin watched as the fo'c'sle was buried by wave after wave, sending a great torrent of water along the decks. He listened as the ship shuddered, its propellers coming clear of the water as they rode the tops of waves. He noted how it was almost impossible to use the 'heads' since the downward motion of the ship threw him from the toilet seat in a state of near weightlessness. If that was not enough, a valve preventing the return of water failed, meaning the sea surged through the drainage pipes, soaking those seated on toilets. Whilst on duty, Robin stood on the bridge, marvelling at the sight, but shivering from the cold. All he could do was listen to the terrible shriek of the wind and pray the storm might pass soon. At one point, the temperature was so low that the bugle froze to his lips, tearing away the skin when he had finished his call.

During breaks between convoys, the *Howe* moored in Iceland, where the teenage bugler received his introduction to small arms. So far he had fought the enemy with no more than a bugle. In Iceland he was trained on a Thompson sub-machine-gun and a Boyes anti-tank rifle. The first time he fired the Boyes, he realized it was misnamed as its recoil propelled the boy firing it three feet backwards.

Generally, life aboard the *King George V* was bearable for Len Chester. Living conditions were not bad compared to older ships. Once at sea, Len lived on a mess deck with twenty-five other marines, all members of the ship's band. It was a far cry from the days when he had lived on the sergeant's mess deck to protect him from paedophile seamen. But life remained basic. He just did his watch, then slept in his hammock, eating meals whenever he could: 'I had to collect my meals on a tray from the galley. It was quite a way from the galley to my mess. And, with the ship going up and down, trying to carry a tray full of food down a ladder was difficult.'

During 1943 the *King George V* moved to the Mediterranean. The ship took part in the bombardment of the Sicilian coast during the Allied landing and, having reached the age of eighteen, Len put in a request to transfer to the ranks. However, this could not be done until they returned to England. Celebrating his birthday at sea made him realize how different he was to other boys of his generation: 'I was a four-year veteran, with two ships and two years at sea.' At home, his old schoolmates were just being called up for military service. It was whilst serving in the Mediterranean that he learned the full power of a battleship: 'The noise! When the guns fire and recoil, it shakes the whole ship. Most of the time they fired salvos – just two guns. If it's a full broadside of all eight guns, it's too much.' HMS *Howe* joined in the bombardment. It was the first time Robin Rowe had sounded 'Action Stations' and the first time he had heard the guns fire in anger. He watched the orange flash of the guns firing, felt the ship shake with recoil, then smelled and tasted the sweet cloud of cordite that filled the atmosphere. Not having closed his eyes, he was temporarily blinded by the flash of the guns. In the following days, the now fifteen year old had a close reminder of the horrors of war whilst in port in Algiers. Following an explosion on an ammunition ship that caused numerous casualties, he saw human body parts floating past. Feeling sick, he moved to the other side of the ship and could not report it. Days later, during a German air raid, one of the *Howe*'s guns misfired. As the cordite charge fell from the gun, it exploded in a ball of flame, burning the turret crew and killing a sailor.

When HMS *King George V* returned to England in 1944, Len left the ship and returned to Eastney to commence training to join the ranks. He was joined in his squad by another ex-bugler, who had trained with him. Peter Baxter had been just fifteen years old when, in November 1941, HMS *Barham* had been torpedoed and then exploded. More than 800 men died in the disaster. He admitted to Len that he had no idea how he had survived: one moment he had been eating a meal, the next he was in the water. Once their training started, Len realized that, despite his youth, he had more sea-time than the instructors. He was pleased to find that, as a 'veteran', the other recruits were eager to listen to him to learn about life at sea. At the same time, Robin Rowe returned to England and found himself back in Eastney Barracks. Two years earlier, he had been a new recruit, sitting there in awe of 'veterans' like Len Chester. Now Len had moved on and he, still just sixteen years old, was the veteran admired by the newcomers. When he went on leave, he found himself feted by his father's friends. In their eyes, despite his youth, he wore a medal ribbon on his breast and must therefore know everything about the Italian campaign. He didn't tell them he knew nothing apart from what he had heard on the radio. When Robin returned to the sea, some of the new marines onboard had come straight from training. The new recruits were nineteen year olds who had never been to sea. It fell to the two sixteen-year-old 'veterans', Robin and his friend 'Whacker', to teach them about life at sea.

With almost every warship carrying a contingent of boys, it meant there were boys involved in nearly every incident of the war at sea. One of the most famous – and important – naval actions of the entire war was marked by the heroism of sixteen-year-old Tommy Brown. Where his story is different to so many is that Tommy was not a sailor but a civilian, a canteen assistant working for the NAAFI. He had lied about his age when he joined the HMS *Petard*, claiming to be seventeen. In October 1942 the ship intercepted a German submarine, *U-559*. Although the U-boat was sinking and had been abandoned by her crew, two British sailors climbed onboard to retrieve the submarine's codebooks. Tommy joined them on the submarine, rowing out to it in a whaleboat, collecting the codebooks and returning them to the *Petard*. Of the three who boarded the *U-559*, only Tommy had escaped when the submarine sank, trapping the other two.

The books and documents were taken back to England where they were passed to the cipher teams at the top-secret Bletchley Park. Once analysed, the documents rescued by the canteen assistant were used to break the 'Enigma' code, giving the Allies a precious intelligence tool that saved thousands of lives in the years that followed. Following his heroic acts, the truth about his age became known and he was sent home to await call-up for military service. The compensation for being sent home was that Tommy was awarded the George Medal for his deeds. Sadly, he did not live to receive his medal. He died in a house fire in 1945, trying to rescue his young sisters.

Another youngster who had a curious experience at sea was sixteen-year-old Jim Hutchison. Jim – the Royal Navy's youngest qualified diver – found himself alone in the sea after his ship was torpedoed off the coast of Africa. After some time treading water, Jim accepted death was imminent. Suddenly he spotted something floating in the water. He swam to the object only to discover it was a shark. The creature had been killed by the torpedo blast but was still floating. Jim hauled himself up on to the shark and hung on until a rescue boat appeared. As he later recalled: 'I bet I'm the only person whose life was saved by a shark.'

Even in wartime, the Royal Navy was full of tradition, with the old hands seemingly a class apart from the newly conscripted men. They had traditional ways of speaking and dressing and were different to the newcomers. As one new recruit, Ray Clarke, later noted:

> I didn't get tattoos – we were hostilities only – only the real sailors had tattoos and beards. You could tell who was who just by looking at them. The old sailors didn't like us. We were regarded with suspicion. And we looked down on them in the same way that the officers looked down on all of us. We had a bit up here – in our heads – they didn't. They were dyed-in-the-wool matelots.

The differences were just as pronounced among officers. Members of the Royal Naval Reserve, wearing the interwoven rings of rank on their sleeves, were easily distinguished from members of the Royal Navy, whose insignia was straight, or the Royal Naval Volunteer Reserve, who wore the waved lines that earned them the name 'The Wavy Navy'. When Derek Tolfree joined the Royal Navy as a sixteen-year-old midshipman in 1942, he noticed a degree of onboard snobbery: 'Most of the other midshipmen were from Navy families. And socially, the RNVR were much closer to the regular officers than the RNR. We were just sailors trying to be gentlemen – they got on together better. They were from the same class.' As a counter to this situation, Derek discovered there was a good reason to remain proud of being a member of the RNR: 'We were better at seamanship. RNR officers were professional seamen – it was their everyday job. On ships, the RNR officer would be the navigator. The Royal Navy spent much of their time on other business, like parading and gunnery.'

When Derek first joined HMS *Nelson*, he found the battleship stunningly large: 'like a floating barracks'. As a midshipman he was the equivalent of an apprentice in a merchant ship: the most junior of the officers who was there to learn how to be a ship's officer: 'I assisted the officer of the watch. There would be a duty lieutenant commander, junior officer of watch, and a midshipman. That way we picked up the trades, learning to steer and so on. Also, the midshipman ran the ship's boats. I also did courses on torpedoes.' Life on the *Nelson* gave him certain reminders of his time on a training ship. Once again, the junior officers were segregated from the senior ones: 'We lived in the gun room – it was just for midshipmen. The ward room was only for commissioned officers. We had a sub-lieutenant to watch over us. He was like a prefect, like we had at school.' He remained with the *Nelson* for six months, escorting convoys to North Africa and Malta. As he later explained, during this period he never felt tense about enemy action. He was more nervous about making mistakes: 'I wanted to keep my nose clean and not cock things up.'

From HMS *Nelson*, Derek was posted to HMS *Westminster*, an ageing destroyer that was part of the Rosyth Escort Force, accompanying convoys along the North Sea coast. It was a far cry from life on a battleship. The officers dressed casually and lived far more closely than on the vast battleship. As Derek noted: 'That was a very happy ship.' However, escorting coastal convoys was not a glamorous role:

> It was a bit of a dreary job. We took ships down to London, which was kept going by coal from up north. The Atlantic convoys came round and mustered at Methil, then we took them down the coast, with others joining the convoy on the way. The convoy dispersed at Southend and went into London. Then we went to Sheerness, refuelled overnight and headed back, picking up another convoy at Southend.

Although not glamorous, coastal work required a high standard of seamanship:

> We had to keep to a narrow, swept channel and it's not an easy coast. There were natural hazards and fog. If you strayed off the paths you

were in trouble. It was strewn with wrecks, you could sometimes see their masts sticking up through the water. I marked the wrecks on our charts, then used ASDIC to ping off the masts and work out our position. Also, we got attacked by a lot by aircraft, E-boats and submarines. Had a few great battles with E-boats and aircraft.

He recalled one attack:

I was on the bridge. The navigator was below, plotting on the charts. I was keeping him informed down the voice pipe. So I was with my head down looking at the charts. I suddenly looked up and there were all these tracer bullets shooting towards us. Bloody hell!

However, the burden of his duties meant the attack did not unnerve him and it was repulsed. During Derek's service on the *Westminster*, the destroyer was credited with three 'kills' as it kept the enemy away from the convoys.

Derek had been lucky. By being posted to coastal convoys he faced fewer dangers than some of his former shipmates from his days training at HMS *Worcester*. He later discovered that one of his mates had gone into the Merchant Navy at sixteen as the member of a tanker crew. His ship was sunk and he spent many days adrift in a lifeboat. The experience convinced him that he would be safer in the Royal Navy and so rejoined the RNR and was called up for service. He was on three ships, all of which were lost. On the third occasion he was lost at sea.

Despite the dangers of life at sea, the former sea-school boys had sailed the world, learned much and matured beyond their years as a result of their sea service. Derek Tolfree found this was particularly evident whenever he went home on leave in the latter years of the war: 'The uniform was smart and you thought you were "Jack the Lad". I would see lads I had been at school with who had just been called up. I was already a sub-lieutenant, when they were just training. I'd been three years at sea. I grew up quickly.'

CHAPTER 17

The Boys on the Home Front

'Time off was for having as much fun as possible, drinking, dancing and partying before being called back to help old Winston win his war.'

Christian Immelman, ship's apprentice

With war came a change in the lives of Britain's youth. As well as an increased spirit of independence, the war years saw a vast rise in youth crime and juvenile delinquency, causing serious concern for those in power. One Home Office report noted it was important not to consider juvenile delinquency a 'pale shadow' of adult crime, rather its progenitor.[1]

Even before the outbreak of war there had been a noticeable rise in criminal activity among juveniles. In 1938, over 36 per cent of all indictable crimes were believed to have been committed by juveniles – 26,000 boys and 1,700 girls. As a result the Home Secretary, Sir Samuel Hoare, commissioned a study of the subject. As Hoare had noted, the numbers of offences by juveniles 'began to assume serious proportion' among overall crime figures.[2] Whereas the early 1930s had seen indictable juvenile offences at 300 per 100,000 of population, by 1936 the figure had risen to 568 per 100,000. However, the fruits of the research were not published until 1942, by which time proposals were already underway for a fresh inquiry entitled 'The Effect of the War on Crime'.[3]

In 1938–9 convictions for indictable offences by children under fourteen had reached 16,208. By 1940–41 that figure had risen by 58 per cent to 25,604. In just the first twelve months of war there were 41 per cent more crimes committed by boys and girls under fourteen. Of particular concern was that offences by girls had risen by 100 per cent – mostly committed by girls under fourteen. The big difference between the boys and girls was that the boys tended to operate in gangs whilst delinquent girls usually acted alone. In the same period, convictions of those aged between fourteen and seventeen had reached 18,694, a 44 per cent rise on the figures for 1938–9. In Essex, juvenile crime rose from 437 convictions in 1938 to 609 by 1942. The MP for Leyton East pointed out that the rising crime levels should be viewed in light of the falling numbers of children in the area as a result of evacuation, effectively magnifying the crime levels.

In April 1941, to address the rising criminality among the young, the Home Office arranged a conference to discuss how the offenders might best be dissuaded from a life of crime. Its concern was that: 'unless effective steps are taken to deal with juvenile delinquency now there might well be a serious increase in adult crime in a few years' time'.[4] The Home Office acknowledged that the rising numbers of offences reflected the changing times. The nation's boys had been gripped by the high spirits at the outbreak of war. With a heightened desire for adventure, many committed low-level offences that reflected a desire to share the adventure they believed their fathers had embarked upon. As the report noted: 'It would be unwise to ignore the effect of the excitement and unsettlement of war on adolescent boys'.[5] It was not just the excitement of war that helped to change society; the horrors unleashed on the nation gripped the minds of Britain's youth. In March 1941 one newspaper described the rise of juvenile delinquency in London as 'perfectly appalling' referring to the 'demoralising effects of violent events on the juvenile mind'.[6]

Furthermore, the initial rise in offences had coincided with the closure of schools as the first wave of evacuations had disrupted young lives. Truancy became an easy option for boys distracted by the experience of war. In some areas truancy and poor time-keeping were considered 'very serious problems and a fundamental factor in juvenile delinquency'.[7] During 1941 the authorities in Birmingham reported 40 per cent truancy rates and suggested that it would be better for the truants to work illegally, earning their wages, to prevent them resorting to crime.

The lack of full-time education was recognized as the prime factor in the rise of juvenile delinquency. In some areas as little as 7 per cent of children were receiving full-time regular compulsory education. In part, this was due to the lack of shelter space at schools as building materials were diverted elsewhere. In Wolverhampton 1,000 children were in part-time education. The council found that local delinquent youths were more interested in working than going to school and were attracted to a scheme that employed them in basic roles such as mending household goods. This and other similar schemes helped lower the local figures for youth crime, leading to the assumption that the youths just needed to be kept busy.

The correlation between crime and school closure was explained by the local authorities in Bristol, where juvenile crime peaked between the ages of fourteen and fifteen. In 1940 the city saw an increase in planned crimes by youth gangs and in the first twelve months of war there was a 41 per cent increase in children under fourteen found guilty of indictable offences. In the fourteen- to seventeen-year-old age group there was a 22 per cent increase in crime. A council report blamed: 'the absence of fathers on military service, the taking up of war work by mothers, the breaking up of home life owing to evacuation and the closing of schools in the early stages of the war'. Also the rising wages for school-leavers and the closing of youth organizations, combined with adolescent boys being excited and unsettled by war, were considered factors. The lower level of youth crime in Bristol than other cities was explained by the fact that there were fewer closed schools than elsewhere in the country.

Noting that the main cause of the high crime levels was a lack of parental discipline and increasingly uncertain home lives, the Home Office recognized the need to provide youths with organized distractions. Similarly, the Department of Education was convinced that male teachers were the best influence to prevent boys falling into crime. In particular, it was the younger male members of school staff who encouraged boys to take part in extracurricular activities, especially sports. However, it was these young male teachers who had been called up into the military, to be replaced by women and older, retired men. In order to prevent delinquency, and to bring the schools back into the centre of the lives of British children, the Department of Education suggested that schools be encouraged to keep their playgrounds open in winter evenings to encourage children to play there rather than risk the dangers of blacked-out streets.

It was not just the children and their teachers that were blamed for the falling standards in wartime. In 1942 Ralph Assheton at the Ministry of Labour blamed parents for the rising levels of juvenile delinquency: 'Since elementary education became compulsory, I suspect there has been a tendency on the part of parents to think they needn't bother to bring up their own children because the state was doing it.'[8] However, officials at the Ministry of Education thought that this couldn't be presented to parents who would simply retort that wealthy families sent their children to boarding schools for thirty-six weeks of the year and were paying for their children to be brought up by someone else.

The changing situation did not just affect schoolboys. School-leavers were confronted by a high demand for their labour, as industry upped production to cope with the demands of the military. These boys found themselves earning wages far exceeding peace-time averages. This often meant they had money to spend rather than save. Magistrates noticed boys appearing before them who

were earning between £3 and £5 a week. As a result of their
new-found wealth, these boys faced 'new temptations', spending
their money 'riotously' and often displaying a recklessness seldom
seen pre-war. As one MP told the House of Commons, high wages
for children meant: 'young people have an overrated opinion of
themselves, and have been able to spend more money than is good
for them'.[10]

The courts and newspapers recorded the behaviour of youth
gangs in parts of London. Teenage gangs were seen roaming the
streets, even during air raids, often flitting from shelter to shelter,
finding the best locations for drinking, gambling or casual encounters with girls. One Army deserter organized a gang, aged between
fourteen and sixteen, to rob shops in south London's Elephant and
Castle area. Soho saw the rise of a teenage gang named the 'Dead
End Kids' who – like the teenage fire-fighters in Stepney –
chose their title in homage to the group of young New York-born
actors who had appeared as a street gang in 1930s films. In Fulham
a gang of twenty youths, mostly aged between sixteen and
seventeen, ruined local dances. They rushed into dance halls,
clutching beer bottles and drove away the dancers. Even when
arrested, their high wages meant fines did not deter them: 'This gang
broke up a dance hall, kicking in the doors, breaking furniture and
windows and pulling away the gas pipes. They are a vicious group.
The use of violence is not unusual. Much of the juvenile drinking in
pubs is done by this small, vicious minority.'[11]

In north London, teenage postman Peter Richards began to
experience a social life with broader horizons than the old days at
the youth club. Increasingly, the boys and girls began to mix and he
no longer laughed at mates who went to dances. The girls were now
not just long-haired creatures who 'danced backwards', but something with a definite appeal. With his weekdays filled by work, sports
and evening trips to the pub, Sunday evenings saw a new form of
entertainment. He began attending a newly opened dance hall: the
Clarence. This was the era in which new forms of dance music

flourished and was embraced by the nation's youth. In the words of George Melly, then a jazz-loving pupil at Stowe School: 'Suddenly, as if by some form of spontaneous combustion, the music exploded in all our heads.'[12]

The Clarence was a weekly club held in a local church hall. It needed club status to avoid the laws limiting dancing. To meet the rules, the local youths all queued up, signed their names on a ledger and received a number. This was, ostensibly, their membership number which they quoted as they paid their entrance fee. Once inside, there was a four-piece band, comprising piano, trumpet, saxophone and drums. Dances included waltzes, foxtrots, quick-steps, then maybe a tango or a rumba. Enthusiastic local singers would join the band onstage to add vocals to the songs as the crowd danced. For Peter Richards, it was a chance for everyone to get dressed up to impress the girls: 'The cinema pushed the latest fashions. We didn't just look like our dads. The youngsters almost wore a uniform. A suit and shirt and tie. Haircut: short back and sides and Brylcreem. We were very conscious of shining our shoes.' As he recalled, looking good was just as important as in peacetime. The particular problem was the restriction placed on clothing, meaning that trousers could not have turn-ups and suits had to be single-breasted: 'There was a lot of subterfuge, especially about turn-ups. The ploy was to get the tailor to cut the trousers with a longer leg so that you had an inch of material to turn up. I used to be very conscious of turn-ups.'

The club was a place for teenagers to dress up and be seen. Girls scraped together whatever make-up they could find, put on their best frocks and paraded for the boys. The boys got changed from their work clothes, put on their best shirts and brightest ties, combed their hair and did their best to impress. It was a world far removed from the stinking dullness of air raid shelters. Although unlicensed, the club offered beer to its customers. This was served not at a bar but in the gentlemen's toilets. The toilet attendant, employed to prevent vandalism, sold it to the boys at a penny more than pub prices. As Peter Richards recalled, it seemed strange that the boys paid 'over the odds' for beer when they could walk across the street and buy a glass.

There was one element that livened up the dances, albeit violently. As Peter remembered: 'What made the Clarence unique was the clientele. The men were a really mixed group, comprising petty villains, "razor boys", lads from the gym and those who might be called ordinary.' The gangs carried cut-throat razors which were opened and wielded at the first sign of trouble:

> There were some vicious fights there. Blood everywhere. It was the usual nonsense: someone said something or looked at someone the wrong way or had pushed them. And they fought over girls. I saw blokes on the floor, with someone just banging his fist into his face, and someone else kicking the person who was doing the punching. The 'razor boys' would cut people on the face, to mark them. The police would raid it from time to time. There'd be people jumping out from the window of the ladies' toilet. But I had a lot of good friends at the club. There were a lot of political types there. We'd discuss politics before breaking off for a waltz or a foxtrot.

As the blood flowed, the gangs practised a form of ritual humiliation in which a rival's tie was slashed off just below the knot, then stuffed in his pocket as a symbol of defeat. Strangely, as Peter Richards noticed, the band never stopped playing despite the unfolding carnage. All those who didn't want to be involved would move to the edge, leaving the gangs to fight until one was victorious. Fortunately for Peter, the gangs only fought among themselves, leaving the more innocent youths unmolested: 'It was a different attitude. If you weren't one of the "razor boys" they left you alone. You didn't upset them though.'

Some observers believed youths seen hanging around cafes were to blame for the rising crime rate, thinking the cafes brought them into the company of disreputable types. Suggestions were put forward that cafes should be licensed to prevent youths using them. Accusations were also made against cinemas and the films they showed. Another target were the 'pin-table saloons' where youths hung around playing pinball. However, the Home Office found no evidence to link films or cinema-going to juvenile delinquency. Instead, cinemas actually kept youths occupied and out of trouble. If anything, American films were aspirational: they showed British youth a world of cafes and restaurants where all manner of food was available. They showed well-dressed people in bright, casual clothes. It was a lifestyle of which the average British teenager could only dream.

Although there was concern that the country was being swamped by a wave of juvenile crime that threatened the very fabric of society, not all were gripped by a hysterical reaction to circumstances that were similar to those noticed during the Great War. As Arthur Norris, formerly the Chief Inspector of the Children's Branch of the Home Office, stressed in a letter to the *Spectator* in May 1941:

> Boys commit mischief because they find nothing else to satisfy their desire, particularly in these days, to be up and doing; their fathers are perhaps on service or employed long hours in munitions or other work, and of even greater import, is that their mothers are also working away from their homes with the result that home influence is lost or diminished and the boys must find their opportunity for activity and adventure, in increasing measure, in the street.[13]

One single factor threatened to change the face of juvenile crime: the availability of guns. Weapons and ammunition were easily available to many children and teenagers. A Home Office report estimated that some 76,000 guns had entered the UK illegally with returning British soldiers. Some had even been posted home by soldiers serving overseas and with around 120,000 packages entering the country each week, it was almost impossible to check each one. Living in York, Peter Gawthrop recalled how easy it was for a curious schoolboy to access munitions:

> We used to cycle out to the air bases. There were ammunition storage places beside the roads. They were supposed to be guarded but they weren't. Me and my friends would go and look at the shells and cordite. The ammo was kept in wooden boxes. The police would come round on their bikes every now and then to inspect them but they didn't come very often. We'd use the cordite to try and make fireworks – we got it to burn but we didn't manage to get it to explode.

In particular there were thousands of households in which guns were stored by members of the Home Guard. In most cases children were able to play with rifles belonging to their fathers. For a responsible child this was like playing 'Cowboys and Indians' with a real weapon. Peter Gawthrop remembered his father's rifle:

> My father was in the Home Guard – and so there was a clip of five bullets in a drawer downstairs – and a rifle in the wardrobe upstairs. I wasn't allowed to play with the rifle, but of course I did when no one else was in the house. Although unlike some I wasn't stupid enough to put a bullet in it. I knew two boys who'd been injured in accidents involving bullets and explosives. One had tried to dismantle a bullet and the other who lost an eye had hit some explosives with a hammer.

Yet other youths had more serious intentions. In 1942 two teenagers ran away from a remand home, broke into a Home Guard storeroom and stole a sub-machine-gun and 400 rounds of ammunition. In Glasgow a group of teenagers stole a box of hand grenades and threw them at an office building, destroying the company boardroom. Some young criminals put the weapons to use: in 1943 a gang – including two seventeen year olds – robbed a cinema using stolen Sten guns. They were jailed for three years for their crimes.

For some, the access to weapons was lethal. In December 1941 seventeen-year-old Colin Sterne was living with his aunt and uncle, Mr and Mrs Turner, at their Gloucestershire farm. Following an argument with his aunt, in which she called Colin's sister a prostitute, he took violent action. Losing his temper, he grabbed a police truncheon that his uncle kept in the house, hitting his uncle: 'Something seemed to go in my head and the next I remember was going to the cart-shed and getting the rifle.'[14] The weapon in question was his uncle's Home Guard issued Winchester rifle, which was kept in the living room. Though unloaded, Sterne found ammunition in a bandolier hanging in the kitchen. Loading the rifle, he went outside. There he found his aunt and shot her. Enraged by having been beaten by his nephew, Mr Turner rushed outside where he was also gunned down. It was a pointless end to a petty argument: one that was only possible because of the easy access to an Army rifle.

By 1945, delinquency became intolerable in some areas. Liverpool was hit by a juvenile crimewave that appalled local people, while church leaders wrote to the Home Office to complain about crime. They reported that children were entering premises, including homes, churches and schools, and deliberately destroying furniture. Goods were stolen from any unoccupied buildings and some empty buildings had been so badly smashed up by youths that they needed demolition. The teenagers smashed their way into shops through roofs, doors and windows. Describing it as a 'reign of terror', the churchmen reported: 'The young hooligans have taken to beating up individuals where their numbers and the locality make the practice safe, and this for no apparent reason other than bravado and fun. In certain areas females are afraid to go out in the evening without strong male escort.'[15] They reported that women, often without the protection of husbands who were away from home on war service, were afraid to complain for fear of reprisals. The problem was compounded by parents who seemed to have no interest in their children when they went before the courts. In October

1945 the Liverpool and District Property Owners' Association passed a resolution regarding 'wanton damage, destruction and thieving which has been done to properties, chiefly by youths and boys who appear to have no respect for law and order, and who are apparently out of police control'.[16]

The local constabulary admitted that these types of crimes had always been an issue in the city, but had got worse in wartime. Offences of breaking and entry, wounding and robbery had increased almost threefold on pre-war levels. Parental control had all but disappeared in some areas due to working mothers and fathers away in the forces. When central government had responded to the need for scrap metal for war production, and relaxed regulations on the sale of metals, Liverpool's youths had responded by increasing the theft of metal. The police also pointed out that some offenders were as young as eight. As the city's Chief Constable admitted, the juveniles they were dealing with:

> become the adults who are responsible for a great part of the serious crime in Liverpool including cases of robbery and serious assaults. They form into gangs which, while not organized as a disciplined body like the American gangs, are yet prepared to assist and protect fellows and at time resort to intimidation.[17]

Though the newspapers were full of news of the antics of fresh-faced would-be gangsters, there were also genuine tales of bravery, dedication and sacrifice by youngsters. One boy who was openly praised was eleven-year old Colin Ryder Richardson. The survivor of the sinking of the SS *City of Benares* struggled to recover from his experiences in the aftermath of the disaster. The boy, described by a fellow survivor as the 'bravest and kindest boy I've ever seen'[18] and noted by the *Daily Mirror* as a hero, needed to settle back into normal life.

In the days following his return to the UK, Colin remained very weak. He later described it as if 'life was passing me by like in a cinema. I was witnessing events as people tried to help me.' Even his arrival in Glasgow, immediately after the Royal Navy had returned the survivors to shore, seemed like a dream:

> At Customs, they asked, 'Where are your passports?' We laughed, we said, 'If you want them, they are 600 miles out at the bottom of the Atlantic!' I had been given the captain's golfing plus-fours to wear. But even though they are short on an adult, as an eleven year old, they were over my feet. So I couldn't wear them. I walked into the Central Hotel, Glasgow. I was in my life jacket and pink pyjamas. I was barefoot, I hadn't any clothes. But nobody raised an eyebrow, or even looked at me. I was just waiting for someone to say, 'What are you doing in your pyjamas at this time in the morning?' But it was as if everything was normal.

Those first days were difficult. At one point, the survivors were taken to a shoe shop where they were photographed trying on shoes. There was, however, one problem: all the shoes were for ladies. There was nothing for an eleven-year-old boy. It was a traumatic time for the whole family. His mother was called north to meet her son. Their meeting was a strange one: 'She looked at me and I looked at her and she said, "What have you done with all your clothes?" I felt responsible for losing it all. A totally ridiculous guilt came over me.' Colin's father first learned of his son's fate at a railway station. He was waiting for a train when he noticed someone reading a newspaper that was celebrating the rescue of the survivors of the SS *City of Benares*. He asked to borrow the paper and the reader asked him why. Colin's father pointed to a photograph in the newspaper and replied: 'I believe that's my son.'

Returning home to Wales, life carried on. Colin was visited by American journalists and photographers, but he never discussed the matter with his classmates at the local school. It seemed that, despite the initial press interest, his mother wanted 'the matter forgotten': 'Her attitude was "Least said, soonest mended". Rightly or wrongly.

It was very strange to say a photographer was going to come into school to photograph me in class.' At times, he thought to himself, 'Was it all a bad dream?' because no one talked about the tragedy.

But if his mother thought the incident could be forgotten, leaving her eleven-year-old son to grow up 'normally', she was in for a surprise. Out of the blue, in January 1941 a letter arrived for Colin from Buckingham Palace. Enclosed was a small certificate, signed by Winston Churchill, informing the eleven-year-old boy that he had been commended for 'brave conduct in the Merchant Navy'.

The wording was curious: he had never served in the Merchant Navy and felt he had done little more than survive the sinking of a ship. As he later recalled:

> I couldn't exactly write back to the King and say, 'Hang on, I wasn't in the Merchant Navy, I was just a passenger on a liner.' I believe it was the ship's carpenter or Professor Day – who had to be tied into the lifeboat to stop him being washed away – who recommended me for the award. I believe Professor Day recommended me for the George Cross. But for that you need to have saved lives, all I had done was help dispose of bodies.

However, he soon received a small badge issued to all recipients of the commendation. The accompanying letter informed him it should be placed 'immediately above the centre of the position in which any medal ribbons are, or would be, worn'. It was a curious instruction for a child whose only uniform was for school and who was seven years too young to be conscripted. This badge was later replaced by an oak leaf emblem along with a message informing him it should be worn on the ribbon of the 'War Medal' – an award he was too young to earn.

The question of how to wear the award was vexing. After all, if in uniform, he would be improperly dressed without his oak leaf: 'I had to wear it. At public school I joined the Junior Training Corps. I had a problem: which side do I wear it? Civilian side, on the right?

Or military, on the left? I thought, "Bugger that, I'll put it on the left."' Despite his mother's desire that he should forget his experiences, Colin developed a curious desire to return to the sea. In 1942, at the age of thirteen, he applied to the Admiralty for a cadetship at a Royal Navy academy, in the hope of becoming a professional seaman. He was rejected on health grounds.

Whilst it was the under-fourteens and their schools which were evacuated by the local authorities, private schools also relocated from the cities into the countryside. As a result, many boys between fourteen and eighteen – mostly from solid middle-class backgrounds – found themselves occupying rural villages. Terry Charles spent the middle years of the war with his relocated London school, the Regent Street Polytechnic, in Somerset. When not at school, the boys worked on local farms, picking apples and other fruits.

Just as in 1939 when he had been privately evacuated to Cornwall, he felt like an outsider and had trouble settling into village life. As a result, it was not always a pleasant experience: 'I didn't feel we were welcome. The villagers didn't want a load of Londoners dumped on them – and we didn't particularly want to be there. It was "us and them". We were teenagers of sixteen and seventeen – the village kids hated us.' As he recalled, whenever the price of beer went up, the schoolboys wrote home for extra pocket-money, a luxury not shared by the local youths:

> There were always fights. Once one of our masters had been down to the village and he came hurtling back into the school. He told us there was a scrap going on. He said, 'Quick, your colleagues are getting murdered down there. They need reinforcements!' So about eight of us piled into his car and he took us down to join the fray.

There were also arguments over girls, with the locals feeling the Londoners were encroaching on their 'territory'. In particular, one girl, described by Terry Charles as someone all the boys knew, was very popular: 'She was very bonny. But she was known as the "village bicycle" – everybody rode her!' The spread of her affections helped to drive a wedge between the locals and the schoolboys.

Apart from fighting with the locals, Terry Charles and his schoolmates found solace in the single village pub, where a 'gentleman's agreement' was established: the pupils had to drink in the public bar whilst the masters used the lounge. Being in Somerset, cider was the favoured tipple of the schoolboys. It was strong stuff: it tasted like apple juice but as soon as the boys stood up and went out into the fresh air they found their legs didn't work.

In the period leading up to D-Day the village filled up with American servicemen. As far as they could see, there was nothing but tanks, trucks and men in uniform. They too became acquainted with the local cider:

> For the first couple of days that the Americans were in the village they frequented the pub. By the third day there was nothing left, they'd drunk all the spirits. They'd drunk the landlord's entire monthly ration. They moaned and groaned, then one of the locals who was sitting there drinking said, 'Why don't you try some of our cider?' They said, 'Na, Pop, we want a man's drink!' But they were forced to drink the cider because there was nothing else. Then a strange thing happened, within about three-quarters of an hour they were passing out. There were bodies all over the floor. They didn't realize how potent it was. From then on they didn't drink anything else.

Prior to leaving school, Terry and his classmates were called back to London to sit the matriculation exam. Just as had happened earlier in the war, he found his return to the city coincided with increased enemy activity:

> We were in a hall at London University. We went in, sat down, they shut the doors and we began. Then the sirens went off. But we weren't allowed to leave – in case we cheated. Because it was a public exam, we still had to sit it. We had to try and concentrate through the air raid, with the sound of bombs going off.

Despite the bombs, he passed the exam.

The middle years of the war saw many youths continuing to show the same enthusiasm that had been shown back in 1939 and 1940. Although the threat from enemy bombers had diminished, there remained a genuine desire for youngsters to play an active role in the war effort. For the teenage boys and girls working in munitions factories or in shipyards, there was already a sense that they were genuinely contributing, but for others there was a need to get involved in more martial activities. For many youngsters, first the Army Cadet Force, then the Home Guard, continued to be ideal. With recruitment set at seventeen, many youngsters found they were able to volunteer much younger, thus earning themselves the right to wear a uniform.

Whilst much has been made of the comic nature of the Home Guard, there was a seriousness that belied its early appearance. Once armed, the force played a genuine role by undertaking guard duties, releasing the regular Army to train and prepare for possible invasion. For youngsters who volunteered for the Home Guard, there was the sense that they were receiving training that they would put to use once they were conscripted. As the war progressed, the Home Guard increasingly trained alongside units of the regular Army, providing opposition during street-fighting exercises. By the time these youths were called up, they had an understanding of life in the Army and the tactics of the modern battlefield. Where once they had appeared as naive youths, in awe of the veterans of the Home Guard who paraded with their chests decked in medal ribbons of long-past campaigns, by the middle of the war these teenagers were ready to prove themselves as soldiers with a far greater understanding of modern warfare than their mentors.

In Aldershot, Dennis Hobbs reached the age of sixteen and was asked to leave the Army Cadets and join the Home Guard. Since Aldershot was a military town, the facilities available to the Home Guard were beyond those available to most local units. As a result, his training was far removed from the comic efforts of 1940: 'The

Home Guard wanted runners and signallers. The signallers would use flags but they also made me learn Morse code. We all knew what we'd have to do in the event of an invasion; I'd have had to run between the commanding officer and the posts taking messages.' For sixteen-year-old Dennis, it was the weapons training that was most attractive:

> There were big rifle ranges nearby – and we went up there to learn to fire Sten guns and Lee Enfield rifles. A rifle nearly knocked me off my feet – as I was only about seven-and-a-half stone at that point. And it wasn't until we'd had a few bursts of the Sten gun that the instructor told us that one in ten of them explode when you fired them!

The Aldershot Home Guard also did hand-grenade and explosives training:

> Whenever we did our training it was up at the camps or in War Department lands – we weren't like *Dad's Army*. One time they even took us up to a camp, made us put on our gas masks and closed us in a room. Then they threw some gas in. Then you had to take the mask off. They taught us to hold your breath then after a minute you were supposed to exhale. That's when everything went – your nose and your eyes. It was horrible. So I got a certificate to say I'd done gas training. It was quite good fun. I'd go back and tell the other blokes who weren't in the Home Guard – 'Look what I did!' Because I was in the Home Guard for two years, I earned a couple of war medals. That was something else you could show off.

Some nights, the teenager was sent to guard the local power station, where he walked around the perimeter with his rifle, trying to look important and brave, rather than belying the truth: that he found it somewhat nerve-wracking to be walking around in the dark, uncertain of what might happen next.

Having earlier worked as a thirteen-year-old ARP messenger,

Roy Finch became one of the new recruits to the Home Guard after, aged sixteen, he found a job as a messenger at Waterloo railway station. He enjoyed the job and found wartime London a fascinating place. His boss sent him out across the city, collecting documents, delivering papers and shopping for tobacco. He enjoyed the street scenes as he made his way across a city still struggling to cope with the occasional bombing raid and the after-effects of earlier raids: 'London was a very interesting place, in an interesting time. It was full of foreign troops. There was the blackout and the bombs. I was queuing up at shops, seeing kids playing in bombed buildings. I thoroughly enjoyed myself.'

He particularly enjoyed watching the American servicemen as they came through the railway station on the way back to base after a day out in London: 'I would see them going back in the afternoon, half-pissed, with a prostitute on their arm.' The station staff enjoyed making fun of the Americans: 'There was a tannoy system in the station. The operator didn't like Yanks. So she would play their national anthem over the tannoy. They all had to try to stand to attention, half-cut, with these women hanging off their arms. "That'll teach them," she'd say to me.'

As he was working there, it was logical that Roy should join the Waterloo station branch of the Home Guard. It was mainly porters, guards and train drivers – all First World War veterans who were too old to be called up. But among them were a handful of messenger boys, like Roy, who were awaiting call-up. The unit underwent regular training at a Home Guard camp, learning drill, doing target practice and being instructed in throwing hand grenades. At other times, the unit were sent to east London where the Army had taken over bombed streets to use as a training ground, instructing the soldiers in street-fighting. Roy and his fellow railwaymen played the defenders as the soldiers practised house-clearing. Roy was given bags of flour that he would throw into 'enemy' vehicles to simulate the explosion of hand grenades. He was entertained by the sight of the umpires telling flour-covered

Grenadier Guardsmen that they had been 'killed' by a Southern Railways messenger boy. On other exercises roles were reversed and troops of Boy Scouts were pressed into service, acting as 'enemy' units in Home Guard training exercises.

However, the Home Guard's main role was to mount guard on Waterloo station:

> We'd do guard duty at the station once a week. You came on duty at six in the evening and patrolled the platforms all night. I was sixteen years old. I'd draw the rifle from the stores, and then I had to sign for two bullets. If a German parachutist had come down we were supposed to confront them. I think if one had actually landed I'd have run back to the sergeant.

At seven in the morning, Roy handed the bullets back in, went for breakfast in the staff canteen and then started work, meaning he remained in his Home Guard uniform for the rest of the day. This had both advantages and disadvantages:

> I strolled around London in my uniform. You'd get the piss taken out of you if soldiers saw your Home Guard badges, particularly if you walked past the Grenadier Guards. But it was a good life. The overcoat didn't have any badges so, as long as you kept your overcoat on, no one knew you were in the Home Guard. If I went into the Union Jack Club with my coat on, I could get a cup of tea and a bun. They couldn't tell it was Home Guard uniform.

Other boys serving in the Home Guard recalled how by keeping on their greatcoats, and appearing to be a serving soldier, they found it easier to chat-up girls.

Up and down the country were thousands of youths just waiting for their chance to serve their country. They had grown up in a world where the passage into manhood was marked by the issue of a uniform. Ray Clarke, a teenager in north London, explained the emotions shared by him and his mates:

I was living in East Barnet – stuck in an office doing electricity accounts. People would come back on leave, in their uniforms, and come round to the office – and I wished I was in their shoes. Being in uniform was glamorous. We used to go round with our pals and someone would say, 'Bill's got his call-up papers – lucky so and so – I wish mine would come.' Then it was the day I'd been waiting for – my call-up – Hurray! At last the day had come. I was going – this meant you'd go somewhere and see the world.

CHAPTER 18

The Good-time Girls

'... vulgar and demoralising literature, certain types of modern "swing" music based on rhythmic tattoos of primitive tribes and with a definite sexual motive.'

Report by Blackpool Council on the falling morality among local youth, 1941[1]

'... young persons who have no moral background and who are out of control and in need of care and protection.'

Ministry of Health report[2]

With the Blitz at an end, the youth of Britain breathed a collective sigh of relief and carried on with their lives. Yet for so many among them, the old social order had been swept away along with the rubble and corpses that had been the legacy of the bombing. Children who had witnessed unspeakable horrors of war, who had sheltered night after night – never knowing if it might be their turn next – could hardly be expected to return to normality overnight. In the summer of 1940 war had gone from being a game to being reality. All over the UK were children and teenagers who had tasted some of the terror previously only known to the men in the front line.

With life so cheapened, it was little wonder the country's youth began to change. The old certainties – the family, school and work – had been replaced by a new reality of dislocation and death. Absent fathers, working mothers, evacuation, closed schools and the ever-present threat of high explosive and incendiary bombs had ruptured the old social ties. Nowhere was this new reality more evident than on the streets of London's West End. It was not long before the press began to make sensationalist claims about teenage girls 'running wild' in the streets of the capital.

Right from the start of war, London had become a magnet for men in uniform. There were Britain's own soldiers, soon followed by men from the Empire and Dominions – by early 1940 some 25,000 Canadian soldiers had already arrived in the UK. Next came the escaping survivors from the armies of the defeated nations, along with civilians, politicians and royal families seeking refuge. From early 1942 they were joined by hundreds of thousands of American servicemen, who soon stamped their distinctive, well-paid – and swaggering – mark across the nation. By early 1944 the UK was home to some 1,400,000 American servicemen. In Northern Ireland the US presence represented a tenth of the 1937 population. In Suffolk, by 1944 there was one GI to every six locals and in parts of Wiltshire the English were, at times, outnumbered two to one.

The American servicemen became the target of young girls seeking adventure. The girls flocked to dances wherever they thought Americans might be found. They copied the latest transatlantic fashions from films and magazines, using their sewing skills in a radical reworking of the 'make do and mend' ethos to dress like their idols. The Americans earned wages at three times the level of their English equivalents and could thus afford to take girls to restaurants that English soldiers could hardly dream of eating in. It was the same in pubs, where English soldiers looked on as Americans were able to keep buying beer as long as stocks lasted. In the parlance of the times, Britain's boys shouted at American soldiers, 'Got any gum, chum?' to hear the reply, 'You got a sister, mister?'

Of course, not all British girls were blinded by the Americans, with their smart uniforms and gleaming white teeth. Jean Redman, who enjoyed the attentions of British boys, was unimpressed: 'I didn't go with any Americans. I found them rather brash compared to our boys who had good manners.'

Whilst there were thousands of respectable girls who were just excited to spend time with the glamorous Americans, there were some whose relationships were shaped by the changing tide of morality that swept the country. With so many thousands of men – far from home – inhabiting Britain, there was a great need for the men to find sexual relief. From kings to lost and lonely cabin boys, from admirals seeking a navy to Lascar seamen seeking a bed for the night, from wealthy New York socialites to all-but-illiterate farmhands, they came in search of excitement as Britain became first a haven, then a playground, for men at war. And with so many new men in town there was one commodity above all others that was in high demand: female company. To ensure the satisfaction of the men flocking to London a whole new wave of British girls turned to prostitution – whether by design or by accident – either on a full-time, part-time or amateur basis. Such was the demand that one recalled working a fourteen-hour day to meet it. To the older prostitutes these men were all the same – whether a medal-wearing hero in immaculate uniform or a gnarled old merchant seaman, they were all, in their language, 'mugs'. To the youngsters, the situation was different, slipping into the 'oldest profession' as a result of a youthful enthusiasm for the excitement and glamour of wartime. The uniforms held a genuine attraction and often gave rise to their introduction to their new career.

To keep the Americans satisfied, London had plenty of prostitutes willing to offer them a few short minutes of female company and some much needed sexual release. Yet, with so many new punters, there was more work than London's pre-war population of 3,000 street-walkers and brothel-workers could cope with. Pre-war it was estimated that most were over thirty years of age and a significant number were foreign women married, conveniently, to British men. By 1941 there were 5,000 girls working the streets. The Blitz had initially seen a fall in numbers of prostitutes working the city's streets as some working girls decided to offer their services somewhere – anywhere – safer. Others changed careers and volunteered for military service, bringing a touch of brassy glamour to the female elements of the armed forces. By 1941 the Metropolitan Police had estimated a significant number of the new working girls were under twenty. The usual haunts of Soho and Mayfair soon became the hunting grounds for a new, younger generation of recruits to the crusade against tyranny. After all, who could not argue that the sexual services they offered played a vital role in preserving the mental stability of servicemen desperate for comfort and company in the face of the prospect of a violently short life?

As prostitution flourished the Air Ministry complained to the Metropolitan Police about a brothel where it was found that married women were earning 'pin money' by having sex with clients, after detectives saw groups of RAF officers entering the building. During 1941 the Metropolitan Police prosecuted the bosses of just seventy-eight brothels, and it was believed that numbers were falling. Senior police officers admitted that the lack of prosecutions was actually a result of the blackout and that with bombs raining down on London, the police had other concerns: it was police policy not to waste manpower on investigating brothels.

By 1944 the figure for brothel prosecutions had risen to 178, with a further 156 cases in which there had been insufficient evidence to prosecute. The police also noted that whenever they took action in one area, the trade simply moved elsewhere. One example was in Eastbourne Terrace, Paddington, an area notorious for prostitution. When the police cracked down on brothels the girls swiftly moved on to nearby Marylebone Lane, where they upset the respectable residents.

The Ministry of Health reported on the 'parade of prostitutes now seen in a number of our better-known streets'.[3] In 1942, a Mayfair resident complained about the behaviour of the girls of Shepherds Market who, he wrote:

> infest the adjoining streets every afternoon, evening and night soliciting everybody who looks like a possible customer for their vile trade and they are supported and encouraged by thugs and bullies who adopt a threatening attitude towards any resident who they think is informing the police.[4]

Appalled residents watched prostitutes lounging around in groups, day and night, leaning against railings and calling out to clients. Some of the girls chose to solicit in less obvious locations. In 1943 the police had to deal with the problem of prostitutes using Warren Street Underground station to pick up punters, annoying the 'residents' who used the station to shelter. Another problem that the police had to confront was that arrests were sometimes made difficult by soldiers who intervened.

Yet the traditional image of ageing, painted, syphilitic whores was far from that of the new generation who aimed to separate the servicemen from their hard-earned cash. For many of the soldiers, sailors and airmen, the girls they picked up were far younger than the pre-war generation of prostitutes. One American general even reported his troops picking up girls as young as thirteen. The Ministry of Health soon recorded that teenage girls were taking up what was described as 'an immoral life' far earlier than they had during the Great War.[5] Official figures recorded a 100 per cent rise in juvenile offences by females during the war years, with a large number of offences related to immorality. The Home Office noted significant rises in the numbers of girls under the age of fourteen appearing among the juvenile crime statistics. A raid on one London brothel found that young girls who had not previously been reported as working as prostitutes were being shared between soldiers. Similarly, a fourteen-year-old Belgian refugee girl was found working as a 'dance hostess' in a London club, whilst a seventeen-year-old absconder from an approved school was found working in an illegal drinking club.

The line between professional prostitutes, amateur 'good-time girls' and young girls just attracted by the glamour of men wearing uniform was often blurred. Across the country, probation officers reported dealing with hundreds of cases of 'wayward' girls; many were under-seventeens who stayed out at night, often visiting Army camps. Rather than take official action, the probation officers attempted to deal with the problem by liaising with parents and most cases never reached the courts. During this period, the Ministry of Health pressed to bring wayward girls before the juvenile courts – hopefully shocking them into modifying their behaviour. In East Sussex the local courts were confused over how to deal with underage girls found to have been behaving 'immorally' with soldiers and seamen billeted in the area. One girl of fifteen came before the courts when she fell pregnant by a soldier. The court excused the soldier since the girl appeared way beyond her years.

It soon became clear to the authorities that the new breed of amateur prostitutes, who swarmed around off-duty servicemen, were not educated in the ways of the trade. In particular, they were responsible for a disproportionate increase in the number of new venereal disease infections. In September 1943 the Joint Committee on Venereal Disease reported: 'the most dangerous sources of infection are the "good time girls" who congregate at places frequented by members of the services in search of entertainment and excitement, and young persons who have no moral background and who are out of control'.[6] By 1943 the rate of venereal disease (VD) in England and Wales had risen significantly since 1939. The figures for gonorrhoea had risen by 63 per cent whilst syphilis infections had risen by 217 per cent.

In Scotland the figures were similarly troubling. For seventeen years leading up to the outbreak of war, new VD infection rates had been falling. Then in wartime cases rose again, with 1,000 new syphilis cases in 1939 rising to 3,700 new cases in 1942. A disproportionate number of these cases were in the fifteen to twenty-five age group. During 1942, ten people a day in Scotland contracted syphilis and sixteen contracted gonorrhoea. In one port the infection rates rose to eleven times the pre-war level. Observers noted prostitutes moving from port to port, seemingly with knowledge of where and when ships were due to arrive.

Whilst 'professionals' understood the need for sexual hygiene, knowing that keeping free from disease was the best way to maintain business, the 'good-time girls' were ignorant and irresponsible. As a result, it was not long before venereal disease infections became prevalent. The Metropolitan Police carried out a series of raids on boarding houses in the Bloomsbury area. It appeared the girls picked up Americans and Canadians in Soho then took them to the streets around Russell Square where there was a plentiful supply of boarding houses offering rooms for £4 a night. Of thirty-six girls arrested by the local police, 25 per cent were infected with VD, with fourteen of them under twenty years of age. The diseased girls were described as 'mostly young and not professionals'.[7]

The authorities reported that VD was spread by 'young persons who have no moral background and who are out of control and in need of care and protection'.[8] The police reported these amateurs were mostly unknown to them, except for a number of juveniles who were regular offenders and were often before magistrates, and were recognized as needing care and attention. In December 1943, Basil Henriques, the Chairman of East London Juvenile Court, gave a speech at Hackney Rotary Club highlighting the social problems he encountered on a day-to-day basis. As widely reported in the press, he reported that child delinquents coming before the courts had increased from between 3,000 to 4,000 a year pre-war to 8,000 or 9,000 a year in wartime. As he told his audience: 'War fever has affected girls far more than boys . . . They are attracted by anybody in uniform, and particularly a soldier who can afford to give them a good time.'[9]

He blamed American films for influencing the girls, noting that their pernicious influence, combined with lack of parental caution and an absence of steadying influence at home, drew the girls into a life of delinquency. In particular, Henriques complained about an American film, *Stage Door Canteen*, that, he suggested, made out that the entire purpose of a soldier's leave was to pick up girls. In his view, these influences meant: 'we should not be surprised at the promiscuous intercourse and even prostitution of girls from 14 to 17'.[10] One of the cases he had dealt with at his court was of a girl of fifteen who had admitted going to central London to sleep with soldiers. He was shocked by the teenager's frank admission of choosing a life of prostitution. After serving one week in custody, she was released and within a few days returned to the West End to continue as a prostitute.

Whilst, during the pre-war years, venereal disease had been found primarily in London and the major ports, between 1939 and 1945 the spread of disease was not confined to these areas. East Sussex medical authorities were placed in a quandary: the issue for the courts was whether a girl was in need of 'care and protection', not whether she carried venereal disease. Thus, the question of treatment of disease only arose once in care. Disease itself could not be the sole reason. They wished to prevent the spread of venereal disease but it was difficult to monitor cases of likely infection due to patient confidentiality. Only if a girl was remanded to care by the local magistrates could they enquire on her medical condition. Otherwise, she would remain free to infect as many people as she chose, until she sought treatment. The Ministry of Health raised its concern that some in Brighton's council were unwilling to take open action against the girls associating with soldiers, and possibly contracting venereal diseases, for fear of sullying the area's reputation as a holiday town.

The question of how to deal with the infected girls was something of a moral minefield. As seen, the courts had limited powers and there was a genuine, long-accepted need for confidentiality. Soldiers were supposed to inform the military authorities of their condition, both in order to ensure treatment and to facilitate the tracking of sources of infection. In itself, this was difficult enough and instead many soldiers had private treatment for disease, concerned that they might have their pay deducted whilst receiving official treatment. Furthermore, it was difficult for men who had picked up both a girl and a disease whilst on leave to recall the girl's name after one night – or a few minutes – of passion. One Canadian soldier failed to follow the correct channels when he reported to the police that he had contracted syphilis through a girl, who was subsequently found to be just fifteen years old. As a result, the Canadian was charged with carnal knowledge of an underage girl. Had he gone through the correct channel, reported to his medical officer for treatment and supplied her details to the authorities, he would have avoided the charge.

In 1942 the Royal Air Force reported a 25 per cent increase in venereal disease cases over its pre-war figures. One Bomber Command station outside Doncaster was found to have the exceptional infection rate of 48 cases per 1,000 men. What was important was that the infection rates were four times higher among aircrew than ground staff, and that Bomber Command had proportionately more cases than Fighter Command. The authorities were clear as to the reasons behind the figures: the hazardous conditions endured by the young airmen risking their lives in the skies over Europe made them casual about their off-duty behaviour. As one senior officer put it: 'youth then feels it is now time to have the last fling before death'.[11] The fatalistic aircrew were seen 'lolling about the messes with an eye on the clock, waiting for the moment when they can dash out of camp and head for the nearest town and bar'.[12]

The 'moral laxity' of these airmen, and subsequent exposure to venereal disease, was reported not to come from professional street-walkers but from local girls the aircrew met in pubs. These were often girls between sixteen and eighteen, effectively 'amateurs' working in factories who found life: 'both amusing and profitable in the company of aircrew'.[13] They were the girls who went on pub-crawls, following the aircrew when they moved from pub to pub as the beer ran out.

By January 1943, the issue of man-hours lost on treating infected aircrews resulted in Air Marshal Sir Arthur 'Bomber' Harris notifying his commanders about it. In particular he noted his concern over how the men removed from operations to receive treatment meant the break-up of crews, resulting in a serious impact upon morale. At a meeting of the Air Council in October 1943 the subjects under discussion included how to prevent the spread of VD. Suggestions included controlling sixteen- to eighteen-year-old girls by introducing compulsory pre-call up training and education in organizations such as the Girls Training Corps. The Ministry of Labour soon pointed out that controlling the movement of girls under eighteen would be impossible to enforce since it would interfere with their work. The raising of the age of consent from sixteen to eighteen, thus placing a legal constraint on sexual relations between the 'good-time girls' and the airmen was also mooted, but this was deemed impossible to put in place since it was enshrined in law that girls could marry at sixteen.

The increasing levels of venereal disease led the American military authorities to attempt to clamp down on both the professional prostitutes and their amateur counterparts, the 'good-time girls', who were described as: 'young girls who were merely out for a good time and knew that American soldiers had plenty of money'.[14] As the police soon realized, it wasn't what the girls had set out to do. It seemed that their behaviour usually started innocently, with teenage girls going out after work to meet soldiers for fun and excitement. The soldiers were just looking for female companionship – anything to break the monotony of living in a barrack-room full of men. Some reports linked the 'easy conquest' of British girls to cultural differences. On 'dates' in the United States girls tended to be heavily complimented and yet, almost by ritual, were expected to end the night with their virtue intact. British girls, not understanding this game, took all the compliments at face value, were easily wooed and succumbed to advances, often to the surprise of American soldiers.

These initially innocent encounters often ended up in sex and, in some cases, spiralled into part-time prostitution and, almost inevitably, venereal disease. For many, prostitution had simply started out as 'an easy means of making money'.[15] Investigations revealed that most VD infections among US servicemen were picked up on leave and around one third originated in London. Medical staff searching for the source of infections found that out of 101 men questioned, 25 named 'Piccadilly Commandos' they had picked up on leave.

A further 27 per cent of American VD cases were contracted in just three locations. The first two, Liverpool and Bristol, were obvious. They were large ports in western England, through which large numbers of American servicemen had entered the UK. In Bristol the Deputy Chief Constable had complained about the behaviour of girls as young as thirteen who threw themselves at soldiers. The third town of the group was a seeming anomaly: Bedford. The small market town, positioned between East Anglia and the East Midlands, was nobody's idea of a hotbed of vice. However, its location had made it the focus of the American military. First had come the military engineers who had constructed the buildings and laid the runways for a swathe of airfields in the region. Once the airfields were operational the town became a place for American aircrew to spend their time. Latterly, the town was home to soldiers living in civilian billets.

Whilst investigating a 1943 murder, local police learned something of the behaviour of the Americans and their girlfriends. When giving a statement one local girl described how she and her boyfriend, Private Hyrum Moody, had gone to a secluded spot beside the river, but had left after they noticed local boys hanging around and peeping out from the bushes. She complained to Private

Moody that there were 'some nosy devils around here'.[16] When interviewed, one of the boys admitted that at the same time, he had been watching another soldier in the grass with a local girl. When he spotted them, he had left his bike then came back to watch them: 'I have been doing this kind of thing for some months every night and on Sunday afternoons and evenings.' He and his mates called watching the couples in the fields 'mooching', and shared stories of what they had seen the couples doing. The boys' voyeuristic enthusiasm meant they sometimes stayed in the fields 'mooching' until almost midnight. As Private Moody told the police, many of his friends had complained about 'peeping toms' and he had himself noticed people watching the couples near a stone bridge on the edge of the town. It was evidence that supported the view of the secretary of the British Social Hygiene Council who had reported that 'men and their girlfriends have nowhere but the streets to amuse themselves'.[17]

Public displays of sex came as a surprise to many. Although it had always been an issue for courting couples with nowhere to go for privacy, the war seemed to have loosened morals. One young schoolteacher, Denys Roberts, filling time between leaving public school and receiving his call-up papers, recalled how the school cricket pitch was his one source of pride. Going out to inspect the wicket he stumbled upon a courting couple:

> To my horror, two figures in the half light were entwined on the ground. What made it far worse was the fact that they were lying just about where a good length ball would pitch. As I approached, I could hear a sound which was rather like acute asthma, following by a series of rhythmical movements and a shout, apparently of anguish, from an unmistakably feminine source.

Upon confronting the couple, he discovered the young lady was the school maid. Despite his complaints, her partner scared the young schoolteacher away.

He subsequently found that the pupils used a telescope to watch her antics. He was also shocked to discover the school's owners knew of her behaviour but did not dare sack her: 'We used to do that ten years ago . . . Not now. We can't afford to lose a maid.' With this clash between his concerns for the cricket pitch and the school's desire not to lose a maid, Roberts left the job. Asking his father to help him find another position, he was told he might get a position in the office of a friend, which was 'full of conscientious objectors, physical wrecks and mental cases. You'd fit in well there.'[18]

In south London, self-confessed street urchin Fred Rowe was one of the local boys who noticed that American soldiers reaped the rewards of their relative wealth. His elder sister had a number of American boyfriends and he enjoyed their visits, especially when they handed out sweets and chocolate or took him for rides in their cars. He also enjoyed the presence of the Americans for other reasons:

> We used to hide in Battersea Park, where the girls would be with the Yanks. There were these little shaded areas where they'd go. We'd be hiding in the trees and watch the Yanks groping the girls. We got a right kick out of that. One local girl had great big tits, me and my mate used to get a hard on watching her tits flop up and down. This Yank had got hold of her and he'd got her tits out. We were watching behind the tree, and having a wank. Two little boys, standing there having one off the wrist! We kept trying to edge nearer, from tree to tree, to get a better look.

Hoping to deal with the spread of venereal disease, in 1943 the American military authorities requested that efforts should be made to clear prostitutes from around hostels operated by the US Red Cross in London and also to keep the main thoroughfares of the city clear. As the Americans pointed out, they were not concerned with the morality of the British girls: they just wanted to keep their soldiers fit and healthy. Whilst officials at the Foreign Office understood the American argument, acknowledging 'disgust that these women should be allowed to swarm round the American Red Cross hostels',[19] there was little they could do. Quite simply, British law would not allow for clearing the streets since there were plenty of females with a legitimate reason to wait outside the hostels. As Superintendent Cole of the Metropolitan Police later noted:

> The 'good time girls' were the source of the trouble, and it was impossible for the police to take any action against them because they were not common prostitutes and did not accost; they simply made it clear that they would welcome advances and this was not a criminal offence.[20]

What the British were able to offer was an explanation of the reasons behind the proliferation of part-time prostitutions: 'war time relaxation of parental control and the appearance of girls who, after their day's work in munitions factories etc, were anxious to have a good time'.[21]

Even if the British had been able to take action, clearing the streets was only the beginning of the problem. Quite simply, the American servicemen were eager for sex, with the military authorities estimating that 70 per cent of their troops were open to advances from prostitutes. As they admitted, the soldiers were often 'young inexperienced men who had probably never spent very much time in a large city and it was natural that they would form an easy prey for the less desirable characters in London'.[22] As had already been noted by the Canadian military, prostitutes were not the principal source of infection of VD for their soldiers, suggesting that the source of infection were the 'good-time girls'. The Metropolitan Police agreed, noting that common prostitutes 'took precautions in their own interests'[23] unlike the teenage girls whose ignorance and irresponsibility spread infection.

Another reason that the police struggled to prevent prostitutes offering their wares was that, as newcomers to the industry, they didn't work the traditional pick-up grounds. The servicemen had little need to solicit the services of girls who openly walked on the streets. Instead: 'All the troops had to do was to go to a Public House, Café, Club, or suchlike place where servicemen congregated, and there find women for whom they bought drinks and then accompanied them home.'[24]

It was not just prostitution that saw a change in wartime morality. Ordinary girls were influenced by what they had experienced and adapted their lives accordingly. The 'live for today' mentality resulted in a degree of promiscuity that had a direct impact upon young lives. As one teenage veteran of the Blitz recalled when asked:

> One has to be a bit careful here. Generally speaking there was a loosening of morals. Lots of people thought, 'I don't care what happens, I might be dead tomorrow.' But we were limited because there was no pill and contraceptives were expensive – You didn't want a girl to get in the family way.

Whilst the girls were understandably attracted to Allied servicemen, there was another, less obvious, source of potential sexual partners: prisoners of war. In south London, one group of prisoners were housed in a timber yard surrounded by a barbed-wire fence, through which they were able to converse with the locals. In the latter years of the war, Fred Rowe watched the behaviour of some of the local girls:

> I was amazed. These girls, fourteen, fifteen, sixteen years old, used to go and give them food and fags. And they would sneak into the wood yard and get knobbed by these prisoners! I'd say to them, 'How can you do it? They've been bombing you!' The prisoners were having a lovely time: there were these young girls going up there, getting their tits out for 'em, and then getting knobbed. I was fucking furious! I went and told one mum but she said, 'My daughter wouldn't do that.' I said her daughter was getting a portion up her!

Fred's reaction was extreme: he asked the mother of one of his friends, who was working in a munitions factory, if she could get him a gun so he could shoot some of the German prisoners. Sensibly, she refused his request. Instead, he and his mates took their revenge more innocently:

> We chucked stones at them. And threw bags of water over them. My mate would offer them fags, when they put their hands through the fence, he'd grab their fingers and bend them back. But they could always get their hands free 'cause we were only boys. And we'd gob in their faces.

One of the main changes seen in wartime was that teenage girls increasingly spent their leisure time in pubs. For the new generation of young women – many working in munitions factories – they worked as adults and expected to live an adult lifestyle. By 1943, three times as many women were drinking in pubs than had done so in 1938 and the percentage of under-twenty-fives drinking in London pubs had increased from 3 per cent to 18 per cent. Surveys showed that from the age of fourteen, London's teenagers increasingly went to pubs independent of their families. Girls between sixteen and eighteen generally went into pubs, taking it for granted that they should do so if invited by a man. One sixteen year old noted: 'We go down to the Hammersmith Palais and if we meet some nice fellows we go out for a drink – nothing in that, is there!' Similarly, a fifteen year old admitted:

> I go in and have one at the local two or three times a week, with my fellow. Usually before and after going to the pictures and when I go dancing with the girls we always go in for a beer. I dance at the Hammersmith Palais. Meet some nice blokes there you do.[25]

As a result, some pubs actually started to look more like youth clubs. One study found around one-third of drinkers at weekends were female. Of these, significant numbers were in their mid-teens. Observers noted large numbers of young girls, well dressed and heavily made-up, going into a pub unescorted. Most were seventeen to eighteen years old and were drinking beer. The pub was so full that it was too packed for dancing. Though a few soldiers and sailors were in the pub, most were civilians. People were pushing through the crowd, elbowing their way to the bar. To those watching, the kids seemed concerned about little except fetching beer and flirting with the opposite sex. It was also clear that the pub's staff were rushed off their feet and had no time to consider whether their customers were underage or not. Amidst the clamour, observers noticed that sex was widely discussed among the youths.

The licensee of one of these pubs noted:

> The young people of today are more sophisticated and advanced in their ways. In fact a girl of 16 thinks, acts, and behaves in every way the same as a girl of 19–20. The war's altered so much of their outlook. You can't keep them down. There's definitely an increase in young people drinking.[26]

The landlord noted that the youth were well paid, their wages giving them an unexpected independence: after all, they were earning more money than most of their parents ever did.

Whilst most of the girls were just out to enjoy themselves – using the pub as an escape from the factory and the threat of death – there was an underlying feeling among the authorities that pub-going by women was related to prostitution. Making this connection was understandable. Both the Home Office and the London Probation Service reported that around 50 per cent of girls admitted to remand homes had been frequenting pubs and clubs, and 'these girls are of a type which would in any case have got into trouble through their associating with American, Canadian or other soldiers, and that drinking has been an incident in the course of their downfall rather than a cause of it'.[27]

Schools also noticed how wartime conditions influenced pupils. Head teachers complained that children attending public dances under war conditions were conducive to immorality and a false understanding of sex. In some areas local politicians blamed the BBC for lowering their entertainment standards. Furthermore, the behaviour of the country's young women did not go unnoticed by its politicians. One MP told the House of Commons that juvenile delinquency was caused by: 'consorting of our young girls with troops ... it is the diseased mentality of some of these young girls that leads them to throw themselves at the heads of the troops, and, in some cases, to affect their lives and future for many years to come'.[28] Another MP reported, 'it has been very disappointing to see young girls, many of whom have probably only just left school, hanging about the places where soldiers congregate'.[29]

In Leicester, the landlord of a pub complained to police about American servicemen bringing in underage girls. Not all landlords were so scrupulous. One south London pub became notorious as a place where the local girls consorted with servicemen. The pub had a bad reputation as one of the toughest spots in the area, and by 1943 it was frequented largely by Canadian soldiers and girls who were under the legal age for drinking. Arriving at the pub, observers noticed a pool of vomit outside the main door. Inside, they were confronted by a room crowded with servicemen and girls, all shouting to be heard over the sound of a piano playing to the accompaniment of five seventeen-year-old girls standing up and singing. A few people were dancing, others were kissing and embracing. One Canadian was seen talking passionately to a seventeen-year-old girl, his body pressed up against her. A considerable number of the crowd were under the legal drinking age. A sixteen year old was sitting on the lap of a Newfoundland private and kissing him. Elsewhere a merchant seaman was kissing a fifteen-year-old girl, whilst a Canadian soldier was overheard asking a sixteen-year-old girl if she would take him home.

In another south London pub, two girls in Sea Scout uniforms were seen waiting to meet soldiers. Across the room a drunken sixteen year old was crying and powdering her face, whilst a Canadian soldier sat with his arms wrapped around her. Apart from the underage girls, there were few civilians in the bar. The behaviour caused a witness to describe London pubs as places 'where extensive drinking by young girls was found in conjunction with picking-up, there was an atmosphere of free-and-easy sex behaviour which might be called exhibitionist'.[30] The connection between the behaviour of girls in pubs and the spread of venereal disease did not go unnoticed. As one London social worker noted in 1944: 'The spreader is the habitually promiscuous woman who evades treatment: often very young, irresponsible, unstable and of poor intelligence; she frequents the bars of public houses and often drinks a good deal.'[31]

The situation was just as extreme in other parts of the country. Some of the pubs around the ports of northern England were described as being little more than markets for women. A 1943 report on venereal disease on Tyneside found that the town's promiscuous women and prostitutes had started early, often before the age of seventeen. The blame for girls turning to prostitution was put on the advertising industry, which promoted a false view of the world. This contrasted sharply with the reality of their lives, being brought up in drab homes with limited opportunities.

At one pub, nestling in the docks of a north-eastern town, unescorted sixteen to eighteen year olds were seen drinking gin and lime. The girls were very young and appeared to prefer sailors, seemingly because they had more money. The pub's middle-aged patrons openly complained about the young girls who they believed to be inviting their own downfall, describing them as 'bloody little bitches'.[32] At one pub, two seventeen-year-old factory girls were seen chatting with sailors. One of the girls said to the sailor: 'Would you like to come and stay with me for the night? I'll be a good little wife to you and you can have it hot and strong.' He replied, 'How much money will you want from me if I come?'[33] The couple then left the bar to conclude the transaction. Other girls openly negotiated the price of a night's company with the sailors.

It was not just the question of preventing teenage girls from sliding into a life of prostitution that vexed the authorities. There was also the question of treating juveniles infected with venereal disease. Normally, females were admitted to isolation wards of hospitals where they remained through the early, infectious stages of disease. However, since a high proportion of the patients were professional prostitutes it was deemed unsuitable. Quite simply, the authorities did not want to put impressionable teenagers in a situation where they would mix with, and possibly be influenced by, older women 'on the game'. Instead, girls were sent to 'approved schools' which had independent treatment facilities. There, they received three months of treatment to cure syphilis, which was followed by periodic treatment for eighteen months as an outpatient. Whilst under treatment, the girls were not allowed ordinary clothes in order to prevent them leaving. During the initial infectious period, the girls were kept segregated from the other patients.

During the war years, the medical facilities of the approved schools had plenty of work. The girls sent to these schools by the courts were the subject of widespread concerns, in particular with regard to their morals. The girls were ordered to the schools for a variety of reasons, including: criminality, being beyond the care of their parents and sexual promiscuity. Those under the age of fifteen were admitted to junior schools, with those over fifteen being sent to senior approved schools. It was intended that these schools would make the girls continue with their education, teach them work skills and social responsibility, allowing them to leave ready to continue a respectable life. Pre-war, the schools had shown a significant success rate, with many girls returning to society and never reoffending. During 1939, 367 girls were admitted to approved schools as being in 'need of care or protection' or being beyond the control of their parents. By 1942, the annual figure had risen 80 per cent to 642.

With the onset of war, accompanied by the influx of glamorous and mysterious foreign soldiers, shifting morality and general uncertainty of life, there were genuine concerns over the behaviour of some of the girls. In 1941, the number of girls entering approved schools with venereal disease was 134, with eleven cases found among girls below fifteen years of age. By 1942 the population of 800 girls in approved schools contained 146 cases of VD, with two cases of syphilis for every five cases of gonorrhoea. In particular, the Ministry of Health reported of the population of approved schools that, 'immorality among girls under 16 is causing much anxiety', and that the 'semi-delinquent type of girl and young woman' was causing a danger to the population by spreading venereal disease.[34]

The Ministry of Health was concerned over girls absconding from approved schools. There were increasing numbers of wartime absconders, both boys and girls, who were attracted by the general excitement of the unsettled situation. In particular, the girls ran away to find 'excitement and keep' with soldiers.[35] During 1942 there were 528 incidents of absconding from senior approved schools, out of a population of 800 girls. Some of these absconded on a regular basis, whilst others returned within hours or days. However, it remained a serious concern and that year forty-two girls were sent to Borstal for absconding. Traditionally, absconding from approved schools meant heading for the 'bright lights' of a big city, but – in wartime conditions – that meant heading straight to the blacked-out streets of London or to areas with many large camps.

The scale of the problem was such that Scotland Yard requested that the schools alert them of girls absconding in order that the policemen on the beats of the West End could try to spot them as soon as they arrived, specifically before they could change clothes and put on their make-up. A police van, known as the 'Children's Wagon', was regularly sent on duty to public parks. Policewomen patrolled railway stations, the main bus stations, milk-bars and late night cafes on the lookout for runaways.

During 1942, 'C' Division of the Metropolitan Police, which

covered London's West End, arrested thirty-seven runaways. Of these, five were under the age of fifteen. More than a third of them – including some of the under-fifteens – had contracted a venereal disease. During one period, of the twenty-six absconders who returned to approved schools with venereal disease, 50 per cent were below the age of fifteen. As one police report noted:

> a good deal of trouble was caused in the West End of London by girls 15–17 who had escaped from approved schools. Such girls, who were often suffering from venereal disease, after absconding, made their way to the West End of London and frequented undesirable cafes where they could strike up acquaintance with American soldiers who had plenty of money. These American soldiers passed the girls on to their friends and in a very short time any one girl could be responsible for infecting a considerable number of people.[36]

As a counter to the concerns, the police took the trouble to stress that not all absconders were likely to turn to prostitution. Some of them just wanted to be in the West End to savour the atmosphere and see what all the fuss was about.

The Ministry of Health noted that the female absconder was likely to contract VD because 'she has absconded with the object of finding sexual excitement or because she is driven by immorality as the easiest means of finding maintenance while at large'.[37] They had no choice but to lead immoral lives because they needed a means of support. The ministry further noted that infectious girls were an 'immediate menace'.[38]

One approved-school runaway, who later became notorious, was Elizabeth Maud Baker. Born in Wales in July 1926, Betty Baker was later described by the headmistress of her approved school, in Sale in Cheshire, as a 'complete misfit' who was 'clever, calculating and attractive'.[39] In February 1940, aged just thirteen, she stole money from her mother's purse and ran away from her home in Neath to Swansea. There she claimed she been sexually assaulted by a man named Phillip Hall. He was charged over the offence but was found not guilty. During the investigations, Betty Baker was medically examined, revealing that, despite her tender years, she was no longer a virgin. Three weeks after the initial incident she was again picked up by Swansea police, this time unconscious in a gutter. Once again she claimed sexual assault but nothing was proven. As her father, given leave from the Army to attend court, admitted, she was 'too old for her years'.[40] She was sent to the junior approved school just days after her fourteenth birthday, as her mother had told the courts that she was beyond control. As the police in her hometown described her, Betty Baker was a strong-willed girl but with loose morals.

Not long after arriving she was reported to be troublesome and a malign influence who was encouraging other pupils to enter her wayward world. As the headmistress noted, Betty was 'a prostitute type and encouraging others in it'. She also noted that her ward was 'fond of the male sex and very untruthful'[41] and 'cold-blooded and completely callous'.[42]

Like so many other girls, attracted to the glamour of wartime, Betty became a serial absconder from the school. On her first 'escape' she took another girl with her and they spent the night in an Army camp. Whilst on the run with Denise Selby, Betty told her that if they wanted money they should 'let soldiers do things to them'.[43] The second time she absconded, Betty headed for Cardiff; on the third occasion it was London. After one of her escapes from school, Betty admitted spending her first night of freedom in a field with a soldier she had just met.

As a result of her 'immoral' behaviour, Betty Baker was 'sent up' to the senior school to prevent any further influence over the younger, more innocent, children in the school. Her behaviour prompted the school's headmistress to suggest that a special centre for sexually precocious girls, between thirteen and fifteen, should be established.

In November 1942, just two months after her sixteenth birthday, the ever-promiscuous Betty returned to her hometown to marry a man she described as her 'half cousin'. More than ten years older than her, and serving in the 1st Airborne Division, Private Stanley Jones was reportedly violently drunk on their wedding night, meaning that the two never lived as a married couple. Instead, she returned to her previous ways. As a married woman, she was released from the care of the approved school and soon headed to London. There, her search for glamour, excitement and the company of soldiers eventually led her into the arms of a man who would change her life. As she later told a policeman, after arriving in London she became a 'bad girl'.[44] By 1944 the approved-school runaway would become of the country's most notorious teenagers.

CHAPTER 19

The Children of Bethnal Green

'I was thirteen years old – and just lucky to be alive.'

Alf Morris

3 March 1943 was a dreary day that started like so many wartime mornings in London's East End. In Bethnal Green the local population stirred at 6 a.m. as they raised themselves from their bunks in the local air raid shelters or the beds of their homes, and prepared to go to work. In the tube station shelter, children folded up their blankets and got ready to return home, have breakfast and go to school. It was just another normal day.

After the horrors of the Blitz and the seemingly endless bombing of 1940 and 1941, a sense of calm had returned to the area. People had grown to accept their situation and learned to live with wartime conditions, and they continued to go about their daily lives. Though the bombers seldom came any more, thousands continued to spend each night in the shelter. The underground existence had become a way of life. Working men went there to ensure they got a quiet night's sleep and mothers wanted their children to be safe.

One of those who had settled into shelter life was Reg Baker. Finally growing homesick after more than two years in a small Oxfordshire village, Baker had returned home in 1942. He was never certain why he had made the decision to go home; quite simply, he seemed to want a change. Even in the dark days of 1940 and 1941, when his parents had endured almost nightly air raids, he hadn't been worried about what was going on at home: 'I didn't think too much about it. The family wasn't affectionate enough to worry. It's still your family but we were still having an adventure, I was with the farmers, out collecting the harvest.'

Back in Bethnal Green he had swiftly adapted to the old ways of city life. Although he was initially shocked to see the vast swathes of destruction, he soon settled down: 'Kids can adjust very easily. One minute I was surrounded by cows and green fields. Next I was back in London, picking up shrapnel from the bombsites.' Though it did not affect him, he soon learned that many people he had known had died. He had to get used to discovering that shops he once frequented were no longer there, replaced by open, empty spaces. Even his own street had changed, with one of the three blocks at Gretton Houses having been destroyed.[1] The empty space had become an allotment where Reg soon put his newly acquired 'green fingers' to use by growing vegetables. Other things had not changed: his mother still spent long hours scrubbing offices in the City and his father lived between work and the pub.

The biggest change of all was the new routine of subterranean life that had emerged since 1940. Some people appeared to live almost entirely underground, only emerging when they had to. For Alf Morris, arriving at the shelter for the night had become part of the routine of wartime life: 'When we went down, there was no need to line up. Mr Hastings, the head of the shelter, just gave us our bunks.' For the people of Bethnal Green, the station had become part of their everyday lives: morale was high; people held wedding receptions and Christmas parties underground; there were toilets, a library and a room for social functions; a priest even performed services in a temporary church. There was a hall for concerts and plays, medical facilities and even a room to isolate children with infections. Families had their own, pre-allocated bunks and a sense of community had emerged. Teenagers like Alf Morris and his mates even found themselves girlfriends among the population of the shelter. It was a far cry from the chaos of 1940 when people had simply staked a place by rushing to the station and laying out blankets. What had been survival had become a way of life.

Settling back into London life, Reg Baker followed his family to the tube station shelter. Every night when the shelter opened its doors, his mother would go down there and settle in. Later in the evening, Reg would join her and then, just before the lights went out, his father would arrive from the pub:

> At night the women would be there in dressing gowns, but the men never undressed. We always slept in the same bunks: Dad in the middle, Mum on the bottom and me on top. One night Dad came down, and he was sozzled. At 11 p.m. lights went down and everything went quiet. In the dark, Dad started climbing into the wrong bunk. Suddenly a woman's voice called out, 'You dirty old bastard!' Everyone could hear it. My dad was embarrassing at the best of times.

The routine of life meant people were always coming and going from the shelter. Families would enter, settle in, then send the children 'up top' with the instruction that they were to come down immediately if the sirens sounded. The local boys and girls would congregate around the junction and lark about. They would play on the pinball tables in a nearby arcade, or go to the baked potato stall, or to a nearby cafe famed for its ham sandwiches. Alf Morris enjoyed the freedom on the surface, playing with his mates and chatting to the girls, but he knew he could not stray far: 'My mother wanted to know where I was. When the raids started we ran down the shelter – and you did run. The door was closed soon after the siren had sounded.' Once safely inside, the 'Alert Sounded' sign was illuminated and people settled down to await the morning.

Yet despite the routine of underground life, there were plenty of concerns about the Bethnal Green tube shelter. It could take up to

10,000 people, with beds for more than 3,000. But there was a problem: everyone entered via a single route. The danger to those attempting to enter the shelter was already well known to the local authorities. In 1941 the Civil Defence Authority had reported:

> The committee are aware in the light of past experience that there is a grave possibility that on a sudden renewal of heavy enemy air attack there would be an extremely heavy flow of persons seeking safety in the tube shelter, and that the pressure of such a crowd of people would cause the wooden structure to collapse and a large number would be precipitated down the staircase.[2]

As was later noted by the Court of Appeal, the civil defence authorities had clearly contemplated the probability that heavy air raids would result in an uncontrollable and dangerous rush of people seeking shelter:

> From the street there was only one entrance, the doors of which opened inwards and led to a flight of nineteen steps. These steps were defective, very faintly illuminated, and, though 10 feet wide, without a hand-rail in the centre. There was no physical means of controlling the crowd and no warden posted there.[3]

One member of London County Council, who in 1942 had tried to enter the shelter at night whilst carrying a baby, recalled having to feel for each step with his feet, telling the local chief warden it was 'a death trap'.[4] It was clear that, with a predicted lapse of seven minutes between the sounding of the alarm and the fall of the first bombs, it would be impossible for thousands of people to safely enter Bethnal Green station.

The authorities were also aware that with a cinema and numerous pubs nearby, and many bus routes passing through Bethnal Green, an air raid at certain times of the day was likely to cause a mass rush to the shelter. Such were the concerns that the local ARP had approached the police to ask that crowds be dispersed from the nearby junction. Yes, there were concerns about the state of the entrance, but this was 1943 – the tide of war had slowly begun to turn, the bombing of London had abated and a sense of normality had returned. The lack of wardens to control access to the tube station was seemingly inexplicable, but the crowds arrived each night in an orderly manner.

Yet 3 March 1943 was not a normal night. All the circumstances that the local ARP had imagined as their nightmare scenario – an unexpected air raid, a large crowd rushing for the shelter, people jumping off buses to seek sanctuary, pubs and cinemas emptying – were all about to come true. It would be a night that left an indelible mark on the area. The local ARP personnel knew that a warden was necessary to control a large crowd, but they had no way of knowing when to expect an unusually large crowd – all the signs were that the bombing was finished anyway and there was no reason to expect a bigger than average turnout on 3 March. They were wrong. For the first time for many months a mass crowd, rather than the usual evening arrivals, tried to enter the shelter.

That evening Alf Morris was at home with his family. The radio had already announced there had been an RAF raid on Berlin the previous evening and the family expected the Germans to retaliate by bombing London. Still, they had been bombed many times before and felt that, if the alarm came, they would be safe in the deep tunnels of the Central line. Then, just before 8 p.m. the radio went off: 'When that happened you knew there was going to be an air raid. This night, my father said to me and Aunt Lill, "You make your way to the shelter and I will fetch Mum and the baby." At that time my sister was three weeks old.'

Picking up the blankets, they left the house and began walking towards the shelter. At this point the air raid warning had not yet sounded, but other families had also started to head to the shelters:

> We walked up Old Ford Road and then the air raid sirens started. We
> reached Victoria Park Square and the searchlight in the Bethnal Green

Gardens came on. It was radio-controlled and went straight on to the plane. You knew the anti-aircraft guns were going to start. We ran down the road. When we reached Green Street we ran across the road and started to go towards the tube.

As the sirens sounded, Reg Baker was a couple of streets away, at home with his father. His mother was already safely in her bunk in the tube station, just waiting for the rest of the family to arrive: 'The siren went and Dad was in the toilet. I said "Shall I run on, Dad?" But he said, "You'd better wait for me." So I waited. We walked through into Roman Road.'

By this time the crowds were beginning to grow. Desperate not to be caught in the raid, people rushed from their homes to the tube station. Alf Morris was in the ever-growing throng that was converging on the single entrance, with its single, dull bulb. Picking up speed, Alf told his aunt: 'Come on, Aunt Lill, the guns are going to start.' He knew it would be safer to get underground before the anti-aircraft guns started firing. The rain of hot shrapnel from ack-ack shells exploding overhead was known to be potentially lethal: 'We got to the station, but still the guns hadn't fired. Everyone was going down the stairs as normal. Everyone was steady – ladies and gentlemen helping each other.' So far, so good: 'I got halfway down and the rocket guns started firing in Victoria Park.'

Not far behind Alf Morris was another local boy, twelve-year-old Peter Perryment. He had been walking towards the shelter when his mother told him and his seventeen-year-old sister Iris and seven-year-old cousin Barbara to run on ahead. Reaching the shelter, they were soon caught in the middle of the heaving crowd. Peter and his sister managed to get through the crowd and on to the stairs.

At that point everything that the authorities had thought could go wrong did go wrong. As the new rocket guns – that no one had heard before – started firing, there was a rush for the shelter. The scream of these new weapons struck fear into the hearts of the locals: was this some deadly new weapon being unleashed on them by

Hitler? Reg Baker was terrified by the sound: 'My dad said, "Get down!" I didn't know what was going on – I'd been in Oxfordshire during the Blitz. I hadn't experienced this. Then we got up and ran to the entrance.'

Two full buses arrived at the stop just outside, disgorging their passengers into the growing crowd. The local pubs emptied as drinkers sought sanctuary. Customers left the local cinema to go to the one place they had felt safe at the height of the Blitz. Seeing the growing crowd, Reg Baker and his father made a fateful decision. Just as they approached the top of the stairs, they realized the crowd was growing too big:

> They were all shoving and panicking at the entrance. A local copper came along, but he couldn't stop people. Everybody was shoving. Dad said, 'Let's run to the shelter behind the pub – under the railway arches.' So we ran across the road and sheltered behind the Salmon and Ball pub. That split-second decision saved our lives.

Not everyone rushed for shelter. Some of the local youths had work to do. As the alarms sounded, fifteen-year-old James Hunt mounted his bike and rushed towards the ARP depot where he had to report for duty. On the way he heard the launching of the anti-aircraft rockets. Such was the blast that he was almost knocked off his bike. He made his way through the crowds to reach the ARP post, where he awaited instructions.

At the tube station shelter, as the crowds grew thicker, jostling to get down the steps, it reached a critical mass. Alf Morris was almost at the bottom of the nineteen steps. Everything seemed normal: yes, it was crowded but he knew every inch of these steps from having walked up and down them almost every day for more than two years. Then it changed: 'As the rockets went up, everyone thought it was bombs coming down. People behind us called out, "There's bombs! There's bombs! Get down!" Those of us on the staircase tried to walk down quicker. But the people behind us pushed us down.' Later, some said an old lady had tripped, falling forward and bringing those behind her crashing down into a deadly heap. Others said it was a woman with a child, who stumbled, fell, picked herself up, then escaped to safety as those behind her crashed down on to the steps. Whatever had happened, those at the bottom fell forward and were crushed by the weight of those behind.

There was sheer panic as the crush grew. Alf Morris could feel the weight of people increasing around him as he was forced forward, his feet lifting from the floor.

> I was holding my aunt's hand. She was moved to the right and I was pushed to the left. I was lifted and carried. I got to the third stair from the bottom. As I got there I grabbed the handrail, along the wall. They pushed me up against the wall. It was all jagged concrete. I was holding the handrail to keep myself upright. With that, people all fell around me.

He was helpless:

> They carried us down. They picked us up, literally – it separated me from my aunt. I was trapped. I didn't know what was happening. I couldn't see my aunt. I was calling for my mother – I was a thirteen-year-old boy! I was calling for Aunt Lill. All the time I was calling out, people were falling around me. I can still see it now. They were building up around me. I kept calling out, but I couldn't move my legs.

As few steps behind Alf Morris was Peter Perryment: 'We got about halfway down the stairs in the middle. I couldn't get no further. I wanted to get out, but I couldn't. They were crushing us. So I put my hands in front of me and curled up in a ball.' As he lay amidst the crushed bodies, he could see his sister but couldn't reach her.

With people dying around him, Alf Morris called desperately for help:

I could move my arms, but not my legs. I couldn't get out. In the commotion – the screaming, the hollering, the shouting – I could see a lady Air Raid Warden who was at the bottom. She was trying to calm everybody, calling out, 'Keep quiet – keep quiet!' But it was beyond her.

Alf was one of the lucky ones. Others were being crushed, the air being forced from their lungs, leaving them unable to cry for help. The pressure had pushed him up against the wall, trapping his legs but leaving him still able to breathe. All around him, within seconds, those in the helpless pile, unable to breathe, began to suffocate, passing out and turning blue. Desperate hands reached out, but with nothing to hold on to, they simply waved in the air, until their owners went limp.

A few were lucky. Alf Morris was among them:

The lady Air Raid Warden, Mrs Chumley, could see the plight I was in. She was a big woman, she laid across these people and her hand went down – wallop! – on my head. She grabbed my hair and pulled and pulled. I screamed. It didn't free me. I was calling, 'Help, Mum! Dad! Aunt Lill.' I was calling for everybody. 'Please, please, help me.' So she laid across the bodies, put her hands under my arms and yelled, 'Come out!' and pulled me out. As I came out I felt my feet going across the faces of the dead and dying. She sat me down and put her finger to my face, 'Go downstairs and you say nothing about what's going on here! Nothing! Go on, downstairs!' Honestly, I was bewildered. I was crying for my mother. I walked downstairs trying to compose myself.

His legs grazed and trembling, his small frame almost crushed, Alf made his way down the escalator.

As the scale of the disaster unfolded, the local ARP post was alerted and those on duty rushed to the tube station. With them was fifteen-year-old James Hunt. He was shocked to see the crushed bodies that were blocking the stairwell. Unable to show fear, he set to helping pull the dead and injured from the mass of tangled bodies. Being young and small he was unable to lift the older people and concentrated on the children. He noticed how the babies and children he carried had turned blue.

Among those who had survived the crush was Peter Perryment: 'I don't know how long I was there. After a while they started moving all the dead bodies behind me. I didn't know they were dead. A policeman got hold of me from the stairs and took me across the road to the railway arches.' As they crossed the road, Peter could see lines of corpses being laid out on the pavement. The corpses were piled on carts then taken to the mortuary at Whitechapel hospital. Once that was full, the bodies were taken to the nearby St John's Church.

Arriving at the safety of the shelter, the policeman gave Peter a clear instruction: 'He told me to wait in the air raid shelter there until the "all clear" goes. So I did. I stayed there till it was time to come out.'[5] It was the same for so many. They were told not to talk about what they had seen and experienced and did as they were told. It was the start of a process that kept the story under wraps for many, many years. After the 'all clear' sounded, Reg Baker and a mate just went home, whilst his father went to the pub, as if nothing had happened. They realized something was wrong but didn't hang around to find out. It was not until the next day that Baker's mate discovered his own sister was among the casualties.

Among the survivors was Reg Baker's sister. She had been out with her boyfriend when the alarm had sounded and had gone to the station to take cover. She had arrived at the entrance just as the people at the bottom had collapsed and the crush had started. She was one of the last to join the crush, having been pushed by the crowd on to the top of the pile of bodies, just one of many whose weight had helped crush those beneath them. As she lay there in the darkness she thought, 'Ain't it soft?', unaware that she was lying atop the dead and dying.

At the bottom of the escalators Alf Morris was:

... crying my eyes out, I was looking for my mother. I pressed the bell and the door opened. He said, 'What's the matter, son?' I was just crying, 'I want my mum!' I just wandered off and walked into an opening and got to my bunk and sat there. I was crying and shaking. I was too frightened to say a word. My legs were all grazed but I was more concerned about my mother and my aunt. I was crying but I wouldn't tell anyone what had happened.

Ten minutes later his aunt arrived: 'She'd also been told to stay quiet. Her stockings had been torn off and her black astrakhan coat and shoes had been left in the crush. We looked at one another and wondered where my mum was. We just held each other and kept crying.' In the fullness of time, Alf realized how important it had been that those who escaped the crush had kept quiet that night. It was vital that further panic was prevented: one disaster was enough.

Although Alf Morris had experienced the horror of being crushed, he still had no idea of the scale of the disaster. The first sign that it was serious came when an air raid warden, a fireman and a policeman appeared from the tunnel, walked past the bunks and made their way up into the station. Everyone wondered why they had come that way. But then, the lights went down for the night and no one said anything else. Instead, they just tried to sleep, their minds full of dire thoughts about what might have happened. For Alf and his aunt, the morning couldn't come quick enough.

Another of the witnesses was sixteen-year-old Bernard Kops. He had not reached the tube station, instead having taken shelter in a doorway as soon as he heard the explosions of the new anti-aircraft guns. As a result, he had missed the disaster, only reaching the shelter once the dead were already being brought out. As he approached, people were talking about what had happened, with the rumour-mill suggesting hundreds were dead. All the teenager could think about was whether his mother and sister were among them.

As Bernard got nearer he could see crowds of rescue workers, policemen and air raid wardens. There were ambulances all around the entrance. Yet for all the evidence of the unfolding disaster, to Bernard it seemed the area was strangely silent. He waited for what seemed like hours as the bodies were brought out, all the time fearing he might spot family members. When he eventually got to see inside the entrance to the tube station, he was struck by the sight of clumps of hair that had been torn from the heads of the victims.[6]

So the night passed peacefully for those within the tube station. The next morning, when the lights went on as normal, people started to go upstairs ready to start another day. Alf Morris and his aunt left the shelter as soon as possible, with her walking barefoot up the stairs. No one made any announcements and there was nothing to suggest what had happened, except for an ominous pile of shoes near the top stairs. Lill stopped and searched for her shoes, put them on and continued the short walk home. Alf continued to keep tight-lipped about what he had seen: 'It was a different era. You didn't ask questions, you said nothing. When you were a boy, you just shut it. We didn't realize that people were missing.'

As they walked back to their home, they had no idea of what they were returning to. All they knew was that something terrible had happened and that the rest of the family had been somewhere behind them. Opening the front door, they were overwhelmed by a sense of relief: the whole family was waiting for them. His mother had heard the guns start firing and had abandoned any idea of reaching the station, instead taking shelter with the baby in the crypt of a Catholic church. His father, who had been last to leave the house, missed her at the church and continued to the shelter, arriving there in time to see that the police and the wardens had sealed off the station. When he asked what had happened, he was sent away. Like his son the next morning, he walked home imagining the worst. For the Morris family, the first sign that something had gone seriously wrong came when an expected visitor did not arrive that morning: 'My mother looked after this girl, Vera Trotter. At eight o'clock she didn't arrive. Mum normally took her to school when her mother went to work.' As the day went on the sense of unease heightened.

Men and women went to work as normal, only to notice that familiar faces were missing. Schoolchildren entered classrooms where there were more empty desks than normal. Yet no one said a thing. Boys like Alf Morris and Peter Perryment, who had been pulled alive from the heaps of crushed bodies, did as they had been told the night before: they said nothing. As Alf recalled: 'Everybody was mystified – people were missing from work or didn't turn up at work. But we just got on with life.'

But the locals soon realized something was wrong. In Reg Baker's class at Cranbrook School two brothers had been killed, part of a family that lost three generations in the disaster. At home he discovered both a neighbour and her grandchild had died. In one class, five children were found to be missing. Because many of the teachers came from outside the area, they had no idea there had even been an incident and started to ask the whereabouts of the missing children. Whilst the children continued to be silent in front of the teachers, by break time that morning they began to ask: 'Where's so and so?'

The failure of Iris Perryment and her seven-year-old cousin Barbara to return home spurred the family into action. Whilst Peter went to school as normal, his eighteen-year-old brother Alfie, who was waiting to be called up into the Army, joined his mother and aunt and went round the local hospitals. But there was no sign of the girls. The mystery went unsolved until Peter's father returned from work:

> He said, 'Where's Iris and Barbara?' We told him we didn't know. So he went to Bethnal Green hospital. They told him that people had died at the tube and they had got some of the bodies in St John's Church. So Dad went there and found my sister. He came home, and my aunt said, 'Did you see Barbara?' He said, 'No,' and told Alfie to go and look. He went there and saw a little black pair of shoes. He told them, 'Turn that one over.' And it was our cousin Barbara.[7]

It was the same situation in the Morris household: 'When my dad got back from work he wanted to know where Vera had got to. We told him we didn't know.' Knowing that Vera's father was away serving in the Army, he knew that something had to be done. It was only right that someone should try to discover if Vera and her mother were among the casualties. At first he toured the local hospitals, but could find neither of them. But as he continued his search, he began to realize the scale of the disaster. So he tried the mortuaries: 'My father had pulled a nail from Vera's shoe a fortnight previous, so he recognized her shoes. But her face was unrecognizable. It was the same for everyone. They only recognized them by their shoes and their clothes. Vera's mother was beside her.' When he got home, he walked up the passage and then sat on the step. What happened next shocked young Alf Morris. In an era when fathers showed little emotion, his father sat and cried his eyes out. Then he turned to his family and said: 'I've found them, they're both dead.'

That experience was shared throughout this close-knit community. In total 173 people had died, sixty of them children. Everyone seemed to know someone who had died. For two weeks there were daily funerals as families laid their loved ones to rest. Mothers were buried alongside children, some of whom had been crushed to death in the arms of the protective parent. All around the world, husbands and fathers serving in the armed forces received the notification that their loved ones had been killed. When Vera Trotter's father was told his wife and daughter were both dead, he asked for compassionate leave, only to be refused on the grounds that he had no one left to go home to. It was a terrible end to a terrible incident. As Alf Morris later recalled, the tragedy had affected so many people in the area and had scarred so many lives: 'It rocked the East End.'

CHAPTER 20

In Every Port . . .

'The best part of going to sea was being able to get a few hours ashore and live it up . . . one did not get a great deal of sleep in places like New York.'

Christian Immelman, ship's apprentice

'It was just one dead town . . . There were no restaurants. There was no food on the shelves, nowhere to have a coffee. It was a bleak, miserable place.'

Murmansk, described by Leslie Forrest,
fifteen-year-old Canadian galley boy[1]

Though still boys, the teenagers of the Merchant Navy and Royal Navy were exposed to a world few could have imagined before the war. Life at sea in wartime soon made the boys grow up. Whether at sea or in port, they started to act like men. Going to sea at sixteen made Raymond Hopkins a regular in the pub whenever he reached dry land: 'I felt grown-up. No one asked me how old I was. I went on the booze a lot. It was our attitude. We thought we'll live today because we might be dead tomorrow. It was the only way. At sea, you had to think that way. If you worried about it you'd get nowhere.' His attitude reflected that of men who'd been at sea for many long years: 'Why worry? It was one of those things. We just wanted to get to the destination and have a drink.' In the words of

Arthur Harvey, who went to sea aged fifteen: 'We didn't have a teenage life, like they have nowadays. We didn't even see the world – we just saw the ports. But we were privileged.'

Reaching foreign ports, the boys marvelled at what they saw and experienced. There was something about arriving in port – whether overseas or on leave – that had them putting on their best uniforms or clothing before going ashore. For boys in the Royal Navy, there was something dandyish about their uniforms: unlike the Army or RAF whose uniforms were modern, sailors were dressed in clothing that had gone unchanged since the nineteenth century. Reg Osborn described dressing for shore leave:

> our tailor-made tiddley, going-on-leave, number ones had wider bell bottoms, the front opening of the jacket cut much wider, and a 'bow wave' carefully introduced to the front of one's cap ... the carefully tied bow of the cap ribbon instead of being, regulation-wise, over the top of the left ear was positioned near to the HMS, or ship's name, as possible.[2]

It was different for merchant sailors, who could wear what they wanted, so suits were pulled from lockers and pressed, shoes were shined and they were ready to 'hit the town'. As they adapted to life at sea, the boys wanted to be like the men they sailed with. On Bernard Ashton's first voyage his ship stopped to refuel at Las Palmas in Tenerife. Eight of the sailors, Bernard included, bought canaries in bamboo cages, paying for them in cigarettes. For the rest of the voyage, the birds all lived in the working alleyway and, as deck boy, Bernard had the job of cleaning out their cages and feeding and watering them. On a later trip, he even took home two monkeys.

As the *Rochester Castle* made its way around Africa, Bernard began to pick up tricks from the old hands on the crew: 'I was quite green – but I learned as I went along.' At some African ports the crew sold spare, worn-out ropes to the locals, making their deals over the rails of the ship. As the saying went, it was 'money for old rope'. In other ports the locals were eager to buy empty jam tins or glass jars. He noticed how his fellow sailors drew all their rations, whether they needed them or not, saving them up to trade in port.

Reaching the Sudan, Bernard began to experience a world he had only previously seen in the books that had inspired him. As the ship was loaded with animal hooves to be taken back to England to make explosives, he watched the men working on the dockside. They were gangs of 'Fuzzy-Wuzzies', skinny, almost-skeletal men, their hair matted with mutton fat. To Bernard, these were men of legend, straight out of the books of his childhood, the warriors who had defeated General Gordon. At seventeen, the poverty in African ports made Edward Ford realize how lucky he had been to have been born British. Even working long hours on a crowded ship for pitiful pay in dangerous waters seemed better than a life of poverty. In Lagos, Edward was shocked to see the method used for loading peanuts. Two planks were positioned between the quay and the ship. Lines of men ran up one plank, poured their peanuts into the hold, then ran down the second plank. The work was relentless: the men were paid by the sackload and were desperate to earn as much as possible.

These exotic, yet shocking scenes, continued once the boys went ashore. Alan Shard recalled the scenes as he left his ship in Egypt:

> Alexandria was a fascinating place full of crooks. Lots of pimps tugging at your arm at every turn. Every nationality practised the ancient trade. The street was named Sister Street. Those who weren't pimps were trying to sell you something else. Stepping outside the dock gates in our whites we were besieged by urchins in the seven to nine age-bracket asking if you wanted a shoeshine in spite of the fact that they were already shining. Didn't matter, they persisted ... they received a kick up their backside. Often as not, this resulted in razor blades being produced and your arms being slashed before they melted into an alley.

The cadet recalled a visit to another Egyptian port:

> three of us were inadvertently steered into a dubious dive just in time
> to witness a riveting demonstration performed by two young ladies.
> We skinned out smartly, with images of 'Cancellation of Indentures',
> but not before sighting the likes of what I had never heard of – nor seen
> since. There was also supposed to have been a performance with a
> donkey, but it was off that night, probably with a 'headache'. Our
> innocence was still intact.

In Cairo Boy Bugler Robin Rowe noticed that, when the sailors
weren't looking, the shoeshine boys threw camel dung at their boots,
thus ensuring they would need to be shined.

Brothels and bars where they could pick up girls were an obvious
lure for the boys. After listening to the lewd tales of their fellow
seamen, it didn't take much to entice them ashore. As an
increasingly confident young cabin boy, John Chinnery attempted
to leave the ship with his crewmates as they made their way ashore
to sample the delights of a foreign port. He thought he was a
good-looking lad and had put on his best uniform, complete with
white scarf, to go out to meet girls in the port. As he was leaving the
ship, the Dutch captain called John back, telling him: 'Not you,
young man: books.' The captain felt responsible for the young
teenager and didn't want him exposed to the dangers of disease or
the attentions of violent pimps. So he was kept onboard to study
seamanship whilst the rest of the crew enjoyed themselves ashore.
In time, he discovered he didn't need brothels and that, as a
handsome and confident teenager, he could find all the female
company he needed without paying. When he joined his crewmates
in brothels he preferred to sit and chat with the madam whilst his
mates availed themselves of the services on offer.

Not all of the senior officers were as attentive as John's Dutch
captain, meaning most youngsters were free to enjoy whatever the
ports might offer. The young seamen, growing ever-more confident,

slipped easily into the lifestyle enjoyed by sailors the world over. Arthur Harvey recalled his first visit to Buenos Aires as a sixteen year old. The port was full of beautiful girls, there were German seamen in many of the bars and there was no blackout. It was a far cry from the ruins of Portsmouth. Most memorably: 'The older men took us into one or two naughty bars. They showed us the world.'

After four years of war, in which he had spent his time in barracks in Portsmouth, moored at Scapa Flow or on Arctic convoys, Len Chester finally got to 'see the world'. During 1943 his ship docked in a number of North African ports:

> We weren't popular in Oran. The people there preferred the Germans, because they were never drunk. With the 'jolly jacks', there were drunks in town every night. In Algiers the Casbah was out of bounds but we went there anyway. If it wasn't out of bounds, we probably wouldn't have bothered to go there! At the time I didn't realize how fortunate I was to see these places. As for the brothels: I only ever went into them for research.

Boy Bugler Robin Rowe was also in the Mediterranean ports during 1943. In Algiers one of his shipmates insisted he accompany him to a brothel. The fifteen year old didn't want to appear an innocent and went along. They chose a nearby establishment, the Sphinx, and joined the queues of sailors and soldiers. As he observed, whilst most people referred to the manageress as the 'Madam', sailors had a more down to earth name for her: 'Mother Judge of Pricks'. The bugler was on such low wages he had to borrow money to pay for the experience. After choosing a girl, he went back to pay the cashier but decided against it. When his mate came out, Robin did not admit he had not gone through with it. He asked the sailor what it had been like. He replied: 'Bit like throwing a banana up an alley.'[3] The innocent bugler had no idea what he was talking about.

Arriving in Calcutta in late 1943, Arthur Harvey received a rapid introduction to Indian life. He had already seen gangs of women loading coal on to ships from baskets carried on their heads. But that was mild compared to what followed. As they sailed up the River Hooghly he was shocked to see corpses floating past. Bengal was enduring a famine that cost the lives of three million people. If he thought the bombing of British ports was bad, nothing could have prepared the seventeen year old for this. People lay in the streets, dying of malnutrition, the scenes becoming so commonplace that people simply walked by. Arthur recalled: 'Wagons used to come round during the day to collect the dead and take them for burning. A horrible smell of death hung over the city for many weeks.'

The situation was compounded by Japanese air raids forcing Arthur to man the ship's guns and supplement the city's meagre defences: 'So we became part of the air defence. We had a 12-pounder and 4.7-inch guns. We were firing away with the Oerlikons. I don't know if I hit anything – I didn't see any of their planes get shot down. But at least we kept them up at altitude.' The only light relief was that a nearby ship was loaded with beer destined for the Army. Each time the Japanese attacked, the ship's crew left the ship unguarded. Arthur and his mates unloaded the beer, carrying the bottles back to their ship. Eventually the local CID was sent to investigate. By a stroke of fortune one of the policemen was from Arthur's home city of Portsmouth. Even more incredibly, he was the former boyfriend of Arthur's mother. He left the ship on good terms with the crew and the matter was dropped.

For seventeen-year-old Stan Scott, there was a certain frustration about being alone in Bombay after having been thrown out of his unit for being underage. With weeks to kill before a ship was due to take him home, he had little to fill his hours:

> I was naive. I had no idea what to do. I had a breakfast, had a shower, would go swimming, sunbathe, then lunch, go to the cinema. I didn't know what to do with myself. One day, I got in a gharry to go down town. Sitting in the corner was this bint. All of a sudden she was pointing at her crotch and looking at me. When I got to where I was

going I got out and the driver asked me, 'You no want her?' I said no. I told the others in the camp and they all laughed at me. But I'd seen the film and lecture on VD when I was training. It was horrible. I didn't want that!

Tattoo parlours became a frequent haunt of youngsters wanting to appear more grown up. Apprentice Alan Shard recalled a stopover in India:

Sighted a tattoo parlour and boldly went in. After flipping a coin Jimmy Pearce went under the needle for a heart with a dagger through it. He did not look very comfortable and Drakley and myself looked at our watches and decided we had better not miss the evening meal, much to the disgust of our shipmate. He was the only one that got a tattoo the whole time we were together.

The trio also displayed a taste for boisterous antics:

On the way to the dock, which was a fair distance, we hailed a gharry – an open carriage drawn by horses. About a hundred yards from the gate we suddenly decided to drop off whilst the gharry was underway and the driver got to the gate before realizing that he had lost his fares. We thought it was great until he saw us and turned on a dime and chased us up a dead end street whilst cracking a fourteen-foot horsewhip. We capitulated and forked out more than we would normally have paid.

Wanting to be like their crewmates, most boys were drawn to pubs and bars where they received their first introduction to drinking. As a seventeen-year-old apprentice from a non-drinking family, Norval Young had a career-threatening introduction to alcohol whilst in port in Italy. He was supposed to be keeping an eye on the MV *Athelvictor* but was invited onboard a nearby ship for lunch. The crew told him they would warn him when his captain was returning so he could get back to his post. However, during the meal he was given a drink that took his breath away: it was his first taste of rum, meaning he was less than steady when he returned to the ship. 'When I got out in the fresh air it hit me. I was a stupid young boy. The captain said my career was over.' Telling the captain he would take any punishment given, Norval was told he was to be sent home:

> I told him if he sent me home, I wouldn't go. I'd run away. I said, 'I dare not go home, my father will give me more punishment. I'd made so much trouble to go to sea, now I'm here, that's it, I've got to stay.' So the captain said for the next six months I was not to leave the ship. Every time we were in port I was to go over the side, strip the hull and paint it with red lead. I had the cheek to say, 'Thank you very much, sir.'

The captain kept to his word, but as Norval later admitted, it was worthwhile: 'It was a steep punishment but if I had been kicked off I would never have got another apprenticeship.'

For the boys, many of whom had joined out of a genuine enthusiasm to 'do their bit' for the war effort, there were many strange encounters. Once in neutral ports they faced the curious experience of coming face-to-face with their German counterparts. Alan Shard recalled his first encounter with the 'enemy' whilst in neutral Goa:

> A half-dozen of us called in at the only 'pub' in the area and spent a really nice evening. About 2000hrs our group started to sing sea shanties and to our surprise at a table at the far end a bunch of white men also started their own sing-song, but in German. Consternation reigned as we weighed our chances, but the second mate stood up and waved them over to our table. I was completely flabbergasted, they all came over except one man who raised his arm in a salute, said, 'Heil Hitler,' and marched out. Whereupon his shipmates all waved their hands at his back as if to say good riddance. What a night: by throwing-out time we were all good buddies.

The many and varied ports of the Caribbean were a constant source of wonder to the boys. Bernard Ashton enjoyed trips to Georgetown in British Guyana, where he was fascinated by the street scenes. The streets thronged with people of all nationalities and he watched barbers with their chairs out in the streets, cutting hair with open razors. The cafes were packed, with music wafting out from their open fronts. Bernard watched as the older seamen filled the bars, spending their wages before their sober crewmates, such as Bernard, had to drag them back to the ship. In Trinidad, he visited the Chinese cafes, watching the hard-working Chinese waitresses as they served beer, curry and rice to gangs of hungry seamen. Another young seaman, arriving in Guyana on his first trip, was told that rum was cheaper than Coca-Cola: 'So I drank rum.'

The West Indies was a source of rum, spices, fruit and cane sugar. As they sailed from port to port, the sailors faced a barrage of locals trying to sell goods to them, and they were soon gorging themselves on bananas. Bernard Ashton joined the routine of trading old jam jars and tins for fresh produce. He learned how the sailors would buy cuts of sugar cane, leaving it to ferment onboard. The old hands showed him how to make toffee using sugar, sucking on it as they worked on deck on their way back across the Atlantic. He also felt a twinge of nostalgia when he noticed his ship's cargo included barrels of pitch from the same company that supplied the Kent coal mine where his father worked.

Whilst many parts of the world seemed exotic, it was the modern luxuries of the United States that most appealed. When Christian Immelman first arrived in the United States in late 1939, he was pleasantly surprised to see a well-stocked store near the oil refinery in Galveston, Texas, where they were collecting fuel:

> Went ashore with a crowd after the evening meal to a general store, in the middle of nowhere, about half a mile up the road from the oil refinery. The store sold everything including boots, saddles, knives, guns, clothing, cooking utensils, milkshakes and beer. It had a jukebox.

We stayed there till late having a musical drinking evening, and sailing early next morning.

Enjoying the opportunities available in the United States became a regular feature of his visits: 'My first call on going ashore in any US port, before hitting the nearest bar with the boys, would be to a drugstore for a fried egg sandwich on beautiful white bread together with a vanilla milkshake.'

His trips to American ports were in direct contrast to his time back in the UK. Between his sixteenth and eighteenth birthdays he received no leave in the UK and thus, despite having sailed around the world, had no contact with his family. In those two years he snatched just a few hours with his mother in Cardiff after she had discovered his ship was due to dock there. Another boy recalled being in Galveston in 1941 when the Japanese bombed Pearl Harbor, bringing the United States into the war. He watched as his openly delighted British crewmates celebrated the United States' declaration of war, telling them, 'You're in now!' and berating them for how long they had taken to enter the war.

The United States was home to one city they wanted to visit above all others: New York. For Christian Immelman, it fast became his favourite:

> Whenever we loaded in one of the refineries in the New York vicinity, after our day's work, we'd head for Manhattan and the bright lights. First stop would often be the British Apprentices' Club in the Chelsea Hotel on 23rd Street. There'd be plenty of snacks, a fruit punch bowl and nice girls to dance with. First-time visitors would be given a gift bag holding a torch, a balaclava and a plug of tobacco. It was a good place to chat with apprentices from other companies. After the club we'd drift up to Broadway. I had a couple of favourite bars: the Wigwam on 44th Street, the Crossroads in Times Square, Jack Dempsey's restaurant for the biggest, toughest T-bone steak you'd ever find. Then there was the Paramount cinema on Broadway, where for

a few cents one could see a movie then an hour of one of the big bands. Also, one was given a packet of Lucky Strike cigarettes free on admission.

On one trip to New York the crew of his ship took two cases of Scotch whisky. They swapped the whisky for two Thompson sub-machine-guns which were taken onboard as additional protection.

Yet for most of their time in New York, such martial thoughts were far from everybody's mind. As seventeen-year-old Ron Singleton later recalled: 'It opened my eyes. Went to see the bright lights of Times Square and everything. It was unbelievable. We could get candy bars out of chocolate machines.' He also found the local population shocked to see him and his mates – three teenage British boys – on the streets of their city. They were amazed how boys so young had braved the Atlantic to reach their city. For Ron it was a strange experience: 'They thought we were real heroes – we weren't.'

At the heart of the gangs of British seamen and boys who experienced life in New York was one particularly lucky group: the 'Distressed British Seamen', those who had been fortunate enough to survive the sinking of their ships and had been sent to the city ready to await another to take them home. By early 1940, the Seaman's Church Institute at 25 South Street had already housed, fed, reclothed and cared for the crews of thirty-eight merchant ships lost in the Atlantic. In late 1940 the staff recognized two of the new arrivals, Towers and Hardie, two eighteen-year-olds who had survived the sinking of the *Blairangus*. Over a year earlier, at the age of seventeen, they had both been among the survivors of the sinking of the *Blairlogie*. Despite their youth, they were true veterans of the Battle of the Atlantic.

The ranks of the 'Distressed British Seamen' in New York were joined by ex-Prince of Wales Sea Training Hostel boy Bernard Ashton after his ship was torpedoed by an Italian submarine in

March 1942. Before reaching New York he had an enjoyable few weeks in Puerto Rico. Having been landed in San Juan, Bernard, his mate Peter Pickett and the rest of the crew were sent to a hotel. To the youngsters it seemed like something from a film. The hotel was built around a courtyard to provide shade, with large open windows, ceiling fans and slatted saloon doors. Sitting out on the veranda, sipping iced drinks, it seemed a world away from the coalfields of Kent or the dirty, bombed slumscapes of British ports.

The first thing the teenagers needed to do was to buy some new clothes – after all, Bernard couldn't go out dancing in his vest, football shorts and boots:

> We went into a store and bought a straw panama hat, and a heavy cotton 'beach suit' – you could wear the jacket as a shirt or wear a shirt underneath it. It was blue with a white stripe and had turn-ups. For underwear, we bought boxer shorts – they were unheard of in England, much better than the baggy old English pants. And we had two-tone shoes. I thought I was Jack the Lad.

They spent their days in a Red Cross canteen, drinking coffee or milkshakes and eating cake. Or they went swimming at local beaches, where they could admire the girls and enjoy the protection of shark nets. At night they would go down the waterfront, sitting outside bars, watching the local girls parading in their finest dresses. After wartime England, everything seemed so alive. In the bars, the jukebox would be playing all night, and Bernard's mate – handsome, six foot tall and an accomplished dancer – was an immediate hit with the local girls. Peter would be dancing, jukebox playing all night. By day they could drink Coca-Cola and, by night, they preferred Cuba Libre cocktails of rum, lime and Coca-Cola. Then after dancing till 1 a.m., the boys would go for coffee and a steak. It was a far cry from the home ports with their beer shortages and bomb shelters.

Through Peter's dancing skills, the boys met some local women who took them out to dances, bars and restaurants. Peter's girl, Christina, had to take a chaperone, so took along her friend, a twenty-eight-year-old married woman. The teenage Bernard felt uncertain in the company of one so mature: 'She was all over me. I was dragged up to the bedroom.' What might have been fun was tempered by the sight of a photograph of her husband: he was in a police uniform and receiving an award for pistol shooting.

After four weeks, the boys had to leave Puerto Rico and head to New York. Having spent all their money in bars and clothes shops, they could not afford suitcases and were forced to carry their possessions in wooden boxes marked 'Heinz Beans', with improvised string handles. In his box, Bernard even carried a white tuxedo jacket that had been given to him by a man who thought it might be useful in New York.

Arriving in New York by liner from San Juan, the seamen were met by taxis which took them to hotels for their first night. Bernard and Peter arrived outside the Times Square Hotel. As they stepped out and looked up in amazement at their accommodation, a uniformed bell boy approached, took their wooden bean-boxes from their hands and led them into the hotel. Once more, the two teenagers had entered an unfamiliar world. From the lift they were taken to their accommodation, an unexpectedly comfortable room with a telephone and a writing desk. Once again, it was a pleasant surprise after the missions and hostels they routinely resided in. As nice as it might have been, there was a whole city awaiting them, and they immediately hit the town: 'We went straight to a dime-a-dance joint. We had our photos taken in a photo-booth, which we had never seen in England. I was wearing my white tuxedo.' In their tropical outfits, the English teenagers were the focus of attention: 'As usual everyone in the joint wanted to dance with Peter.' Walking the streets, they were continually amazed at the contrast to home: 'There were all the lights on in Times Square. The cinemas were lit up.' Of course, it was too good to be true. After just one night in the Times Square Hotel, they moved to the mission in South Street, where they ate their meals at the Merchant Navy club.

At the mission, the staff were struck by the Puerto Rican outfits worn by the boys: 'beach suits' and straw hats were hardly appropriate for New York. When one of the staff asked, 'Is that all the clothes you have?' the boys were taken to a room filled with suits, shoes and hats. Again the boys were in a wonderland. Coming from the land of clothing coupons, New York was stunning. Picking out a brown woollen suit and suitable shoes, Bernard felt correctly dressed for the city. They quickly fell into a routine of going out to dances and restaurants, and once again teamed up with local girls.

After two weeks in New York, the boys left for home. They had enjoyed their time, but were eager to get back to sea to earn some money and to see their families again. As they left New York they had no idea they would be back within days. Shortly into the voyage they were torpedoed off the coast of Florida. Safely ashore, they went through the now familiar routine of replacing all their clothes. At first they chose old clothes from a pile of cast-offs. However, this was just temporary: they were immediately taken to a store and outfitted in a new suit, shoes and hat. Then, within a couple of days, they were off to the railway station and back to New York on the express train: 'Peter had already cabled New York to tell the girls to be there to meet us. And they were at the station waiting. I went back to the seamen's mission to get a new suit. They said, "You were only here the other day!" So I had to explain what had happened.'

Waiting for the next available ship, the boys stayed in New York for another four weeks:

> We had one month's money from the shipping company, so there was plenty for going out. And the girls paid their own way, their fathers told them they had to. We went out like all groups of teenagers: we went out to Coney Island and did all the rides, went on the boardwalk. We would never normally have had the chances to do things like that, but of course you had to go through the hard times first!

As he got friendlier with the girl and her family, Bernard received a tempting offer: 'Her dad wanted me to stay there and marry her. He said he'd set me up with a job on an American ship, then in three years I'd be able to get American citizenship. But I wasn't that keen on my girl and I don't think she was too keen on me.' So, despite the attractions, the two boys returned home.

In 1943, seventeen-year-old Arthur Harvey was sent to the United States as part of a crew to collect a newly built 'Liberty Ship', the *Sampan*. Once in New York they had to wait for two months before their ship was ready. He moved into a hotel on 54th and Broadway and, since he was being paid both his normal wages plus board and lodging, he could enjoy everything the city offered:

> We all got jobs. Some of the lads were store detectives at Macy's. I was an oiler at the Knickerbocker ice cream plant down on West 67th Street. I was earning bloody good money for a kid. I was working on shifts oiling the planks that were used for making blocks of ice. My expenses were all being paid, so what I earned was just pocket-money. We'd walk down to 42nd Street, go to the stage door canteen and get free tickets for all the Broadway shows. I'd do the two to ten shift, go back to the hotel, have a shower, then walk down to Times Square, see all the films and watch all the top bands. You name them, I saw them: Cab Calloway, Harry James, Tommy Dorsey, Jimmy Dorsey, Duke Ellington. There was Radio City, every Thursday night it would be full of bobby-soxers who were there to see Frank Sinatra. So I saw him perform. I was seventeen: a Portsmouth boy in New York.

From New York the crew was sent across the continent to San Francisco to pick up their new ship. Once again, they had a delay before she was ready:

> We had to wait there for two weeks. For beer money, we'd go to the railway station and unload mailbags for a dollar an hour. We'd do an eight-hour day to earn beer money. The next day we'd spend it in a bar. Then we'd work the next day. That went on for two weeks.

After a fortnight combining work and leisure, Arthur and the rest of the crew returned to the docks, the Red Ensign was raised on the 'Liberty Ship' and, loaded with 10,000 tons of cargo and twelve US Army officers, they headed off across the Pacific.

For teenager Alan Simms, too young to drink when ashore in the United States, life was a precious commodity that had to be enjoyed whenever possible. He and his fellow apprentices had to 'fiddle' their papers to ensure they could get served in bars: 'We used to worry – you never knew if you'd get torpedoed, so we used to spend our money on drink. We thought we'd better enjoy ourselves in case we got torpedoed on the way home.'

While the young British sailors enjoyed life in port cities, some ports were more violent than others. Big cities were a great adventure but sailors were often confined to areas populated by other seafarers and dock labourers, and trouble often brewed. Bill Ellis witnessed this violence whilst waiting in Baltimore for his ship to be repaired:

> We'd go down to a cafe near the docks where the bosun liked to sing. One day some Americans had put money in the Wurlitzer jukebox when the bosun started singing. A fight broke out with the boys who'd put the money in – and me and another young lad dived under a table, where we stayed till I was kicked in the ribs. The Americans were all big men – dockers – and we were just boys. I ran to the door to try to escape but the police were called – and all our shore leave was stopped after that.

Whilst in Gibraltar Boy Bugler Robin Rowe received good advice from a shipmate. He was warned to avoid fights with American sailors. It was not the sailors themselves he should worry about but the US Navy shore patrolmen who carried heavy nightsticks and lashed at anyone connected to fights, even bystanders.

Bill Ellis had similar experiences in a Scottish port: as well as feeling like outsiders in overseas ports, the boys of the Merchant

Navy had to get used to British ports in places they might never have
seen had it not been for the war. While it was easy for men and boys
of all nationalities to blend in among the crowds in London, some
of the smaller ports were more insular. Bill remembered his time
based at Greenock in Scotland:

> We used to go to dances in the town hall. My mate was a brilliant
> dancer and, when he started jiving, crowds would form to watch him.
> One day we were at a dance and the galley boy got into an argument
> with two Scots blokes. They had him pinned up against the wall. I tried
> to intervene, telling them, 'Let him go – there's three of us – and just
> two of you!' They let him go and I thought I'd done a good job. I told
> the galley boy to get back to the ship. They gave me a few pushes. I
> said, 'What you going to do?' Then my mate Hazeldene – who liked a
> fight – came over. Next thing, there was the sound of marching feet
> and eight of them appeared – and a fight started.

After the fight had broken up, a soldier approached Bill and asked him
if it was him who had punched the ringleader in the back of the head.
Bill denied it and the soldier replied: 'That's my brother. But we're not
going to do anything now. We'll be waiting outside for you.' Bill asked a
local girl to help him get out without being seen. She put on her long,
loose-fitting coat and he crouched down behind her, hiding in the folds
of the coat, walking through the crowds past the gang who were looking
for him. However, she soon betrayed him to the gang, who chased him
up the street. Eventually, he got away and returned safely to the ship.

The next week Bill returned to the dance hall, this time with a
larger group of men from his ship:

> One of the blokes with us was a hard nut – he'd worked in the circus
> before the war. They announced someone was going to sing 'The
> Bluebells of Scotland'. So my mate stood up and shouted, 'You can
> keep your "Bluebells of Scotland". There'll always be an England!' We
> had to go out through the fire exit – running for our lives.

After being sunk by a submarine in the Atlantic, Christian Immelman landed at Cape Town in South Africa. The crew's rescuers sent them by launch to the quayside where they expected to be met by a reception committee from Shell. There was no one there to meet them and not a soul to be seen:

> There was a light away up the road so we went there and discovered it was a Flying Angel club [seamen's mission]. Luckily for us the volunteer duty man that night also worked for Shell. He took control of the situation, ordered a couple of taxis and took us all to the biggest drinking establishment in town, Delmonico's, settled us there with a few beers whilst he went off to make further arrangements for our stay ... After a couple more drinks he piled all thirteen of us into cabs and took us to the Ritz hotel for the night. At breakfast the next morning I found we had to leave the Ritz because the crew had caused a commotion during the night, chasing chamber maids around the corridors.

The next morning he took the opportunity to send a cable home to his parents: 'Ship sunk. Arrived Cape Town OK.'

When Albert Riddle arrived in Cape Town in 1941, he was stunned by the reception received by British sailors: 'The people were wonderful to us. They lined the dockside with hundreds of cars and the people grabbed us as we went ashore and took us out for the day.' The best part was that the South Africans were able to write home on behalf of the boys. Albert knew his parents would appreciate some knowledge of his whereabouts: 'My parents were baffled – they'd never even been outside the village and suddenly they get a letter from South Africa! They didn't believe it. They'd never even been to Plymouth!' By the time the letter reached his parents, he was far away in Singapore, after the sinking of HMS *Prince of Wales*.

The foreign ports had another advantage. They were a fantastic location for shopping trips, making merchant seamen very popular when they returned home with their 25-lb allowance of food that was available in foreign ports but rationed in the UK. In Buenos Aires merchant seamen were able to purchase pre-prepared boxes of food, designed to provide a selection of goods unavailable at home, including luxuries like tinned ham. As one recalled: 'I would go home with it and Mother would open it up! Fantastic.' The ports of the world offered the teenage Arthur Harvey shopping opportunities of which he had never previously dreamed: 'You could get suits made in India, if you had the money. I got measured in the morning, and the suit was ready by teatime. I also got my shirts handmade.' On his first trip to New York in 1943 he purchased clothes for his baby sister and bought nylon stockings to impress his girlfriends back in Portsmouth.

Neutral ports were also a good place to barter. British seamen who had goods to sell or exchange took items ashore to see what they could get. Ex-*Vindicatrix* boy Bill Ellis remembered a wartime visit to Seville:

> I decided to go ashore on my own and went to a cafe. I had some cheap cigarette lighters that I'd picked up in Lisbon. So I walked up to the counter, asked for a drink and put a lighter down in exchange. There was a woman sitting in there and she wanted to see the lighters. I said OK, if you give me the money. I realized she wanted to buy other things from me. She wanted coffee, which I had onboard the ship, so I agreed to come back the next day with a pound of coffee. She paid me about a pound per pound of coffee – and I got together with her.

When the Spanish soldiers guarding the docks realized he was going into town to trade, they stopped him and demanded cigarettes as a bribe for allowing him to leave port carrying his trade goods.

Sailing the world was an eye-opening experience for all the boys. They not only learned how to enjoy themselves, but also about the iniquities of the world. Bernard Ashton sailed with men of all nationalities, who lived and worked together without concern. On one trip to Australia he was shocked when his friend was refused service in a bar. The seaman, from the streets around London's docks, who Bernard thought of as 'a real Cockney', had been singled out for his black skin. And in the southern ports of the United States, Bernard watched in disgust as policemen beat the feet of black men sleeping in the streets.

One of the least popular ports was Murmansk in northern Russia. It was just fifteen miles from the border with German-occupied Norway, making it uncomfortably close to the front line. Most of the British seamen thought the town cold and dull, with few facilities for them. However, not everybody felt the same. Some appreciated the efforts made by the Russians to entertain them. Jock Dempster, who arrived in Murmansk as a sixteen year old, later described the facilities:

> The authorities had created a social club which we were encouraged to use. Concerts, dances, the occasional ballet and choral renderings. Hard to imagine an audience of unshaven seamen sat watching the classical entertainment but I remember one choral concert which performed to a packed house and a very appreciate audience. The dances were very well attended, and the local militia also used the club. Hostesses – mainly students, teachers and secretaries – were happy to waltz round the floor, but in this instance fraternisation stopped at the main door. The girls would chat, teach us a few words of Russian, talk socially but no more. I have never met any veteran who ever saw a girl home. Respect was observed on both sides. I did learn quite a few Russian phrases and the first two verses of a song I'd heard at one of the concerts, as well as the phrase: 'Can I see you home, please?' The answer was always 'Nyet', but I always received a big smile . . . A bond of mutual respect was created with both sides appreciating the extreme hardships jointly endured. I have never ceased to admire the stoicism shown by the inhabitants living under unbelievably harsh conditions.[4]

The one thing that set the seamen apart from others was that they were able to bring things home. They brought home new suits from

Indian tailors, food from South America, rum from the West Indies, toys from the United States and cloth from around the world for wives, mothers and girlfriends. Most importantly, they returned home dressed in a manner that set them apart from their contemporaries. Bernard Ashton recalled returning home after his epic journey that had seen him buy, then lose, two sets of fashionable clothing when his two consecutive ships were sunk: 'I arrived home in my new American suit. And I had patterned socks. Imagine that in a mining village in 1942! If only I'd come home with my blue-striped beach suit, panama hat and two-tone shoes from Puerto Rico!'

CHAPTER 21

Ready for War

'One chap said to me, "They are training us to kill, we don't even know how to make love yet!" How true that was. We were all immature. We had our rifles but, when it came to women, we didn't have the foggiest. We had missed our teenage life.'

Bill Fitzgerald, 1/5th Queen's Regiment

In summer 1944, with the coming of the long-awaited 'Second Front', many of the soldiers who had volunteered whilst underage finally saw their chance to go to war. In many cases it had been a long wait: Ted Roberts, a volunteer aged fourteen, and Stan Scott, a volunteer aged fifteen, were both now nineteen. Fred Walker, who had joined the Army aged sixteen, and taken part in the Dieppe operation before he reached the call-up age, was now a twenty-year-old veteran of Sicily and Italy. Even his mate John Tupper, who had been just sixteen at Dieppe and who had also fought in the Mediterranean, had finally reached the age of eighteen. They were part of a force that was largely untried, most of whom had only experienced war during the Blitz.

Underage volunteer Eric 'Bill' Sykes spent the final six weeks of 1942 undergoing basic training at Berwick-upon-Tweed, where he celebrated his seventeenth birthday, before being transferred to the

70th (Young Soldiers) Battalion of the Durham Light Infantry. The unit trained incessantly, spending their days marching at high speeds and their nights on guard duty. Bill recalled the marching songs he and his fellow young soldiers sang as they tramped through the lanes of North Yorkshire: 'We are the good ol' DLI. We'll meet the enemy by and by, every man in the regiment is willing to do or die – Cor blimey.' However, Sykes was less than certain about the emotions of the song: 'I don't remember being willing "to do or die" for anyone at any period, then or now.'

However, the proximity of death at any time in the infantry soon became apparent to him. On exercises, live rounds were fired to give the youngsters an idea of what it would be like in battle:

> One exercise involved advancing under a creeping barrage of twenty-five pound artillery shells. On this particular occasion one of the gunners laid back 100 yards, instead of forward one hundred yards, and a shell fell into a group of people and we suffered several losses. I remember that occasion well as I was a member of the burial party for one of the young officers.

Whilst training, Bill noted:

> We did not talk about going to war as we were too busy and at the end of the day too tired to do anything but sleep. As would be usual, the conversation of virile young men would generally turn to girls, sex and the question of when we would get leave to participate in such activities.

In autumn 1943 part of the battalion was detached to act as reinforcements in the Mediterranean. This spurred Bill on to make a move and so, partly attracted by the higher rate of pay, he volunteered for the Parachute Regiment. After a brief, but intense, series of exercises in the Yorkshire Moors, designed by the battalion commander to toughen up the 'Young Soldiers' who had volunteered to be paratroopers, Bill was transferred to the 7th (Light Infantry) Battalion of the Parachute Regiment, joining them at their Physical Training Depot at Hardwick Hall in Chesterfield on 9 September 1943 for six weeks of physical training designed to 'toughen them up' for service as paratroopers.

Having passed the initial course, he was then sent for parachute training at Ringway outside Manchester. Whilst a constant stream of volunteers were 'returned to unit', Bill progressed from tower jumps to a balloon and then finally to an aircraft:

> Our Drop Zone from the aircraft was at nearby Tatton Park and included one drop into trees, and another into water at night. Dramatic experiences for a young teenager who had never been inside an aircraft before, let alone flown in one. Once again the selection process took its toll and only the courageous, or stupid, survived.

Bill was one of the survivors, qualifying as a paratrooper just in time for his eighteenth birthday.

Eric Davies, who had joined the 1/5th Queen's Regiment in North Africa, then served in Italy, was now a nineteen-year-old 'veteran'. Having returned from the Mediterranean, the battalion began to absorb newly conscripted men. In the four short months that he had been in action, Eric had gone from lance corporal to sergeant and seen the full fury of war. He was determined to do all he could to protect the new arrivals by passing on knowledge that might save their lives: 'We kept at it morning and night, trying to instil into them that training was the best way of staying alive.' When they practised working alongside tanks, the veterans taught them to stay safe, pressing home the dangers of standing too close to the lumbering steel beasts. They gave tips on house-to-house fighting; how to stay under cover and not reveal themselves to the enemy; how to dig and cover slit trenches; how to crouch when advancing; how to recognize the sounds that spelled danger. Though Eric was just a year older than the men he was helping to train, he had much to offer.

Among the conscripts listening to these lessons was Bill Fitz-gerald. His previous experience of war had been with the Army Cadets, training to defend London's Paddington station. Now he was an eighteen-year-old infantryman about to join the spearhead of the invasion. After basic training he joined the 1/5th Queen's Regiment. At first he was unsure about being transferred into a veteran unit but soon realized the advantages: 'We felt proud when we sewed on the Desert Rats flash. The veterans were a well-hardened bunch. They'd been through it all. But they were really good – they looked after us. They had to teach us what they knew. They wanted us to be able to watch their backs.' Also joining the Queen's Regiment at this time was Ron Leagas, who had defied his parents to volunteer as a sixteen year old in 1941: 'It was awkward to join the 7th Armoured Division like that – mixing with all the veterans. I found them all right but there was always an atmosphere between us. Some of them had contempt for us, because we hadn't experienced anything – but it wasn't our fault.'

The advice Bill Fitzgerald and his mates received was something they had not been taught in the Army Cadet Force. The new boys listened as the veterans passed on their advice: 'Don't hesitate or you are dead! If you see one, fire. Don't think about who he is or what you are going to do – if you hesitate, he'll get you first.' They asked about hand-to-hand fighting: 'Try never to get to that point. Shoot them before they get that close. If you can see them, shoot them. They might be bigger and stronger than you – you fall over and they'll put a bayonet in you.' It was not just the conversations that helped:

We watched them on manoeuvres: how they moved, how they dug in, how they got out of the way of things. Never run standing up, always crouch – it makes it harder for the enemy to shoot you. Never run in the middle of the road – keep to the sides. In woods, get behind a tree, don't stay out in the open. It probably saved our lives.

As time passed, Bill appreciated the value of being put in a veteran unit: 'We didn't realize what was going on, but we needed to be mixed in with the veterans. Without them, us eighteen year olds would have gone into action and we'd have been wiped out.'

By 1944 the latest batches of soldiers preparing themselves for war was a generation of boys born in the mid-1920s, many of whom had been schoolboys at the outbreak of war. Their teenage years had been marked by war, thousands were former members of the Army Cadets and Home Guard who had taken their first steps in military life as they were hastily assembled to ward off invasion. The youth of this latest batch of fighting 'men' was shown by the fact that some had been schoolboy evacuees in 1939. Among them was Bill Edwardes, who had first heard news of the declaration of war during his first church service as an evacuee.

Aged fourteen, and living in Wales with his mother and her aunt, he told them he wanted to get back to London. With the Blitz having subsided, the family returned to London where he found work:

> I worked in an engineering factory at Highbury Corner. It was a small company with several rows of lathes. They were finishing parts for anti-aircraft guns. It was an alloy mould that needed to be cut and smoothed. So we stood at these lathes, all in a line, and parts would come down the line with each person doing their bit. I would take the part from my basket, pick it up, put it into the chuck, draw the tool into the component, remove it, undo the chuck, then put the piece into the next box. I was doing that all day long.

By March 1943, he was frustrated by life on the production line. The hours were long, the work boring and repetitive, but there were few opportunities for boys whose education had been curtailed by war. With austerity measures affecting everyday life, and little to do except go to the cinema or the pub: 'I was bored to tears with going to work every day. I wanted some excitement: and I got it!' He voiced his frustrations to a friend: 'I said, "I'm fed up with this." He was seventeen-and-a-half. I asked if he was registered for service, but he said they hadn't called his group yet so he was going to volunteer for the Army.' For Bill Edwardes, it was a sudden decision: 'Right, I'm coming with you.' After work they made their way to their local recruitment office and offered their service, with Bill going through the traditional routine of adding more than a year to his age:

> There sat this sergeant. He was ebony in colour, he'd served in India pre-war. He looked very old and wrinkled. He looked up and asked, 'How old are you, son?' 'Seventeen-and-a-half, sir.' 'Don't you call me sir. I'm a sergeant!' 'I'm seventeen-and-a-half, sergeant.' 'Hmm, I'll believe you. Sign here. You'll be called up for your medical in a few days.' Then he gave me a shilling postal order, so I actually took the King's shilling!

On his way home he cashed the postal order and brought a packet of cigarettes. Arriving home, he broke the news to his mother. Shocked, she asked why he had done it rather than wait for his call-up in eighteen months' time: 'Mum, it might be all over before I get a chance to join in.' Knowing that she could march him straight back to the recruiting office and reveal the truth, he asked what she was going to do. She was honest in her answer: 'No. If that's what you want to do, go and do it. You'll never be satisfied otherwise.' However, as he later admitted: 'Many's the time after, when the situation wasn't too good, that I put my hands together and said, "Mum, why didn't you tell them? I don't want to be here!"'

He underwent primary training in Maidstone, with the Royal West Kent Regiment, where he had to learn the ways of the Army. At first it was difficult; standing out as the youngest, most fresh-faced of the new recruits and, being recognized as underage by most of the others, Bill soon learned the need to stand up for himself. At first he faced bullying by one of the conscripts in his barrack hut:

> I looked vulnerable – I was a bit of a weed. And there was one chap who thought I was fair game. He gave me hell and I wasn't very happy.

The chap who was above me in the bunk was very quiet, he never said a word. He had a pug nose and a bruised face – it turns out he was a boxer. One evening the bully was having a go at me. I saw these two legs come over the side of the bunk, he dropped to the floor and went across to the bully. He pulled him from his bunk, pushed him up against the wall and put his fist up to his face: 'Leave the kid alone or I'll knock your fucking head off!' Then dropped him. So I had a mate after that.

Apart from learning the basics of soldiering, he also needed to learn that being a soldier was about more than marching and firing rifles. On one occasion he was slouching past the company office with two of his mates when he heard a booming voice: 'You three, come here at the double!' It was Regimental Sergeant Major (RSM) Tasker, a small but fierce man, with a tremendous reputation. 'In my office now!' The three recruits doubled into his office in the expectation of some punishment:

> He lined us up and changed immediately from being a martinet to an avuncular old man: 'Boys, you really disappoint me. You are soldiers now. I don't want to see you slouching about. When you get leave – if you get leave – and you go home, you'll be marching down the street where you live. Children will run into their houses and shout, "Mummy, there's a soldier coming." They'll all come out to look at you.

Then the RSM reverted to type: 'Get out of here! Don't let me see you slouching like that again!'

Having overcome the bullying, Bill Edwardes proved the RSM right and became determined to remain an infantryman, rather than opting for one of the other arms of service. At the end of primary training he was called into the company office and told he had been selected for training as a signaller. He was swift to reply: 'Oh no, sir, I want to go into the infantry.' However, as he later realized: 'What a bloody fool I was!' Back in London on leave he confirmed that the ageing RSM had been right. He was proud to be in uniform and swaggered through the streets. The uniform meant he was no longer a child: at home he was no longer the baby of the family, even if his mother did cry to see her little boy dressed in his khaki. When he met up with his old mates some thought he was crazy to have volunteered when he could have been living in London and working in a factory. But Bill knew that he had grown up, whilst the others still seemed like children: 'I walked up Holloway Road thinking I was Jack the Lad. I went and had my portrait taken, and being the lad I was improperly dressed with my collar open.'

Bill Edwardes was then transferred to the 1st Battalion of the Worcestershire Regiment, where he joined C Company. The following months were a whirl of activity as the troops underwent heavy training in preparation for the inevitable invasion of Europe. For sixteen-year-old Bill, the training was hard-going since he lacked the physical strength of the older men. In sessions where they alternated between marching and running, Bill struggled to keep up and was seen by his officers to be in difficulty. To remedy the situation, he was sent to a special training camp where under-strength recruits were put on a special diet and training regime to increase their strength and stamina. It worked: after two weeks Bill returned to the Worcesters and rejoined his company.

In the final weeks of training before D-Day, an accident befell Bill Edwardes. Whilst crossing a ploughed field, he fell and gashed his knee. Needing stitches, he was sent to hospital where he remained for two days. Returning to the camp he discovered the entire battalion had left. Sent to a holding camp, he was desperate to get back to his regiment, knowing that if they were going overseas he wanted to be alongside the men he had trained with:

> Every morning the sergeant would call our names out and send men off to certain battalions. After a couple of days he said, 'I want three volunteers to go to the 1st Worcesters.' I was up there like a shot. He said, 'Wait a minute, son, you don't know what it's for.' I said, 'That's

my battalion and I want to go back.' So he told me, 'Right, son, from now on you are a stretcher-bearer.'

For the next few weeks he learned the basics of first aid. The training was based on the principle of the 'Three Bs':

> Breathing – is he breathing? If not move on. Bleeding – check the blood flow, fit dressing and tourniquets. Bones – check for broken bones. We were shown how to cope with bones sticking through the skin. If they were alive our job would be to stem the blood flow, make him comfortable and get him back to the Regimental Aid Post. I took to it like a duck to water.

With just a few weeks' training, and little practical experience, he prepared for war. He knew that it would be his role to decide who could be saved and prioritize their evacuation, effectively carrying out battlefield triage. It was a heavy responsibility for a seventeen year old.

In the final days before going overseas, sixteen-year-old Ken Durston – serving in the Devonshire Regiment – was given embarkation leave. He had joined the Army because he was unhappy at home, having constant arguments with the father of the evacuees who had lived with the family since 1939. At first he had accepted the boys, but when their mother had been killed in an air raid, the father had also moved in with them. Deciding to join the Army, he had gone to a recruitment office but admitted he was underage. The sergeant simply told him the date of birth to put on the papers and his problem had been solved.

At home on leave Ken told his mother that he would soon be going into action. She was unhappy that such a young boy would be putting his life on the line when he was two years away from being called up. Her doubts had an immediate effect:

> When I got back to camp there were orders for me to report to the CO. He said he'd had confirmation that I was underage. You had to be

eighteen to go overseas and my unit was going to north-west Europe. He was going to discharge me but I said I was happy where I was and didn't want to be discharged. He said, 'I can't let you go abroad with the draft,' but he did say he'd keep me on the permanent staff of the holding battalion until I was of age and then we could get it sorted.

He realized his mother must have written to the regiment but knew he could do nothing about it.

In the final days before D-Day, a few young boys joined the invasion fleet. Among them was Thomas Osborne, a fifteen-year-old pupil from the London Nautical School. At school, he had been asked if he would like to volunteer to go to sea as a member of the crew on a rescue tug. No one told him he would be taking part in the biggest amphibious operation in history, yet he could not believe his luck to have been asked. Normally he would have needed to study for a further two years and then obtain a cadet apprenticeship before going to sea. When he arrived at HM Rescue Tug *Assiduous*, he was approached by the chief officer who told him he was going to have to sign papers stating he was a volunteer.

On 1 June, the tug fuelled at Southampton and the crew had their last night ashore, where they went to a pub: 'And I was served with my first full glass of beer. The proprietor did not want to serve me as I was underage, but a Canadian noted my silver Merchant Navy badge and argued with him that service on a ship in wartime rules over drinking regulations.' Thomas felt the landlord only agreed to quieten the other soldiers who joined in the argument. He was then hoisted on to the shoulders of an American soldier and the whole room cheered as he drank the beer. 'I think I must have been the happiest and proudest boy in the whole of England that night.'[1]

Still just seventeen, Roy Finch was part of the infantry element of the 8th Armoured Brigade that assembled for D-Day. As his unit prepared to board the ship that would take them across the Channel, he was confronted by a senior officer who called a group of a dozen youngsters together and said: 'The thing is I know you are all under eighteen and you are not allowed to go overseas.' Roy was unsure of what would happen next: 'I suppose we all looked a bit miserable. We were with all the blokes we had joined up with and trained with, we wanted to go.' He was then shocked to hear his officer say: 'But if you actually get on to one of the landing ships and we leave, we won't be able do anything about it!' As the officer turned away, Roy and his young comrades fell in with the rest of their unit and boarded the ship: 'I should have stayed back in the UK. Everyone knew we were underage, but apart from that officer, no one said anything. It was so exciting – but our parents would have killed us!'

CHAPTER 22

The Boys in Normandy

'I woke to hear the throbbing sound of diesel engines; hundreds of landing and escort ships were moving toward the open sea. Overhead, aircraft of every type were moving in unending streams towards France.'

Fifteen-year-old Thomas Osborne,
onboard HM Rescue Tug *Assiduous*[1]

Among the first 'men' to land in France on D-Day was Eric 'Bill' Sykes. As a paratrooper in the 7th Battalion, The Parachute Regiment, Bill and his comrades were to be dropped east of the Orne River, on the far left flank of the invasion area. Their job was to reinforce glider-borne units that would seize the road and canal bridges. Taking these bridges would allow seaborne forces to move through the next morning, holding the high ground above the river and preventing German reinforcements reaching the invasion bridgehead. The plan was simple but relied on the paratroopers being dropped in the correct location.

Having been in the Army since the age of sixteen, it was easy to forget that, had he waited for his call-up papers, by June 1944 he would still have been undergoing basic training rather than parachuting into France. He recalled his emotions:

As a very young man, I of course felt invincible and if anyone was going to die it certainly wasn't going to be me. I had anxious moments and was at times a little nervous but certainly never felt in need of the services of a psychiatrist. Remember, I was a street-savvy youth and a survivor.

In reality, his chances of survival were slim. As he waited to board his plane ready for take-off, Bill Sykes talked to the crew: 'When I questioned them about the drop zone, they assured me that they had flown over the area in Normandy several times in the preceding weeks and "knew the exact field" on which we were to be dropped.' The journey was calm, until they reached the Normandy coast:

All hell broke loose. The parachute exit door in the floor at the rear end of the aircraft was now open and the inside of the fuselage was continuously illuminated by the explosion of far too close for comfort anti-aircraft shells which were peppering the outside of our aircraft with shrapnel.

Soon the order came to jump, and Eric 'Bill' Sykes found himself floating down into an apple orchard. He landed alone, with no sign of other members of his unit: 'Remember the crew of the plane who "knew the exact field"? Well, they may have known the exact field but they sure as hell didn't know the right river.' He heard firing going on in the distance and realized he had landed far from his drop zone, although at the time he didn't realize just how far away. He later discovered he had been dropped near the mouth of the River Dives, rather than the Orne, and was nearly twenty miles off target. After some searching, Bill joined up with eight others from his plane. For nearly two weeks they attempted to reach the Allied lines. They engaged in 'hit and run' encounters with the enemy, dodged the unwanted attentions of Allied fighter planes, and took shelter with French civilians. Two of the group were killed in action, but it seemed they were getting no closer to their objective of rejoining their unit.

On the morning of D-Day, whilst Bill was desperately searching for his comrades, the invasion went ahead according to schedule. Among those in the invasion force were a number of underage volunteers. Onboard a Royal Navy rescue tug, fifteen-year-old Thomas Osborne had his first taste of the war at sea. He could see and hear the warships firing, and heard the same shells exploding inland. He watched as a landing craft blew up. Exhausted, he went below decks to his hammock, but was soon awoken by a slap and told they were under attack:

> I ran back to the boat deck and two of the older members of the crew made a place for me near the shelter of our gun pit. They put their arms around me; I realized that I was trembling. Now it was a question of my mind's endurance and the return of my conscious self. The desperate truth is a child cannot find comfort from frightened adults and I was still a child.

From the deck he could see tracer bullets from the anti-aircraft guns arcing across the sky as they engaged swiftly moving targets.[2]

Thomas Osborne was not the only schoolboy with the invasion fleet. Just prior to D-Day, the Royal Observer Corps was asked to provide volunteers to join ships to act as lookouts against attacks by enemy aircraft. Those volunteering had to undergo a cursory medical examination, then a rigorous test on aircraft recognition, to select those suitable. Three seventeen-year-old boys were chosen. Ian Ramsbotham, Wally Shonfield and Jack Thompson were then given the temporary rank of petty officer in the Royal Navy, and sent to ships in the invasion fleet. Once their invasion duties were complete, they returned to England and immediately returned to civilian life. For Ian that meant returning to school.

Also heading towards the French coast was seventeen-year-old Stan Whitehouse, a private in the 1st Buckinghamshire Battalion, part of No. 6 Beach Group. Their role was to land on Sword Beach and secure the beachhead, preparing predesignated areas as fuel and ammunition dumps. When he had joined the Army he had promised his parents he had joined a boys' battalion, and would not be sent overseas until after his eighteenth birthday. The reward for his deception was to be among the first to land in France.

As Stan approached the beach, he noticed his unit was landing alongside the commandos. If they – the elite fighting-force of the British Army – had yet to hit the beach, it was a sign he was about to be thrust into the heart of the action. The run in to the beach provided a vivid introduction to war as the seventeen year old watched the invasion unfold before him: planes fell from the sky; boats sank; battleships fired broadsides; and corpses floated in the water. Ahead on the beach, he could see soldiers advancing, crouching as they came under fire. He watched as some were hit and fell to the sand. When he had changed his date of birth to join his father's old regiment and escape the monotony of life in a factory, this was not what he had imagined; his perceived adventure was something very different. This was real: this was war.

Among the commandos landing on Sword Beach was Fred Walker. No longer a green sixteen-year-old volunteer, he was a veteran of Dieppe, Sicily and Italy, who could say, with the certainty of a veteran: 'What's the colour of blood? If it's brown, you're bleeding to death.' He had come a long way since the days of the Blitz, when, as a civilian in a bombing raid, you had no control over your destiny. It made him think of his mother in the Blitz of 1940 who had refused his pleas to take cover, telling him, 'If we get hit, we get hit.' She may have accepted that her destiny was out of her hands, but he realized that, as a soldier, there was always something he could do to try to stay alive.

For Fred controlling his destiny was simple: get off the beach, reach the objective, win. And keep doing it – for as long as it takes:

> I was in front of our mob on the beach. I got up that beach so fast. There was a unit in front of us. They'd never been in action before. They were fodder for the guns. Half of them were terrified – well we

were terrified, but we'd done it before. They were even digging in by the sea. With the water lapping beside their holes! As we went by we were saying, 'Get off the beach, son!' But they couldn't fucking move. We went across a swamp. The noise of the German mortars was awful, they frightened the life out of us. But they were sinking in the swamp and not doing any damage when they exploded.

Although incoming mortar bombs frightened him, Fred was just glad he had a definite objective: 'There was nothing worse than mortar fire. I would always rather be walking forward than sitting in a slit trench under mortar fire. You were just waiting to be hit.'

Also with No. 3 Commando was Stan Scott, finally getting an opportunity to do what he had always dreamed of when he had volunteered for the Army as a fifteen year old. Approaching the beach, all he could think of was reaching the unit's objective, the bridges over the Orne Canal and River where they were to reinforce airborne units: 'I felt nothing. We'd done it so many times in training, so many different ways, that I felt OK. One thing was in our heads: 3 Troop, 3 Commando, you will get to the bridges. You will not stop for anything. No fighting, just go round trouble.' To achieve the necessary speed to reach the bridges, Stan was carrying a bicycle, to which was strapped a case containing mortar rounds. As they approached the beach, Stan felt the landing craft was a death-trap. It was confirmed when he saw a nearby craft take a direct hit, then slide beneath the waves.

His mind returned to the task ahead when he heard the order to load weapons. Then, suddenly, it was the moment for which he had been waiting for so long:

Hit the beach, down went the ramps. Whack! Next thing I hear is someone saying, 'Get up, Scotty, you're not hurt.' Got up, picked my bike up and ran up the beach. The two men beside me had been hit. Straight over the road, straight into the swamp. We couldn't stop. There were already bodies lying there – Jerry started hitting us with rockets. I saw a German mortar crew firing on the beach, but we followed their instructions and skirted around – still thinking of the bridges and the instructions not to get into a fight.

Struggling out of the swamp, Stan and his mates stopped to clean their bicycles before heading off to their target. The journey was uneventful, the roads seemed to be empty and they reached the village without incident. Still on their bikes, they raced down to the bridge and crossed it, quickly receiving orders to move through to the village of Amfreville. The rest of the day passed in a blur of activity:

> When things start happening, you are too busy to think about fear. Any worries, you think about them after. One of my pouches had been shredded by bullets or an explosion – I don't know when it happened, I couldn't remember . . . There was a sense of apprehension. You can't say you're not scared, but you look around at your mates and they all look OK. Of course, you can't see the inside.

Buoyed by the sight of his comrades' resilience, Stan moved forward, with bayonet fixed and 'one up the spout'.

The commandos took Amfreville, but only after coming under machine-gun fire that inflicted significant casualties. It was the first time Stan Scott had encountered death and wounding:

> Captain Westley was sitting there bandaged up. We sent him back. Les Hill had a bullet in his head. Dixie Dean was dead, he died in my arms. Abbott had his leg taken off by the machine-gun burst. Harnett had a bullet through his arse. Coaker got it in the head.

It was a story that was repeated in each unit that landed that day.

In the later waves came seventeen-year-old Roy Finch. He found the approach to the French coast strangely exciting:

> I thought I was immortal – you think you are the 'King's whiskers'. If I'd have known what I know now, I might have thought differently.

Now I think I was bloody stupid. At the start of the war I'd been armed with a whistle, shouting 'Take cover!' during air raids. Then I'd been a Home Guard in Waterloo station armed with just two bullets. Then all of a sudden I'm going into hell.

As they got closer to the beach the excitement increased:

All hell was going on. There were planes coming over the top. Battleships were firing over us on to the shore. The sergeant said, 'When we hit the beach, run like hell and spread out.' The landing craft beside us blew up. I saw tanks coming off and just sinking. We stepped off into nine feet of water. I couldn't swim. I had 250 rounds of ammunition round my neck – I had full Bren gun pouches. I went straight down and lost my rifle. The Sergeant got me to the shore. I was soaking wet, I'd lost everything, and I was in no fit state to take on the German Army. It was crazy. But I survived.

He marvelled at the sight of officers from the Royal Navy directing troops and vehicles. He looked at dead bodies but tried to ignore them: 'I didn't think it could be me. I thought I'd survive.'

As the commandos fought their way inland, seventeen-year-old Stan Whitehouse was hard at work consolidating the bridgehead. He soon had his first introduction to seeing shell-shocked soldiers who had suffered a psychological breakdown within minutes of landing in France. Worst was to come. He helped stretcher-bearers as they assisted horribly wounded men, including some of Stan's comrades. He watched as one mate went pale and bled to death, killed by a tiny shrapnel wound that had punctured his vital organs. But, most importantly, he was learning the lessons that would keep him alive: when to duck; when to take cover; when to run.

Within days of landing in France, Fred Walker came under heavy mortar fire. His unit had been constantly in action since landing, but this was some of the most intense and accurate fire he had experienced:

We'd just made an attack and the mortar bombs were coming down on us. Three of us were lying down in a little hut and all of a sudden – crash – the hut was hit. It blew my Tommy gun to pieces, but my mate Johnny Tupper copped the lot. He was killed next to me. He was sixteen at Dieppe, but he looked older. He was only eighteen when he died. The other bloke got hit in the backside. All I got was a long, thin piece of shrapnel in my foot. I only had minor injuries, but I was sent back to England.

Arriving in France on D-Day Plus Two, Ted Roberts was one of that lucky breed of soldiers able to accept that death was a likelihood:

If you lived, you lived – if you died, you died. I believe that when your time comes there's nothing you can do about it. I was fatalistic. I didn't worry about a thing. It doesn't mean I wasn't scared – because I was. Only mad men and liars weren't frightened. You'd be talking to someone, you'd walk away and turn around and he's dead. You can't live like that for twenty-four hours a day without being scared. But you accept it and learn to live with it. It makes you careful.

Within hours of arriving in France he was introduced to the importance of luck, when his unit was called to a halt: 'I went down on one knee, like they taught us to do. Suddenly a great big chunk of shrapnel hit the ground in front of me. I thought, "This is for real!" After that I always dug in as quick as I could.'

It didn't take long for him to identify the fate that awaited so many of his comrades:

The first dead body I saw was when we came to the bottom of a road. There was a jeep with half a body underneath it, burnt to a cinder. You think, 'Oh Christ!' but you carry on. It's a funny feeling that you can't really explain. It gives you a bit of a shock but you realize that's what it's going to be like. After a while, you see a dead body and you don't even think about it.

For Ron Leagas, the first encounter with the realities of war was a similarly shocking, and sobering, experience. Moving inland in advance of his first action, his carrier was the third in a column: 'When I looked up, the front carrier had gone. It had been blown to pieces by an 88 mm gun. I turned my carrier and got out of there.' After the enemy gun had been destroyed, Ron was ordered to advance: 'We said, "How can we go forward over that lot?" and pointed out the wreckage of the carriers and the bodies of the crew. They'd just been killed – we didn't want to drive over them.' The officer in charge found a simple solution:

> We had to get out of the carrier with shovels and clear up the mess. It was horrible. There a boot with a foot in it. I saw a bloke with his brains mashed up inside his steel helmet. We had to shovel up all these bits into blankets and leave them for the graves' registration people. That brings it home to you.

It reminded him of his father's words when Ron had volunteered aged sixteen: 'He's made his bed, he's got to lie in it.' Having volunteered for war, he could hardly start complaining.

Having encountered death, Ted Roberts had to grow accustomed to killing. Fortunately, most of the action was long range. Rather than firing at what he could see, he simply fired where he was told:

> You don't normally see the enemy – except for dead ones. We were getting machine-gun fire from a copse. You couldn't see nothing – just a little puff of smoke. We fired at that. That was all we could do. We couldn't see the Germans. But the first time you open fire isn't the big thing that makes an impression: it's when they start firing back at you!

In the last week of June, the 1st Battalion of the Worcestershire Regiment arrived in France. With them was seventeen-year-old stretcher-bearer Bill Edwardes. Immediately after landing he encountered his first casualty. As yet uncertain how he would react to the sight of the dead and wounded, he discovered how effective his training had been and found he reacted exactly as taught:

> I had learned the 'Three Bs' by rote – Breathing, Blood, Bones. The first casualty was a guy in a cab of a truck, leaning over the steering wheel. The top of his head had gone. I'm a bit ashamed that I didn't think, 'Poor Bugger.' Instead, I looked at him and thought, 'I won't have to check his breathing.'

Within days Bill got his first opportunity to find out how he would react when he was dealing with seriously injured men. In the weeks ahead, he would be part of a team, spending some time at the Regimental Aid Post (RAP), then with the rifle companies on rotation. As he later noted, the rotation system had a positive benefit: he never spent long enough with a company to get attached to the men. It also meant that by the time he was attached to C Company, where he had earlier served, most of his mates had already been killed or wounded and he never found himself treating friends: 'I lost touch with people. You'd get reinforcements in the morning but they'd be gone by the evening.'

Like all young soldiers, his first battle had a profound effect. It was his first chance to prove himself. He recalled the first time he heard the call, 'Stretcher-bearers!' and advanced to treat the wounded:

> It was the attack on Mouen. We were just behind the infantry, crouched in a cornfield. We watched, saw someone go down and went to them. The first one was the company commander. He had quite a severe neck wound. He lived, but he was badly wounded. I held his back and head as my mate bandaged him. I was able to say things to him that I didn't dare say when I was in his company.

Bill was pleased to discover he had not panicked when he encountered the wounded officer. He was also pleased that the company commander remained stoic, accepting his wounds in silence.

In the days ahead, Bill learned that not all the wounded were so stoical. Some cried for their mothers, others screamed in agony. Some men were grimly determined to survive, whilst others accepted their fate, telling him, 'Bugger it, I've had it.' Day after day, he witnessed scenes he could never previously have imagined. At one point he was called to a group of five officers hit by mortar fire:

> With a group you have to look and make your own judgement. Leave the man with the bullet in his leg, to deal with the man with shrapnel in his back. You learn to prioritize and go to the one who is worst off. If someone else complains, you tell him to shut up and wait his turn. As a medic, you are in charge.

When dealing with the officers, Bill realized there was a certain irony that, while still a boy, he was saving the lives of his officers:

> There was me, a seventeen-year-old boy, cradling these senior officers: men in their late twenties or their thirties. Holding them in my arms, looking after them. I'd tell them, 'You're lucky, it's a "Blighty wound", you'll be going home.' But knowing full well they might not last the day.

As he later noted: 'The casualties didn't care how old I was.'

Bill Edwardes had entered a hellish world. The shout of 'Stretcher-bearer!' – often from the mouths of dying men – was a constant accompaniment to his waking hours. His was a world of blood and bandages: a place where he rushed forward to help wounded men only to find they were already dead. His life was dictated by binding wounds, as he listened to men screaming in pain. He administered hundreds of shots of morphine to badly wounded soldiers, marking a bloody 'M' on their foreheads. The seventeen year old used his discretion as to how much should be administered, anything was worthwhile to diminish the pain of the most badly wounded men: men who pleaded for the relief that only drugs could bring.

Having seen so many horrible wounds, Bill Edwardes began to get a better understanding of his patients and their behaviour:

> Back wounds affected me the most. I could see the damage but the casualty couldn't. A man could see his leg, even if it was severed, and he knew the extent of the damage. You could tell him what you were doing – 'I'm going to put a tourniquet on now. Stand by, I'm going to really pull it tight!' But when chaps got flying shrapnel in their back, they'd be in pain but they didn't know what was wrong. Sometimes I'd be asked to put an end to it, to put a bullet into them. But I couldn't do that. I told them I wasn't armed. How could you put them out of their misery? That worried me.

The situation was always different when the battalion was in a stationary position, in particular when they were 'dug-in' during the night, and came under bombardment. It was these occasions that tested Bill Edwardes' mental strength:

> You'd hear the call 'Stretcher-bearer!' The last place you wanted to be was outside your own hole, among the bombs. But you knew you had to go. It was a question of duty. Your mates were depending on you. You'd go out into the dark, following the call. You'd find the casualty in his slit trench. You had to get him out, not knowing what further damage you were doing, and sort him out as best you could. If they were ambulant you just pointed them in the direction of the aid post – if not, you'd get them out on a stretcher, carried them there.

Such incidents put pressure on the bearers, as they risked their lives to rescue those in need. As they worked they listened to the whine of incoming German mortar bombs, counting them and just hoping to survive until the sixth and last bomb of the barrage had exploded.[3] After each such action Bill found himself feeling under strain: 'I was OK whilst I was working, but when I got back to the hole the shakes would start. I looked at my mate and said, "Bugger that. Let's not hear the next shout." But when it came we always went out to it.'

As someone who had not been physically strong when he joined the Army, Bill Edwardes always found carrying stretchers with the dead weight of a wounded man was a genuine strain. Trudging through fields, half crouching from incoming fire, he could feel his arms, then back and neck, tighten as the burden increased with every step. The only respite came when they stopped to take cover from heavy fire. The biggest shock came when he reached the aid post. As soon as he put down the wounded man, he began to feel lightheaded, feeling as if he had been spinning in circles: 'As a nine-stone weakling I found the carrying of a stretcher by just two men extremely difficult, and would stagger round like a drunkard for a few moments, after putting the stretcher down!' Then, as the strain wore off, he moved forward again, back to treat more wounded and – hopefully – carry them back to safety.

The dedication of the bearers, the medics and the doctors made the difference between life and death for so many soldiers. A generation of young men, including so many who had been schoolboys in 1939, were among those who needed the services of the medics. One was Bill Fitzgerald. It was four years on from when he had trained to defend London as an Army Cadet; now he finally faced the enemy in France. He immediately realized how important the training he had received from the veteran 'Desert Rats' had been:

I saw chaps being hit. And I knew what I was there for. I had to keep my mind clear. Remember – don't think about men being hit, but about the men firing at you. You have to suppress them. I saw them in the distance – it's either them or me. Shoot. It was a weird feeling to know you are hitting someone. But all the training came back. No hesitation. I had to do it.

However great the veterans' skills at teaching the ways of the battlefield, they were still as vulnerable as their pupils:

When the corporal got killed it was the first time I'd ever looked at a body. I began to feel the pressure. He was a chap who had been helping me for the last year or so. He'd been all through the North African and Italian campaigns. I thought, 'Why him?' Then one of the other veterans said to me, 'Just keep going forward.'

Bill's time in Normandy lasted just ten days. His unit was in a wooded area when it came under artillery fire:

They shelled the life out of us. They blew the bloody place to pieces. All I can remember is going up in the air. Then crashing on to my back. I was hit on the head and I could feel blood on my leg. I knew something was wrong. I was helpless and I was dead scared. The shells were coming over and another soldier grabbed me, put his arm across me, put a helmet across my face, and said, 'Keep still!' I don't know who he was, I call him my 'unknown saviour'. He stayed with me until the bearers turned up. I couldn't move. I didn't realize my femur had been broken by shrapnel.

Within minutes he was picked up by the bearers, filled with morphine and sent to hospital. He arrived back in England within days and he was encased in plaster to keep the leg and lower body from moving. When he was finally discharged from hospital more than a year later, one leg was two inches shorter than the other. All that mattered was that he was alive.

As the days and weeks passed, Ted Roberts became accustomed to life in the front line: he snatched catnaps where and when he could, never really falling into a deep sleep. He hardly ever ate hot food, mostly living on sandwiches. He endured the diabolical stench of rotten flesh, from the bloated corpses of dead cattle and men. In the slit trenches and dugouts around him, Ted became accustomed to the look of fear on the faces of his comrades. He listened to their prayers and watched the tears of those whose spirit was being eroded by the whine of incoming mortar and artillery fire or the distant rumbling threat of enemy tanks. Above all else, he learned that the battlefield was a lonely place: 'Although you were in a crowd – you were on your own.'

He also began to learn the nature of courage: 'Just to be there was brave – everyone was risking their lives. You just do what you've got to do at the time.' He was convinced most of the men he saw performing acts of tremendous bravery were hardly aware of what they were doing. It seemed they were running on adrenaline. Every day seemed to bring out displays of courage that went unnoticed and unreported. For every act of heroism that earned a medal, plenty more were unrewarded. Like so many others, Ted put himself in danger, hardly thinking of what his actions meant: 'I went out with another chap and pulled in a wounded sergeant. It was just something you do. We couldn't leave him there, he was wounded and under fire. He was only about fifty yards away, but we could both have got killed. But we did it.' His motivation was simple: 'You hope someone would do it for you.'

It was time to learn that all normal concerns had to be put on hold for the duration of the war: 'One minute you are having a laugh and a joke, the next you are under fire and thinking, "Oh Christ! Am I going to be killed?" My emotions and attitudes changed by the minute.' It was an experience that no amount of training could have prepared him for: 'You lived as raw as you possibly could. We were just existing.' No one talked about what was happening, they quietly got on with achieving their own aim: 'All you want to do is be alive when the battle is over.'

But most of all, Ted Roberts was learning to kill, up close:

> One time the enemy were really close. I was behind a barn and I put me rifle to the side as I was lighting a cigarette. I looked around the corner and saw two Germans running towards the barn. We looked at each other – it seemed like it was for hours – I grabbed me rifle, they turned away and I fired. I know I got one of them and I think I got the other as he was going over the hedge. It was a really personal thing, you didn't get that very often.

Despite the vicious, sometimes personal, nature of the combat experienced by infantry in Normandy, Ted Roberts never lost sympathy for the enemy. Yes, he had volunteered aged fourteen, but he did not go into battle consumed by hatred:

> I never felt hatred to the average German soldier. We hated the SS because of their atrocities. They'd shoot anyone – including women and children – I could never do that. But I had no animosity to the average German – he was trying to kill me, I was trying to kill him. What's the difference?

Looking back he noted: 'Yes, I have killed people, but I'm not proud about it. It's not a thing to be proud about.'

Ironically, for someone who had volunteered aged fourteen, Ted had one particular concern: he hated the prospect of coming face to face with the child-soldiers of the German Army:

> I worried about the Hitler Youth Division, who were on our front. They were fanatics. They'd been trained from school kids. Now if a thirteen- or fourteen-year-old kid had stepped out in front of me with a rifle, I don't know if I could have shot him. Thank Christ, that never happened, because a split-second delay can cost you your life. I saw lots of youngsters – dead, wounded and prisoners – but I never came face to face with one. I was glad about that.

For many of the troops fighting in Normandy, there was a feeling that this was an opportunity to pay back the enemy for what they had witnessed during the Blitz on Britain's towns and cities. Looking back, Patrick Delaforce – who had spent his school holidays with his grandmother in London during the early years of the war – felt the experience had influenced his feelings once in battle: 'It helped to confirm that, whatever nasty events might happen in the future, "soldiering on" was vital. The Blitz and the wholesale slaughter of innocents almost certainly made me callous during the campaign in north-west Europe.'[4]

In the midst of the horror, Stan Whitehouse – still five months away from his eighteenth birthday – found time for relaxation. He became friendly with a local girl and at night would creep away to meet her. At first they bartered, exchanging army rations for fresh, local produce. Then they grew closer, kissing and cuddling in the hedgerows. As he later recalled, every time his hands strayed, he received a slap across the cheek from the sixteen-year-old French girl. Stan may have been doing a man's job, but when it came to romance he was still a boy.

Thirteen days on from D-Day, Eric 'Bill' Sykes and his small squad of lost paratroopers encountered the enemy near the coastal town of Cabourg:

> We were engaged by heavy machine-gun fire and pinned down in a water- and mud-laden ditch. After what seemed to be an eternity, the machine-gun firing stopped and a couple of grenades were thrown into the ditch ... Luckily we were far enough away to avoid most of the blast except, of course, for the shower of mud, water and other debris. As we were at an obvious disadvantage it appeared futile to attempt to fight our way out of our predicament through the one point of exit as it appeared that we would certainly be killed so unfortunately we had no other solution than to surrender.

In the hours that followed, Bill and his mates were stripped naked, lined up in front of a firing squad, reprieved, then sent for interrogation, during which he refused to answer questions. At the end of his interrogation, the German officer reprimanded him for the youthfully flippant manner in which he had approached the interrogation: 'The major was quite right, I was a very young and very foolish young man who apparently didn't realize the possible consequences of my flippancy.' Transferred to Paris, and then to Germany, he spent the final year of war in captivity.

As June turned into July, Bill Edwardes had little respite. His battalion was at the forefront of two of the most vicious battles in

Normandy: Hill 112 and Mont Pinçon. During the latter battle he
found himself under counterattack at the objective, a hilltop
junction, recalling: 'It was hell at those crossroads. The enemy didn't
want us to have them.' Such days were the norm for Bill and in two
months of fighting he had just three days' rest. When the chance
came to get away from the front line, he and his mates decided they
should go to Bayeux:

> I was a virgin. One of my mates said, 'Do you fancy going to a brothel?'
> I said, 'Why not?' I wanted to be like the lads. We had been given an
> address and the three of us scoured the streets. We found it in a row of
> terraced houses. It didn't look very likely but we rang the doorbell. The
> door opened, and the entire doorframe was filled by a military
> policeman. He looked down and said, 'What do you want?' Quick as
> a flash, I said, 'Sorry, I thought this was a cinema.' He told us to bugger
> off. We never knew if we'd been set up, or if the MPs had a franchise
> on it. So no luck there. I had to wait until later.

Back in the front lines, the days simply blurred into one another:
each day he survived meant he did not dwell on the events of the
preceding days. In those weeks his entire life changed. It was more
than just growing up:

> It's surprising how quickly a seventeen year old gets hardened – not
> indifferent, but detached. You got accustomed to wounds and death.
> But you didn't get used to it. After a very short time and seeing some
> serious wounds, you tended to think, 'I've seen worse than this – and
> they have survived.'

In those few weeks he had managed to close his mind to the raving
and crying of seriously wounded men. Where once the sound of a
man crying for his mother had affected him, he could now ignore it.
   His experiences also gave him a full understanding of his own
mortality:

You came to the conclusion that how could you possibly survive when so many people were going down around you. In the morning you'd wake up and you'd think to yourself, 'Maybe it's today?' You'd say to your mate, 'If it is, I hope it's quick. I just want to be wiped off the face of the earth. I don't want to go through what some of these blokes are going through.' You didn't want to have a piece of red-hot shrapnel travelling at about 100 miles an hour into your back.

Added to the sense of mortality was the fear that he might suffer a mental breakdown. He had seen enough soldiers unable to cope with the pressure: men who broke down in battle and who he had sent back for the medical officer to examine. It was terrible to see his comrades, men he had admired and respected, cracking under the strain: men crying, their heads hung low, or sitting in the open, paralysed with fear. He could understand their suffering. Countless times, he too felt he could not take any more. But after a few hours' sleep, he gathered up enough mental strength to continue another day.

Eventually, after almost six weeks of fighting, Ted Roberts reached a point he had long expected would come. Having captured a village, his unit came under a fierce counterattack from Germans just across the road from his position. Desperate to bring forward the mortars of the support company, an officer ordered one man back to find them. Ted watched as the man rushed across open ground, only to be cut down by enemy fire. Knowing their survival was dependent on getting support, the officer called forward the next man. His gaze fell on Ted:

'You! Go back and fetch the carriers.' I started to run across the orchard. I could hear the whip-crack of two bullets. I got down and waited a few seconds. Then I started running, zigzagging so I didn't make myself an easy target. But a bullet hit my arm in one side and came out the other. It spun me round – my tin hat went one way, my rifle went somewhere else.

Out in an open field, there was little he could do, except hope the wound was not too bad:

> When the bullet first hit me I didn't feel pain. It was just like someone had given me a good push. But as I lay there it was a burning sensation. It felt like having your arm too close to a fire. I couldn't move the hand or the arm. The bullet had taken a chunk out of the bone and bruised all the nerves.

Having come under accurate fire, Ted knew a sniper had spotted him. He knew that if he moved, he would be shot again. All he could do was play dead. He couldn't even move his hand across to hold his wounded arm. Trying to staunch the blood with a field dressing would have brought a potentially fatal shot:

> If the sniper had seen me move he'd have killed me. I was lying there, I couldn't move and I couldn't see anything – I could only move my eyes. I was wondering what was happening, 'cause they were giving our boys a bashing. I thought, 'This is it, I'm going to be a prisoner or be killed.'

Unable to move, Ted heard an ominous sound: the rumble of tank tracks. As the ground shook beneath him and the noise grew louder:

> I thought: 'Are they ours or are they theirs?' Out of the corner of my eye I saw this tank. Then the tank swung around towards me. They weren't fussed about running over bodies! I was getting more and more agitated. When it got to my side I thought, 'Sod it!' I wasn't going to let it squash me. I was going to move, regardless of whether it meant I got shot again. So I started to move. Then this head pops out of the turret and says, 'Where are all these effing Germans you lot are shouting about?' I'm not ashamed to admit it, I was petrified.

Once the tanks had repulsed the German attack, Ted was able to get treatment. Firstly, a corporal gave him a cigarette but within seconds he passed out from blood loss. When he awoke, he was slumped in a Bren-gun carrier with a wounded officer on his lap and another man propped up beside him. From there, he was driven back to the Regimental Aid Post, then to a field hospital where he was taken inside a tent and placed into a hole in the ground. Although the hole was for protection, it seemed more like a grave. Despite his concerns, he was finally able to relax: 'I could hear bombing but they weren't aiming at me. So I did a lot of sleeping.' He was soon sent back to England, then by train to Preston. Only in Preston was he was finally able to change out of his stinking, blood-stained uniform and have his original wound dressing replaced. From there, he was taken to Blackburn where the long process of recovery commenced.

For Stan Scott, the battle for Normandy developed into an endless round of reconnaissance patrols, fighting patrols, probing attacks and deadly battles to hold ground. As his unit was depleted by enemy action, Stan became increasingly resigned to the notion that it would be his turn next. He had seen friends and comrades die, one after the other. Men had died in his arms or he had seen their guts blasted out of them: 'After a few days you stopped worrying about it. If it's going to happen, it's going to happen. Especially in your hole at night, under mortar fire. You think, "Where's the next bastard going to land?" But you survive it.' While he grew accepting of the likelihood that he might be killed or wounded, he remained convinced he would not succumb to battle fatigue: 'I never thought I would break down – I felt too streetwise.' The nearest he came to failing was while under fire from an enemy tank:

I'm not going to hide it, I froze. We were out in the open, suddenly there was an almighty bang and screech – clods of earth flying everywhere. Christ! What was that! It was a tank everyone had missed. But we were too close, it couldn't depress its guns enough to get us. But I was gone. My mate said, 'Move!' He kicked me up the arse. That got me moving! I had completely frozen. I thought this is it!

His brain and body were shocked back into activity and he swiftly rejoined his mates, and returned to a world where being tired, hungry, dirty and slightly 'bomb happy' was the norm.

With casualties mounting, the front-line units became desperate for reinforcements. As a result, the Beach Groups that had landed on D-Day were stripped of men, who were then sent to front-line units. Seventeen-year-old Stan Whitehouse opted for the 1st Battalion, Black Watch. He would remain with the battalion for the rest of the war, one of the growing number of Englishmen serving in Scots regiments.

In the midst of the fighting in Normandy, the King's Own Yorkshire Light Infantry were ordered to advance on Tessel Wood. The fighting was bitter and bloody. The infantry struggled to fight its way uphill and into the woods only to be forced back out and down the hill again. With them was eighteen-year-old Private John Longfield, who a year earlier had volunteered for the infantry from his headmaster's study. In the weeks of fighting he had grown into an experienced Bren gunner and had seen all the horrors of war. What he saw that day was to haunt him forever.

As John retreated down the hill he spotted one of his comrades. He was lying on the ground with his helmet down over his face. He appeared unwounded so John leaned over and spoke to him. He didn't react. So John decided to take a look. He lifted his helmet. What he saw shocked him: 'The front of his head was missing and there was a grey mash of brains mixed with blood. The poor lad was only seventeen years old. He had got into the Army by falsifying his age. What a dreadful waste.' All John could think about was that this boy shouldn't be in Normandy, fighting a vicious war, when he was too young to even go into a pub and order a beer. As he recalled: 'It is difficult to forget. Out of all the deaths I saw that summer – out of all the corpses – the seventeen year old was the one I remember the most.'[5]

As the Allied armies slowly advanced, there was a growing sense of exhaustion enveloping the British Army. The long days and short nights, hardly offering more than a few moments to snatch sleep, pushed the infantrymen to the very limit of their endurance. The hideous cocktail of smells – the stench of dead men and animals rotting in the sun, the sickly sweet aroma of cordite, the appalling smell of tank crews being scorched inside their burning tanks – assaulted their senses, overwhelming the stink of their sweat-soaked uniforms, rotten socks and dirty boots. Everywhere they looked were signs of war: twisted bodies, ruined homes, burned-out vehicles. The noises of war gave them no peace: the distant rumble of advancing tanks, the terrifying whine of incoming mortar bombs, the cries of the dying and wounded. And that was on top of the fear of almost certain death. Teenage infantry sergeant Eric Davies, who was desperately trying to keep himself and his men alive, later wrote: 'We decided that hell was paradise compared to Normandy.'

The vicious nature of the fighting in Normandy changed many of the soldiers forever. Most learned to become callous, readily killing in a desperate attempt to stay alive. At one moment they could show tenderness and mercy to wounded enemies, at the next they could be extreme and brutal to anyone who threatened their lives. Death became a daily routine, with friends, enemies and innocent civilians all losing their lives. In the charnel house world of the infantryman there was little space for civilian morality. This was not a gentleman's war, but a fight to the finish. For Eric Davies the fighting in Normandy led to a new brutality, one that he had not known in Italy: 'There was an unofficial rule that the SS would not take any "Desert Rats" prisoners, and the same way, we would not take any SS prisoners.'

During one advance in Normandy, Eric and his men put this rule into practice. His unit was advancing along a road in preparation for an attack. As they advanced, Eric could not help but be reminded of photographs he had seen of France as a child. The scene – with its long, straight, tree-lined road – was an image he had long imagined was typical of the French countryside. As he reflected on how this road might have looked in peacetime, his momentary idyll was shattered. Mortar bombs and artillery shells rained down among the advancing infantry, causing heavy casualties. Rapidly advancing through the fire, Eric took his carrier forward and located the German observation post that had been directing the fire: 'It was manned by SS men who had infiltrated into the area during the night. As you can imagine, there were no prisoners taken.'

Whilst the battle for Normandy raged, and teenage infantrymen fought and died, the boys of the Merchant Navy continued to show the same dedication that had allowed them to prevail in the Battle of the Atlantic. In June 1944 one new recruit arrived off the coast of Normandy ready for his introduction to war. Bristol-born Alfred Leonard had left home six months earlier on his sixteenth birthday and, after a few months at a nautical training school, he joined his first ship, the *Empire Cricketer*, an oil tanker converted to carry water. His motivation for joining the Merchant Navy had been simple:

> It was getting towards the end of the war and I wanted to get in and rather than wait to be conscripted – it would have taken another two years – I managed to get into the Merchant Navy. If you want to go, you've got to go. I'd got the urge to go abroad. It opened up opportunities for me.

Though his parents had not welcomed his decision, his determination meant there was little point in trying to stop him.

Arriving off the coast of Normandy and taking up station within the Mulberry Harbour at Arromanches, his ship soon set to work. For three months they shuttled between the harbour and deep-sea tankers at anchor in the Channel, topping up and then returning to the coast to provide water to any ship that needed it. Alfred recalled: 'On the invasion, everything was happening so rapidly I didn't really think about anything. But once I'd been away a while I got a bit homesick – even though I wasn't that far from home.'

It was not just homesickness that entered the youngster's life. Whilst the latter war years saw the enemy threat to ships on the

Atlantic convoys diminishing, the Normandy coast was less than comfortable. As the *Empire Cricketer* made its way from the harbour out to sea to be restocked, it was regularly shelled by long-range enemy artillery, causing sixteen-year-old Alfred to become increasingly aware of his mortality: 'We got hit once by the shells. Another time we went over an acoustic mine but because we were fast we avoided the worst of the blast. But everything on the ship moved forward. For a sixteen year old it was quite an experience.' Despite the dangers he relished the freedom of being at sea:

> It was a complete adventure. I had been working in an experimental aircraft factory – doing secret work on engines – and it had been like working in a prison. You went through the gates, they checked your pass, everything closed behind you and you worked undercover. So being out on the sea was more open and more lively.

Having survived D-Day, the rescue tug *Assiduous*, whose crew included fifteen-year old Thomas Osborne, travelled back and forth across the Channel, towing vessels back for repair and taking the concrete blocks across to build the Mulberry Harbour. Whenever they came under air attack, he stood on deck and passed ammunition to the gunners. The hours were long and the work hard. To cope, he was issued with Benzedrine tablets: 'I slipped into a disembodied feeling, a feeling of my body being forced on and on. The slightest motion seemed exaggerated, yet all I had witnessed was stamped forever in my mind.'[6] In September he returned home on leave, where he celebrated his sixteenth birthday. He was then paid off: 'The war is almost over and when it is I shall travel the world to see if there is a place where I can find a new life.'[7]

For Peter Richards, who as a teenager had closely followed the Communist Party line and argued for the opening of a 'Second Front' to help relieve pressure on the Soviet Union, once he arrived in Normandy the realities of war were found to be somewhat different:

I was absolutely enthusiastic about it. We had got carried away a bit. We really thought that when we opened the 'Second Front' the Germans would collapse. Suddenly you realize that, after all this gung-ho approach, you can actually get killed. You see a bloke wearing the same uniform as yourself and he's dead. It was quite a shock. The first one I saw was lying there covered with a groundsheet with his boots sticking out. Of course, they were the same boots as mine, that really hit me. I realized we were playing for keeps. Then you see bodies with no legs and so on. I saw a dead German. The corpse was rotten – it was as black as the ace of spades, with maggots coming out of his nose. And the smell – dead animals, dead bodies – that's what's always missing from war films.

He went into battle carrying a copy of the selected works of Karl Marx. It was a heavy, hardback book that he stuffed inside his battledress blouse – just as others carried a Bible. When he later looked back at carrying the book, he was amazed by his arrogance: 'How bloody stupid. We were fighting the SS, who were the most viciously anti-communist. Imagine if they had captured me. Maybe I thought I was going to convert them!' However, carrying the book did pay dividends: one day a large piece of shrapnel tore open his blouse and carved into the book, preventing it from piercing his chest and killing him. There was a delicious irony in being saved by this book: many old soldiers told of being saved by a Bible so it seemed perfect that a book from the new 'religion' had saved Peter Richards.

Having lived through the Blitz, he realized that rather than help prepare him for war, his experiences had used up part of the store of courage every man was thought to have within him:

You went through phases. The first phase in action you didn't know if it was two o'clock or Thursday. Then you saw dead bodies and thought, 'That could happen to me!' You jump at every little bang – you get very scared. Then you get to a state when you are a bit cocky. I was fed up with being scared. I just wanted to carry on.

The sense of cockiness developed by Peter cost him dear. He was riding his motorcycle along a country lane, when the road came under mortar fire: 'I'd been warned about the mortars but I kept going.' The bombs fell in a salvo of six but as they fell he kept riding until the last moment. He dived to the ground, hoping to find shelter, hugging the ground – 'with a greater fervour than I have ever hugged a woman' – just hoping the firing would pass. It didn't: the final round landed beside his right leg. He later described it as being like a savage blow with a red-hot hammer that shattered his leg. In that moment his war was finished. One thing was certain, he was closer to being the subject of one of the telegrams he had delivered to the families of dead servicemen than he was to the youth who had defied the Blitz by taking training runs through the shrapnel-strewn streets of London. He had used up his luck and it would be a long time before he would run again. Indeed, it would be a long time before he could even walk unaided: almost a year later he was still wearing a calliper to support his damaged leg.

For Stan Scott, the inevitable happened as the commandos entered the town of Honfleur. They made a deadly mistake and let their guard down. Thinking the town empty, they sauntered in without employing their usual tactics of rapid movement. Stan found himself in the town centre: 'We thought it was all over, that was our undoing. We were too casual. We were bloody stupid. I don't know what hit me. The last thing I saw were fishing boats and fishing nets everywhere.' Then he spotted an 88 mm gun. The next thing he knew he was lying on the ground some distance from where he had been standing. He heard the words, 'He's dead,' someone reply, 'No he isn't,' and then he passed out. He awoke to find himself in hospital. A few days later he was released from hospital and made his way back to England to rejoin his unit, which had been withdrawn from France.

The same fate awaited another north London boy. During the fighting in Normandy, Ron Leagas had been lucky. At one point he returned to his carrier to discover it had been blasted up into the air and over a cemetery wall. Another time the gunner on his carrier had accidentally bounced machine-gun bullets off the top of his helmet when they hit a bump in the road. Even in a face-to-face encounter with an enemy soldier, when his weapon jammed, leaving him defenceless, the German soldier turned and ran away.

But his luck couldn't last forever. Reaching Lisieux, his unit dug in for the night, expecting a quiet evening:

> All of a sudden we heard this droning noise. It was a German six-barrelled mortar. I thought, 'Some poor bastard's going to get it in a minute.' Then I heard: Bang! Bang! Bang! Next thing I know, I'm waking up inside a tent. I heard the surgeon say, 'I can't treat this man here.' But I had no idea how I got there or what was wrong with me.

He was immediately labelled, put in an ambulance, then flown back to England and put in hospital for six weeks:

> So I realized something must have happened. My ear was all swollen and hanging right down. And my nose was burned on the inside – it was all stuck together. And I smelled of burning hair. But it was just burns and I think I had concussion. I knew nothing about it. I still don't know what happened to the corporal who was with me.

After the long and costly battle for Normandy, which saw so many eager young men sacrificed, the German forces were finally driven back, encircled and destroyed. Yet for the British Army there was one final effort to be made: to force a crossing of the River Seine, hold the far bank long enough for bridges to be built, then allow the Allied armies to drive across northern France, into Belgium and the Netherlands, then finally into Germany. The spot chosen for the crossing was the town of Vernon. The crossing was bloody, with German machine-gun fire cutting swathes through the assault formation as the force motored across the river in boats. The battered units made their way up the opposite bank, slowly advancing despite their losses. The British came under fierce counterattacks that left them under no illusion that their hold was tenuous. Some units were cut off, then destroyed or captured. As the engineers raced to construct bridges for the armour, the infantry fought on alone, desperate for support.

The 1st Worcesters crossed the Seine and began their advance up a winding road towards the top of the valley. The battalion HQ and Regimental Aid Post was set up beside the road, and Bill Edwardes tried to cope with the ever-increasing number of casualties. From the hillside above him he could hear the sounds of battle as his comrades attempted to hold off the counterattack. At one point he heard the roar of incoming artillery, as one of the advance companies called down artillery fire on their positions to force back the assaulting enemy. It was a sure sign of their desperate situation.

For Bill Edwardes, this was more intense than anything he had previously experienced:

> I have very stark memories of Vernon. We met very fierce opposition going up that escarpment. They had Tiger tanks and some very hot infantry. The lay-by was the only place on the road where the battalion HQ and the RAP could set up. We were tucked in beside the road. The woods above us were full of German infantry.

The sound that came from ahead was one that filled their hearts with fear: the rumble of tracks and the roar of a tank engine:

> These Tiger tanks were coming down. A tank-hunting group went out with PIATs [handheld anti-tank weapons] but they didn't have much effect. We didn't have any armour with us: they were trying to bring tanks across on rafts. We had two six-pounder anti-tank guns. These were set up to cover the bend in the road ahead of us. The first tank edged its way around the corner and at one crucial point it was sideways on. The anti-tank gun got him with the first shot – under the turret – and knocked it over the side of the road.

As Bill watched, the second tank continued to advance towards him: 'He now knew what to expect. As soon as he came round he went "Bang! Bang!" and took out the anti-tank guns, killing the crews. It started to come down the road, sweeping the roads with machine-guns.' Fearing the worst, he watched as the tank continued its merciless advance: 'A man went down in the road and two stretcher-bearers went out to get him in. All three were killed. A tank machine-gun picked them out and shot them.' With the anti-tank guns knocked out, and the Germans showing no mercy to the stretcher-bearers, Bill realized it would take a miracle if they were to survive: 'The German tanks were only twenty yards from us, it was frightening, they were just sweeping the road with their forward machine-guns.' He knew that the rest of the unit could pull back, but he would have to remain with the wounded regardless of the situation.

Then came their salvation:

> It was just like the cavalry arriving – up the road came two Sherman tanks. The German tank commander knew he could take out the first one, but then the second one would get him before he could reload. So he withdrew and the day was saved. It was that close. They were trying to drive us back to the river. We would have been overrun. I was terrified.

The tide of battle had turned and the Worcesters continued their advance. The riverbank was held and it was time to begin the advance north towards Germany.

CHAPTER 23

The Return of the Blitz

'I saw a bloke who'd lost an eye. And a woman with her hair burnt off. It was fucking awful. Before that, we had thought the war was over.'

Fred Rowe, on seeing the damage done by a V2 rocket
when he was eleven

Though civilian suffering had greatly abated since the dark days of 1940 and 1941, war remained an ever-present danger – as the children of Bethnal Green had found to their cost. The occasional air raids had continued to strike towns and cities – such as the bombing of a school in Catford, south-east London, that cost the lives of some thirty-eight pupils when a bomb crashed through the side of the building. Out in the countryside there were military vehicles driving on once-peaceful lanes, where children expected to roam in safety. There were large numbers of deadly weapons in homes all across the land. There were unexploded bombs and the risk of aircraft crashing. In West Wickham four boys died when they picked up unexploded mortar bombs from an Army training ground. In the ruined cities, children risked their lives to play on bombsites, with the ever-present danger of buildings collapsing on them. They also swam in emergency water tanks in the basements of ruined buildings. And there were minefields all along the coast that were a particular threat to children who dreamed of being able to play along the nation's beaches. On Merseyside, one boy – thirteen-year-old Frank Smith – was killed and his friend, Robert Adams, injured after going into a minefield to retrieve a tennis ball. It transpired that the shifting sands had buried a stretch of wire and obscured the words of a warning sign. In one particularly tragic accident, a young boy died when he was run over by a bus carrying American troops: he was chasing the bus hoping to get some sweets.

Whilst such incidents were a result of war, they were not caused by enemy action. And then, in the summer of 1944, the enemy returned with a fury. On the morning of 13 June the people of east London heard a sound in the sky unlike anything they had ever heard before: a low constant drone, described as being like a motorbike engine without a silencer. Then, without warning, the noise stopped. As the engine cut out, the flying bomb nose-dived and plummeted down towards the ground. Striking a bridge carrying the railway between Liverpool Street and Essex, it caused considerable damage to the bridge and the tracks. A number of nearby houses were destroyed and six people were killed. In nearby Bethnal Green, Reg Baker heard the explosion: 'It was in Grove Road. I heard the fire engines. So I ran there – they hadn't blocked it off yet. Six people were killed. It was 13 June 1944. It was the first V1 to land in London.'

Five days later a flying bomb landed at the Aldwych in central London, close to the office where Peg, a south London teenager, was working in an office. Back in the Blitz she had defied her mother by going out into London with her friends. Then she had been lucky; this time war came closer.

The sirens had gone but I needed to go to the Post Office. I went across the road but it was full. I thought, 'I can't stand it here' – so waited a bit then ran across the road to the office. I walked up the stairs and nearly reached the second floor when – Whoosh! Bang! Crash! – I was blown all the way down the stairs to the bottom. I couldn't see a thing.

All I could hear were people screaming, whistles blowing – shouting.
There was brick-dust everywhere. What do I do now?

The doors to the building had been blown off so she followed the
light and went out into the street:

I was covered in dust, my hair was a mess. I came across a man on the
pavement with some corrugated iron on top of him. So I bent down
and said, 'I'll help you.' I pulled it off him and saw his legs were
missing. I just froze. I was sixteen years old! A policeman put his hands
on my shoulder and said, 'All right dear, we'll see to this.' They took
me to hospital. It was full of casualties on stretchers. A doctor asked me
how I was feeling. I said I was OK, just shocked. He sent me home. I
was on the tube to Tooting Broadway. Everyone was looking at me.
My hair had gone frizzy. I was covered in filth and dust. I felt awful. I
didn't get home till about ten o'clock. My mother was going berserk,
she'd heard this flying bomb had dropped in the Aldwych.

In the first two weeks of the V1 campaign some 1,600 people were
killed and 4,500 injured. The difference between these attacks and
the 1940–41 Blitz was that parts of suburban London suffered
disproportionate damage. The outer London boroughs of Croydon,
Bromley, Lewisham, Bexley and Orpington became known as
'bomb alley' since the flying bombs approached from the south-east
and often cut out in that area. By mid-July 1944 some 200,000
homes in 'bomb alley' had been damaged.

The worst hit London borough was Croydon, which was struck
by 10 per cent of all V1s. Starting on 16 June 1944 and ending in
January 1945, some 148 V1s and four V2s landed in Croydon,
killing 215, wounding 2,000, destroying over 1,000 homes and
damaging another 70,000. Although thousands of children were
swiftly evacuated, it seemed the population could not escape the
horror. For the first time since 1940, life became a lottery. Local
people stared up into the sky, eager to see the V1s pass overhead,

willing them on to land further north. One teenage girl, who had first been bombed out in 1940, recalled her first experience of this new weapon:

> You didn't get any warning of the flying bombs coming. Suddenly you heard a horrible noise. The first one we ever saw came over at night. We wondered, 'What is that strange noise – it's not like a usual German plane?' I looked out and there was a red fire coming out of the tail. Then the noise cut out – and it was coming down – that was the first one I'd seen.

On another occasion, she watched as a V1 sailed towards her:

> I noticed a flying bomb coming over – my mother and I ducked into the shelter – then I looked out and I could see this thing coming over. Then it cut out and it seemed to be coming straight towards us – which was frightening. Quickly I ducked back into the shelter but it had turned and it actually hit a junior school not far from us.

Fortunately none of the children were hurt as they were safely hiding in the school's air raid shelter.

In South Croydon, eleven-year-old Colin Furk experienced the deadly effect of the new weapons. Four years earlier he had witnessed the effects of a parachute mine that had sheared off the back of his home. But this was different: he was older and had acquired a greater understanding of what war was about. However, he was still young enough to find it exciting to be 'almost clobbered' by a V2 rocket that landed in a nearby park: 'It was Sunday afternoon and we were getting ready to go out and everything was silent. Suddenly all the net curtains came flying at me.' As the blast hit, he heard the sound of the explosion:

> I fell to the floor and was wrapped in the curtains. I was covered in glass but the curtains had saved me. My sister had been on the stairs –

and the big heavy front door was blown up the stairs and she was taken up with it. It wedged in front of her. A large amount of damage was done to the house. It was a lucky thing as we had no warning.

There was a sudden shout: 'My father came rushing out of one of the bedrooms just as a heavy light came crashing down from the ceiling, right in front of him. My mother was in another room – and we were all unhurt. I'd have been shredded if it hadn't been for those net curtains.'

It was not his only encounter with the effects of the new bombing campaign:

My grandfather was living with us – and he asked me if I would go down on my bike and collect some shoes he had in for repair. When we got there – there was nothing – the whole row of shops had been taken out by a flying bomb. We had to go back empty-handed.

He returned to his grandfather, telling him: 'I think your shoes have had it.'

Just like the Blitz of 1940, this new wave of bombing brought a new understanding of survival. People quickly learned that if they heard the motor running, they were safe – for the moment. Only when the engine cut out did it mean the flying bomb was about to crash to earth. People stared up into the sky, charting the course of the unmanned aircraft, waiting for danger to pass. Then they could let out a sigh of relief – they were safe until the next bomb came over. However, if the engine could be heard to cut and the weapon began to fall, it was time to take action. Just as in 1940, Terry Charles, now seventeen years old, had returned to London from evacuation just in time for the bombing to start: 'You hit the ground. You developed hair-trigger reflexes. If something untoward happened, you didn't stand there, scratch your head and say, "Now I wonder what that is?" No way. You hit the ground. It was self-preservation.'

As in 1940–41, the children of London swiftly adapted to the new routines. After almost five years as an evacuee, Kathleen Stevens had returned to London in order that her older sister could continue her education. She arrived just in time to experience the devastation that took place near her flat on an estate in Elephant and Castle, where her father was the caretaker: 'My dad wouldn't let us go down to the local shelters because they were in such a state – people would shit on the floor.' Staying in their flat, the family developed a routine for when the flying bombs came over:

> It was about teatime and my mum was making doughnuts in the flat. We all had specific jobs to do in the event of a raid. When there was danger we'd go out into the corridor of the block where there were no windows. I had the job of opening the windows in the flat – so they didn't smash with the blast. I went into the room to open the window and before I could Dad shouted to me to get down and I did. I heard the explosion – and the glass blew in all over the doughnuts – and all this black stuff came through the windows. My dad went downstairs to see what needed to be done and I went with him – and there were all these old ladies sitting out on chairs in the corridor just shaking.

The image of these shaking old ladies became her overriding memory of the period.

By summer 1944, fourteen-year-old Roy Bartlett had left school and taken up employment in the stores at the nearby AEC engineering plant. His job was to drive around the factory delivering parts to where they were needed. He was forbidden to carry passengers, but he liked carrying the young post girls around the factory. They would sit on the back and dangle their legs over the side. As he later admitted: 'They were much more attractive goods to carry.' Whilst working there he grew used to the arrival of the V1 flying bombs:

I was very brave one day. There was an open space between the buildings. I was trundling along, carrying this very pretty girl, and a flying bomb was approaching. We could see it in the distance. We knew that if it cut out it could glide for a while until it landed. It kept coming and kept coming. I had one eye on the flying bomb and one on the girl. Then it stopped. I didn't wait to see where it was going to land. We both jumped off on to the side of the road. I gallantly threw myself on top of her – and remained there for the next half an hour. You have to be chivalrous. That happened several times – but not always with the same girl.

On another occasion he had a strange encounter with a flying bomb while he lunched outside. The workers could all see the 'doodlebug' approaching but ignored it. They waited to see if its engine was going to cut out before taking cover. To their relief it passed overhead and disappeared. Suddenly a shout resounded across the grounds: 'It's coming back!' Somehow the V1 had turned and was heading back towards them. They watched as it again passed over their heads, then the engine spluttered, cut out, and it plunged to the earth just hundreds of yards away. As he watched the smoke rising, Roy saw a man jump up and start running, screaming about his wife being at home. He had seen where the bomb had landed and knew his own home had been beneath it.

One of those wounded by flying bombs that summer was Betty Baker, the promiscuous Welsh teenager who had run away from approved school, married at sixteen, then separated from her husband and moved to London. Arriving in January 1943, still aged sixteen and buoyed by a weekly allotment of money courtesy of her estranged husband, she had initially found employment in Paul's Café, Hammersmith, West London. In the summer of 1944, as she approached her eighteenth birthday, Baker was living in lodgings in Edith Road in Hammersmith. When a V1 flying bomb landed nearby, the house was rendered uninhabitable, forcing her to seek alternative accommodation. Having abandoned her old name, by early 1943 she had taken her husband's name, changed her middle name from Maud and was calling herself Elizabeth Marina Jones. Five-foot-five tall, good looking and appearing far older than her years, the newly christened Elizabeth Jones had also taken to speaking with a North American accent, utilizing the memory of her early years in Canada. The accent gave her an air of glamour that belied her background in the juvenile courts.

For a teenager in search of male attention and glamour, a Hammersmith cafe was far from an ideal workplace and she swiftly moved on, working as a barmaid, chambermaid, cinema usherette and cashier. Then, craving attention and the show-business lifestyle, Betty set out to become a dancer. Once again, she acquired a new name to go with her new position, calling herself Georgina Grayston. She soon found employment as a dancer at the Cabaret Club in Beak Street. However, the now seventeen year old's promiscuous lifestyle soon caught up with her. The club's costume mistress discovered stains on one of her stage costumes, leading to concern that she had contracted a venereal disease. As a result, the club's owner sent her for medical examination by a Harley Street doctor who confirmed the diagnosis. The club's owner also discovered that 'Georgina' was frequenting the Strand Corner House, a location he had designated 'out of bounds' to the club's employees. As a result, her employment was terminated.

Her next job in the entertainment industry was as a striptease dancer at the Panama Club in Knightsbridge and the Blue Lagoon Club in Carnaby Street. These jobs were the potential source of wages of £14 a week. However, Harry Adams, the clubs' owner, considered her stage act to be unsatisfactory and in February 1944 the employment was terminated. Through the rest of 1944 'Georgina' lived on the thirty-five shilling allowance from her estranged husband and what she could earn from 'encounters' with servicemen she met in the pubs and clubs of London. This behaviour contrasted with her claims that she was training to be a dancer. On the positive side, 'Georgina' was well dressed, young,

pretty, relatively tall and slim, with a glamorous foreign accent –
even if it wasn't her own. However, the other side of her life was that
she had a criminal record, had failed as a dancer, was falling into
prostitution and had contracted both a venereal disease and scabies.
On top of that, in the summer of 1944, she faced the same dangers
as every Londoner and was forced from her lodgings when the
building was damaged by a flying bomb.

She then took lodgings at 311 King's Road, Hammersmith. When
she first arrived, she still sported bandages from the slight injuries
sustained in the bombing. Bizarrely, she failed to tell her landlady
that she had been injured just a few streets away. Instead, she
claimed she had been wounded at an Army camp in Essex. The lies
were compounded when 'Georgina' told her new landlady that she
was a Canadian. Her fantasy world caught up with her on 3 October
1944. Her search for glamour and excitement brought her into the
company of an American officer calling himself Lt Richard 'Ricky'
Allen. Yet both were living a lie. He was no more an officer called
Ricky than she was a dancer named Georgina. Despite his uniform,
he was in fact Private Karl Gustav Hulten, an American soldier
absent from his unit. Hulten had arrived in the UK in early 1944 but
had been arrested for possession of a concealed weapon. Escaping
from confinement, he had stolen an officer's uniform and gone on
the run in London.

Elizabeth Jones was immediately attracted to Hulten. He told her
about his life back in Chicago where he claimed he had been a
gunman for the 'Mob'. He also claimed to run a gang in London and
to have killed people in both cities. He later said that he had made
up these stories to 'build himself up' in the eyes of his new girlfriend.
At the same time, he showed off his gun, a .45 pistol. Elizabeth was
attracted to his bogus story of the excitement of the gangster lifestyle
and wanted to be his 'gun-moll' like those she had seen in films.
What Hulten gave her was exciting, but dangerous, as they
embarked on a series of violent, and almost pointless, crimes.

First they tried to hold up a taxi, only to find it was carrying an

American officer. Not daring to chance a shoot-out, Hulten and Jones fled the scene. Their next crime was similarly pathetic. Whilst driving a stolen vehicle, Hulten pushed a young woman from her bicycle. As she lay on the ground, the would-be gangsters robbed her. Their next victim was an eighteen-year-old girl on her way home to Bristol. The pair offered her a lift to Reading. On the way Hulten faked a breakdown. Dismounting from the car, Jones distracted the girl whilst Hulten hit her with a car jack. She stumbled forward and was felled by a second blow. While Jones held her legs, Hulten throttled her, only letting go when her body went limp. Then they robbed her. The girl survived the assault and was discovered wandering by the roadside.

The pair's next victim was less fortunate. Thirty-four-year-old George Heath was a taxi driver. On 6 October 1944 he was looking for fares at a firm which gave him regular work but, with no fares forthcoming, he was about to head for home in his grey Ford. Hardly the perfect target for a heist, Heath was carrying a wallet containing just £8. Hulten and Jones hailed the taxi and directed him out of London. Near Staines, Hulten finally took action. Sitting behind Heath he fired a single shot that entered the driver's back, one inch from his spine, and exited through his chest, killing him. As Heath lay dying by the roadside, Hulten took his wallet, whilst Jones took his pen, watch and even the pennies from his pocket.

Leaving the corpse in a ditch, Hulten and Jones returned to London in the grey Ford. It was a foolish act that characterized their poorly planned and hastily executed crimes. Although it was three days before Heath's body was discovered, Hulten had not yet got rid of the car. Their failure to erase the trail of clues was their undoing. An alert was issued and the police located the vehicle. Officers watched and waited, hoping the driver would return and on Monday, 9 October 1944, as Hulten approached the car, the officers rushed him, pinned him against a wall and arrested him on suspicion of murder. As they searched the car, Hulten's Remington pistol and ammunition were found. When questioned that morning

Hulten told the police he had spent the previous night with a 'commando' – or prostitute – named Marina Jones.

The trail then led to Elizabeth Jones. Interviewed by police, she soon incriminated herself – first denying any involvement and then saying she looked tired because of what she had seen. Later she admitted she had been there when Hulten shot Heath. She also admitted to robbing Heath's body. On 23 January 1945 they were both sentenced to death. When the sentences were passed, she was led screaming from the court. Six weeks later King George VI signed a conditional pardon and her sentence was commuted to penal servitude for life. Prisoner 11393 K. G. Hulten was executed at 9 a.m. on 8 March 1945 at Wormwood Scrubs. He was twenty-two years old.

Four years on from his own early forays into criminality, eleven-year-old Fred Rowe hoped the flying bombs might give him an opportunity to loot food. He rushed to the scenes of explosions in the hope of filling his ever-present shopping bag. Once again, the scenes of carnage made a terrible impression upon him:

> What a fucking mess they made! Even behind a wall you could feel the blast. All the debris would come down from the sky: bits of wood, windows, glass. It was like a rain of bricks and mortar. Then a dust cloud came down. There were people running around with blood pouring out of them. I remember one old bloke with no arm. It was just tattered flesh hanging there. It was pumping out blood. He fell down and died in front of us. There was a kid running about with half an arm hanging off. I felt so fortunate 'cause I'd never gone in the shelters, and that had never happened to me. It was only as you grow up that you realize the risks.

Just as the threat of the V1s began to recede, a new threat entered the airspace above London and the south-east: the V2 missile. This arrived silently and so couldn't be predicted. There was no time for those in its path to take cover. It simply raced down from the sky and unleashed its fury. There was none of the old tension of sitting in air raid shelters listening to bombs coming closer. It was instant and deadly, causing levels of destruction previously unseen by single bombs. The four missiles that landed in Croydon each damaged an average of 500 homes.

The speed with which this new missile travelled meant that few people ever actually saw one. Terry Charles was one of the few to witness the missile in action:

> I actually saw one arrive. I couldn't hear it, but I did see it. As I was walking home after school I crossed a bridge over the railway lines behind Paddington station. It was completely overcast, clouds were filling the whole sky. I was thinking of nothing in particular. Suddenly in the sky a hole appeared in the clouds – a red ring. I knew instantly what it was – a V2. I hit the deck and stayed down. Seconds later it landed a mile or so away.

In a similar experience, Reg Baker saw what he thought was a falling star and – following the old superstition – he thought a new baby must have been born. Then he heard the explosion and realized it had been the glow of a V2 rocket.

Growing used to the destruction, Roy Bartlett became curious about the rockets and missiles and so, whilst with friends, he heard the boom then blast of a falling missile and decided to investigate:

> We grabbed our bikes, thinking can we do something? It was about a mile away. We rushed down and found it had struck the Packard Car Company on the Great West Road. By the time we got there US servicemen were helping out and had set up a mobile hospital. There was nothing we could do. One of my most vivid memories is seeing the bodies being laid out on the pavement outside and the blood running into the gutter. I was terribly upset.

Thirty-two workers were dead and more than a hundred were seriously injured in the explosion. The scenes that he witnessed stayed with Roy: 'Tragedy and trauma making an indelible imprint when the young brain is at its most retentive.'

Fred Rowe also witnessed the aftermath of a V2 rocket attack:

> I've never heard such a massive noise in my life. I was at least half a mile away. The sky was filled with glass and debris. People who weren't that close were wounded. I saw a bloke who'd lost an eye. And a woman with her hair burnt off. It was fucking awful. Before that, we had thought the war was over.

He soon found that the destructive power of these new weapons undermined his criminal ventures: 'It was ghoulish, but we went there to see what we could nick from the shops. But these places were pulverized. There was nothing left. Where was the grub? There was nothing left to nick.' On 24 March 1945, just weeks before the war in Europe came to an end, the final V2s fell on England. One landed in Orpington, causing a single fatality. The other hit a block of flats in Vallance Road, Stepney, killing 134 people. It was less than two miles away from Grove Road where the first V1 had landed.

When the flying bombs had first appeared thousands of children had once more been evacuated but, with the threat over, London's children flooded back to the capital. In the spring and summer of 1945 the Metropolitan Police reported children being responsible for a new wave of juvenile crime, in particular petty theft from shops and vandalism. The police station at Lavender Hill in south London noted: 'Since the return of the evacuees, a very marked rise in this class of offence was recorded at this station.'[1]

What was noted was the extreme youth of some of the offenders. A nine year old and an eleven year old were found in a bomb-damaged Battersea house that was being repaired. The children were discovered painting the bath, having pierced several tins of paint. The paint then seeped through the floor and ruined the freshly plastered and painted ceilings in the rooms below. Similar cases went through the juvenile courts. In June 1945, a group aged six, eight and ten broke into a shop and spread foodstuffs over the walls. A storeroom at a goods depot in Battersea was forcibly entered and extensive damage caused to building materials. Paint tins were punctured with nails and chimney pots, which were to be used to repair bombed houses, were smashed up. As the police reported, it was 'obvious that the place had been used as a playground'.[2] The suspects were aged between seven and ten.

The exasperated local police reported on the source of the crimewave: 'There is little doubt that the increase of crime on this section is due to the returned evacuees, who look upon bomb-damaged property as a legitimate playground, and during their leisure time gain access to other property adjoining and commit offences.'[3] In particular, two young brothers – returned evacuees – were blamed for a large number of crimes.

The truth was that it was not just the returning evacuees who were destroying the buildings. Local boys who had remained in London throughout the war were also responsible. Twelve-year-old Fred Rowe was among them:

> We wrecked the places. We smashed up everything. It was all due for demolition. The 'spivs' were coming around taking all the nice doors from the houses, or the lead. They'd kick us out, or tell us to be quiet until they'd gone. They didn't want the Old Bill coming down. When they'd gone, we'd come back and start it all again. The Old Bill were worried about the houses falling down on top of us and killing us. Of course, we didn't see the dangers. We thought, 'Fuck it! Bosh!' There were gangs of us. There were about fifteen of us in my gang. We'd do a whole street. The Old Bill would come and we'd shriek with delight and run off. They'd try and catch us on their bikes.

Having witnessed so much horror and destruction, often having themselves been bombed out, the local kids saw no value in the wrecks of what had once been their homes:

I used to love to wreck stuff. It was a joy to see a house collapse and
think you'd done it. You'd kick the floorboards in, get a stout piece of
wood and start hitting the window frames out. It was lovely – I used to
nick my dad's hammer to smash stuff up. Brilliant – excellent stuff. We
used to cut through the roofs. One time we were running through a
house and my mate fell through the floorboards, landed a floor below
and twisted his ankle. We'd go home rotten – filthy and dirty. I'd get
a clip round the ear for that.

The rising crime levels inspired the local police station to request
permission to take positive action. They visited schools, many of
which had recently reopened after repairs to bomb damage, to give
talks on vandalism. The talks attempted to make the children
understand that the police did not blame them for their actions, but
simply wished them to think about what they were doing. The talks
opened with the words: 'A boy or girl who has never got into mischief
has never been a boy or girl.'[4] It was an attempt to engage with the
children, in particular the returning evacuees, and empathize with
their shock at returning to a landscape utterly transformed by war. The
talks highlighted the natural, and understandable, desire of children to
break things, telling the audiences: 'Boys like breaking things . . . in the
same way as puppies like gnawing old shoes or pieces of wood.'

But the tone of the talks changed, pointing out that smashing up
abandoned buildings was criminal: 'Many of these things start quite
innocently, but might end up in some little boy or girl appearing in
front of a magistrate.' The lecturers gave the example of a boy who
just wanted to impress his mates: 'He thought he would not get
caught. Of course he got caught. They all get caught sooner or later.'
More importantly, there were warnings about the genuine dangers
of collapsing buildings, especially for lone vandals: 'It is possible no
one will find you until it is too late to help you'. The police warned
that, if the young vandals continued in that manner, they would
eventually find themselves in prison. It was a warning Fred Rowe
should have heeded.

CHAPTER 24

To the Bitter End

'At last we were "going up". We had been destined for this moment ever since we had been kids in short pants . . . Now we, too, were going to do our bit, as the phrase of the time had it. We were going to fight the battle that would achieve victory for our country.'

Charles Whiting, who volunteered for the Army aged sixteen,
describing his approach to the front line just days
after his eighteenth birthday[1]

With the Battle for Normandy completed, the British Army broke out from the bridgehead across the Seine at Vernon. For seventeen-year-old Bill Edwardes, who had seen so much suffering and sacrifice in the weeks leading up to the crossing of the Seine, the aftermath of the battle was a wonderful period. His unit's transport was taken away and they were left far behind the line, 'licking their wounds' and enjoying a brief respite from the horrors.

Far ahead, other units drove forward towards Germany. This rapid advance, christened 'The Swan' because the Army was 'sticking its neck out', took them sweeping across northern France, into Belgium and up to the Dutch border. Most importantly, it took them through the areas being used to launch the V1 rockets that had been raining down on London and south-east England. Former

Home Guard Geoff Pulzer, by now serving in the 11th Armoured Division, recalled: 'The advance was calm but exhilarating. It was amazing how the population came out to meet us. We were in the lead all the way to Antwerp. There were lots of clearing-up jobs on the way.' Upon arriving in Antwerp, Geoff's tank went straight into the city centre where they engaged the enemy: 'We were almost in the centre of Antwerp. There were Germans in dugouts on a bombsite on top of a little hill. We ferreted them out of their positions with our machine-guns. They came out holding white shirts above their heads. We took them prisoner.'

Nearby, in a block of flats, two British teenagers heard what was happening and realized that they might soon be free. The Vanhandenhoeve sisters, who had been stranded in Antwerp since 1940 when their ship was sunk, watched the scenes unfold: 'We saw the tanks rolling in. It was great excitement.' However, with British troops occupying the city and the docks becoming operational, war soon returned to Antwerp as the Germans targeted the port with V1 flying bombs and V2 missiles, as Yvonne Vanhandenhoeve later recalled: 'I hated that. You could hear them coming then it went quiet. It really frightened me. We didn't have shelters or anything. We just had to put up with it – we didn't get any time off school.' Meanwhile, her younger sister Julienne had little idea of the impact the arrival of the 11th Armoured Division would have on her life when she finally returned to England.

As the British Army prepared itself for the inevitable assault into Germany, there was a desperate need for fresh infantrymen. The heavy toll of casualties on the battlefields of Normandy left the Army needing thousands of new recruits. Older men who had spent years at depots across the UK were briefly retrained and sent to the front and the hospitals were scoured for men fit for service. However, not all those who had recovered from wounds were considered suitable for service. The Worcestershire Regiment discovered that one of its wounded 'men' was a boy of just sixteen. He was taken before officers and told that he would not be allowed to return overseas. Hearing this, the soldier informed them that he would simply desert and re-enlist. A compromise was reached: he was allowed to rejoin the regiment as a cook, but not allowed on to the front line. He eventually stayed on with the regiment, retiring from the Army with the rank of major.

In September 1944 the British launched 'Operation Market Garden', the ill-fated attempt to use airborne troops to capture a series of river bridges between the Belgian–Netherlands border and the town of Arnhem. During the final stages of the battle, as British infantry attempted to push north between Nijmegen and Arnhem, the 1st Worcesters were thrown back into action. Bill Edwardes, still two months away from his eighteenth birthday, was among them: 'The day we attacked Elst was the worst day of the war for me. It was key for both sides to retain it and so it was a fierce old battle.' He was at the battalion HQ whilst the infantry held a vital crossroads they had been ordered to occupy. However, the divisional commander, General Thomas, arrived and issued new orders:

> He was ranting and swearing – 'I don't want you to hold crossroads! Get into Elst – now!' It was just one hour before darkness, but the lads climbed on to Sherman tanks and advanced. They reached the edge of town, bunkered down for the night, then the battle started in the morning. We were unprepared. There was no real plan, just a head-on assault. We should have encircled the town, but there were not enough troops, and the boot of the commanding general was behind us.

During the following day's battle, Bill found himself thrown back into the world of bullets, blood and death that he had so violently encountered in Normandy. He worked tirelessly to save and evacuate the wounded, and watched as some twenty-seven men were killed. The only difference between this and the fighting in Normandy was that there were now plenty of walls to shelter the wounded behind. Watching the carnage, he soon returned to his fatalistic mindset: 'It'll happen one day, so I might as well just get on with it.' He once again found the ability to make light of their situation. By seeing the funny side of what was dangerous and horrifying, he felt better able to cope with war than many of his comrades.

Arriving in the Netherlands, Eric Davies had an encounter that recalled the life he had enjoyed before war had engulfed his world. Near Tilburg he had a chance encounter with Gareth Evans, an old school friend, whom he had not seen for many years. In the lull of battle, they took the chance to catch up, talking about the old days back in south Wales: 'We stood talking at the corner of a house – he was on one side, I was on the other. After a while he stopped talking. I went down on all fours and looked around the corner. He had been shot and killed by a sniper.' One moment Eric had been recalling his school days, the next he had reverted to the soldier he had become. Fetching his carrier and a tank, they opened fire on the house he believed the sniper to be in, destroying it and sniper within.

For Eric, it seemed that he had been unbelievably lucky. He had somehow survived the campaign in Italy and then managed to last for months in north-west Europe without being killed or wounded. He had seen friends and comrades wounded or killed and had again been promoted, reaching the rank of sergeant major while not yet twenty years old. In peacetime such rapid promotion would have been unthinkable, in wartime it seemed inevitable. He had survived many close shaves and felt luck had been on his side. On more than one occasion he had made sudden decisions to move the carrier, only to see the spot they had been waiting in hit by a shell. Such moments gave him a feeling that a guardian angel was watching him, but deep down he knew there was little chance he would get through the campaign unscathed.

The moment he had been waiting for came during an advance over open ground to occupy a village, followed by an attack on some woods occupied by an SS unit. Due to the roads of the village being blocked, Eric had left his carrier behind and advanced on foot. Reaching the edge of the woods, all hell let loose:

> The Germans came out of their trenches and came at us with bayonets fixed . . . I caught a glimpse of something shiny, I turned my head to see a Jerry charging at me with his bayonet. I immediately shot him but his impetus carried him on enough that his bayonet caught my face. I remember bleeding like a pig and then I passed out.

Eric awoke to discover his face had been bandaged and he had been evacuated. He felt certain his war was over – that he would be sent home to a hospital and spend months recovering. His hopes were dashed when he was sent to a hospital in Belgium where surgeons worked to reconstruct his face. First they stitched his face from inside and then used a form of liquid skin to heal his wounds.

For the next few weeks he languished in hospital, his face wrapped in gauze. The sterile world of the hospital was a shock to the soldier who had endured months of living in slit trenches and ruins:

> I had come out of hell – unshaven, smelling of death and blood. A world of continuous noise, shell bursts, mortar bombs – all the time having to go forward. I cannot explain what it was like to sleep in a bed, to have food at a certain time, to have no noise and smell.

This peaceful interlude gave him an opportunity to look back on all he had endured since volunteering for the Army as a seventeen year old: 'I had time to think about the last two years and it did not make for nice thoughts. To think that I, who was from a church-going family, could kill not only with rifle or pistol, but with my bare hands.'

If the psychological burden of war had not already proved enough for Eric, he now had to endure leaving hospital and returning to the front line: 'The time arrived for the gauze and bandages to come off. I looked in the mirror and did not recognize the person looking back at me. What a shock!' His once smooth skin was torn and scarred. Despite the brilliant work of the surgeons, he felt disfigured. The shock was emphasized when he returned to his regiment: no one recognized him and they refused to believe it was the same person. He felt dreadful, realizing that he felt like an outsider in the place that had become his home: 'You can imagine my state of mind having to start all over again – into hell.'

In the weeks and months that followed D-Day, Stan Whitehouse continued to learn about life in the infantry. On his first day with the Black Watch he had seen packs waiting at the HQ. He assumed the packs were ready for him and his mates, the reinforcements. He went to check, only to discover the neat lines of sixty-four packs belonged to the men they were replacing. He grew used to long days without food, to the constant struggle to control his fears, to the sight of death and destruction. Most importantly he grew accustomed to the 'kill or be killed' mentality necessary to endure life in the front line. Seeing friends die became a gruesomely routine part of his life: as routine as shaving in the morning and cleaning weapons after an action.

By November 1944 Stan and his unit were in the Netherlands. One night he found himself and his mates defending a crossroads when they came under attack by the enemy. The Germans fired anti-tank rockets at them, with the Black Watch responding with hand grenades. Within minutes the enemy were upon them, and hand-to-hand fighting ensued. Stan found himself in a water-filled ditch, beating an enemy soldier over the head with a sub-machine-gun, before his mate shot the German. It was a swift and bloody encounter that had seen Stan only just survive. The following morning he asked his platoon commander the date; it was only then that he realized the battle had taken place on his eighteenth birthday.

The final weeks of 1944 were a difficult time for the British soldiers. As the winter weather engulfed them, a wave of illness and low spirits surged through the Army. As much as they enjoyed the fact that the advance had slowed and there was little action, they hated the cold and damp. For Bill Edwardes, it was a time when, rather than treating bullet wounds and digging shrapnel out of bloodied soldiers, he was dealing with men suffering from trench foot, influenza or pneumonia. It was also time for him to finally celebrate his eighteenth birthday, something the Army thought he had done some two years before. Yet living in a small Dutch town in the middle of wartime, there was precious little chance to celebrate his birthday. After seeing so much action in the previous few months, he simply celebrated surviving another day.

Winter 1944–5 saw Stan Scott's return to the continent with No. 3 Commando. After two-and-a-half months fighting in Normandy, Stan was a veteran. As an experienced soldier, he was shocked by the expectations of a replacement officer who arrived with his unit. He had been asked to act as a bodyguard to the officer, who kept on addressing him brusquely: 'Pick up my valise! Where's my room?' Stan replied: 'You doss down where you can!' The officer continued by asking Stan to polish his boots for him: 'I told him, "I ain't got time to clean me own bloody boots! Everyone looks after themselves here, mate!" I thought to myself: Where did they find him?'

For Stan, there was no place for such behaviour in the commandos. Discipline was something a commando soldier had through their personal way of behaving – it was not something that could be enforced by inexperienced officers giving pointless orders. Stan had seen enough friends die or be wounded, and seen enough of their replacements go the same way, to be clear in his understanding of the possibilities that lay ahead of him. Survival was simply a matter of fate. There was nothing a junior officer could do to him that was worse than what he expected to experience in the battles that were sure to follow. Fortunately, the first months were relatively easy, compared to what he had experienced in Normandy. There were a series of minor exchanges with the enemy, a number of villages to be cleared and patrols to be conducted, but nothing on the scale they had known.

Early in 1945, the British and Canadian armies launched an operation to drive the enemy from the west bank of the Rhine. As the Canadians advanced through the riverside plains, the British pushed through the Reichswald forest. The weather was cold and damp, the enemy resistance was fierce and the landscape unforgiving. They fought from tree to tree, often unable to see the enemy, just responding to the flash of weapons and the sound of incoming fire. They fought up to their knees in mud and were often face down in the tangle of tree roots and broken branches. For many it was the worst fighting they had known. With them was Bill Edwardes: 'Things got heavy again. But I was more or less continuously in the RAP. I think it was because I was a survivor. The medical officer was a great guy, and he kept me with the team. So I didn't go out to the companies a great deal.' He was lucky: casualties among the stretcher-bearers continued to be high.

> We had a turnover of four or five a month. They would come in to the RAP for the first week, then go out to the companies. I would tell them what to do and what to watch out for. And I was just a pimply nosed kid! The new chaps were turning to me for advice. I was just eighteen – younger than any of them – but I was already hardened. I should have just been called up. If I'd have waited, I wouldn't have gone over as a reinforcement until the very end.

In the final months of war, Stan Whitehouse somehow managed to survive both the battle against the enemy and his own battle to remain sane. Every time he saw the twisted corpses of his friends, it seemed to subvert the remnants of his morale. Just eighteen years old, he was a veteran of seemingly endless battles, yet was younger than the reinforcements who came to replace his dead and wounded mates. He grew nervous and irritable, yet managed to control himself even when others deserted or gave themselves self-inflicted wounds as an excuse to get to hospital. As he later wrote of his mental state, he was 'hanging on by the slenderest of threads'.[2]

Somehow he held on. In early 1945 Stan was luckily given leave in Brussels. It was the perfect opportunity to relax, do his best to forget war and recharge his batteries. Overstaying his leave, he was sentenced to twenty-eight days' detention, resulting in him missing the crossing of the Rhine and the battles that followed. In one incident following the Rhine crossing most of Stan's platoon was wiped out. It was awful for him to later learn the fate of his comrades, but he had survived.

Another underage volunteer who survived was Fred Walker. He had seen plenty of action since D-Day, been wounded and sent home for treatment once already, seen other boys die alongside him and spent winter patrolling in the snow-covered wasteland of the Netherlands. Having grown used to war, Fred coped well with the pressure. He allowed himself the luxury of being positive about the weather. As he later recalled, he had occupied a slit trench with the frozen corpse of a German soldier. Rather than worry about living alongside a corpse, he simply acknowledged that the freezing cold meant the body was not rotten and did not stink – unlike all the corpses he had seen in Sicily, Italy and Normandy.

His war ended when a jeep came towards him on an icy road. Skidding on the ice, the jeep slid towards him: 'I was lucky. I tried to get out of the way but it hit my knee and fractured it. I had to walk back for a mile using my rifle as a crutch. It was lucky – a "Blighty wound". That was my war finished.' Despite the injury meaning he would miss the final advance into Germany, Fred was eager to get back to his unit. He was sent to a rehabilitation unit and worked hard to get his injured leg back to full strength, in the hope of rejoining No. 3 Commando. He despaired at the men around him, who had no intention of getting fit and were just hoping the war would be over before they recovered. It made Fred realize the difference between an all-volunteer unit and one comprised almost entirely of conscripts: 'We were volunteers. We wanted to do it.'

Whilst war took an increasing physical and mental toll on many soldiers, some managed to remain calm. For Geoff Pulzer, who back in 1940 had defied the Blitz to carry out his Home Guard duties as a seventeen-year-old volunteer, even the hellish conditions in Normandy had not fazed him:

> I was never frightened in the Blitz – I was never frightened in the war. That's why governments always recruit youngsters. I was young – I wasn't going to get hurt. I wasn't going to get killed. It concerned me when I saw people being bombed out in the Blitz. It was awful, but it wasn't me. When people were killed it was very sad, I was very sorry – but life goes on. It was their bad luck. I never thought it was going to be me.

It was only in Germany in spring 1945 that he was suddenly struck by the idea that he might be mortal: 'I was lying there sunbathing – the guns were firing – and a piece of shrapnel landed six inches from my head. That woke me up to the danger.'

It was a good time to be gripped by a sense of mortality. With war fast approaching its end, attitudes began to change. Many units reported their soldiers taking increasing care, avoiding any senseless risks and relying on fire power to solve all their problems. Why assault a defended position, when they could call down artillery fire, air support or flame-throwers? As a member of the medical staff, Bill Edwardes noticed the overwhelming desire among his battalion not to be the last casualty:

> There was a definite reluctance to put one's head above the parapet. Our officers must have seen what was going on. The medical officer could see the change. Men were coming to us with trivial things, claiming to have pneumonia and asking to be sent home. This one chap came in, claiming he was having an attack of malaria. He asked us to give him bed rest for a couple of weeks, by which time it would all be over.

As the war approached its seemingly inevitable conclusion, the situation for prisoners of war became increasingly uncertain. With the Reich ever shrinking, the deliveries of Red Cross parcels to POW camps became even more irregular and rations plummeted. Then, with the prisoners facing starvation, many thousands were removed from their camps and sent on forced marches into the heart of Germany. Those in camps far in the east were the first to be evacuated, with men leaving the work camps and beginning the long journey towards home. In January 1945, in the midst of winter, John Norman, who had been captured aged just sixteen, was finally released from the Silesian mine that had been his home for five years and marched for hundreds of miles back into the heart of Germany. As they marched through the snow, in long straggling columns, he witnessed the murder of fellow prisoners who were unable to keep up. He watched as older, weaker men – wracked by sickness, hunger and exhaustion – collapsed and died by the roadside. It was one of the times he was pleased to be young. After five years of heavy work, he was strong and able to endure much hardship. Spending his teenage years as a miner, living in conditions of virtual slavery, had also given him the mental strength to push him forward, never succumbing to hunger and exhaustion.

Eventually the column of increasingly desperate prisoners came face to face with advancing American troops who threw food to them and arranged for them to be transported to the rear. Within days, John Norman was back home in England. He later described how shocked he was by the scenes of devastation in London and how he faced an uncertain future in a country that seemed to be 'on its knees'. Released from the Army, he also faced the uncertainty of finding work: having spent five years as a prisoner, and having no education, he was qualified for nothing other than manual work. However, only one thing really mattered: he was home and alive.

In the final days of the war one teenage soldier had an encounter with a German prisoner of war that brought home the reality of how far war had taken him. By spring 1945 Reg Fraser was an eighteen-year-old infantryman with the 5th Battalion of the Wiltshire Regiment. For six months he had been in the front line, fighting in Belgium, the Netherlands and now Germany. In his very first day of battle he had seen his friend's head blown off. Since that point he had realized he was lucky to be alive. Yet with the end of war approaching, he could see how far he had come in the last five years. In 1939 he had been evacuated from London with the children's home he lived in. In 1940 he had joined the Army Cadets, a year later he had joined the Air Training Corps, then the Home Guard, until finally he had been conscripted into the Army. One war, four uniforms – and the obligatory evacuee's paper label. Somehow, boys like him had progressed to a stage where they were able to defeat the once dreaded German Army. The absurdity of this became apparent when he was dealing with a batch of prisoners. He fell into conversation with a German prisoner who spoke perfect English, a conversation that reminded Reg of the dark days of 1940 when, as an unarmed cadet, he had trained to repel any invaders:

> He told me he had trained for the invasion of England. I said I thought it was a good job they didn't come. And I told him, I was only fourteen at the time, but I had been waiting for him armed with a broom handle. He just said, 'You English have a strange sense of humour.'

In early April 1945 Stan Scott was shocked by the intensity of the fighting in northern Germany and wondered what the Germans were fighting so hard to defend:

> I was in the leading patrol. We were in a position off the side of the road. All of a sudden we heard marching feet. Down, quiet. Along the road comes this column of Germans, marching in threes. They didn't have a clue we were there. I had the Bren, and Ossie had a Thompson. Blimey! We let them get close then he gets up and shouts, 'Halt!' The leading ones opened fire on him. He fired. I opened fire, and emptied the magazine. There was no more marching column.

As the Germans scattered, the commandos took positions in a wooded area where they were counterattacked by German marines. Attack after attack hit their positions as the Germans attempted to drive them out of the woods. Stan watched as men who had survived the hell of Normandy were killed and wounded around him, all of the time using his Bren gun to hold back the enemy. He was soon down to just half a magazine for the Bren gun and two magazines for his Colt pistol. After that he would have nothing left but his commando knife:

> We watched through the trees as the Germans formed up for the final attack. Suddenly we heard an almighty wail, like a banshee. There were splintered trees and flying bodies. Christ, what a noise! Then the Vickers machine-guns opened up and we watched as No. 6 Commando carried out a bayonet charge on the Germans.

He soon learned why the Germans had been fighting so hard. As his patrol advanced, Stan and his mates turned to each other: 'What's that bloody smell?' They soon found out the source of the smell: 'We could see the barbed wire. We saw this little kid – a girl in a tattered dress – walking down the road. Then we reached the gate and saw a camp. We didn't know it, but it was Bergen-Belsen concentration camp.' The commandos were ordered not to enter the camp, instead moving on to their main objectives and leaving the guards and inmates to be dealt with by other units.

Having landed in France aged just seventeen, Roy Finch had got through the campaign relatively unscathed. He had taken part in many actions, yet had experienced few close shaves and never felt himself to be in particular danger. He was simply one of the lucky ones. The enemy had been encountered as distant movements that he fired at but never knew if he had hit them, or had been corpses left behind as the battle moved on. The first time he ever got a close look at the enemy was in the final weeks of the war when they had begun surrendering en masse.

With Belsen under British control, Roy had an experience he –
and the rest of the world – would never forget:

> We were in northern Germany. The company commander said, 'I
> want thirty men.' They just picked us out and put us in a truck. They
> said we were going to help the medical orderlies at a repatriation camp.
> The lorry took us to Belsen concentration camp. That was horrifying.
> To see those people, and the piles of dead bodies being shovelled up
> by bulldozers. You realized there was hatred for the Germans. We
> were told, 'If you see any of the German soldiers not doing their work,
> just shoot them.' I was eighteen years old, that was my education. I
> can't tell you what emotions I went through. I couldn't believe what I
> was seeing. OK, you see a dead soldier on the battlefield whose head
> has been squashed by a tank, you take that as part of war. But to see
> all these emaciated people begging you for food, and you can't touch
> them because of concerns about disease, was awful. To see what the
> Germans had done to all sorts of ordinary people. It's still in my mind.
> The engineers had masks on just shovelling human beings into pits. I
> can't forget it, even now I find it horrifying.

This was not war as he had trained to fight it:

> If you went into action you had your mates beside you. You watched
> each other's backs, but if someone copped it, you walked by. You just
> carried on. You'd say, 'Bill's caught it. What rations did he leave
> behind?' War was not like that in Belsen, where there were so many
> people. It took a lot of believing. The hostility we had for the Germans
> grew. We would have shot anybody who stepped out of line. I didn't
> do it, but some of the others did. They just chucked their bodies into
> the pits with the rest of them. We were merciless and we felt hatred for
> them. It was the first time we felt like that. There was a great
> resentment. We didn't know what was going on until we went there.
> To see the bodies and the rats, that were feeding on them, was horrible.

For the witnesses to the horrors of Belsen, there was a sense that nothing could be the same after this. Most changed, became harder and perhaps more cynical. Stan Scott recalled how one of his mates told him: 'At that time the war was a big adventure, but after Belsen – anything German I wanted to smash it.' German prisoners had to be careful to avoid the attentions of their captors, who became increasingly willing to swing a rifle butt at surrendering soldiers. At the end of April, Stan and his comrades took control of a slave labour camp, contained within a Germany military base. The slave labourers were immediately released and their guards were forced into one of the labourers' filthy, cramped huts. A German officer dared to complain about their treatment. He was told, in no uncertain terms, that his complaints were falling on deaf ears: 'If you don't shut up, we'll get some petrol and burn down the hut with you in it!'

For Roy Finch, Belsen was an education that also made him look at himself:

> Our attitude towards the Germans was, 'You made this shit, get on and clear it up.' If it was a question of hitting them in the guts with a rifle butt, you did it. I can't explain, it wasn't anger, it was unbelievable to see it. It made ordinary human beings turn nasty. It made you think about yourself. What type of people were these German guards? Could I have done it?

His question was valid, after all this war had started when he was a schoolboy, one who was excited to be armed with a whistle to give the alert during air raids. Five years on he was a veteran soldier and a witness to the greatest crime the world had known.

In the final weeks of war Eric Davies once again came face to face with his old foes of the SS. He had told the new recruits about the dangers of revealing themselves on the battlefield, but with the war just days from its end, a group from his regiment rushed forward to accept the surrender of a group of German soldiers. With the British soldiers exposed the Germans dropped to the floor and SS machine-gunners opened fire from behind them. To the horror of Eric and his fellow veterans, seven of their comrades were cut down by the bullets. Once again, Eric knew there would be no SS men taken prisoner in the days ahead.

Just days later he found himself in the village of Vahrendorf outside Hamburg. In a day of vicious fighting, the 1/5th Queen's and the 2nd Battalion, the Devonshire Regiment took control of the village against heavy counterattacks by the SS, German marines and Hitler Youth. At the end of the battle a group of around forty surrendered Germans, mainly Hitler Youth, were executed by the British soldiers. Later estimates suggested the average age of the German dead was just seventeen – exactly the same age Sergeant Eric Davies had been when he joined the British Army two years earlier. It was an indication of the terrible price paid by both sides – youths who had been schoolboys in 1939 had grown up to massacre each other in the final days of war.

In the final weeks of the war, the advancing Allied armies finally approached Milag, the camp for interned merchant seamen. With the sound of fighting getting ever nearer, John Brantom – who had spent the years between the ages of fifteen and nineteen as a prisoner of war – decided to escape from captivity. Using a homemade ladder to cross the barbed wire, John and a group of other men escaped from the camp. However, the youngster ripped open his arm on the barbed wire. Whilst the others made their getaway, he remained in the forest before taking refuge with a local couple on whose farm he had worked whilst a prisoner. Using a 'liberated' motorcycle, he made his way towards the front line where he eventually found a British regiment. Within days he was home in Swansea.

For those who remained in the camp there was an overwhelming sense of uncertainty. Large numbers of RAF prisoners, transferred from other camps, had arrived at Westertimke. To make room for them in Marlag, the camp for captured Royal Navy personnel, around 700 naval ratings were transferred to Milag, soon crowding out the facilities. Despite the overcrowding, the prisoners were able to sustain themselves on the knowledge that they would soon be liberated. That long-awaited moment came on 28 April 1945. With the Guards Armoured Division advancing in the area, the Germans dug in around the camp. On 26 April the Germans had requested a truce to allow the prisoners to leave the area. However, events moved too fast and the British quickly closed on the camp. As the prisoners did their best to dig slit trenches to protect themselves from the developing battle, the British laid a smokescreen and advanced on the German positions, destroying their heavy guns and opening the route for the tanks of the Scots Guards. The prisoners sheltered as German mortar bombs flew over their heads in one direction and machine-gun bullets whistled above their trenches from the British positions.

With the British finally in control of the area, the gates to the camp were opened and the relieved seamen were free to head out into the countryside. Leslie McDermott-Brown was sleeping and awoke to find that, after more than four years in captivity, he was finally free: 'I rushed outside to see troops around the wire with real British helmets on. Everyone was talking, trying to find some soldier who came from the same town as himself.' He recorded the emotions in his diary:

> Oh, did they realize what they really meant to us? The end of five weary long years ... I looked at many people whom I hadn't seen smile for long enough, their faces were just about cracking, new light in everybody's eyes. White bread came into the camp. Yes, real honest-to-goodness white bread. It tasted like cake.[3]

Whilst they all had reason to celebrate and make up for lost time, some rougher elements among the seamen were reported to have abused their new-found freedom. There were chaotic scenes as they entered villages in search of food, alcohol and loot. All manner of transport was 'liberated' – cars, bikes, horses – as they armed themselves and then roamed through the countryside collecting whatever they wanted, safe in the knowledge that the local population could not resist. A few among them broke into German homes and abused the population, beating up German civilians. As a result of the excesses, a 'riot squad' was formed from Royal Navy personnel to deal with major incidents.

One boy who had much to celebrate was John Hipkin. The day of liberation was the eve of his nineteenth birthday. Once outside the camp, the first thing he did was to approach a foxhole. Inside was a dead German; hardened by his time in the camp, John took the man's water bottle and mess tin, knowing he might need them in the days before he got home.

Yet the experience of war – complete with all the horrors of those final weeks – had not hardened everyone's hearts beyond repair. In the final days of war, No. 3 Commando entered a German town alongside an American unit. Stan Scott was searching a German home when he heard a whimpering noise. He looked into the room and was shocked by the scene:

> A Yank was there. His rifle and kit were on the floor. His trousers were round his knees. He's got this bird on the floor. She was 90 per cent undressed and scared out of her life. You could see what was going to happen. I said, 'Don't do it, Yank!' He said he'd got to have a woman, but I told him, 'If you do, I'll bloody shoot yer!'

He wasn't joking and the American knew it. Two commandos arrived and dragged the American away, while the girl got dressed and ran away to safety. Just days later, the war in Europe was over. When Stan Scott heard the news, he sat down, smoked a cigarette, drank a cup of tea and had a well-deserved sleep.

Elsewhere in Germany, there were mixed emotions. Many soldiers were simply too exhausted or too emotionally drained to celebrate. Instead, they simply wanted to relax, finally allowing themselves a night of deep sleep. On the other hand, some men did celebrate their survival. In this group was Geoff Pulzer. Five years earlier he had been a teenage Home Guard volunteer, whose military career had started with little more than an armband as a uniform. In the intervening years he had watched tanks exploding, seeing their crews emerge in flames, realizing his friends were dying around him. He had endured the sweet stench of death at Falaise, where his tank had rolled along roads lined with the corpses of men and animals. Now he was a veteran able to exact revenge for the interruption the war had brought to his life:

> We raided a liquor store and I drank a whole bottle of brandy. It didn't do me any good at all. We were shooting off German chimney pots with machine-guns. There was a bit of mayhem. Fortunately we didn't get into trouble. Even though I'd drunk all this brandy, I woke up feeling fine. Then I ate breakfast. For the next two days I was violently ill.

It was not just the end of the war that was celebrated across Britain. In thousands of households, the end of war did not have the same impact as the return of a son, especially those who had been prisoners of war. One such returning prisoner was John Norman, who had been captured in 1940 aged just sixteen. Just after arriving back in England he met his future wife Sylvia Bowman, a seventeen-year-old girl living in his street. They met at a street party held in honour of his return. Like so many of the returning prisoners of war, John appeared extremely shy. The experience of so many years living in isolation made them uncomfortable, particularly with the opposite sex. A few days later he visited her home and asked her father's permission to take her out. He was surprised by the young man's quiet and polite manner and agreed. John later told her he wanted a girlfriend who lived nearby since, after his experiences on the long POW march, he didn't want to have to go too far to walk a girlfriend home. Regardless of his shyness, John and Sylvia fell in

love, married and went to live in Germany where John – still a
serving soldier – was based. Shortly after returning to England, John
had a medical and discovered that he had, at some point, suffered
from tuberculosis whilst in the prisoner-of-war camp. He was told
he was healed but within four years the disease re-emerged,
resulting in him spending four years in hospital and a sanatorium.

Another who had left home as a boy and returned as a man was
John Hipkin. He had spent most of his teenage years in a
prisoner-of-war camp and was desperate to get home to Newcastle.
He was flown home, spent twelve hours getting to Newcastle,
arrived home at 2 a.m., had a cup of tea with his mother, then went
to bed. He awoke the following morning to the sounds to
celebrations: he was nineteen years old, he had been away for four
years, now he was free. It was VE Day.

The familiar images of the VE Day celebrations – vast crowds,
dancing and drinking, flag-waving, surging through the streets –
masked the reality of the overt sexuality on display in some areas.
As one youngster recalled: 'People were shagging one another all
over the place on VE Day. It was a complete letting down of hair –
and trousers! Pretty much any girl who was around must have lost
her virginity – if she still had it.' But for many, the reality was that
they had no cause to celebrate the end of an event that had caused
so much pain and heartache. Parents who had lost children had little
to be excited about. Those orphaned by war felt similar emotions.
Those with family members still fighting in the Far East felt
aggrieved that such celebrations should erupt whilst their loved ones
were still fighting and dying. Some youths felt cheated that war had
come to an end before they had had a chance to join in. Others had
little to celebrate since they knew they would soon be called up for
National Service.

For many it was simply a time of confusion. War had become their
normality and its end bred uncertainty. In London, seventeen-year-
old John Sweetland watched the VE Day celebrations with a friend.
His words encapsulated the feelings of many of his generation:

I didn't feel like celebrating . . . The war had begun when I was eleven and, now being seventeen, the whole of those six years, despite every hardship, had been the only real and normal life that I could recognize, for I was a child before September 1939. So it was that I felt a complete outsider, observing only the dancing, singing and general merrymaking taking place in the West End . . . Now in the early hours of the morning, VE Day was over. We made our way home both wondering what life held in store for us.[4]

In east London there were large parties to celebrate the end of the war, but not everybody was able to enjoy them. As a fifteen year old, Reg Baker felt left out: 'I remember dancing with some girls but I spent the night sitting on the allotment behind the house. I was too old for the kids' parties but too young for the adult ones. Some people were out celebrating, but it was mainly for the little ones.' Conversely, another fifteen year old, Roy Bartlett, found the experience was improved by being a teenager. In the daytime he hung around on the fringes of a street party for children, making himself look pathetic and being given food by sympathetic mothers. At night he did the same at the adults' party, hanging around so that men passed him glasses of beer. As he later recalled: 'I only have a vague recollection of the evening, so I must have had one beer too many.'

Of course, there were thousands of men and boys who were in no position to relax. The Merchant Navy – the service that had suffered so many casualties – was not able to stop and celebrate. Their war was over but they were now back at work. However, the boys of the Merchant Navy could finally relax, safe in the knowledge that there were no more submarines prowling the deep in search of their quarry. For John Chinnery, it was the end of a long, eventful and dangerous war – one that had taken him to the edge of a psychological precipice. He had served throughout the conflict, been sunk by submarines in the Atlantic, taken convoys through the Mediterranean and endured frostbite on the Arctic convoys. Yet as war came to an end he was just eighteen years old. Having been through six years of danger, he was just old enough to buy a beer and be called up for National Service.

After spending the entire war at sea, Christian Immelman – who had started the war as an apprentice and the youngest member of his crew, and finished the war as a third mate – felt something was missing. He was mid-voyage when the news came through that the war in Europe was over: 'Not being able to join in the end-of-war celebrations in London was the second biggest disappointment of my war service, the first was my not getting home to see the family after my first trip.'

For some, the announcement meant that, as the youngest and most inexperienced crew members, it was time to face practical jokes, as seventeen-year-old Norval Young remembered:

> The bosun said to me, 'Get up the top of the mast and clean it off. That's brass up there.' It was blowing a force-eight wind at the time but I put the cleaning stuff inside my shirt and started climbing. I got halfway and moved on to the wire ladder. Then I heard the 'Old Man' shouting, 'What the hell are you doing up there?' I told him the bosun had asked me to polish the top of the mast and he shouted at me to get down. I think the bosun got a rollicking for that.

For other young seamen, the war's end was celebrated not with pranks but with victimization. Sixteen-year-old Tony Sprigings was onboard his second ship, heading out to the Far East ready for the invasion of Japan when news arrived that the war was over. However, the news did not reach him for days:

> Captain Armstrong was known as an absolute tyrant. He was mad. We had just entered the Gulf of Aden. He had the only radio onboard and heard that the Japanese had surrendered. So he sent for the first officer and told him to knock the crew off for a week in celebration. But turn the apprentices to, in their stead. We were told we had to paint the

decks black with bitumen paint. I was on the fo'c'sle head with a roller on a long pole. I heard this scream from the bridge. It was the captain. He came flying up the foredeck and said, 'What do you think you're doing?' He grabbed the pole, hits me with it, then throws it over the side. He says, 'You'll paint like the others.' It was with a round brush, on my hands and knees. After three or four days of this I had the 'screamers', I was in a terrible state.

Sick and barely able to continue, Tony was inspected by the ship's doctor who told the captain that if he didn't stop forcing the apprentice to paint the decks he would die. The captain simply replied: 'He'll finish the bloody job first!' Unable to force the captain to change his mind, the doctor gave Tony some cotton wool to mop himself down with whilst he kept working. The apprentices finally finished the job: 'Then the captain announced, "By the way, the war is over." He had let us all go for a week before telling us. People always said, "If you can sail with Harry Armstrong, you can sail with anyone." But the war was over, and things started to improve.'

With the war in Europe coming to an end, there was still much fighting to be done in the Far East. Merchant ships continued to head east to supply the Army ready to push the Japanese back. They were escorted by the Royal Navy, with some of the ships proceeding to the Pacific to support American landings. Robin Rowe, now seventeen years old and a veteran of three years at sea, was on HMS *Howe* as it supported the landings at Okinawa. There he was witness to Japan's last-ditch effort to defeat the Allies. He watched as kamikaze attacks were launched against the fleet. Planes came from all directions, surrounded by the black clouds of shell bursts, seemingly weaving their way through the arcing lines of tracer bullets as hundreds of anti-aircraft guns opened fire. He saw Japanese planes crash into the sea and, horrifyingly, saw them crash into ships, exploding into balls of flame. In the aftermath of the action, he noticed how the crew appeared more strained than he had ever seen. He realized as he watched the kamikaze attacks that he had become indifferent to the fact that each explosion on other ships meant death and wounding for men and boys just like himself. He later wrote: 'My senses had become accustomed to the ferocious sight and sound of war, rather as if I were at the cinema.'[5] His exuberance was diminished when a pilot switched course and aimed for the *Howe*. It was just 300 yards away, and heading directly for Robin's position when it was hit by anti-aircraft fire, veered off course and flew over the ship, just 100 feet from where Robin was standing. As it passed he could see the lifeless body of the pilot. Later that day, as he ate his meal, Robin noticed that his hands were shaking.

After the battles at Okinawa, the *Howe* returned to South Africa. Whilst there, the Americans dropped the world's first atomic bombs on Hiroshima and Nagasaki and the war came to an end. Three months after the end of hostilities, Bugle Boy Robin Rowe was marched before Major Ross, the senior marine officer onboard HMS *Howe*. He stood before the officer as the sergeant spoke: 'Boy Bugler Rowe requests to be rated Bugler, sir!' The officer granted permission and Robin marched from the office. He'd been at sea for over three years. He was a veteran of Arctic convoys, had bombarded Sicily and survived attacks by the Japanese kamikaze aircraft: it was his eighteenth birthday.

CHAPTER 25

The New Order: Post-war Britain

'From when I was fourteen in 1939 until I was twenty, the war absorbed me completely – winning the war, surviving the war, what will I do after the war? It absorbed my life in a way young people today would find hard to understand. A lot of my friends were killed. It was a total absorption.'

Anthony Wedgwood Benn

For a generation which had known little but war, peace had a profound effect. There was something unfamiliar about this strange new world in which bombs were no longer falling. To the younger children, war was all they had known. Older children could remember the peace of the pre-war years, but it seemed distant after the monumental changes they had experienced. For many, the war years had been a combination of trauma and excitement, and they had enjoyed freedoms they might otherwise never have known. At the time, most youngsters enjoyed the disruption of their schools and teenagers had enjoyed the benefits of high wages. For those who had volunteered for service before their time, they had exchanged their youth for an unforgettable experience.

Whether good or bad, few of the nation's children and teenagers had been unaffected by war. The social catalyst of evacuation, bringing together people from all backgrounds and mixing them with the population of the small towns and villages, changed the face of the countryside. There was also the political catalyst, this sense that the nation should not return its children to the slums in which so many had been raised. As one author noted: 'Are they, when the war is over, simply to return to the slums, there to resume life as they lived it before, after this glimpse of a better and healthier and freer life?'[1] This sense that the country deserved better changed the entire post-war political landscape, bringing the Labour Party to power in 1945, seeing the creation of the welfare state and improving the lives of millions of ordinary people. The generation that had sacrificed so much in wartime felt they deserved reward and protection. The children who had been bombed from their homes now wanted new homes to bring up their own children. Those whose education had been curtailed by war wanted their children to benefit from free education. Those who had seen doctors and nurses give everything to save the victims of war wanted the same protection to be freely available to all. Regardless of party political allegiances, nobody wanted to go back to the pre-war society. As former evacuee Reg Baker put it:

> I get sick of the older generation talking about the good old days. They were horrible ... Pre-war I was always hungry; I always seemed to have the arse out of my trousers; always had holes in my shoes ... So please let's have no more about the 'Good Old Days'. I lived in them, there was nothing good about them.[2]

One youngster for whom the political and social changes in wartime were an unforgettable influence was Anthony Wedgwood Benn. At fourteen he had been excited by war and been keen to do his duty. In 1940 he had written to his father:

> That at eighteen I'd go into the RAF, be commissioned by nineteen and, if I were still alive after the war, I'd go to Oxford. And that I'd die

aged eighty-two. I had a very clear view of what I'd do. It was my way of having a scheme. I volunteered for the RAF as soon as I could do so – at seventeen but I couldn't join until I was eighteen in 1943.

As war progressed he found that whoever he spoke with talked of the future: 'During the war there was only one topic of conversation: what do we do after the war?'

The experience of war had a profound influence on his later political life. Having joined the Labour Party aged seventeen, he was asked to stand as a parliamentary candidate at the first post-war election, but declined the offer. Onboard a troopship headed for pilot training in South Africa, he joined in political discussions:

> We had a riveting discussion. I remember one lad said in the 1930s we had mass unemployment but we don't have unemployment in wartime – he said if you can have full employment killing Germans why can't you have full employment building a society. It was a simple point but it explained why in 1945 the public voted for the Labour Party manifesto . . . People didn't vote against Churchill, they voted against the pre-war years' Conservative Party in favour of something better. It wasn't an ideological shift, it was common sense.

Returning from South Africa aged twenty, he also realized that many of those who had fought so hard for victory had no say in their future: 'When I got back from the war I couldn't even vote – you had to be twenty-one. All these men my age who had come back from fighting still couldn't vote.' It was not just his sense of social justice that was developed by the experience of war: 'My hatred of war began at that time – I was keen to take part because I thought we might get invaded, but my dislike of war and what it does to people was growing.'

Despite all the criticisms of the UK's youth, there were many in authority who recognized the sufferings, sacrifice and positive contribution the boys and girls of Britain had made to what was a 'total war'. In November 1945, as part of a Parliamentary debate, members gave thanks for this contribution. Jack Jones, the member for Bolton, pointed to the independence given to children by war and stressed that the rise in delinquency was not universal: 'It is not a bit of use decrying the rottenness of our young people, and forgetting the millions of splendid characters there are in this country.'[3]

The member for Harrow East, Mr Skinnard, went even further, noting that a youthful sense of adventure was central to the issue of delinquency. He told the house that youth needed to be guided into using its talents legitimately and the energy of youth should not be wasted. He also felt that war had nurtured the talents of the young, turning potential delinquents into heroes: 'If they had been six years younger, many of the young VCs and DSOs would have been in Dartmoor, Borstals or remand homes, for exercising the very same valuable instincts of initiative and courage for which they have been rewarded in the Services.' Mr Skinnard announced that he was pleased to see crowds of young people in dance halls enjoying themselves. He admitted that he found the area he had earlier worked in had changed beyond recognition, with war bringing responsibility to working-class areas that had once been plagued by violence and delinquency. 'We have taken these young people into our confidence and tried, during this war, to put square pegs into square holes, and to harness all their energy, courage and resource. We encouraged youth because the country was in desperate need on account of the war.'[4]

Six years of war had made an indelible impression upon all the children and teenagers who had lived through it. As underage volunteer Eric 'Bill' Sykes put it: 'Anyone who goes to war and survives is lucky. Anyone who goes to war and survives with their life and whole body and mind is extremely lucky.' He was right. Thousands of youngsters carried a resounding emotional and physical burden. For some it was just regret that evacuation had split their families and that war had taken them away from the places they knew and loved. For others there was a pride that war had challenged them, they had responded and they had used the experience to build upon. But for many there was a deep darkness. What of boys like John Chinnery, who served six years at sea, yet was just eighteen at war's end and who had been driven to the brink of suicide by his experiences? Or Roy Finch, still seventeen when he went to France as a soldier and just eighteen when he witnessed the indescribable horrors of Belsen concentration camp?

What memories must it conjure up for former Royal Marine bugler Len Chester to hear the notes of 'The Last Post': the first time he played it at a funeral, he was just fourteen years old, already on active service, standing in tears beside the graves of six sailors:

> When I am walking along the street, I look at people and think, 'None of you know that I was at war aged fourteen.' When I go on Royal Marine parades I don't see anyone else of my era. Everyone thinks of the marines as commandos, they all wear the green beret. I wear a white beret in memory of the merchant seamen who died on the Arctic convoys. No one else ever wears it. That is the one that means the most to me.

Asked about going to war at such a young age, he has no regrets: 'I'm still here. I'm eighty-six years old. I've got a family. If I hadn't joined the marines at fourteen, I would have been called up at some point. I could be lying dead under the sand of the Libyan desert. How can I have regrets?'

The survivors of the SS *City of Benares* struggled to come to terms with their experiences. While fully occupied childish minds found plenty of distractions, they could not remain occupied forever. Dreams and nightmares about the sinking were a regular feature for the survivors. Despite their maritime sufferings, a number of the *Benares'* boys made a curious decision: Derek Capel served seven years in the Royal Navy; in 1944 Ken Sparks joined the Navy as a 'boy sailor'; Billy Short and Fred Steels also chose to do their

National Service with the 'Senior Service'. The lure of the sea also called Colin Ryder Richardson who did his National Service in the Royal Navy. When he joined the Royal Navy, Colin was told that, at all times, he should wear the 'oak leaf' emblem he had been awarded in recognition for his bravery following the sinking of the *Benares*. Again, this was a shock: 'On parade, I was the only one with anything to show.'

It was whilst serving in the Royal Navy that the nineteen-year-old survivor of the SS *City of Benares* first became able to assess the tragedy he had so narrowly survived. After developing an infection at sea, he was sent to an isolation hospital:

> I was told just to lie in bed. It was the first time I had really been able to grieve. How could it have happened? Why did it happen to me? Once the infection had cleared I was told to get out of bed. I couldn't get up. What had happened was that I had lain there grieving away and my blood had stopped flowing. I had got deep vein thrombosis. I was taken to Chatham naval hospital and spent a few months there. Then they discharged me from the Navy.

Colin came to understand why it had taken so long for the grief to affect him: 'My mother had told everyone not to talk to me about my experiences. She wanted me to get over them. There was no understanding of "post-traumatic stress" – you just got on with life.'

Sometimes just getting on with life had its shocks. Having been bombed out from Clydebank, Ella Flynn and her parents settled in Glasgow. The move meant she never learned of the fate of the people she had known until years later:

> Mum and I were in a shop in Glasgow when my mum was suddenly rooted to the spot. She said, 'My God, that's Mrs Wade.' We had understood that Mrs Wade, a tall red-haired woman, had been killed in the bombing. She had a teenage son and a daughter called Marion. The lady my mum was looking at had snow white hair and was not like the Mrs Wade I remembered.

After a tearful reunion, they heard her story: 'Mrs Wade and her son and daughter had been in the shelters behind their house. They were buried under the rubble for three days – her son had died first and then her thirteen-year-old daughter Marion had said to her, "Mummy, Jesus is coming for me," and died.' Mrs Wade had eventually been pulled from the rubble. A girder pinning her shoulder had kept the heavy brickwork from suffocating her. Everyone else in the shelter was killed.

For Peter Richards the war had been a very personal journey. It was the same for his old schoolmate, John Cotter, with whom he had listened to the declaration of war. At the time they had thought themselves on the brink of a great adventure: 'This was to prove true, with the award of a Distinguished Flying Cross for John, who successfully completed a tour of bombing operations, and a year in hospital for me after my marginal efforts to liberate France.'

He could not forget all he had experienced. Though never a pacifist, Peter remained resolute, knowing that war could never be treated lightly. Whenever he heard people treating war as a gung-ho episode his mind turned to the poor, bereaved relatives to whom he had handed telegrams revealing the fate of their sons or husbands. Even seventy years after the Blitz, just to hear the news of the deaths of soldiers continues to haunt him:

> When I hear one or two soldiers have been killed in Afghanistan, people think it's just one or two men. But I think of all the grieving families and friends. It's not just the immediate family; it affects all the other people. I try not to dwell on it, but I still remember it. I just can't listen to the 'Last Post' on Remembrance Sunday.

Whatever people say about the Blitz on British cities, with some observers claiming it was as hard for civilians as for soldiers at the front, Peter Richards knew that this was untrue. He had seen both. He had cycled and run through the streets of London and delivered post through the City as it lay in smouldering ruins. Yet all the time there was one consolation:

during the Blitz one knew that death and destruction were coming
mainly from the skies, allowing of course for delayed action bombs and
falling buildings, about which there was usually some warning. During
the hours of daylight, one knew that one was comparatively safe. But
at the front one never felt secure, for danger was ever-present.

Another soldier who endured a prolonged period of treatment in
order to recover from his wounds was Ted Roberts. His shattered
arm, 'was dead for about eighteen months. That's why I never went
back into battle. I had to get the nerves to work again.' The
treatment included hot wax baths to build up a protective coating
on his arm, allowing the wounds to heal. Electrodes were placed
either side of the wound to stimulate the working of damaged
nerves. Eventually he started on physiotherapy: first weaving a
small carpet to get his fingertips working again, then doing exercises
to build up strength in the arm. All the time, he was uncertain
whether full movement would return to his arm.

In the post-war years, Ted Roberts was lucky never to be plagued
with nightmares. He often dreamed about being in the Army, but
never about the fighting. Despite not suffering trauma he remains
able to recall almost every moment of those six weeks in the front
line. Looking back, he has no bitterness towards the enemy and
certainly not to the man who shot him: 'If I had been in the position
of the German who shot me, I would have done the same thing. If
I could meet him now, I'd buy him a drink. He did me a favour –
the wound saved my life.' He was right: the long months in hospital
meant he never returned to the front line.

For some of the boys who had seen service in wartime, there was
an unexpected surprise awaiting them: the prospect of having to do
National Service now they had reached eighteen. Leaving the
Merchant Navy after four years at sea, Alfred Leonard was told that
he still faced conscription, despite having served on a merchant
vessel as a sixteen year old. To prevent being called up he joined
the Royal Navy Volunteer Reserve, ensuring if he were conscripted

he would at least return to the sea. He couldn't understand why he should face such a situation. After all, he had been awarded campaign medals for his Merchant Navy service: surely he had already done 'his bit'?

In later years, such matters were of less concern. What mattered was that he was proud of his service:

> Without a doubt, I really started to grow up when I went to sea. My mother and father said, 'You went away a boy and came back a man.' You really had to toughen up at sea. I'm a World War II veteran but I am as young as you get. When I joined the veterans' club they told me I didn't look old enough. I was only sixteen in Normandy and seventeen at the end of the war.

For John Chinnery, who finished six years at sea in wartime at just eighteen years of age, the post-war years did not see his memory wiped clean of all the bad events he witnessed while in the Merchant Navy. In the immediate aftermath of war he was asked to represent the Merchant Navy in the victory parade through the streets of London but refused. He also knew that he had to remain at sea since, as an eighteen year old, he faced being conscripted for National Service despite his wartime service at sea. Not only that, but he realized he had grown up quickly whilst at sea and had outgrown his contemporaries who were only just starting out on an independent life.

Despite growing up quickly and developing a precocious confidence, John also carried the emotional scars of all he had experienced. In later life he admitted to his wife Daphne that chatting to her over the morning cup of tea had become a form of therapy. He said that as a child between twelve and eighteen years of age, he had been unable to take in all that he had experienced. Somehow, his youth and the circumstances of life at sea in wartime had cushioned him. He admitted to her that he carried the emotional burden of memories that he didn't want to recall to anyone and was frank in realizing that, if he had admitted this to himself in wartime, it would have proved too much. He believed he would have killed himself or died of shock at the horrors he had witnessed.

John Hipkin, who was a prisoner of war from the age of fourteen to eighteen, did not return to the sea. Instead, he returned to education and trained as a schoolteacher. Looking back on his four years as a teenage prisoner of war he remained remarkably upbeat: 'It sounds silly, but we had a great time. We were boys but we were treated like men. But I had missed a lot. When I got home at the age of nineteen I had a lot of time to make up.' Despite his light-hearted outlook on the seemingly wasted teenage years, there was a darker side to his homecoming:

> We were never getting enough of the right food. You put adolescent boys in a prison camp and make them work, well by the time we were liberated we were as skinny as can be. The doctors checked me and said I had been malnourished. I still get a war pension as a result of the lack of food I suffered. The grown men had an easier time of it.

After retiring, he became interested in another group of servicemen: the underage volunteers of the Great War who were executed for cowardice and desertion. As he told a local newspaper: 'I'm fighting for the boys.'[5] He established the 'Shot at Dawn' campaign, fighting for a pardon for British and Commonwealth soldiers executed between 1914 and 1918. In 2006 the campaign reached its climax when the queen granted pardons to the executed men.

Like so many, Geoff Pulzer kept his wartime experiences hidden for many years. He had witnessed the Blitz on the City of London, joined the Home Guard as a sixteen year old, then served with a tank regiment from D-Day to VE Day. Yet he felt this did not compare to the horrific experiences of his wife. When Geoff Pulzer had entered the Belgian city of Antwerp with one of the liberating units, he had no idea that his future wife was just a few streets away as they engaged the remaining German defenders. Fourteen-year-old Julienne Vanhandenhoeve, whose war had started when her ship had been sunk as she attempted to return to England, was similarly unsuspecting.

As Geoff recalled:

> I didn't know it at the time but I had virtually liberated her. Funnily enough, in Antwerp there was one little battle I was involved in. We were ferreting some Germans out of their positions on a bombed area on a hill. They were dug in and we were firing on them with our machine-guns – until they came out holding white flags. We took them prisoner. I later found out it was only a hundred yards away from where Julienne had been living.

The two finally met some years after the war when they were both working in London. As he recalled: 'Word got round among the boys that there was a pretty Belgian girl joining the department. So I went and told her I had liberated her!'

Julienne's sister Yvonne also returned to England. The experience of growing up in German-occupied Belgium had made a profound impression upon her:

> My husband used to say he could never get a true answer out of me. I had it engrained in me that you should not say anything out loud, because you didn't know if your friends were collaborators with the Germans. So all my statements would be very guarded and I didn't give a straight answer. He found it very frustrating.

She was also affected by both the sinking of the ship and the later bombing of Antwerp: 'I have never talked to my children about my experiences in Antwerp. It left me very worried about loud noises. I couldn't stand thunder and lightning. I've got a bit more used to it now. I still won't watch films with guns firing – I switch them off. I don't like violence.'

For Bill Edwardes, who served as a stretcher-bearer in an infantry regiment from June 1944 to May 1945, war was the making of him. Just sixteen when he volunteered, seventeen when he was sent to France and eighteen when war ended, he was forced to grow up:

> Was I daft? Yes and no. Consider this, I was something of an urchin. I wasn't very well educated. I joined the Army. I did my primary training and within three months I'd learned to ride a motorbike, drive a Bren carrier, to shoot, to fire all sorts of weapons – I was as happy as Larry – I was having a whale of a time. When I joined I was slim, but I ate well and put on weight. It did me good. It was just the fighting bit that came later that didn't do me good.

Yet Bill can never escape the memories of Normandy. Something in the back of his mind takes him back to the sights and sounds of the battlefield: 'One abiding memory is the smell, the stench of dead cattle, cordite and rotting bodies. It was an awful, and constant, mixture – I can still smell it now. There was no getting away from it. There is nothing else like it.' Even in his mid-eighties, the memories return: 'I sometimes do battlefield tours – for the Territorial Army, the regular Army, or trainee officers – then I come home and for a few days I have nightmares. My wife wakes me up and tells me I have been shouting and raving.' The one memory that returns is the battle at Vernon:

> It spooks me. The sight of the Tiger tank coming towards us, just yards away, sweeping the road with its machine-guns. The sound of the tank rumbling and its tracks clattering on the road. The whole area was dark and eerie. I can still see it all in my mind. It was horrifying.

It is not just the bad memories of war that remain. The experience changed him and gave him skills that stayed with him throughout his working life:

> I was very much calmer in difficult situations. In my career there were situations when someone needed to take a grip, take charge, and I could do it automatically. I saw the need and just did it. I was at one factory and just stopped the production line down because things were getting out of hand and nobody wanted to take charge. I put that down to having to react quickly when dealing with casualties. It was like triage. I was self-reliant. I am still not frightened to help people who are hurt or taken ill. It doesn't worry me. When I went into the Army it was a huge benefit to me as a person. It turned the boy into a man. I was given jobs that as a boy I would never have had a chance to do. I learned all sorts of new skills.

He carries the feeling that the whole experience was worthwhile, that his youth was not wasted:

> I was twelve when war broke out and I was eighteen when it finished – people say to me, 'that was all your youth gone'. It didn't go, it was just spent in a different way. I don't regret it one bit. It was an experience that saw me through the rest of my life. The only time I regretted it was when I was actually in battle, thinking I could have been back in the factory, doing that boring job. But I was doing something positive, I was saving people's lives.

For all the horrors he experienced, Bill Edwardes was of a generation old enough to make the choice to go to war. Naive, maybe, but they had sought out war, not waited for it to come to them. For the younger children who were sucked into conflict and saw it at its most violent, there was no escape into celebration of their service. All they had were memories of the darkness that had engulfed their childhood. Like Alf Morris, who 'bottled up' the memory of his experiences at Bethnal Green, keeping them to himself until he finally felt he had to tell the world about the horrors.

For more than fifty years he didn't talk about his experiences at Bethnal Green tube station. However, being pulled alive from a pile of 173 bodies – including those of many people he knew – deeply affected him. Yet even his family were not aware of how close he had been to death. Even Alf's wife Vera, who had been living in the same street as him in 1943, knew nothing about his experiences. Yet the memories are always with him:

> It was a small incident in a big, worldwide event – it stays in your mind forever. I can't get rid of the memory of the sound of people dying around me. People who haven't been through it can't understand. I just bottled it up. I never told anyone. I never told my wife. But I thought about it all the time. When I was eventually asked about it, I said I was there, and Vera said, 'What?' She didn't know. My kids never knew about it. But I had dreams about it. I'd wake up and be unable to get back to sleep. Sometimes I'd shut myself in the toilet and have a little cry about it. Just to let it out.

Eventually Alf Morris decided that a memorial should be erected in memory of the dead and a charity, the Stairway to Heaven Memorial Trust, was started to raise funds for one. 'I feel I owe it to the dead to have a permanent memorial to them. I won't be happy until I see the memorial erected. These people have got to be remembered.'

In later life, Alf's experiences gave him sympathy for the suffering of others around the world. However, the depth of his experience – having been 'bombed out' from four homes and narrowly escaping death in Bethnal Green tube station – meant he remains convinced it was correct for the Allied air forces to have inflicted huge devastation on Germany in revenge:

> We didn't want to go to war. I was only a kid, but I can remember it all. It was forced on us. At first, we took a hammering. Then, when we got going we did what we had to do. They showed us what they could do, and we gave it back, but better. But when it was payback time people don't like it. It wasn't nice – they started it, but we finished it properly.

For one underage volunteer, who preferred to remain anonymous, the post-war years were marked by a struggle to settle down in civilian life. As he admitted in the final years of his life, he had grown used to killing and had eventually grown to enjoy it. After service in the Mediterranean and north-west Europe – first seeing action as a seventeen year old – killing became a routine part of his everyday existence. At times the violence had been intensely personal, having killed Germans with a knife whilst engulfed in fury at the news of his brother's death.

Aged just nineteen at war's end, he returned home to marry 'the girl next door', only to crave a return to the excitement he had known whilst overseas. He soon escaped the boredom of post-war Britain and returned to Germany to find employment with the British element of the Allied Control Commission.

This was followed by an itinerant existence, at some times hitching lifts around Europe, even illegally entering the Soviet Bloc and making his way to Russia. He later found work as a taxi driver, taking American war-widows to the site of their husband's deaths. For a while he also drove a water-taxi in Venice, before finally returning home almost twenty years after the end of the war. Only after those itinerant years did he finally find stability, settling down with a new wife and family. Even in the final years of his life he refused to divulge the details of the worst of his war experiences to his family, and the extent to which growing to enjoy killing had influenced his life.

He was not alone in being turned from a boy into someone who found killing easy. For Fred Rowe, just seven years old when the Blitz hit London, the horrors shaped his entire life. It seemed that every day for the next thirty years was influenced by the experiences he had in the Blitz and his childhood looting expeditions. In 1944 he passed the 'Eleven Plus' exam and started at the local grammar school. Yet his time there was uncomfortable. The self-confessed street urchin didn't fit in with many of the other boys and was soon expelled for fighting.

In 1950 he was called up for National Service, joined the infantry and was sent to Korea. His experiences in Korea were shaped by what he had seen in wartime London, and he was reminded of the violence he had seen in the streets around his home: 'It was nothing new. There were dead bodies everywhere, but I'd seen it all. There were kids my age with me in the Army who had been evacuated during the war. They hadn't seen anything. In Korea, they'd see a body and be revolted. I could look at it and think nothing of it.' In the increasingly bitter conflict, he began to learn the ways of the battlefield, especially that he could expect no mercy from the enemy: 'The North Koreans never took prisoners. We'd find blokes who'd been nailed to a tree, left there, then starved to death. It was awful.'

Fred turned into a soldier without pity for the enemy. On one occasion his officer told him: 'You are a cold-hearted bastard, aren't you, Rowe?' With utmost honesty, he replied: 'I'm a realist. I'm going to survive. I come through one fucking war as a kid, I ain't going to die here.'

On one occasion, he witnessed scenes that reminded him of being back in London during the Blitz, and brought home to him the difference between him and his comrades who had never experienced bombing:

> We were on a hill. It was winter. You've not had a winter till you've had a Korean winter. It was fucking perishing! There was a platoon of us in this wooded area waiting for their patrol to come. Patrol! There must have been a thousand of them coming towards us. The officer said, 'When they appear we'll start shooting.' I saw all these Koreans coming towards us, looked at me gun and thought, 'That ain't gonna be any good!' So the officer got on the radio and called up air support. Napalm! What a lovely fucking weapon! That sorted them out. Three jets came over and dropped their bombs on the Koreans. It cooked them all. You could smell it from where we were. It was a massacre. Hundreds of them done in seconds. We were safe: what a fucking

blinder! I'd smelt burning bodies like that before, back in 1940. The others were moaning about the smell. I said, 'What's the matter with you? Do you want to fucking die?' All I thought about was the threat they posed to me.

Fred Rowe had seen death close up at an impressionable age and grew realistic about his chances of survival. It was a kill or be killed world, where he would do whatever he considered necessary to survive. On one occasion his unit captured a North Korean intelligence officer. The Korean was needed back at headquarters for interrogation:

> The officer said to me, 'Rowe. Take him back to HQ.' He gave me two new blokes – rookies – to escort the prisoner back. When we got about a hundred yards out of our camp I said to these two rookies, 'I'm going to kill this cunt!' I told them the North Koreans were probably watching us, and we'd never get to the HQ.

He justified what he was suggesting by telling the rookies that the Koreans might appear at any moment, shoot them, and help the prisoner escape. He was convinced the Koreans knew they were holding the officer and would not let them get him safely to headquarters:

> I asked the lads if they wanted to die. No. So we had to make it look good. I told them to say the prisoner had made a run for it so we had to shoot him. So I told the prisoner to go. He knew what was happening, he wouldn't go. So I got a pistol, held it up and said, 'Fucking go! Or I'll do it here!' So I kicked him away, then I shot him in the back of the neck.

After their report of the prisoner's escape and death a Court of Enquiry was held to determine the facts. Fred Rowe and the two other men stuck to their version of events and the matter was closed.

After the hearing, his officer approached and spoke candidly to Fred: 'I know what went on. I saw your face.'

Another time he was asked to search a barn:

> The sergeant said there was a Korean in there. I said, 'Fuck him, throw a hand grenade in.' The sergeant said no. So I went in. I had a pistol. The Korean was in there. He put his hands up and said, 'No. No.' I took his gun off him and searched him. I said, 'Come.' He said, 'No.' So I put the gun to his nose and shot him. It blew the back of his head off.

After leaving the Army, he returned home and slowly fell into the criminal fraternity. Starting with snatching wage bags, escaping on stolen motorcycles, he graduated to safe-blowing, earning his nickname 'Spider' for his ability to scale the outside of buildings. He enjoyed the lifestyle. He made good money, spent it on cars and women, waited until the money was exhausted and then returned to crime. Prison was an occupational hazard that he grew to accept: after all, it was his own choice. Eventually he progressed to armed robbery. After a number of short spells in prison – all of which devastated his family – he was finally given a ten-year sentence.

And so his criminal career continued until a fateful day in 1974 when Fred encountered a neighbour in his south London flats. The neighbour was a would-be artist and musician named Ian Dury. After a hesitant start, the two became firm friends. Fred would later credit Dury with helping him 'go straight'. When Fred was offered employment as Dury's driver he took the chance and never looked back. In the years that followed, Fred Rowe was Dury's constant companion, setting up equipment for his bands, introducing Dury on stage, acting as a minder and, above all, being there as a friend. The exposure to this unfamiliar world, working around the world with bands, meeting the type of people he hardly knew existed, opened his eyes to another world. Though all his old criminal mates didn't believe he would be able to, he changed his life and 'went straight'. More than thirty years after he had first looted the bombed-out shops of south London, Fred Rowe had finally broken the cycle of criminality and settled down to a 'normal' life. Up until that point, he didn't know any other life and – apart from his family – had no contact with 'straight people'. As he later admitted: 'Ian turned my life around. He was in the right place at the right time.'

So what had made Fred Rowe the man he was? Whilst serving his ten-year jail sentence, he underwent an examination by a psychiatrist, who tried to understand what had made him into a career criminal. After all, he was from a loving family, his parents were both hardworking people and all his siblings were respectable. What had made him a criminal, in and out of prison, year after year? After listening to Fred's story he came to a conclusion: he was like that because of his experiences as a wartime street-urchin. Every time his mother had accepted looted food from her seven-year-old son, she had encouraged him. Her acquiescence, in order to put food on the table, had made him view criminality as something acceptable.

He makes no excuses for his career as a criminal or for the killing of prisoners in Korea, nor does he ask for sympathy. Instead, he simply states:

> It was a tough old life – but I brought it all on myself . . . World War Two prepared me for it. Things don't shock you so much. It wasn't a good way to live, but I was thrown into it . . . Now, I'm really ashamed of my criminal life because I know how good life can be.

Of course, not all young witnesses to the violence of war were hardened by their experiences. Some were profoundly affected by them, never escaping the memories of the turmoil. One such victim was John Norman, who became a prisoner of war aged just sixteen, experiencing five terrible years as a slave labourer in a Silesian coal mine. He and his wife Sylvia retired to Canada in the 1980s. In the latter years of his life he underwent tests on his heart that revealed he had suffered something unusual at some point in his life. He realized this was the massive electrical shock he had endured whilst a teenage prisoner of war working in a German coal mine. When he developed Parkinson's disease, he wondered whether the effects of the electrical shock had been responsible for the development of the illness.

In the final years of his life, Sylvia noticed how he seemed to suffer from 'flashbacks' in which he was unable to differentiate between reality and his earlier experiences of deprivation and suffering as a teenage prisoner of war. He would simply stop and stare into the distance, as if lost deep in thought. As the situation worsened, he became deeply suspicious of outsiders. At one point she discovered he had moved bottles of alcohol. When asked where they were, he replied: 'I've hidden all the drinks in the garage so that the guards won't find it.' Sometimes he got up at night, staggered from his bed and sat in the hall, telling his wife he was waiting for his shift in the coal mine to start. When he heard his neighbour's dog barking, he was convinced it was a German guard dog. As his dementia increased, he was convinced he was still in a prisoner-of-war camp and kept asking his wife where the rest of the prisoners were. He shouted out: 'Where is everybody? They've all gone home! I want to go home!' As Sylvia said: 'My beloved husband was reliving all the horrors he had experienced as a POW.' Eventually, after suffering a number of falls, he was admitted to hospital and found to be suffering from Post-traumatic Stress Disorder. His past had caught up with him. He died in a care home aged eighty-five.

Notes

Preface

1. Winston Churchill, quoted in *The 1940s House* (Channel 4, 2001).

Chapter 3: A Phoney War?

1. *Ourselves in Wartime* (London: Odhams Press Ltd, 1944).
2. Sarah Gertrude Millin, *World Blackout* (London: Faber & Faber, 1944).
3. 'Pilgrimage for Hearts of Oak; Scapa Flow survivors remember fallen colleagues', *Glasgow Herald* (15 October 2004).
4. Millin, op. cit.
5. The youngest member of the armed forces to die on active service was Royal Marine Boy Bugler Peter Avant, who died aged fourteen when HMS *Fiji* sank at Crete in 1941. He was one of eight 'Boys' lost on the *Fiji*.

Chapter 4: Eruption – May 1940

1. Quoted in Norman Longmate, *The Real Dad's Army* (London: Arrow Books, 1974).
2. Ibid.

3. 'Prince Takes Final Dunkirk Veterans' Salute', Press Association (4 June 2000).
4. Jay Iliff, 'It Was the First Time I'd Ever Seen a Dead Body', *Daily Express* (30 May 2000).
5. *Ourselves in Wartime.* op. cit.

Chapter 5: London's Burning

1. Bernard Kops, *The World is a Wedding* (London: MacGibbon and Kee, 1963).
2. *Britain Under Fire* (London: Country Life Ltd, 1941).
3. Sam Greenhill, 'Now that's the spirit: 70 years on, veterans of the Blitz gather to remember start of their darkest hour', *Daily Mail* (8 October 2010).

Chapter 6: The Water Babies

1. Quoted in Tom Nagorski, *Miracles on the Water* (London: Robinson, 2007).

Chapter 7: The Blitz Spreads

1. Imperial War Museum archives: Ray Peat (97/40/1).
2. *Ourselves in Wartime*, op. cit.
3. Imperial War Museum archives: Ray Peat (97/40/1).
4. Ibid.
5. Name changed on request of interviewee.

Chapter 8: Heroes and Villains of the Blitz

1. National Archives WO32/9849.
2. Details taken from an unpublished photo – story by Bert Hardy for *Picture Post*, April 1941.

3. 'Coventry's Wartime Heroines', *Coventry Evening Telegraph* (7 February 2005).

4. Ibid.

5. 'Wartime women honoured at last', *The Times* (10 July 2005).

6. 'Forres woman's heroism in the Blitz marked by plaque at her old school', *Aberdeen Press and Journal* (22 February 2002).

7. 'Heroines of War Finally Remembered', *Sunday Express* (30 January 2005).

8. 'Bravery of a very plucky teenager', *Kent & Sussex Courier* (28 January 2005).

Chapter 9: Boy Soldiers

1. David Fraser, *And We Shall Shock Them* (London: Hodder & Stoughton, 1983).

2. National Archives WO32/9848.

3. National Archives WO32/9849.

4. Ibid.

5. Ibid.

6. National Archives WO32/9848.

7. Ibid.

8. Patrick Davis, *A Child at Arms* (London: Hutchinson, 1970).

9. Imperial War Museum archive: C. T. Framp (85/18/1)

10. Imperial War Museum.

11. National Archives WO32/9848.

12. Ibid.

13. Ibid.

14. Ibid.

15. Ibid.

16. Ibid.

17. Ibid.

18. National Archives WO32/9727.

19. Ibid.

20. Imperial War Museum archive: Captain P Collister (83/46/1).

21. Imperial War Museum archive: C. T. Framp (85/18/1).
22. National Archives WO32/9848.
23. Ibid.
24. Ibid.
25. National Archives WO32/10470.

Chapter 10: Going to Sea

1. Quoted in Peter Elphick, *Life Line – The Merchant Navy at War, 1939–1945* (London: Chatham, 1999).
2. Reg Osborn, *Trust Me . . . I'm An Old Sailor* (London: Banyan Books, 2006).
3. Ibid.
4. HMS *Worcester* deteriorated during the war and in 1945 was replaced by the TS *Exmouth*, which had returned south from Scapa Flow. She took the *Worcester* name and remained in service until the 1970s.
5. Many years later, at a reunion, Bill Ellis met the woman who had run the stores. She complained that she could never work out why the bread rations were short. Bill had to admit he had been responsible.
6. Robin Rowe, *Sticky Blue – A Boy and a Battleship* (Devon: Devonshire House, 1995).
7. Ibid.

Chapter 11: Flyboys

1. Quoted in James Taylor and Martin Davidson, *Bomber Crew* (London: Hodder & Stoughton, 2004).
2. National Archives HO45/20250.

Chapter 12: Fighting Back

1. Quoted in Robin Neillands, *The Raiders – The Army Commandos 1940–1946* (London: Weidenfeld & Nicolson, 1989).

Chapter 13: The World Turns

1. Quoted in Ben Wicks, *Waiting for the All Clear* (London: Bloomsbury, 1990).
2. Peter Richards, *Bombs, Bullshit and Bullets* (London: Athena Press, 2007).
3. National Archives WO32/9847.
4. Ibid.
5. National Archives ED 11/248.
6. National Archives HO45/20250.

Chapter 14: Merchantmen and Boys

1. Osborn, op. cit.
2. National Archives T335/30.
3. Ibid.
4. *Daily Mail* (10 May 1994).
5. The Commonwealth War Graves Commission names these boys under the age of fifteen who died on active service: Cabin Boy Vincent Cook; Mess Room Boy George Corlett; Deck Boy William Hills; Cabin Boy Alfred Hunt; Steward's Boy Robert Jones; Mess Room Boy Kenneth Lewis; Mess Room Boy John Ostrich; Galley Boy Alfred Page; Mess Room Boy Robert Robinson; Mess Room Boy Bernard Sexton; Sailor Sydney Smith; Mess Room Boy John Watson; Engineer's Boy Thomas Watson.
6. 'Fight for a medal; Bureaucracy has denied teenage sailor killed in wartime the honour he clearly deserved', *Daily Post* (5 September 2005).

Chapter 15: Boys Behind the Wire

1. Imperial War Museum archive: Leslie McDermott-Brown.
2. Ibid.
3. Ibid.

4. Ibid.

5. Paul McMillan, 'This soldier panicked and ran. The German soldier shot and killed him. I had never seen anybody die. I was just 14', *Evening Chronicle* (20 June 2006).

6. Ibid.

7. James Diffley, 'Justice Looms at Last', *Evening Chronicle* (7 March 2006).

8. Imperial War Museum archive: Captain F. W. Bailey (95/35/1).

9. *The Prisoner of War. The Official Journal of the Prisoners of War Department of the Red Cross and St John War Organisation*, 2: 16 (August 1943).

10. Ibid., 2: 15 (July 1943).

11. Rob Kennedy, 'The commandant hated us like we were poison. If anyone didn't work, he punished them', *Evening Chronicle* (12 January 2006).

12. 'A tide of memories', *Journal* (27 October 2005).

13. McMillan, 'This soldier panicked and ran', op. cit.

14. Mel Mason, 'My teenage years in a prisoner of war camp', *Northern Echo* (1 March 1996).

15. *The Prisoner of War. The Official Journal of the Prisoners of War Department of the Red Cross and St John War Organisation*, 2: 25 (May 1944); 1: 12 (April 1943).

16. 'I was 15 and thrown into the Jap factory of death', *Daily Record* (14 August 1995).

17. Imperial War Museum archive: Leslie McDermott-Brown.

18. Ibid.

Chapter 16: A Boy's Life on the Ocean Wave

1. Imperial War Museum archive: W. M. Crawford (92/27/1).

2. Len Chester, *Bugle Boy* (Ebrington: Long Barn Books, 2007).

Chapter 17: The Boys on the Home Front

1. National Archives HO45/20250.
2. National Archives HO45/19066.
3. National Archives HO45/18716.
4. National Archives HO45/20250.
5. Ibid.
6. Ibid.
7. Ibid.
8. National Archives ED 11/248.
9. National Archives HO45/20250.
10. Ibid.
11. Ibid.
12. George Melly, *Owning Up* (London: Weidenfeld & Nicolson, 1965).
13. National Archives HO45/20250.
14. National Archives HO144/22160.
15. National Archives HO45/25144.
16. Ibid.
17. Ibid.
18. Quoted in Nagorski, op. cit.

Chapter 18: The Good-time Girls

1. National Archives ED138/92.
2. National Archives MH55/2317.
3. National Archives MH55/2325.
4. National Archives MEPO3/2139.
5. National Archives MH102/1149.
6. National Archives MH55/2325.
7. National Archives MEPO3/2140.
8. National Archives MH55/2317.
9. National Archives MH102/150.
10. Ibid.

11. National Archives AIR2/5995.
12. Ibid.
13. Ibid.
14. National Archives MH55/2317.
15. National Archives MEPO2/6622.
16. National Archives MEPO3/2277.
17. National Archives MEPO2/7012.
18. Sir Denys Roberts, *Yes Sir, But ...* (Chichester: Countrywise Press, 2000).
19. National Archives MH55/2317.
20. Ibid.
21. Ibid.
22. Ibid.
23. Ibid.
24. National Archives MEPO2/6622.
25. Mass Observation Report on juvenile drinking, June 1943: National Archives HO45/25144.
26. Ibid.
27. Ibid.
28. National Archives HO45/20250.
29. Ibid.
30. Mass Observation Report on juvenile drinking, June 1943: National Archives HO45/25144.
31. National Archives MH71/104.
32. Mass Observation Report on juvenile drinking, June 1943: National Archives HO45/25144.
33. Ibid.
34. National Archives MH102/895.
35. Ibid.
36. Ibid.
37. Ibid.
38. Ibid.
39. National Archives HO144/22159.
40. National Archives MEPO3/2280.

41. National Archives HO144/22219.
42. National Archives MEPO3/2280.
43. National Archives HO144/22159.
44. National Archives HO144/22219.

Chapter 19: The Children of Bethnal Green

1. This bombed block was the one Alf Morris had been living in.
2. *Annie Amelia Baker v Mayor, Aldermen and Burgesses of Bethnal Green* [1945] 1 All ER 135.
3. Ibid.
4. Ibid.
5. Peter Perryment met the policeman again fifty years later at an event to mark the anniversary.
6. The experience stayed with Bernard Kops for many years. In 1975 he wrote a television play, *It's a Lovely Day Tomorrow*, about the disaster.
7. When Peter Perryment's mother died forty years later, they found the coat Iris had worn that night in her wardrobe.

Chapter 20: In Every Port . . .

1. 'Merchant sailor witnessed world at war', *Kitchener-Waterloo Record* (2 January 2008).
2. Osborn, op. cit.
3. Rowe, op. cit.
4. *The Scotland-Russia Forum Review*, 20 (December 2008).

Chapter 21: Ready for War

1. Imperial War Museum archive: T. Osborne (04/35/1).

Chapter 22: The Boys in Normandy

1. Imperial War Museum archive: T. Osborne (04/35/1).
2. Ibid.
3. German multi-barrelled 'Nebelwerfers' fired a volley of six mortar rounds. They were notorious among the Allied infantrymen who grew to fear, and respect, the destructive power of their barrages.
4. Patrick Delaforce later used his experiences to write a series of acclaimed divisional histories telling the story of the 1944–5 campaign, telling the story from the point of view of the officers and men in the front lines.
5. Sixty years later, John Longfield and his wife visited York Minster to see his regimental chapel. As he entered he glanced at the Book of Remembrance. There on the open page was the name of the seventeen-year old soldier whose death had haunted him for so long. After so many years, it was a shocking and a moving experience to see the name of the boy again.
6. Imperial War Museum archive: T. Osborne (04/35/1).
7. Ibid.

Chapter 23: The Return of the Blitz

1. National Archives MEPO3/1965.
2. Ibid.
3. Ibid.
4. Ibid.

Chapter 24: To the Bitter End

1. Charles Whiting, *The Battle of the Bulge – Britain's Untold Story* (Stroud: Sutton Publishing, 1999).
2. Stanley Whitehouse and George B. Bennett, *Fear is the Foe* (London: Robert Hale, 1995).

3. Imperial War Museum archive: Leslie McDermott-Brown.
4. Imperial War Museum archive: J. Sweetland (97/21/1).
5. Rowe, op. cit.

Chapter 25: The New Order: Post-war Britain

1. Douglas Reed, *A Prophet at Home* (London: Jonathan Cape, 1941).
2. Letter to the *East London Advertiser* (26 March 1998).
3. National Archives HO45/20250.
4. Ibid.
5. James Diffley, 'Justice Looms at Last', *Evening Chronicle* (7 March 2006).

Bibliography

Ted Barris, *Juno: Canadians at D-Day* (Ontario: Thomas Allen, 2004).

George Beardmore, *Civilians at War* (London: John Murray, 1984).

Will Birch, *Ian Dury* (London: Sidgwick & Jackson, 2010).

Patrick Bishop, *Fighter Boys* (London: HarperCollins, 2003).

Britain Under Fire (London: Country Life Ltd, 1941).

Angus Calder, *The People's War* (London: Literary Guild, 1969).

—, *The Myth of the Blitz* (London: Jonathan Cape, 1981).

E. R. Chamberlain, *Life in Wartime Britain* (London: B. T. Batsford, 1972).

Len Chester, *Bugle Boy* (Ebrington: Long Barn Books, 2007).

John Costello, *Love, Sex and War* (London: Collins, 1985).

Patrick Davis, *A Child at Arms* (London: Hutchinson, 1970).

Peter Elphick, *Life Line – The Merchant Navy at War, 1939–1945* (London: Chatham, 1999).

Robert Fabian, *London after Dark* (London: Naldrett Press, 1954).

David Fraser, *And We Shall Shock Them* (London: Hodder & Stoughton, 1983).

Norman Gelb, *Scramble* (London: Michael Joseph, 1986).

Richard Hough and Dennis Richards, *The Battle of Britain* (London: Hodder & Stoughton, 1989).

Ludovic Kennedy, *Pursuit. The Sinking of the Bismarck* (London: William Collins, 1974).

Bernard Kops, *The World is a Wedding* (London: MacGibbon and Kee, 1963).

Wing Commander Asher Lee, *Blitz on Britain* (London: Four Square Books, 1960).

Norman Longmate, *The Real Dad's Army* (London: Arrow Books, 1974).

Kenneth McAlpine, *We Died with Our Boots Clean* (Stroud: History Press, 2009).

Martin Middlebrook, *Convoy* (London: Allen Lane, 1976).

Drew Middleton, *The Sky Suspended* (London: Martin Secker and Warburg, 1960).

Sarah Gertrude Millin, *World Blackout* (London: Faber & Faber, 1944).

H. V. Morton, *I Saw Two Englands* (London: Methuen & Co Ltd, 1942).

Tom Nagorski, *Miracles on the Water* (London: Robinson, 2007).

Robin Neillands, *The Raiders – The Army Commandos 1940–1946* (London: Weidenfeld & Nicolson, 1989).

Reg Osborn, *Trust Me . . . I'm An Old Sailor* (London: Banyan Books, 2006).

Ourselves in Wartime (London: Odhams Press Ltd, 1944).

Douglas Reed, *A Prophet at Home* (London: Jonathan Cape, 1941).

David Reynolds, *Rich Relations* (London: HarperCollins, 1996).

Peter Richards, *Bombs, Bullshit and Bullets* (London: Athena Press, 2007).

Robin Rowe, *Sticky Blue – A Boy and a Battleship* (Devon: Devonshire House, 1995).

Jon Savage, *Teenage* (London: Chatto & Windus, 2007).

W. C. Berwick Sayers, *Croydon in the Second World War* (Croydon: Croydon Corporation, 1949).

Stan Scott and Neil Barber, *Fighting with the Commandos* (Barnsley: Pen and Sword, 2008).

James Taylor and Martin Davidson, *Bomber Crew* (London: Hodder & Stoughton, 2004).

Donald Thomas, *An Underworld at War* (London: John Murray, 2003).

Adrian Weale, *Renegades – Hitler's Englishmen* (London: Weidenfeld & Nicolson, 1994).

Stanley Whitehouse and George B. Bennett, *Fear is the Foe* (London: Robert Hale, 1995).

Charles Whiting, *The Battle of the Bulge – Britain's Untold Story* (Stroud: Sutton Publishing, 1999).

Ben Wicks, *No Time to Wave Goodbye* (London: Bloomsbury, 1988).

—, *Waiting for the All Clear* (London: Bloomsbury, 1990).

Philip Ziegler, *London at War* (London: Pimlico, 2002).

Documents Held in the
National Archives

ADM1/9839 Loss of HMS ROYAL OAK: report on rescue and subsequent assistance to survivors

ADM1/9840 Loss of HMS ROYAL OAK: report of Board of enquiry

ADM1/11593 Summary of defences of Scapa Flow and Section 1 of report of board of enquiry into sinking of HMS ROYAL OAK

ADM1/14083 Training of sea cadets for RN communications branches under Bounty Scheme: appointment of RNVR (Sp) Officers as administrators of scheme and instructors

ADM1/14704 Welfare and recreational training in Open Units of Sea Cadet Corps

ADM116/4181 Boy and Sea Scouts and Sea Cadets in service as messengers, etc. with Naval Units: remuneration

ADM1/14737 Recruitment of boy buglers in Royal Marines: consent for sea service to be obtained prior to entry

ADM199/158 Loss of HMS ROYAL OAK, 14 Oct 1939: board of enquiry

ADM205/1 Committee of Imperial Defence. Chiefs of Staff Sub-Committee. Acceleration of defence programme 1939. Loss of HMS ROYAL OAK, etc.

AIR2/3942 British Social Hygiene Council prevention of venereal disease: enquiry from Mr Amery, MP

AIR2/5995 Control of venereal diseases in R.A.F. proposed defence regulations

AIR49/365 Venereal Diseases: miscellaneous reports

ASSI36/72 Murder: Bailey, Ernest George

CRIM1/482 Defendant: Jones, Elizabeth Marina, Hulten, (Private) Karl Gustav Charge: Murder of George Heath, taxi driver

CRIM1/585/137 Pardon: Jones, Elizabeth Marina

CRIM1/1615 Defendant: ARMITAGE, Guy Hamer Charge: Procuring and living on the earnings of prostitution

ED11/248 Juvenile delinquency

ED124/6 Juvenile Delinquency. Issue of joint Home Office and Board of Education Circular 1554 "Juvenile Offences". Reports from Standing Conference of National Juvenile Organisations, various local education authorities, youth committees and others. Welsh Youth Committee questionnaire and report on "Drinking amongst young people in Wales"

ED138/92 Juvenile delinquency. Extracts from Department's files

ED147/32 Juvenile delinquency 1947–1949

FD1/6518 Venereal diseases amongst British Forces

FD1/6805 Ministry of Food: salmonella infection in poultry

FD1/6556 Foam and human thrombin

HLG57/295 Extension of venereal disease: services to meet war-time needs; certification of grant claims

HO45/18118 CHILDREN: Increase in juvenile crime statistics

HO45/18716 CHILDREN: Incidence of juvenile crime

HO45/19066 CHILDREN: Enquiry into juvenile delinquency on behalf of the Home Office under the supervision of the London School of Economics and Political Science

HO45/20250 Conference on Juvenile Delinquency 1941

HO45/21055 Juvenile Courts: publication of names of juveniles in newspapers

HO45/21119 Juvenile Courts: composition; age of magistrates

HO45/21120 Juvenile Courts: composition; age of magistrates

HO 45/21223 Official history of World War II: juvenile delinquency and other matters relating to children

HO45/23119 Proposal for training young offenders for the army or navy as an alternative to Borstal training

HO45/23766 Juvenile, member of British Union at 13 years of age, district leader East Leyton branch: detention

HO 45/25144 Juvenile delinquency: drink as contributory cause; problems met by juvenile courts; assistance by voluntary organizations; problems in Liverpool

HO45/25599 Venereal disease: proposal to introduce compulsory treatment under a new defence regulation. Joint Committee on Venereal Disease: minutes of meetings; investigation into the incidence of venereal disease in the RAF

HO144/21905 Borstal treatment for young female offenders

HO144/21619 Contraction of venereal disease by members of HM Forces

HO144/22002 Reverend Martin Kiddle convicted of importuning male persons for an immoral purpose: free pardon granted after sentence of imprisonment quashed

HO144/22219 HULTEN, Karl Gustav Convicted at Central Criminal Court (CCC) on 23 January 1945 for murder and sentenced to death. JONES, Elizabeth Marina nee BAKER Convicted at Central Criminal Court (CCC) on 23 January 1945 for murder and sentenced to death (commuted)

HO187/477 PERSONNEL: Venereal disease

HO213/811 Venereal diseases in merchant seamen

HO144/21808 Treatment of girls aged 14–17 brought before juvenile courts

HO144/22159 CHILDREN: Elizabeth Maud Baker (later known as Elizabeth Marina Jones): committed to approved school on account of her not being under proper care of guardianship and falling into bad associations

HO144/22160 CHILDREN: Colin Chester Sterne, aged 17 sentenced to be detained during HM Pleasure on a charge of murder

LAB8/109 Position of prostitutes

LAB19/98 Conference on juvenile delinquency

MEPO 2/6216 Extracts from minutes of Senior Officers Crime Conference: suggested action to reduce juvenile delinquency

MEPO2/6622 Reports and statistics on prostitution: post-war increase in convictions before passing of Street Offences Act, 1959

MEPO 2/6626 Attendance of police representatives at meetings on juvenile delinquency organised by St. Pancras and Richmond Councils

MEPO2/7012 Organisations interested in promoting conditions to reduce the prevalence of venereal diseases: police assistance requested

MEPO2/7146 Prosecution in cases of gross indecency and importuning: opinion by Metropolitan Police Solicitor

MEPO2/8859 Activities of homosexuals, soldiers and civilians: co-operation between the army and the police

MEPO3/758 The Caravan Club, 81, Endell St, W.C. 1: disorderly house, male prostitutes

MEPO3/770 The Arch Social Club, 67, Bryanston Street, W.1: keeping a brothel

MEPO3/994 Mitford Brice: attempting to procure a boy aged 15, to commit an act of indecency

MEPO3/988 Album of foreign prostitutes: its purpose and restricted distribution

MEPO3/1939 Venereal disease: compulsory treatment under the Defence Regulations

MEPO 3/1961 Power of Juvenile Courts to order birching of offenders over 14 years of age

MEPO 3/1965 Police appeal to educational authorities in preventative measures of juvenile crime

MEPO3/2135 Suspected brothels, male importuners: Statistics

MEPO3/2138 Prostitution in the West End of London with special reference to American troops

MEPO3/2139 Prostitution in Mayfair, London: complaints, police action and statistics

MEPO3/2140 Police action to prevent allied servicemen contracting venereal disease from prostitutes

MEPO3/2141 Women suffering from venereal disease: first conviction under Defence Regulation 33B

MEPO3/2142 Women suffering from venereal disease: procedure under Defence Regulation 33B

MEPO3/2277 Murder of Robert George Smith by Kenneth William Gribble (age 16) in a spinney at Kempston, near Bedford on 6 August, 1944

MEPO3/2297 Murder of Ivy May Philips by Peter Joseph Jarmain (age 18) at the Red Arrow Garage, Thornton Heath, on 28 June, 1945

MEPO3/2298 Murder of Daphne Jean Bacon, (age 14) by Ernest George Bailey, a soldier at Aldringham, near Leiston, Suffolk on 8 July, 1945

MEPO3/2331 Gross Indecency: importance of legal aid in cases likely to cause publicity

MEPO3/2967 Prostitution in London: research by British Social Hygiene Council

MH51/412 Protection of defectives from acts of sexual immorality; procuration

MH55/1341 Defence Regulation 33B: importation of venereal disease by Service personnel; wartime conferences

MH55/2317 Control: solicitation by prostitutes of United States servicemen based in London; Joint Committee on Venereal Diseases

MH55/2325 Joint Committee on Venereal Diseases: minutes of meetings and papers

MH71/104 Advisory Sub-Committee on Venereal Diseases: minutes, correspondence and report

MH96/1137 Treatment of venereal disease with penicillin

MH102/895 Girl absconders from approved schools soliciting American soldiers in the streets and spreading venereal disease

MH102/1117 Approved school accommodation: provision of new school to deal with girls suffering from venereal disease

MH102/1129 Publicity about Home Office schools: film on juvenile delinquency, comments by Scottish Education Department, also press cuttings

MH102/1134 Publicity about Home Office schools: film about juvenile delinquency involving the work of juvenile courts; recommended by the Institute for the Scientific Treatment of Delinquency

MH102/1146 Treatment of venereal disease in approved schools for girls: meeting of the Case Sub-Committee of the Brighton Probation Committee; letter to Home Office Children's Branch concerning young girls associating, often immorally, with soldiers

MH102/1147 Treatment of venereal disease: juvenile delinquency in Blackpool; minutes by National Youth Committee police reports and general correspondence

MH102/1148 Treatment of venereal disease: Shirley Remand Home for girls; suitability of use as place for treatment

MH102/1149 Control of venereal disease: minutes of conference held at the Home Office; reports made by Joint Committee on Venereal Diseases

MH102/1150 Juvenile delinquency in young girls: parliamentary question on statement made by the Chairman of the East London Juvenile Court

MH102/1151 Venereal disease in juveniles: letter from Warwickshire County Council to the Ministry of Health asking whether sick juveniles should be brought before a juvenile court as being in need of care and protection

NSC9/407 Director General's Office: notes of a meeting held at Headquarters to discuss policy regarding the prosecution of juvenile offenders against the Post Office (Includes memo on the law and procedure applicable to the prosecution of children and young persons)

PCOM9/413 Venereal disease: women prisoners

PCOM9/435 Young offenders in prisons: treatment and privileges

PCOM9/1034 DAVIDSON John Gordon: convicted at Manchester 1 May 1944 of murder and sentenced to death

TS27/549 Hereford Juvenile Court: enquiry by Lord Justice Goddard into the conduct of the Court in proceedings against Dennis Harold Craddock and others

TS335 – Merchant Navy Awards

WO32/9727 Battalions: Young Soldier Home Defence Formation

WO32/9847 Junior Training Corps Intelligence Scouting for boys under 15

WO32/9848 Young soldiers battalions

WO32/9849 Pre-military training for youths

WO32/10470 Age for drafting overseas

WO32/10471 Age of drafting overseas

WO32/10473 Young soldiers training camps

WO32/11187 Organisation post-war training

WO32/11519 Formation of General Service corps

WO166/14163 2 Young Soldiers Trg. Centre

WO199/919 Conferences: reorganisation of Home Defence and Young Soldiers Battalions

WO365/81 Young soldier battalions: disposal of unsuitable personnel

WO379/102 Guards Training Battalions; Guards Armoured Training Wing; Young Soldier Training Centres/Training Battalions

WO379/110 Special Training Units: Stamford Practical Training Area; Young Soldiers Training Units, later Special Training Units

WO379/124 Young Soldier Training Centre: Primary Training Centres affiliated to infantry Depots

Acknowledgements

This book was originally inspired by the tales I heard from my parents and their siblings. Although they were fortunate enough to live in a small town, it was not untouched by war – at first it was filled by evacuees, then later by American servicemen. My mother was fascinated by both groups since my grandmother first took in a Jewish family evacuated from London, then later made space for GIs to be billeted in their home. My father experienced the freedom of growing up in wartime: he left school aged just thirteen to take a well-paid job that had been vacated when the local men had been called up. Whilst researching this book I heard vivid tales that filled in some of the gaps found in stories contained within official reports. Unfortunately I have to offer thanks to my parents posthumously.

A number of veterans whom I had interviewed for previous books helped inspire this story. When I first started thinking about youth in wartime I recalled how John Longfield, whose memories had helped colour both *To the Victor the Spoils* and *T-Force*, had volunteered for the Army after a row with his headmaster. The idea of boys leaving school to join the Army soon became firmly fixed in my mind. I also recalled the stories of Ted Roberts, whom I first met whilst he was selling poppies in a Croydon shopping centre, and who had told me tales of being thrown out of the Army aged just fourteen. I revisited Ted to hear more of his remarkable story.

Thanks must also go to Marion Davies, who shared the notes made by her late husband Eric, who had earlier assisted me when I was researching *To the Victor the Spoils*. From Canada, Sylvia Norman (née Bowman) shared stories both of her wartime experiences and those of her late husband, John, whose story I had earlier told in my books on prisoners of war.

A few years ago I attended a reunion of prisoners of war whose experiences I had related in my books *Hitler's British Slaves* and *Dunkirk: The Men They Left Behind*. Also at the event was the Evacuees Association. Among its members I met Reg Baker who shared tales of his wartime experiences in Bethnal Green. We later met up so he could expand on his memories. Reg then kindly introduced me to Alf Morris who continues to work hard to raise funds for a memorial to the dead of the Bethnal Green tube disaster. From Reg and Alf I was able to get a vivid image of life in the bombed streets of east London.

Once again, *Wartime News* and its editor Marilyn Ward was a great source of information and interviewees. Through Marilyn's help I was able to locate Colin Ryder Richardson, Roy Finch, Roy Bartlett, Terry Charles, Ken Durston, Dennis Hobbs, Geoff Pulzer and his wife Julienne, as well as her sister Yvonne Stanford (née Vanhandenhoeve). I must thank them all for responding to my appeal.

I must offer sincere thanks to Tim Brant and John Rix of the Merchant Navy Association who kindly published an appeal for me. This generated a tremendous response and put me in contact with: Bernard Ashton, Robert Ball, Ron Bosworth, Bill Ellis, Stuart Henderson, Raymond Hopkins, Christian Immelman, Arthur Leonard, Anthony Longden, Douglas Morse, Albert Mulholland, Alan Shard, Alan Simms, Ron Singleton, Herbert Taylor, Jim Thomas, Derek Tolfree and Norval Young. Following this appeal Daphne Chinnery contacted me to share tales of her late husband, John. My thanks go to them all. I just hope this book helps further the understanding of the tremendous sacrifice made by the Merchant Navy, whose contribution has been too often ignored.

Tim Essex-Lopresti, Tim Hissey and Robin Woolven at the Civil Defence Association are owed my gratitude for putting me in touch with Sidney Ties.

Thanks to Jason and Helen for putting me in touch with Albert Riddle. My thanks also go to Moyra Alison, Tony Benn, Len Chester, Jean Ceiriog-Jones, Ray and Jean Clarke, John Cotter, Patrick Delaforce, Edward Ford, Reg Fraser, Colin Furk, John Hipkin, Michael Howard, Ron Leagas, Agnes McBarron, Tony Moynihan, Thomas Nagorski, John Osborne, Dr Brian Phillips, Peter Richards, Peter Rowlands, Dilip Sarkar, Kenneth Toop, Kathleen Walder and Gillian Wheeler. Thanks also to Stan Scott, both for sharing his story of volunteering for the Army aged fourteen and for putting me in touch with Fred Walker. I am also extremely grateful to Will Birch for putting me in touch with Fred Rowe, whose stories injected a genuine sense of the horrors of growing up in wartime London.

As ever, thanks go to my editor Leo Hollis, all at Constable and Robinson, my agent Andrew Lownie and my wife Claire (who has once again endured my disappearing around the country on the quest for the perfect story).

Appendix

Colin Ryder Richardson

Colin (photographed in 2009) narrowly survived the sinking of SS *City of Benares* whilst being evacuated to the USA aged eleven. He received a commendation for his brave conduct in the Merchant Navy. He later credited his traumatic childhood experiences with giving him the mental strength to successfully battle against cancer.

Peter Richards

Former telegram delivery boy Peter (photographed in 2009) with the copy of the *Selected Works* of Karl Marx that he carried inside his tunic whilst serving as an infantryman in Normandy, 1944. The cover still carries the scar where it was hit by shrapnel.

Whilst working as a telegram boy in wartime London, he wore motorcycle gauntlets with the communist slogan 'Second front, Now' painted on them. After the war he returned to the Post Office and remained a loyal member of the Communist Party throughout the post-war years, only leaving the party in the 1990s.

John Cotter DFC

John (photographed in 2009) joined the RAF aged seventeen after a friend told him that he would be able to get sweets and cakes in the NAAFI. He completed a tour of duty piloting Lancaster bombers and was awarded the Distinguished Flying Cross. He then became an instructor. He continued to serve in the RAF, post-war, and later worked at the Air Ministry (close to the Foreign Office where he had been an unarmed teenage 'Home Guard' during the Blitz).

He later became an airline pilot and travelled the world before retiring to Brighton.

Sadly, his brother who volunteered for the RAF, aged just fifteen, did not survive the war.

Arthur Harvey

Arthur (photographed in 2010) with a model of the 'Liberty' ship, the *Sampan*, that he served on during the Second World War. He remained in the Merchant Navy and became a Master Mariner. After retiring from the sea, he established a shipping company, leasing containers used to ship goods worldwide.

Below: Arthur (left) as a teenager in the wartime Merchant Navy.

Ron Bosworth

Ron Bosworth (photographed in 2010) joined the Merchant Navy in 1938 aged fifteen. He was at sea when war broke out and was sunk three times before his eighteenth birthday. He remained in the Merchant Navy post-war, until retiring from the sea to work in the docks at Avonmouth.

Tony Sprigings

Tony (photographed in 2009) joined the Merchant Navy aged sixteen after his father arranged an apprenticeship for him. He eventually retired as a Master Mariner, having captained ships of all sizes around the world.

Bill Edwardes

Bill (photographed in 2010) joined the Army aged sixteen and served as a stretcher-bearer in Normandy at seventeen. He had managed to convince his mother to let him join whilst 'underage' because he feared the war would be over before he had a chance to join in.

During his post-war career in industry, he credited his military service, in particular having to remain calm whilst treating men with serious wounds, with the ability to remain calm and clear-headed, whatever the circumstances.

He later became the Chairman of the 43rd Wessex Division Old Comrades Association.

Geoff and Julienne Pulzer

Geoff and his wife Julienne Vanhandenhoeve (photographed in 2010). She was trapped in Antwerp in May 1940 after the ship bringing her back to England was sunk. Geoff took part in the liberation of Antwerp in 1944. When they met in London post-war, he introduced himself with the words 'I liberated you'.

Left: Pulzer in his pre-war army cadet uniform. He joined the Home Guard aged sixteen and used the skills he had learned in his school cadet unit to teach middle-aged Home Guard volunteers to shoot and carry out rifle drill.

John and Sylvia Norman

Frank (John) Norman and his wife Sylvia celebrating their sixtieth wedding anniversary at their home in Orangeville, Canada. They met at a party to celebrate his homecoming after his release from a German prisoner-of-war camp. He is believed to be the youngest British soldier to have been captured during the Second World War. After five years of captivity, he was still just twenty-one years old.

Below: The Normans in post-war Germany after their marriage.

Sidney Ties

Sidney (photographed in 2010) was a teenage Londoner who had originally wanted to train as a doctor. As a First Aid volunteer, he treated casualties in the streets around his London home on the first night of the Blitz. When his home was bombed, he was evacuated to Guildford and served in the Civil Defence. He later became an instructor. Post-war, he continued his Civil Defence role and at the time of the Cuban Missile Crisis, found himself in a local government bunker plotting wind patterns to monitor fall-out in the event of a nuclear war.

John Osborne

John (photographed in 2010) joined the RAF aged sixteen. He was partly inspired by the film *Target for Tonight* and partly by the tension between his parents.

Being colour blind, he was unsuitable for either aircrew or to work as an electrician, as had been his original intention. Instead he served as a driver. At one point he even acted as the driver for the same pilot who had featured in *Target for Tonight.*

The RAF only discovered his true age when he had to submit his birth certificate in order to get permission to marry. He had not only lied to the RAF, he had also told his fiancée he was three years older than he really was.

Derek and Peg Tolfree

Derek Tolfree and his wife Peg (photographed in 2010). He had joined a nautical training college aged fifteen. At sixteen, he took the opportunity to transfer to the Royal Navy. He went to sea with the rank of midshipman and served on North Sea coastal convoys at the age of seventeen.

Peg was a typical London teenager who defied both her parents and the Luftwaffe to go out in London at the height of the Blitz. In 1944 she narrowly escaped death after being blown down three flights of stairs and out into the street by the blast of a V1 rocket which landed opposite her office.

Ron Leagas

Ron Leagas (photographed in 2010) joined the Army aged sixteen. He volunteered after an argument with his mother which culminated in her throwing a stew over him. He had to forge a letter from his father giving his age as eighteen. When the Army discovered his true age, Ron successfully pleaded with his commanding officer to be allowed to remain in the Army.

He was wounded in Normandy and spent the rest of the war in relative comfort at a base in Gibraltar.

Roy Finch

Roy Finch (photographed in 2010) volunteered for the Army aged seventeen after his seriously wounded brother was repatriated from a prisoner-of-war camp. With his brother back home, he felt it was his turn to serve. After he volunteered, his brother took him back to the recruiting office telling them he had given a false age. The sergeant refused to release him and Roy landed on D-Day as a seventeen year old.

He witnessed the horrors of Belsen concentration camp when it was liberated, an experience that had a deep emotional impact upon him.

Len Chester

Len Chester (photographed in 2010) holding the German bullet that nearly hit him when he was serving as a Royal Marine 'boy bugler' on a warship in 1940, aged just fourteen.

The first time he ever attended a funeral was in 1940 at the burial of six sailors. As he tried to play *The Last Post*, he broke down in tears and was consoled by an admiral attending the funeral.

He remained in the Royal Marines post-war and completed eighteen years' service.

Left: Len (right) aged fourteen, with his father and brother after qualifying as a bugler.

Ted Roberts

Ted (photographed in 2010) had always wanted to be a soldier, like his father and brothers. He volunteered for the Army in 1940 aged just fourteen.

He was thrown out after six months when his true age was revealed. He rejoined, only to be thrown out for a second time when his mother wrote to his commanding officer in an attempt to prevent the sixteen year old being sent overseas.

He was eventually successful and served in Normandy where he was seriously wounded, taking a year to recover strength and movement in his wounded arm.

Stan Scott

Stan (photographed in 2009) volunteered for the Army in 1940 aged fifteen, but was released after ten days when his true age was uncovered. He rejoined within six months and served overseas, only to be sent home when it was revealed he was just seventeen.

He later served as an instructor before joining the commandos and landing in France on D-Day.

Post-war, he left the Army, only to join the Territorial Army as an instructor in 1970, serving for twenty-four years. He also spent nine years as a civilian instructor teaching Army Cadets.

Below: With his father in 1942.

Fred Walker

Fred Walker (photographed in 2009) joined the Army aged sixteen after being sacked from his job demolishing bombed buildings in London. He volunteered for the commandos and served at Dieppe, then Sicily and Italy, before landing in Normandy on D-Day. He is now a 'Chelsea Pensioner'.

Below: Members of No. 3 Commando shortly before the raid on Dieppe (Walker fourth from left). Among the group were other underage recruits, including John Tupper who served with Walker in Sicily and Italy and was killed beside Walker in Normandy.

Left: John Tupper.

Above: Tupper's grave. He was aged just eighteen when he was killed in Normandy. He had already served at Dieppe, Sicily and Italy by the time of his death.

Albert Riddle

Albert Riddle (photographed in 2010). Albert joined the Royal Navy aged fifteen. He served on HMS *Prince of Wales* during the pursuit of the *Bismarck*. In 1941, aged seventeen, he narrowly escaped from the *Prince of Wales* when she sank. He was also fortunate enough to escape capture by the Japanese when Singapore fell a few months later.

After retiring from the Royal Navy, he became a farmer in Cornwall and devoted many years to his role as Chairman of the Royal Cornwall Show, living on the showgrounds at Wadebridge in Cornwall.

The Bethnal Green Disaster

Above: Alf Morris (photographed in 2009) at the entrance to Bethnal Green tube station where 171 people were crushed to death in 1943. Alf was pulled alive from the bottom of the stairs.

For many years he refused to talk about the tragedy. He eventually decided to confront the painful memories and dedicated himself to raising funds for a permanent memorial to the dead through a charity, 'Stairway to Heaven'.

Left: Reg Baker (photographed in 2009). Reg was fortunate to narrowly escape the disaster. When the air raid siren sounded, he was delayed since he had to wait for his father who was in the toilet. He has always credited this delay with saving his life.

Left: Fred Rowe (photographed in 2010). Fred started his criminal career looting from bombed shops during the Blitz. It was only after meeting the singer Ian Dury during the 1970s, and becoming his driver and personal assistant, that Fred decided to 'go straight'.

Right: Tony Benn (photographed in 2010). After experiencing the Blitz on London, he moved to Scotland where – despite being aged just fourteen – he was recruited to the local ARP unit on the grounds that he was the only person to have actually experienced an air raid.

Left: Bernard Ashton (photographed in 2010). Joining the Merchant Navy aged fifteen, Bernard was sunk three times before his eighteenth birthday, two of these being on consecutive convoys. He made a career in the Merchant Navy and his home still overlooks the docks at Dover.

Still devoted to the Merchant Navy, he flies the correct flag for the nationality of visitors to his home. When the author visited him, he flew the British merchant fleet's 'Red Ensign'.

Above: Jean Redman (photographed 2010). Aged fourteen, she left school to work in her local town hall, helping find homes for evacuees. Many of the evacuees were only just younger than her. She wanted to serve in the military, but at the age of sixteen she realized that her parents would refuse permission. As a result, she volunteered for the Land Army and spent the rest of the war on a farm. After the war she resumed the career path that war had interrupted and trained to be a teacher.

The author believes that Jean was one of the staff who organized for an evacuee family to move in with his mother's family.

Below: Bill Ellis (photographed in 2010). Bill joined the Merchant Navy aged sixteen after being rejected by both the Army and the Royal Navy. He experienced the full horrors of war whilst serving on a hospital ship in the Mediterranean. After retiring from the Merchant Navy, he became a butcher in Somerset.

Index